KINGDOM in the WEST

The Mormons and the American Frontier

Will Bagley, series editor

VOLUME 5

George Q. Cannon, about the time he served as editor of the *Western Standard*.
Courtesy, Utah State Historical Society.

DEFENDING ZION

George Q. Cannon and the California Mormon Newspaper Wars of 1856–1857

Edited by
Roger Robin Ekins

THE ARTHUR H. CLARK COMPANY
Spokane, Washington
2002

LIBRARY OF CONGRESS CATALOG CARD NUMBER 2002034794
ISBN-0-87062-321-4
ISBN-0-87062-274-9 (entire series)

Library of Congress Cataloging-in-Publication Data

Defending Zion : George Q. Cannon and the California Mormon newspaper wars of 1856–1857 / edited by Roger Robin Ekins.
p.cm. — (Kingdom in the West ; v. 5)
Includes bibliographical references (p.) and index.
ISBN 0-87062-321-4 (alk. paper)
1. Cannon, George Q. (George Quayle), 1827-1901. 2. Mormon press—California—San Francisco—History—19th century.
3. Church of Jesus Christ of Latter-day Saints—Apologetic works—History and criticism. I. Ekins, Roger Robin. II. Series.

BX8695.C255 D44 2002
289.3'794'09034—dc21

2002034794

In memory of my loving father,
V. Ross Ekins,
and his mother,
Eva Eudora Broadbent—
a daughter of polygamy

Contents

Illustrations

Foreword

In the wake of the gold rush, an obscure religious weekly waged a remarkable newspaper war with the leading journals of California. George Q. Cannon, one of the most eloquent and perhaps his era's brightest defender of the Mormons, or Latter-day Saints as they still prefer to be known, manned the battlements of the *Western Standard,* the herald of the young religion on the Pacific Coast. This book chronicles the attacks and counterattacks, and the victories and defeats, of this extraordinary conflict.

George Q. Cannon was the most able defender of Mormonism in the nineteenth century. Born and educated in England, he joined Joseph Smith's revolutionary religious movement as a child. By age sixteen he was living in Nauvoo, Illinois, having lost his mother on the voyage to America and his father shortly after his arrival. He worked for his apostle-uncle, John Taylor, as a printer's apprentice at the *Nauvoo Neighbor,* learning the skills he would employ over the next six decades as his religion's leading political and intellectual champion.

By the time he was thirty, Cannon had been a printer's devil, a religious refugee, an 1847 Utah pioneer, a member of the great trek of 1849 across the southern Great Basin to California, a gold miner, a Latter-day Saint missionary to the Hawaiian Islands, and finally, editor and publisher of the San Francisco *Western Standard.* In an unequal contest, the eloquent young believer was the sole Mormon combatant in a fiery newspaper war in a day when media meant print. The *Standard* single-handedly engaged the enemies of Mormonism and the leading newspapers of frontier California in a stout defense of the principles of religious freedom and toleration and the political doctrines of popular sovereignty and states' rights. These abstractions sprang to life in controversies raging over the fledgling theocracy on the shores of Great Salt Lake, in charges that Mormons joined American Indians in "depredations" against overland travelers, and in the heated debate over a man's right to have as many wives as the Lord thought appropriate.

San Francisco, which only ten years earlier had been a tiny hide-trading village sprawling sparsely over the hills above Yerba Buena Cove, was by 1856 a burgeoning metropolis boasting 30,000 citizens, most of them young males in hot pursuit of fortune. Few then or now realized how instrumental the Mormons had been in building the city. The arrival of some 230 Latter-day Saints aboard Samuel Brannan's ship *Brooklyn* in 1846, as H. H. Bancroft observed, made the settlement "for a time very largely a Mormon town." A little more than a year later Brannan recalled, "When I landed here with my little company there was but three families in the place, and now the improvements are beyond all conception, houses in every direction, business very brisk and money plenty." He predicted in 1847, "Here will be the great Emporium of the Pacific and eventually of the union." Within a decade, the explosive growth of what historian Gunther Barth has called the "instant city" had proved Brannan right. The municipality was the most vibrant, resplendent, diverse, violent, and corrupt city in the United States, the result, the authors of *The Annals of San Francisco* claimed, of "exalted intellect, unexampled energy, and toilsome industry."

To the young true believer, California was a hard country, but Cannon was determined to spread the message of his faith even in the "Sodom of the Pacific." As he told Daniel H. Wells, "My continual desire and prayer is that the honest in heart may be brought in contact with the truth." The youthful energy and doctrinal dynamism of Mormonism attracted few converts as the Gold Rush came to its end, and among the worn-out placers prospects for the new religion were bleak. As Cannon told Brigham Young, "San Francisco seems to be the most difficult of all fields in which to awaken the people."

In a portrait taken about 1857 (frontispiece), an intense loyalty, conviction, and ambition burn in the eyes of the thirty-year-old editor. Beneath an already expansive brow and above a carefully trimmed Van Dyke, Cannon's grim-set mouth appears ready to burst into exhortation—or laughter. He is dressed as a gentleman, or perhaps more accurately as the consummate businessman he had already become. He looks spry, but unlike many of his contemporaries—including some of his Mormon brethren—it is hard to imagine this youthful thinker in a fist-fight or shootout. Yet this unwavering young religious stalwart was a champion brawler in one of the most fiery battles of all the newspaper wars in early California. He took on all—and they were many—who had the "intention of pulling down 'Mormonism'" and lining their "own pockets by the operation."

Throughout his California career, Cannon stoutly defended Brigham Young, exploiting the "spirit of curiosity to know more about this wonderful man" who drew endless and bitter attacks from the press. The controversies surrounding the Mormon prophet, the most successful empire builder of his day, commanded not only the pages of the *Western Standard* but consumed oceans of American ink as Young used his fiery oratory and office as governor of Utah Territory to defy the federal government. Cannon was totally devoted to "Bro. Brigham," and fought to preserve him "from every evil and the machinations of the enemies of the kingdom of God." Unlike other Mormon editors, officials, and propagandists, Cannon never advised Young to watch his words, and he handled the Mormon firebrand with a finesse and diplomacy that foretold the brilliance of his subsequent political career. In print confrontations, Cannon devised a defense of Young still favored by devout Mormon historians: the wonderful man was simply misunderstood.

Roger Robin Ekins has done a yeoman's work in rescuing Cannon's early writings from obscurity. They paint a vivid picture of the 1850s, an often-forgotten period in California's colorful past, and again reveal how obscure Mormon sources shed light on the history of the wider West. The editorials, articles, and letters collected in this volume deal with frontier justice, vigilantism, politics, journalism, religion, violence, overland emigration, "White Indians," Danites, and even sex. Polygamy inspired a host of scandalous tales of how "the crafty elders of Salt Lake" lured their young victims into sexual slavery. "Perhaps you may have some knowledge of a certain Mr. Brenchley who lived several years in the Sandwich Islands," Brigham Young gossips, "where he kept native men and women to minister to his wants and pleasures." The editorials brim with the puns and wordplay of the time and thunder with its rhetoric. More importantly, these primary accounts chronicle the bitter controversies that eventually led President James Buchanan to send a military expedition to Utah so costly that it almost bankrupted the republic on the eve of the Civil War. The army's arrival changed life in Deseret forever, for as Jane Richards told Emily Bancroft in 1880, "It has never been the same place since."

Like most good biographers, Roger Ekins shows great empathy for his subject. Unlike other recent studies of George Q. Cannon's life, he acknowledges that as a human being, Cannon was less than perfect and was not universally beloved, especially after he became one of the great powers in Mormon society. Yet in dealing with the controversies that surrounded Cannon's early years, this study is an honest defense of this Defender of the Faith, a fitting approach when dealing with a fearless but hopelessly outnumbered soldier in one of the frontier's most bitter newspaper wars. As a contribution to the documentary record of frontier Mormonism, *Defending Zion* presents the most cogent arguments of the religion's best nineteenth-century champion. To understand the passions that surrounded this new religious movement, such a perspective is more than desirable: it is essential.

A less sympathetic evaluation would emphasize that Cannon was neither a great thinker nor theologian: he was an apologist. Some of the principles he held dear stand discredited, such as polygamy with its heritage of heartbreak, and states' rights, which the South used to promote and foster slavery just as the Mormons hoped to use it to defend polygamy. He usually picked easy targets and avoided examining the religious loyalties that Latter-day Saints put ahead of obedience to civil law. Cannon could never acknowledge the brotherhood of the blood of Israel he and his fellow Saints claimed with the remnant of Israel in the New World, the American Indians. He did not yet belong to the highest echelons of the Mormon hierarchy and at times appears to have lacked knowledge of his church's actions and true policies, particularly its occasional authorization of violence. "To pretend that there were no holy murders in Utah and along the trails to California, that there was no saving of the souls of sinners by the shedding of their blood during the 'blood atonement' revival of 1856, that there were no mysterious disappearances of apostates and offensive Gentiles," Wallace Stegner observed in *Mormon Country*, is "bad history."

Cannon brilliantly exploited the errors and excesses of his opponents, and he knew "the more the work is opposed the more it will spread." He could be eloquent, witty, ironic, subtle, bitter, brilliant, and biting in demolishing the arguments of his opponents, but his defense sometimes lacked perspective and credibility. His writings for the *Western Standard* represent his honest views, but throughout his life Cannon demonstrated a willingness to serve as a defender of the faith without regard for the practical truth that any good journalist seeks to uphold. "Cannon served higher truth, an end that justified the means," historian David L. Bigler has observed, "and was ever ready to conjure up whatever justification might be needed."

Brigham Young elevated Apostle Cannon to the First Presidency, the triumvirate at the top of the Mormon hierarchy, in 1868; Cannon's son Frank observed that his father was "the only one of the younger generation who ever won his entire confidence." Reading the older Cannon's letters as Utah Territory's congressional delegate is a revelation. His correspondence (sometimes written in Hawaiian) with Brigham Young and other Mormon authorities is full of intrigue—ciphers, blind references, and code names—and demonstrates the remarkable extent of the delegate's influence. Much of it came from the cash he used freely to buy political support or kill legislation that threatened Mormon interests, but Cannon's knowledge of the system and personal charm was perhaps more important in protecting his religion. Still, these letters raise ethical questions. Cannon told D. H. Wells in 1872 he thought he could defeat a bill by "giving a few thousand dollars. What is your mind? Shall we try?" In another context, Cannon expressed doubts about such largesse: "we might well pause and ask whether it was exactly the right thing to do, to take the peoples' money and give it to such characters." Especially troubling is Cannon's ability to condone some of the worst examples of Utah's violence, such as when he joked with Brigham Young about how John Dawson "had been half emasculated" during his brief tenure as Utah's territorial governor. Someday a bright historian will use this material to expand our knowledge of the practical operation of congress in the Gilded Age.

As a man of enormous influence during the Latter-day Saint struggle for survival in the nineteenth century, and as a religious authority who probably did more to shape modern Mormonism than anyone except Wilford Woodruff, Cannon remains sadly unappreciated. In a labor extending over several years, Roger Robin Ekins has collected his writings from the *Western Standard* and the editorials and articles of the opposition press, along with the young missionary's correspondence with Brigham Young, John Taylor, Wilford Woodruff, and Daniel H. Wells. He has done Cannon's memory and Western history a great service. These documents paint a vivid picture of the heated debate that raged over the new religion as it approached one of its greatest crises, the Utah War of 1857–1858. The intensity of the battles in Cannon's two-year newspaper war, in which some of his adversaries called for the extermination of an unpopular religious minority, reminds us that in 1857 the very survival of the Mormon kingdom was an open question.

Beyond his vast and talented progeny, perhaps the greatest legacy of George Q. Cannon is the astonishing success of Mormonism in the twentieth century. In a fiery crucible of bitter controversy, he was instrumental in forging the faith of modern Latter-day Saints. The religion owes much to this true believer, who never doubted that "the Lord being on our side we must triumph, if we only stick to His kingdom."

WILL BAGLEY
Salt Lake City, Utah
June 2002

Preface

I wish to express my gratitude to all those who have made this study possible. First, I thank a fellow rare book collector, Gary Manwill, for having talked me into paying the princely sum of $600 for a lovely copy of *Writings from the Western Standard,* the reading of which sent me on this fantastic journey. Thanks also to my employer, Butte College, which—in its eagerness to return me to full-time teaching—provided me with the time necessary to begin this project as well as a subsequent sabbatical leave, so that I might complete it. I am grateful to Ron Watt and his associates at the Family and Church History Department of the Church of Jesus Christ of Latter-day Saints for their generous assistance as well as those who helped me find newspapers, photos and other resources at the California History Room of the California State Library in Sacramento, the Bancroft and Doe Libraries at U.C. Berkeley, the Utah State Historical Society, and the Special Collections Libraries at Brigham Young University and the University of Utah. Thanks to Shirleigh Coronado and especially Kevin Scot McCarthy, former and current Butte College librarians, for helping with internet research and interlibrary loans and to Ardis E. Parshall for sharing some of the marvelous resources she has assiduously collected from LDS Archives. I appreciate the efforts of Michael Yockey, librarian of the Swedenborg House of Studies in Berkeley and Carroll Ohdner, Library Director of the Swedenborg Library at Bryn Athyn College, who helped locate what may be the only photograph of John Hyde, reproduced herein for the first time. I am also indebted, in more ways than one, to my mother, Soni Ekins and my son, Adam, who selflessly assumed the role of research assistants when I could not get back to Utah to check on items I had overlooked. I am especially grateful for Lisa Clewett West, a former Butte College

Honors student, promising writer and good friend who graciously volunteered to copy-edit early versions of the manuscript.

I owe a special debt to the late Leonard Arrington, a great man of great faith who tried to tell it like it was, and also to his friend and associate, Davis Bitton, for their support and encouragement. I am also grateful to my colleague, Dan Barnett, who helped me out of more computer glitches than I care to admit, to my friend Ric Machuga, who helped me understand that my "true function" is as a teacher and writer rather than as an administrator, and to other friends and colleagues who read progressive stages of the manuscript, offering excellent advice, at least some of which I was bright enough to accept. These include Liz Dulaney, Glen M. Leonard, Michael N. Landon, Floyd A. O'Neil, and David L. Bigler. David J. Whittaker, and William P. MacKinnon were particularly insightful and gave me numerous suggestions for further reading.

Of course none of this would have been possible without my publisher, Robert A. Clark, and my sensational editor and biggest supporter, the irrepressible Will Bagley. Will added much more than I could ever adequately acknowledge to this venture; his interpretations do not always coincide with my own, but this book would not have been nearly as interesting or as informative without his superb contributions. Most of all, I express my love and gratitude to Helen Leonard Ekins, my eternal companion, for her encouragement and criticism, both of which helped make this a better book than it would have been otherwise.

Editorial Procedures

I have organized this collection along topics critical to the ongoing struggle between the Mormons and their Gentile neighbors. The newspaper wars chronicled in each chapter are organized in roughly chronological order. Where appropriate, excerpts from related letters to the editor are included. Historical details on the newspapers and their editors can be found in the appendix. In the concluding chapter I summarize Cannon's life and substantial leadership role following his relatively brief stint as editor of the *Western Standard*, while assessing his victories and defeats in California. I also attempt to examine some of the larger questions raised through the battles of the remarkable newspaper wars of 1856–1857 that raged on in the Golden State.

Throughout each chapter is found amplifying commentary drawn from modern scholarship as well as nineteenth-century sources. Several of the early sources are so obviously biased that one of my colleagues asked why I have included such "discredited" material. I have done so because it graphically reveals the deeply held prejudices George Q. Cannon and other defenders of the Mormon faith were called upon to combat. Besides, it makes for fascinating reading. Most importantly, as John Stuart Mill made clear through his classic work, *On Liberty,* truth best emerges from the clash of opposing ideas.

One of the most important lessons I learned through this project is that writing Mormon history is like walking through a mine field: you never know what members you are going to lose. By its very nature, this material is highly controversial and I might as well admit that "objectivity" (if such a thing is even possible) has not been my chief goal. Rather, I have strived for intellectual honesty in my editing of material both supporting and attacking the Church of Jesus Christ of Latter-day Saints. There will be much here to both delight and infuriate those on either side of the modern Mormon divide. Perhaps if no one is completely satisfied that will be an indication I have done a good job in my roles of observer, reporter and interpreter of historical perspective.

The material is organized into chapters, sections, and documents. Each document contains an abbreviated heading identifying the source and its location. Full citations for these items, including manuscript numbers, are found in the bibliography.

I have taken the liberty of occasionally editing the text of these various newspaper editorials to eliminate undue repetition, exercising caution in my use of ellipses to avoid changing or distorting the original meaning or context. Despite this editing, a certain degree of repetition is unavoidable for several reasons. First, nineteenth-century prose tends to be wordy and sometimes even melodramatic, especially compared with modern-day journalism. Even George Q. Cannon's admiring biographer, Davis Bitton, complains that many of Cannon's editorials are "prolix, unnecessarily protracted."[1] Second, the very nature of journalism demands a constant restating of preceding events, particularly when those events occurred several days or even weeks earlier. Cannon could never be sure his readers had seen the rival editorial to which he was responding, and therefore inevitably found himself paraphrasing or quoting that which he was about to attack. Finally, each of these California newspapers tended to be critical of many of the same things—the supposed autocratic rule in Utah and the infamous principle of polygamy, to name but two. As a result, they often raised the same objections to Mormonism, constantly replaying variations on the same theme. Notwithstanding, I have made every effort to select this material with the modern reader in mind.

Where they differ from modern usage, nineteenth-century spelling, punctuation and paragraphing have been retained to preserve the flavor of the original newspaper text. Such words as "cotemporary" and "contemporary" were used interchangeably, and many words had variant spellings—all of which were considered quite proper. Therefore, I have inserted *"sic"* only in those cases where a clear typographical, major spelling or other error appears in the original printed source. Spelling in letters is left unchanged. Underlining is reproduced in italic, but bold lettering and ~~strikethroughs~~ in quoted material are reproduced as found in the original source. I have italicized and capitalized "the" when a newspaper's name consists of a single word, such as *The Pacific* or *The Messenger.*

For the most part, my transcriptions had to rely on microfilms—rather than original copies—of the newspapers. A few films were badly scratched and/or unfocused, making accurate transcription very difficult. Where the context permitted an educated guess, I have provided what I believe is the correct text, followed by a question mark in brackets; in the rare case where the text is completely illegible and therefore indecipherable, I have so indicated.

The Journal History of the LDS church, a daily "scrapbook" of Mormon history consisting of journals, minutes, letters, and articles extracted (and expurgated) from church records by Andrew Jenson, is cited as Journal History. The holdings of the extensive collections,

---

[1] Bitton, *George Q. Cannon, A Biography,* 86.

including the George Q. Cannon and Brigham Young papers and other items, at the Archives of the Church of Jesus Christ of Latter-day Saints in the Family and Church History Department at Salt Lake City, Utah, are cited as LDS Archives.

Footnotes cite published sources by author, title, and page number. While some of the newspaper articles are cited by page/column (e.g. 1, 2/3), most are listed simply by the title of the article or editorial. The bibliography contains a complete listing of all the books, articles, newspapers, journals, and manuscripts referenced in the footnotes. I have italicized book titles and put article, thesis, and dissertation titles in quotation marks. Manuscript citations appear in plain text without quotation marks.

Introduction

When I first read George Q. Cannon's 1864 book, *Writings from the "Western Standard," Published in San Francisco,* I was immediately captivated by the powerful and uncompromising prose of this young, twenty-eight-year-old Mormon newspaper editor—a journalist destined to become one of the most influential men in the development of the American West. Here was a person who not only possessed an articulate command of English, but the strength of character to speak plainly and take no prisoners in his newspaper wars with the frontier California editors of his day. How unlike the usually careful, polite discourse of most journalists and religious leaders today, I thought. Here was a man of another century, taking on his world with humor, sarcasm, and often-brilliant rhetoric.

How many people have read these editorials? Long out of print, *Writings* is a rare book to which very few have access. My first thought was that someone should issue a reprint, but it occurred to me that it would be even more interesting to read Cannon's editorials in context with those to which he was reacting. To what extent had he quoted his nemeses accurately? Had he been scrupulous in his quotations, providing a fair context for his rebuttals? What about his editorials that he chose not to include in the book—were some of the more interesting ones left within the pages of his long-forgotten and short-lived Mormon newspaper? And how did those other California editors of the mid-1850s react to him? Who had gotten in the final word and in the end, who had won or lost these often bitter newspaper wars? Perhaps most importantly, what do these newspaper wars reveal about the settling of the American West?

What was needed, I concluded, was someone to research those newspapers meticulously in order to provide interested readers with a side-by-side contrast of George Q. Cannon's fascinating editorials with those of San Francisco and Sacramento newspapers of 1856 and 1857. With a semester off, I suddenly had some free time as I prepared to resign as dean of instruction and return full time to the classroom to teach English and the history of ideas. I soon found myself hunched over microfilm readers in half a dozen libraries in Utah and California, digging out the answers to these questions myself. This book is the result of those questions and the labor that followed, supplemented by a year's sabbatical and virtually every spare moment I could find over the next couple of years.

Since times have changed so radically, what is the value of reading old newspaper editorials, written by people long dead? Why struggle through often archaic and verbose prose written about issues that, for the most part, are no longer relevant? For one thing, far too many of us are ignorant of history. As time passes, the details fog into generalizations and events evaporate into vague recollection, if not misunderstanding or—even worse—historical amnesia. Few Mormons—more than half of whom reside outside the United States—are even aware of these events of 1856 and 1857, and those people not connected with the LDS church are often amazed to learn what a tumultuous period this was, not only in the history of Mormonism but in the shaping of the American West. It is precisely through the study of primary sources, relatively free from the interpretive biases of those who would pre-select our history for us through extensive editing—that we can gain a more complete understanding of the past.

There is, I hope, much here for the modern reader, Mormon and non-Mormon alike. The whole question of polygamy continues to be a fascinating conflict of social and sexual mores. Issues concerning the separation of church and state and the ethical role of journalists continue to haunt us to this day. Is what passes between consenting adults the business of the public? To what extent is governmental intrusion into deeply held religious values justified—then or now? What is the legal and moral responsibility of newspapers for the editorial positions they take? One cannot help ponder current debates about these issues when reading editorials from the newspaper wars that erupted so forcefully in California in 1856 and 1857.

The 1850s were exciting years for journalism in general and for California newspapers in particular. The decade following the 1848 discovery of gold in California was a free-wheeling one in which vigilantes thrived and newspaper editors sometimes gunned down one another in broad daylight. George Q. Cannon found himself in the middle of the colorful newspaper racket of early California, when journalism played the role in that new state that the rule-less internet plays in American life today. Newspapers were the source of the latest joke, the latest news, and the latest rumor. Constrained by few rules and tempted by endless possibilities, newspaper editors—few of whom were experienced professionals—took on the world, often heedless of the consequences. Reading these editorials provides a rollicking, first-hand view of mid-nineteenth-century America, with a particular focus on the Western frontier.

Moreover, the newspaper wars that form the heart of this study provide insight into the relationships between Mormons and non-Mormons as the Church of Jesus Christ of Latter-day Saints assumed its central role in the development of the West. Why did Californians, especially, feel so threatened by and preoccupied with the Mormons? What was the relationship between religion and politics in the West just prior to the Civil War? How did the excesses of Utah's religious reformation of this period affect the relationships among Indians, Mormons, and other white settlers? How real was the perceived rebellion in Utah Territory that prompted President Buchanan to replace Governor Brigham Young and send in federal troops? To what extent can California newspapers be credited or blamed for the Latter-day Saints' decision to abandon their colonizing footholds in California and other parts of the West outside of Utah Territory? This study does not provide definitive answers to such questions, but it presents the primary sources (heretofore unavailable) which form the foundation to scholarly probing of these questions. In the process, this book explores these and related issues by presenting letters, editorials, and excerpts from books of that period.

For those interested in the development of the American West, it is critically important to understand how the Mormons saw themselves and were seen by others. One of the major premises of this series on the

Kingdom of the West is that the Mormon story is not just a saga of Utah, but rather pervades most regions and events of the American frontier. What better way to experience the political and social turmoil of the time than through these fascinating newspaper duels, which reveal so much about the mores and prejudices of the day? Nineteenth-century newspapers engaged in toe-to-toe journalism hardly known today except, perhaps, in the tabloids of the United Kingdom. Both libel laws and subtle "spin" were virtually non-existent, and Cannon and his various nemeses responded to one another with raw emotion. It is when we are most angry that we are most likely to drop our guards, betraying our true feelings. There is therefore much truth to be found between the lines of these often-bitter editorials—truths that reflect on both sides of "the Mormon problem."

It must be emphasized that many of Cannon's editorials dealt with matters no longer sanctioned by the Church of Jesus Christ of Latter-day Saints. In no case is this truer than in his defense of polygamy, a practice officially abandoned by the LDS church in 1890. Nor is the tone with which Cannon confronts his "enemies" that which is generally employed by official defenders of Mormonism today. But it is precisely through this fiery rhetoric of mid-nineteenth-century journalism that one can best understand the zeal with which the church was both attacked and defended. This foment ultimately contributed to events that continue to influence Mormonism to this day, such as President James Buchanan's controversial decision to send federal troops to Utah in 1857.

We cannot forget that history has an uncomfortable habit of repeating itself, albeit in forms and combinations that defy accurate prediction. Reviewing California's ancient newspaper battles might help us confront the more subtle appearances of bigotry and prejudice today. If a group of Americans could once be actively persecuted—and very nearly destroyed—primarily because of their strange beliefs and provocative defiance of the power and authority of the U.S. Government, how safe are those who march to the beat of different drums today? Have we really progressed all that much from the time of George Q. Cannon? Perhaps a study of the events of his day can better help us understand—and guard against—the Wacos and Ruby Ridges of our own time.

Cannon was not always right. He rejected out of hand the reports of Mormon complicity in the massacre at Mountain Meadows, completely unaware of the dark truth. Nor did he hesitate to employ virtually any rhetorical device—including the occasional argument *ad hominem*—to help him drive home a point. But in terms of sheer brilliance of intellect and precision of writing, George Q. Cannon stands in a class by himself as the greatest public defender of the Mormon faith of his time. It is no wonder that in subsequent decades he took on the leadership of the United Kingdom's *Millenial Star* and then returned to Utah to become, in effect, publisher to the entire church while rising in influence as a politician, businessman, and counselor to four presidents of the Church of Jesus Christ of Latter-day Saints.

Chapter I

"A NEWSPAPER DEVOTED TO THE CAUSE OF TRUTH"

In a live television interview with talk-show host Larry King on 8 September 1998, Gordon B. Hinckley, the fourteenth president of the Church of Jesus Christ of Latter-day Saints, was asked by a viewer/caller why his faith did not respond more aggressively to its critics in the media. Hinckley, who had spent years in public relations activities, responded, "We do come out sometimes. But you have to know this, that if you get into a fight with somebody, you just excite more curiosity and create more problems than you settle."[1]

This response by the man the Latter-day Saints regard as a "prophet, seer and revelator" was totally consistent with earlier pronouncements, including the often-quoted simile popularized by a late Mormon Apostle.[2] Bruce R. McConkie wrote, "The Church is like a great caravan—organized, prepared, following an appointed course. . . . What does it matter if a few barking dogs snap at the heels of the weary travelers? Or that predators claim those few who fall by the way? The caravan moves on."[3]

Remaining above the fray has been the general position of the LDS church since the early twentieth century, and was sometimes the position of the church in its early days. Consider the advice from President Brigham Young to the son of assassinated Apostle Parley P. Pratt in 1859. Pratt had apparently asked how the Saints should react to a popular anti-Mormon book written by Benjamin G. Ferris. Young was unequivocal in his response:

---

[1] Interview with Larry King, aired 8 September 1998, transcript courtesy of CNN at www.cnn.com.

[2] At the top of the hierarchy of the Church of Jesus Christ of Latter-day Saints is a president, assisted by two counselors. They, in turn, are assisted by a quorum of twelve apostles. For all intents and purposes, this was the same structure in place during Brigham Young's day.

[3] McConkie, "The Caravan Moves On," 85.

> Ferris' book is not worthy of any notice, for it is difficult, if not impossible, to touch *pitch* and not be defiled, and as *notoriety* is what the world are after the more his book should be noticed by us the greater would be its sale, and the more noted would be Ferris, which is what he is after, hence the *let alone policy* is the one to be pursued in this matter both *publicly* and *privately.*[4]

This was not always Young's position, however, especially with respect to the "Gentile" world. The term Gentile was used then, and to some extent still is used—though typically in lighter, or humorous contexts—to designate all non-Mormons, including Jews. Early usage also generally carried a negative connotation. As a leading non-Mormon scholar has written, "Gentiles, early on, were more often than not castigated as enemies and persecutors. For many decades, the term *Gentile* was rarely simply a descriptor indicating nonmemberhip; it meant a potential or actual adversary, unless a person somehow qualified as friendly."[5] In the early days of the Church of Jesus Christ of Latter-day Saints, the term "Jack-Mormon" referred to "a man opposed to illegal violence against the Mormons," though today it typically refers to a backsliding Saint.[6]

Perhaps one reason the term Gentile has lost much of its bite today is that it is easier to be magnanimous and to disregard one's critics from a position of power, prominence, and influence as is the case as the eleven-million member LDS church enters the twenty-first century. But in the middle of the nineteenth century, when Mormonism was literally fighting for its life, the eye-for-an-eye doctrine of the Old Testament was often much more the rule than Christ's admonition to love one's enemies.

At that time, the Saints of Utah were still licking their wounds from their forced expulsion from Missouri and Illinois and were under attack almost daily in the national press. This was due to several factors, including their theocratic government (perceived as un-American), their communal economic practices, and most visibly, their 1852 public acknowledgment of polygamy—a hitherto vociferously denied and secret practice that virtually all other Christians regarded as morally repugnant. Most Americans did not trust Mormons, and the sentiment was more than reciprocated as first the new Republican party, and soon the Democrats as well, united against a common threat—Mormon polygamy.

---

[4] Young to Pratt, 19 October 1859, Archives of the Family and Church History Department of the Church of Jesus Christ of Latter-day Saints (hereafter cited as LDS Archives).

[5] Shipps, *Sojourner in the Promised Land,* 128.

[6] "Fatal Affray at Carthage," 19 July 1845, *The Messenger,* 22.

With the exception of an average of eighty elders called each year to serve missions,[7] Brigham Young encouraged his people to withdraw from the Gentile world, to avoid outside business dealings as much as possible and to build up Zion within the remote regions of the West. Nonetheless, it was also apparent to that astute leader that such isolation could not last and that there were great advantages in convincing the nation that Utah was worthy of statehood. From the earliest settlement of Utah, the clear preference for statehood over territorial status was simply an extension of the desire for self-rule, expressed by Brigham Young as early as 1846 in a letter to President Polk:

> Resolved, that should we locate within the territory of the United States, as we anticipate, we would esteem a territorial government of our own as one of the richest boons of earth, and while we appreciate the constitution of the United States as the most precious among the nations, we feel that we had rather retreat to the deserts, island or mountain caves than consent to be ruled by governors and judges whose hands are drenched in the blood of innocence and virtue, who delight in injustice and oppression.[8]

When he wrote the above letter, Young was unaware of the political strings attached to territories; it was Col. Thomas L. Kane, Young's most important non-Mormon ally, a Philadelphia lawyer and the son of a powerful Democratic judge, who helped him understand that his original objective—political autonomy—could better be met via statehood.[9]

Whether officially designated as a state or territory, the Mormons wanted their own kingdom in the West as they prepared for Christ's Second Coming and the establishment of His Kingdom of Heaven on earth. This goal could never be achieved simply by turning the other cheek whenever someone lashed out at the struggling church. An important element of Young's public relations campaign was to establish newspapers in key cities in the United States and then turn them loose to promote a strong defense of Mormon doctrines—particularly polygamy and theocracy—through an unrelenting offense directed at its many critics.

The press had always been important in the history of the LDS

[7] Whittaker, "Brigham Young and the Missionary Enterprise," 89. The title "elder" was and is a priesthood office, applied specifically—but not exclusively—to missionaries.

[8] Cited in Larson, *Prelude to the Kingdom*, 72.

[9] Walker, "Thomas L. Kane and Utah's Quest for Self-Government," 111. For a brief sketch on Kane, see Arrington, "In Honorable Remembrance."

church, beginning with the first printing of *The Book of Mormon* in 1830. To help spread the restored gospel, as well as to answer the attacks from its growing number of enemies, the most vicious and dedicated of whom were often disaffected former members, the church sponsored a series of newspapers. This began with *The Evening and the Morning Star*, published in Independence, Missouri, during 1832-1833; after a mob destroyed the press, the paper was published in Kirtland, Ohio, during 1833–1834. Still, prejudice and persecution followed the young religion throughout its wanderings from New York to Ohio, Missouri, and Illinois. One of the most grievous attacks against the Mormons was the demolition of its printing press in July 1833. Arguably the single most significant contributor to the final attacks on Joseph Smith was the destruction of the opposition newspaper, *The Nauvoo Expositor*, in June 1844—an act ordered by the Nauvoo City Council, under the leadership of Joseph Smith in his capacity as mayor.[10]

The *Expositor* was published by Mormon dissenters who, though still believing in *The Book of Mormon* and other basic doctrines of the church, had concluded Joseph Smith was a fallen prophet. As suggested by the name of their newspaper, it was their objective to expose the "religious despotism" they believed had crept into the Church of Jesus Christ of Latter-day Saints.[11]

According to Gustive O. Larson:

> The publication of the *Expositor* put Smith in a dilemma. If he did not stop its publication, exposure of the secrets of polygamy and the political kingdom of God might well rend the church asunder and leave it a prey to the Gentiles. If he closed the paper, he faced charges of flaunting one of the most sacred of American liberties, the freedom of the press . . . If the Mormon prophet could not afford to tolerate an apostate newspaper dedicated to the exposure of practices and principles which—at least for the present—had to remain secret at all cost, he had no recourse but to silence the press by force.[12]

[10] Legal scholar Dallin H. Oaks (now an apostle in the LDS church) concluded that while "alternative means might better have been employed . . . the common assumption of historians that the action taken by the city council to suppress the paper as a nuisance was entirely illegal is not well founded. Aside from the damages for unnecessary destruction of the press, for which the Nauvoo authorities were unquestionably liable, the remaining actions of the council, including its interpretation of the constitutional guarantee of a free press, can be supported by reference to the law of their day." Oaks, "Suppression of the *Nauvoo Expositor*," 903. See also Oaks and Hill, *Carthage Conspiracy*, 14–15.

[11] "Introductory," *Nauvoo Expositor*, 7 June 1844, 2.

[12] Larson, *Prelude to the Kingdom*, 158.

Regardless of the legal issue, the destruction of this press proved a grave mistake, setting in motion events that led to the murder of Joseph Smith and his brother, Hyrum, on 27 June 1844 at Carthage, Illinois, and the Western exodus of the Mormons two years later.

Once safely in the Great Basin, the church established its own weekly newspaper in Great Salt Lake City in 1850, the *Deseret News*,[13] while continuing its support of the *Millennial Star*, which had published continuously in England since 1840. Both of these media organs were, quite literally, playing to the choir. What came to be needed were outlets of Mormon opinion in the wider world. Brigham Young established additional journals and newspapers in four major American cities, three of which were at gathering centers for converts immigrating to Zion. This was an act of considerable foresight for a man who often commented that he had only eight days of formal education.

The first of these Mormon-owned publications was *The Seer*, a journal published by Orson Pratt in Washington, D.C. from 1853 to 1854. This was immediately followed by *The St. Louis Luminary*, edited by Erastus Snow from 1854 to 1855. *The Mormon*, published from 1855 to 1857 in New York City, was the forthright title of the journal edited by John Taylor, who later became the third president of the church. The fourth, the *Western Standard*, published and edited by Taylor's nephew, George Q. Cannon, is the focus of this book.

The eldest of seven children, Cannon was born in Liverpool, England, on 11 January 1827, three years before Joseph Smith organized what later became known as the Church of Jesus Christ of Latter-day Saints in upstate New York. The Cannon family learned of what was purported to be a restoration of Christ's original church through one of its twelve modern apostles, John Taylor, Cannon's uncle. By the time George was approaching his sixteenth birthday, the family was en route to Nauvoo, Illinois, the new capital of the Mormons. Tragically, his mother died on the voyage and was buried at sea.

As a young man, Cannon experienced firsthand the many tribulations and persecutions visited upon the Mormons by hostile neighbors. Two

[13] For an interesting treatment of the early *Deseret News*, including some discussion of the newspaper wars that developed within Utah Territory—some continuing today—see McLaws, *Spokesman for the Kingdom*. The word "deseret" appears in the *Book of Mormon* (Ether 2:3) and is translated as "honey bee." The Mormons hoped their state would be named the State of Deseret and to this day, a beehive appears on the official seal for the state of Utah.

months after the martyrdom of the prophet Joseph, Cannon's father also died, leaving him an orphan under the care of his apostle-uncle. Together with one of his sisters, they migrated from Illinois and then Iowa to the Salt Lake Valley, arriving in October 1847, three months after the first pioneer company.

In fall 1849, George Q. Cannon and a few others were called by the church's new leader, Brigham Young, on an unusual mission, or long-term religious calling, to California. Notwithstanding Young's hostility to mining as an activity appropriate to the Saints, their assignment—driven by the church's economic necessity—was to mine for gold to help build up the Kingdom of God on earth and provide income for destitute church leaders. "There was no place that I would not rather have gone to at that time," Cannon recalled, "than California."[14] His first experience in El Dorado was not a happy one. Cannon and his party nearly perished on their way to the Golden State, and his time there was one of life's chapters he wished to forget.[15]

After a miserable year in California, Cannon accepted a second mission, along with nine others, to preach to the natives of the Sandwich Islands, or Hawaii. Here he enjoyed incredible success. Not only did he and his companions baptize some four thousand native islanders, but he quickly learned Hawaiian and accepted the heavy responsibility of translating *The Book of Mormon* into the native language. On his way home, after serving in Hawaii for four years, Cannon was hired by an old family friend, Apostle Parley P. Pratt, to assist as a copyist with the writing of Pratt's autobiography in San Francisco.

Almost immediately after his return to Utah in spring 1855, Cannon was called by Brigham Young to return to California. The calling came at the behest of Pratt who had made it clear to Young that Cannon would be indispensable to publishing *The Book of Mormon* in Hawaiian and to starting a San Francisco newspaper.[16] This time Cannon's bride, Elizabeth Hoagland, and two assistants, Matthew F. Wilkie and Joseph Bull, accompanied him.[17]

---

[14] Cannon, "Twenty Years Ago," 13.

[15] Landon, ed., *The Journals of George Q. Cannon, Vol. I,* 82.

[16] Pratt to Young, February 1855, LDS Archives.

[17] Later, in response to Cannon's request, Young sent Cannon's brother David—then only fifteen years old—as another assistant. Still later, William H. Shearman, a California Missionary, also joined the staff.

Brigham Young traveled with Cannon and his companions at the beginning of their journey through Utah on the southern route to California. Before bidding adieu to his president and prophet at Cedar City, Cannon asked for a priesthood blessing. He retrospectively recorded a synopsis of that blessing in his journal for Sunday, 20 May 1855.

> I spoke to Br. Brigham about having him bless myself and Elizabeth before we parted; he told me he would, and to come down to Bro. [Isaac] Haight's in the evening. We went down, and listened with great pleasure to his remarks elicited during an evening's visit. He blessed us, Bro. [Jedediah Morgan] Grant [Young's second counselor] & himself laying on hands, and said, they thanked the Lord for the wisdom He had given me already even in my youth and that he would still continue to give me wisdom and when I should take up the pen to write I should be blessed with wisdom should be blessed in writing and publishing, and that the Lord would inspire me with thoughts and ideas that what I should write and publish should be acceptable to the people of God. To open my mouth and lift up my voice and not fear for I should be borne off victorious. I should be prospered greatly and have all the desires of my heart; should accomplish a mighty work, and return again to enjoy the society of my friends in the midst of the mountains . . . Bro. Brigham told me to practice writing as much as I possibly could. Bro. Jedediah told me to let them know I was a Cannon & to roar.[18]

In addition to eventually replacing Parley P. Pratt as President of the Pacific Mission, Cannon was given two primary responsibilities: to print copies of the Hawaiian *Book of Mormon* and to establish a newspaper.[19] While yet hard at work on the translation, the twenty-eight-year-old Cannon set his sights on establishing the newspaper through which he would indeed learn how to roar.

Cannon was no neophyte to the printing business. He had been exposed to it for five years as a youth while assisting as a compositor, or typesetter, for his uncle, John Taylor, who had been the editor and publisher of the *Times and Seasons* as well as the *Nauvoo Neighbor* (previously, the *Nauvoo Wasp*). Nonetheless, this was a daunting challenge.

In a letter to Brigham Young, dated 31 August 1855, Cannon laid out his plans for the newspaper, anticipating some of the difficulties that lay before him—particularly his inability to hire much-needed additional

---

[18] George Q. Cannon Journal No. 1, May 10 1855—February 1856, California, LDS Archives.

[19] For more on Cannon's assignment to both translate and then publish *The Book of Mormon* in the Hawaiian language, see Whittaker, "Placing the Keystone."

help—while characteristically asserting optimism. He credited Apostle Orson Hyde, the presiding authority in Carson Valley, with the suggestion for the name of the paper (which Pratt had originally planned to call *The Mormon Herald*[20]) and, though anxious to begin work on it, felt it best to delay until his Hawaiian translation of *The Book of Mormon* was printed.[21]

If Cannon's secret hope was that President Young would authorize him to hire more men to launch the paper, it was quickly dashed when Young responded by agreeing whole-heartedly to delay publication to reduce costs, clarifying his expectation that the paper would be self-sufficient:

> We fully coincide with you in relation to deferring the publication of the paper so as to obviate the necessity of hiring more hands. I think it a good suggestion as it becomes necessary especially in these hard times to keep within our own resources and not run into debt. It is our wish that your office may meet its own expenses and be sustained by the brethren in that region.
>
> We have written to our brethren at San Bernardino[22] to patronize our paper when it shall appear, and we trust that you will be sustained as you go along by pursuing the course above mentioned as suggested by you; at all events it is proper for you to keep as much as possible within your present resources, and never go beyond a fair and reliable prospective.[23]

Two months later, Young restated his aversion to debt while clarifying what he felt the purpose of the newspaper should be:

> I do not feel in the least that you have been dilatory in not publishing a paper. I would prefer its still further postponement than have you involve yourself in debt. 'Tis true we would like to see a newspaper devoted to the cause of truth, sending forth the testimony of the gospel in California, and think that we will through the blessings of the Lord be able to accomplish it . . . The Lord will open the way before you, even as He has in times past;

---

[20] Cannon, *Writings from the "Western Standard,"* vii.

[21] Cannon to Young, 31 August 1855, LDS Archives.

[22] San Bernardino, from its foundation as a Mormon colony in 1851 until its abandonment in the face of the Utah War in 1857, was the major stronghold of the Saints in California during this period. While Cannon did not have any ecclesiastical authority over the settlement, it was an important source of support for the *Western Standard* and all Mormons in California. For histories of San Bernardino as a Mormon settlement, see Cowan and Homer, *California Saints,* chapter 10 and Lyman, *San Bernardino.*

[23] Young to Cannon, 30 October 1855, LDS Archives. In this and other letters, Young was responding to Cannon's specific request for "any counsel you may feel to give." Cannon to Young, 1 October 1855, LDS Archives. Although he gave such counsel from time to time, it is clear that Young had great confidence in Cannon's ability to make most decisions himself: "So far as I am informed, I cordially approbate your course and policy . . . ." Young to Cannon, 29 November 1855, LDS Archives.

and if He does not work in the hearts of the people, and aid in the dissemination of truth through his servants, but little will be done that will be worthy of attention. The press is a powerful lever or agency through which the Lord can reach the minds of the people . . .[24]

Meanwhile, Cannon had completed printing the initial run of 2,000 copies of the Hawaiian translation of *The Book of Mormon* and was ready to launch the newspaper. On 4 January 1856, its prospectus was printed and widely circulated:

PROSPECTUS

OF THE

WESTERN STANDARD

It is the intention of the Subscriber to commence the publication of a Weekly Newspaper bearing the above title, the first number to be issued about the middle of February next, to be devoted to the interests of the Church of Jesus Christ of Latter-day Saints—to be an exponent of its doctrines, and a medium through which the public can derive correct information in relation to its objects and progress. Its columns will also contain items of general intelligence and the current news of the day, both foreign and domestic, which, from our position, situated in the Queen City of the Pacific, we will be able to obtain at the earliest dates and in ample detail.

It will be our aim to make "The Western Standard" an interesting and instructive sheet; and, as its columns will be enriched by the correspondence of the Elders of the Church, who are labouring in different portions of the earth, and by choice selections from the leading papers of the United States and Great Britain, we trust it will be satisfactory to our subscribers.

To the Saints, the announcement that another publication is being issued, under the sanction of the First Presidency of the Church, that will be found on the side of truth, defending it and heralding it forth, will be received with pleasure, and will, no doubt, meet with their hearty co-operation and support.

As a medium of advertising, the columns of "The Western Standard" present unusual facilities to business men and general dealers, as it will be extensively circulated among the emigrating portion of our Community.

GEO. Q. CANNON.

San Francisco, Cal., January 4th, 1856[25]

In a letter to President Young, the youthful editor forwarded a copy of

[24] Young to Cannon, 30 January 1856, LDS Archives.

[25] *Latter-day Saints' Millennial Star,* 18:171. Copies of the Prospectus were also printed in the initial edition of *The Western Standard* and were widely circulated via various means both within California and Utah, with varying subscription costs, as noted below.

the prospectus. He suggested that in consideration of the economic stress being experienced by the "Saints in the Vallies," their subscription rate be only half that of the five dollar per annum which was the going rate for weeklies in California. His plan was to sell enough subscriptions in California to cover the costs of a printing office and then "have the proceeds of the Subscriptions in the Territory placed at the disposal of the Church, as the [Deseret] 'News' is at present." He noted that he had found it necessary to incur considerable debt in amassing the materials necessary for production, "but I feel quite hopeful that, with economy and faith, we will be able to liquidate it, and also be able to avoid it in future."[26]

On 1 March, Cannon again wrote to Young and modestly announced that the first edition of the paper had been issued on 23 February 1856, but not without difficulty:

> It has taken longer than I anticipated, yet we have not been dilatory. We had to get a great many little things both of material and furniture that we did not need for the Book, which occupies time; and as we had no funds to draw upon, only such as I contrived to get in very small amounts, we had to keep planning to 'make ends meet.' We have now quite a nice *little* office, of course we have not every thing as convenient as they have in large offices, yet we think it first rate, and we are able to do our work with but little bother. We think it a pretty close approximation to the sectarians' idea of the Lord's creation of the earth—out of nothing. The Lord be praised for it; his hand has been over us for good from the time of our leaving the valley up to the present, and I feel assured that nothing but His power could have supported us.
>
> Since the paper started we have been kept very busy and have had but little time [to] spare. We find that it is [as] much as three of us can get along with; the brethren set it up and Bro. Wilkie works it off, while I keep myself busily employed, writing, selecting, *devil*-ing,[27] putting up and folding papers, etc. We all feel in good spirits being contented and happy, and can realize that, whether in the Valleys of the mountains, on the islands of the sea, or in California, so long as we are in the line of our duty we can enjoy the Spirit of peace and happiness.

Cannon may have been subtly complaining, but it is clear that he was sincere in the humility with which he approached the greatest challenge of his young life—not only to preside over the Pacific Mission,[28] but to

[26] Cannon to Young, 30 January 1856, LDS Archives.

[27] A "printer's devil" was another term for the apprentice to a printer and "deviling" referred to the various tasks assigned to that apprentice. Cannon began his newspaper career in Nauvoo as a printer's devil to his uncle, John Taylor.

edit and publish a weekly newspaper with little or no financial assistance. He concluded:

> I rely greatly on the prayers offered up so unceasingly by yourself and the brethren in behalf of the elders; I never felt my own weakness and the great need of the assist of the Lord so much as at present, and I should be tempted, did I not realize that the Lord can bestow strength sufficient on all those who put their trust in Him, to shrink from the position which I at present occupy.
>
> I shall be pleased to hear from you often, and shall be obliged if you will continue to suggest and give us counsel on any thing that may appear needful. If there is anything in the arrangement or in the spirit of the articles that you wish altered—as I know I lack wisdom and experience in these things—I hope you will not fail to mention it and I will try and profit by it.[29]

Young's next letter to Cannon made no mention of the newspaper because he had not yet received his copy, which had to be sent by steamer to San Pedro and from there overland to the Mormon outpost of San Bernardino and then on to Great Salt Lake City. Young noted that he "was much rejoiced in receiving a copy of Hawain [*sic*] Edition of the Book of Mormon." He related news from home, noting some recent troubles with some of the Indians, and described the territory's poverty. "My self as well as nearly every body around me have rationed their families to a half pound (of flour) each per day and by frequent fastings save considerable amount even from this allowance to give to the poor."[30] Little wonder that Brigham Young later used Cannon's ingenuity and frugality as an example to support his policy of sending missionaries to distant parts of the world without financial support or—as the phrase went—"without purse or script."[31]

Cannon had overcome great obstacles in establishing a newspaper in San Francisco. Parley P. Pratt had given up the project and even some of the more active and prominent California Mormons opposed his efforts from the outset. Forty-three years later, Cannon reminisced about his initial efforts in California:

---

[28] Although Cannon confined his activities almost exclusively to northern California, the Pacific Mission also included Oregon and Washington territories and the British and Russian American possessions to the north.

[29] Cannon to Young, 1 March 1856, LDS Archives.

[30] Young to Cannon, 3 April 1856, LDS Archives.

[31] Brigham Young, "Testimony to the Divinity...Satan Angry," 31 August, 1856, *Journal of Discourses*, 4:36, quoted in Newquist, "The Western Standard," 238–39; and Flake, *George Q. Cannon: His Missionary Years*, 107.

> Well, I was but young, and I looked younger than I really was; and the Saints in San Francisco said, "It is no use." One of the leading men said to me, "If you have got a thousand dollars, you can open an office here." They said everything almost to discourage me. I said, "The Lord has sent me here; I am going to publish a paper here; I am going to publish the Book of Mormon here." I need not rehearse to you the particulars of how the Lord opened the way. For many weeks we lived on bread and water. Shortly afterward, I having opened an office and commenced the publication of the book, the officers of the branch and conference asked me if I would not attend a meeting that they were going to hold. I supposed that they, seeing how destitute we were (myself and the two Elders who were with me, and my wife), were going to do something to assist us; but instead of that, they notified me that they would not be responsible for any debt of my contracting. They saw I was going ahead, but they did not want me to deceive myself with the idea that I could fall back on them and expect them to pay any debts that I might contract. You can imagine what effect that would have on any of you. It stirred me up a good deal, and I prophesied to them—for I had the spirit of prophesy—and told them to get out of my way and not impede my work. They told me to shut up the office. I said to them, "I am sent here to do a work, and with God's help I will do it; and if you do not want to help in this, the Lord will raise up others that will." And He did. In a very short time I was able to send to President Young nearly two thousand dollars in cash tithing.[32] Money was offered me by the thousands to assist me in my work. I did not avail myself of the [loan] offer, because I knew if I did I would not be able to return it for a while. But I published the Book of Mormon, and sent 2,500 copies to the Sandwich Islands; and I published a paper, and did so till the Buchanan war broke us up.[33]

Part of the reluctance of the California Saints to contribute to the establishment of the *Standard* may have stemmed from a disastrous investment in a "vessel designed to sail between San Francisco and the Sandwich Islands for commercial purposes and also for the emigration from the islands to Utah of the native Saints." The boat sank, along with the confidence many investors had demonstrated in the leaders who had promoted the idea.[34] Nonetheless, even the Mormon apostate Sam

[32] Flake, citing Evans and Cannon, eds., *Cannon Family Historical Treasury*, refers to a gift of $3,000 from "a wealthy Hawaiian planter" that was subsequently sent to Brigham Young by Cannon, resulting in a great relief to the church at a time of "serious financial crisis." Ibid., 100. It is probable that this is the source of the $2,000 to which Cannon refers; whether the $3,000 figure is in error or whether Cannon found it necessary to use part of that gift for local purposes is unknown. See also Whittaker, "Placing the Keystone."

[33] Cannon, "Discourse at the Utah Stake," *The Deseret Weekly*, 17 April 1898.

[34] Cummings, "Shining Lights," 127; cited in Flake, *George Q. Cannon: His Missionary Years*, 105.

Brannan, who was Cannon's landlord at the time, donated a fifty-dollar gold-piece in support of the *Western Standard*.[35] By May 1856, Cannon could report to Brigham Young that "agents in Cedar City, Parowan, Manti, Nephi, Palmyra and Pleasant Grove, forwarded their orders, which amount, in the aggregate, to 147 copies for these six settlements."[36] It would be some time before the newspaper was out of debt, but Cannon steadfastly refused any financial assistance from Salt Lake. Cannon specifically requested Daniel H. Wells, who replaced the late Jedediah M. Grant as Young's second counselor, not to credit "wheat, etc., forwarded to the Tithing Office as pay for the 'Standard.'" He explained, "I feel it would be wrong to draw one dollar out of the Hive for the support of a paper here."[37]

The venture started slowly, but by fall 1856 more than eight hundred subscriptions had been sold in Utah alone.[38] Eventually, the paper began to realize a modest profit. The growing amount of space given to paid advertisements gives some indication of the financial success of the *Western Standard* over the nineteen-month life of the paper. From the outset, Cannon was not shy in hawking advertising space, and over time, merchants in San Francisco, San Bernardino, and Great Salt Lake City began to buy space in the fledgling newspaper. Nowhere was Cannon's bid for advertisers more clear than in the following "Notice to Potential Advertisers" that appeared in the first issues:

> To Merchants and other Advertisers: As the Standard will have a very large circulation among the inhabitants of Utah Territory, independent of its extensive circulation in this State, strong inducements are offered to business men of this vicinity to favor us with their advertising patronage. There is at present an immense amount of goods purchased by the people of Utah, and San Bernardino County Cal., into this city; at the former point also, the Standard will be read by the hundreds of emigrants who sojourn at that place on their way from the east. We call particular attention to Hotel keepers and others to these facts. Those merchants who are already aware of the great and constantly increasing trade between the two cities of Great Salt Lake and San Francisco, can appreciate the advantages that are offered. The cost of advertising will be made as low as can possibly be afforded.

---

[35] Cannon to Cannon, 7 January 1921, cited in Bitton, *George Q. Cannon: A Biography*, 75–76.

[36] Cannon to Young, 26 May 1856, LDS Archives.

[37] Cannon to Wells, 4 March 1857, LDS Archives.

[38] Young to Cannon, 27 September 1856, LDS Archives. The Utah subscriptions consistently outstripped those Cannon was able to sell in California.

The masthead of the *Western Standard,* designed by T. C. Boyd. It features an imagined Mormon temple in the heights of the Rocky Mountains, to which people from all nations are gathering by land and by sea. *Courtesy, LDS Archives.*

The first issue contained but a single advertisement, for T.C. Boyd, Wood Engraver. This ad ran for an entire year, probably because it was Boyd who engraved the *Western Standard's* striking masthead, and it was printed not as a paid advertisement but one that was bartered for services rendered. Nevertheless, the newspaper attracted some twenty advertisers by its peak in May 1857. One of these, "John Baptist, Manufacturer of Trusses of all Kinds and Sizes," advertised "Riding Belts, Suspensories, Knee Caps, Laced Stockings, Wooden Legs, Abdominal Belts, Chest Suspenders, Dr. Linton's Side Splints, etc."[39] Verplanck and McMullin made themselves available as "Jobbers and General Dealers in Groceries, Provisions, Wines, Liquors, etc." The firm of "Graves and Smith, Coppersmiths, Plumbers and Hose Makers" advised the public of their "Worms, Brew Kettles, Heaters and Stills made to order." Their ad was accompanied by a prominent illustration of a state-of-the-art still.

I Had a Load on My Shoulders

Arriving in San Francisco only to find that Pratt had already returned to Utah was a shock to Cannon, for he had assumed he had been called

[39] Morgan, *The Great Salt Lake,* 274–82, tells of the notorious career and subsequent demise of one Jean Baptiste, who might possibly be this John Baptist.

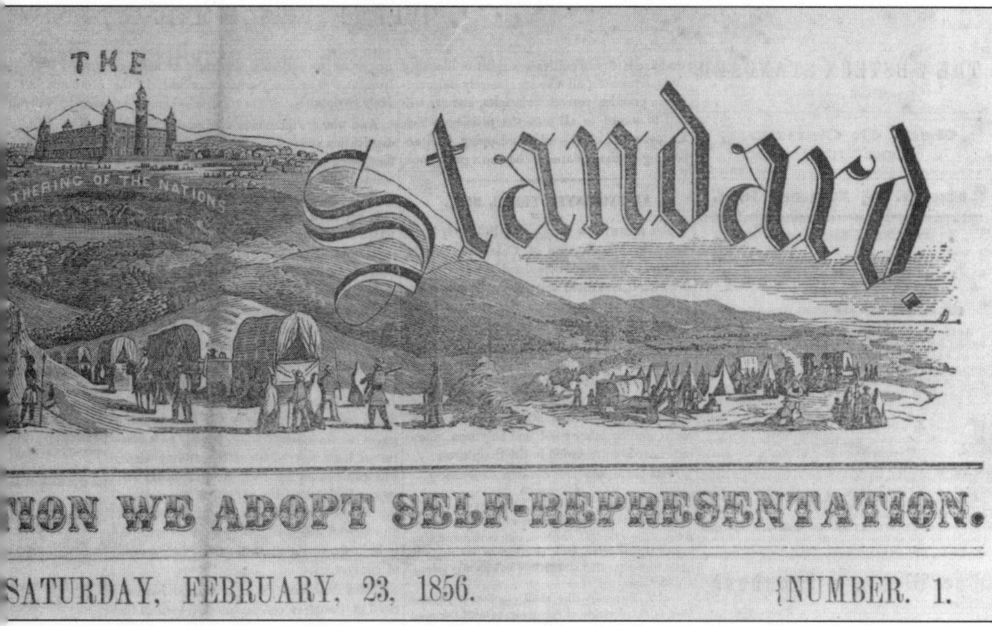

to assist his older and more experienced friend rather than assume responsibility for the entire enterprise. Writing to Brigham Young in July, Cannon expressed his concerns but also revealed his confidence in his own talents and the ultimate success of his mission.

GEORGE Q. CANNON TO BRIGHAM YOUNG, 27 JULY 1855,
LDS ARCHIVES.

San Francisco, July 27th, 1855.
Dear Bro. Brigham:

As another mail leaves to-morrow for the valley I take the liberty to write you a few lines to assist in keeping you informed in relation to matters and things in this country and in relation to our proceedings and success since our arrival here.

We were prospered on our journey after parting with you at Cedar city as well as could be expected, although we did not make as quick a trip by several days as was talked about before we left you – we arrived at San Bernardino in 16 1/2 days from Cedar city, without the loss of an animal. We found it very hot on the last deserts before we struck the Mohave river. Hearing, when I arrived in San Bernardino, that Bro. Parley was thinking of returning to the valley on or about the 1st of July, I made all the haste possible to arrive in San Francisco before he left; and we were ~~by the~~ enabled, by taking steamer at San Pedro, to reach here by the 24th of June. Bro. Parley had crossed the Bay a few days before, intending to stop at Bro. [John] Naile's until the 25th of June when he would start for the Valley. Leaving the brethren who accompanied me in San Francisco, I started for Bro. Naile's, and succeeded in meting with Bro. Parley at his place the evening prior to his departure; he appeared to be glad to see me, and had been looking anxiously for my arrival. He had written letters containing all the necessary counsel and information and left for me in San Francisco. I was pleased to have a personal interview with Bro. Pratt as it was much more satisfactory.

The press, type, paper, &c. was stored in this place, and the new debt which the press, in its transportation ~~of the press~~ from Honolulu with the cartage storage &c., had incurred, amounted to a little rising of $100. Upon examination of the press we found the ribs broken and before the press could be put up they had to be recast or repaired; and after some little trouble, we succeeded in getting new ones cast.

Two or three days after my ~~arrival~~ return from my visit to Bro. Parley, Bro. O. Hyde arrived here and brought with him a joint letter written by himself and Bro. Parley – he having met with Bro. Parley between Sacramento and Stockton – in which I was instructed to obtain a suitable building here, and proceed with the publication of the Hawaiian translation of the Book of Mormon; the publication of the paper was to be deferred until further instruction from you Bro. Hyde having written to you for fresh counsel. Bro. H. staid three days and then returned to Carson Valley. After Bro. H. left we were successful, after considerable search for a suitable place at a reasonable rent – in obtaining two rooms in a fire proof brick building on Montgomery St., belonging to S. Brannan; his brother has, however, the renting of all his buildings.

We soon removed our press and material from the place of storage to our new office and got tables, stands &c. made and used the utmost economy dispensing with everything that was not absolutely indispensable. We found everything, with the exception of the broken ribs, in tolerably good order. Our title letter was not what had been ordered, not being suitable for book work, but it will be useful for a newspaper. We expected a better quality of paper but what we have answers tolerably well. They sent a regular fount of type with sorts suited to English printing and did not send any extra sorts, as ordered to do, suitable for a publication in the Hawaiian language but we have got along very well – having quite a large fount – with everything but lower case k's, a letter very frequently used in that language, occurring as often as e's in ours. In consequence of the small quantity of this sort we have been obliged to issue an octavo instead of a half sheet of sixteens, but hope to be able in a few days to raise sufficient for such a form, as we have sent to Sacramento, where they use more of this kind of letter – Long Primer – than they do here, – to get them. I send you herewith a copy of the two first forms, which we have struck off; the title page, testimonies &c. we have reserved until the last as there may be a few odd pages at the last and it will save extra work.

When I look at the progress we have already made – although it is but little – I feel that we are realizing your blessings; for when I learned the situation of affairs here, and that Bro. Parley, with pretty much all those who had the power and the disposition to assist, had gone, I felt that I had a load on my shoulders, but when I took hold with the determination by the help of the Lord to effect something, gleam after gleam of sunshine shone in my path dispersing the gloom, and giving me fresh testimony that God was still mindful of His servants, however weak and insignificant they might be. The saints here who have any disposition to assist are quite poor and there are but few of them and as the office at present brings in no income we have to depend on donations to sustain by economising we have been able to the present time to sustain ourselves and I feel sanguine for the future. In all my efforts and labors I have found the brethren who accompanied me – Bros. Bull and Wilkie – always on hand and enjoying a good spirit and I feel comforted in their society. –

Bro. Amasa[40] is here, having been sent out with some 75 or 80 others to preach &c. in this upper country and collect means for the liquidation of the mortgage on the Rancho. Bros. N.V. Jones, Fotheringham and Luddington, are here from the East Indias; they are well and in good spirits and intend returning home this fall.[41]

The brethren all join as well as my wife, with me in love to you and to Bros. Heber [C. Kimball] and Jedediah [Grant] and to the brethren of the Twelve, Bros. [Daniel H.] Wells & [Albert] Carrington & the brethren in your office. I shall [be] happy to hear from you at any time and receive any counsel or instruction you may have to give.

With prayers for your success and prosperity I remain as ever, Your Brother,

Geo. Q. Cannon

Aside from the accelerating financial success of the enterprise, what were the responses of both the Mormon and non-Mormon readership to this latest San Francisco newspaper? Many of the editors of competing newspapers eventually launched vicious attacks on both Cannon and the church he represented, but initial reactions were more friendly.

[40] Initially called to California as one of the church's "gold missionaries," Amasa M. Lyman, who years later apostatized as a spiritualist, was an early leader of the church in California. With fellow-Apostle Charles C. Rich, Lyman established the important colony of San Bernardino in 1851, which continued as the primary settlement in southern California until it was abandoned in 1857. See Cowan and Homer, *California Saints,* 125–33, 168–86.

[41] Nathaniel Vary Jones was a Mormon Battalion veteran and had served as president of the mission to India, along with William Fotheringham, a pioneer of Lehi, and Elam Luddington, a former Mormon Battalion lieutenant.

San Francisco, as it appeared in 1856 from Rincon Point,
from an engraving by F. N. Otis.
Courtesy, California History Section, California State Library.

According to his granddaughter-biographer, Reva Scott Stanley, even though he had gone home, Pratt had paved the way for Cannon by establishing good will with at least one editor of an influential San Francisco newspaper:

> The *Daily Alta California* of about December 7, 1854 [*sic*], gave him a favorable write-up and was open-minded about his teachings and beliefs. "Mr. Parley P. Pratt, for whom we have considerable respect as a man and as a teacher, coupled with as much admiration of his talents as the doctrines which he employs to defend it will admit of—Mr. Parley P. Pratt appears to have walked into the temples of our money changers in this city, and fairly put to flight all reason and philosophy by the boldness of his attack upon the Christian Church."[42]

A close reading of the original source, however, suggests that Stanley may have been over-eager to cast Pratt in a favorable light. The *Alta Cal-*

[42] Stanley, *A Biography of Parley P. Pratt: the Archer of Paradise,* 290.

ifornia paid only grudging homage to Pratt, bemoaning the fact that "no David has gone forth against this Philistine." The paper acknowledged Pratt's argumentative powers and that the law, regrettably, appeared to be on his side, but the *Alta* mercilessly attacked Mormon polygamy. It challenged the city's ministers to take on Pratt in vigorous debate: "Missionaries are sent to the heathen, and why should discussion be denied heathenistic doctrines when they are brought to our very doors?"[43]

Even though the press was generally opposed to Mormonism and universally to its doctrine of polygamy, at least one of the initial responses to the *Western Standard* was supportive. Although its friendly relationship with the *Western Standard* was to be short lived, the *Sacramento State Journal* was one of the first papers to pass judgment, complimenting the typesetters and editor while carefully avoiding commentary on the content: "We have received a copy of this new Mormon weekly paper, published at San Francisco. In beauty of typographical appearance it is unsurpassed by any other weekly paper in the State, and it is, apparently, edited with considerable ability." Cannon reprinted this review in his second issue, together with the following response: "We accept the above as quite a compliment, Mr. Journal, as we are of the opinion that California is unequaled by any State in the Union in the typographical finish of their newspapers."[44]

The *Sacramento Union* dispensed its compliments much more indirectly, if not reluctantly:

> We are in receipt of the first number of a large and handsomely printed newspaper, published in San Francisco, bearing the name of the *Western Standard*...
>
> The editor, Geo. Q. Cannon, in his introductory address . . . asserts that the Mormons have been maligned, vilified and misrepresented, while the good they have done has been withheld from the world. Paradoxical as it will appear to our readers, this arbitrary exponent of faith which has for its object the undermining of the very foundations of our civil and religious government, the disruption of family ties, the utter repudiation of the commandments of holy writ, the encouragement of a system of licentiousness more impure than that of the Turkish harem, thus coolly defines his position in the salutatory . . .
>
> The first shot from this editorial Cannon is a bomb shell. . . [The *Union*

[43] *Daily Alta California*, 11 December 1854. For a fine overview of Pratt's relationship with the various San Francisco newspapers of the day, see Grow, "Parley P. Pratt and the San Francisco Press, 1854–55."

[44] *Western Standard*, 1 March 1856.

> quotes from Cannon's criticism of a bill introduced in California by Senator Norman to declare polygamy illegal.] The above 'isn't a priming' to the charges preferred by this great Cannon of polygamy. Look out for more explosions after his next load is fired off.[45]

Not surprisingly, the reactions from the Mormon community were enthusiastic, especially with respect to the editorials. They appreciated the hard-hitting, uncompromising stance of the editor and hoped that the *Western Standard* would play a major role in disabusing the nation in general and California in particular of its misconceptions and prejudices concerning the Church of Jesus Christ of Latter-day Saints.

Like the editor of the *Sacramento Union,* Mormons wrote several letters to the editor that could not resist making puns on Cannon's name, but they complimented him on the doctrinal fusillade he had fired upon the Gentile world. A letter from a missionary, Wm. H. Shearman, writing from Salmon Falls, ended with this observation: "Though but *one* 'Cannon' may you prove an effective, invincible and powerful 'Battery,' which the enemies of the kingdom shall find it impossible to silence or captivate."[46] Orson Hyde joined in: "May its 'CANNON,' well charged, ever be planted on the ramparts of truth, and directed by a 'single eye' to the magazine in the fortress of error, that every successive discharge may tell for the triumph of right and downfall of wrong."[47] G. Clements observed, "I look upon the 'W.S.' as a powerful champion of Truth; and its 'Cannon' a powerful auxiliary in moving forward the great cause."[48]

Several of those who wrote to compliment Cannon on his publication were particularly impressed that such prose would come from a man so young in age and lacking in experience. One early subscriber, G. M. Miller, was so impressed by the quality of the newspaper that he offered to pay for subscriptions for those who could not afford the $5.00 per annum cost.[49] A Mormon missionary, writing on behalf of an aged, destitute couple, took him up on the offer.[50]

---

[45] The *Sacramento Union,* 25 February 1856.

[46] *Western Standard,* 8 March 1856.

[47] Ibid., 22 March 1856.

[48] Ibid., 2 August 1856. Cannon's name, of course, just begged to be appropriated by punsters. I am indebted to Bill MacKinnon for pointing out an especially intriguing use of the name "Cannon." Though it is unknown whether a specific allusion to George Q. was intended, Thomas Dunn English included an Army officer, Captain Cannon, as a character in his three-act play set during the Utah War. If the allusion was intended, then "Captain Cannon" was certainly placed on the wrong side of the conflict. See English, *The Mormons; or, Life at Salt Lake City.*

[49] Ibid., 14 June 1856.

[50] Ibid. 28 June 1856.

The *Standard's* primary sister-paper, the *Deseret News,* consistently showered praise upon Cannon and his associates. The *News* was especially impressed to find quality writing and editing from such a young and relatively impecunious staff:

> The Western Standard, Nos. 18 to 23 inclusive, came to hand per last Cal. Mail, and were full, as they always are, of interesting and useful matter, greatly to the credit of br. George Q. Cannon and his assistants brs. Joseph Bull and Matthew F. Wilkie, all of whom are quite young and, heretofore, measurably inexperienced in the conduct of business so arduous and difficult.
>
> That they started from here without capital to go to San Francisco (where the expense of living is so high and 'Mormonism' so low) to set up a press, to print the Book of Mormon in the Hawaiian language, into which it had been previously translated by Elder Cannon, and to edit and publish a weekly newspaper, are well known facts.
>
> That they have printed a large edition of the Hawaiian Book of Mormon and successfully issued a very excellent paper, amid so many disadvantages, and that too without incurring liabilities to be paid by the Church, or even by individual brethren and friends, beyond what they expect to personally and promptly meet, is a strong manifestation of the attendant blessings of our God, and that he does and will open an effectual way for the accomplishment of the duties devolving upon those who earnestly strive to fulfil his purposes, as counselled by those whose right it is to counsel.[51]

Mormon leaders in Utah were equally pleased with their newest newspaper—only one of a reported 3,754 being published nationally at that time.[52] Brigham Young, in a letter reprinted in the *Standard,* declared, "We perceive from your papers that you are still prospering, and feel gratified with the eminent success which appears to crown your efforts. One thing is certain, whether you obtain sufficient patronage to sustain you or not, your paper is every way worthy of it, and I rejoice to have a journal so ably conducted, devoted to the interests of Zion, in California."[53] Wilford Woodruff, in his role as an assistant church historian, praised Cannon in a letter to Orson Pratt: "I am very much pleased with the appearance of the *Standard,* it is ably conducted, and I think it will prove a benefit to the Saints, and help to keep at bay some of our vile calumniators, who will not be so barefaced in their attacks, when they see we have a paper that will defend our cause."[54]

---

51 "California News," *Deseret News,* 10 September 1856, 213.

52 Cited in Zboray, *A Fictive People,*128. (This accounting, by Aleksandr Lakier, was in 1857.)

53 *Western Standard,* 12 July 1856.

54 *Latter-day Saints' Millennial Star,* 9 August 1856.

The *Western Standard* was more than simply a means to support and defend Mormonism. It was also a *news*paper in every sense of the word, apprising the citizens of San Francisco of the latest events about town. Though not much interested in his landlord, Samuel Brannan (officially disfellowshipped from the church five years earlier), Cannon nevertheless paid wary attention to the resurgence of the "Vigilance Committee" Brannan had been instrumental in organizing in 1851. Cannon reported and sometimes editorialized on the extra-legal activities of the Second Committee of Vigilance. He apprised his readers of the numerous shootings, knifings, and beatings so common in the rough-and-tumble town of San Francisco, increasingly contrasting such mayhem with the peace and order to be found in the valleys of Utah. He summarized one particularly tough week:

> City Morality.—Our readers may form some idea of the morality of our City when we inform them that no less than sixty-six cases were on the docket of the Police Court on Monday last. Among this motley group might be found gentlemen and ladies celebrated as drunkards, thieves, vagrants, pugilists, swindlers, perjurers, and other professions too numerous and degrading to mention.[55]

Though George, and no doubt Elizabeth, disliked California immensely, he maintained his sense of humor about his home away from home. Even while reporting on some of the violent tendencies of the denizens of San Francisco, Cannon could not resist an opportunity to place his own "spin" on the news of the day. In his "City Items" column, he reported on two local altercations:

> A Duel.—A difficulty between two *gentlemen* was brought to a successful termination on Friday last by a chivalrous appeal to arms.—The quarrel originated in a conversation about Odd Fellowship. The challenged party chose double-barreled shot guns, at thirty paces!—They met, attended by their seconds and a surgeon, in the suburbs of the city, and banged away at each other once; but to their great relief, without injury to either party—one fired too high and the other too low. Their honor being satisfied, and both having shown their courage, they shook hands and agreed to an amicable settlement."

> ANOTHER QUARREL.—A couple of draymen feeling much aggrieved at each other's conduct, determined to settle it, in company with their seconds

[55] *Western Standard,* 18 October 1856.

> and as many spectators as chose to be present, at Meig's Wharf on Monday evening. Their only weapons were those furnished by Nature. After fighting two rounds, and losing several teeth, and one's jaw being broken, they expressed themselves as being perfectly satisfied! Most strange and brutal ways men have of satisfying their peculiar notions of honor![56]

As was typical of newspapers of the day, the pages of the *Standard* sought to keep pace with the latest scientific discoveries throughout the world, often as first reported (though not always credited as such) in other newspapers as "exchanges," particularly articles drawn from the *Deseret News*.[57] A perennial area of interest was health and medical subjects. A sampling of headers for columns designed to equip the *Standard's* readers with the latest knowledge for acquiring and maintaining sound health includes: "Horrors of Opium Smoking," "Colored Candy is Poisonous," "How to Purify Water," "Effects of Overwork," "Danger of Eating Full Meals at Night," "Heat and Cold Phenomena—the Cause," "Necessity of Sleep," "Excessive Use of Salt," "Philosophy of Sneezing," and the ever-popular "A Certain Cure for a Rattlesnake Bite or Spider Sting."

Following the custom of other nineteenth-century newspapers, Cannon liked to regale his readers with "filler" that touched on the strange customs of other countries and the latest scientific advances (or pseudo-scientific frauds) of the mid-nineteenth century.

Many of these subjects are today quite humorous, but it was all reported as straight journalism with nary a tongue in cheek. This is not to suggest that the *Western Standard* did not engage in conscious humor. Much of the filler was devoted to puns, riddles, jokes, and humorous anecdotes, all of which apparently enjoyed the approbation of Brigham Young, who wrote Cannon, "I like a little fun and rich anecdot[e]s, (you know I think they do no harm to any paper)."[58]

This joke of the day, from the paper's inaugral issue, reflects deeply held cultural values: "'I can't bear children,' said Mrs. Prim. Mrs. Partington looked over her spectacles mildly before she replied—'Perhaps if

[56] Ibid., 29 May 1857.

[57] Various U.S. Postal Acts, beginning in 1793, allowed free carriage of newspapers through the postal system among newspaper offices. Because it was a common practice to copy out material from other newspapers as "filler," original attribution was often impossible to determine and was therefore rarely given. See Whittaker, "The Web of Print," 16–17. This practice of using filler, of course, encouraged the promulgation of sensational stories about the Mormons and other sub-cultures, the veracity of which was often difficult to determine.

[58] Young to Cannon, 29 April 1856, LDS Archives.

The editorial and production staff of the *Western Standard. Left to right* are Joseph Bull, David H. Cannon, George Q. Cannon, William H. Shearman, and Mathew F. Wilkie. Photograph by R. H. Vance, June, 1857.
Courtesy, Utah State Historical Society.

you could, you would like them better.'"[59] Another relies on the time-honored tradition of the pun: "The substance of a verdict of a recent coroner's jury on a man who died in a state of inebriation, was, 'Death by hanging—round a rum shop.'"[60]

While some might expect an ecclesiastical leader like Elder George Q. Cannon to maintain a rather stuffy sense of propriety, his humor was remarkably unrestrained:

> Mr. Jones, after having spent an evening over his bowl, went home a little "how come you so." He was fortunate enough to find his better-half asleep. He went to bed, and after a moment's conversation, he thought it would be policy to turn over, lest his breath should betray him; when Mrs. Jones opened her eyes, and in the mildest manner in the world, said—"Jones, you needn't turn over—you're drunk clear through."[61]

[59] Ibid., 23 February 1856.
[60] Ibid., 5 April 1856.
[61] Ibid., 31 May 1856.

Cannon maintained his sense of humor to the end. Even in the final issue, as he was preparing to close down the newspaper so he could join his brethren preparing to confront the federal army on its way to Utah, Cannon joked: "A rogue asked charity on pretense of being dumb. A lady having asked him, with equal simplicity and humanity, how long he had been dumb, he was thrown off his guard, and answered, 'From birth.' 'Poor fellow!' said the lady, and gave him a dollar."[62]

In spite of the worldly information and fun found within its pages, the motto, "To Correct Mis-Representation We Adopt Self-Representation," summarized the purpose of the *Western Standard*. The newspaper printed LDS missionary tracts, poetry dealing with religious themes, "News from Utah," letters from the elders laboring in California, minutes of the semi-annual general conferences of the church, pronouncements and letters from LDS church authorities, and other matters of general interest to Mormons. Above all, the amazing editorials in which George Q. Cannon defended his religion while attacking its enemies, at times with merciless precision, were the heart and soul of the *Western Standard*.

George Q. Cannon published many—but not all—of his editorials in his 1864 book, *Writings from the "Western Standard."* In the preface he noted that his primary objective in re-publishing those editorials was for the benefit of his posterity, but that he had been encouraged by "the Brethren" to produce enough copies for others who might be interested. The often humble, self-effacing Cannon suggested that his writings were "destitute . . . of literary merit and other qualities." He also excused himself, as "These articles were written so hastily—there being, in the beginning, but Brothers Bull, Wilkie and myself to do the selecting of extracts, editing, type-setting, proof-reading, folding and mailing—that the first portion of nearly all of them was in type before the latter portion was written."[63]

Cannon was far too modest. He did revise some of the titles of his editorials for *Writings*, but he made very few other changes and none of substance. Either he wanted to bequeath his children an accurate picture of his earlier work, or he did not feel his writing was in need of great revision. His prose is typical of the best journalists of his time and is sometimes a challenge to the modern eye and ear. Yet today's reader will find his style clear, unambiguous, and forceful. He is sometimes sarcastic, often persuasive, and almost always entertaining.

[62] Ibid., 6 November 1857.

[63] Cannon, *Writings from the "Western Standard,"* iii–iv.

Samuel Brannan, circa 1860.
From Shuck, ed., *Representative and Leading Men of the Pacific Coast. Courtesy, California History Section, California State Library.*

Chapter 2

"Two Wrongs Never Will Make a Right"

Sam Brannan and the Vigilantes

By some accounts, the *Western Standard,* edited and published by George Q. Cannon in San Francisco from 23 February 1856 to 6 November 1857, was not the first "Mormon" newspaper in California. Sam Brannan, a newspaperman and Mormon convert, had helped Joseph Smith's brother, William, and then Parley P. Pratt, put out *The Prophet* (later named *The Messenger* to reflect a more secular orientation) in New York City from 1844 to 1845. In 1846, Brannan took the press used to print these publications with him to California on the ship *Brooklyn,* along with about 230 Mormons. Six months after his arrival in Yerba Buena, later to be called San Francisco, he began publishing the first newspaper in San Francisco, the *California Star.*[1]

Although many presume that this press was the property of the LDS church, there is evidence that it was Brannan's personal property by the time the *Brooklyn* set sail. In a letter to Brigham Young, Orson Pratt remarked that "Bro. Brannan thinks it will be difficult to take his printing establishment and go to California unless he goes away dishonorably without paying debts. If he could sell he could pay his debts. He feels very anxious to go and is willing to do anything he is counseled." Brannan was more than happy to sell his press for the right price: "He says that the church perhaps would consider it wis-

[1]The first newspaper in California was the *Californian,* published on the old Mexican government press in Monterey by Robert Baylor Semple and Walter Colton, making its debut on 15 August 1846, nearly six months before Brannan's press was up and running. The *Californian* was later moved to San Francisco where it eventually merged with the *California Star.*

dom to buy his establishment & still keep up the paper [in New York]."[2]

The Control of Public Opinion May Be in Our Hands

Though the *Star* is listed in *The Encyclopedia of Mormonism* as a "church newspaper,"[3] that was not how Brannan represented it. Edward C. Kemble, a non-Mormon who had worked with Brannan on the *Prophet,* accompanied him to California, and later took over the *California Star,* said the following of that early newspaper: "It is not known if the original intention was to print an organ of that sect [the LDS church] on this coast; it is more likely that a secular paper was intended."[4] In his "Extra from the California Star," published on 1 January 1847 and then reprinted in the *Millennial Star,* Brannan began by addressing the Saints in England as "Beloved Brethren" and concluded with "Yours truly, in the bonds of the everlasting Covenant, S. Brannan, President." Nonetheless, nothing in this publication suggested that he was about to publish a newspaper on behalf of the church. On the contrary, Brannan announced that "We shall commence publishing a paper next week, which will be the government organ by the sanction of Colonel Freemont [*sic*], who is now our Governor, and is at the present time on a campaign to Lower California to subdue the Spaniards, who have lately taken up arms."[5] Shortly later, Brannan made it clear that his newspaper would distance itself from both political *and* religious influence.

From the outset, Sam Brannan appeared to make his paper independent from the church, just as he was soon to make himself so independent from the Mormons that he was finally "cut off," or disfellowshipped. Among other charges, Brannan was accused of collecting tithes from the California saints, only to deposit them in his own

---

[2] Orson Pratt to Young, 21 October 1845, LDS Archives. Moreover, in his prospectus for the *California Star,* Brannan noted that he had "purchased and brought with him to California a press and all the necessary materials" to start his newspaper. See *California Star,* 9 January 1847 and subsequent issues.

[3] Ludlow, ed., *Encyclopedia of Mormonism,* 1663. This same apparent error is found in Lambert, *Printing in California,* 10.

[4] Kemble, "The History of California Newspapers," *Sacramento Daily Union,* 25 December 1858, 2.

[5] *Millennial Star,* 15 October 1847.

pockets. Or, as Bancroft put it, Brannan "was a leader in Israel as long as it paid."[6]

Brannan's early communications with Brigham Young indicated his eagerness to serve Mormon interests and goals through his paper, but his published pronouncements were contradictory.[7] This may have reflected his practical conclusion that it would prove more effective to advance his church's political influence in a secular rather than an overtly religious newspaper. Regardless, the *Star's* promotion of Mormonism was soon so covert as to be hardly detectable, and it was not until an indisputably church-owned press was shipped to San Francisco in 1855 that George Quayle Cannon established an unabashedly "Mormon" newspaper.

Brannan's contributions to early California extended beyond bringing the first shipload of American emigrants to the province and launching one of its first newspapers. He relentlessly advanced the prospects of the newly conquered territory, and it was a promotional issue of the *Star* that carried first word of the gold discovery to the eastern United States. Arguably, his dramatic announcement of "Gold! Gold from the American River" on a beach at San Francisco in May 1848 launched the gold rush, although the discovery days earlier of trace gold in John Sutter's mill race by veterans of the Mexican War's Mormon Battalion obviously was foundational. Not only did he become California's first millionaire through land speculation and cagey business ventures, but as one of the leading businessmen of early California, Brannan organized the first Committee of Vigilance in 1851. He was also involved with the resurgence of the vigilante movement when the second committee was reborn in 1856.

Contrary to popular opinion—largely resulting from early treatments sympathetic to the vigilante movements in California[8]—it was more than rampant predatory crime and inadequate law enforcement that led the good citizens of San Francisco to take the law into their own hands.

---

[6] Bancroft, *Popular Tribunls,* 2:116. Nonetheless, Brannan was finally disfellowshipped in 1851 "for his personal sins, general apostasy, and involvement with the vigilantes" as opposed to defalcation of tithing funds. Bagley, ed., *Scoundrel's Tale: The Samuel Brannan Papers,* 297.

[7] See Brannan to Young, 29 March 1848, LDS Archives, in Bagley, ed., *Scoundrel's Tale,* 246.

[8] See Bancroft, *History of California* and *Popular Tribunals*; and Soulé, Gihon, and Nesbet, *Annals of San Francisco.*

Although a secondary factor in 1851, Richard Maxwell Brown and Kevin J. Mullen have demonstrated that business and political interests were the primary instigators of the much larger resurgence of Brannan's original Committee of Vigilance in 1856.[9] Regardless of the motives behind their actions, both the 1851 and the 1856 committees hanged four alleged miscreants and frightened away many more while simultaneously bringing about significant changes to the political and fiscal life of San Francisco.[10]

Interestingly enough, the event that gave Brannan and his cohorts the excuse to seize political power was the assassination of one newspaper editor by another. James King, of William, one of the leading members of the first vigilance committee in 1851, was the editor of the *Daily Evening Bulletin.* (King used the "of William" to refer to his father, thereby distinguishing himself from another James King with whom he grew up in Georgetown.) He had come to California in 1843 and as a result of his business and banking connections brought to his editorial work a fearless resolve in his assaults on corruption.

The citizens of San Francisco were generally delighted by King's attacks on the "power elite" of the city. As a result, Kemble informs us, the *Bulletin* "'took' like fire runs. In six months the daily edition had grown to the before unexampled circulation (for California) of seven thousand copies. It became a power in the State; King was the idol of a large portion of his readers."[11]

George Q. Cannon, in a footnote in his *Writings from the Western Standard,* commended King: "In the short space of a little over seven months, he had, as editor of that paper, by his remarkable fearlessness and the vigor and pungency of his articles, made his name familiar to every reading man in the State of California."[12] Reflecting on King some fifty years

[9] Brown, *Strain of Violence*; and Mullen, *Let Justice Be Done.*

[10] For additional insight into these fascinating events, see Bancroft, *Popular Tribunals*; Valentine, *Vigilante Justice*; Lotchin, *San Francisco, 1846–1856: From Hamlet to City,* chapter IX; Royce, *California: From the Conquest in 1846 to the Second Vigilance Committee in San Francisco,* chapter V; Brown, *Strain of Violence,* chapter 5; Mullen, *Let Justice Be Done*; Stone, *Men to Match My Mountains,* 167–71 and Bagley, *Scoundrel's Tale,* chapter 11.

[11] [Kemble,] "The History of California Newspapers," *Sacramento Daily Union,* 25 December 1858, 6. For more on King and the 1856 Vigilance Committee from the point of view of an early newspaperman, see Young, *Journalism in California.* For this and other stories of "pistol packin' editors," see Dary, *Red Blood & Black Ink,* chapter six.

[12] Cannon, *Writings from the "Western Standard,"* 108n.

James King, of William, editor of the *Daily Evening Bulletin.* His assassination by James B. Casey ignited the Second Vigilance Committee movement of 1856. *Courtesy, California History Section, California State Library.*

later, Josiah Royce added that "it was his life to assail official, business, and social corruption of every sort, and that not impersonally . . . he not infrequently felt a good deal of personal spite against the public sinners that he assailed."[13]

As might be expected, such an outspoken "champion of the people" gained numerous enemies. After King accused J. P. Casey of being not only an ex-convict, but of having gained a seat on the Board of Supervisors by stuffing the ballot-box, Casey mortally wounded him in broad daylight on 14 May 1856.[14]

This effrontery to civilization was too much for even the hardened citizens of San Francisco and provided the momentum for the old Vigilance Committee to reorganize and regain *de facto* control over the law enforcement system of the community, hanging Casey and one other miscreant on the same day as King's funeral. The *Bulletin* became the primary champion of the vigilantes and the most popular newspaper in

[13] Royce, *California,* 434, 432.
[14] For an extract of the offending article, see Ibid., 109.

town, while those competitors that did not immediately support the committee lost popularity—and advertisers—almost overnight.

Inexplicably, Kemble failed to mention that King's assassin, James P. Casey, was highly regarded as an editor of a rival newspaper, the *Sunday Times,* at the time of their altercation. Casey was such a frequent contributor to the *Times* that he was widely perceived to be its editor.[15]

THE MOST INTENSE EXCITEMENT: CANNON AND THE VIGILANTES

George Q. Cannon's attitudes towards the Vigilance Committee of 1856 reveal much about the popular attitudes of San Franciscans in general, especially in his earliest editorials. They also tell us something about how Cannon saw these events within the larger context of the "latter days."[16] The *Western Standard* covered the rise and fall of "popular tribunals" in San Francisco from the shooting of James King to the disbanding of the Vigilance Committee. There were no newspaper wars on that subject, for the only newspapers that publicly disagreed with the vigilantes soon found themselves without subscribers.

"AN ATTEMPT TO ASSASSINATE AN EDITOR," *WRITINGS FROM THE "WESTERN STANDARD,"* 17 MAY 1856, 108–12.

SAN FRANCISCO has been in a state of the most intense excitement since Wednesday afternoon, in consequence of an attempt having been made by James P. Casey, editor of the *Sunday Times,* to assassinate James King of Wm., editor of the *Evening Bulletin.* It appears that an article appeared in Wednesday's issue of the *Bulletin,* in which Mr. King alludes to Mr. Casey in the following language:—

"The fact that Casey has been an in [*sic*] inmate of Sing-Sing prison in New York, is no offence against the laws of this State; nor is the fact of his having stuffed himself through the ballot-box as elected to the Board of Supervisors from a district where, it is said, he was not even a candidate, any justification for Mr. Bagley to shoot Casey, however richly the latter may deserve to have his neck stretched for such fraud on the people. These are

---

[15] Young, *Journalism in California,* 19.

[16] The frequent reference among Mormons to the "latter days" was, and to some extent still is, reflective of the belief that Christ's Second Coming was near at hand. The phrase was included in the official name of the church after April 1838 to distinguish it from the ecclesiastical organization established by the Savior during his earthly ministry.

acts against the public good, not against Mr. Bagley in particular, and however much we may detest Casey's former character, or be convinced of the shallowness of his promised reformation, we cannot justify the assumption by Mr. Bagley to take upon himself the redressing of these wrongs. This case of Bagley's has caused us much anxiety, and we should have been pleased to have withdrawn, cheerfully, his name from the list alluded to, but we cannot conscientiously do more than express our gratification at the assurances we get of his present conduct, in which we trust he will persevere. As to the Casey fight, we suggest to Mr. Bagley if he can explain that away, it would not be amiss to do so, and he can have the use of our columns for that purpose."[17]

After the publication of this article, Mr. Casey called at the editorial room of the *Bulletin,* and asked the editor what he meant by its publication; telling him that he was willing that all his acts since he had been in this country should be investigated, but was not willing that his previous acts should be raked up. King asked him if he was done; if he was, to leave. Casey then told him that he should say through the columns of his paper what he pleased, and, if necessary, he should defend himself; and then left. Shortly afterwards, Mr. King left his office, and was met by Casey near the corner of Washington and Montgomery streets. As King approached, Casey cried out, "Draw and defend yourself," and, immediately throwing off a short cloak which he wore, presented a navy revolver, when they were but a few feet apart, and shot King in the breast, the ball passing through his body. When he received the wound he exclaimed, "I am shot," and staggered into the Pacific Express Office. Casey was immediately hurried off to the station-house and locked up. In a few minutes after the assault, the street was densely packed with men, all in the highest state of excitement; and, as soon as it was ascertained that the assassin was at the station-house, a rush was made there by the whole crowd, with cries of "hang him," "hang him," etc.

For greater security he was carried in a carriage, by the officers, from the station-house to the county jail; and to defend himself while in the carriage, he was armed with a brace of revolvers! During the evening the most tremendous excitement prevailed throughout the whole city. On Montgomery street, where the people had assembled in immense crowds, several exciting speeches were delivered, and strong appeals made to the people to avenge the blood of their fellow-citizen who had been so inhumanly shot down. From there they adjourned to the Plaza; but for want of leaders, no organization was effected. The military were called out, and repaired to the jail, where they remained throughout the night, and, by their presence,

[17] J. W. Bagley, clerk of the San Francisco Board of County Supervisors, was arraigned with four other men on 25 October 1855 "for an assault with knives and pistols on Mr. James P. Casey, in the course of an election riot." See Soulé, Gihon, and Nisbet, *Annals of San Francisco; Together with the Continuation,* 71.

deterred the people, who had assembled in large numbers, from making an attack upon it. On Thursday morning the old Vigilance Committee met together, and came to the conclusion to have the names of those who wished to join, registered. Thousands signed their names, pledging their honors to carry out whatever determination the majority should come to. Great reliance was placed by the populace in the action of the Vigilance Committee. On Thursday afternoon the following placard was posted up:—

> "EMERGENCY OF THE MOMENT!— TO THE PEOPLE!—FRIENDS AND FELLOW CITIZENS, LEND ME YOUR EARS!—The time was, when, in San Francisco, many among us, law-abiding men, regretted the acts of the Vigilance Committee, and were willing to hope that if the law of the land had been duly supported the guilty would have met with their deserts. Since then, better experience has convinced us that the Law is here a MOCKERY; that the weak, the poor, the stranger, may pay his misdeeds in the forfeiture of his liberty or his life; but the rich villain, the powerful gambler, supported by his rich confederates, laughs at the impotence of the law, and stalks through our streets with bowie knife or revolver to work out his wicked will, conscious of a 'friend at court,' who will screen him from his deserts!
>
> "Patience is a virtue, but there is a point beyond which it degenerates into cowardice. Obedience to the law is the duty of every citizen; but when the law is effete, or its protection becomes tyrannical, RESISTANCE becomes the duty of FREEMEN!
>
> "Such is the PRESENT EMERGENCY, to our view. The Law and its Courts are a farce; murder stalks amongst us, AND MUST BE CHECKED. Then up, friends, and let the majority of the people TRY THE PRESUMED MURDERER, and then, if he be guilty, EXECUTE!
>
> "BRUTUS."

The streets have been lined with people from morning till night, the scenes of the past few days being the only topics of conversation. The bulletin boards of the different papers have been surrounded by throngs of eager people, anxious to learn all they can in relation to the action likely to be taken in the matter. All feel that the time for action has arrived. It has now to be decided whether peaceful and law-abiding citizens can be shot down with impunity in the streets like dogs, and their murderers allowed to go forth uncondemned and unpunished, or whether the majesty of the laws shall be vindicated, and the assassin receive the just punishment of his demerits. The people have now to decide, whether they will rise in their majesty and strength, and thoroughly cleanse the judgment seats and courts of justice of the land from the impurity, injustice and corruption which now abound there, or whether they will submit to have things continue as they have been. If they are but firm and united, and are determined by the expression of the popular will to hurl these office holders, who do not respect either the laws of the land or their constitutional obligations, from the positions of trust and responsibility which they now occupy, a change for the better will soon be apparent, and matters will mend. But if these things are not done, if vice and crime are allowed to thrive unmolested and unchecked, if the blood of the innocent and unoffending can be spilled without restraint, and the murderer be permitted to again go at large and seek fresh victims, as has been the case heretofore, then woe unto this city and this country, for the Lord will not permit the blood of the guiltless to cry from the earth unavenged. The cries of the widow and the fatherless, made so by the demoniacal psssions [*sic*] of men, will not ascend to his ears in vain; he will visit, with scourges, the people who will permit such things to take place in their midst without taking means to remedy them.

We have but one opinion of the diabolical attempt there has been made to take the life of Mr. King. With order loving men there can be but one opinion. It was a dastardly and atrocious attempt to silence a man, whose "faults" have been to speak the truth, on many subjects, too plainly to be palatable. We do not think that Mr. King is faultless, or that he has not been injudicious, in some respects; we would be doing him injustice, however, did we not give him credit for fearlessly and manfully speaking out, regardless alike of the smiles or frowns of the corrupt, in opposition to every thing that he deemed wrong. He has battled earnestly and zealously to expose iniquity and to defend the rights of the people, and if he has erred, it probably has been for lack of knowledge, and not from a disposition to intentionally do wrong. Mr. King, throughout the whole of Thursday, was quite rational, and hopes were entertained that he might recover. Yesterday, however, the physicians made an examination, and pronounced his situation, critical. He is surrounded by kind and anxious friends, and his wife, though in a delicate situation, has been unremitting in her attention upon him ever since he was wounded.

"The Only Safe Plan of Reform," *Western Standard*, 24 May 1856.[18]

. . .The behests of the Vigilance Committee have been complied with, and a terrible retribution has been exacted for the blood which was so recklessly shed. Men imagine, now, that the stream of crime will be arrested, and that, henceforth, justice will be impartially administered; they look for good order to prevail, and expect that the leaven of iniquity, which has been so long at

[18] Reprinted in Cannon, *Writings from the "Western Standard,"* 112–14. See also "Events of the Week" in the same issue of the *Western Standard* for an objective summary of the various events that had taken place to date with respect to the King murder.

work, diffusing its poisonous influence throughout the society, will be effectually neutralized. The question naturally arises, are the measures that have been adopted in the present instance sufficient to counteract the baneful influences that are at work, producing anarchy, confusion and bloodshed in our midst? Is the remedy sufficiently powerful for the disease? Men predict an entire change for the better, and the inauguration of a new era, dating from this revolution. There will, most assuredly, we trust, be a change, and the open violation of the laws in so flagrant a manner will no doubt be checked; but will this be permanent? Have the causes which produced this almost universal corruption in high places, been removed? Are men any more honest, or any less revengeful and likely to take life, than they were previous to the organization of the Vigilance Committee and the enforcement of its decrees? The little effect these stringent measures have had in restraining the effusion of blood upon slight provocation, was apparent a few days ago, when, for a blow with the open hand, pistols were drawn, and blood would undoubtedly have been shed had not the bystanders interfered. Until these feelings are eradicated—until men reform and put away every evil thought far from them, these things will continue to be. We have no hesitancy in predicting that, unless this reform does take place, and the people do repent of their sins with full purpose of heart, turn to the Lord their God, and seek to do his will, these evils will continue to increase, despite the Vigilance Committee and every other measure of the like kind, until a man that will not take up arms to defend himself against his neighbor, will have to flee, or perish. It is plain to be seen that this state of things is fast being brought about, and no other plan than that laid down by Jehovah can avert it. If men really want reform, let them begin at home, and seek to cleanse and purify themselves—forsaking sin, and bowing themselves down in humility and meekness before the Lord in obedience to his commandments. . . .

"EVENTS OF THE WEEK," *WESTERN STANDARD*, 21 JUNE 1856.

The past week has passed off more tranquilly than ordinary, and business has been attended to as though no such organization as the Vigilance Committee was in existence. The only very perceptible change is the decrease of crime; not that we think the people are more virtuous and orderly than they were previous to the commencement of the exciting transactions of the past few weeks, but such characters are overawed by the attitude of the Committee, and the summary manner in which they deal out justice. Many of the most notorious for evil have been arrested, notified to leave or have left for more hospitable quarters; and other cities and countries will now receive the *benefit* of their talents.

Although most accounts of the Second Vigilance Committee do not directly mention Sam Brannan, it is clear that he was one of the primary instigators in re-establishing his old committee from five years earlier. As suggested by Bancroft, "Mr. Brannan was just the man to incite a revolution, but he was not the man to conduct one."[19] Even before the assassination of James King, Brannan was arrested for "inciting to riot" when he publicly advocated the hanging of Charles Cora. This incident was recorded in retrospect some thirty-three years later in the *San Francisco Examiner:*

> Previous to the latter date, in November, 1856 [1855], Brannan brought himself prominently into notice in connection with the killing of United States Marshal Richardson by Charles Cora, the Italian gambler. Cora shot down his man about 6:30 o'clock on the evening of the 17th. Then he delivered himself up to the officers of the law, feeling as confident, perhaps, as did the mass of the indignant populace, that thus he secured his ultimate safety. But the bells began to ring and the crowds to gather, and above the throng at the Oriental Hotel was seen the form of Sam Brannan, his voice ringing out over the turmoil, urging the instant execution of Cora. The Sheriff commanded him to desist, but he refused. Then the official arrested him and started with him to the Station-house. A howling and hooting mob followed the two, and a rescue was about to be immediately effected. But Brannan restrained his friends, and at the Station-house the officials made a virtue of necessity and released him on his own recognizance.[20]

Cora, a professional gambler, had already outraged the sensibilities of some of San Francisco's more genteel citizenry by openly living with a New Orleans prostitute. (In this, he foreshadowed the license taken by Judge W. W. Drummond of Utah, to be discussed in chapter 9.) Mrs. William H. Richardson, wife of the United States Marshall, complained to her husband when Cora flaunted his relationship with Annabelle Ryan by conspicuously sitting with his "Belle" in an open box during a performance of the American Theatre. The marshal and the gambler had already been feuding, and when General Richardson accosted Cora about this perceived breach of etiquette, Cora drew a pistol and shot the allegedly unarmed marshal dead.

Brannan was arrested because, it was argued, criminals like Cora should be dealt with by the law, not by mob action. But Brannan and his follow-

---

[19] Bancroft, *Popular Tribunals,* I: 245.

[20] "The Pioneer at Rest," *San Francisco Examiner,* 7 May 1889, 1/3–4, in Bagley, ed., *Scoundrel's Tale,* 425.

ers felt they had good reason to mistrust the law. Cora had friends in high places and, as it turned out, his murder trial resulted in a hung jury. This, in turn, generated a series of blistering editorials by James King, which only further incited the spirit of vigilantism. When King was also killed—this time by an Irish-Catholic—the stage was set for the creation of the biggest and best-organized vigilante movement in American history.

While it would be foolish to disregard the emotional impact these two murders had upon the populace of San Francisco, eradicating crime was not the only agenda of the Second Vigilance Committee. Many of San Francisco's civic leaders—Sam Brannan among them—sought to challenge the political machine of David C. Broderick and his Southern-oriented wing of the Democratic Party. Broderick was not above stuffing ballot boxes (one of the primary charges King levied against County Supervisor Casey) and employing Irish-Catholic "shoulder strikers" to pressure voters as he aggressively challenged both the anti-Catholic Know-Nothings and the Whigs for control of the city. Graft, corruption and a mounting municipal debt accompanied huge payoffs to the Broderick machine.

It came as a surprise to no one, then, when William Tell Coleman and other leading merchants immediately re-constituted the Vigilance Committee on the very night of the King shooting. By noon of the following day some fifteen hundred men acceptable to Coleman had signed up, with another five hundred added to their ranks by nightfall. Three days later, the committee claimed to have eight thousand members.[21]

The group leased a building on Sacramento Street and immediately fortified it with an eight-foot enclosure of gunny bags filled with sand, thereby giving the nickname to their new headquarters of "Fort Gunnybags." After adopting the same constitution the group had used under Brannan's leadership in 1851, twenty-five hundred vigilantes marched on the jail, cheered on by fifteen thousand citizens. The mob successfully seized Casey and then Cora as Major General William Tecumseh Sherman of the state militia watched helplessly from the roof of the International Hotel with the city's mayor and the state's governor.[22]

[21] For a brief discussion of the actual number, estimated at from 6,000 to 8,000, see Brown, *Strain of Violence*, 359–60n21.

[22] Ball, *Army Regulars on the Western Frontier*, 103. At this point in his career, Sherman was a resigned West Point First Lieutenant who was the California agent of a New York and St. Louis banking house while simultaneously playing a senior role in the state militia.

Lithograph depicting the seizure of Cora and Casey by the vigilantes prior to their summary execution. *Courtesy, California History Section, California State Library.*

On 20 May 1856 Casey and Cora were tried by a jury of twelve vigilantes and convicted of murder, with the date of execution set for the same day as King's funeral. Before being led to his death, Charles Cora was allowed to marry "Belle," thus making an honest woman of her after all. Both men were hanged until dead from hinged platforms outside the second floor of Fort Gunnybags as every church bell in San Francisco tolled in memory of that fearless editor, James King, of William.

Before their work was done, the Second Vigilance Committee of 1856 hanged four men they had convicted of murder. Over two-dozen petty criminals and political malefactors (many of whom were Broderick's henchmen) were sent into exile. In doing this, the committee brought about much-needed fiscal reform and smashed the political machine of David C. Broderick.

Nonetheless, everything the committee did was completely illegal. In spite of the general support of the populace, the vigilantes inevitably came into conflict with state and federal authority, which they held in open contempt. During their reign of terror, "Law-and-Order" Gov. J. Neely Johnson declared that San Francisco was in a state of insurrection and called out the county's militia, which refused to respond. Army General John E. Wool refused to honor his promise to arm General Sherman's militia. The vigilantes seized state arms and ordnance and the city's arsenals, and Johnson complained to President Franklin Pierce that he was powerless to protect citizens and punish the committee's "lawless acts of aggression and disobedience."[23]

Before disbanding, the vigilantes instituted a political reform movement under the name of the People's Party. Whereas the extra-legal activities of the vigilantes terminated after only three months, the legal legacy of that movement lasted much longer, and the People's Party retained political power in San Francisco for the next decade.

With the disbanding of the Committee of Vigilance came Cannon's last editorial on the subject, published five days after the vigilantes' final grand review and parade.

"DISBANDMENT OF THE VIGILANCE COMMITTEE,"
WRITINGS FROM THE "WESTERN STANDARD," 23 AUGUST 1856, 190–93.

The exciting topic of the past week has been the disbandment of the Vigilance Committee, or more properly termed, perhaps, their retirement from active service. On Friday morning of last week their fortifications were demolished, and the bags of sand emptied into the Bay. And on Monday, previous to the resignation of their power, they determined to marshall all their forces and display to their friends and enemies their numerical strength and military appearance. No pains were spared to make the parade and review as imposing as possible, that it might have the desired impression on their opponents and the outsiders. . . . The arrangements for the procession were well planned and admirably carried out, and every thing passed off to the satisfaction of those engaged in it. After the procession had moved through the principal streets they repaired to Headquarters, and there disbanded. Various estimates have been made as to the number under arms; those favoring the Vigilance Committee state that according to the official reports from Headquarters there were five thousand men under arms; their

[23] Ibid., 104–05.

opponents, on the other hand, assert that by actual count from different points as they passed they did not exceed two thousand eight hundred. Several arrests were made during the day, and the parties were lodged in the cells of the Committee.

It is presumed that whenever necessity shall again occur for the re-organization of this formidable power, a call to that effect will be promptly responded to by all its members. Many of the bands of which it is composed will, it is quite likely, form themselves into permanent independent companies, and retain their present organization complete; this will enable them to speedily resolve themselves into a Vigilance Committee of the most formidable character at any moment; and if they can keep their arms and maintain their present state of discipline and the unanimity of the feeling which they have heretofore had, it will be a task of no small magnitude for any force, independent of the U.S. troops, to put them down, or prevent them from carrying into effect any measure they may deem proper to adopt. Since their organization, a period embracing exactly three months, they have pursued and carried out their objects with a remarkable degree of moderation, and the success which has attended all their movements, the unanimity that has characterized their organization, will embolden them, whenever in their opinion it shall be needed, to have recourse to the same measures, with the expectation, of course, that it will be attended with the same results. We have many doubts about the same unanimity and moderation characterizing future organizations of this kind. When the majority of the people are pure and upright, persons possessing those qualities will be the kind of men they will elevate by their suffrages to offices of trust and power, and when such men are in power there is no need of organizations being formed unknown to and unrecognized by the laws. If the majority of the people, however, desire wickedness and corruption prevails in their midst, their officers will be men who have but little regard for their constitutional obligations or for the laws which they are chosen to administer, and an organization ostensibly formed for the purpose of carrying out the laws will confer no real benefit upon such a people. The organization must of itself be composed of the same element, and be actuated by the same motives, as the mass by which they are surrounded, or they can not maintain their supremacy. Here, in our opinion, is the danger of such associations, for if the majority of the people are desirous of seeing the laws properly enforced they have the power, by the mere expression of the popular will through the ballot box, and without violence, to place such men in office as will mete out justice impartially, irrespective of rank or position; but if the majority are corrupt, and those of them who desire justice and right are in the minority, it will at once be perceived that such an organization would be used to oppress the minority—however unjust and contrary to right it might be—by carrying out the wishes of the majority. We look upon an organization of this kind as a bad

> and dangerous precedent, though the objects may, as in the present instance in this city, be praiseworthy. Its danger is not so apparent so long as the people are actuated by good motives; but when the bounds of law are overstepped, there is no barrier to restrain the masses, only their own will and the ideas they may happen to have of right and wrong. This may not be productive of much harm while the popular voice is heard in favor of the right; but a precedent is established that may be adopted, as such, by the people at some future time, when they might desire to band together for unworthy objects—objects that they might think could not be effected by the law. We confess that we have seen so much of these popular demonstrations acting independently of the law, and, in fact, in direct opposition to it, that we cannot help viewing such movements with distrust, though, at the same time, we may freely and willingly give, to many engaged in them, credit for being actuated by pure and correct motives. Under our form of Government, the people have everything in their own hands; they are the sovereign power, and the expression of their will is indisputable and supreme. If the laws are inefficient, they have the power to remedy them; and, if there is any fault in the administrators of the law, it is also their prerogative to remove them, and fill their places with those who are honest and capable, and who will faithfully fulfil their obligations. We cannot conceive of any case that can arise, if the people will only remain honest and true, where there will be a necessity for any organization or association antagonistic to the laws. The people may have to suffer, for awhile, in some instances, but it is better to suffer wrong than to do wrong. "Two wrongs never will make a right;" and, in seeking to escape the evils with which we may be threatened, we cannot be too careful in abstaining from such moves as may place us in a worse position than that which we already occupy.

What a fascinating evolution of position. Cannon began by cheering on the Vigilance Committee, literally calling his fellow citizens, "in their majesty and strength," to arms. A week later, after Casey was summarily executed, Cannon still supported the committee, but suggested that ultimate reform would have to be based on a return to true religion. After the passage of another month, Cannon acknowledged a decrease in crime thanks to the vigilantes, while hinting that this had come at a high cost—"the summary manner in which they deal out justice." Finally, once the committee had officially disbanded, Cannon became quite open in his criticism. Had he changed his mind from the outset? Was it only now that he came to see the Vigilance Committee as a "bad and dangerous precedent"?

THIS DELUDED PEOPLE: THE *WESTERN STANDARD* VS. *THE PACIFIC*

Curiously, throughout the entire vigilante affair and indeed, throughout his tenure as editor of the *Western Standard,* Cannon seldom mentioned his former brother in the Gospel, Sam Brannan, the vigilante leader who had made such a huge impact on the development of California. But when *The Pacific* took a potshot at the LDS church, suggesting that only its apostates (with Brannan undoubtedly at the head of the list) had managed to make and keep money in California while its faithful members were now paupers, Cannon rose to the defense of his people. Before the exchange had ended, perhaps unable to perceive the beam in its own eye, *The Pacific* undertook to cast out the mote from Cannon's, taking him to task for the tone of his editorials. In doing this, the Congregationalist editors of *The Pacific* had apparently forgotten the motto on their own masthead: "First Pure, Then Peaceable—without Partiality and without Hypocrisy."

"TEMPORAL EFFECTS OF MORMONISM," *THE PACIFIC,* 12 FEBRUARY 1857.

There is a singular, but significant fact connected with the history of the Mormons in this city, strongly suggestive of its blighting effects on, at least, the secular interests of mankind; and which ought to speak with practical force to the judgment of that generally honest, but universally ignorant and misguided people. They came to California, as is well known, at an early day—at a period prior to the discovery of gold. They settled in this city at a time when hundreds of vara lots were to be had almost for the asking.[24] A state of things they were not backward in turning to their worldly advantage; so that, when this species of property came to be valuable, they were mostly owners of real estate—many of them to a large amount. They were among the first parties into the gold mines, after their discovery, and being a hardy and industrious class, had the best possible chance for making money; and they did make money, more, perhaps, than any other class in the diggings. In fact they were quite notorious for their success in this respect. Being adventurous and hardy, they were always pushing forward into new and rich localities, from which, having taken the cream, they went on still to others. In this

[24] A vara is a traditional Spanish unit of distance, generally equivalent to about 33 inches. The vara is still the official unit of measurement in the General Land Office of Texas.

way they took out large sums, and were, for the most part, careful of their earnings. We well remember that in '49 they were nearly all well off, being the owners of much real estate, and also cattle and money. This was but seven years ago, and yet what is their pecuniary condition, as a people, to-day, in San Francisco? They are the poorest white men among us. Most of them are reduced to the verge of poverty, in fact, most of them are abjectly poor. Their broad acres of city lots are gone; their houses and money are gone; their accumulated wealth is dissipated. Why is this? Have they suffered more from fire than the rest of our citizens? No, generally less, their property being mostly removed from the localities that have been visited by that element. Have they undergone more sickness and disease than others? They should not have done so, seeing their Elders, of whom they are never without a plentiful supply, are able to cure every species of malady by the simple imposition of hands. Have they suffered more from bad laws and insecure titles than their neighbors? No, generally less. Owing to the early creation of their titles, and the districts where located, they have been disturbed even less than elsewhere; and yet with all these advantages they are impoverished. There are but two or three of their original number who can any longer be called rich, and they are now apostates from the faith.[25]

Why should it be so? Why should a healthy, frugal and industrious people, so favorably situated, have gone steadily down from affluence to poverty? It cannot be mere accident. It will not do to attribute it solely to mischance, or the disasters incident to business. There must be some hidden reason—some cause not yet wholly apparent to the world, nor even to this people themselves. Did it never occur to them to inquire into this matter? To ask how it is that with all their economy and labor they have been going constantly down from wealth to want? Why this mysterious wasting away of their substance? Why this slipping through the tightening grasp of their lean and meagre fingers of their goods, their lands and the homes of their children? There must be some special cause for all this. What it is we do not profess to wholly understand. It may be the vampyre of priestly cunning that is sucking their life-blood, while they sleep. It may be the burdens secretly imposed upon them by the church, or it may be the workings of some dark and deadly principle inherent to the system itself. This depletion may be caused by the outward leeches on the people, or it may be some consuming evil, lodged deeply in the soul. It may be the tithings and tribute exacted by the church,[26] or it may be the spirit recoiling from a faith that a

[25] This included Samuel Brannan, who was widely acknowledged in 1857 as the richest man in California. Brannan was cut off from the LDS church in 1851 but had not yet been reduced to poverty due to his drinking, costly divorce, and poor investments.

[26] "Many contemporary observers charged Brigham Young with being particularly arbitrary in his use of church funds, but there seems to have been remarkably little objection registered by church members themselves. Most of them seem to have felt, as Young himself undoubtedly did, that he was simply doing

feeble intellect has suffered to be imposed upon it. Whatever the cause, the fact is such as we have stated, and we trust it will stimulate this deluded people to inquire why it has been so.

"FALSE STATEMENTS OF THE 'PACIFIC,'" *WESTERN STANDARD,* 14 FEBRUARY 1857.[27]

In an article of some length in the *Pacific* of Thursday, headed "Temporal effects of Mormonism," the wonderfully astute and sapient editors of that paper make the announcement of a grand discovery they have made, in regard to the blighting effects of "Mormonism" on its followers. This discovery, which is announced with a grand flourish of trumpets and gratuitously set forth by this brace of lynx-eyed reverends for the consideration of the deluded "Mormons," is something that has been strangely and unaccountably overlooked by all writers on this subject until the present. For the *Reverend* J. H. Brayton and the *Reverend* S. V. Blakeslee, editors of the *San Francisco Pacific,* have the great honor of discovering [that] this mare's nest [has] been reserved! By the exercise of their extraordinary penetration they are in a fair way to immortalize themselves and earn unfading fame! Their discovery applies particularly to the first "Mormon" settlers of San Francisco and California; but, if true in regard to them, will doubtless be applicable to "Mormons" elsewhere. The article states that. . . [Cannon then extensively quotes from the above article, ending with "Their broad acres of city lots are gone; their houses and money are gone; their accumulated wealth is dissipated."] Assuming this last statement of theirs to be correct, they ask,— Why is it? The remainder of the article consists of a series of questions and answers, which they, of course, expect to be conclusive in convincing their readers, and perhaps, "this generally honest, but universally ignorant and misguided people," that poverty and want are the natural attendants of belief in "Mormonism."

They do not attempt to reconcile the apparent discrepancy which exists between their first statements in regard to their proverbial industry and success, and their last respecting their present extreme poverty. They were "Mor-

---

what the inexorable logic of his position dictated. A popular contemporary expression reflects this view: 'He is a Prophet, because he is of Profit to the people.' The president's attitude throughout thirty years of service as trustee-in-trust was that it was the duty of the Saints to pay tithing, and his responsibility to see that it was spent in the interests of the Kingdom." Arrington, *Great Basin Kingdom,* 141–42. Even though Young made some attempts to separate his personal assets from those of the church in his will—as recommended by Thomas L. Kane—his propensity for mingling his personal business interests with those of the church, coupled with the need to assign church assets to its "trustee in trust" to protect them from federal auditors, made settling Young's estate during 1877–1879 an especially difficult and vexing task for his successor, John Taylor. Even the final settlement was challenged in court, resulting in the ex-communication of seven of his heirs.

[27] Reprinted in Cannon, *Writings from the "Western Standard,"* 339–341. (In *Writings,* the date of this editorial is incorrectly listed as 14 February 1856.)

mons"—believers in "Mormonism"—in the days of their first settlement of this country; how came it, then, if the assertions of the *Pacific* be true that the temporal effects of "Mormonism" are abject poverty and want, that they should be so signally prospered beyond their fellows in those days, as to have it become notorious and proverbial throughout the country? Every reader of the *Pacific* possessing a grain of common sense, and bestowing the slightest reflection on the subject, will perceive in a moment that the story is absurd and badly constructed. If, as the *Pacific* hints, present poverty and want are attributable to the vampyre of priestly cunning that is sucking their life-blood while they sleep; or to the burdens secretly imposed; or to the tithings and tribute,—how came they to prosper and rapidly acquire property in those days at any subsequent period? Now, we have the evidence on hand to prove, that these *reverend* editors have basely and maliciously *lied* when they stated as a fact that the "Mormons," who in '49 were nearly all well off, and who owned real estate, cattle and money, are in a state of abject poverty, to-day, in San Francisco. It may be termed a religious lie, and be justified under the circumstances as necessary to prejudice the people against "Mormonism," and to prevent its spread; but still it is a lie. What are the facts about the first "Mormon" settlers? Do not the editors of the *Pacific* know that the "Mormons" are continually gathering to Utah, and that it is one of the most prominent doctrines of their belief? And do they not also know—which if they have been acquainted with the affairs of this country since the early settlement they must know—that these early settlers, with few exceptions, have left San Francisco, and either gone to Utah or San Bernardino? We fearlessly assert, and we do it on our own personal knowledge, that the editors of the *Pacific* cannot put their finger on a man in this city, who belongs to this Church, that in early days was well off and is now reduced to the verge of poverty. They must have been aware when they penned their article on this subject that they were stating a falsehood and from that falsehood drawing incorrect and unreliable deductions. When men resort to such despicably low measures as the editors of the *Pacific* have done in this instance, to injure and counteract the influence and progress of a system and community, they are in a pitiable condition. The "Mormons" in San Francisco are not particularly noted for the abundance of this world's goods in their possession; but we do not know of an individual among them that is in a state of abject poverty. We would think it no disgrace, however, even if they were, so long as they are honest; and that they are thus honest, frugal, hardy, adventurous and industrious, the editors of the *Pacific* have freely borne testimony to. We wish that we could bear the same testimony in regard to *their* honesty; but, setting aside their honesty in regard to pecuniary matters, upon which we at present express no opinion, they have manifested gross dishonesty in robbing truth of its good name, and in falsifying and misrepresenting it to the world.

The good qualities which were possessed by the Latter-day Saints at the time of the first settlement of California, and which produced success and prosperity then, are still theirs and produce now the same results, as evidenced in the prosperity of San Bernardino in this State, Carson Valley in Western Utah, and the thrifty and well established settlements in the Valleys on the Eastern side of that Territory. Why not extend your researches in regard to the "temporal effects of Mormonism," Messrs. Editors, to these settlements? Are poverty and want the concomitants of "Mormonism" in Southern California or in Utah? You know they are not. You also know, if as conversant with history as you should be, that when permitted to dwell unmolested we have never suffered from poverty and want. These are not the effects of "Mormonism," though often endured by "Mormons," but are the effects of mobocracy, aroused and fanned into a flame by the exertions of priests and editors, who think it no harm to fabricate and publish lies about this system.[28]

"The Mormon Paper, Western Standard," *The Pacific,* 19 February 1857.

Last week's Pacific contained an article on the temporal effects of Mormonism, to which the Western Standard has since offered a coarse reply. In the first place, we have to say that the article in question was written, not by our selves, but by a gentleman who has suffered, not a little, in his own family, from the tampering of Mormons with the domestic relations, and who may, therefore, be supposed to know something about themselves and the practical workings of their miserable system. And secondly, we are not inclined to demean ourselves by any controversy with men whose first resort, towards those who differ from them, is the free use of such epithets as lying, liars, &c.

We should want no better evidence against Mormonism than the tone maintained by its standards. We have noticed particularly in any controversy among the Mormons, the ready and free bandyings of the charge of lying, just as others would charge unintentional error. What must be the moral training, or moral state of men who cannot conceive of opposite sentiments and endure opposing statements without the charge of falsehood? We suspect them as we always suspect those who are profuse in their suspicions and

[28] During his initial (1859–1850) sojourn among them, U.S. Army First Lieutenant John W. Gunnison was astonished by the relative lack of poverty among the Mormons in Utah: "Their comparative comfort and degree of prosperity is significantly shown by the fact that they canvassed the country, to ascertain how many inmates there would be for a poor-house, and finding only two disposed to ask public bounty, they concluded that it was not yet time to build a house of charity: and this among the thousands who, three years before, were deprived of their property, and could, with the utmost difficulty, transport their families into the valley." Gunnison, *The Mormons,* 34. This was corroborated by Stansbury, *Exploration and Survey,* 133.

charges against mankind in general. In the slang of the Standard against other papers in this city, we have noticed too much of the profane elegance of the bogus prophet, Brigham Young.

With such men we have little to do, nor can they pick any difficulties with us whatever. A few months since a Mormon elder [John Hyde] lectured in this city. From what we heard of him we were inclined to respect him. We sent and reported one of his lectures that we might have their own words from which to reason whenever we had occasion to refer to the subject. But a few weeks had elapsed when we received from that man a recantation of the errors into which he had been drawn when but a boy of fourteen years of age. He is now holding up the beauties of practical Mormonism as seen in the city of the saints. The days of that delusion are numbered. At first a system of ignorant pretence, it has grown to be a hot-bed of pollution, and deserves to be execrated from the face of a Christian land.

"Shifting the Responsibility,"

Writings from the "Western Standard," 21 February 1857, 349–51.

Our contemporaries of the Pacific, when they are pressed to the wall or have their veracity impugned, have a very unique and convenient way of dodging the issue. We have a fair specimen of this before us, in their paper of Thursday last. It will be remembered by our readers that, in our last week's number, we took the liberty of contradicting, in rather plain language, statements made in an editorial article of their paper of the 12th instant relative to the "temporal effects of Mormonism." We branded their statements in that article as false, and said that we had the evidence on hand to prove them to be such. In an editorial, written in allusion to this subject, in their paper of this week, they, in the first place, disclaim the authorship of the article, and say that it was written by a gentleman who has suffered not a little from the "Mormons." And in the second place, they are not inclined, they say, to demean themselves by any controversy with men whose first resort towards those who differ from them is the free use of such epithets as lying, liars, etc. They neither substantiate nor deny the false statements and deductions which they have so freely made, but as a convenient way of avoiding either, fall back on their dignity! They do not wish to demean themselves, they say, by any controversy with men who freely use such epithets as lying, etc.! The editors have truly strange ideas about what is demeaning. It is not demeaning to publish false statements, but it would be to get into controversy with the individual who calls these statements false, or in plain, mountain English—lies! It is not demeaning to shift the responsibility of an editorial article containing those unblushing falsehoods on to the shoulders of some unknown individual, who has "suffered not a little from the Mormons," as though his sufferings gave him a right to traduce and defame "Mormonism" and every "Mormon!" It is not demeaning after these statements are publicly contradicted to maintain the most profound silence in regard to them, neither withdrawing them by acknowledging in a frank and manly manner that they were based upon incorrect information, nor attempting to support them! We must confess that the ideas of the editors of the Pacific and ours differ very materially as to what is demeaning. We would rather be charged with the too free use of such epithets as lying, etc., than be accused of the free indulgence in false statements, which are virtually lies. And should we, during our editorial career, ever advance anything that is calculated to misrepresent and malign a system or a community, we trust that we may never be so destitute of honor as to shun the bold and open withdrawal of such statement, upon becoming aware of its tendency.

As to their remarks that we are ready and free in the charge of lying, where others would charge unintentional error, and that they have noticed "too much of the profane elegance of the bogus prophet Brigham Young" in our remarks, we have a few words to say. We have never hesitated to style such statements as those advanced by the Pacific—which, to view them in the most charitable light could never have originated in unintentional error—as lying, and every man who has any perception of right and wrong would do the same. But we have ever been careful, in all controversy with our contemporaries, to discriminate closely between unintentional errors and wilful perversion and misrepresentation of truth. The bluntness and "profane elegance" of Brigham Young and other servants of God, is as much of a stumbling block to this generation as the bluntness and plain habit of the speech of Jesus and his apostles. It shocked and offended the Pharisees, doubtless, to be called hypocrites, murderers, liars, and children of the devil, etc., as much as it does the editors of the Pacific to be told that the statements published in their columns are false.

By what process of ratiocination these editors have got the idea that, because we deny their unjust assertions, we wish to pick a difficulty with them or draw them into a controversy, is a mystery to us. If they wish to escape our notice, they must confine themselves to the truth when they speak about "Mormonism" and the "Mormons." If they do this in future, we can assure them that they will have but little cause to complain of us trying to pick a difficulty with them; if not, they will find us both ready and willing to defend our religion and ourselves from every aspersion they may publish. The day is past, and we thank the Lord for it, for us to sit tamely by and have detraction and unmeasured abuse heaped upon us without daring to resent it or to hurl the falsehoods back in the teeth of the men who utter them.

"Mormon Tone—How It Should Be Judged," *Writings from the "Western Standard,"* 21 February 1857, 343–46.

A religious contemporary, in an article to which we allude in another column, says, that it wants no better evidence against "Mormonism" than the tone maintained by its Standards. It is not an unfrequent thing for objections to be raised by the professedly pious and religious against the tone of the "Mormon" speeches and articles. Everything said by the Latter-day Saints is so devoid of that sanctimonious twang and affectation of piety, so popular in the religious world in these days, that many who are disposed to measure their neighbor's religion by the amount they display of these qualities, set the "Mormons" down as an irreligious and impious community. The school in which the Latter-day Saints have been trained is a very different one from that in which the people by whom we are surrounded have been; and the difference to be observed between us and the religious world is in consequence of the difference in our experience. Men, to pass a correct judgment on "Mormonism" by the tone of its professors or of its Standards, should first become acquainted with the circumstances which have produced this peculiarity in their tone; for, were the writings of many of the prophets and apostles to be judged by their tone alone, without their peculiar and bitter experience being remembered or the circumstances taken into consideration under which their records were written, Christianity or the gospel of Jesus—the system to which they belonged—might be condemned. But remembering the trials and suffering which they endured because of their adherence to the gospel of Jesus, our hearts are filled with sympathy for them, and we intuitively perceive and acknowledge that all they said and wrote, though it might be considered harsh and offensive under some circumstances, was perfectly justifiable and proper.

So it is in regard to the Latter-day Saints. Though many of their contemporaries may condemn the tone of their remarks and writings, yet posterity, when the history of this age is spread before them, will be astonished at the forbearance and meekness they manifested; and they will readily acknowledge that nothing but the assistance of a superior power, could have aided them in enduring, in so wonderful a manner, the dreadful sufferings and wrongs that have been heaped upon them. Every species of enormity and oppression that the mind can conceive, or the most malignant inhumanity devise, has been unsparingly inflicted upon them, and by those, too, who should have been foremost to extend the hand of sympathy and friendship. Men, before they find fault with or condemn the tone of "Mormon" remarks and publications, should read their history, and ponder over their murdered men, their ravished women, and their homes made desolate by the ruthless hand of persecution. They should follow them in their wanderings,—driven from city to city, from county to county and from state to state; plundered of their property and violently expelled from their inheritances; seeking in vain for a spot in the land of their nativity, sheltered by the constitution of their fathers, in which they could dwell in peace and quietness. Let them reflect on these things, the list of which is so dreadful that the mind almost shrinks with horror from the contemplation, and then ask themselves what they think of the tone of "Mormon" speeches and writings. If they are reasonable and humane men their only wonder will be how human nature ever endured it. The bare remembrance of these scenes, when we permit our mind to recall them, causes emotions that we prefer at present to repress. When we see the same spirit indulged in by individuals now, who, had they the power, would re-enact those scenes of violence and persecution, we feel indignant, and we freely express it. The Latter-day Saints, when they became acquainted with the principles of their holy religion, were filled with an intense desire to impart the knowledge unto others, and with hearts overflowing with love and joy, they made known these things to all by whom they were surrounded. In the simplicity of their hearts, when they first became acquainted with the Work, and perceived the beauty and excellency thereof, they imagined they would only have to open the Bible and point to the promises contained therein to have all men ready to embrace it; but how cruelly were they deceived! The men who ought to have received it with joy, were the very men, in many instances, to fan the flame of persecution and incite and head crusades against them. Ministers and professors of religion have been their most zealous and unrelenting persecutors, from the days of the early rise of this system until the present. They have looked on approvingly while every imaginable indignity has been heaped upon the "Mormons," and have witnessed their expulsion from the haunts of civilization without extending a hand to prevent or raising a voice to rebuke so foul and flagrant an outrage upon the rights of man, and yet they find fault with the tone of the Latter-day Saints' remarks! They strain at a gnat and swallow a camel!

If our cotemporaries, religious or otherwise, desire to avoid for the future the charge of uttering and publishing falsehoods they must learn to keep within the pale of truth; if they will forsake the society of the truthful and respectable to mingle with the vicious and depraved throng, they have no right to complain if they receive the same treatment as those they associate with. A thin-skinned non-combatant should keep out of the fray; and it is only a miserably contemptible and dastardly spirit that would prompt a man to insult and outrage the feelings of another, and then rely upon his professedly peaceful character to protect him from the indignation and punishment he so richly merits. We wish the world to understand that we, as a people, have submissively and patiently endured, without resenting, all that the Lord requires of us to submit to. We have been smitten on one cheek, times without number; and have meekly and repeatedly turned the other, only to experience similar treatment. How long the world would think that we should submit to this treatment without any change in our demeanor or tone, we know not; but this we do know, that there is a point beyond which submission, even by a Latter-day Saint, would cease to be a virtue.

The Veriest Liar That Ever Trod the Earth

While the vigilantes were generally well received in San Francisco, their extra-legal activities appalled many Americans who had all too frequent experience with mob violence. Although the Mormons and the vigilantes had no connection, the temptation to link them was too much for some of their critics to resist. Ten months after the disbandment of the Second Committee of Vigilance, Cannon found it necessary to combat charges that not only Sam Brannan, but Parley P. Pratt and Mormons in general were behind the recent lawlessness in San Francisco. Pratt had first arrived in San Francisco in July 1851, staying for less than two months, as the first vigilante movement burned itself out. His single reference to these events came when he noted in his journal that his congregation had withdrawn Mormon fellowship from Brannan "for a general course of unchristianlike conduct, neglect of duty, and for combining with lawless assemblies to commit murder and other crimes."[29] Brannan had been a founding spirit of the first Committee of Vigilance, but he was not a primary leader of its 1856 revival. Although he had advocated hanging Cora on 17 November 1855, Brannan was either in Europe or en route when Cora and King were executed on 20 May 1856. Pratt was in Utah.

Utah territorial justice W. W. Drummond, a bitter enemy of Mormonism and the "popular tribunals" that posed a direct threat to his livelihood as a jurist, was the likely author of an anonymous letter published in the East under the pseudonym of "Verastus," a name perhaps selected to imply "veracity."[30] Drummond had left Salt Lake City on 17

[29] Stanley and Charles, eds., "A Mormon Mission to California in 1851," 176.

[30] Furniss, *The Mormon Conflict*, 59, concluded the style and content of the Verastus letters "bore evidence of Drummond's hand."

May 1857 and spent August in San Francisco, where he claimed to be an eyewitness to the activities of the vigilantes.[31]

The San Francisco *Alta California* picked up the presumed Drummond letter, originally published in a Washington, D.C., newspaper,[32] whereupon George Q. Cannon again put on the whole armor of God in defense of Zion.[33]

"The 'Mormons' and the Vigilantes,"
Writings from the "Western Standard," 12 June 1857, 439–42.

The *Alta California,* true to its instincts, still continues to utter its threats and denunciations against the "Mormons," and appears to be determined that its puny efforts shall not be wanting to aid in bringing to pass the destruction of which it has talked so much of late. In its issue of Monday we find another long tissue of slanderous charges against the people of Utah, which is extracted from an anonymous communication published in the Washington *National Intelligencer,* purporting to have been written by a man who spent, it is said, nearly twelve months in Utah, and was engaged in business connected with the transit of the mails to and from that Territory. This communication is written over the *nom de plume* of "Verastus," and has neither the date, nor the name of the place where written attached to it, and does not afford the slightest clue, except the peculiarities of its structure, by which its writer can be identified. It may have been written in Great Salt Lake City, in Washington, or San Francisco; though if we were to judge by the article itself, we should say that it was written from California by a certain notorious United States ex-Associate Judge of Utah Territory. Every characteristic of the letter bears the impress of ex-Judge Drummond's handiwork. But whether he be the author of this communication or not, makes at present, but little difference; the communication itself affords another very striking instance of the evidence that is brought to bear against "Mormonism." The editor of the *Alta* no doubt thinks it irresistible, and publishes all the charges that are made, accepting them as a further confirmation of what has already been published by Drummond. But does it not strike that sapient gentleman that a good, loyal, honest man would certainly affix his name, place of residence, etc., to a document of such importance as this. Who is this man that condemns a whole people as being traitors,

[31] Fielding, *Unsolicited Chronicler,* 340. In a 21 April 1857 letter to the *New York Times,* Drummond reported seeing vigilante activities. See Ibid, 242n35.

[32] "The Modern Sodom," *The National Intelligencer,* 20 April 1857, 2/1–2.

[33] Along with the following editorial, Cannon printed a companion piece titled "Treasonable Sentiments of the Alta," not reproduced here, in which he argued that the *Alta* was hypocritical in having supported the vigilantes while condemning the Mormons for their own alleged rebellion against the Government.

disloyal, etc. and recommends the Government in such earnest language to exert its power in breaking them up? Does the editor of the *Alta* know his name? If he does, let him make it public, that all men may know the amount of credibility to be attached to his statements, and that we may know the antagonist with whom we have to cope. If he does not know his name, nor who he is, why does he say that the denial of the advocates of "Mormonism" goes for naught in the face and eyes of his testimony? He may be the veriest liar that ever trod the earth, and the editor of the *Alta* not know it, if he only knows him by the *nom de plume* of "Verastus."

That the editor of the *Alta* knows that the statements of "Verastus" are false, is evident, or why did he keep so mum about his tale concerning the Vigilance Committee and the "Mormons"? If the dear public must believe one part of his letter they certainly should the other; and if they believe the whole, what conclusions must they draw? Why, that the editors of the *Alta California*—the most loud and violent advocates of the Vigilance Committee—were acting in concert, while in that movement, with Brigham Young and the "Mormons" to overturn the Constitution and laws of the United States! Are the editors of the *Alta* prepared to endorse this? Hear what he says on the subject:—

> "Now permit me to conduct you to San Francisco, California, on the ever memorable 18th day of August, 1856, and behold the streets of that ill-fated city thronged with men and arms. The Federal Constitution has been upheaved, the laws overthrown, and the 'Committee Vigilantes' have instituted a reign of terror. The Committee lays down its power and calls out its adherents to celebrate its retirement to law and order. The streets are decorated and hung with flags,—but, alas, the star-spangled flag of the free was set aside! 'The all-seeing eye over the crescent' on which was inscribed 'Vigilantes,' occupied the foreground, with a United States flag on either side. Immediately in the rear of these, also in the centre, hung the Mormon emblem (worn by them as military badges) of 'bee-hive and bees;' in the rear of these, between other United States flags, was the 'Lone Star' on blue ground, surrounded by a constellation. These are the prominent ensigns of Mormonism.[34] No one knew the object of the secret order—'Vigilantes'—but those who recognize Brigham as their prophet, priest and king.[35] The Vigilance Committee of 1851 was an *experiment* of Mor-

[34] Mormons used both the all-seeing eye, also a Masonic symbol, and the beehive, but the vigilantes' similar use of the same images appears coincidental.

[35] There is compelling evidence that Joseph Smith, Brigham Young, and John Taylor were each anointed as "King on earth" by the Council of Fifty. See Hansen, *Quest for Empire*, 66; Quinn, *The Mormon Hierarchy: Extensions of Power*, 238–39; Quinn, "The Council of Fifty and Its Members, 1844 to 1945," 185–87; and Ehat, "'It Seems Like Heaven Began on Earth,'" 255–57.

> mon strength, headed by Samuel Brannan, Parley P. Pratt, and others; and the Vigilance Committee of 1856 may be regarded in the same light. If not Mormon, let some one assign reasons for the setting aside of the United States flag and the display of ensigns of Mormonism."

Not only are the editors of the Alta California included in this category but every one of the originators of the "Vigilance Committee;" for "Verastus" says, that "no one knew the object of the secret order 'Vigilantes' but those who recognize Brigham as their prophet, priest and king." Must the public receive this portion of the testimony of "Verastus," Messrs. Editors of the Alta? Must the public believe that the Executive Committee and the leading men of the Vigilance organization are numbered among the 200,000 spies and emissaries that "Verastus" says the "Mormons" have in the adjacent States and Territories? What a dilemma this short-sighted editor of the Alta has got himself into by his endorsement of the truth of "Verastus" stories!

It would be useless for us to make an elaborate denial of these statements of "Verastus" to the people of San Francisco or California. Falsehood is palpably written on their face, the endorsement of the Alta to the contrary notwithstanding. The idea of mixing Governor Young's or Parley P. Pratt's name in the organization of the Vigilance Committee of San Francisco, is so absurd that our only wonder is that any sane San Franciscan could be found to endorse, and publish as correct, the testimony of a man who would make such statements. We presume the editor thought, when he wrote that endorsement, that it would pass unnoticed; of course, nobody would think of looking in the National Intelligencer to see the remainder of the letter, and the opportunity to belabor the "Mormons" being too good to be lost, he concluded to risk it. Before he sits down again to pen anything upon "Mormonism," however, we advise him for the sake of his credit, to examine and scrutinize the character of his authorities. If he do this, he will not be so apt to publish such false statements as occasionally appear in the columns of the Alta, and he may, perhaps, save himself considerable mortification. His experience as an editor ought to have taught him, that anonymous communications containing such wholesale and reckless charges, as are made in this instance, are not to be relied upon. We have repeatedly exposed the falsity of the charges which have been published through the Alta California, and have shown them to be entirely devoid of foundation, and, in the most of instances, to be the coinage of the brains of wicked and unscrupulous men whose words are entirely unworthy of credit; but the editor has never yet manifested enough common honesty to withdraw or qualify the reckless and false statements to which he has given publicity; on the contrary—as if enraged at the ample refutations with which these statements have been met—he has seized every opportunity of publishing, without distinction, all the base and improbable stories that have come under his notice, and commented upon them to suit his own purposes. Such a course may be in keeping with his ideas of modern journalism; but it is untruthful, unmanly and dishonest, degrading to himself and attended with pernicious effects to the public who peruse his paper. The adoption of such a policy by him may be injurious for a time to the Latter-day Saints; their character, which he so assiduously blackens and misrepresents, may be lowered in the estimation of those who may lend a ready credence to his accusations; but this cannot last long; in taking the course which he does he injures himself and his readers far more than he does the Latter-day Saints, and the day will undoubtedly come when he will receive convincing proof of the truth of what we here state.

To Shoot and Hang Their Scores and Hundreds

The Mormons continued to perceive themselves as being different from the rest of the Christian world, which of course they were. They particularly loved to contrast themselves with what they perceived to be the lawless vigilantes of "Christian" California. Writing to Cannon in July 1857, Apostle Wilford Woodruff made that contrast particularly clear:

I have noticed from the papers that there is one singular characteristic with all men who either go out of Utah, or go through it, who are enemies to this people, and that is "they just *barely escape with their lives!*" yes, they do really escape with their lives, and so many of them too! this is singular, when we consider that the Mormons are such a desperate, blood thirsty people, as our enemies would fain make the world believe, but would these characters report this, and feel that way, if they did not really believe that if justice had been done them, they never would have left Utah with their lives? I think not, but really has there not anybody been killed in Utah? If there has not, I think the people are sadly to blame, for since the opening of the gold mines of California, the whole country from California to Oregon has been so infested with murderers, robbers, and thieves, that the good Christians of California have found it necessary to shoot and hang their scores and hundreds, without judge or jury according to law; and no one has called them in question for it, or held the governor responsible; and it would be strange if there was not any one in Utah that should get killed without judge or jury, but then I will acknowledge there is a great difference; for the people in Utah are mostly Mormons, and they have a Mormon governor, and the Christians would of course think that a Mormon governor should be held

> responsible for the death of any man, and any crime committed in his Territory; while any man would at once be considered only fit for the insane asylum who should make any such demand, or require any such responsibility, of any governor in any other state or territory: but this is an item of difference between Mormons and anti-Mormons. There is more crime committed in one day in many cities of the United States, with the same amount of population than there is in Utah in a year, but that is performed by Christians and ours by Mormons, *that makes the difference.*[36]

Cannon's private opinions about the committee were always ambivalent. Something had to be done about hooligans like Cora and Casey and the corrupt politicians who were shielding them, and Cannon, like most of San Francisco, was undoubtedly happy to see them dispatched. But in a letter to Brigham Young, written less than two weeks after King's assassination, Cannon expressed his deep concerns:

> California is a hard country. As you will see by the accompanying papers which I send you, there has been a recurrence in San Francisco of the terrible scenes for which California has been so noted. A committee, styling themselves the Vigilance Committee, the ruling power, or executive of which, is composed of twenty-nine men, whose acts are entirely secret and unknown to the remainder, and whose word is law to the remainder, hold the supreme power here at present. They have taken the law in their own hands, and are determined that it shall be magnified; so far, the majority applaud and uphold their course, as they have acted with circumspection and order in the execution of their plans. But how terrible a situation for a people to be in, and how replete with evil and danger such a subversion of law and order: they think the exigencies of the case demand it; but they cannot see the difficulties by which they are surrounded, or the abyss upon whose verge they stand. All the officers, with scarcely a single exception, are notoriously corrupt; and the people are in a dreadful dilemma, for if they eject them, they know not where to turn to select men more honest and competent to fill their places. It needs but little of the spirit of prophecy to see what the result of these things will be; the wicked are determined to slay the wicked; and it seems, to look around California at the present time, that the word of the Lord through Bro. Joseph, stating that the man who would not take his sword to fight against his neighbor, would have to flee to Zion, is very near its full accomplishment; in fact, it has commenced already. The

---

[36] Woodruff to Cannon, 8 July 1857, *Western Standard,* 7 August 1857, 3. This was a favorite argument of the Mormons. For example, the *Deseret News* made a similar point in March 1857 in describing the election riots in Baltimore and New York City surrounding the 4 November 1857 presidential elections in contrast to the peace and quiet of Salt Lake City.

> editor, King, who has been lately killed, was the only public man in town that I have heard of who would not fight a duel; and he has been killed.[37]

Given the hard experience of the Mormon people with mob violence, it was perhaps inevitable that the spectacle of the vigilante's rough justice would at last appall Cannon and his fellow Latter-day Saints. Nor would the movement's public contempt for the rule of law and its defiance of the federal government escape the young editor when he had to answer charges of lawlessness and treason leveled against the Mormons.

---

[37] Cannon to Young, 26 May 1856, LDS Archives.

Chapter 3

"Hang 'em Up—Like Pirates!" The Mormons: Saints or Sinners?

Though they called themselves "Saints," the Mormons never thought of themselves as perfect. Many of Joseph Smith's revelations reminded them of their individual and collective shortcomings. Nonetheless, they considered themselves God's chosen people and firmly believed it would be through their efforts that the Lord's Second Coming would soon become a reality.

Their enemies—old as well as new—accused the Latter-day Saints of every foul deed imaginable. There was nothing new about the crimes attributed to the Mormons by the California newspapers. Witness the following list, compiled by the infamous John C. Bennett—formerly mayor of Nauvoo, major general of the Nauvoo Legion, and assistant president of the church—in his 1842 attack on his erstwhile brethren:

> It appears from the mass of evidence in this Exposé that the Mormon Hierarchy are guilty of infidelity, deism, atheism; lying, deception, blasphemy; debauchery, lasciviousness, bestiality; madness, fraud, plunder; larceny, burglary, robbery, perjury; fornication, adultery, rape, incest; arson, treason, and murder; and they have out-heroded Herod, and out-deviled the devil.[1]

Given his own questionable character, Bennett's charges are highly suspect. Whether a fallen believer or a conniving opportunist, Bennett had been excommunicated for many of the moral lapses he denounced, and his objections to Joseph Smith's polygamous relations were less the result of moral outrage than of jealousy. Still, the depredations allegedly committed by Joseph Smith's Danites and Brigham Young's Destroying Angels provided plenty of smoke, if not fire, to blacken the name of early Mormonism.

---

[1] Bennett, *The History of the Saints,* 257. For the best biography to date on Bennett, see Smith, The Saintly Scoundrel.

By 1856 there was no lack of controversial topics useful in attacking the young religion. As the voice of the LDS church in California, Cannon had to fend off charges involving the handcart disaster, the character of Joseph Smith, missionary efforts in Hawaii, the misbehavior of reputed missionaries, and scandalous tales of young women abducted into sexual slavery by "the crafty elders of Salt Lake."

The venomous political controversies of the time, driven by sectionalism and battles over slavery cloaked as "popular sovereignty," often fueled the blasts frontier editors leveled against Mormonism in general and the *Western Standard* in particular. At the very least, the Saints were vulnerable to the charge of prevarication. As both sides denounced each other as liars throughout the California newspaper wars, the Mormons were at a disadvantage, having steadfastly and often heatedly denied the practice of polygamy prior to their belated acknowledgement of that "peculiar institution" in 1852. Wanting to be perceived as completely honest in all matters, in spite of this history of obfuscation, led to some interesting rationalizations. Joseph F. Smith, son of Joseph Smith's brother, Hyrum, and future president of the church, tried to justify his father's early denials of polygamy: "There is a difference between telling a lie and not telling the truth. Webster says: 'Polygamy, a man having several wives, or a woman having several husbands.' The latter part my father meant to deny, and not the former; therefore he did not lie."[2]

Thomas B. Marsh, who would have been at the head of the twelve apostles in place of Brigham Young had he not apostatized, claimed Danite founder Samson Avard "advocated LYING for the support of their religion, and SAID IT WAS NO HARM TO LIE FOR THE LORD!" Following the model set by Joseph Smith's public denials of polygamy, Mormon leaders on the frontier felt perfectly justified in "lying for the Lord" to protect their embattled religion.[3]

The Utah Land of Abominations

When the San Francisco *Pacific* reprinted a richly imaginative story

---

[2] *N. Y. Semi-Weekly Tribune,* 14 September 1869; quoted in Green, *Mormonism,* 440n.

[3] Bennett, *The History of the Saints,* 321. For a well-developed essay on this topic, see Hardy, *Solemn Covenant,* Appendix I, 363–88.

about the crimes and moral degeneracy reigning in Utah Territory, George Q. Cannon immediately responded, launching a lengthy newspaper battle that eventually drew in the *Daily California American.* The episode affords a glimpse into the psyche of Americans in general and Californians in particular as they tried to make sense of the theocratic, "communalistic," and "polygamic" system known as Mormonism. Westerners—especially those living on the borders of Utah Territory—perceived this encounter with the "other" as a clear and present danger as is obvious from the unrelenting editorial opprobrium Western newspapers hurled at the Saints. Whether Cannon truly believed he could deflect such criticism by pointing out the logical fallacies of his opponents while often returning their vituperation is an open question. But he did not shrink from his mission to portray his people as "more sinned against than sinning."[4]

"Mormonism," *The Pacific,* 6 November 1856

Among a party of nine hundred Mormons, who recently left comfortable homes in England to surrender to the sway of Brigham Young and his hopeful associates, came two girls, whose transfer to the Utah land of abominations has very much the character of kidnapping. The story of their flight, as related in the English papers, is as follows:

Their father was a man in middle life, well to do and industrious. His labors had placed his family, consisting of a wife and several children, in a state of decent competence and happiness. Satan came among them in the guise of a Mormon cmissary, [*sic*] and beguiled the eldest son, who made a pilgrimage to the land of rougues [*sic*]. True to their instinct, the crafty elders of Salt Lake made Mormonism so delightful to the neophyte, and advanced him so very rapidly in their fraternity, that he returned to England as a preacher of the delusion. The father, whose employment took him away from his family for periods of a week at a time, returned to the house one Saturday from a business excursion, to find it deserted. His whole family had disappeared with whatever portables they could lay their hands upon; and his wife had stolen his money to no inconsiderable amount—all that she could collect or pilfer. He traced the fugitives to Liverpool, and reached that place to discover that they had embarked, under the persuasions of his Mormon son, in an emigrant ship, the Enoch Train. The distracted father chartered a steam-tug, and, taking with him a police officer, overtook the vessel. After an infinite deal of persuasion, aided by the master of the ship,

[4] Shakespeare, *King Lear,* 3.2.60–61.

and opposed by the Mormon leaders, he succeeded in inducing his wife to go back with him. He also, as a matter of great favor, obtained the surrender of his infant children. But his two eldest daughters refused to return with their parents, and the heart-broken father went without them. Their fate, going thus unprotected to Utah, may well cause a shudder.

A community thus replenished is maturing measures to apply for admission as one of the States of this confederacy. We were never among those who calculated the value of the Union, or who dreamed that the possibility of its being sundered was among contingencies to be considered in any case. But the possibility that our fathers may have fought to establish a shield for a community of adulterers and bigamists, and their progeny, makes us pause. That all which we hold sacred in religion, or virtuous in social and family relations, may be trampled under foot by a State represented on equal terms with those founded by Penn and the Pilgrims, by Oglethorpe and the Cavaliers; that the Old Dominion and the land of the Puritans may be allied with a fraternity of licentious and debauched rogues—these possibilities, should they become facts, will leave no value to the Union for any body to 'calculate.' Nothing has cast so great a doubt over the future of this country as the Mormon plague-spot. And if the State of Utah is to be admitted into our constellation, the sign will lose its present proud significance, and stand—as stars sometimes do in an equivoque—the representatives of something too foul to be spoken or written.

And all this evil, if it be consummated, will be fairly chargeable upon the absurdity of squatter sovereignty—a demagogue's figment to serve a party purpose, carried to its legitimate deductions by knaves, operating through the instrumentality of zealots, fanatics, fools and lechers. We have no patience with the Mormons, and as little with temporisers who leave the evil to increase, until at last literal and bloody war may be forced upon us to crush what common sense and a just idea of the power of the general government might have averted. The contact with the Mormons of such settlers of the West as have just ideas of purity and decency, will be terrible whenever the tide of emigration reaches them. And if the descendants of the wretches now wallowing in Mormonism—modern vermin perpeuating [*sic*] their kind in the disgusting ratio of other loathsome creatures—if, we say, these children of such paternity do not form a Pariah race in our country, it will be because this bad leaven taints the whole moral mass. Extremes meet. We have enjoyed a high order of social virtue in this republican country, because no corrupt royalty and nobility have made illegitimacy tolerable, and recommended the bend sinister as a badge of honor, provided that the blood, no matter by what questionable vein it descends, be 'honorable.' But if squatter sovereignty, and liberty, deteriorating into licentiousness, produce the same results, we have only substituted Fitz-Youngs and Fitz-

Mormons for Fitz-Jameses and Fitz-Clarences;[5] and certainly have not gained much by the exchange.—*Philadelphia American.*

"'PACIFIC,' 'POST,' AND MORMONISM," *WESTERN STANDARD,* 15 NOVEMBER 1856.

The *Pacific* of last week, and the *Pathfinder and Post* of the 12th inst., contain an article on Mormonism extracted from the *Philadelphia American,* which exceeds in bitterness, vituperation and filthy epithets, any thing we have seen upon the subject for a long time, and which exhibits the deep corruption of the heart and brain of the writer. The language it contains would be much more becoming frequenters of the "Five Points" in New York, or "Billingsgate" in London,[6] than the mouth of an American editor, and we are surprised to see any paper in this State disgrace its columns by its insertion; we can only account for its appearance on the supposition that some of the California editorial fraternity, being destitute of the necessary amount of brains to concoct stories about the Mormons, have been compelled to have recourse to "foreign aid," in order to gratify their malicious propensities towards us. We do not profess to be so expert in the use of slang phrases and low vulgarisms as the editor of the *American,* nor do we wish to degrade ourselves to his level by adopting his course, for says the wise man, "Answer not a fool according to his folly lest thou be like unto him." There is one thing, however, which we would remind gentlemen of, and that is, that selecting all the scurrilous and abusive words from a dictionary and arranging them in consecutive order, though it may exhibit a certain degree of smartness, is not *argument,* and though it may pander to and please the passions of the vulgar, unthinking crowd, it will not only fail to convince, but will disgust every sensible and reflecting man and woman. There is not an objection raised in the article to which we allude, but what could be easily and satisfactorily answered, but we do not consider it worthy of a reply, for it carries its own refutation on its face, and the only reason we notice it is, because it shows the mean, cowardly, underhanded course which certain editors in this city are determined to pursue towards us and our principles, and because it is also a tolerably correct criterion of their taste: crows flock to carrion, but its very scent is sufficient to drive away birds of cleaner tastes and purer instincts.

[5] Anti-Irish and anti-Catholic bias was a national obsession in the 1850s—a prejudice from which Brigham Young and other church leaders were hardly immune. Although relatively few Mormon converts were of Irish extraction and there were huge disparities between Mormonism and Catholicism, these three entities were often linked by critics of the Saints. See Bunker and Bitton, *The Mormon Graphic Image, 1834–1924,* 82–86.

[6] Five Points was a lower Manhattan neighborhood of New York City, notorious as a den of iniquity. Billingsgate was a gate, wharf, and fish market below London Bridge. The unpolished dialect of the local inhabitants resulted in the use of "Billingsgate" as a synonym for coarse language.

Why is it gentlemen, that you are compelled to resort to such means to sustain your position? We are here to debate with you the principles of Mormonism on their own merits, and to answer your objections against them, if you have any. We invite discussion; we court inquiry. Bring forth your strong reasoning; show us our errors; prove Mormonism to be false, either from the Bible or Nature—we are willing to meet you on these grounds. But no; instead of pursuing this manly, consistent, straightforward course, you sneak away behind the invincible barrier of some absurd story that has been hatched up by some charitable, disinterested man as the editor of the *American,* from three to ten thousand miles away, and about which, neither of us know as much as a monkey does of algebra, and then you valiantly stick your heads out of your hiding places, and call upon us to refute these ridiculous offshoots of a diseased brain, when you well know that it is impossible for us to obtain the necessary proof to do so. Shame on such a contemptible subterfuge. We again ask, why is it that you pursue such a course? We are compelled to conclude, that it is either because you have learned by past experience that reason is not a weapon that can be used against Mormonism—that no sound argument can be brought to bear against it; or else, that you really do not know enough to conduct an argument on the subject. If the latter *is* the case, we advise you not to open your mouths again until you have something to say, but to remember the fable of the Ass, who, when attired in the skin of a Lion, passed very well for that noble animal, until he attempted to imitate his roar, when his bray betrayed his true nature.

The Propagators of Such a Monstrous Evil

As "one of the first propagators of 'Mormonism' on the Sandwich Islands," it is hardly surprising that Cannon responded forcefully when the California press attacked Mormon missionary efforts in Hawaii. As he often would, Cannon used an eloquent defense of American liberties to decry his opponent's ill-considered call to "hang 'em up like pirates," and to point up the unfortunate effects Protestant[7] missionary efforts had on Polynesian culture and morals. Taking the bait, the editor of the *California American* tried to defend his "somewhat exaggerated" language, providing Cannon with another opportunity to blast this intemperate "burst of indignation."

[7] Although clearly a non-Catholic form of Christianity, the Church of Jesus Christ of Latter-day Saints never thought of itself as Protestant. Rather, the Mormons consider their church a restoration of primitive Christianity, with authority coming directly from God rather than through a split from the original church established by Christ.

"'MORMONISM' IN THE SANDWICH ISLANDS," *WESTERN STANDARD*, 6 DECEMBER 1856.[8]

"The Mormons are preaching their accursed doctrines in the Sandwich Islands, of all places in the world needing the prevalence of just the opposite principles of social conduct. The great obstacle in the way of civilization in that quarter has always been the strong tendency of the people to licentiousness. It has been in some measure surmounted, and might soon be fully overcome, but for the advent of this new *ism into* that region. The propagators of such a monstrous evil as Mormonism would be in the Islands—emerging as they are from a semi-civilized condition, and after so many years of patient labor on the part of the better classes of the natives to advance the general welfare,— *ought to be hung up, like pirates*" [emphasis added by Cannon].

The above is an editorial item from the columns of a Sacramento paper, (the *California American*) of Saturday last, and is strikingly indicative of the spirit of murder and bloodshed which dwells in the breasts of many who hold themselves up as guides of public opinion, and teachers of virtue, good order and peace. Every honest, peaceable and upright man must be disgusted with such sentiments, and cannot but execrate the spirit that would dictate their utterance. Men that will permit themselves to be actuated by such feelings, are unworthy of the society of their fellow-men, and should be shunned as enemies of their race. Had they lived in the days of Christ they would have been in the crowd who cried, "crucify him, crucify him;" or, had they been present at the execution of Stephen, they would doubtless have rubbed their hands in glee, should they have lacked the courage to throw the stones. Such men filled the cells of the Inquisition with victims, and caused the streets of Paris to flow with the blood of those who dared to think differently from themselves; and, had they the power to-day, they would have another St. Bartholomew and the Latter-day Saints as their victims.[9] If the Latter-day Saints are preaching "accursed doctrines" on the Sandwich Islands, they are preaching "accursed doctrines" in California; for we preach but the one doctrine wherever we go.[10] And as, in the opinion of the editors of the *California American*, the penalty for propagating "Mor-

---

[8] Reprinted in Cannon, *Writings from the "Western Standard,"* 280–83.

[9] The stoning of Stephen is described in Acts 7: 54–60. Bartholomew, one of the original twelve apostles and generally identified with Nathanael, is the subject of many legends of Christian martyrdom.

[10] Mormon missionaries were instructed *not* to introduce the doctrine of polygamy into the Sandwich Islands at this time, a policy which began with Cannon, during his earlier mission to Hawaii in 1854. See Flake, *George Q. Cannon, His Missionary Years*, 83. However, when the doctrine of polygamy was attacked in the local press, Benjamin F. Johnson, one of Cannon's fellow missionaries, wrote and distributed 400 copies of a pamphlet defending the principle. See Whittaker, "Early Mormon Polygamy Defenses," 50–51.

monism" there should be *"to be hung up like pirates,"* if they would but express their feelings, they would advocate the visitation of the same penalty upon its propagators here; and, as its believers all become propagators the moment they become acquainted with it, the hanging process would have to be extended to every member of the society throughout the earth! Are the editors of the *California American* prepared for such a consummation?

We had the honor to be one of the first propagators of "Mormonism" on the Sandwich Islands, and we were the first individual who preached, what the editors of the *California American* are pleased to term, the "accursed doctrines" of "Mormonism" to those Islanders in their own language; before they go, therefore, to those lands to execute the sanguinary vengeance they have decreed against the "Mormons," they had better commence with us, as we have not only been "guilty"of propagating "Mormonism" there, but are also engaged in the same delightful occupation here, and, the Lord being our helper, intend to follow the business for the remainder of our life and throughout the endless ages of eternity. Before they commence, however, they had better weigh well the consequences of such a movement, and be prepared to meet them, as the shedding of the blood of one Latter-day Saint will be the seed from which such an abundant harvest will be raised that the extirpation of their system would be impossible. We know that the doctrines taught, both on the Islands and here, and, in fact, throughout the world by the "Mormons," are not "accursed," only in the estimation of Satan and his agents; neither is their system "a monstrous evil." As we have been a propagator of these doctrines there, it is but reasonable to suppose that we have a little knowledge on this subject. The people were, and are now, being taught to believe on Jesus Christ, the Son of God, with all their hearts; do the editors of the *California American* think this an accursed doctrine? They have been shown that baptism for the remission of sins was necessary; is this what they would phrase an accursed doctrine? They have also been exhorted to walk uprightly, to deal justly and to forsake and abhor everything licentious or corrupt; do they term these doctrines accursed? These are the doctrines taught by the Latter-day Saints to the Sandwich Islanders, Californians and people of every land for their obedience, and every doctrine antagonistic to this *is not* "Mormonism." The *American* says truly, that "the great obstacle in the way of civilization in that quarter has always been the great tendency of the people to licentiousness;" but the writer betrays great ignorance, when he says that "it has been in some measure surmounted, and might soon be fully overcome, but for the advent of this new *ism* into that region," as every person who is in the least acquainted with the history of those islands knows, that licentiousness, instead of being in some measure surmounted, has increased to an alarming extent since the first attempts of the Protestant missionaries to civilize them. The evil practices which the people of those islands indulged in before the advent of the missionaries were very bad; but, since their appearance there, the old licentiousness has manifested itself in new and more dreadful forms. Repressed in one direction, by the well-meant but ill-advised and unwise measures of the missionaries, it has broken out in other directions, and we do not assert too much when we say, that the depopulation of the Islands is inevitable, unless "Mormonism" be obeyed; and if it should be obeyed, the effects produced by obedience to it in Utah and elsewhere will be produced there—industry, good order and virtue will increase on all hands.

It is a poor plan, and a very great evidence of weakness for men to recommend the *hangman's rope* as an argument to arrest the progress of "Mormonism." Though very potent in its way, it is not very apt to show men their errors, or to cause men of firmness to abjure them. Such an *argument* in the hands of tyrants and despots may be a terror to slaves and sycophants; but when used by an American editor towards freemen, the only feelings it gives rise to, are those of pity and contempt for the man who would so far forget himself as to use them.

"MORMONISM," *DAILY CALIFORNIA AMERICAN*, 9 DECEMBER 1856.

[The *California American* began this editorial in the same way Cannon began his—by quoting the controversial paragraph from its earlier issue, ending with the phrase, "ought to be hung up, like pirates."]

The above paragraph appeared in the editorial columns of this paper, a week or ten days ago, and was the result of a momentay [*sic*] burst of indignation, upon reading, as an item of news from the Sandwich Islands, that the monstrosity of Mormonism was gaining a foothold in that region. The language is somewhat exaggerated, it is true, for we could hardly be supposed to be literally in favor of publicly executing Mormon preachers, detestable as they all undoubtedly are, and however well deserving the fate of common felons; for, however beneficial it might be to the interests of humanity to extirpate, by law, so monstrous an evil as Mormonism from the face of the earth, yet it would be dangerous to the Rights of Man and to the great doctrine of liberty of conscience, to establish in this government, or any other, such a precedent. A departure from the great republican principle of a free toleration of religious opinions, in a solitary instance would endanger the principle itself, and tend to revive in its full force a policy which the past experience of civilized nations has shown had better be allowed to slumber among "the things that were." For the Mormons themselves we have no respect—we mean the leaders of the sect—but we do respect the great principle under which they seek shelter, which like the rain from Heaven, that falls upon the just as well as the unjust, is for them as well as for any other class of men. Had we the power to control our national legislation, we would restrain the hand of destruction aimed at the Mormons, odious as they are and repugnant to every sentiment of decency within us, not for their sake, but for the sake of the country. We would not strike them down, for the same reason that we would not tear down a splendid monument to the genius of architecture, whose massive pillars and sky-reaching dome the labor of a century had reared, for the purpose of extracting or putting to death a miserable reptile that had hid within its walls. No; rather let it live on, though it should issue forth at times to hiss, and stink, and strike at all it met.

So much we would not do, and so far do we qualify the language of the paragraph above quoted. But we do not hesitate to say, that could it be done with safety to the principle of which we have spoken, the propagators of a general system of licentiousness like that of Mormonism—so open, shameless and indecent in its every day workings, so destructive of every quality that most ennobles man and distinguishes him from the brutes—*ought* to be hung up, every one of them, as the common enemies of mankind.

We have thus taken the pains to explain our precise meaning in the paragraph in question, because it has been taken up as a text by the *Mormon Standard* at San Francisco—of Saturday's issue—upon which to write a long article denouncing us for the expression of such a sentiment. The editor of that sheet affects to suppose that we are *literally* in favor of hanging up Mormons, or of making it the policy of the country to do so, and intimates that, if such a course is to be pursued, we had better begin with him, as he has preached Mormonism both in the Sandwich Islands and in California. We do not deny that, were we engaged in such a business, we should consider the editor of the *Standard* a fit subject for our attention; and we take occasion to say to him, since he seems to desire our notice, that, while we pity a poor, miserable fanatic, who knows no better than to be led by the nose into the filthy slough of a most foul and monstrous superstition, we scorn, with every feeling of manhood that is in us, the lying hypocrite, who *knows* that what he preaches is false, and not only false, but destructive of the very best interests of society, as it is the deadliest blight upon virtue and morality. We know well enough that the Mormon leaders expect to thrive upon what they call *persecution,*[11] and that they would delight in getting into controversies

[11] Perceptive contemporary observers argued that persecution was responsible for much of Mormonism's growth and strength: "Persecution has aided it: men who have been two or three times driven from their homes, and driven from all inhabited country for their religion's sake, if at first but half believers in it, are sure to be thoroughly so after suffering for it; and such men have some right to say they are not mere impostors." Chandless, *A Visit to Salt Lake*, 173.

with respectable newspapers, but we will, nevertheless, so far humor them on this occasion, as to tell them, in plain terms, what they are—at any rate, how they are estimated by decent people. They are considered hypocrites and impostors—a foul blot upon humanity which ought at once to be wiped out; and that they are tolerated at all, is owing not to any regard for them, but for the principle of *religious tolerance* under which, with all their loathsome vileness, they have sense enough to know that they can be protected. The sledge-hammer which is to knock out their brains is not legislation, but public opinion, and we are satisfied to let it do its work.

"'CALIFORNIA AMERICAN' ON 'MORMONISM,'" *WESTERN STANDARD,* 20 DECEMBER 1856.[12]

In our issue of the 6th instant we re-published an item from the editorial columns of the *California American* of Scaramento [*sic*?], headed "Mormonism in the Sandwich Islands," in which it was stated by the editor of that paper that the propagators of "Mormonism" on those islands "*ought to be hung up like pirates.*" In our comments upon the article we expressed our unqualified condemnation of the spirit and sentiment which it contained, remarking that if hanging *ought* to be the penalty for preaching "Mormonism" there, we were equally liable here, as "Mormonism" was the same wherever taught. The editor of the *American,* in another article on this subject in last week's paper, states that the item in question was the result of a momentary burst of indignation, and that he would not wish to be understood as being literally in favor of publicly executing "Mormon" preachers. He then delivers his opinion on the benefits of free toleration of religious opinions etc., and what he would do for the "Mormons" had he the power to control "our national legislation"—that he would restrain the hand of destruction aimed at the Latter-day Saints, not for their sake, but for the sake of the country. So far he attempts to qualify the language of the paragraph in question. But he has no sooner finished his qualifying remarks than he says that, could it be done with safety to the principle of free toleration, the propagators of a system like that of "Mormonism," "*ought* to be hung up, every one of them as the common enemies of mankind." And again, he says that they are "a foul blot upon humanity which ought at once to be wiped out." Was it another "burst of indignation" that called forth these last sentiments? We suppose that we must set it down as such, and consider the "language somewhat exaggerated," as there is so little difference between these sentiments and the sentiments of the paragraph which he has attempted to qualify, and which he says was the result of a momentary burst

[12] Reprinted in Cannon, *Writings from the "Western Standard,"* 283–85.

of indignation and contained language somewhat exaggerated, that we can scarcely detect any difference. We are pleased that the editor has informed us that he is subject to such fits when he reads anything about the progress of "Mormonism," as we shall be able, hereafter, to overlook any "exaggerated language" that he may indulge in when treating upon this subject.

Still under the influence of this "burst of indignation," however, he goes on indulging in some very vulgar and ungentlemanly language towards ourself, giving us his opinion of "Mormons" in general and ourself in particular informing us what he would do with us were he *hangman*—that if that were his business, he would consider us fit subject for his attention—all of which, after the explanation he has given, we conclude to be the unmeaning, exaggerated ravings of a man who has a strange habit, whenever the progress of "Mormonism" is alluded to, of writing about hanging men up like pirates, when in reality he does not wish to be so understood! Not being subject to "momentary bursts of indignation," nor being in the habit of dealing in "exaggeration," we confess that we cannot compete with the editor of the *American* in the use of low, abusive and ungentlemanly epithets. In this he excels us. His past education and experience have given him such ready command of ribaldry that we must for ever despair of being able to emulate him. Our sense of self-respect and neighborly courtesy, if nothing else, would forbid the attempt. But as the editor of the *American* is probably not aware of the fact, that slang and abuse do not pass among sensible and well bred people for argument and ability, we take the pains to enlighten him, and to inform him, also, that the use of such terms as *lying hypocrite—miserable fanatic—impostor—filthy monstrosity—foul superstition,* etc., only betrays a mean and ignoble spirit that, by its proficiency in vulgarity, would endeavor to hide its lack of sense. He is of the opinion that the Latter-day Saints expect to thrive on persecution, and that they would delight in getting into controversies with respectable newspapers; insinuating, of course, that he is *respectable!* and that we ought to submit quietly and resignedly to any insults or abuse to which he may give vent whenever he is seized with one of his "bursts of indignation." That is the idea conveyed throughout his whole article. He has said the "Mormons ought to be *hung* up like pirates." We have had the temerity to condemn the sentiment, though uttered by the editor of the *California American*! and because we have done this we must be bespattered by the filthy emanations of the brain and pen of a man who calls himself *respectable.* Now, we wish the editor of the *American* to distinctly understand that, whenever he shall so forget himself as to give utterance to a sentiment similar to that with which we found fault, and which he attempted to qualify, we shall unhesitatingly condemn and expose it. We do not seek either persecution or controversy; but if they are to be the consequences of our condemning odious, tyrannical and unrighteous sentiments, let them come, and we will do our best to prepare for them. We have been educated to believe that we have an equal right, with every other citizen of this Republic, to express our dissent to everything arbitrary and intolerant, and the fact that we are a Latter-day Saint will never hinder us from exercising it. The religious tolerance of which he speaks, and under which he says we have sought protection, is not a *privilege* granted unto us, neither is it anything for which we should be thankful to him or any other man; it is our inalienable *right*—our birthright—bestowed upon us by the Deity himself, and though we may be deprived of it by despots, it is still a right for which we shall ever contend.

"The Mormons Again," *Daily California American*, 22 December 1856.

[The editor of the *California American* began this rebuttal with a quotation of several lines from Cannon's editorial of 20 December 1856.]

. . . the editor of the *Standard* accuses us of using low, abusive and ungentlemanly epithets, and says something about our "past education and experience" fitting us for ribaldry. Those who know us—and not strangers—are the best judges of our "past education and experience," and they will at least bear us out when we say that our past "education and experience" never led us into any such vile and shameless conduct as is the every day practice of Mormonism, whatever may have been our "past education and experience"—and of that, as we have just intimated, we leave those who know us to speak.

In regard to our using abusive and ungentlemanly epithets, we can only say, that we generally call things by their right names. We consider the Mormon leaders *lying hypocrites,* and can find no fitter words to convey our meaning. We look upon the actual believers in Mormonism as the dupes of impostors, and regard their faith as a foul and monstrous superstition, and must so express ourselves. If there is a more elegant and gentlemanly way of signifying the same thing, we have no objection to adopting it. But a skunk is a skunk, and it would not change the nature of the animal, were we to call it an odoriferous digitigrade carnivorous mammal.

"The 'California American' Again," *Western Standard,* 3 January 1857.

Our article headed the "California *American* on Mormonism," published in the *Western Standard* of the 20th ultimo, has called forth a rejoinder from the editor of that paper, which we feel disposed to notice, though at the risk of being again charged by him with a desire to covet his attention. We have an aversion to newspaper warfare, but when assailed in the manner we have been by the *American* we should be, in our opinion, recreant to the cause with which we are identified and to every duty incumbent upon us, were we to allow it to pass unnoticed. [Cannon here summarizes at some length the newspaper war between the *Western Standard* and the *California American* to date.]

Gentlemanly courtesy will never prompt a man to call another a liar, and publish it abroad, unsupported by anything but assertion; much less will it influence him to denounce a whole community as lying hypocrites, impostors and dupes without advancing the slightest shadow of proof, other than his bare opinion, to support the charge. What would the editor of the *American think* were we to call him a driveler, a political trickster, a man who would advocate any measure or support any candidate, if he should only be paid enough? Were we to make such statements and publish them upon no other evidence than our mere say so, the mildest terms men could use to us would be that we were low, abusive and ungentlemanly, and the plea, that we "generally called things by their right names," would avail us but little. Yet this would be equally as consistent and honorable a course as the one he has taken towards us in his articles. We have, for nearly a year past, been disseminating and advocating "Mormonism" through the columns of this paper; this is the only object we had in view in publishing it. It may be presumed, therefore, that a tolerably correct idea of our doctrines can be gathered from its contents. Now, we defy the editor of the *American* to bring forward a single instance from it, or indeed from any of our publications or teachings, where licentiousness or immorality is taught and sanctioned. If "Mormonism" be such a system as he represents it to be, so vile and shameless in its everyday workings, he surely will have no difficulty in proving it be such from our writings; but we wish him to bear in mind that his idea of what is vile, shameless and fanatical will not be the standard by which we must be measured—that standard must be God's word and not man's opinion. We hope our cotemporary will not run away this time with the idea, because we have noticed him again, that we covet his attention; we want him to be undeceived on this point. We have lived thus far without the attention of so "respectable" a paper as the California *American,* and we are not yet quite so low as to be under the necessity of resorting to it. The editor of that paper may rest assured, however, that whenever he gives vent to such sentiments as he has lately advanced regarding "Mormonism" and the "Mormons," we shall never hesitate, by the assistance of that Being to whom "Mormonism" owes its origin, to expose and condemn them.

Such a Drunken Dog: the Mormon Preacher

A short article in the Sacramento *State Journal* promulgated the common assumption that Mormon women were virtual prisoners to polygamy who would happily escape Utah if only given the chance. Cannon apparently felt he could ignore this attack, but a second article recounting the crimes of a purported Mormon missionary on the same page of the same issue, provoked a pointed yet humorous response from the "editor of the Mormon *Standard.*"

In spite of Cannon's relatively gentle rebuke, the *State Journal* continued to regale its readers with articles and editorials uncomplimentary to the Mormons. The final straws for Cannon were apparently the *State Journal's* refusal to accept the fact that the infamous Mr. Willis was not an acknowledged representative of the church and its particularly vicious reporting of the unexpected death of one of Brigham Young's counselors and the mayor of Great Salt Lake City, Jedediah M. Grant. Without referencing the specific articles that provoked him, Cannon's final word on the *Journal* was to dismiss it as "the most mendacious and corrupt" newspaper in California.

"MORMONS AND THE RAILROAD," *DEMOCRATIC STATE JOURNAL,* 15 DECEMBER 1856.

The San Francisco Sun has a leader advocating the construction of a railroad from this State to Salt Lake City. It thinks that if the isolation of the people in that locality could be destroyed, it would be the most legitimate and effective way to change the order of things there. The article expresses the opinion that the Mormon "wives" would break for California by the herd, if there were such a facility.[13] The leaders of the Mormons will join heartily to the work, as it will greatly increase the value of their large tracts of land.

"A MORMON PREACHER IN THE CHAIN GANG," *DEMOCRATIC STATE JOURNAL,* 15 DECEMBER 1856.

We mentioned a day or two since that a fellow named Willis was convicted of stealing a carpet-bag and contents from a negro at one of our hotels.[14] He had hoped to escape by the refusal of the Court to receive the

---

[13] The advent of the transcontinental railroad hardly resulted in Mormon women breaking for California "by the herd." On the contrary, the Rev. Leonard Bacon lamented that the railroad "has added millions to the wealth of the Mormon chiefs; it has facilitated the going forth of emissaries from Salt Lake City to the ends of the earth, and the coming in of the wretched dupes by thousands to swell the Mormon population and the Mormon vote, not only in Utah but in the neighboring Territories." See Froiseth, *The Women of Mormonism,* 305.

[14] Not enough information about Willis is available to identify him. There are a number of candidates: Lt. W. W. Willis, who led a Mormon Battalion detachment to Pueblo in 1846; Joshua I. Willis, who settled Toquerville, Utah; Sidney Willes, a battalion veteran and one of the discoverers of California gold at Mormon Island (whom Cannon knew personally); Sidney's brother, Ira, another battalion veteran and author of a popular guide to the gold mines; and John Willis, later implicated in the Mountain Meadows Massacre. (These and other names are indexed in Robert's *Comprehensive History* and in Jenson's *Latter-day Saint Biographical Encyclopedia.*) This Willis does not appear to have been any of these men or even a member of the LDS church.

testimony of the person robbed, but there was other evidence, and he was sent to the chain-gang for thirty days. He was sent by Vicegerent Young from Salt Lake on a mission to convert the Sandwich Islanders. Willis lectured on phrenology in this city in 1852, and afterwards became such a drunken dog that his wife, who had accompanied him, left in disgust and went back. She is probably now safe in the bosom, not of Abraham, but Brigham, Jedediah, or some of the bogus prophets. Young, in one of his late elegant addresses, remarked that he didn't intend to send decent men on missions, for he wanted them to stay there and attend to their business, but he chose to send away the poor "cusses" that were of no use at home. He certainly hit the nail on the head in this case, and in some others that could be named. The editor of the Mormon Standard and his brother missionaries must feel highly complimented in being placed in such a category, by their lord and master, the mighty Brigham.

"An Untruthful Statement," *Western Standard,* 20 December 1856.

Under the head of "A Mormon preacher in the Chain gang," the Sacramento State Journal of Monday last has a city item, detailing the arrest of a man by the name of Willis for stealing a carpet-bag from one of the hotels, and his sentence to the chain-gang for thirty days. The writer of the item in question states that Willis was sent from Salt Lake by "Vicegerent" Young on a mission to convert the Sandwich Islanders, and after his arrival in that city lectured on phrenology, etc. He finally became such a drunkard that his family, who it seems accompanied him from Salt Lake, left him and returned there.

At the risk of spoiling so good an item, we take the liberty of informing the State Journal that when it states that this man Willis is a Mormon preacher, or that such an individual was ever sent to the Sandwich Islands on a mission it states a falsehood. If there ever was a person of that name who lectured in Sacramento on phrenology, or got drunk, or stole a carpet-bag, or worked in the chain-gang, he certainly deceived the Sacramentans when he said he was a Mormon preacher, for no such person, bearing such a name, has been sent either to the Sandwich Islands or to California as a preacher from Salt Lake. So much for the "Mormon preacher in the Chain-gang." If this fellow ever was in Salt Lake Valley, he no doubt found that the society there was exceedingly uncongenial to a man of his tastes, and concluded he would strike for California where there is so much encouragement and protection for men of his stripe.

"Willis, the Mormon Preacher," *Democratic State Journal,* 15 January 1857.

This "divine," who has served out his term in the chain-gang, got into another scrape yesterday. He had a "revelation" that certain cunning artificers in timber were laboring in a new dwelling-house erected at the corner of L and 8th streets, and that said hewers of wood were in the habit of leaving their tools about when they went to dinner. He accordingly proceeded to that field of labor and laid tithes upon the property spoken of to the extent of two hand saws. Unluckily for the man of many wives and other sorrows, the carpenters could not be made to receive the doctrine of running saws upon them, and the Elder was trotted to the Station House. As there has been an unjust attempt to deprive Willis of the honors of his Church, we would simply invite those who see fit to deny the position of this pillar of the faith, to call on the Reporter of the Journal.

"BEFORE HIS JUDGE," *DEMOCRATIC STATE JOURNAL*, 15 JANUARY 1857.

Jedediah Grant, the second person in rank[15] in the Mormon Church at Salt Lake, died on the 1st of December last. This person had at the time of his death more women living with him in the degraded state countenanced by that community, than any member of it except Young, the leader. The forty or fifty[16] poor, foolish, simple, betrayed females are left behind with their characters blasted forever in the estimation of all reasonable, respectable and honest persons. It is a fearful thing to go into the presence of the Almighty with the load of guilt that this polluted soul carried with it; with the groans and tears of these wretched beings who have long ere this seen the folly of their conduct; with the curses of many a wretched parent, brother or husband, (for such as him do not scruple to break the most solemn obligations previously formed, when it suits their lustful purposes,) bowed with grief and shame at the seduction of those they once so well loved, by this priestly profligate. The absurd abstractions with which those leaders in this abhorred iniquity have been defended, will never avail them at the bar before which one of their fellow culprits may be now standing. Let those who advocate and excuse such horrid crime beware, for their time must also come, and their guilt is little inferior.

[15] Grant, whose various nicknames were "Mormon Thunder" and "The Sledgehammer of Brigham" as well as the more affectionate "Jeddy," was the second, not the first counselor to Brigham Young. He was a puritanical reformer and fiery orator whose mission in life was to call his people to repentance: "May all the sluggards and the drones who will not do this, be bit by bed-bugs, and tormented by the nightmare, and have their bodies clogged with a conscience clear as mud." Sessions, *Mormon Thunder*, 167. Grant was arguably the one person most responsible for the good, as well as the excesses, of the Utah Reformation of 1857.

[16] A gross exaggeration—Quinn lists but seven plural wives of Grant. Perhaps the *Journal's* editor was thinking of Brigham Young's other counselor, Heber C. Kimball, who married some forty-four women, though many of these marriages were apparently never consummated. See Quinn, *The Mormon Hierarchy: Origins of Power*, 549 and 557.

"Mendacity of the 'State Journal,'"
Western Standard, 24 January 1857.[17]

Whether it is because there is nothing to be gained at present by keeping quiet on "Mormon" topics, or for some other reason, the Sacramento *State Journal* has, of late, taken particular pains to publish every low, scurrilous article that could be found about the "Mormons." Not content with republishing everything of this kind that could be selected, the editors have been to the pains to manufacture items to suit, thinking it no disgrace to utter barefaced lies to make a good story. The unenviable notoriety which this paper has recently gained throughout the State for being the most mendacious and corrupt sheet published within its limits, makes its slanders on "Mormonism" and the "Mormons" comparatively innocuous. The editors are in a position somewhat similar to the shepherd boy in the fable, who so completely lost his character for truthfulness by giving false alarms, that his cries, even when there was a good cause for them, were heard unheeded. Were "Mormonism" and the "Mormons" even to become so bad as they depict them to be, they can never make the public, who are acquainted with the late course of their sheet, believe that there can be any reliability attached to their statements; and, like all slanderers, they will find that their efforts to defame and blacken the characters of an innocent people, will result in their own discomfiture and disgrace.

Cannon might have been referring to characters such as the unidentified Willis when he complained that "One thing that has tended in no small degree to lessen 'Mormonism' has been the conduct of some who pass as Mormons, and who when they get into any mean, nasty scrape, must have . . . the name of 'Mormon' or of 'Mormonism' dragged in."[18]

While it might appear highly unlikely that such a character would have been sent on a mission by Brigham Young, this report from a San Francisco newspaper was not entirely inaccurate:

They admit, however, that Brigham Young did say, in one of his speeches, and that it is a custom in the church, when a man is troublesome, or drinks or gambles, or is full of chicanery and deceit in his dealings with his neighbors, or with church property entrusted to his care, and in Young's words 'gets to be too bad for Salt Lake,' to send him off on some distant mission to preach and gather converts. This, they say, gives him a last chance to reform and become useful; but if he continues to do ill, the elder or presi-

[17] Reprinted in Cannon, Writings from the *"Western Standard,"* 324.

[18] *Deseret News*, 14 November 1855, 286, quoted in Flake, "George Q. Cannon's Mission to California," 89.

> dent of the branch where he is sent, reports him at once, and he is immediately cut off forever, though upon giving satisfactory evidences of a true repentance and reform, he may be received again. This way of getting rid of troublesome characters they regard as a very smart piece of management; but, they add, there are very few sent out on missions under such circumstances, and they said they knew of only one batch of preachers of that kind, who left Salt Lake last year.[19]

Anti-Mormons charged that Brigham Young routinely sent his greatest rascals on missions. One argued that "it is the Mormon custom to send all who are unruly and hard to manage, or who have committed crimes, on a mission. It is thought that by 'bearing the pure vessels of the Lord' to such poor wicked wretches as the Gentiles, they will perchance themselves become purified."[20] Yet another argued that "men who are disposed to be turbulent, and who may exercise an influence dangerous to the reigning prophet, are sent to distant parts of the globe, to keep them out of the way. Some, too, who have become miserable sots, and otherwise burdensome, are sent off, in the hope that they will die or reform."[21] The woman who dared divorce Brigham Young named names: "Joseph A. [Young's son] was sent because his father did not know what else to do with him; he had become so dissipated and caused so much trouble at home."[22]

On one occasion, Brigham Young essentially conceded the point. "We have at times sent men on missions to get rid of them; but they have generally come back," he said at a church conference in 1860. "Some think it is an imposition upon the world to send such men among them. But which is best—to keep them here to pollute others, or to send them where pollution is more prevalent?"[23] More typically, Young admonished his missionaries to achieve and maintain personal worthiness: "If the Elders cannot go with clean hands and pure hearts, they had better stay here and wash a little longer . . . be pure from the crown of the head to the soles of your feet; then live so every hour. Go

[19] "Talks with the Mormons," *Evening Bulletin,* 25 August 1857.

[20] Waite, *The Mormon Prophet and His Harem,* 192.

[21] Ferris, *Utah and the Mormons,* 337.

[22] Young, *Wife No. 19,* 170. See also *Mormonism,* 191-96.

[23] Brigham Young, "Appointment of Elder Cannon to Fill Up the Quorum of the Twelve—Remarks To Departing Missionaries," 7 April 1860, *Journal of Discourses,* 7:228–29. See also Whittaker, "Brigham Young and the Missionary Enterprise," 85–106.

in that manner, and in that manner labor, and return again as clean as a piece of pure white paper. This is the way to go; and if you do not do that, your hearts will ache."[24]

Whether an Elder Willis was sent on a mission for personal reformation or simply to get rid of him, as president of the California Mission Cannon would have known of any accredited missionary by that name. Cannon argued that Willis was no saint, his actions were not in harmony with the teachings of the Church of Jesus Christ of Latter-day Saints, and that the church should therefore not be judged by such an individual. That did not stop those who—for whatever reason—had a need to demonize Mormonism. David M. Stuart, one of Cannon's young missionaries, complained of the effect such sentiments were having on the missionary work in California:

> They have substituted the word "Mormonism" for "Hell," it answers their purpose admirably. The other night we stopped with a Mr. Simmonds at Hillsborough, Washington Co., O.T. [Oregon Territory]. His wife had never seen a Mormon before, and she sat up all night for fear the Mormon elders would run off with her. An old lady told us her minister said we were spies come to take the country and run off with the women. They have scared the women round here so that they won't come out to hear us.[25]

Jedediah M. Grant, on the other hand, was convinced that "Hell" was exactly what most Californians were interested in. Trying to console George Q. Cannon for his relative lack of success in bringing people to Zion, Grant wrote, "If you can satisfy the people that in the Territory of Utah, they will find in every city, village and hamlet gambling houses, houses of *approved fame,* tippling influences, secret and French customs and fashions, plenty of well written novels, all the luxuries of life easily obtained, then you might get them from Babylon."[26]

The critics of Mormonism perceived the religion as a very real threat to what little social stability existed in the West during the middle of the nineteenth century. As the Mormons themselves tried to understand just

[24] Brigham Young, "Necessity of the Servants of God Being Pure in Heart and Deed . . .," 28 August 1852, *Journal of Discourses,* 6:273.

[25] "From Oregon Territory, Extracts of a letter from Elder David M. Stuart to Elder Wm. H. Shearman," *Western Standard,* 17 July 1857, 3.

[26] "Letter from President J. M. Grant," *Western Standard,* 12 September 1856, 3.

why they were so unpopular, many simply shook their heads in disbelief, echoing the words of David Taylor, a contributor to the correspondence page of the *Western Standard:*

> That there are bad men in every society none will deny, nor do we attempt to deny that many such join the Saints . . . I have been told that some have done wrong; but it is not reasonable to condemn a people because some of their associates are wicked; upon this principle of reasoning, who would be able to stand?
>
> . . . I am no respecter of persons and contend that every man who respects himself should be respected, whether he be a christian or an infidel. I do know that the Latter-Day Saints have done some things which are commendable, and deserving the praise of any people. They have settled the western wilds, and caused the wilderness to blossom as the rose, and where, but a few years ago, the rude savage held dominion, there may now be seen growing cities and fields of waving grain; where the Indians once danced around their council fires, and sung their songs of war, there, where the Sabbath of the Lord was once unknown, may be seen congregated people from every clime, and with smiling faces and happy hearts, singing sweet anthems of praise to the everlasting God.
>
> With all these facts staring him in the face, how can any enterprising man help admiring Mormon character? Every reflecting man should admire virtue, industry and intelligence wherever it may be found, and judged upon this principle, the Saints will bear investigation, and their character come out bright from scrutiny.[27]

Language So Beastly and Degraded: Brigham Young's Profanity

Brigham Young's coarse and often inflammatory rhetoric—which John Hyde, the subject of a later chapter, was able to quote with such effect—posed a host of problems for Mormon newspaper editors and diplomats charged with defending their religion in the press and the halls of congress. Critics had a field day with the extemporaneous and folksy sermons of LDS leaders, attacking both the style of Mormon orators, which was laced with plain language and generally mild oaths, and its political content, which sounded treasonous to many Americans. The fiery discourses of leaders such as Jedediah Grant, Parley P. Pratt,

[27] "Why is Public Sentiment Hostile to the Mormons?" Ibid.

and Brigham Young often seemed designed to provoke outrage outside of Utah.[28]

This language, along with polygamy, proved to be a particular stumbling block to the faith of Frederick Margetson. While frontier newspaper editors overlooked their own "salty" language, they were not used to hearing or reading of extemporaneous and often rough vernacular from the pulpit or, as the LDS phrased it, "the stand." The editor of the *Daily Evening Bulletin* found apostate Margetson's objections to Brigham's language a perfect excuse to point to the supposed hypocrisy of Mormonism.

"Another Witness Against the Mormons," *Daily Evening Bulletin*, 3 July 1857.

Frederick G. I. Margetson, a converted Mormon, has sent us a long communication from Los Angeles, in which he seeks to expose to the world some of the "Horrors of Mormonism." His paper is too long and too loosely written to admit of its publication entire. We are, therefore, forced to give the gist of his statements in a more condensed form; in which shape they will the more readily meet the eye of the reader.

Mr. Margetson says he was only fourteen years old when he was converted to Mormonism, and connected himself with the Church of Latter Day Saints, which he did in his own country. He warns the public against the missionary agents of the Mormons, and exposes their mode of proselyting the young of both sexes. He says these missionaries labored pertinaciously to undermine his principles; they continually represented the necessity of embracing their doctrines—this was demanded by his spiritual and eternal happiness and welfare; nor did they fail in holding out temporal inducements and rewards. These missionaries promised him land in unlimited quantities, to be free of taxation, if he would but go to Utah. They represented in glowing colors the advantages of a residence among the "Saints"—the parental care and supervision that would be bestowed upon him; how he should be nursed when sick, and cherished and restored to health by the loving priesthood. These arguments and temptations proved sufficient to lead the youthful mind of Mr. Margetson estray [*sic*]. He embraced Mormonism, and set out for Salt Lake City, where he arrived as he was entering his sixteenth year. He had not long been there, however,

[28] For analyses of this problem, see Jones, "Brigham Young's Rhetoric"; Keele, "A Doctrinal Group Counterattacks: An Analysis of the Oral Rhetoric of the Mormons in the Utah War"; Poll and MacKinnon, "Causes of the Utah War Reconsidered," Walker, "Raining Pitchforks"; and Parshall, "The Many Voices of Brigham Young."

before the scales fell from his eyes, and he saw that he had been deluded. We give his own words:

Young as I was when I arrived in Utah, it was not long before I discovered, that all I had heard, and been taught to believe by the Missionary Agents, were misrepresentations. I found discord and confusion amongst the very body itself—saint arrayed against saint, priest against priest, elder against elder; laws imperfectly administered, the vile system of polygamy in all its hideousness prevailing, the peace of families destroyed, and the priesthood, illiterate and ignorant, generally profane swearers and reprobates; Brigham Young himself, in the pulpit, often using language so beastly and degraded, that at this distance of time I cannot bring the subject to my recollection without an emotion of horror. And as to the worldly or temporal inducements—in vain. I sought for land, or the care and attention I had expected in the hour of sickness. I found the same cold, callous world I had left behind me—no soothing voice to cheer, no saintly supervision, but all heartless and dreary.

Our correspondent charges directly, that not content with polygamy, the heads of the Mormon Church are now seeking to legalize marriages between the children of a father and the children of a wife by a former marriage, thus establishing almost incestuous intercourse between brothers and sisters. He relates an instance of one man, whom he is ready to name, marrying at the same time a mother and her young daughter; and another, of an elder marrying three sisters. And he says a very well known case occurred while he resided in Utah—during the illness of a Mormon's wife in childbed, the husband compassed the ruin of a young girl attending upon her, which coming to her knowledge, so acted upon her enfeebled frame that it produce insanity, and subsequently death.

Brigham Young is represented by our correspondent as being a man of information and vigor of intellect, but extremely illiterate. He is profane and blasphemous in his language, and this vice is particularly exhibited in the pulpit, where he boasts he "does all his swearing" to impress upon his audience the force of his doctrines!

Mr. Margetson is undoubtedly in earnest in his declarations about Mormonism; and we hope that his warning may not be without its effect.

"Another Witness Against the Mormons," The *Western Standard*, 10 July 1857.[29]

In the *Evening Bulletin* of Friday last, we find another of those articles for which that paper has lately become so noted. It is headed "Another witness against the Mormons," and is based upon a "long and loosely written" com-

[29] Reprinted in Cannon, *Writings from the "Western Standard,"* 472–75.

munication sent by one Frederick G. I. Margetson, of Los Angeles, to the editor of the *Bulletin*. . .

The *Bulletin,* whether in consequence of the known proclivities of its editor, or some other cause, has been extremely unfortunate in its choice of correspondents and witnesses against the "Mormons;" and in no instance has it been more so than in bringing forward the testimony of this man Margetson. To those who know the man it will appear highly ludicrous, and they will certainly conclude that the editor of the *Bulletin* is desperately eager to obtain evidence of any kind and from every source against the "Mormons," or he would never publish this. Throughout the Great Salt Lake country, Margetson was well known during his residence there as a most incorrigible loafer—a man too lazy to make the necessary exertions to support himself. During a few months' residence in Great Salt Lake City, during the winter of 1854-5 we had an opportunity of knowing something relative to the course of this "deluded young man." He had friends there who were willing to do all in their power for him; but his habits of laziness (he may call them principles) were so confirmed that they found it impossible to undermine them, and they gave up the attempt in disgust. Of course, it would be in vain for a man of this description to seek for land there; he had not energy enough, during his residence of three years and a half, to accumulate sufficient means to purchase cultivated and improved land; and to go to a new settlement, where he could have any reasonable amount by fencing and taking care of it involved too much labor.

The missionaries whom he heard, told the truth when they said that land could be obtained readily in Utah. At the time he went there it could be obtained in many places in unlimited quantities by paying for the surveying and recording. Hundreds who went there after he arrived, obtained all they wanted; and hundreds more will obtain all they can cultivate and they will expect it to be taxed. No missionary would be so simple as to tell them that real estate would be free from taxation; because every man and boy of reflection would know that it would be indispensably necessary for the development and improvement of the country. Had he investigated "Mormonism," as he should have done before embracing it, and exercised the common sense with which nature endowed him, he would never have imbibed the idea that when he landed in Utah he would have no occasion to labor or exert himself, neither would he have expected the people there to have carried him in their arms. A boy of eight years of age, gifted with an ordinary capacity, would see, upon reading the history of "Mormonism," and inquiring into the work yet remaining which it had to accomplish, that, if he connected himself therewith, he must exert himself with all his energy for his own sustenance, and must also expect nothing more from others than he himself would be willing to bestow. As to his statement that he did not receive that care and attention there that he expected, he must have had very unreasonable expectations or he would have been satisfied. We know that he was treated kindly in Utah, and received every encouragement that any reasonable man could have expected. Even after he left Utah, in the spring of 1855, and came to this country, he was befriended by the "Mormons," among whom he made great professions of faith in "Mormonism." In fact, it was through "Mormon" influence and aid that he was enabled to go from this city to Los Angeles. He had not money enough to pay the regular fare on the steamer; but a gentleman connected with this office, taking pity on him, and thinking he might do better under the care of his parents, who reside in Los Angeles, mentioned his case to a party of Latter-day Saints, who were going to San Bernardino and he was taken along at a reduced rate.

We knew that Margetson was a drone; his communication convinces us that laziness is not his only bad quality. He has written base falsehoods,—things which he knew to be false; but the idea that the testimony of such as he should be adduced against the "Mormons," will be as amusing to the people of Great Salt Lake City, who know him, as it was to us when we saw it. We only condescend to allude to him and his communication, to give the editor of the *Bulletin* an insight into the character of his new witness against the "Mormons." When the gentleman receives any more communications about the people of Utah, we would advise him to inquire a little into the antecedents of the writers. A few minutes conversation with us might enlighten him, and might save him considerable labor in patching up "long and loosely written" communications, and making them presentable to the public and telling against the "Mormons."

Regardless of Margetson's basic character, he was not the only person to comment on Mormon leaders swearing at the pulpit. "Nearly all the newcomers attended our church or rather theatre, for more amusement is exhibited there than the play-house can furnish," Joseph P. Hamelin, Jr., wrote during his 1849 visit to Salt Lake. "Brigham Young then arose and went on in a string of blasphemy which would put a blush on a Five-point bully.[30] He insulted every member of his church, cursed, swore, and used the most vulgar language. Every decent person must have been much disgusted."[31] J. H. Beadle, who edited an anti-Mormon newspaper in Corinne, Utah, for fifteen months in 1869 and 1870,[32] professed shock at the language he heard from the pulpit: "For the first time in my

[30] See chapter 3, note 6.

[31] Hamelin, Jr., Journal, 23 September 1849, Beinecke Library.

[32] For an overview of Beadle's association with the *Salt Lake Reporter*, see Dary, *Red Blood & Black Ink*, 198–201.

life I heard the Government and people of the United States denounced, ridiculed and cursed, and the very name of American made a hissing and a byword; for the first time I heard professed preachers swearing in the pulpit, and such expressions as 'd——d apostate' flung recklessly about by so-called apostles and priests."[33]

Lt. J. W. Gunnison offered a contemporary analysis of this predilection for cussing:

> Much has been said of the Mormon profanity, in the pulpit and out of it. But what is considered profanity by the world, is not thus considered with them—for they take their vain oaths without taking the name of the Supreme in connection with the words.
>
> They curse or condemn with man's curses whenever they please, and such rough language sounds gratingly in refined ears, when it becomes usual in ordinary conversation—how they have learned to consider it innocent, we cannot imagine . . .
>
> When, therefore, we hear that their apostles and prophets have outraged decency in their temple language, let us bear in mind their education and instruction is to make a distinction between the most denunciatory words applied as expressions of dissent or emphasis, and taking the name of Jehovah in connection with the epithets, whereby they become blasphemy, and subject to severe civil penalty.[34]

Jedediah M. Grant excused the "Hyperbolic Fancies" found in many of the speeches of the Mormon leaders as part of a "style of speaking all our own."[35] Brigham Young apparently saw no problem with swearing, so long as it was not blasphemous and was done to serve a holy purpose: "I swear some, my brethren and sisters; but it is always in the pulpit,—never anywhere else."[36] According to John C. Bennett, this proclivity for swearing can be traced all the way back to Joseph Smith: "Joe is notoriously profane, but he says God will not notice him in cursing the DAMNED GENTILES!"[37]

One especially humorous example of Young's use of salty language—which may very well have been colored through the re-telling and/or

---

[33] Beadle, *Life in Utah*, 285.

[34] Gunnison, *The Mormons, or, Latter-day Saints, in the Valley of the Great Salt Lake*, 73–74.

[35] Letter to the *New York Herald*, 8 April 1852.

[36] Quoted in Waite, *The Mormon Prophet and His Harem*, 102.

[37] Bennett, *The History of the Saints*, 94.

recording—is found in the 8 July 1858 diary entry of John D. Lee. The context is the Utah War negotiations between Young and other Mormon leaders and Gov. Alfred Cumming and the peace commissioners, Lazarus Powell and Ben McCulloch:

> Pres. Young seeing the obstinacy on the part of the government officers gave them to understand his fee[l]ings re[l]ative to the matter, by relating an anecdote of a man that was tried by a prejudice[d] court. The Judge anounced the Sentence verry gravely which was as follows: The Prisoner Shall be hanged until he is dead; dead; dead; The Prisoner knoing that inJustice had been done Replied as gravely, Kiss my Ass; kiss my ass; kiss my ass.[38]

He Speaks from the Heart: Brigham Young's Rhetoric

Beyond whatever troubles Brigham Young's choice of language created, his heated political rhetoric raised a host of problems for Mormon defenders, particularly when it appeared in national newspapers, far removed from its cultural context. Outsiders who understood that context and took the time to get to know Young were often capable of considerable indulgence. Two sophisticated Europeans, the French botanist, Jules Remy and his scholarly traveling companion, Julius Brenchley, expressed their appreciation of Young's folksy speaking style after visiting Great Salt Lake City in 1855:

> Brigham exercises great influence as a preacher. An orator he certainly is not, in the classical sense of the word; his sermons are stuffed full of puns, jokes, buffooneries even, which remind us more of the curate of Meudon than of the eagle of Meaux, of Rabelais rather than of Bossuet,[39] and would most certainly revolt our European fastidiousness; but, then, he is not addressing himself to the charming penitents of the Madeleine, he has to do with quite a different public, and as, in all probability, he instinctively knows that the first condition of a speaker's success is to place himself on a level with his audience, he has done so with his, and so much to their satis-

[38] Cleland and Brooks, eds., *A Mormon Chronicle*, I:175. See also Jones, "Brigham Young's Rhetoric."

[39] François Rabelais (1483?–1553) was a French humanist and satirist best known for *Gargantua and Pantagruel*. As a Benedictine monk, he spent his last years as the curate of Meudon. The eloquence of Bishop Jacques Bossuet (1627–1704) won him the nickname Eagle of Meaux.

> faction that they allow themselves to be persuaded and convinced, which is always the true sign and object of eloquence. Moreover, he has qualities which are everywhere favourably appreciated. His manner in the pulpit is simple, agreeable, and perfectly devoid of affectation; he speaks from the heart and the fullness of it. He does not preach, he converses . . . It is impossible not to admire his tact, and on leaving him, we carry away with us a feeling of respect, and a better opinion of Mormonism, at all events, to say nothing of human nature.[40]

American humorist Charles F. Browne, writing under the name of Artemus Ward, had this to say about the lack of piety of the Mormon prophet, often inferred from his sometimes profane language: "Brigham Young is a man of great natural ability. If you ask me, How pious is he? I treat it as a conundrum, and give it up. Personally he treated me with marked kindness throughout my sojourn in Utah." (This despite Browne's earlier imaginary interview with Young in which he concluded that Salt Lake was a "2nd Soddum & Germorrer, inhabitid by as theavin & onprincipled a set of retchis as ever drew Breth in eny spot on the Globe.")[41]

Brigham Young was well aware of the problems his forthright statements raised but he was typically blunt in dismissing those who thought he should keep the Lord's inspired directives to himself.

BRIGHAM YOUNG, 6 OCTOBER 1855, *JOURNAL OF DISCOURSES*, 3:48–49.

> I have wise brethren around me who will sometimes say, "Don't speak so and so, be very careful, now do be cautious;" and I have been written to from the east; I have package after package of letters, yes, a wheelbarrow load of them, saying, "O, brother Brigham, I would beseech and pray and plead with you, if I only dare, to be careful how you speak. Would not this or that course be better than for you to get up in the stand, and tell the Gentiles what they are? Would it not be better to keep this to yourself?"
>
> Do you know how I feel when I get such communications? I will tell you, I feel just like rubbing their noses with them. If I am not to have the privilege of speaking of Saint and sinner when I please, tie up my mouth and let me go to the grave, for my work would be done.
>
> It was for this that they killed Joseph and Hyrum, it is for this that they wish to kill me and my brethren; we know their iniquity, and we will tell of

[40] Remy and Brenchley, *A Journey to Great-Salt-Lake City*, 1:498–500.

[41] Browne, *The Complete Works*, 219, 76. (The original misspellings were for comic effect.)

> it when the Spirit dictates, or talk about this, that, or the other person and conduct at the proper time.

Were the Mormons of mid-nineteenth century America "saints" or "sinners"? The answer would have to be an unqualified "both." Like any people, the Mormons had plenty of the good and the bad among them. To judge the entire religion—either for bad *or* for good on the basis of a single individual would be completely unjust. Nonetheless, that is exactly what happened in the frontier West. Far too often, those who did the judging did so on the basis of second- or third-hand information, often from those who had once been members of the church, but who had left with hurt feelings and personal grudges.

On the other hand, Brigham Young's inflammatory anti-government pronouncements, laced as they often were with profanity, contributed to the perception that the Saints had turned against American values in general and the government of the United States in particular. As a powerful religious leader, the Superintendent of Indian Affairs, and the Territorial Governor, Young made a serious error in speaking as freely as he did. While his wry wit and contempt for his perceived enemies played well at home, his provocative rhetoric only exacerbated the general prejudice against the Mormons, thereby contributing to a volatile momentum that seemed inextricably headed towards war.

The only known image of John Hyde, as a Swedenborgian minister shortly before his death in 1875.
Courtesy, Swedenborg Library, Bryn Athyn College.

Chapter 4

"THE PUSILLANIMOUS RAILINGS OF AN APOSTATE MORMON" The Strange Case of Elder Cannon and Mr. Hyde

Just as many Americans and most Westerners perceived Mormons as a threat to their culture and religion, the Mormons often perceived those who had become disaffected with their religion as their greatest threat—and not without reason. From the outset, the faith's most dedicated and dangerous enemies were those who had once enjoyed the hand of fellowship among the Saints. As Kimball Young put it, "apostates are the religious equivalent of political traitors."[1] Whether in Kirtland, Far West, or Nauvoo, the defectors left the Mormons but could not leave the Mormons alone. They wrote the exposés, the damning histories, and furious letters to the editor that created so many problems for Joseph Smith and his struggling but ever-growing band of believers. "What has been the starting point of all your afflictions?" Brigham Young asked the Saints in 1853. "They began with apostates in your midst; these disaffected Spirits caused others to come in, worse than they, who would run out and bring in all the devils they possibly could. That has been the starting point and grand cause of all our difficulties, every time we were driven."[2]

This pattern did not end with the western hegira of Brigham Young and his followers. The harsh conditions under which Mormonism survived in the American West and the challenges that Brigham Young presented to converts to "live their religion" generated a host of apostates.

---

[1] Young, *Isn't One Wife Enough?*, 3.

[2] Brigham Young, "Joseph, a True Prophet—Apostates—Dream, Etc.," 27 March 1853, *Journal of Discourses*, 1:82.

Caught up in a spiritual reformation beginning in fall 1856 that eschewed lukewarm Saints, members of the Church of Jesus Christ of Latter-day Saints soon found themselves either becoming more committed to Brigham Young or increasingly alienated from a religious and social system that had little tolerance for dissent. In frontier Zion, one was either a part of the church or apart from it. One of the most prominent and ultimately influential dissenters from Mormonism at this time was Elder John Hyde, Jr.[3]

TYRANNY AND WRONG, CORRUPTION AND SORROW, VICE AND CRIME

Later characterized by Edward W. Tullidge as the "the ablest intellectual apostate of the Mormon church,"[4] John Hyde was born in England in 1833. He joined the Mormons at age fifteen and almost immediately engaged in missionary work, joining John Taylor in France in 1851. With about four hundred other converts this gifted and classically-educated young man sailed from Liverpool in 1853 and crossed the plains to Zion, where he married and began teaching school. Early in 1854 he was "initiated into the mysteries of the 'Mormon endowment,'" which included "the most solemn oaths, accompanied by frightful penalties." As noted by Leonard J. Arrington, Hyde "could not bridge the gap between his own mystical vision of God and the crude reality of the kingdom of God in the mountains."[5] The inconsistencies he perceived in Mormonism, along with the dramatic temple rites, apparently began to erode his faith, for he soon resolved to leave Utah for California. Hyde was subsequently called on a mission to Hawaii, probably because Brigham Young felt that immersing Hyde back into the spiritual life of

---

[3] For the best treatment to date on Hyde, see Jorgensen, "John Hyde Jr., Mormon Renegade," 120–44.

[4] Tullidge, *Tullidge's Histories,* 2:445. Tullidge compared Hyde to Satan: "the young man was brilliant, eloquent, his mouth full of words, luminous like Lucifer, with his own light, like him proud of his intellect and ambitions, self-conscious that he could reach the pinnacle, if the chance were given him, and the pinnacle by right of his native excellence belonged to him."

[5] Arrington, "Centrifugal Tendencies in Mormon History," 171. In discussing Hyde's dramatic exposé of the temple rites, Edward W. Tullidge suggested "The burlesque is his own; certainly not of the Mormon temple and the august revelation of creation." Writing in 1889, Tullidge found Hyde's sensational description of the ritual to carry a "spirit of blasphemy, which sufficiently shows the apostate malice in the telling." *Tullidge's Histories,* 2:437, 439.

the mission field would help him regain his enthusiasm for the gospel. He accepted the call, either as an opportunity to get to California in spite of his poverty or thinking that "perhaps, as I was told, I had 'grown rusty'" and that "to be actively employed in the ministry might waken up my old confidence; that in the effort to convince others, I might succeed in reconvincing myself." He later wrote, "I tried hard to believe it true."[6] In all likelihood, he was responding to both of these motives in accepting this mission call.

The *Western Standard* had published Hyde's inspirational poetry and a couple of newsy letters, and while on his way to Hawaii he lectured on the virtues of polygamy in San Francisco.[7] As he sailed west, *The Pacific* printed lengthy extracts from Hyde's pro-Mormon lecture, but by the time he had reached the Sandwich Islands, he had decided to publicly renounce Mormonism.

The Pacific was only too happy to print his retractions and publicize his anti-Mormon lectures. Perhaps sensing how much damage Hyde could do to the LDS church, Cannon took immediate and particular pains to denounce his newfound enlightenment as nothing short of shameless hypocrisy.

"RENUNCIATION OF MORMONISM," *THE PACIFIC*, 27 NOVEMBER 1856.

We are happy to publish below, a letter from Mr. John Hyde, Jr., recently an Elder in the Mormon Church. When we published a few weeks since, in the Pacific, the report to which he alludes, of a lecture delivered by him in San Francisco, in favor of polygamy, we did it knowing that he was regarded as one of the most talented members of the Mormon community, and wishing to give the strength of their own arguments in the language of a believer. The impression which he made was that of a candid man, seeking not so much to make proselytes as to arrive at truth. It is with great pleasure that we learn of his renunciation of an error, into which, when but a youth an enthusiastic nature caused him to be led. . . . We are thankful that he intends visiting this State and also England. May Providence make him instrumental in opening the eyes of multitudes to the abominations and pollutions of their so-called religion. While the nation is pondering how to meet the evil threatening us, in the existence of the anomalous community in Utah, Providence may thus be raising up instrumentalities, seemingly insignificant, like

[6] Bancroft, *History of Utah*, 152n11; and Hyde, *Mormonism*, 20–22.

[7] Hyde's poetry appeared in *Western Standard*, 19 July, 9 August, 23 August, 20 September, and 1 November 1856; for his letters, see the editions of 12 July and 23 August 1856.

David with his sling, yet really more powerful than legislation and armies to overthrow the legions of a false prophet.

[Letter from John Hyde, Jr.]

SIRS:—I feel it my duty to make this intrusion on your time and attention. In your issue of Sept. 18th ult. you have reported at some length a lecture delivered by me on the Sabbath evening previous. The ground I there took was, the scripturality and morality of polygamy. Since leaving Salt Lake, and even at the very time of my delivering those two lectures, my mind had been severely tried as to the truth of the claims and pretensions of the Mormons. In the hurry and occupation of a trip across the plains, the constant excitement of meeting small parties to support the positions assumed by the Mormons, while at San Francisco, besides feeling a warm and strongly prejudiced desire to be able to see Mormonism as I once saw it, I had but little leisure calmly and carefully to investigate and reconsider my position. The God of truth has led me I believe to perceive many of their and my errors. Gradual doubt and darkness grew upon me, and led me to examine. Investigation confirmed instead of dissipating the cloud—it grew into loss of confidence—still grew, and I determined to cease preaching that which I could not feel. As an expiring effort, and far more, to endeavor to satisfy myself than to convince others, I delivered the lectures, one of which you published; doubt however renewed its power, and I sank under a cloud that I now begin to feel was of reason and truth.

The scriptures stand as they are, but God never gave a law to make men miserable or degraded. I solemnly, calmly assert, that the practice of polygamy at Salt Lake does not make men or women happy nor elevated—that on the contrary it does degrade and deprave them,—that it does make wretched women, destroys home, engulfs home pleasures, renders children wicked, rebellious, neglected and precociously vicious; and that to judge it as a cause from the effects that follow it, it cannot come from God.

I have resolved utterly and forever to forsake my error and renounce Mormonism. My former friends reproach me with inconsistency—they appeal to my pride. I hope I may never be so proud as to be unwilling to renounce falsehood; and I hope I may ever be proud enough to receive and turn to truth. To say I have erred is but to say that I am a man; to say I have forsaken my error is to say I am a wise man. That philosophy that teaches adherence to falsehood in spite of conviction, for the sake of consistency shows a state of the heart and an amount of mind from which I pray ever to be delivered.

Perhaps your report of my lecture may have inflicted some injury on some one. I trust this renunciation of that and the other errors and heresies of Mormonism, may effect greater good than that has accomplished harm.

Please consider this as entirely at your disposal to use in any manner you think fit.

And believe me yours respectfully,

JNO. HYDE, JR.

"'UTAH AS IT IS,' TO THE EDITOR OF THE POLYNESIAN,"
THE PACIFIC, 27 NOVEMBER 1856.

It is ignoble to attack the weak; and foolish to meddle with the ridiculous.

Mormonism, however, is not weak. Between 2000 and 3000 professors of this cruel delusion will have arrived before this date at Salt Lake, as this year's immigration; it is not therefore decreasing.[8] A system that has sufficient pretence of truth to obtain the acquiescence of a hundred thousand men and women of different countries, persuasions, abilities and prejudices; to combine them into one active cooperative body, and from 40,000 to 50,000 persons, who are gathering in one location, knocking at the gate of the Union, demanding admission as a state, is certainly not ridiculous. Its religious pretensions are too arrogant and presumptuous to deserve any thing but contempt; but the attention it has attracted, the abominations it practices, the moral depravity and religious ruin it is consummating in its many devotedly deluded followers, demand more serious consideration.

The Mormons accuse the rest of mankind of adultery, prostitution and corruption—point to misery and disease as their consequences—offer a better plan, polygamy, for the salvation of the world, the purification of our morals, the increase of our happiness, and to prepare, say they, for the coming of Jesus Christ. If their plan be effectual, surely it must result in good at *home.* There, in the paradise begun of Utah, we may expect to find a fair illustration of the workings of the system. Of course in the support of such high pretensions we must find superior evidences of moral purity, domestic happiness, social elevation of woman, and consequently a more holy race of children, drinking in, as they pretend, the streams of direct revelation from God through thier [*sic*] prophets and apostles. But if we find them more corrupt, men and women less happy, more degraded, and the children more depraved, we must reject the system as false and their claims to divine inspiration as infamous blasphemy.

It becomes, therefore, a question of fact. The Mormons, of course, all claim the affirmative. From pulpit and platform, from the highest in authority and oldest in standing to the lowest and youngest in the church, in private council meetings and in public assemblies, in their printed organs and published circulars—polygamy was furiously and strenuously denied until

[8] According to the best expert, 4,684 people migrated to Utah in 1855, while the number declined to 2,400 in 1856. See Unruh, *The Plains Across*, 120.

lately. Orson Pratt, one of their ablest men, and an apostle, called it an abominable doctrine. John Taylor, another apostle styled it "idelicat, *(sic)* obscene, and disgusting, such as none but a corrupt and depraved heart could have contrived." (Taylor's Discussions at Bosiogne, page 8.) All denied it; their very pretended revelations opposed it. Doctrine and Covenants, Sec. XII, p. 7: "Thou shalt love thy wife with all thy heart and shalt cleave unto her and none else; and he that looketh upon a woman to lust after her shall deny the faith, and shall not have the spirit, and if he repents not shall be cast out." And again, Sec. CIX., "Inasmuch as the church has been charged with the *crime* of fornication and polygamy we declare we believe that one man should have one wife, and one woman one husband; except in case of death when either is at liberty to marry again."[9] These two extracts from their Book of Commandments have been handed about as statement of doctrine to rebut the charge of polygamy, when those very men knew that it had been practiced since 1843, according to their tardy acknowledgment, and if they would confess it—*before that date.* On the 7th April, 1852, polygamy was publicly avowed, and a pretended revelation of J. Smith's, commanding its practice was read and commented upon: since then this principle has formed a part of their public preachings.[10] The whole of the apostles abroad had lied in denying it; positively, deliberately, wilfuly lied,—wrote lies,—published and circulated lies,—the heads of the church sanctioned and commanded them and claimed for it the approval of that Being who "cannot lie"! What confidence can we place in the statements of such men, or the pretensions of such a system?

The men who for nine years hesitated at no assertion to enforce or cover up their falsehoods, will not be very scrupulous in the means they adopt today to conceal what they do not wish told, or deny what another may reveal. Their testimony as to the workings of their polygamy therefore, is inadmissible. A liar of nine years' standing certainly cannot be depended on, notwithstanding all his claims to inspiration, divine authority and a holy priesthood. The testimony for the defence being inadmissible, the contra testimony remains intact; and what is it? That polygamy owes its rise to the lusts of Joseph Smith; that it is subversive of man,s [*sic*] happiness; that it is degrading to the women, who feel bitterly their degradation; that it is not productive of peace, but heart-wringings, anguish and despair; that it pro-

---

[9] Hyde's rendition contains some minor errors, but the original wording of this scripture condemned polygamy in no uncertain terms. Well after the practice was publicly acknowledged, this section of the *Doctrine and Covenants* was replaced by what is now Section 132, in which Abraham, Isaac, Jacob, and David are cited as precedents for plural marriage. (Interestingly, the revelation is still found in modern editions of this scripture even though the LDS church routinely excommunicates anyone who practices polygamy today.)

[10] The doctrine of plural marriage was first publicly preached on 29 August 1852.

duces an unruly, swearing, lying precocious and profligate race of children; that it is not beneficial to the increase of population nor improving to the physical or mental development of their offspring, and that instead of purifying and elevating man, it is a most depraved curse.

I who have been an eye witness and an ear witness to its practical operation at Salt Lake City, am prepared to substantiate these eight assertions; and may perhaps at another time, do so at a greater length than afforded by the space of a newspaper.

The Mormons demand admission into the Union as a State, claim to have over 70,000 inhabitants in the Territory of Utah and set forth that as a reason why the right to make their own laws, elect their own officers and regulate their own affairs should be accorded to them. Their census is a *monstrous perjured falsehood!*[11] Any United States appointed officer who would take the real census list of inhabitants, would find it little, very little more than the half of their representation. In the Cache Valley district, for an instance, only occupied by a few church herdsmen, they have represented hundreds of inhabitants. In the Battle Creek district, they have put down many who are dead, many who never even came to America, many who never had an existence and never will have; and in simalar [*sic*] manner through most of the other districts. The district reporters deliberately made affidavit and swore that these census returns were correct; knowing as they did, and as many since have privately and boastingly acknowledged, they were extravagantly and intentionally false! The testimony of such wilful perjuries would not be received on the simplest case—and how can they expect to be believed when speaking of the purity of their morals, the divine authority of their revelations, the divine authority of their prophets and apostles, or the holiness of their lives?

Last Spring I left Salt Lake for these Islands, dissatisfied and unhappy.[12] On recalling to my memory all that I had witnessed; what I had seen of tyranny and wrong, corruption and sorrow, vice and crime—what I had heard of contradictions and inconsistencies in doctrine, ridiculous preten-

[11] There was an incentive to exaggerate Utah census figures, since a territory needed a minimum population of 60,000 eligible voters to qualify for statehood. See Lyman, *Political Deliverance,* 7. Moreover, the more eligible voters a territory had, the more the political parties became interested in bringing that territory into their fold. The self-declared 1856 population of 76,335 was probably twice the actual count, fraudulently including both deceased citizens as well as Europeans who had yet to emigrate. The federal census for Utah Territory in 1860 totaled only 40,273. See Powell, ed., *Utah History Encyclopedia,* 431. Mormon historian B. H. Roberts analyzed population statistics in *Comprehensive History of the Church,* 3:487–88n.

[12] As one graphic example of anti-Mormon "spin," note how J. H. Beadle later characterized Hyde's decision to leave Utah: "the Mormons claim the right to slay all who commit adultery, 'or violate a sanctified oath,' and for this cause Elder John Hyde was compelled to flee from the Territory." Beadle, *Life in Utah,* 304. Nowhere in Hyde's book, which Beadle had read, did Hyde allege any such threat to his life. He apparently made a calm, deliberate decision to abandon his faith while en route to Hawaii.

sions, miserably supported, outrageous imposture and intolerant bigotry, I determined to forsake this system. My reasons have been repeatedly asked, and by many persons. I have selected, Mr. Editor, your columns as my means of communicating the above brief sketch of some of them and am sir,

Yours respectfully,

JON HYDE, Jr.

Honolulu, 14th Oct., 1856

"An Apostate and His Endorsers," *Western Standard*, 29 November 1856.[13]

The *Pacific* of Thursday comes to us laden with articles against "Mormonism." They consist of a communication from John Hyde, jun., to the editors, in which he renounces "Mormonism," and terms its doctrines errors and heresies; another from the same individual, entitled "Utah as it is," published in the Sandwich Islands *Polynesian,* and copied from that paper into the *Pacific,* in which he gives his reasons for forsaking "Mormonism". . . and an editorial on the same subject from the pen of the editor of the *Pacific,* in which he expresses his happiness at learning of Mr. Hyde's renunciation of this error, and indulges in the hope that, though an insignificant instrument, he may yet prove really more powerful than legislation and armies in overthrowing "the legions of a false prophet." Our readers will have already learned, by a perusal of our Sandwich Islands' correspondence of last week, that Mr. Hyde has also been engaged in Honolulu in lecturing against "Mormonism." The arrival of another vessel from the Islands puts us in possession of a synopsis of this lecture. As in his communication, entitled "Utah as it is," this lecture charges the "Mormons" with stealing, perjury, and lying, and is very bitter in its opposition to polygamy and its fruits. . . . The only opinion that any person can have of another who would act with such hypocrisy is, to quote his own words, that "he positively, deliberately, wilfully lied—wrote lies—published and circulated lies," and used all his power to make people believe and embrace that which, he now says, he knew at the time to be a lie.[14] And yet this is the insignificant David whom the editors of the *Pacific* think may prove more powerful than legislation and armies in overthrowing "the legions of a false prophet!"

No man who had a spark of love for his family, and knew that such cor-

---

[13] Reprinted in Cannon, *Writings from the "Western Standard,"* 255–59.

[14] Had Cannon had access to the journals of James H. Hart, he would have further exposed Hyde's hypocrisy. Contrary to Hyde's implication that he had never heard of polygamy until his arrival in Utah, Hyde himself—along with most other Mormon missionaries who knew of the principle—had lied about the "spiritual marriage doctrine," taking great pains to keep it secret while serving as a missionary in the Channel Islands and Havre-de-Grace prior to his emigration to America. See Hart, "John Hyde Junior—An Earlier View," 305–12.

ruptions and abominations existed among the Latter-day Saints which he says he did, would have left them in such a nest of profligates as he describes the "Mormons" to be. Neither could as honest, wise and pure man as he would fain represent himself to be through the *Pacific,* possibly have lived for the length of time he did in the midst of so much abomination as he says exists in Utah. Such an individual, had such a state of things really existed there, would have made but a short stay, and then, in leaving, would not have left his family behind, nor have left in the character of a missionary! Again, if he knew of the existence of these evils and abominations while in Utah, he certainly could not have been ignorant of them while he was in California; there was not the slightest necessity of his taking a sea voyage of upwards of two thousand miles to find them out; and if he knew of their existence while here, why did he preach lies, solemnly testify to lies, and use every exertion to palm them off upon the people of this city as truths? Why did he not, instead of publicly testifying to the truth of "Mormonism," testify to its falsehood? "As an expiring effort," he says in his communication, "and far more to endeavor to satisfy myself than to convince others, I delivered the lectures, one of which you published." To endeavor to satisfy himself of what? To endeavor to satisfy himself that polygamy was abominable? That, he states, he was satisfied about long before he left Utah. To endeavor to satisfy himself that a system which he knew to be abominable was not abominable—to endeavor to satisfy himself that a system which countenanced perjury, stealing and even murder, was good and virtuous? The lectures he delivered here were on the Scripturality and morality of polygamy; has he weakened either the Scripturality or morality of polygamy as practiced by the ancients, by anything he has yet published relative to its practice by the Latter-day Saints? . . . though he saw with the clearness of a line of light, after this lecture, that it was nothing but a system of imposture, he suffered a week to elapse, and then, instead of avowing his unbelief, sat down and wrote a letter to the *Pacific,* correcting the report of his lecture, strengthening his positions in favor of polygamy and reaffirming his entire confidence in "Mormonism." He now "solemnly, calmly" asserts that he knows "Mormonism" to be false, and predicates his assertion on the effects which it produces in Utah. The practice of polygamy there, he now says, degrades and depraves women, makes them wretched, destroys homes, produces an unruly, swearing, lying precocious and profligate race of children. He must, then, while here have acted the part of a consummate hypocrite, and have deliberately, wilfully and corruptly lied; for in his last lecture, a short sketch of which was published in the *Pacific,* he states that its effects were good and immeasurably superior to the effects which followed monogamy. He then stated, that "he had seen more obscenity, licentiousness and crime in this city in one night, than during the whole of his stay of several years in Utah." A liar of years' standing cannot be depended upon. "His testimony is inadmissible." "The testimony of such a wilful perjurer would not be received on the simplest case." Yet this man, who has told, published and circulated such glaring, unblushing and palpable lies, the editors of the *Pacific*. . . think will be likely to annihilate "Mormonism," and convince every honest Latter-day Saint of his errors. Bah! the idea is absurd.

The course taken by the *Pacific*, in this instance, is but another illustration of the folly and imbecility men will indulge in to bolster themselves up in their opposition to "Mormonism." Had Mr. Hyde continued to be a believer in "Mormonism," and continued to testify in the most solemn manner to its entire truthfulness, his testimony would not have received the slightest attention from these gentlemen; but having invalidated his own testimony, and proved to all men that his word is utterly unreliable and that he has been acting the hypocrite for years, they suddenly become enamored with him and are profuse in their expressions of sympathy for his deliverance. If the editors of the *Pacific* can find any comfort and support in publishing such a mass of ridiculous falsehoods, contradictions and inconsistencies as are contained in the articles we have alluded to, and imagine that by these means they will be able to counteract the "threatening evils" of "Mormonism," we are perfectly willing they should have their wish; but, after a little, they may learn that the apostasy of a "Mormon" and his declaration that polygamy is immoral, does not make it so—that his unbelief neither destroys its Scripturality, nor blots out a single syllable in its favor from the word of God; and that it would still stand out bright and pure, as a doctrine approved by the Lord and believed in and practiced by his ancient servants, though every Latter-day Saint should apostatize and deny its truthfulness.

We understand Mr. Hyde intends revisiting this city on his way to England; if he should, and conclude to lecture on this subject, . . . we have no doubt but his efforts will be productive of more real good to "Mormonism" than his most active exertions in its favor could have been, so long as he preached in the spirit that he evidently did while here.

The Rise, Progress and Corruptions of the Mormon Fanaticism: John Hyde in California

True to his stated intention, upon his return to California from the Sandwich Islands John Hyde immediately commenced lecturing again upon Mormonism, this time as an opponent. When he arrived at Placerville, a representative of the local paper (who now gave Hyde the title of Reverend, rather than Elder) eagerly reported on his lectures. So did at least one Mormon missionary, Elder William Cooke, who immediately entered into the fray. First, Cooke attempted a direct rebuttal at one of Hyde's lectures, but when he was not allowed to continue the debate, he appealed to a more sympathetic audience in a letter to the editor of the *Western Standard.*

"LECTURE ON MORMONISM, BRIGHAM YOUNG, ETC.," *MOUNTAIN DEMOCRAT,* 7 MARCH 1857.

The Rev. Mr. Hyde, an Intelligent and pleasing speaker, a seceding Mormon Elder, lectured in our town on Saturday, Monday and Tuesday nights, to crowded, attentive and delighted houses, on the rise, progress and corruptions of the Mormon fanaticism—to call it religion would be a misnomer. If half what he asserted be true a viler or more depraved sect never polluted the earth. He quoted freely from the sermons of Brigham Young, published by authority in the *Deseret News,* to sustain his positions. He gave them credit for great patience, industry and perseverance. He frankly confessed that Brigham was a remarkable man—energetic, shrewd, penetrating, intellectual—a deep thinker, a plausible, insinuating speaker, and thoroughly understanding of human nature. He was a man of iron will and dauntless courage—more of an enthusiast than knave. He was hospitable, generous, sociable—fond of society, frank to a fault; but tolerated no opposition to his imperial will. His sermons were more forcible than elegant—more passionate than profound—destitute of religious fervor, but abounding in vigorous passages. His comparisons were often vulgar, sometimes blasphemous, but never weak or obscure. [Heber C.] Kimball was a weak, vain, ignorant, scheming, deceitful, fawning scoundrel. The Mormons generally were ignorant, superstitious, fanatical—implicitly believing in what their Elders taught, and slavishly submitting to the most intolerable bondage. The Elders discouraged education, and kept the converts busily employed to prevent them from thinking.

On Monday night a Mr. Cook [*sic*], an elderly man, an Elder of the Mormon church, after Mr. Hyde had concluded his lecture, asked permission to reply to him, which was readily granted. His language was so outrageous and disgraceful that the audience, out of self respect, were compelled to stop him. Filth flowed from his mouth as freely and as offensively as from the sty of a hog. He refuted not one of the arguments of Mr. Hyde—controverted not one of his assertions. He injured the cause he advocates, and convinced all who heard him that if we are to judge of the fruits of Mormonism by the language of its teachers, it is depraved beyond redemption. Mr. Hyde, in perfectly respectful language, replied to him, but his sarcasm was withering, and every word fell with the force of a sledge hammer, blistering and burning like red-hot iron.

On Tuesday evening Mr. Hyde lectured to the largest audience we have ever seen in Placerville on a similar occasion. Every seat in the Theatre, long before the lecturer arrived, was occupied, and every available spot was taken up. He confined himself exclusively to an exposition of the impostures, inconsistencies and contradictions—flagrant and absurd in the extreme—of the book of Mormons. He traced its history from its first appearance up to the present time, and proved to the satisfaction of all present that that portion of it which was *not* stolen, was the silliest, weakest, shallowest of humbugs. He has evidently studied his subject carefully and understands it thoroughly. He read a verse from the book, in which a fearful curse is pronounced against polygamy, and stated that in England the Mormons indignantly deny that it is part of their creed. They contradict their own words—repudiate their own book. Many of the wretched beings now at Salt Lake, having awakened from their delusion, would willingly leave it, but they cannot get away. The best way to root out Mormonism, in his opinion, is to settle the country round them with inhabitants of a different persuasion. He deprecated violence, and said, we use his own language—"At no time, under no circumstances, can mob violence be justified. Any and every infraction of the laws must, sooner or later, be atoned for." Men who censured us not a year ago for using similar language, cheered it when uttered by another, so vacillating is public opinion.

[LETTER FROM WILLIAM COOKE], *WESTERN STANDARD*, 20 MARCH 1857.

Weber Creek, Near Placerville
March 9th, 1857

DEAR BROTHER CANNON:—

The enclosed slip, giving an account of a course of lectures given in Placerville against Mormonism by the apostate Hyde, I have cut from the *Mountain Democrat* of the 7th inst.; and as the Editor has made free use of my name in connection therewith, I will give you an account of the "filth" which he says flowed so "freely and offensively" from my mouth, for the amusement of your readers, if you think it will not sully the pure pages of the *Standard* by an insertion . . .

When I ascended the pulpit to speak, the Rev. Mr. Frear told me that ten minutes would be allowed me. I told him that I could not say what I wanted in that time, and that if I could not be allowed longer I would rather defer it and take an evening on purpose if he would allow me the use of the church. He told me the Trustees would not consent to that; but desiring to make the best use of the present moment, I arose, and was introduced to the audience. I told them I had yet to learn that Mormonism professed to introduce any new principles, that it was eternal, immutable truth, and claimed to be nothing more or less than the ancient gospel restored, and that it was either what it claimed to be or it was the most stupendous delusion which had ever been visited upon the world; and of its truth or falsity they could every one satisfy themselves by honestly yielding obedience to its requirements. I gave them a short sketch of my own experience and connection therewith, and how I had come to a *knowledge* of its truth; stated Mr. Hyde said those principles which were preached by the elders were only to throw dust in the eyes of the people, we must go to what was peculiarly Mormon, to the Book of Mormon, but he had not proved that that Book was not what it professed to be—a divinely inspired Book co-equally so with the Bible. We must go to their polygamy, but he had not produced the first scriptural or rational argument to prove polygamy as practiced by the ancient Patriarchs, and as restored to, and practiced by the Mormons, was not a pure and a true doctrine. Had brought forward instances of the alleged mis-conduct of individuals, (Abraham, Rachel, etc.,) which did not at all affect the truth of principles, and of which they were entirely independent; neither had he shown us that a better state of things existed in what is called the Christian and civilized world than existed in Utah. He had asked, why, if it be lawful for one man to have many wives, it is not lawful, upon the same principle, for one woman to have many husbands? I would answer him that question, by saying, because from well known physical laws it would engender disease instead of children, as was abundantly verified by practical experience in the world. I would give them a few facts as proof that had come within my own knowledge.

There are some things says Mr. Hyde that it will hardly do to mention, but nevertheless *they exist,* and as such it is proper to mention them. I then commenced the following narrative: I left San Francisco for Australia in the spring of 1853, in the bark *Galatea.* There were three hundred passengers on board composed of individuals from various countries and climes, of various creeds and churches, also amongst them some professed Infidels, Atheists and Deists. They were about a fair specimen of such material as compose the world, neither better nor worse. Their common conversation was about their connection with women. We made a stay of eight days at the Sandwich Islands, and to judge from their conversation, they were not only like the sailor who is said to have a different wife in every different port, but a many of them seemed to have a different wife every different night; and soon after we left there, as a natural result of such practices, seventy-five of them were on the doctor's list, undergoing medical treatment for a foul disease engendered thereby. Here the Rev. Mr. Frear and Mr. Hyde stopped me, and said I could not be allowed to make use of such language as that. I wanted to put it to vote of the congregation if I should be allowed to proceed, but Mr. Frear said, "there can be no vote taken on this question," and one or two persons cried put him out. Had I been telling the same things about the "beastly Polygamic Mormons" it would have been received with thundering plaudits, as were Mr. Hyde's narratives, but as the truth was coming too near home it was "filthy and offensive." I told the audience I was not permitted to go on as I desired—and that if they wished to know the principles of Mormonism I should be happy to lay them before them as long as I remained in the neighborhood, if they would furnish me a place to preach in. And I remarked Mr. Hyde had laid before them a paradox. He said the Mormons sent out the biggest rascals they had on missions to preach the gospel, confer the gift of the Holy Ghost by the imposition of hands and to gather them to Salt Lake; but he had not told us why he was sent on a mission; why he had left a wife and child[15] to the tender mercies of such a wicked people; why he had, no later than last August and September at San Francisco, repeatedly testified publicly that he knew Mormonism to be true and of God; had preached in favor of polygamy and testified that the morals in Utah were pure compared with those of the world, and that he had witnessed more licentiousness in San Francisco in one night than he had done in Utah in all the years he had lived there. . . .

Expecting to be with you at the coming Conference,

I remain your brother in the covenant, WM. COOKE

"MORMONISM," *MOUNTAIN DEMOCRAT,* 28 MARCH 1857.

The *Western* (Mormon) *Standard* of the 20th inst. contains a lengthy and characteristic letter from our pure and saintly Mormon friend, Elder Cooke, who evidently imagines himself "some punkins" in reply to our strictures on his indecent language and the lecture of Mr. Hyde. With unusual modesty, which takes us completely by surprise, he confesses that his communication is "filthy," and hopes—an unnecessary hope—it "will not sully the pure pages of the *Standard* by an insertion"! Of course, not, Elder; nothing better was to be expected from you, and its "filth" was its chief recommendation. It is a precious *morceau*, and will give you a free entry into the refined society of Salt Lake City. You must be aware that it takes an extra quantity of "filth," and evidently there is an abundance of it in the city of the Saints, if we are to judge by the language of the Elders it sends out among the Gentiles, to "sully the pages" of a Mormon paper, or the reputation of a Mormon Elder.

We confess that we have not been initiated into the fascinating mysteries of Mormonism, nor do we know much about it, but the little that we do know is not creditable either to the doctrines taught, the teachers, or the

[15] No record has been found of a child being born to John Hyde, Jr. and Lavinia Hawkins.

members of the church. From our limited knowledge of it, and from Mr. Cooke's own admissions, it is admirably adapted to suit the tastes of depraved men, and if the great Mormon leader Brigham Young do not slander his brethren, a greater set of graceless scamps, liars, thieves, swindlers, perjurers, bloats, gamblers and libertines never polluted the earth than are to be found at Salt Lake, in the very bosom of the church. Mr. Hyde read an article from the *Deseret News,* written by Brigham, in which he boasted that the Mormons could "beat the world at bragging, lying, cheating, swindling, swearing, drinking," &c. &c. We do not make these charges—we only quote the *authority of the church.* We do know, however, that Mormonism, when it was tolerated in Illinois, blighted the fair name of the State, and drove many respectable families from it, who could not be forced to believe that prostitution was a virtue or blasphemy religion. Elder Cooke says:

"I told them I had yet to learn that Mormonism professed to introduce any new principles, that it was eternal, immutable truth, and claimed to be nothing more or less than the ancient gospel restored, and that it was either what it claimed to be or it was the most stupendous delusion which had ever been visited upon the world."

You did tell them so, and Mr. Hyde proved that you either did not understand or were wholly and inexcusably ignorant of the Mormon doctrine. He named a number of "new principles it introduced," disgraceful and repulsive as new, which you tacitly admitted. If it be eternal, immutable truth, why does it so frequently contradict itself? It cannot be true and false at the same time. Mr. Hyde read a number of passages from what is termed the Mormon bible, flatly and positively contradicting each other. Truth is not inconsistent, but the Mormon bible certainly is. If it "introduced no new principle," said Mr. Hyde, "there is no necessity for it; if it has introduced new principles let us investigate them and see if they are good and worthy of inculcating." *He,* not Elder Cooke, for the Elder was too *prudent* to mention some of the *slight vagaries* of Mormonism, named a number of the "new principles introduced" by the Mormon Book, every one of which was in direct opposition to decency and religion. Mormonism, according to *its own authority,* cannot be what it claims to be, and must therefore be in the graphic and truthful language of Elder Cooke, "the most stupendous delusion that has ever cursed mankind. . . ."

"Society in Utah.—Misrepresentations," *Western Standard,* 3 April 1857.[16]

. . . An apostate-"Mormon" lecturer states that the Latter-day Saints are a bad people, a set of graceless scamps, and reads from the words of

[16] Reprinted in Cannon, *Writings from the "Western Standard,"* 382–85.

Brigham Young, published in the *Deseret News,* to prove it. The editor of the *Democrat,* who attends the lecture, thinks that "*Brigham ought to know,*" and, therefore, what this lecturer says must be so. He knows so little about "Mormonism" that he thinks everything evil that can be said about it must be true, and that it would not be in the least strange if Brigham Young should "write" an article to the *Deseret News,* boasting that the "Mormons" were the biggest rascals in the world! He knows so little about "Mormonism" that this does not strike him as being at all inconsistent. He does not stop to examine the statement or to inquire whether it had been qualified or not, but swallows it greedily, without investigation, and thus becomes the ready and willing dupe of a designing knave. This is the most charitable view that we can take of the case; for if the gentleman has not been duped, he has published that which he must know is a garbled report of the language of the prophet Brigham.

The following remarks, we presume, are what the editor has reference to, and upon the authority of which, he says, he represents the state of things existing in Utah to be so bad. As he lays a great deal of stress upon them, quoting them as reliable testimony to support him in his assertions, we give them with the context:—

"What fault can the world justly find with this people? Some have passed through here to California to dig gold, but they have received nothing at the hands of this people but kindness. What do they know about us? They can not charge us with one evil. Suppose there are wicked men here; I say the kingdom of heaven is like unto a net that gathers fish both good and bad, and I say this because it is true. Suppose I was preaching in the world and they should allege that some of the people in Utah swore, stole, and were wicked in many ways, I would acknowledge it to be the case. They might inquire,—'Why do you say that you have got the gospel of salvation? and why do you come to us to preach, seeing that your own people do wickedly?' I would reply that the kingdom of heaven is like unto a net that gathers fish of all kinds, therefore we must have the good and bad in Utah, or else it can not be the kingdom of heaven. As to the great argument against the kingdom of God, because there are some evil doers in the church; I will take the principles and doctrines taught by Jesus and his apostles, and show that these go to prove and substantiate the fact that this is the kingdom of God. Why? Because we can produce the meanest curses there are on the earth,—those who take all the revelations given by the Almighty and every influence and revelation they can get from the devil, and make use of them to add sin to sin. This fact is also another proof that all hell is against this people, for there is not a person in the world that gives way to wickedness but what has antipathy against this people. We can produce the best men and the worst; the best women and the worst; and thus prove, according to the sayings of Jesus Christ and his apostles, that this is the kingdom of God, or at least answers to the Savior's description of that kingdom. There are many of the men and women now before me who have looked for a pure people, and have supposed that that was a proof of the truth of our doctrines, but they will never find such a people until Satan is bound and Jesus come to reign with his saints. The doctrine we preach is the doctrine of salvation, and it is that which the elders of this Church take to the world, and not the people of Utah. Some of the elders seem to be tript up in a moment, if the wicked can find any fault with the members of this Church; but bless your souls, I would not have this people faultless, for the day of separation has not yet arrived. I have, many a time, in this stand, dared the world to produce as mean devils as we can; we can beat them at anything. We have the greatest and smoothest liars in the world, the cunningest and most adroit thieves, and any other shade of character that you can mention. We can pick out elders in Israel right here who can beat the world at gambling, who can handle the cards, cut and shuffle them with the smartest rogue on the face of God's footstool. I can produce elders here who can shave their smartest shavers and take their money from them. We can beat the world at any game. We can beat them, because we have men here that live in the light of the Lord, that have the holy priesthood and hold the keys of the kingdom of God."

His remarks sufficiently explain themselves, and give a very different idea of "Mormon" morals than that given either by the lecturer whom the editor of the *Democrat* heard, or by the editor's own remarks on the subject. Brigham Young says that the gospel net gathers the bad; but he also says it gathers the good. Though there are adroit rogues and bad people in Utah, yet the best people in the world are to be found there. Come, Mr. Editor, why not publish to the world upon the authority of Brigham Young, that the most meek, peaceable, united and God-fearing people that can be found in the world, are in Utah, as well as to say "that Brigham Young boasts that the Mormons can beat the world at bragging, lying, cheating, swindling, swearing, drinking, etc., etc."? Why not contend that the people of Utah are a good people—a people that can beat the world in good deeds and righteous works, because Brigham Young says so, as to contend for the opposite? If his testimony is reliable on one point why not on the other? Or, would this be giving the "Mormons" too fair a representation?

You were, without doubt, as much deceived also, Mr. Editor, by this apostate-"Mormon" lecturer in the passages which he read from the "Mormon book," and which you say flatly and positively contradicted each other, as you were in the quotations he gave you from Brigham's sermons. Had you given us a clue by which we might have known what "new principles introduced by the Mormon book, every one of which was in direct opposition to decency and religion" he pointed out to you, we doubtless could have given you proof of this. The apparent ease with which the apostate "Mormon" has duped you, corroborates the truth of the statements made by Brigham Young in the extracts above. This man has hoodwinked you, and made you believe his lies were the truth so smoothly and adroitly, that you have the proof in your own case, that when a "Mormon" elder does turn round and give heed to the adversary, he can beat the world in deception and cunning.

The Sudden Going Out of This Twinkling Star

In his battles with John Hyde and other defectors from Mormonism, Cannon held the advantage that loyalists have over traitors to a cause. As Hyde himself acknowledged, "to have been a Mormon, is to be an object of suspicion. To be an apostate, is to be regarded with distrust. To be an apostate Mormon, is to be doubly suspected."[17] Hyde's personal history and evasions raised other questions that Cannon exploited masterfully, pointing out that Hyde had "invalidated his own testimony, and proved to all men that his word is utterly unreliable and that he has been acting the hypocrite for years."

Hyde's public lectures financed his return to the East to publish *Mormonism, Its Leaders and Designs* the following year. The text was largely drawn from sources such as Bennett, Howe, and Ferris and repeated many classic anti-Mormon charges, including the now-debunked Spaulding theory, which claimed Joseph Smith and Sydney Rigdon had plagiarized *The Book of Mormon* from Solomon Spaulding's unpublished romance, "Manuscript Found."[18]

More tellingly, Hyde painted a fascinating and detailed portrait of Brigham Young, demonstrating a grudging admiration for his avowed enemy. The book was dedicated to "Honest Believers in Mormonism" whom Hyde hoped to lure away from falsehood and error through a series of arguments, some of which were ingenious while others were

[17] Hyde, *Mormonism, Its Leaders and Designs,* 13.

[18] Fawn Brodie analyzed the Spaulding theory in Appendix B of *No Man Knows My History*. For a comprehensive study, see Bush, "The Spalding Theory Then and Now," 40–69. Bush followed the incorrect "Spalding" spelling used in Eber D. Howe's *Mormonism Unvailed* [*sic*]. A modern reprint of the work in question, with an introductory essay by Rex C. Reeve, Jr., is in Jackson, ed., *Manuscript Found.*

strained. Although he never mentioned Cannon by name, Hyde responded to many of his arguments, even agreeing that "there are less [*sic*] robberies, murders, arsons, rapes at Utah, than in any other place of equal population in the world." Of Cannon and his assistants at the *Western Standard*, Hyde said, "They publish a weekly sheet at San Francisco, California. Its editor, workmen, and even devil, are all 'on mission;' get nothing but food and raiment; but are 'therewith content.' Their sincerity can not be doubted, whatever be said of their intellect."[19] Hyde's book appeared shortly after the president ordered troops to march for Utah, and in July 1857 the influential *Harper's Weekly* published the apostate's article on Mormon leaders.[20] Hyde's work provided *post hoc* justification for Buchanan's decision to send federal troops to the territory, for Secretary of State Lewis Cass read his book and the president concluded it "contains much valuable information."[21]

As might be expected, Hyde's about-face caused quite a stir among the Mormons. Most, however, remained philosophical. Writing from Honolulu, where Hyde had first announced his change of heart, Edward Partridge commented on his apostasy:

> There has been more talk about the Mormons and Mormonism in this place the last few days than I have heard for some time. It has been occasioned by our once respected brother John Hyde, who upon reaching these islands, renounced Mormonism, wrote a piece for the *Polynesian*, and this evening, by request of several of the most bitter opposers of Mormonism, delivered a lecture in the Bethel before a full house, giving his reasons for taking the course that he has. It was a rich feast for the clergy and all those who are bitter against the Latter-Day Saints. They no doubt think they have achieved a great victory over the "poor Mormons," and consequently will have but little more to apprehend from that quarter. I presume they have an idea that all there now remains for us to do is to pick up and leave the islands; still they should have known us better than to think that we would be scared by the pusillanimous railings of an apostate Mormon.[22]

Before leaving the islands, Hyde published an anti-Mormon pamphlet in the Hawaiian language.[23] Partridge reported, "I have not been

[19] Hyde, *Mormonism, Its Leaders and Designs*, 113, 131.

[20] Hyde, "Salt Lake and Its Rulers," *Harper's Weekly*, 11 July 1857, 440–43.

[21] Furniss, *The Mormon Conflict*, 80.

[22] Letter from E. P. [Edward Partridge], *Western Standard*, 22 November 1856.

[23] See Hyde, *No ka aoao Moremona*, copy at BYU Library Special Collections.

able to perceive that John Hyde has done any injury to Mormonism, altho' I will give him credit for doing all he could in the way of lying and slandering us as a people, and trying to make our doctrines, or the doctrines which we have embraced, appear in an unfavorable light to the public."[24] Writing on 12 December, a missionary who had traveled to the islands with Hyde optimistically concluded that "his apostatizing will give a new impetus to the work of God on these lands; the Lord has not sent us here for nothing."[25]

Writing Cannon from San Bernardino, Amasa Lyman provided his view on Hyde's apostasy:

> By letters published in the STANDARD I see that Elder John Hyde has become weary in well doing. The indications of what has transpired with him were unmistakably manifest in that egotistical vanity that, fed by a little superficial learning, led him to suppose that he was the light that illuminated the world, and that, in case he should withdraw his light, all would be in darkness; so John went out . . . What, then, is the consequence of the sudden going out of this twinkling star, that while it shed its doubtful and uncertain light along the pathway of the Saints, gave slight promise that at some future day it might brighten into the effulgence of a son and become fixed in the house of his Father? Alas, instead of the birth of a son the star has set in its own darkness, and in proof that the Saints were wrong he owned he had lied! What a jewel is consistency! But poor John! He is more to be pitied than despised.[26]

George Q. Cannon reported to Brigham Young on a chance encounter he had with Hyde upon the latter's return to San Francisco:

> John Hyde is here at present, and I understand contemplates lecturing against us. If he should it will be very likely to cause many to investigate who otherwise might not be aroused. He seems to have abandoned himself completely to the power of the evil one, and is filled with bitterness and hatred. I met him this morning in the street; if his countenance be any index of his heart he must be a walking hell, for I never saw a man that looked more utterly miserable than he did. There is one glorious consolation that we have, that every thing such men can do will be for us; the Lord being on our side we must triumph, if we only stick to His kingdom. Hyde has already so pal-

[24] Letter from Edward Partridge, *Western Standard*, 29 November 1856.

[25] "From the Sandwich Islands," letter from Thomas A. Dowell, *Western Standard*, 31 January 1857.

[26] "Correspondence of President A. Lyman," *Western Standard*, 27 December 1856.

pably proved himself a liar that every honest person will be disgusted with him; those that are not honest we care nothing about.[27]

Young agreed that Hyde would not likely do great damage to the cause: "Your picture of John Hyde is true I believe, & his course will soon be run, & if in this he can procure hearers, the investigation, will result favorably to the honest in heart & the Kingdom of God."[28]

Hyde remained in California delivering anti-Mormon lectures until April 1857. David J. Whittaker has pointed out that Cannon's printing of twelve-hundred copies of "Scriptural Evidences in Support of Polygamy" (based on Parley P. Pratt's earlier tract, "Marriage and Morals in Utah") may well have been a response to Hyde's activities.[29]

Mormonism, Its Leaders and Designs met with considerable success, going into a second American edition. An English plagiarist calling himself John Benjamin Franklin incorporated large sections of Hyde's book in a "clumsy parody" of a pamphlet, *The Horrors of Mormonism,* adding lurid details of his own. Franklin's potboiler went through at least five editions in the two years following its publication in 1858.[30] John Hyde, Jr., carried on his career as an author and lecturer, using his experiences in Utah to write an unpublished novel, "Infatuation: A Fiction Founded on Fact."[31] He also published a biography of eighteenth-century religious philosopher Emanuel Swedenborg (1859), whose revelations on the afterlife resembled Mormon beliefs, and several lectures and books, including *The Angels* (1875) and *Our Eternal Homes, by a Bible Student* (1877).[32]

"The role of traitor is not one which in any wise brings credit to the performer, either from one side or the other," California historian H. H. Bancroft observed. "However great the service he may render us, we cannot but feel that he is false-hearted and vile." Nonetheless, Bancroft held Hyde in higher regard than other dissenters: "Quite different from any

[27] Cannon to Young, 3 January 1857, LDS Archives.

[28] Young to Cannon, 31 January 1857, LDS Archives.

[29] Whittaker, "Parley P. Pratt and the Pacific Mission," 69.

[30] The text of Franklin's pamphlet appears with an insightful analysis in David A. White's invaluable documentary collection, *News of the Plains and the Rockies,* 3:240–66.

[31] BYU Library Special Collections, Vault MSS 509, is a 346-page typescript of Hyde's novel.

[32] For a list of Hyde's publications, see Arrington, "Centrifugal Tendencies in Mormon History," 172.

of his brother apostates is John Hyde, Jr. who cannot by right be placed in the category of vulgar ranter or hypocritical reformer. I regard him as an able and honest man, sober and sincere. " In fact, Bancroft's major complaint was that "Hyde's book would be quite useful were he not so loose about his dates; it would appear from the way he throws statements together that in the absence of a date he guessed at it."[33]

Years later, in a publication for Mormon youth, Cannon elaborated on his opinion of Hyde's character:

> He [Hyde] had been called, at a Conference (April, 1856) at Salt Lake City, to go on a mission to the Sandwich Islands. He came to San Francisco on his way. I was then publishing the *Western Standard* and presiding over the California mission. It was with a feeling akin to disgust that he spoke to me about his mission. If he had only been called to go to France, to England, or to any of the so-called enlightened nations, he said he would have gone willingly; but to go to a degraded, heathenish people was entirely beneath him. A man with his talent and acquirements would be thrown away upon them.
>
> He apostatized while on the voyage to Honolulu; or, to state it more properly, he made up his mind while on the sea to dissolve his connection with the Church. He was an apostate in heart and feelings before he left San Francisco. But can any one, who understands this work, wonder that a man who felt thus should lose the Spirit and apostatize? It would be a wonder if he did not.[34]

In spite of his obvious disgust in and disdain for his former friend, Cannon rather remarkably chose to publish one more of John Hyde's poems, "Farewell Hymn." Perhaps it was the irony of the title that persuaded Cannon to publish the poem on the front page of the *Western Standard's* last issue of 1856, appearing more then a month after Cannon learned of Hyde's defection. If so, there is even further irony in the opening lines of the poem: "Zion, yes, I truly love thee, / Prophet, Priesthood, great and true."[35]

Mormon authorities excommunicated John Hyde, Jr., on 11 January 1857. As part of these proceedings, Heber C. Kimball delivered Hyde

[33] Bancroft, *History of Utah*, 150-52n11.

[34] Cannon, "My First Mission," in Nibley, *Three Mormon Classics*, 178.

[35] See Hyde's "Farewell Hymn," published on 27 December 1856. In addition to those published in the *Standard*, several of Hyde's poems appeared in the *Deseret News*.

"over to Satan to be buffeted in the flesh" and announced he had "lost his family, and forfeited his priesthood." Kimball pointed out that the action would not affect his spouse:

> The limb is cut off, but the Priesthood takes the fruit that was attached to the limb and saves it, if it will be saved. Do you understand me? His wife is not cut off from this church, but she is free from him; she is just as free from him as though she never had belonged to him. The limb she was connected to is cut off, and she as though she never had belonged to him. The limb she was connected to is cut off, and she must again be grafted into the tree, if she wishes to be saved; that is all about it.[36]

Although Hyde had assured people in Hawaii that he expected his wife to join him in St. Louis, Lavinia Hawkins Hyde remained in Utah and married Joseph Woodmansee on 24 July 1858. Apparently Lavinia did not share her former husband's aversion to polygamy: she was not the only branch to be grafted onto the tree of Woodmansee, for her new husband also married Amelia Ann Smith on the same day.[37]

The full story of John Hyde, Jr., has yet to be told. He was an extremely talented, sensitive, ambitious, guilt-ridden, jealous, productive and contentious crusader. Naturally, Hyde was not the only Mormon defector of the period. Many dissenters found the well-ordered, highly regulated nature of life in Utah too stifling. Others, who had used the LDS church to escape European poverty, found conditions no better following Utah's repeated crop failures and were quick to seek greener pastures. The harsh demands of life in the Mormon kingdom and golden lure of California tempted many away from Zion, where the press was only too happy to report on those who publicly renounced Mormonism in general and Brigham Young in particular. But few of these defectors had the enduring impact of that disillusioned seeker, John Hyde, who died in 1875 at the age of forty-three, still searching

---

[36] Heber C. Kimball, "The Body of Christ...Expose Each Others' Follies," 11 January 1857, *Journal of Discourses,* 4:165.

[37] This information is available in the Joseph Woodmansee records available through the FamilySearch Ancestral Internet Genealogy Service: www.familysearch.org. For a discussion of Hyde's later unsuccessful attempt to divorce Lavinia from England, see Cannon, "A Strange Encounter: The English Courts and Mormon Polygamy."

[38] For additional details on Hyde's life, with an emphasis on his later year as a Swedenborgian minister, see his obituary, "The Rev. John Hyde" 460, 468-77.

This wood engraving is typical of the sensational treatment given to alleged Danite activity. *Harper's Weekly, 26 February 1859.*

Chapter 5

"The Bandits of the Plains"

Red Indians, White Indians, Lamanites, and Danites

In pioneering the Great Basin, Mormons and other settlers encroached on the traditional lands of the Ute, Shoshoni, Paiute, and Gosiute nations. The Saints shared the common American belief, derived from *philosophes* such as Emmerich de Vattel, that those who tilled the land should own it, a revolutionary concept in Enlightenment Europe but one fraught with danger for American Indians.[1] Along with the popular concept of Manifest Destiny, the Latter-day Saints claimed a special justification, believing that the land belonged to God and, by extension, to His chosen people, who would make better use of it than the "fallen" Indians. Inevitably, this attitude of presumed inheritance led to conflict in the West, just as it had many years before with the old settlers in Missouri.[2]

Out of these conflicts came a variety of charges, notably assertions that disloyal Mormons were actively alienating Indians from other Americans. More sinister stories claimed that they disguised themselves as "white Indians" and led raids against overland travelers. Many quickly linked such activities with the Danites, the legendary band of "Avenging Angels" that carried out the will of their prophet with violent fanaticism. Naturally, both subjects provided ample ammunition for a protracted newspaper war in California.

---

[1] Swiss legal philosopher Vattel's 1758 *Le Droit des Gens* profoundly influenced the views Franklin, Washington, and Jefferson held on Indian rights. Nations were "obliged by the laws of nature to cultivate the ground," Vattel argued, and nomadic people who "disdain to cultivate the earth, and choose to live by rapine, are wanting to themselves, and deserve to be exterminated as savage and pernicious beasts." See de Vattel, *The Law of Nations*, 92.

[2] The major book-length treatments of Mormon/Indian conflicts are Gottfredson's *History of Indian Depredations in Utah* and Peterson's much more scholarly *Utah's Black Hawk War*.

Mormon religious beliefs about American Indians profoundly influenced their relations with their new neighbors in the Great Basin. The "very purpose" of *The Book of Mormon* was to bring the "knowledge of their fathers, and also the knowledge of Jesus Christ" to America's first nations, the people the book identified as "Lamanites."[3] Mormon scripture linked American Indians with the Bible's "remnant of Jacob," while Brigham Young identified them as Ezekiel's "stick of Joseph," descendants of the Israelite tribes of Ephraim and Manasseh, the sons of the biblical prophet Joseph "who came across the waters to this continent."[4] Of powerful significance to a people who believed in the imminent return of Christ, "before the great day of the Lord shall come," the Mormons would redeem the Indians, and "Jacob shall flourish in the wilderness, and the Lamanites shall blossom as the rose."[5] Mormons believed that together, the righteous descendants of Ephraim (white Mormons) and Manasseh (converted Indians) "shall become exceedingly angry, and shall vex the gentiles with a sore vexation." Righteous Latter-day Saints were sometimes promised that "when the remnants of Jacob go through the Gentiles like a lion among the beasts of the forest, as the prophets have spoken, thou shalt be in their midst and shall be a captain of hundreds."[6]

The Saints believed that besides their common destiny, literal blood ties bound them to the Lamanites, for they both shared the sacred blood of Israel. "It is Ephraim that I have been searching for all the days of my preaching, and that is the blood which ran in my veins when I embraced the Gospel," Brigham Young preached. "When we send to the nations we do not seek for the Gentiles, because they are disobedient and rebellious. We want the blood of Jacob, and that of his father Isaac and Abraham, which runs in the veins of the people. . . . It is the house of Israel we are after." Young believed that those who converted to Mormonism were largely descended from the tribe of Ephraim, while the Lamanites were of the blood of Manasseh. "We are of the House of Israel, of the royal seed, of the royal blood," he said. The occasional convert who

[3] 2 Nephi 30:5.

[4] Isaiah 10:21, Ezekiel 37:19, and Brigham Young, 29 May 1870, *Journal of Discourses,* 13:175.

[5] *Doctrine and Covenants,* 49:24.

[6] Peterson, *Utah's Black Hawk War,* 24; and Journal of John Borrowman, in Bigler *Forgotten Kingdom,* 65. See also Micah 5:8 and*Book of Mormon,* 3 Nephi 16:15, 20:16 and 21:12.

lacked this royal blood would have to be physically transformed. Joseph Smith had taught Young "that the Gentile blood was actually cleansed out of their veins, and the blood of Jacob made to circulate in them; and the revolution and change in the system were so great that it caused the beholder to think they were going into fits."[7]

Brigham Young was not only the president of the LDS church, commander of the Nauvoo Legion, and governor of Utah Territory from 1850 to 1857, but in his role as superintendent of Indian affairs, he was uniquely situated to set policy.[8] Typically, that policy was a mix of Young's idealistic religious vision and his hard-headed practicality. As one historian put it, "The relations of Brigham Young with the Indians were a blend of his social-religious-humanitarian philosophy and practical measures that he thought necessary for establishing the Mormon kingdom of God on earth."[9] He was driven to prepare the way for the Lord by redeeming the remnant of Jacob, but he "had little time to waste on recalcitrant Lamanites who did not wish to give up their wild ways and be reformed into proper Old Testament figures." He told Utah Valley settlers in 1849 that the older natives could never be saved, "but they will die and be damned," and the next year his militia general issued orders there calling for "exterminating such, as do not separate themselves from their hostile clans, and sue for peace." The Mormons set about filling up the country and waiting for a new generation of righteous Indians to arise.[10]

But generally speaking, Brigham Young was averse to the shedding of Indian blood.[11] "Experience has taught us that it is cheaper to feed Indians than to fight them—a statement that has been so often repeated that it has become a recognized axiom among us," Brigham Young said in

[7] Young, "The Blood of Israel and the Gentiles," 8 April 1855, Journal of Discourses, 2:268–69. Doctrines associated with "blood," or family and group relationships, had a now-forgotten significance in early Mormon doctrine, and a strange obsession with blood pervaded Brigham Young's public speech during the 1850s.

[8] For a revealing examination of Brigham Young's conduct as territorial Indian superintendent and the resulting conflicts with federally appointed Indian agents, see O'Neil, "Of Pride and Politics," 236–50.

[9] Coates, "Brigham Young and Mormon Indian Policies," 428. For insight into Young's beliefs about the Kingdom of God, see Brigham Young, "The Kingdom of God," 8 July 1855, *Journal of Discourses*, 2:309–17.

[10] Bigler, *Forgotten Kingdom*, 65, 70.

[11] For insights into Young's general aversion to bloodshed, see Walker and Esplin, "Brigham Himself: An Autobiographical Recollection," 19–34.

1866.[12] The axiom was less a prophetic revelation than the practical conclusion of a man who had tried both approaches before making a decision based primarily on economics. Nonetheless, the Mormons sincerely believed they acted in the best interest of their neighbors. After allowing for the paternalistic "white man's burden" mentality found among even the most progressive nineteenth-century thinkers, Mormon attitudes toward the Indians were unusually sympathetic for the time. As Brigham Young told Cannon:

> The accounts of Indian hostilities in Washington and Oregon are truly painful, though we expect that the Indians have more cause for their feelings and acts than is generally known. When will the people learn to treat Indians as they themselves would like to be treated, to do unto them as they would like to be done unto, to make allowance for their ignorance, habits of life, traditions, and instead of treating them like dogs and wolves, learn to treat them kindly, and like human beings, to abstain from gratifying their own inordinate and hellish lusts with the squaws, and from destroying the reason and intellect of the Indian with their bitterest foe—the fire water, and from plundering him of his effects under the name of trade? When will the whites refrain from shooting them down for mere pastime? Rather expensive sport they begin to find out, though the guilty are not the ones that most generally suffer in consequence of all these criminal practices. But who can blame the Indians for resenting such injuries, and upon what principle of enlightened and christian humanity can they be made responsible to the white man's law, before they are made acquainted with its obligations?[13]

The Fate of the Red Man

Believing that American Indians were, as revealed in *The Book of Mormon,* the fallen remnant of several Israelite families who had migrated to the Americas, the Mormons were eager to accept them as their benighted brethren. Joseph Smith sent the first men he called to preach the gospel on a mission to the Delaware Indians who had been forcibly relocated to the western borders of Missouri by the U.S. Government.[14]

---

[12] "Governor's Message to the General Assembly of the State of Deseret," *Millennial Star,* 17 March 1866, 163. Young had begun this policy during a confrontation with the Omahas in 1848. See Coates, "Brigham Young and Mormon Indian Policies," 433.

[13] Young to Cannon, 30 May 1856, *Western Standard,* 12 July 1856, 3.

[14] See Allen and Leonard, *The Story of the Latter-day Saints,* 53–54.

Neither the first mission to the "Lamanites" nor subsequent proselytizing efforts with the tribes of the Great Basin yielded many true converts. Hundreds if not thousands of Indians were nominally baptized, but the cultural gap between the Mormons and the natives was too wide for many in either group to bridge completely. Nonetheless, the very effort to gain converts among the Indians fostered suspicion and resentment among many whites. Indian agent Garland Hurt, though not opposed to missionary work *per se,* was concerned that the Mormons were actively seeking to turn the Indians against the rest of white society, creating a distinction in their minds between the "good Mormons" and the "bad Mericats." Noting Hurt's complaint, Brigham Young explained the practice to Utah Territory's congressional delegate:

> The most Dr Hurt complains of is the distinction made between "Mormons and Americans" by the Indians it having as he alleges been taught them by the Mormons ... Tis nothing of any consequence [for] as far as we can learn and as regards Mormons & Americans the Indians themselves made the distinction when the California emigrants first made their appearance in this Territory in 1849 & 50. ... [The Indians] being in the habit of being shot ~~at~~ by Emigrants and other travelers to California when we met by them finding that the Mormons fed them and clothed them instead of killing them soon learned to inquire of every part they met whether they were Mormons or Americans—a distinction which they have and probably always will make. The rumor here about the Americans having war with Mexico and also that we as a people were driven out from the United States by the Americans.[15]

Although both sides in the Utah War alternated between attempts to keep the tribes neutral and manipulating them to the advantage of first the Mormons and then the U.S. Army, the lingering suspicion that Mormons were recruiting the Great Basin tribes as allies against the government exacerbated an already volatile situation.[16]

George Q. Cannon was among those who attempted to bridge the cultural gap between white society and America's Indians. In the pages of the *Western Standard,* he wrote frequently about the plight of the Indi-

---

[15] Young to Bernhisel, 4 November 1856, LDS Archives.

[16] See O'Neil and Layton, "Brigham Young as Indian Superintendent," 246–49 as well as MacKinnon's forthcoming volume in this series. "In 1857 President James Buchanan submitted nearly sixty documents to Congress to justify his decision to dispatch American troops to Utah . . . three-fourths [of which] came from files of the Office of Indian Affairs." Bigler, ed. *A Winter with the Mormons,* 114.

ans, echoing the sentiments of Brigham Young and always arguing for a more compassionate response to their "depredations."[17] Consider his answer to the question, "What is to be the fate of the red man?"

"The Indians and Their Future,"
Western Standard, 19 April 1856.[18]

What is to be the fate of the red man? The commonly received opinion is, that they, whose forefathers once held undisputed possession from the east to the west sea, are to be hemmed in by the advancing civilization and, finally, exterminated. The past history and experience of the race would favor such a supposition, circumstances at present transpiring around us strengthen it, and it has become an almost settled conviction that fate has so willed it, and, therefore, it must really be inevitable. In the northern territories there seems to be a disposition very prevalent to assist fate in disposing of these troublesome neighbors; and many of the people appear to think that it is actually obligatory upon them, and they are conferring a benefit upon humanity by killing these poor wretches off. Such a spirit is in the highest degree reprehensible. There have been, no doubt, causes which have tended to produce these feelings of antipathy and hatred on the part of the whites in those territories; they have suffered, and suffered keenly too, in the loss of their relatives and friends, in the destruction and loss of their property and stock, and in the complete stagnation of their business. These are events to be deplored. But if the causes which have produced these terrible results were to be traced and equitably decided upon, we are of the opinion that the whole of the blame would not be laid at the door of the Indians. Had they the facilities we have of making their grievances known to the world, what a catalogue of injustice and wrongs received at the hands of the whites, they could present! Despoiled of their lands, driven from the graves of their fathers, and from reservation to reservation, until there is scarcely a spot left that they can call their own, or where they can be free from the obtrusive footsteps of the hated white man, theirs has been a dreadful and pitiable fate. Who can really blame them, when they take all the circumstances into consideration, for feeling as they do? For, although they have not had the means that we have had to perpetuate the tale of their sufferings and the injustice they have experienced, yet the oral traditions of these things, handed down from generation to generation, have been sufficiently impressed upon their memories to make them indelible.

We have no idea that the Indians, as a people, will ever be exterminated, neither do we have an idea that there is any necessity for it. If a conciliatory

---

[17] See also "The Indians in the North," 26 July 1856; and "The Future of the Red Man," 13 December 1856.

[18] Reprinted in Cannon, *Writings from the "Western Standard,"* 70–72.

policy were adopted, and the Indians were treated as human beings, possessing feelings like ourselves, though they may be untutored, very different results would soon be apparent. Let them not be judged and condemned in their ignorance, as we would judge and condemn each other were we guilty of their deeds. Neither ought we, with our enlightenment and knowledge, to condescend to their level, and be guilty of the same acts which we condemn so much in them. Yet it is done; the papers teem with instances of white men wreaking indiscriminate ve[n]geance on the innocent and the guilty, because they are of the same color! Innumerable peaceable and friendly Indians have been shot down like dogs, and left to rot unchronicled and unmourned, because, perchance, their murderers have lost a friend or an animal at some previous time in their lives while among Indians of a different tribe. And yet, as likely as not, these same individuals,—if a poor, ignorant and debased Indian, whose every instinct is grovelling, and whose education has taught him to look upon the shedding of blood as a trifling thing, should be guilty of precisely the same offence—would be filled with resentment and indignation, and would, if it were in their power, exterminate him and his whole race. Can these things pass unnoticed and unpunished by the Father of all? Is not the life of an Indian of any value in His sight? As true as He lives, and has made of one blood all nations of men, and has said by the mouth of His Son, that the measure we mete out shall be measured to us again, such deeds will have to be atoned for, sooner or later, and they can not pass unnoticed nor unpunished. There is an unlimited amount of sympathy expended in favor of the negroes, and many go so far as to assert that a curse will rest upon our nation because slavery is tolerated within our borders; but we candidly think that a greater curse and more terrible retribution will rest upon the nation for its treatment of the Indians, unless they pursue a different policy, than can possibly result from the present treatment of the slaves. We imagine there is a great responsibility resting upon this nation in their treatment of the red men. The Lord, in his wisdom, has permitted us to discover and occupy their land, and we have been placed as a foster-parent over them. Their fate has to a certain extent been in our hands, and we have had the power to exercise an influence upon them for weal or woe. How this power has been abused and prostituted to accomplish base purposes, is well known. It is not too late, however, to adopt a different policy; we yet have the opportunity of exhibiting our boasted philanthropy, enlightenment and zeal for the elevation of fallen humanity, by our treatment of the Indians, and we yet have the power to atone in part for previous missteps, inattention and abuse.

Cannon's spirited defense of the "red man" earned him the opprobrium of many fellow Westerners, who generally agreed with General

Phil Sheridan's later statement that the only good Indian was a dead one. His voice blended with a few others—often ministers of other religions—who called for a more humanitarian approach to the "settling" of the American West.

While there were significant exceptions, the Mormons generally found it was not only cheaper but more in keeping with their religion to feed rather than fight the Indians. The happy results of this policy were reflected in a letter from G. Clements of Utah published in the *Western Standard*:

> The Indian tribes around us are friendly and peaceably disposed. The wise and sound policy displayed by Governor Young in relation to the red men, has produced the happiest results. The progress of civilization in every Territory throughout our wide spread Union has been marked by the blood of the red man, except Utah. The Indians here feel that we are *their friends.* Many of them are forsaking their idle, pilfering habits and turning their attention to the cultivation of the soil.[19]

To Join with the Indians: White Indians

Even before the Mormons arrived in the Far West, Marcus Whitman blamed much of the violence along the Oregon Trail on American desperadoes. Some of the Indians, he wrote, "are already well known to be led by desperate white men and Mongrels who form banditti in the difficult passes and are at all times ready to cut off some lagging emigrant." As knowledge spread "that large quantities of valuable property and considerable sums of money are yearly carried over this desolate region," Whitman stated, "it is to be feared that organized Banditti will be instituted."[20]

Many, if not most, of the violent incidents attributed to Indians in the 1850s were the work of Americans, common criminals called "White Indians" who were notorious for their brutality.[21] As early as 1850 William Bedford Temple concluded that "the savage Indians"

[19] Clements to Cannon, 30 June 1856, *Western Standard,* 2 August 1856. Clements' letter overlooked such brutal conflicts as the battle with the Utes at Provo in 1851 and the Walker War of 1853.

[20] Whitman to Secretary of War, late 1843, in Drury, *Marcus and Narcissa Whitman,* 2:397.

[21] Munkres, "The Plains Indian Threat on the Oregon Trail before 1860," first noted the major role white criminals played in violence on the overland trails.

between the Platte River and Missouri were "afraid to come near the road," and "near all the stealing and killing is done by the Whites following the Trains."[22] As William Renfro Rothwell noted near the same spot on 20 May 1861, "The 'White Indians' are more dangerous than the Pawnees."[23] If "not for the white traders and outlaws who were among the Indians, leading them on to depredations, emigration could pass through unmolested," overland emigrant William Smedley concluded.[24]

Utah Indian Agent Jacob Holeman reported as of May 1852, "The *white* Indians, I apprehend, are much more dangerous than the *red*. The renegades, deserters and thieves, who had to fly from justice to California, have taken refuge in the mountains, and having associated themselves with Indians are more savage than the Indians themselves."[25]

Brigham Young denounced such activities in July 1854. "The emigration leaving Bear River must be prepared to run a still harder gauntlet, for it is reported that a numerous and well-organized band of white highwaymen, painted and disguised as Indians, infest several points on the road, and drive off stock by wholesale, and recent murders are rumored from that quarter." Young blamed the havoc on a "robber band" made up of "the Arkansas murderer, and a large number of associated outlaws and fugitives."[26] Almost everyone else in the West believed the "White Knives" were Mormons, and any number of California newspaper reports fed this prejudice.

"JUSTICE ON THE PLAINS," *ALTA CALIFORNIA*, 10 SEPTEMBER 1854, 2/4.

A gentleman who has just arrived with stock, informs us that a man was accused of stealing a horse at Thousand Spring Valley. He was tried by a jury of six men, who, after hearing all the circumstances, condemned him to death. The choice of the manner of death was left to the prisoner, who preferred to be shot. It was, however, somewhat difficult to find persons willing to execute the deed, but after long delay, four young men stepped forward and expressed themselves ready to serve the demands of justice. The

22 William Bedford Temple to "Wife and Littleones," 2 June 1850, Oregon Historical Society.

23 Rothwell, Papers, Beinecke Library.

24 Smedley, *Across the Plains in '62*, 35, 44.

25 Morgan, *The Humboldt*, 214.

26 Brigham Young, "Emigration: From the East to the Pacific, and the Land Sharks of Utah" *Deseret News*, 13 July 1854; reprinted *New York Times*, 8 September 1854.

> sentence was about to be executed, when the person from whom the horse was stolen interposed, and an altercation arising, the prisoner escaped. He was afterwards picked up by a portion of the same party, and severely whipped. During his trial he confessed that he was one of the many sent out by the Mormons, instructed to join with the Indians in the stealing of horses and stock.—*Grass Valley Tel.*

California emigrants often claimed that Mormons led attacks on wagon trains, but the evidence for most of these charges were entirely circumstantial. William Smedley described meeting an 1852 trail veteran who recounted his party's "capture of a white man in Indian paint and costume." The man claimed to be a Mormon "but could not be made to say that Brigham [Young] had any knowledge of or had anything to do with his present business." A man whose family had been murdered nearby put a revolver to the robber's head. He "turned his face away and fired — killing the unfortunate desperado on the spot." While the man may not have been guilty of the murders, Smedley felt justice had been done, since he "was in league with hostile Indians, leading them on to depredations for which the Indians received entire blame and perhaps chastisement."[27] In a letter home, one overlander complained, "The Mormons is stealing a great many sto[c]k. They are a great deal worse than the Indians."[28]

After the Utah War broke out in 1857, overland travelers had no doubt who was behind such assaults. The "Mormons are closely leagued with the Indians, providing them with arms, and furnishing [them] with provisions."[29] Richeson Abbott complained that for three hundred miles "the immigrants had to run the gauntlet of Indian attacks and Mormon treachery." After an attack at City of Rocks, he was "satisfied the attack was led by Mormons, as they heard them cursing in regular Mormon slang, and calling out to them to get out of the country, as they had no business there." They threatened that the Mormons "would kill them all." Hundreds of emigrants had been killed, and it was "an undoubted fact that the Mormons were at the head of most of these outrages, and instigated the Indians to commit the mur-

[27] Smedley, *Across the Plains in '62*, 35, 44.

[28] P. H. Ferguson, in Mattes, *Platte River Road Narratives*, 473.

[29] "More Testimony against the Mormons," *Daily Alta California*, 9 November 1857, 2/5, copied from *San Andreas Independent*.

ders."[30] Louis Fine claimed men from Arkansas "were attacked near City of Rocks by Indians, led on by white men they supposed to be Mormons." For the next three hundred miles "they were fired into or attacked almost every day." The emigrants "all appeared to have more fear of the Mormons than of the Indians; and the general feeling among them is that the Mormons led the Indians in their attacks and murders."[31]

The perception that the Mormons and the Indians were allies frightened many Americans. Travelers and mountaineers sometimes tried—through action or rumor—to bring enmity between them. B. F. Matthews' story reveals the suspicion and mistrust that existed between the Mormons and the emigrants who passed through their kingdom in the West.

B. F. MATTHEWS TO GEORGE Q. CANNON,
WESTERN STANDARD, 15 MAY 1857.

I presume the misfortune which befell me on my return to the [Salt Lake] Valley with a company last year, has become pretty generally known. I refer to the existence of the small pox in my company, and its consequent introduction among the Saints in the Territory.

I saw a notice of it in the *Mormon*, stating that a train of emigrants on their way to California, picked up a bead near an Indian camp, which was stuffed with cotton impregnated with small pox virus, and had been put there by the Mormons to introduce that disease among the Indians, and thereby effect their destruction. This is a lie of the blackest dye, and is one of the contemptible and abominable methods by which our enemies are seeking to create excitement about, and embitter the feelings of, the people towards us, and thereby arouse them to hostility against this people. I perceive that they have a great deal to say about the people of Utah, and a great many stories are circulated about the mistreatment of the California emigrants in Salt Lake Valley, which I know to be false.

With relation to the bead containing the poisoned cotton, and the subsequent breaking out of the small pox, the facts are these:

When about seven miles from Green river, near the forks of the road, one of my company picked up a large bead, stuffed with cotton, and gave it to a little boy of Mr. Wight's, about six years of age, who had been run over by a wagon a few minutes before and quite seriously injured, to play with. His aunt picked out the cotton with a needle, from curiosity, and about five days

30 "More Mormon Massacres," *Daily Alta California*, 1 November 1857, 2/2.

31 *San Francisco Herald*, 2 November 1857; reprinted in *The California Farmer*, 30 October 1857, 128:1/2.

afterwards he was taken sick, as I thought, with the fever, nor did I know any better until he broke out with the small pox, which did not take place until after we arrived in Salt Lake City.

This, of course, created a great deal of excitement in the Valley, and many long lectures were given about it, and as a natural result, much prejudice existed against myself in consequence of this sad occurrence, which thus introduced this terrible disease among the inhabitants of Utah. My supposition was, and is, that a company of California emigrants who were ahead of us, threw out the bait for us and we bit at it and were caught, and my humble opinion is, that this bead was placed there by them for *us* instead of the Indians, as it was known we were a Mormon train bound for the Valley.[32]

Many Americans perceived Mormons and Indians as dangerous enemies with whom peaceful co-existence was impossible. As a result of the general, though sporadic, peace that existed between the Mormons and their Indian neighbors, they were often lumped together, and not completely without cause.

The Danite Band, or the Avenging Angels

Reports of Mormon/Indian collusion were inevitably linked to tales of "Danites" or "Destroying Angels." Its history is murky, but this shadowy organization evolved in Missouri as the "Brothers of Gideon," "Daughter of Zion," "Sons of Dan," or "Danite Band" and was led by Sampson Avard for five months in 1838. Apostle George A. Smith later claimed that the Danites had only existed for some six weeks and "was used to know each other" but "their has been none for the last 19 years."[33] Though not, perhaps, without some justification,[34] some of the members of this secret organization participated in extralegal actions against perceived enemies of the Church of Jesus Christ of Latter-day Saints during one of the most tumultuous periods in its early history. The extent to which Joseph Smith knew of and approved of their vigilante activities has long been debated, but it is unlikely that the group existed without at least implicit sanction from higher authority

[32] Matthews to Cannon, 19 April 1857, *Western Standard,* 15 May 1857, 3.

[33] Utah Stake Minutes, 30 August 1857, 668–69, LDS Archives.

[34] See Anderson, "Atchison's Letters and the Causes of Mormon Expulsion from Missouri," 3–47.

than Avard—perhaps Sidney Rigdon of the First Presidency.[35] The Sons of Dan first attacked Mormon dissenters but soon turned its attention to external adversaries. "The riches of the Gentiles shall be consecrated to my people, the house of Israel," Avard vowed, "and thus you will waste away the Gentiles by robbing and plundering them of their property."[36]

After Avard turned against the Mormons in return for immunity from prosecution, church leaders excommunicated him in March 1839.[37] Though he was left behind when the Saints moved west, the Mormons could not leave behind persistent rumors of loyal Danites doing anything and everything their prophet commanded.

Shortly after settling in the Great Basin, Brigham Young (who ironically had helped expose Avard) organized a force of "Minute Men" to recover stolen cattle. The group, which naturally included many veterans of the Danite episode, evolved into the Nauvoo Legion, the Utah territorial militia, and law enforcement agencies such as the Salt Lake City police and the county sheriff's office. "Although they do not maintain their organization, being generally merged into 'Brigham's Life Guards', yet without the same name," John Hyde observed with some accuracy, "they have performed the same deeds." The American public identified men such as Bill Hickman, Porter Rockwell, Ephraim Hanks, and Howard Egan with the Danites or as "Brigham's Destroying Angels." Utah residents referred to these hard-bitten men as the "be'hoys," but there is no evidence to indicate they had any formal organization.[38] In what may well have been the nation's first published interview, newspaper editor Horace Greeley asked Young in 1859, "What do you say of the so-called Danites, or so-called Avenging Angels, belonging to your church?" Young snapped back, "What do *you* say? I know of no such band, no such persons or organization. I hear of them only in the slanders of our enemies."[39]

---

[35] "The influential role of the Danites and the presence of Mormon leaders within the organization supports the witnesses' testimony that the First Presidency approved of and encouraged the group's activities. There remains a question, however, regarding the extent to which Joseph Smith actively directed the Danites." LeSueur, *The 1838 Mormon War in Missouri,* 208.

[36] Roberts, *History of the Church,* 3:180. Information on the founding of the Sons of Dan is drawn from Schindler, *Orrin Porter Rockwell,* 34–65.

[37] Smith, Jr. *History of the Church,* 3:284.

[38] Hyde, *Mormonism,* 105; and Brooks, ed., *On the Mormon Frontier,* 653n21. The B'hoys were a notorious gang in New York's Five Points district.

[39] Greeley, *An Overland Journey,* 214

Regardless of whether the Danites were ever officially organized and directed by Mormon leaders, they became the scapegoats for any number of crimes, real or imagined, that were laid at the feet of Utah Mormons. Arthur Conan Doyle continued as late as 1886 to perpetuate stories of the fantastic crimes attributed to the "Avenging Angels" of Mormondom in his first Sherlock Holmes adventure. Doyle invented a charge against the Latter-day Saints beyond the imagination of even the most creative anti-Mormons:

> The supply of adult women was running short, and polygamy without a female population on which to draw was a barren doctrine indeed. Strange rumours began to be bandied about—rumours of murdered immigrants and rifled camps in regions where Indians had never been seen. Fresh women appeared in the harems of the Elders—women who pined and wept, and bore upon their faces the traces of an unextinguishable horror. Belated wanderers upon the mountains spoke of gangs of armed men, masked, stealthy, and noiseless, who flitted by them in the darkness. These tales and rumours took substance and shape, and were corroborated and re-corroborated, until they resolved themselves into a definite name. To this day, in the lonely ranches of the West, the name of the Danite Band, or the Avenging Angels, is a sinister and an ill-omened one.[40]

Responsibility for violence on the Mormon frontier has been one of the most divisive topics in LDS church history. Early treatments tended to be sensational exposés or defenses of the faith, and writers either found Danites under every sagebrush or tried to deny their very existence. Fortunately, recent scholarship has been more balanced.[41]

Experience had taught Cannon that it would only be a matter of time before virtually any criminal activity in the West would be blamed on the

[40] Doyle, *A Study in Scarlet,* 135, 157, 154. See also Homer, "'Recent Psychic Evidence,'" 264–74; Cornwall and Arrington, "Perpetuation of a Myth," 160–63 and Homer, "The Mormon Subplot in *A Study In Scarlet* and *Angels Of Darkness,* 166–90. Doyle's racist, unpublished play, *Angels of Darkness,* is based on the second half of *A Study in Scarlet* and is even more melodramatic in its vilification of Mormon Danites.

[41] Classic accounts of the Danites are found in Corrill, *A Brief History,* 30–32; Bennett, *The History of the Saints,* 265–72, 324–28; Waite, *The Mormon Prophet and His Harem,* 261–63; Hickman, *Brigham's Destroying Angel;* Reid, *Sketches and Anecdotes,* 34–54; Lee, *Mormonism Unveiled;* Roberts, *Comprehensive History,* 1:500–508; and Kelly and Birney, *Holy Murder.* For more recent scholarship, see Schindler, *Orrin Porter Rockwell;* Gentry, "The Danite Band of 1838," 421–50; Allen and Leonard, *The Story of the Latter-day Saints,* 121–24; Arrington and Bitton, *The Mormon Experience,* 53–55; LeSueur, *The 1838 Mormon War in Missouri;* and Whittaker, "The Book of Daniel in Early Mormon Thought," 166–73. One of the most recent church-sanctioned histories of the Mormons briefly acknowledged the offensive, as well as defensive, role of the early Danites. See Leonard, *Nauvoo,* 26-28.

Mormons. In a 31 July 1857 editorial, he responded to several articles that had appeared in the Los Angeles *Star* and other papers that complained that a "formidable banditti have taken up their quarters in the San Bernardino mountains."

"THE BANDITTI," *WESTERN STANDARD,* 31 JULY 1857.

This brings forcibly to our mind the organized bands of horse-thieves and robbers who located themselves in the neighborhood of Nauvoo, and committed numerous depredations upon the property of the neighboring inhabitants. Of course, the Mormons got the blame for every theft and other rascally act committed within a given distance of their city, and that circumstance was one of the causes of the angry feelings which the old citizens cherished against us.

We are apprehensive that a similiar [*sic*] feeling will be stirred up in the lower country, unless decisive and vigorous measures be adopted to ferret out and effectually break up this nest of outlaws. Unless this be done, it will be supposed that they remain by sufferance, and the Saints will be charged with connivance at their villainies. Sheriff Clift is a man of the right stripe to see this matter accomplished, and we know him well enough to say, He will attend to it without delay.[42]

THE MYSTERIOUS AND BLOODY BAND OF "DANITES"

Outraged by attacks apparently committed against overland emigrants by white men in league with Indians, the San Francisco *Weekly Chronicle* engaged in a little investigative journalism and identified a couple of supposed Mormons, Peter and Alfred [Albert] Haws, as Danites who were not above disguising themselves as white Indians. Following the *Chronicle's* accusations, Cannon launched his usual spirited rebuttal.

"THE BANDITS OF THE PLAINS," *WEEKLY CHRONICLE,* 22 AUGUST 1857.[43]

Our readers will recollect that in the accounts of the depredations committed upon the immigrants mention is made of two men by the names of Haws; they are, we believe, Peter Haws and Alfred Haws, and have for some

[42] Robert Clift served as a lieutenant in the Mormon Battalion and as alcalde of San Diego in 1848. The first sheriff of San Bernardino County, Clift was killed by Indians in Ruby Valley, Nevada, while carrying mail in 1859.

[43] The newspaper is erroneously dated one week later than the actual date of publication. For another, similar, complaint of "Indian attacks and Mormon treachery" in this vicinity, see *Los Angeles Star,* 7 November 1857, 4/1.

time been known to those familiar with border life as a brace of ruffians, who should have long since graced a gallows. As long ago as when the Mormons were in Nauvoo, these Haws were domiciled among them, and were notorious for their horse stealing and counterfeiting operations. And ever since that time they have followed the track of the Mormons, as the jackal follows the track of the lion, for the purpose of snapping up such little prey as escapes the jaws of the larger monster. Whenever danger threatens them, and they wish to hide for a time, they seek the protecting wing of the Mormon Church, under which they repose for awhile, when they again sally forth in search of plunder.

These men belong to that class of renegades who consort with the Indians for the purpose of robbing and murdering the whites, and who are in reality the cause of four-fifths of the robberies and murders occurring on the Plains and near the border settlements. When the Mormons took up their abode at Salt Lake the Haws, among other renegades, accompanied them, and for a long time were members of the famous band of "Danites," whose murderous exploits have made them notorious. They went so far, even in this band, that it was thought proper to remove them, and consequently they have been engaged ever since, in company with others, in plundering the immigrant trains while in the vicinity of the Humboldt.

It appears these fellows are located somewhere in the Walker River country, where they are joined from time to time by the outlaws from this State. They are ostensibly engaged as Indian traders, and furnish the Indians with whisky, arms, ammunition, etc. Of course they adopt nearly the manners of the Indians, and have succeeded in obtaining considerable influence over them; and their red friends are never backward in engaging in any scheme of plunder which may be pointed out to them.

Their plan of operations appears to be this: To embrace every opportunity of plundering the immigrants of their stock and stores while along the Humboldt, and then run the stock off to the southward, across the range of hills or mountains into the valleys along Walker's River, through which the immigration seldom, if ever, passes. Here the stock is kept in tolerable security, and allowed to recuperate until along in the fall, when it is driven through by the southern route around Salt Lake into Salt Lake City. Here the cattle, horses and mules are kept for the use of the inhabitants; or perchance in the spring, if they are not needed at the Lake, they are driven into this State by parties and sold.

Heretofore the Indians have been alone blamed for the outrages committed on the plains, but recent developments have conclusively established the fact that these renegade white scoundrels are the real criminals. There appears to be but one feasible plan of ridding the country of them, and that is to have a good company of dragoons or mounted riflemen, stationed say at Genoa or some other point in Carson Valley, which shall frequently scour the the [sic] Walker River country, and then through the hills north to the Humboldt; and whenever they come across a band of these villains, destroy them without mercy. If some such plan is not adopted soon, it is very evident that these outrages will increase instead of diminish, and immigration will be deterred from seeking our State. It is a subject which should receive the earliest attention of the United States Military authorities, as it is one of great importance not only to the people of this State, but to those who risk their lives and property on the Plains.

"From Carson Valley and the Plains," *Western Standard*, 21 August 1857.[44]

The intelligence received from the eastern side of the Sierra Nevada confirms the accounts, previously received, of the existence of an organized band of robbers composed of Indians and whites, who are seriously annoying the immigration. One desperado has been killed, who proved to be a fugitive from justice in California. A man named Brown and two others named Jones, ostensibly traders, were seen at Gravelly Ford, on the Humboldt, on the 30th of July, since which time they have not been heard of. Some surmise that they have been killed; but the probability is that they are in league with the Indians. On the 19th of July, the train of Messrs. Holloway & Rector was attacked by Indians and whites. This occurred at the head of Goose creek, where the road leaves the canon. They (H. & R.) are confident that this attack was led on by white men, for they distinctly heard the voices of three who spoke English freely. They also swore in English vociferously. A train known as Buster's train was, while crossing the plains, attacked by about thirty Shoshones. Twenty-four of the Indians were killed, and one white man who is supposed to have been the leader of the band. All the Indians who were seen near the camp of Holloway & Rector had new rifles, and it is thought that Tooley and the two Haws carried to them this season a whole wagon load of arms and ammunition. The Chronicle represents the Haws as having been "hangers-on upon the Mormon camp," and, finally, members of the mysterious and bloody band of "Danites," but were ejected from that mythical body because of their extraordinary villainy. This imaginary Danite band has been a terror to certain editors and priests, whose superstitions transform shadows into giants and posts into hobgoblins. The Danite band was neither more nor less than the creation of the Missouri robbers aided by "Mormon" apostates, and applied in the first instance to the militia of the "Mormon" county of Caldwell, whose only obligation was to preserve the peace and maintain the supremacy of

[44] Reprinted in Cannon, *Writings from the "Western Standard,"* 498–500.

the Constitution and the laws. This name became notorious because of the fearful oaths which were supposed to bind them together, and the horrid crimes said to have been committed; and was afterward applied to the police of the city of Nauvoo, whose oath in nowise differed from the usual oath of policemen, and is now applied to the police of Great Salt Lake City. This is all the Danite band that we ever knew of,—and we have been a member of the Church of the saints for the last twenty years. These Haws, are not nor never were members of the Salt Lake City police, but had they been, and were detected in villainy and dismissed from that body as the Chronicle infers, it reflects credit upon that body, and gives the lie to the wretched yarns about the supposed Danites. We should have been less particular about this, did we not perceive a latent desire to shift the responsibility of the outrages committed upon the immigrants from the guilty parties to the "Mormon" people, and thus increase persecution against the saints in California. There can, however, be no doubt that white men are in league with Indians to rob and murder immigrants; and it is quite possible that some of those men may have been as jackals prowling around and in the "Mormon camp." But the people of this State may depend, if they fall into the hands of the citizens of Utah, they will meet with certain and adequate punishment.

With respect to crimes and misdemeanors, the situation of the saints is in some respects the opposite to that of Christians.[45] Among the latter, if a crime be committed, no one is held responsible but the perpetrator. But if a "Mormon" be guilty of crime, the whole Church must bear the blame. It matters not whether he is a member of the Church, or not,—if he has been a member and has apostatized or been cut off for his misdeeds, or if he has been amongst our people, whatever crime he may commit thereafter is sure to be charged upon the entire Church. There is such a manifest injustice in this, that one would suppose that a people professing the liberal sentiments of American citizens, would be the last to be guilty of it. But experience has taught us, that whatever of courtesy, honor, justice, humanity or right which Christians freely accord to each other, it is by no means intended that such neighborly dealing shall be extended to the Latter-day Saints. Consequently the Church must expect to bear the blame of the wicked acts of apostate "Mormons," "hickory Mormons," etc., until we attain unto a position before the world, that will demand the observance toward us of at least the common courtesies of life.

---

[45] Today, the Church of Jesus Christ of Latter-day Saints goes out of its way to emphasize that its members are, indeed, Christians. In Cannon's day, however, the LDS church often made a distinction between the Latter-day "saints" and the Gentile "Christians." "Mormon," on the other hand, was a name that Cannon did not particularly appreciate—hence his use of quotation marks most of the time he refers to "Mormons" or "Mormonism." Even today, the church tries to downplay this nickname.

Quite Too Many for the White Indians

The Peter Haws identified by the *Chronicle* and implicitly acknowledged by Cannon was not only a Mormon, but a member of the Council of Fifty.[46] On their way to Salt Lake, European sojourners Jules Remy and Julius Brenchley stayed at his homestead and trading post on the Humboldt River, some four hundred miles west of Salt Lake, from 3 to 14 September 1855.

Remy learned that Haws had been one of the earliest Mormon pioneers to settle in Salt Lake, where he had been in the whisky making business. Haws allegedly left the valley because he could not get along with his leader: "A dispute he had with the new Prophet, Brigham Young, disgusted him, and he resolved to withdraw from the society to entertain the holy doctrines in his own way, without having to bow to the authority of the President of the Church."[47] Young, in turn, did not think much of Peter Haws. He reminded Cannon of his distrust and commented on "Lord" Brenchley's sexual proclivities in a chatty letter informing him that the European sojourners had arrived in Salt Lake.

Brigham Young to George Q. Cannon, 29 April 1856, LDS Archives, 722–25.

Elder George Q. Cannon
Dear Brother,

Your note of the lst Ultimo. came duly to hand on the 28th inst. We also received the first six numbers of your paper, this being the first arrival in this region. We had looked for your paper with some interest and anxiety, and feel exceedingly gratified at its appearance in manner, matter and form. Your heading tho' well conceived is not quite so well executed as I could wish. The

[46] Quinn, *Origins of Power,* 523. Joseph Smith organized the Council of Fifty in Nauvoo as a highly secret brotherhood forming the "living constitution" of the political structure that would rule the world after the Second Coming of Christ. Although not officially part of the Church of Jesus Christ of Latter-day Saints, most of its original members were Mormons, many of whom had earlier served as Danites. Klaus Hansen's pioneering work, *Quest for Empire,* first pointed out the importance of the council. See also Clark, "The Kingdom of God, the Council of Fifty, and the State of Deseret"; Andrus, *Joseph Smith and World Government*; and Ehat, "'It Seems Like Heaven Began Earth.'" One of the major reasons Haws withdrew from Brigham Young was because of a differing understanding of the authority of the Council of Fifty relative to that of the twelve apostles. See Quinn, "The Council of Fifty and Its Members, 1844 to 1945," 182–83. The Council is further discussed in chapter 8.

[47] Remy and Brenchley, *A Journey to Great-Salt-Lake City,* 1:139–40. Like fellow Council of Fifty members John D. Lee, Charles C. Rich, Amasa Lyman, and Orson Hyde, Haws settled at a critical location on the network of wagon roads leading to California.

temple should be a little higher to show a symetrical proportion being too large for its height. If this was not aimed to be the crowning feature in Vignetts it would be less matter ~~and~~ but does very well as it is.[48] The selections are good, I like a little fun and rich anecdot[e]s, (you know I think they do no harm to any paper). I am pleased to see that you pursue a cautious course, it is much the best and very frequently avoid back action to which so many of the publications of the day subject themselves.

The English Lord, as he represented himself, and his french valet, Dr. Remy turned out as I expected. The frenchman was exceedingly anxious to be baptized while here, but I suppose he has forgotten his proclivities for Mormonism. It would almost seem strange too if we were not used to such things. They came here in the company of Peter Haws, as they state themselves, a man you are aware in whom we have reposed no confidence for many years; and wished to see me alone, they enquired if I could speak french, I told them I could not, they then commenced talking french in my presence to each other, I told them I had no room for private conference with them and walked out of my office as I felt insulted by their conduct, they followed me out and walked along with me tell they could get to speak to me privately, and then asked to borrow money of me. They came here as any other loafers would, without money or recommends. The Englishman represented himself as having an income of some Eighty thousand per year in England, which tho' he seemed anxious still found it difficult to spend. further than this I know but little about them. Subsequently to their first call they apoligised for their rudeness and solicited another interview, which I granted; but I could not see as they had any business further than to gratify an absurd & impudent curiosity. When Mr. Remy sent in his request soliciting me to baptize him I declined doing it, but returned for answer "that if he really wished to be baptized that any of the elders would do it for him" As to the mormonism of him or his aimable friend and pitcher who sustains him I know nothing more [inserted] about it or them, neither cared no more than now. You handled the matter very well so far as I have noticed. I merely mention these facts to post you a little in regard to them, there are plenty here who are better acquainted with them than me and perhaps you may have some knowledge of a certain Mr. Brenchley who lived several years in the Sandwich Islands where he kept native men and women to minister to his wants and pleasures. Well this is the same man, only he has picked up this french Remy to attend him in his pregrinations and pander for him. . .

Praying that the Lord may bless and prosper you, the boys in the office and all faithful Saints

I remain,

Your bro. in the Gospel of Christ
Brigham Young

---

[48] Cannon did not make the suggested change, perhaps due to the cost of a new engraving.

Even though Young had "no confidence" in Haws, Remy and Brenchley were favorably impressed with him and found Haws to be a faithful Mormon. Remy described him as being about fifty years of age (he was sixty at the time—a bit old, perhaps, for the life of a desperado). He was living with his wife, a ten-year-old daughter, and a daughter married to one Carlos Murray. Apparently neither of Peter's sons—Alpheus Peter nor Albert H. (not Alfred, as reported by the *Chronicle*)—was living there at the time.

Both of Haws' sons had bloody reputations and were at least partly responsible for the rumors described in the *Chronicle*. After a killing spree in which he shot several lawmen in Nevada and Utah, Albert Haws died in May 1870 under the guns of a posse that included Porter Rockwell. Alpheus Haws was born in Canada on 15 October 1825 and had served as a sergeant in the Mormon Battalion. In 1854 he "had the Indians on the Humboldt River and Ruby Valley Banded together with secret signs and pass word, like the robbers of old," Mormon diarist O. P. Huntington charged, "and he laid a plan to murder me."[49] During the explosion of violence on the California Trail in 1857, California papers charged

> Alph Hawes, who left this State last spring, took with him twelve dozen muskets which he furnished to the Indians, and it is these guns with which they are shooting the emigrants with [*sic*]. The Hawes had a partner, whom some of the emigrants caught and shot, putting thirty bullets through him, and would have served Hawes the same way, had he not escaped them.[50]

In spite of the evidence to the contrary, Alpheus Haws steadfastly denied that he and his brother were involved in these depredations upon emigrants, branding such "disreputable allegations" as untrue.[51] Alpheus Haws ultimately settled in Berkeley, California, and died at Sonoma on 3 November 1906.[52]

Renegades such as Return Jackson Redden and Carlos Murray joined the Haws family in their depredations. Indian agent Jacob Holeman reported in 1852 that Redden was "associated with a company of white men and Indians who are stationed near Carson Valley, and that their

[49] Schindler, *Orrin Porter Rockwell*, 216n66, 355. Huntington met Alpheus Haws in California in 1899 and recalled, "We chatted together like other men but he could not hold his gaze on mine."

[50] "Arrival of Emigrants.—Myers' Train," *Stockton Daily Argus*, 17 October 1857, 2/2. Citation courtesy of David Bigler.

[51] "From the Plains—Mr. Hawes' Statement," *Alta California*, 19 October 1857, 2/1.

[52] Larson, *A Database of the Mormon Battalion*, 119.

object is to rob and plunder the emigrants." Redden had once been a Mormon and had warned a friend "to paint the horns of his cattle so that he may be known, as they do not wish to molest the brethren," but he was "now held by them in utter contempt, and looked upon as a great scoundrel."[53]

Carlos Murray, a nephew of Heber C. Kimball, was an especially rough character. Murray and Peter Haws accompanied Remy and Brenchley for a few days on their journey to Salt Lake. While the travelers were glad of the company of Haws, they developed an "unaccountable aversion" for Murray, who acted suspiciously, as if he were waiting for an opportunity to engage in some kind of mischief against them. Their suspicions were later confirmed when they learned that in addition to killing at least one Indian, Murray "had murdered two pale-faces to secure their money, and the Mormons suspected that more than one other victim attributed to the Shoshones should be laid to his charge." When these European adventurers did not arrive in Salt Lake according to their previously announced schedule, many assumed they had "fallen victims to the much dreaded Carlos."[54]

Remy and Brenchley maintained full confidence in Peter Haws. Although they had approached his homestead with trepidation ("was it not rather the abode of some wretched pale-face, located among the savages to urge them on to plunder for his benefit?"), they quickly warmed to this "advanced sentinel . . . of Mormonism in the desert." Regarding him as "among those of the worthiest of men that we have met in the course of our wandering life," and being "worthy of being cited and admired," Remy and Brenchley believed Haws was completely unaware of the nefarious character of his son-in-law, Carlos Murray.[55]

Haws apparently told Remy and Brenchley that he had been authorized by federal Indian Agent Garland Hurt, "to call upon the Indians

[53] Morgan, *The Humboldt*, 213–14. Return Jackson Redden had served as bodyguard to Joseph Smith and as a scout for Brigham Young's 1847 pioneer camp. Whatever his status in 1852, he later settled in Utah and was a justice of the peace in Tooele and Summit counties. Redden died at Hoytsville, Utah, in 1891. See Bagley, ed., *The Pioneer Camp of the Saints*, 343.

[54] Remy and Brenchley, *A Journey to Great-Salt-Lake City*, 1:137–38. After he was tried and acquitted by a Mormon jury for murdering an Indian, Murray and his wife were killed by the Shoshonis. For more on the Haws family, Murray, Jackson, and other alleged Mormon renegades see Morgan, *The Humboldt*, 213–21; and Hickman, *Brigham's Destroying Angel*, 110–11. For depredations on the southern route, see Lee, *Mormonism Unveiled*, 270–72; and *Los Angeles Star*, 24 October 1857, 2/1; and 7 November 1857, 2/1–3.

[55] Remy and Brenchley, *A Journey to Great-Salt-Lake City*, 1:122, 138, 148, 150.

to punish those emigrants who should commit any offence against the natives."[56] Whether or not Haws properly understood whatever authority he had been given, he regarded himself as an agent of the U.S. government in such activities—at least that was what he told his European visitors.

Cannon read into the *Chronicle* article the charge that the Haws had been named as "members of the Salt Lake City police" when the only allegation was that they were "Danites." The Salt Lake police force included members of the original Nauvoo Legion and police force, many of whom had been affiliated with the Danite band back in 1838. Having denied the very reality of a Mormon Danite Band, there was no point in Cannon denying that the Haws family had been members of that organization. Rather, he denied their membership in the Salt Lake City police.

Rumors of Mormon complicity in Indian violence began as early as the late 1830s, during the Missouri persecutions.[57] For the most part, later reports of white Indians can be traced to either non-Mormon mountain men or thugs who had been excommunicated from the Church of Jesus Christ of Latter-day Saints.[58] One of the earliest to debunk the inevitable exaggerations of the activities of Mormon "white Indians"—at least until the Mountain Meadows Massacre, to be discussed in chapter 12—was William Chandless, writing in 1857:

> Some other of the doctor's stories had a little of the cock-and-bull nature: *ex. gr.* that Brigham had a number of sham Indians (*i. e.* white men in disguise) to attack and kill those trying to leave the territory, and 'one of them,' said he, 'lives in that house opposite' . . . That some special offenders or known enemies may have been secretly dispatched is likely enough, but the number who leave for California without 'counsel,' and though on one pretext or another notoriously with no *animus revertendi,* are quite too many for the white Indians.[59]

Cannon often dealt with rumors of Mormon white Indians assassi-

---

[56] Ibid., I:124.

[57] See Bennett, *The History of the Saints,* 309–10; Hollon, *Frontier Violence,* 30–34; and LeSueur, *The 1838 Mormon War in Missouri,* 18.

[58] Anderson, *Desert Saints,* 127–28; and Unruh, *The Plains Across,* 193–97.

[59] Chandless, *A Visit to Salt Lake,* 239–40. Chandless was a well-to-do English visitor to the United States who traveled to California from Missouri as a common teamster in 1856 but did not publish his experiences in the U. K. until the following year.

nating apostates and other undesirables in editorials that addressed a host of similar charges. In May 1857 he cleverly caught the attention of his readers by using the same sensational headlines he was about to refute, contrasting the law-abiding citizens of Utah with those non-Mormons who had recently supported vigilante justice in San Francisco. He also had a field day when a typographical error confused apostles with apostates.

"LATER FROM SALT LAKE — BR. YOUNG'S DESTROYING ANGELS! — THE MORMONS BREAKING UP IN A GRAND ROW — HUNDREDS OF APOSTLES RUNNING OFF — FRIGHTFUL REPORTS,"
WESTERN STANDARD, 22 MAY 1857.

Under the above caption, in yesterday's *Globe,* we found a summary of the latest intelligence received from G.S.L. City, and Carson Valley. It says, quoting from an interior paper: "Two of the apostates had arrived in Carson Valley, having ran away from Salt Lake on the sixth of April, and swam Bear river, near by, to make good their escape."

From this very reliable source, they learn that the dissensions among the Mormons have come to an issue; three hundred who had become disgusted with the rule of Brigham Young have left for the Atlantic States, and six thousand more are anxiously awaiting a safe opportunity to escape, but are prevented from doing so by a band of bravoes employed by Brigham Young, and known as the "Destroying Angels." They report that dead bodies are being constantly found about that place, said to be murdered by Indians, but whose death is, by this brace of apostates, charged to the Mormons. And all this is greedily swallowed on the *rumored* testimony of *two* men, of whose character and antecedents they are ignorant, and whose evidence has not been given in person. It is customary to confront the accuser and accused, and hear the testimony on both sides before judgment is pronounced; but we suppose the "Mormons" are considered outside the pale of humanity, and are not entitled to the common rights of mankind—but we must tamely submit to every outrage, insult and slander that may be heaped upon us, and if we dare to reply or defend ourselves, men affect to be astonished at our "audacity" and "unblushing effrontery."

How did it sit upon the stomachs of our "Mormon-eating" cotempo-raaries [*sic*], when, upon the appearance and testimony of such men as Mulligan and Duane, during the recent Vigilance excitement, the sympathies of the New Yorkers and others were enlisted in their favor, and the San Franciscans were denounced as a horde of mobocrats and ruffians, and enemies to their country and government? Yet there was far more foundation for such charges against the citizens of San Francisco then, than there is for the reports concerning the insubordination and disloyalty said to exist in Utah now. We think any suggestions to put down rebellion in Utah, even supposing it to exist, comes with a very bad grace from those who so recently violated every principle of law, held the authorities of the State at defiance, and even went so far as to prepare to resist the forces of the General Government had they been called into requisition.[60] When thousands of the citizens of Utah are seen in hostile array against each other, and seizing the arms and stores of the Federal Government to use against its authority, and to prevent its officers discharging their duties—then it will be time enough to cry out about the disloyalty of the Mormons, and even then, unless devoid of shame, San Franciscans might well blush to say anything about it.

We do not expect, however, always to have undisturbed peace at Salt Lake. The wicked and the righteous cannot dwell harmoniously together; but though we should have as much trouble in our midst as the Israelites had on their journey from Egypt to Palestine, it would prove nothing against the principles we teach.

But these stories carry their own refutation with them. *Six thousand* men are anxious to leave Salt Lake, but dare not for "fear of the "destroying angels'," while *two* make their escape to California and three hundred to the east—how consistent! *Hundreds* of Apostles leaving, when there are but *twelve*! The Mormons have broken up in a grand row; and yet, hundreds of them are showing their confidence in the principles and the authorities, by starting on missions to the States and elsewhere, dragging handcarts after them.

But you did the best you could, gentlemen, under the circumstances. It's a hard matter to make a lie look like the truth."

Mr. Haws Has Managed to Secure the Confidence of the Indians

Before Cannon had fired his first broadside to refute charges of Mormon-Indian collusion or Jules Remy had traveled up the Humboldt River, Apostle Orson Hyde wrote to Albert Carrington, editor of the *Deseret News*, from Peter Haws' ranch. Hyde, who had served on the original Council of Fifty with Haws, was on his way to take command of the Mormon settlements at Carson Valley. The apostle provided a detailed description of the California Trail and then gave Peter Haws' perspective on the "unjust and cruel" charges that he preyed on overland emigrants.

[60] Cannon referred to the Second Vigilante Committee's defiance of federal authority in 1856.

"LETTER FROM ELDER O. HYDE; HAWS RANCH, MAY 31, 1855," *DESERET NEWS*, 27 JUNE 1855, 128.

. . . Mrs. Haws prepared us an excellent supper of the best of potatoes and beets of their own raising, some fresh antelope meat nicely broiled and served up according to "gunter." If the traveler want a good meal, let him call at Mr. Haws', and he will get it. Not only tea or coffee "but cream into it too."

Mr. Haws has managed to secure the confidence of the Indians to a great degree. He appears to apprehend no danger from them. His stock roams unherded and unguarded without molestation, unless by some strange and transient Indians. He keeps no locks upon his doors; but the strings hang out day and night. He has succeeded in restraining them to a good degree from committing depredations upon the whites as they pass, but he says they are getting "tobuck" angry, because Major [Jacob] Holeman, a former agent, promised them pay for horses stolen from them by the emigrants, and a reward for six Indians, whom the whites killed without provocation. With these promises the Indians were induced to give up 700 sheep and some cattle, which they had taken as an indemnity. Major Holeman soon left, and Major Bedell succeeded him in office; but his health being poor, he was not able to visit them, and soon died. The words and promises of Major Holeman have not been fulfilled.[61]

Mr. Haws is very anxious that the agent come out here with his own interpreter, and stay during the season of emigration, and make himself acquainted with things as they are, as some have felt to censure him with being colleagued with the Indians in robbing emigrants.

This, so far as I can discover, is unjust and cruel. At any rate, if the agent will come out with his interpreter (Shoshonee), and inquire into the full state of affairs, he will be quite satisfied. He feeds many Indians, and has induced them to labor. They want plows, and seed grain, and the usual implements of husbandry: and as game is nearly all killed and frightened away by the emigrants, they must raise from the soil what they will require, or steal and rob in order to live.

I think that a small appropriation by government to open some farms under the management of judicious men, furnish them seed grain and farm-

[61] One of two sub-agents appointed in February 1851 to assist Superintendent of Indian Affairs Brigham Young, Kentuckian Jacob H. Holeman arrived in Utah on 9 August. Holeman felt "that no Mormon should, officially, have anything to do with the Indians." See Holeman to Lea, 28 November 1851, in U.S. Senate, "Massacre at Mountain Meadows," Sen. Exec. Doc. 42 (36–1), 1860, Serial 1033, 129. He claimed the Mormons were trying "to form an alliance with the Indians, to resist the Government, should it be determined to force authority on the territory." See Holeman to Lea, 29 March 1852, in Morgan, "Washakie and the Shoshoni," *Annals of Wyoming* (July 1953), 184. His successor, Edward A. Bedell, died in office.

> ing utensils, would be a step, not only satisfactory to the Indian, but highly advantageous to them.
>
> The Indians up and down this river feel that they are neglected, and they have become angry, turbulent, and very annoying to travelers. I hope the agent will visit this section, and look into things, and the condition of the Indians. Something must be done for them, or no man can travel with safety up or down this river. . . .

Desperate Men, Often Fugitives from Justice

As Cannon pointed out repeatedly, it was impossible for his opposing editors to prove "the wretched yarns about the supposed Danites," and it is equally difficult for historians to connect white Indian incidents with Brigham Young in particular and Mormon leaders in general. Nonetheless, it also proved impossible for Cannon to stop the flood of ink California newspapers devoted to tales of Mormon-Indian depredations.

Amid the confusion, however, reasonable voices occasionally emerge from Western records. The government dispatched engineer Frederick West Lander in 1857 to assist in opening an overland wagon road that avoided Utah. His reports contain some of the best informed and most balanced views on Mormon-Indian relations. Lander blamed the many trail depredations on whites "who purchase the stolen property, and sometimes join the Indians in making their attacks on trains." There were plenty of "desperate men, often fugitives from justice," in the Rocky Mountains who were "ready for any enormity." Lander found, "It would be a hard thing to say that these are all Mormon outrages, but the property stolen certainly often finds its way into the upper Mormon settlements." Lander, however, thought the Saints were thrifty and industrious, "and, I believe, law-abiding citizens." He concluded that Secretary of War Marcy's claim "that the Mormons are never molested by the Indians" was "grounded on false intelligence." He recommended stationing agents on the road to "prove who the instigators of these murders are, and whether Gentiles or Mormons, they could be brought to justice."[62]

Compared to the puzzles surrounding white Indian incidents, the realities and consequences of Mormon Indian policy pose few myster-

[62] Sen. Exec. Doc. 42 (36–1), 1860, Serial 1033, 130–31.

ies. As historian Howard Christy observed, Brigham Young's "Open Hand and Mailed Fist" presented native peoples with a choice between becoming dependent clients of their white neighbors or death.[63] "As a result," David L. Bigler noted, "Mormon treatment of the natives in Utah vacillated unpredictably between generosity so open-handed it imposed on white settlers a 'most oppressive burden,' according to one early Indian agent, and extermination campaigns that sometimes failed to discriminate between hostile and friendly."[64] Ultimately, the Ute people found their history "had not been so different from the experience of other tribes."[65]

In spite of Young's and Cannon's expressions of empathy and concern for the indigenous tribes, the impact of Mormon Indian policy—the displacement of the region's native peoples and the appropriation of their lands—differed little from the story of self-interested paternalism, cultural destruction, and Indian survival told throughout the American West. Nonetheless, as David J. Whittaker has argued, "it seems reasonable to conclude that the Mormon-Indian frontier had elements of both *conflict* and *cooperation,* and that when interpreting the Mormon-Indian experience, historians would do well to set aside polarities for models of human complexity and diversity. The breadth of data cannot be encompassed otherwise."[66]

---

[63] Christy, "Open Hand and Mailed Fist," 216–35 and "'What Virtue There is in Stone,'" 300–319.
[64] Bigler, *Forgotten Kingdom,* 65.
[65] O'Neil, "A History of the Ute Indians," 188.
[66] Whittaker, "Toward a Reconstruction of Mormon and Indian Relations, 1847–1877," 36.

Chapter 6

"The Grossest Form of Human Depravity" Polygamy and the Relics of Barbarism

Throughout its brief history, the Church of Jesus Christ of Latter-day Saints had been very much aware of its political power. The Saints tended to vote as counseled by their leaders, and where they achieved sufficient numbers to influence local elections, politicians of every persuasion were anxious to court their increasingly critical bloc vote. At times this worked to the church's advantage, but the practice ultimately proved disastrous as disappointed politicians—who felt they had been played for fools—turned against the Mormons.[1] Once the Saints found themselves in the Utah Territory, they lost entirely the power of the bloc vote that had given them substantial political influence in Illinois. Early Utah's popular elections were astonishingly unanimous, but western Mormons were at the mercy of the politicians the President and Congress appointed to govern the territory.

By the time the Saints were well established in what they hoped would become the State of Deseret, the nation was already approaching civil war. President Franklin Pierce threw his support behind the Kansas-Nebraska Act in 1854, which effectively nullified the Missouri Compromise of 1820. With its demise came an end to restrictions on slavery in the territories and the revival of sectional conflict over that peculiar institution. "Border ruffians" from Missouri swarmed into Kansas the next year in a successful attempt to install a fraudulent pro-slavery terri-

[1] Fawn M. Brodie describes several examples of each situation in *No Man Knows My History*. For a self-serving, yet nonetheless revealing, glimpse of how one early political figure interacted with the Mormons, see Ford, *A History of Illinois*, chapters 10, 11 and 13.

torial legislature. Free-state settlers responded with their own antislavery constitution, and bleeding Kansas began to hemorrhage deeply in the summer of 1856.

Peace was briefly restored and the Democrats won a close national election, but a new party, the Republicans, emerged as northern Whigs, Free-Soilers, disaffected "anti-Nebraska" Democrats, and a handful of abolitionists came together in support of a common cause. While the 1856 Democratic platform paid lip service to the concept that the people of the states and the territories should control practices such as slavery through popular sovereignty—the equivalent of today states' rights—the Republicans embraced a free-soil platform that put the Democrats on the defensive.[2] It also moved the issue of Mormon polygamy to the forefront of national politics.

Though considered most binding on those men who could afford more than one wife—particularly those in significant ecclesiastical callings and those who hoped to be worthy of such—Mormons in the 1850s were expected to support the "principle" of plural marriage. Even prior to the blistering rhetoric of the Reformation, Brigham Young made it abundantly clear what would be the fate of those who refused: "Now if any of you will deny the plurality of wives, and continue to do so, I promise that you will be damned."[3] Still, as Kimball Young so eloquently put it, "it should not be forgotten that plurality of wives was a permissive, not a mandatory, feature of their lives. It was an additional aspect of the larger scheme of celestial marriage. True, to practice the Principle gave one added status, here and in the hereafter; but one was not, strictly speaking, compelled to practice polygamy."[4]

To achieve the highest degree of exaltation in the Celestial Kingdom, the Saints were expected to "do the works of Abraham," using polygamy to bring forth numerous offspring, many of whom were presumed to be the "great and mighty ones, reserved until the dispensation of the fulness of times, to come forth upon the face of the earth, through a noble parentage that shall train their young and tender minds in the truths of eter-

---

[2] Stampp, *America in 1857*, 4–7.

[3] Young, "Plurality of Wives.—The Free Agency of Man," 14 July 1855, *Journal of Discourses*, 3:266. For additional statements stressing polygamy as a binding commandment, see Gordon, *The Mormon Question*, 92.

[4] Young, *Isn't One Wife Enough?*, 106.

nity."[5] At least this was the primary rationale offered by Orson Pratt when the church finally announced to the world that they were, indeed, practicing polygamy, all previous protestations to the contrary notwithstanding.

As time passed and George Q. Cannon and other defenders of the faith responded to the pointed criticisms of Victorian America, numerous rationales for the practice of polygamy emerged. These included arguments that polygamy was a more "natural" and more efficient way to "multiply and replenish the earth"; that it discouraged prostitution and other moral vices; that it provided more women with opportunities for an honorable marriage; that it assured waiting spirits of appropriate opportunities on earth; and that it promoted better health, improved genetics, and happier family life. But the primary justification for members of the church continued to be that the doctrine of plural marriage was the result of a revelation from God.[6]

The Approaching Storm & Tempest

The political ramifications of polygamy increased and complicated the importance of the Mormon territory in the Great Basin. Writing from New York, where he was editing *The Mormon*, Cannon's uncle and future LDS church president, John Taylor, informed Brigham Young of a particularly troublesome plank in the new Republican Party's platform:

> Immediately after the departure of the last mail, political affairs took a very sudden change, in relation to us. At that time indications of a favorable reception were prevalent throughout the country. The Democrats, particularly, were in our favor or, if not decidedly for us, they were not, at least, against us. This was only, however, a prelude to a coming act, or lull in the political atmosphere; or calm before the approaching storm & tempest. The

[5] Pratt, "Celestial Marriage," 29 August, 1852, *Journal of Discourses*, 1:60, 62–63. For a discussion of that address, see Whittaker, "The Bone in the Throat: Orson Pratt and the Public Announcement of Plural Marriage." Pratt went on to formulate the most extensive and systematic contemporary defense of polygamy, published in the journal he edited, *The Seer*, from January 1853 to July 1854. See also Orson Pratt's arguments in support of polygamy found in *The Seer* as well as those appearing in other Mormon newspapers of the time including the *Deseret News*, the *St. Louis Luminary*, and *The Mormon*.

[6] For discussions of early rationales for polygamy, see Whittaker, "Early Mormon Polgamy Defenses" and Bitton, *The Ritualization of Mormon History*, 34–53. This latter source also offers some useful parallels between the polygamy issue and that of slavery. For arguments on the other side, see Cannon, "The Awesome Power of Sex." For general bibliographies on polygamy see Bitton, "Mormon Polygamy: A Review Article" and Scott, "Mormon Polygamy: A Bibliography, 1977–92."

> Republicans knowing the position of the Democrats, in relation to us introduced opposition to Polygamy, as well as to Slavery, as one of the planks of their platform denominating,—"Slavery & Polygamy, as *twin* relics of barbarism,"—thus throwing the onus of protecting & sustaining both onto the Democratic party, which although a mean dastardly act, is nevertheless in good keeping with other political moves of the present day; is greedily swallowed by religionists of all parties, & is a good hobby, in the absence of others, for our political roisterers to ride.[7]

Whether or not this provision of the Republican Party was a "mean dastardly act," it was "in good keeping with other political moves of the present day," for it effectively placed the Democrats on the horns of a dilemma. "If Congress did not have the power to curb the marital excesses of the Saints, how were they to be checked?" asks historian Richard D. Poll. "And if Congress did have such power, might it not also be exercised to exclude the 'peculiar institution' of the South from the territories?"[8] Regardless of the Democrats' position on popular sovereignty, it was one thing to support slavery but quite another to support polygamy. Slavery enjoyed widespread support, but there was no love for polygamy except in the politically powerless Mormon country. Both major parties began to compete in denouncing the least popular of the twin relics. Polygamy became everyone's whipping boy.[9]

The other relic of barbarism, slavery, had been a major source of conflict between the Mormons and their neighbors in Missouri. The pro-abolitionist sentiment of its mostly northern members, as Cannon remarked in his pamphlet, *The History of the Mormons,* meant that early Mormons were:

> recognized as "Yankees," were accused of secreting and "stealing" negroes, and were hated as abolitionists with all the bitterness that the men who lived on the border of the slave states at that time felt for adherents of that doctrine. This was held up as a most grievous offense, and they were driven out at the point of the bayonet. No charges of immorality then! No talk of *imperium in imperio!* No holy abhorrence of polygamy . . . Because they did not have slaves and did not want them, they were abolitionists.[10]

---

[7] Taylor to Young, 12 July 1856, LDS Archives.

[8] Poll, "The Mormon Question Enters National Politics, 1850–1856," 117.

[9] For a discussion of the linkage between polygamy and slavery, see Gordon, *The Mormon Question,* 47–58.

[10] Cannon, *The History of the Mormons,* 3.

In 1836 citizens in Clay County, Missouri, drafted a report listing their concerns about the Mormon immigrants. "They are *non*-slave-holders, and opposed to slavery, which in this peculiar period, when abolitionism has reared its deformed and haggard visage in our land, is well calculated to excite deep and abiding prejudices in any community where slavery is tolerated and protected."[11]

The gathering to Zion brought members from the South as well as the North to Utah. Given the enormous political pressures encroaching upon the territory as it applied for statehood, some church leaders became much more sympathetic to Southern viewpoints, denouncing the abolitionists and defending slavery as a "divine institution." Moreover, with only one or two early exceptions under the presidency of Joseph Smith, Blacks were prohibited from holding the priesthood (a policy not changed until 1978) and Brigham Young and others brought African-American "servants" with them to Utah, which became the only slave territory in the West.[12] Nonetheless, following advice from their political mentor, Thomas L. Kane, the Mormons avoided taking a clear position that would place them on one side or the other of the sectional controversy. Writing to Kane in 1849, Willard Richards, a counselor to Young, assured him that "Of slavery, anti-slavery, Wilmot provisos, etc., we, in our organization, have remained silent."[13]

There were any number of issues George Q. Cannon would have preferred to write about, but time and again he was forced to defend the principle of polygamy. Although he was at the time a newlywed monogamist, his religion had openly admitted its return to Old Testament polygamy in 1852. It now fell to the Defender of the Faith to convince his fellow Westerners that Mormon polygamy should be assiduously protected as a tenet of religion by the constitution of the United States. Not surprisingly, Cannon's opening salvos in the first issue of the *Western Standard* were directed against an early attempt to outlaw plural marriage in California.

---

[11] Smith, *History of the Church,* 1:450.

[12] Bush, "Mormonism's Negro Doctrine." Dr. Lester E. Bush, Jr., now a physician with the Central Intelligence Agency, examined the historical roots of the priesthood ban in 1973. See also his "Writing 'Mormonism's Negro Doctrine: An Historical Overview' (1973): Context and Reflections, 1998"; and Taggart, *Mormonism's Negro Policy*. For revealing insight into Young's views on slavery, see his speech to the Joint Session of the Legislature, 5 February 1852, in "Brigham Young Addresses."

[13] Richards to Kane, 25 July 1849, Journal History, quoted in Walker, "Thomas L. Kane," 113.

"AN UNCONSTITUTIONAL BILL," *WESTERN STANDARD*, 23 FEBRUARY 1856.

The following is a copy of a Bill lately introduced by Mr. Norman, of Calaveras, into the [California] Senate. We were considerably surprised in perusing it, and could scarcely credit our senses, or believe that any man in this country would be so intolerant as to propose such a measure. After rubbing our eyes once or twice, however, we finally were convinced that it was no delusion, and that a Bill had in reality been introduced, proscribing men who believe in certain doctrines, believed in and practiced by the patriarchs, and by other good and holy men, whose acts have been recorded in the Scriptures . . .

When a man, elevated by the suffrages of the people to fill a dignified and highly honorable office, so far forgets his constitutional obligations and the position which he occupies, as to engage in a crusade against a body of people whose only crime is a firm belief in the words of divine revelation, we think such an attempt is in the highest degree reprehensible, and ought to be frowned upon by all honest and independent men. It is, indeed, an unjust, tyrannical and unconstitutional abuse of power.

If the "Mormon" elders in this country had been guilty of marrying men or women already married, to others, and such things were notorious, there might then be a slight pretext for a measure like the above. But it is a well known fact, that however much we may believe in polygamy and theorize upon it, yet, an elder of our Church who would presume to marry such individuals, or a member who, with a wife living, should marry or take another female to wife, in this country, would, upon the fact being known, be immediately severed from the Church. The rules of the Church are strict upon this subject, and order has to be observed by elders and members, or they forfeit their standing.

What is the difficulty with the "Mormons"? Are their political sins of such a nature that they, out of all the people of the State, should be singled out and disfranchised and their religious belief used as a pretext to accomplish it? The "Mormons" believe that the course taken by Abraham, Isaac and Jacob, with other Bible worthies, in regard to polygamy was not in violation of any law of God; but, that there is every evidence to believe, it was practiced by them under His immediate sanction. They also believe that God has the undoubted and indisputable right to reinstate this order of things, whenever He thinks proper. These principles are identified as a portion of their religious belief, and they are compelled, so long as they believe in the authenticity of the Scriptures, to believe as they do. Can they be blamed for this?

If such an Act can be passed and enforced—an event that we have too much confidence in the patriotism and justice of the Legislature to think ever will be the case—it would deprive a large portion of the citizens of California of the right of representation. The people of San Bernardino, in the county of San Bernardino, one of the most thriving places in the southern portion of the State, and which has the reputation of being as moral, orderly and well behaved a city as there is in this country, would be excluded from the polls. There are numbers also of "Mormons" scattered throughout the State, located at various places, farming, mining, dealing in merchandize, etc., living as other citizens, and quietly pursuing their business without interfering with their neighbors,—these, of course, if they do not deny their faith, would also be denied the right of suffrage, and be included in the proscription.

Is it expected that they will tamely submit to this unjust and unheard of deprivation of their dearest rights as freemen, rights purchased by the blood of their fathers, and rights, too, which in the words of the Declaration of Independence, are inestimable to them and formidable to tyrants only? Would this be liberty—the blessing for which the heroes of the revolution spilled their blood? Let this state of things be brought to pass, and liberty will exist only in name. What, disfranchise men for believing the Bible! Tell it not in Sacramento, publish it not in San Francisco, let not the sound reach Europe, that, in the nineteenth century, a Senator in the free and enlightened State of California, introduced a Bill, into the body of which he was member, proposing to withhold the right of suffrage from men whose only crime was belief in the Holy Scriptures.

And who are these men who must suffer this deprivation and proscription; are they aliens or foreigners, traitors or disloyal? The honorable Senator has no doubt forgotten that to this very people, whom he would proscribe, considerable credit is due for many of the blessings which he, in common with the rest of us, enjoys; that they have been, in fact, instrumental, to a very great extent, in establishing the freedom and independence of this State. Many of the men who, by the passage of this Bill, would be deprived the right of suffrage, have crossed the burning deserts and scaled the lofty mountains, with their muskets on their shoulders, in the service of their country, enduring privation, fatigue and suffering in almost every imaginable form, to rescue this land from the grasp of the enemy; while others, an adventurous band, have doubled the stormy Cape, and contributed by their thrift, industry and energy to develop the abundant resources of this highly favored land. They have occupied a prominent and honorable position in bringing to light the auriferous and agricultural wealth of the country.[14]

If the "Mormons" are in error, and have arrived at incorrect conclusions in regard to the Scriptures, would it not be wiser, more Godlike, Christian-like and worthy of a great and enlightened people, to send men well posted up in these matters—close reasoners and profound logicians—to inform them of their errors, and to bring them back to the path the world has trod-

[14] Cannon referred to church members who had come to California with the Mormon Battalion and ship *Brooklyn*.

den so long? We unhesitatingly assert, that if such a course were pursued, it would be attended with far more beneficial results than the course proposed by the honorable Senator. When, in the history of mankind, have persecution and proscription been successful in curing men of their errors; or when, on the contrary, has a merciful, charitable and loving spirit failed to accomplish the desired end?

The "Mormons" are a living example of the futility of persecution—of its inefficiency to convert men to the views of the persecutors. Who can say that "Mormonism" does not owe its present position and influence to the persecution so perseveringly and unsparingly dealt out by those who thought to crush it? The martyrdom of the Prophet, an event which its enemies fondly hoped would accomplish the entire overthrow of the system, only tended to establish it more firmly; and since his death the Work has spread with a rapidity unprecedented in the previous history of the people.

The past teaches an important lesson. Be warned by it; and if the "Mormons" are fools and fanatics, their folly and fanaticism will soon be apparent in the eyes of the world. Such folly and fanaticism, as they are sometimes represented to possess, can not long exist in the midst of an enlightened Republic like ours. They are the minority; and if, we say again, they are deluding and being deluded—are the perpetrators and victims of as gross an imposture as "Mormonism" certainly is, if not a true system, then there need be no apprehensions entertained as to the result; it can not hold together, but must certainly crumble to pieces, and be overpowered by the light of truth and the overwhelming influence of the majority.

But, we would ask, why this sensitiveness in regard to the "Mormons"? Are they the only persons who practice "incorrect principles" or are they to be made the scapegoat to bear off the sins of others more criminal, that they may obtain a reputation for purity and sanctity which they are far from possessing? If the suppression of immorality is to be the object attained, and that is the motive which caused the honorable gentleman to introduce the Bill, then, we think, a few other clauses might with great propriety be introduced. Suppose, for instance, an additional test of eligibility to vote and hold office be inserted, not confining it to the mere belief in polygamy alone, but including the *practice of fornication and adultery,* crimes that, when compared with the belief and practice of polygamy as taught by the "Mormons," make the latter practice (even if incorrect, which we do not admit) appear honorable.[15]

We have an alternative left to preserve one of the rights of freemen, that is, to deny our faith, and avow with our lips what our reason and convictions can not assent to. And if we could so far forget our lineage, and be so despi-

---

[15] The Mormons took sexual impropriety seriously. One of the first five ordinances created by the Saints en route to the Great Salt Lake basin was one for "adultery or fornication. Such culprits were to be given up to 39 lashes on the bare back and fined not to exceed $1,000." See Anderson, *Desert Saints,* 85.

cable and entirely lost to the sense of all that is manly, as to barter away our freedom of conscience for the right which we already possess by inheritance, dearly bought by the blood of our fathers, what assurance have we then, that this once obtained, another encroachment will not be made, and another concession demanded, until, deprived of all that makes existence tolerable, we sink into abject serfdom.

We have no disposition to find fault with constitutional enactments; and if there were the least shadow of justice or reason in such a measure as has been proposed, we would be the last to complain; but this is not the case; it is an abridgment of the rights of the subject, in direct contravention of the Constitution, is obnoxious to the spirit of our institutions, and, therefore, we raise our voice against it.

Let a precedent of this kind be established, and men of every creed and belief will have cause to tremble for the safety of their liberties. A religious test would thus be instituted; and we hazard an assertion, that if such a measure is ever carried out, it will not long be confined to the "Mormons," but will continue to spread until anarchy will cover the land.

How antagonistic the spirit of this Bill to the spirit which pervades the following letter, written by the immortal Washington soon after the formation of the Constitution, and addressed to the "Central Committee of the United Baptist Churches in Virginia."

> GENTLEMEN:—If I could have entertained the slightest apprehension that the Constitution framed by the convention where I had the honor to preside, might possibly endanger the *religious rights* of ANY ecclesiastical society, certainly I would have never placed my signature to it; and if I could conceive that the General Government might ever be so administered as to render the liberty of conscience insecure, I beg you will be persuaded, that no one would be more zealous than myself to establish effectual barriers against the horrors of spiritual tyranny and every species of religious persecution. For you doubtless remember I have often expressed my sentiments, that any man conducting himself as a good citizen, and being accountable to God alone for religious opinions, ought to be protected in worshiping the Deity according to the dictation of his own conscience.

Mormon Elders with Their Wives and Concubines

Cannon's first fusillade made clear that the young journalist had listened carefully to the blessing he had received from Brigham Young while on his way to California. He was unafraid to open his mouth and roar. He was, however, less than accurate on several points.

In arguing that Mormons had not "been guilty of marrying men or women already married," he either did not know of or chose to overlook the highly unusual polyandrous marriages of Joseph Smith and the technically bigamous marriage of Parley P. Pratt that would eventually get him killed.[16] His generally accurate claim that the Mormons were not "aliens or foreigners" overlooked his own status as an immigrant from England, perhaps because he already considered himself a naturalized citizen.[17] Ironically, the charge that many of the emigrating Mormons—Cannon among them—were aliens soon become a major political issue. One manifestation of anti-Mormon xenophobia can be seen in a humorous piece by the acidic Wyoming journalist, Bill Nye:

> Yesterday's train No. 7 was loaded with some more Mormons, who had been proselyted by the bunko steerers of the church of Jesus Christ of Latterday Saints from the various poorhouses and lunatic asylums of creation.
>
> Most every one who don't know much about Mormonism thinks that the church is simply ignorant, with a morbid desire among its communicants to get married.
>
> The plain, stub-toed truth, however, is that the average Mormon not only wants to get married at every available opportunity, but he is a man who glories in the clothes he wore ten years ago, and who brings with him the dust and dirt of foreign climes.
>
> He comes among us from every benighted land under the sun, bringing with him the flavor of his native hog pen, and the choice fragrance of the steerage passenger. He lands upon our shores unable to speak our language or to adopt our style of soap. The first words he learns are those necessary to ask some cross-eyed old hag with a wen on her nose to marry him, and he goes on inducing the old condemned hens of Zion to be sealed to him till a merciful providence cuts him down and he leaves a herd of snorting widows with feet like a sack of flour and complexions like an old hair trunk . . .
>
> If Mormonism, and a wild and frenzied longing to marry every wappy-jawed woman in Christendom, be a stench in the nostrils of the president, what must it be here within a hundred miles of polygamy, bigamy, trigamy and pigamy.[18]

---

[16] See Compton, *In Sacred Loneliness: The Plural Wives of Joseph Smith*. For details on Pratt's marriage to Eleanor McComb McLean, see Chapter 10. In a technical, doctrinal sense, Mormons could—and occasionally did—argue that if non-Mormon baptisms were invalid, then the validity of non-Mormon marriages, performed by those without proper priesthood authority, was also in doubt. However, while such an argument might have been used to justify Pratt's marriage to Mrs. McLean, it does not explain Smith's marriages to women already wedded to other faithful Mormons.

[17] Cannon's status as a "foreign immigrant" continued to haunt him as he later attempted to claim his seat in Washington.

By emphasizing the patriotism and suffering of the members of the Mormon Battalion and Sam Brannan's shipmates on the *Brooklyn,* Cannon failed to point out that not all their motives were completely altruistic. Both groups demonstrated great courage and sacrifice in coming to California, but self-interest and not patriotism inspired them to move west. Brannan was looking for a way for the Mormons to leave persecution by leaving U.S. jurisdiction and had even brought a new flag, featuring the Virgin and twelve stars, presumably to raise over an independent Mormon nation. When he saw Old Glory flying proudly over the newly conquered San Francisco Bay, Brannan was reportedly less than thrilled.[19]

The Mormon Battalion came about as a result of church initiative—not simply as a patriotic response to a government request or as a countermeasure to foil a plot to exterminate the Saints, theories later passionately advanced by Brigham Young. The struggling church was in desperate need of cash if it hoped to transport its thousands of faithful to the Rocky Mountains, so Young's agents initially proposed that the U.S. government hire the Mormons to build posts along the Oregon Trail. After the outbreak of war with Mexico, Jesse Little sent President James K. Polk a thinly veiled threat that if their own government failed them, the Mormons might find it necessary "to receive assistance from a foreign power."[20]

The threat worked. "The main object of taking them into service would be to conciliate them," Polk wrote, "and prevent them from assuming a hostile attitude towards the U.S. after their arrival in California." The president offered to enlist "a few hundred" Mormons as volunteer soldiers, though his original plan was to have them join the army after arriving in California.[21]

Ann Eliza Young, the most prominent defector from a Mormon "harem," and a woman with an obvious ax to grind, complained that "this war put twenty thousand dollars in Brigham Young's pocket; and yet he is very fond of talking about the cruelty and tyranny of the United States government in *forcing* five hundred of the ablest Mormon men into its service at a time when they were the most needed, and leaving the weak and

---

[18] Nye, *Forty Liars, and Other Lies,* 148–50.

[19] [Kemble], "Flag of the Twelve Stars," *Sacramento Daily Union,* 22 May 1858; Stellman, *Sam Brannan,* 55. For an intriguing discussion of other possible designs for and uses of a special Mormon flag, see Quinn, "The Flag of the Kingdom of God."

[20] Little to Young, in Bigler and Bagley, eds., *Army of Israel,* 34.

[21] Quaife, *The Diary of James K. Polk,* quoted in Ibid, 36..

helpless to cross the plains without sufficient protection."[22] Families left without their men suffered great privations, but it was hardly the case that the Mormons were drafted against the will of their leaders. Nonetheless, the Mormon "priestess" and poet Eliza R. Snow contributed to that historical position: "one of the most remarkably unreasonable requisitions came officially to President Young, from the United States government, demanding five hundred efficient men to be drawn from our traveling camps . . . it was a heavy tax—a cruel draft—one which imposed accumulated burdens on those who remained, especially our women."[23]

Cannon found himself constantly responding to a host of complaints in the California press related to Mormon polygamy. Although many editors pretended to be more shocked by this "licentious" practice than they actually were, bashing polygamy played well to their readers and helped sell newspapers. Nineteenth-century America was both fascinated and repulsed by the idea of a man having more than one wife, and it became Cannon's job to defend what for most was simply indefensible. His exchanges with the editors of the *Golden Era* show that he did so with sarcasm, humor, and almost always with an air of righteous indignation.

"MORMONISM AND ITS PROFESSORS," *GOLDEN ERA*, 20 MARCH 1856.

> . . . Snugly nestled among the mountains of Utah, the Latter Day Saints are now a little world of themselves, living up to their armpits in the greatest immoralities that unrestrained licentiousness and a disregard for every social decency can desire. With missionaries in every quarter of the globe, preaching to the needy millions "corn and wine," not Mormonism, they are pouring into Deseret a constant tide of immigration; and with a consciousness of increasing strength, hurling treason into the face of the General Government, and forcing their doctrines into every community. To attempt to establish in the broad day-light of the nineteenth century the divine origin of the book of Mormon, is almost too great a scandal upon the intelligence of the age to be tolerated, but when we find that same book being quoted as authority for the commission of crime and outrage, it is time to

[22] Young, *Wife No. 19*, 165.

[23] Quoted in Tullidge, *The Women of Mormondom*, 315. See also Bigler, ed., *A Winter with the Mormons*, 153, 165–66. For an analysis of how money from battalion recruits helped the Mormon exodus, see Arrington, *Great Basin Kingdom*, 21–22. Numerous books have been written on the Mormon Battalion. Five of particular interest are Tyler, *A Concise History of the Mormon Battalion in the Mexican War, 1846–1847*; Roberts, *The Mormon Battalion: Its History and Achievements*; Golder, Bailey, and Smith, eds., *The March of the Mormon Battalion from Council Bluffs to California, Taken from the Journal of Henry Standage*; Ricketts, *The Mormon Battalion: U.S. Army of the West, 1846–1848*; and Bigler and Bagley, eds., *Army of Israel: Mormon Battalion Narratives.*

come to some understanding as to how far the National Constitution will permit a foul-mouthed and insulting religious faith to override every sense of decency and justice. The Mormon Elders with their wives and concubines, point to an article of the amended Constitution, and smile at the threatened interference of law. We admit that the Constitution guarantees to all the full exercise of their religious belief; but when Washington, Franklin, Hamilton, Gerry and Madison put their names to that document, they had too good an opinion of their fellowmen to provide for a contingency as unlooked for as that now presented in Mormonism; they did not think it possible that a religion could exist and flourish with the tenets of amoral hue so dark and damning as to be found in conflict with the wisest of legislative enactments, with the holiest of social laws. There are crimes which human depravity sometimes perpetrates, of so heinous a nature that they are not only without a name but without a penalty, and there are outrages committed with impunity under the protection of the perverted sense of an enactment, or a constitutional right, which, held out in the fair sunlight of justice, would take a name as foul as guilt expresses.

This is the shape in which we are fed Mormonism. Sanctioning the commission of crime under the cloak of a protected religious faith, protected by the Constitution, it presents a nice point for adjudication. It is the first instance since the organization of the Government, in which law and religion have been brought to conflict, and the decision [illegible] importance from the precedent it will establish, which will be received as authority for the future. If the Mormons have the right to outrage law because their religion teaches it, then have thieves and murderers an equal right to practice their callings unmolested, by announcing themselves the chosen of heaven and the executors of its decrees. There must be a dividing line somewhere between the religion to which the Constitution guarantees protection, and the rank imposture that may shield itself under its provisions. Viewed in this light, Mormonism is not a religion, nor is it entitled to the consideration of a recognized religious belief. It is an imposture, whose origins can be traced, and whose career is written in lines of unblushing rascality and outrage against law and decency. Let the Mormons renounce polygamy and turn honest men, for the time will come, and shortly, too, when their flimsy religious pretexts will not protect them from an insulted sense of right or the strong arm of law.

"Mormonism and Its Professors," *Western Standard*, 5 April 1856.[24]

In a leader under the above title the editors of the *Golden Era* most unmercifully pitch into the Latter-day Saints, and give them, as the writer no doubt supposes, a severe flagellation for their misdemeanors. If we had

[24] Reprinted in Cannon, *Writings from the "Western Standard,"* 59–64.

not heard such thunder before, and to such an extent as to have become accustomed to it, we might possibly have paid more attention to the exhortation and prediction which the article contains, and "have renounced polygamy and turned honest man" to avoid "the insulted sense of right and the strong arm of law" which the editors predict will be visited upon us. Not having the fear of the wrath of the *Golden Era* before our eyes, however, nor confidence in the prediction which the editors have uttered, we are still so "recklessly depraved" as to be guilty of "bidding defiance to our enemies and comfort to our people," aye, and even still attempting to sustain, in the broad day-light of the nineteenth century, ("scandal though it be on the intelligence of the age,") the divine origin of the Book of Mormon with the doctrines which it contains. Were we to condescend to the language and *arguments* used by the editors of the *Era* in this article, we would think our writings extremely profitless and unworthy of notice. Thousands of men as honest, intelligent and discriminating, no doubt, as the editors of the *Era* are, have united themselves with the system called "Mormonism;" thousands of others to whom "the missionaries in every quarter of the globe are preaching 'corn and wine'," are likely yet to ally their fate with it; and to stop the progress of this system and break it up, will require stronger arguments than mere assertion—the only arguments the *Golden Era* has produced; more particularly is this the case when the old and oft-refuted stories of horse and cattle thieving are resorted to.[25]

This article states that we are guilty of quoting the Book of Mormon as authority for the commission of crime and outrage. . . . We do no such thing. Neither are we guilty of abetting and justifying men in committing crime. We suppose, from the tenor of the article, although it is not stated, that the writer alludes to the doctrine of polygamy when he accuses us of authorizing the commission of crime. If this is the principle he thinks criminal, he ought to know that we do not substantiate it from the Book of Mormon, but from the Bible, and King James' translation, too. There is no necessity for us to refer to anything else for proof; it contains all that we need. If, because the "Mormon" elders attempt to support this doctrine as not being opposed to the laws of God, their tenets are to be considered "dark and damning," with how much more consistency and propriety can we retort that we consider the tenets and ideas he would advance, while condemning polygamy, as "dark and damning," and utterly opposed to Scripture and reason. Witness

[25] Accusations of Mormon horse stealing were often clear fabrications, as evidenced in the journal of Nathan Tanner Porter (53–4). Nonetheless, Bill Hickman was a notorious horse thief who, according to John Bennion, was protected by one Mormon authority on at least one occasion: "Br. [Orson] Hyde said, speaking of the [horse] stealing, that a man may steal and be influenced by the spirit of the Lord to do it—that Hickman had done it years past—Said that he never would institute a trial against a brother for stealing from the Gentiles, but stealing from his brethren, he was down on it." Quoted in Cleland and Brooks, eds., *A Mormon Chronicle*, 328n67. See also Hickman, *Brigham's Destroying Angel*, 141–47.

the results of the two systems,—polygamy, and the one which he no doubt would have us embrace when we "renounce polygamy"—and without searching for any further evidence, we think that every unprejudiced man will admit that polygamy, as believed and practiced by the Latter-day Saints, when contrasted with the popular system of Christendom and its concomitants, is in every way superior, and that if either merits the title of "dark and damning" it must be the latter. Shall we, then, be governed by the tenets of the *Golden Era,* or the tenets of the Bible?—the popular ideas of *pseudo*-Christianity of the nineteenth century, or the plainly written and well sustained ideas of the people of God and of the Savior, himself, contained in the Scriptures? It will require but little time to make the choice. . . .

The reason that thieves and murderers have not an equal right with the "Mormons" to practice their callings is, simply, that such practices are wrong, and in direct contravention of every law, human and divine; while "Mormonism" is not, but is in strict accordance with all the practices of holy and just men, whom we recognize in these days as men of God and patterns of piety. This is the reason, and an all-sufficient reason also, we think, why such characters should not have an equal right with the Latter-day Saints to practice their views. As to the dividing line "between the religion to which the Constitution guarantees protection, and the rank imposture that may shield itself under its provisions," that is very easily defined so long as we acknowledge the Scriptures to be the text book of a pure and holy system of ethics, and the basis upon which the Constitution was framed. So long as this is acknowledged—and who can deny it?—instead of polygamy being a crime—an outrage against the laws, and its professors and believers condemned, the religion which possesses and practices it as a pure and holy doctrine ought to be the religion to which the Constitution will guarantee full and complete protection; while those systems in which it is not incorporated, and whose propagators affirm that it is an incorrect doctrine, ought to be reckoned as rank impostures, calculated in their tendencies to abrogate the system of pure and holy morality, set forth by the book on which the Constitution is based. That the "origin of Mormonism can be traced," we are well aware—and, in our opinion, it is its chief recommendation; but we boldly deny that it can be traced as an imposture, or that "its career is written in lines of unblushing rascality and outrage against law and decency." What law, in the name of common sense, do the "Mormons" outrage by the teachings of their religion? Does "Mormonism" justify men in the practice of any impure or unholy principle? The question is already answered by our writings, scattered broadcast through the length and breadth of the land.

A few years ago the absurd story of the "Mormons" "turning horse and cattle thieves in the name of the Lord" might pass, and some people might believe it; and if they were told "that the only thing that kept them together while in Illinois and Missouri was plunder, and that the majority of their converts were refugees from justice, and cut-throats" they might have believed that statement also; but in these days, the conduct of the Latter-day Saints in Utah, their good order, morality and indefatigable perseverance and industry, in a country where they had no one to steal from, except, indeed, the poor Indians, is so world-renowned, and has been so often borne testimony to by hundreds of disinterested men, that we wonder at the editors of the *Golden Era* imposing so gross and palpable a falsehood upon their readers as a truth. If they had given the subject the attention needed and proper before writing such an article, we feel confident that they must have been aware that this statement was utterly false and without foundation, as it has been so often refuted, not only by ourselves, but by hundreds of others who do not believe in "Mormonism," that our opponents have long since ceased to assert it in relation to us. The article betrays unpardonable ignorance on the part of the writer in relation to our history; he makes the "saintly Joseph" flee from New York and settle in Nauvoo! and also places the exodus across the plains as following immediately after the expulsion from Missouri! The mobbing and disgraceful proceedings of Missouri are ascribed to the rascalities of the "Mormons," "which had become so intolerable that the people of Missouri were obliged to rise in arms and expel them from the State." Volumes of testimony have been accumulated by the Latter-day Saints, proving beyond successful contradiction that we were unrighteously, illegally and inhumanly expelled from our houses and lands in Missouri, and robbed of the hard earnings of years without the least shadow of justice. We chose to serve God in accordance with the dictates of our own consciences, and this could not, of course, be permitted. We were a feeble and comparatively insignificant people, and we had to submit because "might made right." Since that time another people have come in contact with the same state of Missouri. Unlike us, their views were the views of a large portion of the Union; but, powerful as they were, the bordermen of Missouri have not hesitated to attempt to use the same weapons and resort to the same method, so successfully carried out in the case of the "Mormons," to expel them also. We would ask, Messrs. Editors of the *Golden Era,* if the rascalities of the Free Soil men have become so intolerable to these *immaculate* individuals that they can no longer restrain their virtuous indignation, but must also expel or exterminate them, as they did the Latter-day Saints?[26]

Our sufferings, expatriation and present situation, "snugly nestled among the mountains of Utah," can, to a very great extent, be attributed to such men as the writer of this article, who, hearing stories to the prejudice of the "Mormons," without stopping to investigate the truth or falsity of

[26] In the conflict over slavery, the abolitionist Free Soil Party was formed in 1848 and was absorbed into the Republican Party in 1856. The "bordermen of Missouri," also known as the "border ruffians," were Missourians who crossed over into Kansas in 1854, using para-military force against the free-soil set

the charges, are ready to catch up the cry, and re-echo vociferously every thing evil that they may hear about the people. All their instincts seem to be corrupt; and if there should be an extenuating circumstance that might be advanced in palliation of the "Mormons'" supposed guilt, it is very carefully suppressed. We are willing that our belief, doctrine and practices should be investigated, and, if evil, condemned. It is no light thing, however, to class a body of people, comprising the whole of the inhabitants of a territory (a thing that the *Golden Era* has not hesitated to do,) as *"knaves," "plunderers," "horse and cattle thieves," "refugees from justice, and cut-throats"* and wish these things to be believed because they assert them. We have not language to express the contempt which we have for the principle that would actuate a man to make such sweeping charges against an innocent and unoffending people. If we are to be condemned, let us be condemned upon evidence, not assertion. . . He has only to prove his assertion—"that it has not a solitary proof of anything like divinity"—and there will be no further need to exhort us to "renounce polygamy and turn honest men" to be protected from "an insulted sense of right or the strong arm of law;" for let this be proved and sustained, and "Mormonism" will soon be numbered among the things that have been.

"THE WESTERN STANDARD," *GOLDEN ERA*, 13 APRIL 1856.

THE WESTERN STANDARD, the Mormon organ on the Pacific, dropped down upon us with a two-and-a-half column leader, in its issue of the 4th inst., in reply to an article in a previous date of this paper, entitled "Mormonism and its Professors." The editor disputes many of our assertions, without disproving any; therefore, we have nothing further to add in relation to the disagreeable subject, except that we can substantiate our position throughout, and are prepared, if necessary, to acquaint the world with many facts bitterly unpalatable to Mormonism generally. We did not examine the Mormon doctrine as a religion, for we do not recognize it as such—but as a disgusting canker upon our social system, which it behooves the surgery of law to radicate [*sic*] and cleanse. We do not deal with religions, but with morality when religion comes in contact with it.

"'MORMONISM AND ITS PROFESSORS' AGAIN," *WESTERN STANDARD*, 19 APRIL 1856.[27]

The editors of the *Golden Era*, in their paper of the 13th inst., in an article of about eighteen lines length, disingenuously try to *creep out* of the position which they so fiercely assumed two or three weeks ago in their leader entitled "Mormonism and its Professors," by saying, that they "have noth-

tlers to attempt to influence the political process in favor of slavery. The ruffians burned several buildings, destroyed two anti-slavery newspapers, and killed at least two persons, acts that contributed to John Brown's radical abolitionism.

[27] Reprinted in Cannon, *Writings from the "Western Standard,"* 72–73.

ing further to add in relation to the disagreeable subject;" and then very opportunely append the threat that they *could say something,* "if necessary, that would acquaint the world with many facts bitterly unpalatable to Mormonism generally." Wonderful clemency and forbearance! Messrs. Editors, you are really too magnanimous! A few strokes of the pen are only needed to annihilate a system, nine-tenths of whose numbers are *"knaves," "horse and cattle thieves," "refugees from justice, and cut-throats,"* and yet the editors of the *Golden Era* think that it is not necessary to expose them! What better or more Godlike employment can men be engaged in than in exposing iniquity, and in eradicating and cleansing a "disgusting canker upon our social system?" Come, Messrs. Editors, you will never have so good an opportunity again of immortalizing yourselves. Annihilate "Mormonism" by exposing its errors and corruptions; bring forward your strong reasons why it should not be believed by the good and honest, and, our word for it, you will find that portion, which according to your own admission is, at least, one-tenth, deserting it, and rallying around the standard of truth that you will erect. But be warned by the futile attempts of your predecessors, and do not substitute *assertion* for *proof*; for, be assured, it does not pass current among the "Mormons"...

We have met their assertions with counter-assertions, and we have requested them to furnish evidence, if they have any, of the truth of their statements. This, we imagine, we have the right to demand, but they have, so far, utterly failed to advance a solitary proof to sustain their caluminations; and we are forced to conclude that their last assertion, "that they can tell something bitterly unpalatable to Mormonism generally," is as destitute of substantial foundation as their former ones were.

The Coinage of a Poetical Lunatic

Cannon's battle with the *Golden Era* soon capitalized on the paper's charge that Mormonism was "an imposture, whose origins can be traced, and whose career is written in lines of unblushing rascality and outrage against law and decency." Cannon claimed he had "no disposition to get into a newspaper war," but once in the fight he quickly demolished his opponent's argument that "among the intelligent, Mormonism makes no converts." His challenge "to prove that Mormonism is founded upon imposture" forced the *Era* to concede, "Religion can neither be substantiated nor contradicted."

"MORMONS AND MORMONISM," *GOLDEN ERA*, 27 APRIL 1856.

Our Mormon friend of the *Western Standard* requests us to prove that Mormonism is founded upon imposture, and is unworthy the belief of the honest and intelligent. We have never assumed the province of building up religions, nor shall we devote ourselves to the task of pulling them down. We leave such pastime to the organs of the different religious sects, whose duty it is to proselyte [*sic*] to their respective doctrines by proving themselves right and their neighbors wrong. Religion can neither be substantiated nor contradicted. Enshrouded in mystery at is [*sic*] origin, time but exaggerates its virtues and obliterates the doubtful circumstances of its birth. The Mormon doctrine is of such recent origin, however, that its progress is not as much a matter of history as of remembrance. All the tricks resorted to by Joe Smith in the workings of miracles are still fresh in the minds of many. Still, Mormonism cannot be proven to be false, although much, very much, may be told to favor such a position, for it is useless to attempt to prove a man in the wrong who is determined to believe himself right. Among the intelligent, Mormonism makes no converts, although it finds shrewd adherents. Argument cannot shake the faith of those who believe the writer of the Book of Mormon to have been inspired! Then why should we sum up the evidences against it? Why prepare ourselves to prove that the Book of Mormon was the coinage of a poetical lunatic, and was found, altered, and elaborated by Joe Smith? Why expose the miracles of the great founder, who resurrected the dead by burying live men in coffins, with tubes through the earth for supplying the subject with air, and walked on the water by ingeniously arranging a plank platform two inches below the surface? Why speak of their lawless operations in the Western States, previous to their expulsion, or of the foul-mouthed profanity with which the immortal seventy-wived Brigham interlardes [?] his religious discourses? We attacked Mormonism because it countenances polygamy, which, as one of its tenets, it may practice under the protection of the Constitution. We attempted to show why it should not be recognized as a religion, and, we believe, with complete success.

"'MORMONS' AND 'MORMONISM,' AND THEIR OPPONENTS," *WESTERN STANDARD*, 3 MAY 1856.[28]

In the last issue of the *Golden Era* we notice another article of the series of editorials on "Mormonism and the Mormons."... In their second article on this subject they threateningly said, because we presumed to dispute their assertions made in a previous article, that "they were prepared to acquaint the world with many facts bitterly unpalatable to Mormonism gen-

[28] Ibid. 94–96.

erally." Not wishing, by our silence on the subject, to tacitly admit the existence of such facts, and desirous also of defending ourselves against the wicked and unfounded calumnies to which they gave utterance, we called for these facts so "bitterly unpalatable," if they really were in their possession, and wished them to give these things publicity; but all that they have produced is what has been alluded to. If, by the reiteration of these old, ridiculous and oft-refuted stories, or by their bare statement that the polygamy of the "Mormons" is dark and damning, they imagine that they have shown with complete success why it should not be recognized as a religion, we are compelled to acknowledge that we are fully of the opinion that it must be to their own satisfaction alone, as we think that, so far, their attempt has proved a decided failure. Do they have the idea that by repeating these slanders they prove the assertions contained in their articles to be true? Would they consider the truth of the doctrines of Christ invalidated by the recital of that well-told lie, perpetrated and perpetuated by the pious old Pharisees, that, instead of Jesus having risen from the dead, as his disciples said he had, the latter had come by night, while the guard slept, and stolen the body away? In those days this passed for as complete a trick to humbug the people, as Joseph Smith's walking on the water or raising the dead; but it would be considered absurd at the present time to produce such lies—the stealing of the body of Jesus, etc.—as arguments to disprove Christianity; and yet it is no more absurd than it is to adduce these fabrications about the "tricks of Joseph Smith," which they hint at, as arguments against the system of Jesus—or "Mormonism" as it is frequently called—which he taught. The one story is equally false with the other.

It would seem, from some of the remarks of the writer of the article in the *Era,* that he is an infidel in his views; but we miss the tone of research and reasonable argument evinced by the generality of infidels in their writings upon such subjects. He deals largely in assertion and condemnatory remarks, but avoids proving the wholesale, sweeping charges made in the previous articles, by saying, "It is useless to attempt to prove a man wrong who is determined to think himself right!" But, admitting that the "Mormons" are composed of this class, (which, however, is by no means the case,) are there not others who might be benefited by the production of these evidences? If the grave charges they have made have any foundation in truth, there must be an abundance of evidence to support them. A system that is composed of "knaves, cattle and horse-thieves, and who sanction the commission of crime in their teachings," surely give ample room for criticism in their published works. Evidences must abound in their writings, if all these charges are true, that will be sufficient to condemn them, without having recourse to these trumped-up stories, which have been rebutted and disproved times without number, and the falsity of which has been made apparent to every candid, unprejudiced man, by the whole course of the people from their rise up to the present time. "Mormonism" can not be proven to be false upon the evidence of such inventions; neither can the "Mormons" themselves be persuaded that the system they have embraced is wrong, if the doctrines are not disproved. They did not embrace it on such evidence, neither can it be expected that they will forsake it on such; unless, indeed, through transgression of the laws of the Lord, they lose the Spirit which obedience to His commandments bestows. People who may be inclined to investigate the doctrines of the "Mormons," will not be deterred by his talk about their all being "rascals, thieves, cut-throats," etc.; their intercourse with the people will speedily disabuse their minds in relation to these falsehoods, and they will see that they have been belied and misrepresented; and they will, therefore, look with suspicion and distrust on the remainder of these stories, and not allow them to have any weight in their minds. Men gain nothing, therefore, by such attacks. "Mormonism" is not in the least injured or retarded by it. They may struggle against it, and use every effort to put it down; but it is the truth of heaven, and, therefore, will progress and fulfill its predestined mission. And, as sure as the Lord lives, and reigns in the heavens, every plan that may be laid to thwart or stop its progress, will be the means of accelerating its onward march.

When we answered their articles we had no disposition to get into a newspaper war, although we by no means dreaded it; but to have permitted their assertions to have passed unnoticed and unchallenged would have been, in our opinion, criminal in us. When we called for those facts that were so unpalatable, with which they had threatened us, we were satisfied that they would not be forthcoming; we really expected more, however, than has been advanced. They have made broad and unqualified statements, which cannot be authenticated, because they are utterly false.

The Harems of the Priesthood

It was popular to imagine that since the Mormons had abandoned morality with the introduction of polygamy, it must follow that they were generally immoral. Not surprisingly, one of the concomitant charges against them was of general dishonesty. However, many non-Mormons who visited Great Salt Lake City during the gold rush agreed with Cannon that the Saints were anything but dishonest. "In the whole of our intercourse with them, which lasted rather more than a year, I cannot refer to a single instance of fraud or extortion," Capt. Howard Stansbury wrote after exploring Utah in 1849 and 1850. "I strongly incline to the opinion that the charges that have been preferred against them in this respect, arose either from interested misrepresentation or erroneous information."[29] Later travelers such as William Chandless agreed, acknowledging that he had "met at Salt Lake with two or three proper scoundrels; but, taking the people all round, I consider them as moral, industrious, fair-dealing, and hospitable a set, as one is apt to fall in with.[30] By their own reckoning, European sojourners Remy and Brenchley concluded that at the time of their visit in 1855, there were some twelve thousand Mormons living in the city with fewer than a hundred Gentiles. Yet it was the latter whom they perceived as the greater threat to civility: "During our sojourn at the Salt Lake we were robbed twice, and each time it was found to be by the Gentiles."[31]

Several months after its initial skirmish with Cannon, the *Golden Era* published yet another commentary on the Mormons based on Benjamin G. Ferris's *Utah and the Mormons,* the book Brigham Young counseled Parley P. Pratt, Jr., to "let alone." Ferris served without particular distinction as secretary of Utah Territory for six months in 1852 and 1853. By his own admission, his primary interest in accepting the post was a "curiosity, long cherished, to visit a portion of the world about which many marvelous accounts had been given."[32] Once he and his wife had acquired sufficient material for their respective books, they returned to the East via California.

Ferris' wife, Cornelia, published two books, the second a variant edition of the first: *The Mormons at Home* and *Female Life among the Mormons.*[33] "If I could make myself a Caligula, and hold the sword of the executioner over these detestable villains, having but one neck for the convenience of a single blow," she wrote in an example of the bitter enmity she and her husband felt for the Mormons, "I should be sorely tempted just now to undergo the transformation." She was particularly credulous, believing every outrageous story that came her way that reflected poorly on the Mormons, including one alleging that Parley P. Pratt once

[29] Stansbury, *Exploration and Survey,* 134.

[30] Chandless, *A Visit to Salt Lake,* 196.

[31] Remy and Brenchley, *A Journey to Great-Salt-Lake-City,* 1:199

[32] Ferris, *Utah and the Mormons,* vii.

[33] Cannon reprinted an unfavorable review of *The Mormons at Home* from *Reynold's Miscellany* in *Western Standard,* 8 November 1856.

swapped one of his "over-stocked" wives to the Ute chief Wakara for ten horses.[34]

As scurrilous as the Ferris books were, they provided great copy. *The Golden Era,* which prided itself as being a literary journal, was not above using it to attack polygamy.

"MORMONISM AS IT IS," *GOLDEN ERA,* 23 NOVEMBER 1856.

Joe Smith, the Prophet, in his early visions, condemned polygamy; but in his latter days, after decreeing a special wife to himself, proceeded to lay down the general law, as it is now received by the Mormons, as the prime article of their faith and the corner-stone of their social polity. . . .

Let us look a little at the practical workings of the system, as seen and described by Mr. Ferris in his book—

DOMESTIC ECONOMY: "Polygamy," says Mr. Ferris, "is introducing a new style of building at Salt Lake City. A man with a half dozen wives builds, if he can, a long, low dwelling, having six entrances from the outside; and when he takes in a new wife, if able to do so, adds another apartment. The object is to keep the woman and babies, as much as possible, apart, and prevent those terrible cat-fights which sometimes occur, with all the accompaniments of Billingsgate, torn caps and broken broom-sticks. As the divine institution extends, these buildings increase, and in a few years the city will look like a collection of barracks for the accommodation of soldiers. Some have separate buildings in parts of the city remote from each other, and others have farm houses, and the wives are thus kept separate, the husband dividing his time between them all."

EFFECT OF POLYGAMY UPON POPULATION: "The effect of polygamy upon population is decidedly deleterious. The prophet Joseph had over forty wives at Nauvoo, and the rest of the priesthood had various numbers, corresponding to their standing and inclinations; and nearly all the children of these polygamous marriages died at that place—indeed, it is alleged by Mormons that not one was taken to Utah. Brigham Young has 30 children, of whom eight are by his first and second lawful wives; the remaining twenty-two are by his *spirituals.* He has about fifty wives, some of whom were widows of Joseph Smith, and are probably past the time of having children; but, supposing him to have thirty who are capable of having issue—which is below the true number—the twenty-two children would be less than one child to a concubine. If each of these degraded females could have been the honored wife of one husband, the aggregate number of children, according to the usual average of four in a family, would be one hundred and twenty, showing a loss in population of ninety-eight.

[34] Ferris, *The Mormons at Home,* 164, 166.

"The children are subject to a frightful degree of sickness and mortality. This is the combined result of the gross sensuality of the parents, and want of care toward their offspring. As a general rule, the saintly pretenders take as little care of their wives as of their children, and of both less than a careful farmer in the States would of his cattle; and nowhere out of the Five Points in New York city, can a more filthy, miserable, neglected looking and disorderly rabble of children be found than in the streets of Great Salt Lake City. The Governor, again, whose attention to his multifarious family we are bound to suppose greater than the average, affords a fair illustration. He was twice lawfully married, and has eight legitimate children, who are all living. He has had a large number of children by his concubines—no one knows how many—it is only known that there are only twenty-two surviving. These females do not reside in the 'Governor's house,' so called, but in different establishments, from one up to a dozen in a place."

PROGRESS OF INDECENCY: "Their system of plurality has obliterated nearly all sense of decency, and would seem to be fast leading to an intercourse open and promiscuous as the cattle in the fields. A man living in common with a dozen dirty Arabs, whether he calls them wives or concubines, cannot have a very nice sense of propriety. It is difficult to give a true account of the effects which have resulted from this cause, and, at the same time, preserve decency of language. The Saints are progressive. In the year 1852, they seriously discussed the subject of introducing a new order into the church, by which the wives of absent missionaries might be sealed to Saints left at home. There are a number of cases in which a man has taken a widow and her daughter for wives at the same time. One has a widow and her two daughters. There are also instances of the niece being sealed to the uncle, and they excite no more attention than an ordinary case. How far the plague-spot is to spread in this direction remains to be seen.

Brigham Young stated in the pulpit, in 1852, that the time might come when, for the sake of keeping the lineage of the priesthood unbroken, marriages would be confined to the same families; as, for instance, the son of one mother would marry the daughter of another by the *same father*. There has been some talk of going even beyond this, and allowing the father to seal his own daughter to himself."

THE HAREMS OF THE PRIESTHOOD: "The high priest dignitaries of the church are exceedingly skillful in procuring young girls for wives. They inculcate the idea that elderly members, who have been tried and found faithful, are surer instruments of salvation than the young, who may apostatize, and as marriage to one who remains steadiest is essential to escape from the fate of being mere angels, a great many young women are fooled into this bubbling and seething cauldron of prostitution.

"Elder Wilford Woodruff, one of the twelve apostles, has a regular system of changing his harem. He takes in one or more young girls, and so manages, after he tires of them, that they are glad to ask for a divorce, after which he beats the bush for recruits. He took a fresh one, about fourteen years old, in March, 1853, and will probably get rid of her in the course of the ensuing summer. These maneuvers are practised more or less by the whole gang, the girls discarded by one become sealed to others, and so travel the entire rounds; and when they accomplish the whole circuit, and are ready to start anew, they have a profoundly 'realizing sense' of female modesty, to say nothing of some of its adjuncts."

THE MORMON WIFE: "A *wife*, in Utah, cannot live out half her days. In families where polygamy has been introduced, she suffers an agony of apprehension on the subject which can scarcely be conceived, much more described. There is a sad complaining, suffering look, which is obvious to the most ordinary observer, which tells the story, if there were no other evidence on the subject."

"OUR NEIGHBOR, THE 'GOLDEN ERA,'" *WESTERN STANDARD*, 29 NOVEMBER 1856.[35]

Cannot the editors of the *Golden Era* secure, upon reasonable terms, the services of the *Herald's* invaluable correspondent on "Mormonism?" If they could by any means secure the aid of his pen, such obsolete stories as those they published last week, under the head of "Mormonism as it is," from the goose-quill of the emasculated Ferris, would never again disgrace their columns. You evince but little taste, gentlemen, in the selection of such stale, thread-bare stories. We feel confident that the inventive brain and unscrupulous pen of *"Amicus Curiae,"*[36] would be of great importance to you in furnishing bright, sparkling and amusing scraps direct from the mint, on Utah and the "Mormons." When our contemporaries become so hard-pushed for extracts on this subject as to be compelled to resurrect such antiquated stuff as that which *dis*-graced the columns of the *Era* last week, and are unable to secure the services of a competent correspondent, they had better give us a call, and we will try and supply them with something more suitable, as we contrive to keep a few items of this kind on hand. To publish articles on "Mormonism" of so old a date as those written by Ferris and wife, in this progressive age, is an imposition on the public; they require something new, spicy and interesting, mixed with considerable romance, about this ever-advancing system of "Mormonism." From the specimens we have seen of

[35] Reprinted in Cannon, *Writings from the "Western Standard,"* 264–65.

[36] Another Latin pseudonym for Utah Territorial justice W. W. Drummond, whose charges Cannon refuted elsewhere.

> the ability of "*Amicus Curiae*" in romancing, we should think he would be the very *hombre* to suit our neighbors of the *Era*. As we think the business would suit him and he would be likely to attend to it on reasonable terms, we would suggest the alliance. He can doubtless be found in San Francisco or vicinity.

While Ferris was wrong about much of what he had concluded through his very short observation of the Mormons, his claim that Joseph Smith had "over forty wives at Nauvoo" was not far off the mark. The intense secrecy that surrounded polygamy during the 1830s and 1840s makes it difficult to ascertain the number of women the first Mormon prophet was sealed to during his lifetime. The latest scholarly work lists thirty-three definite and another eight possible plural wives of Joseph Smith during a ten-year period, beginning as early as 1833.[37] Ferris' estimates of the number of wives of Brigham Young, however, were wildly inaccurate. Young eventually married fifty-six women and had fifty-seven children by sixteen wives. He cared for nine "temporally," but many such marriages—if not all—were presumably not connubial relationships. Thirty women were sealed to him "for eternity only."[38]

It was common for nineteenth-century critics to assume, with Ferris, that "gross sensuality" was the main motive behind polygamy. (Even today, the generally conservative—even prudish—modern polygamists are constantly offended by people asking if they all share the same bed or engage in group sex.[39]) At least one early non-Mormon spent enough time with the Saints to understand such was hardly the case: "the sacrifices to be made, and the hardships to be overcome before practicing [polygamy], are such that no sensualist would be much tempted."[40] As time went on, the critical emphasis on sensuality diminished. In her study of popular literature about the Mormons for a hundred-year period beginning in 1860, Jan Shipps concluded, "of the total number of references to polygamy, only about 10 percent were ref-

---

37 Compton, *In Sacred Loneliness*. 4–8.

38 The best expert on the Young family, Jeffery O. Johnson, identified fifty-five wives in "Determining and Defining 'Wife': The Brigham Young Households," 58, but has since increased the total by one. See also Arrington, *Brigham Young: American Moses*, Appendix C. For data on the number of children polygamous wives tended to have, see Embry, *Mormon Polygamous Families*, 37. For a general overview of Young's complex family, see Jessee, *Letters of Brigham Young to His Sons*, xxi–xli.

39 For revealing insights from women who practice polygamy today, see Batchelor, Watson, and Wilde, *Voices in Harmony*.

40 Chandless, *A Visit to Salt Lake*, 175.

erences to sexual debauchery or other overt sexual concepts. This seems to indicate that the 'gross sensuality' aspect of plurality was not nearly as important as the way it seemed to threaten the institution of marriage and the nuclear family."[41]

Ferris's claim that the aging Mormon hierarchy inculcated the notion that young girls could best assure their salvation by marrying older, "proven," men had some basis in truth. As early as 1853 one observer noted that Mormon fanaticism "makes paradise appear more certain in the train of an apostle or high priest than trusting their salvation to an ordinary saint whose own claims to a seat in heaven are less certain or even doubtful."[42] Ann Eliza Young suggested that this argument was used with considerable effect: in the Reformation, LDS leaders advised girls "to choose for their husbands men of experience, who would have the power of resurrecting them, rather than a young man whose position in the church was not fixed. They carried the practice of this doctrine to the same extreme that they carried everything else. One enthusiastic elder secured for a wife a girl of eleven years, and brides of thirteen and fourteen were often seen, especially in Southern Utah, where the excitement was most intense, and rose almost to frenzy."[43]

According to another apostate, Fanny Stenhouse, Apostle Heber C. Kimball counseled his young missionaries "not to pick out from the flock the young, fair, and tender lambs," but to bring them home safely to Zion—presumably so that Kimball and other members of the Mormon hierarchy could have first pick.[44] One of the most extreme examples of age disparity can be seen in the last polygamous marriage of President John Taylor, the successor to Brigham Young, who married a girl fifty-one years younger than himself. Apologists argue that the marriage was performed primarily because the ailing Taylor needed a nurse and it would be unseemly for anyone but a wife to attend to him. Perhaps one of the factors that led to the divorce between Brigham Young and Ann Eliza Webb was the difference of forty-two years in their ages.

As young Mormon women married older, more established men, this resulted in some hard feelings among the younger, less wealthy males.

---

[41] Shipps, *Sojourner in the Promised Land,* 71.

[42] Schiel, *Journey through the Rocky Mountains,* 84.

[43] Young, *Wife No. 19,* 322–23.

[44] Stenhouse, *"Tell it All,"* 202.

Kimball Young characterized this as "poaching in its worst sense"[45] and Horace Greeley observed that "it certainly looks to me as though a rich dignitary in the church has a freer and fuller range for the selection of his sixth or eighth wife than a poor young man of ordinary standing has for choosing his first. And I infer that the more sharp-sighted young men will not always be content with this."[46]

Although this was not a phenomenon restricted to polygamy,[47] there were many instances of older polygamist men marrying much younger women. While her study of polygamy in three southern Utah counties suggests that these "December/May" marriages were rare, Jessie Embry concluded that "men chose women for their second, third, or fourth wives who were approximately the age of his first wife at the time of their marriage even though he was ten to thirty years older."[48] The biggest problem with age disparity was not so much the difference in age between the husband and his latest wife as it was the difference in age between the first wife and the last.[49]

As to the charge of uncles marrying nieces, the Mormons were indeed vulnerable even though this was not a common practice. Ann Eliza Young made three such allegations. After accusing George D. Watt, one of her husband's clerks, of having married his half sister, she complained that Bishop Smith of Brigham City married two of his nieces and that Bishop Aaron Johnson of Springville married six of his.[50] Kimball Young relates how Mary Jane Ruge justified her marriage to her much older uncle, John Zimmerman. "None of the young men appealed to me so much as did my uncle," she wrote. "He was kind and joyous and everyone liked him."[51]

The often-repeated charge of incest was partly a result of the relatively frequent practice of marrying sisters. Joseph Smith had married at

---

[45] Young, *Isn't One Wife Enough?*, 139–40.

[46] Greeley, *An Overland Journey*, 239.

[47] Stanley S. Ivins demonstrated that "such marriages were not much more common with the Mormons than among other groups." See his essay on this and related subjects, "Notes on Mormon Polygamy," reprinted in Quinn, *The New Mormon History*, 169–80.

[48] Anderson, *Desert Saints*, 398–406; Embry, *Mormon Polygamous Families*, 34. See also Burgess-Olson, "Family Structure and Dynamics in Early Utah Mormon Families."

[49] Young, *Isn't One Wife Enough?*, 176–77.

[50] Young, *Wife No. 19*, 310–11. This second claim, along with several others, was also made five years earlier in Beadle, *Life in Utah*, 367–71.

[51] Young, *Isn't One Wife Enough?*, 184.

least three pairs of sisters; five sets were included among the forty-five wives of Heber C. Kimball and Brigham Young married two pairs; of 1,642 polygamists studied by Ivins, 10 percent married one or more pairs of sisters.[52] Cannon himself married Emily Hoagland, sister of his first wife, in 1881, when she left Jesse C. Little for a man of higher standing in the kingdom.[53] Women who already knew and loved one another as literal sisters often found it much easier to share a common husband than those who did not already enjoy strong family ties. In several cases men had their wife's mother sealed to them, but rarely was such a "marriage" consummated. Still, some very strange relationships grew out of polygamy. One resulted when a young wife of John D. Lee asked for a divorce:

> I told her that if [I] could not make her happy that she should have her liberty, and if there was any other man that she could be more hapy with, to say so & I would use my endeavors to have her seald to that man. She replied that she could love me and respect me as a Father but not as a husband, and that she wantd my oldest son for her companion & that she loved him more than any other Man that She ever saw. Upon reflection I answered that her request Should be grantd. Under those considerations I married them at the time above specified, and I gave them a sumptious Supper and Social Party in my Family Hall to which I invited all the inhabitants of Harmony, who all participated in the rich festival.[54]

Thus, Lee's eldest son married one of his numerous stepmothers. While most of these strange intermarriages fall short of true incest, Kimball Young was correct in arguing that "these alleged incestuous matings probably served to induce hostility, fear, and determination to uproot this system as much as any single item in the long repertoire of alleged Mormon crimes and vices."[55]

According to Ferris, a polygamous wife was doomed to an artificially short and unnecessarily tragic life. Every time he looked at a Mormon

---

52 Ivins in Quinn, *The New Mormon History,* 174–75. Another study suggests a figure of 19 percent. Young, *Isn't One Wife Enough?,* 111.

53 Bagley, ed., *Scoundrel's Tale,* 370–71. This divorce apparently led to Little's alienation from Mormon leaders. He complained to Brannan that they "gathered up Money among the people to pay Bonds men $45,000.00" to raise bail for Cannon, but "they would not give me 45 cents."

54 Cleland and Brooks, eds., *A Mormon Chronicle,* 191.

55 Young, *Isn't One Wife Enough?,* 18. Curiously, the Saints had no qualms about marrying a woman and her daughter from a previous marriage in spite of the Jewish proscription against such liaisons. See Lev. 18.17.

woman, it seems he encountered "a sad complaining, suffering look." Even the most faithful polygamous women often admitted that the practice was a tremendous trial, but the popular view that Mormon wives were virtual prisoners in their own homes was simply untrue.

Non-Mormons generally presumed that the Mormon women—if given the chance—would bolt for freedom. While a hundred reportedly left with Col. Steptoe's troops in 1855 and a like number accepted Gov. Cumming's offer of protection and left Utah when the Utah Expedition arrived three years later, the mass exodus that many had hoped for never materialized.[56] "There are today from fifteen to twenty-thousand mothers and daughters within the territory," one purported victim of polygamy asserted in 1857, "suffering under a cruel enslavement within those Mormon harems, who would make any sacrifice for freedom."[57] As a result of these widely believed claims, Cornelia Paddock and others associated with the Utah Commission lobbied Congress in 1886 for $100,000 to establish the Industrial Christian Home Association. The home was to provide shelter for women desiring to escape the evil clutches of Utah polygamy. After receiving an allocation of $64,000, the shelter was built in 1889, but only a few women ended up living there and it was never made clear how many of these—if any—were actual refugees from the last remaining relic of barbarism. Most were apparently the wives of apostates.[58]

This should not have come as too much of a shock following the 1870 mass meeting of more than three thousand Mormon women in the Salt Lake Tabernacle to protest anti-polygamy legislation. "To the surprise of those who assumed Mormon women to be unwilling victims of a priestly dominated polygamic system, there was general denunciation of proposed measures to interfere with plural marriage."[59] Even the

[56] Mexican War hero Maj. Edward Jenner Steptoe, a veteran of the Cherokee removal and the Seminole Wars, commanded a U.S. Army party that wintered in Great Salt Lake City in 1854–1855. He conducted a frustrating investigation and prosecution of the Gunnison massacre. In Young's mind, many of the women who left with Steptoe had been seduced by the soldiers and were simply going to California "to whore it." Brigham Young, "Utah Delegate to Washington—U.S. Government and Officers," *Journal of Discourses*, 2:322. For details on the evacuation of 1859 as well as earlier departures of apostates, see Aird, "Escape from Zion."

[57] Green, *Mormonism*, 323.

[58] Larson, "An Industrial Home for Polygamous Wives," 263–75.

[59] Larson, *The "Americanization" of Utah for Statehood*, 223–28 and 67–69.

then-ex-communicated Edward W. Tullidge described the mass meetings held throughout Utah in tandem with the passage of the Utah female suffrage bill as "probably the most remarkable woman's rights demonstration of the age."[60]

Just as Ferris and the *Golden Era* characterized Mormon women as "dirty Arabs," many newspapers of the time attacked polygamy by denigrating the women who embraced the practice. Samuel Bowles, editor of the *Springfield Weekly Republican,* offered an either/or proposition with respect to the character of Mormon women: "There is certainly none of that 'loudness' about the Mormon ladies, that an eastern man cannot help observing in the manners of our western women generally. And I hardly think the difference is to be attributed to the superior refinement and culture of the sisters of the Salt Lake Basin; it rather and really is the sign and mark of their servitude, their debasement."[61] Bowles, like most critics of Mormonism, could not allow himself to perceive "refinement" in Mormon women, so he assumed their quiet demeanor was the result of the servitude that *must* accompany polygamy.

Characteristically, Samuel Clemens could not resist lampooning polygamy by making fun of the Mormon women:

> With the gushing self-sufficiency of youth I was feverish to plunge in headlong and achieve a great reform here—until I saw the Mormon women. Then I was touched. My heart was wiser than my head. It warmed toward these poor, ungainly and pathetically "homely" creatures, and as I turned to hide the generous moisture in my eyes, I said, "No—the man that marries one of them has done an act of Christian charity which entitles him to the kindly applause of mankind, not their harsh censure—and the man that marries sixty of them has done a deed of open-handed generosity so sublime that the nations should stand uncovered in his presence and worship in silence."[62]

Nor was an earlier German traveler, Jacob Schiel, particularly impressed, closing his account "with a great incivility to the women of Utah":

> I make this transgression in the interest of consoling those of my countrymen who may look with silent envy and perhaps secret desire upon the prerogatives of the saints. In the entire valley I saw not a single beautiful woman, or even one approaching it, and only one girl who, while quite pretty, was not

[60] Tullidge, *The Women of Mormondom,* 379.
[61] Bowles, *Across the Continent,* 127.
[62] Twain, *Roughing It,* 117–18.

> the type to 'shake the saintship of an anchorite'; yet she can await salvation with certainty, for compassion still lives in Utah. May all the daughters of Utah forgive me that I have no better opinion of their charms.[63]

It is entirely possible that the perspectives recorded by male visitors of Mormon women had much to do with how long they had been out on the trail. Back in 1851, William Kelly was much more charitable: "the softer tints of female loveliness prevailed to a degree that goes far to prove those 'Latter-Day Saints' have very correct notions of angelic perfectibility . . . and I hope I may say, without any imputation of profanity, a more bewitching assemblage of the [female] sex it has rarely been my lot to look upon."[64]

Were "cat-fights" more common in polygamous homes, as Ferris suggested? Perhaps, but most Mormon patriarchs would find such conduct unseemly and not to be tolerated.[65] Writing to Cannon in early 1857, Samuel Pitchforth, a former co-worker in the *Nauvoo Neighbor* office, testified:

> I have seen less quarrelling in the same number of families where there are more wives than one, than in those who lived in the practice of the monogamic system, the wives living in union; they do not fight like Kilkenny cats, and the husbands have peace. Now this is the truth, and could be proved by a thousand respectable witnesses. But there are exceptions to all general rules and there are some who do not live happy; but it is their own fault, for God never would have revealed any thing to make His children unhappy.[66]

A favorite nineteenth-century argument against polygamy, only hinted at in Ferris, was that it must necessarily produce defective children afflicted with physical deformities, mental instability, and even general unruliness.[67] An observer as objective as Horace Greeley, while noting the scarcity of "idiotic or malformed children," charged "their phrenological developments were, in the average, bad."[68] This was related to the belief that the offspring of such sensualists must necessarily be raised as immoral and undisciplined. One early observer remarked:

---

63 Schiel, *Journey through the Rocky Mountains*, 94.

64 *An Excursion to California*, quoted in Mackay (Mayhew), *The Mormons*, 267–69.

65 See both chapter 9, "Plural Wives in Competition and Conflict" and chapter 10, "Cooperation Among Wives," in Young, *Isn't One Wife Enough?*, 191–225.

66 Pitchforth to Cannon, 10 January 1857, *Western Standard*, 28 February 1857, 3.

67 See Froiseth, *The Women of Mormonism*, 207–12

68 Greeley, *An Overland Journey*, 242.

Because the latest polygamous wife was nearly always younger than the others, it is understandable that the other wives often received her with less than unqualified enthusiasm. From *Young, Wife No. 19.*

> Were men the subjects and women the objects of sensuality, or were the latter looked upon as mere concubines, even if the mother's love were not debased, children would stand a great chance of neglect and ill-treatment. Probably no people (speaking collectively) set a higher value upon their children than Mormons do . . . they are brought up carefully enough: certain newspaper paragraphs about "the terrible immorality, blasphemous language, and ungovernable temper of the rising generation in Utah," I look upon as so much sheer nonsense.[69]

A Flagrant Sin against God and Nature

With older men marrying multiple wives, often much younger than themselves, some of whom were even relatives, Cannon had a full plate when it came to convincing nineteenth-century America that the Mormons were not sexual degenerates. Given the sensibilities of the times, they were deviants, far outside the norms of polite society. What to the

[69] Chandless, *A Visit to Salt Lake,* 192, 205.

Mormons was a simple return to Old Testament morality was to the rest of the nation a grossly immoral blot on its honor and more than enough reason to deny statehood.

The *Alta California*—arguably the most powerful newspaper on the West Coast for decades—was quick to frame the ultimatum that eventually contributed to a major change in Mormon policy: abandon polygamy or forget about being admitted to the Union.

"ADMISSION OF UTAH—LEGALIZATION OF POLIGAMY [SIC],"
ALTA CALIFORNIA, 8 JANUARY 1857.

One of the most important questions of domestic policy that will come before Congress at the present session, will doubtless be the application of the territory of Utah to be admitted as a State, under the constitution formed a year or two since. The question is important, as involving an issue never before raised under the Federal Constitution—the power of Congress to refuse to admit a State upon moral grounds alone. It is equally important in view of the ultimate effect upon our system of government, of admitting, as a member of the Union, a people who tolerate and sanction, as a divine institution and a part of their religious faith, a practice revolting to the moral sense of the nation, and contrary to the laws of God, man and nature.

The constitution of Utah, as originally framed, and as it will, we presume, be presented to Congress, comes within the requirements of the Federal Constitution; it is undeniably republican in its character, neither sanctioning nor forbidding anything repugnant to civil or religious liberty, or contrary to the moral or political principles underling [*sic*] our whole system of free government. Therefore, the application of Utah cannot be rejected for anything contained in her constitution. Yet it is notorious that the civil and ecclesiastical polity of the territory are now, and would, under her constitution, continue to be identical; both resting upon, as a fundamental principle, the revolting pretence that poligamy [*sic*] is the proper condition of human society, and that it is expressly ordained by the Almighty. Thus, the grossest form of human depravity known to our race, is blasphemously held to be a divine institution, constitutes a leading article of religious faith, is defended as the purest and holiest domestic relation, cherished and practiced as the most exalted Christian virtue, and protected in all its shocking deformity by the civil law. This is the relation in which the people of Utah, as a territory, stand to poligamy [*sic*]; it is not pretended by them that that relation will or can be changed by their admission into the Union; on the contrary, they deny the right or power of Congress, under the constitution, to take cognizance of ther [*sic*] horrible debaucheries, because they constitute a part of their religion, and that their religious freedom cannot be circumscribed.

If the admission or rejection of Utah as a State, with all the iniquities of Mormonism, only involved a question of morals and policy, the difficulty would be of easy solution. That it would be both right in itself and politic to reject the application, there could be no doubt. But, as the event must turn upon the abstract right of a Territory, presenting a republican form of government, to be erected into a State of the Union, it will devolve upon Congress to determine if a flagrant sin against God and nature can be set up as an article of religious faith, or a religious ceremony, and whether it is entitled to protection as religious liberty under the Federal Constitution. This will open a wide range of philosophical and metaphysical discussion, which will result or at least should result, in the conclusion that the adoption of the principle of religious freedom in our form of government did not contemplate the tolerance, much less the encouragement, of any practice detrimental to the well being of society, or repugnant to the principles of Christianity or morality as understood and practiced by the whole civilized world. The ecclesiastical theories of Mormonism, however conflicting with revealed truth, and absurd as theological tenets, cannot be made the subject of investigation, either by the legislative or judicial authorities; and the people professing the heretical faith are entitled to all the latitude of thought they choose to take, and their civil rights and liberties cannot be abridged in consequence. But the maintenance of their spiritual faith is in no manner dependent upon the maintenance of the degrading social system which they choose to hold as a religious principle. The moral ulcer of polygamy can be exterpated [*sic*] without affecting their church dogma, or entrenching upon their religious freedom. Their claim to admission into the Union with all their doctrines and practices intact, cannot, therefore, be maintained upon the ground that a debasing physical habit is entitled to the protection guaranteed to theological belief.

But they tell us flatly that they will come in with their sails set and colors flying—priestly tyranny, polygamy and all, or else they will not come at all; that if we will not admit them on their own terms, they will bid defiance to the power of the United States, declare their independence, and propagate Mormonism by fire and sword. Whatever this threat may amount to, Congress will have to consider it in connection with the policy of admission, the abstract constitutional right being disposed of. That the Mormon people will declare themselves independent of the General Government, in the event of the rejection of their application, we presume there can be no doubt. That the General Government would permit them to maintain themselves in independence, can hardly be imagined, though to compel them to submission, would cost a protracted, bloody and expensive war. To admit them as a State, with all their present revolting depravity, would implicate the whole people of the nation as the supporters of legalized polygamy and all its attendant horrors and crimes. It would be an insult to the moral sense of mankind, and would fix a stain upon our national escutcheon that time could never obliterate. We cannot imagine that under any circumstances Utah can be admitted, unless her constitution is remodeled, and made to prohibit expressly the practice of polygamy, and to guarantee to all people absolute religious freedom.[70]

"THE 'ALTA CALIFORNIA' ON 'MORMONISM,'" *WESTERN STANDARD*, 17 JANUARY 1857.[71]

A leading article under the heading, "Admission of Utah—Legalization of Polygamy," appeared the latter part of last week in the *Alta California* of this city. The writer discusses at some length, in a very bitter, biased, one-sided manner, the question of Utah's admission with her present institutions into the Union; and concludes that, if Congress do right, and decide the question, as in the opinion of this writer it should be decided, she will not be admitted, unless her constitution is remodeled, and made to prohibit expressly the practice of polygamy. More silly, baseless arguments we never saw advanced by any writer than have been advanced by this one in support of his propositions. He admits that her constitution, as originally framed by her delegates in convention assembled, comes within the requirements of the Federal Constitution, and is undeniably republican in its character,— "neither sanctioning nor forbidding anything repugnant to civil or religious liberty, or contrary to the moral or political principles underlying our whole system of free government." Therefore, he says, the application of Utah cannot be rejected for anything in her constitution. But she must be rejected for the revolting pretence of her inhabitants that polygamy is expressly ordained by the Almighty. The gist of his argument amounts to this: polygamy, "the grossest form of depravity known to our race," being blasphemously held to be a divine institution, and cherished, practiced and defended as the purest and holiest domestic relation by the Latter-day Saints, it would be an insult to the moral sense of mankind, and an ineffaceable stain upon our national escutcheon to admit them as a State. Our constitution being eminently and purely republican, and unobjectionable in every particular, we cannot be rejected on the ground of any fault in that instrument; and the whole question, therefore, according to his ideas, hinges upon the decision of Congress whether such a flagrant sin against God and nature, as he asserts polygamy to be, can be set up as an article of religious ceremony, and whether it is entitled to protection, as religious liberty, under the Federal Constitution.

According to our view of the case, Congress has nothing to do with the

[70] Ironically, Cannon ultimately supported the constitution that secured Utah's statehood, which guaranteed "perfect toleration of religious sentiment" but prohibited "polygamous or plural marriages" forever.

[71] Reprinted in Cannon, *Writings from the "Western Standard,"* 313–16.

decision of this question. Polygamy is already admitted and recognized to be a part of our religious belief, and Congress and all the world know this to be the case. Congress, therefore, cannot say whether it shall be set up as an article of religious faith, for it already is such, and their decision would not affect it one way nor the other. The editors of the *Alta* think it a flagrant sin against God and nature, and that it should not be recognized as a portion of religion. They have equally as good a right to entertain this opinion, if they so wish, as we have to indulge in the opinion that the practice of monogamy is productive of misery, wretchedness and crime, and is in direct contravention of physiological laws. But Congress, in their legislative capacity, whether polygamists or monogamists, have no right to so express themselves; they are restricted by the Federal Constitution from making any law respecting an establishment of religion, or from prohibiting the free exercise thereof, and are expressly required to guarantee a republican form of government to every State. The question for them to decide, and the only question pertinent to the subject will be, is the constitution of Utah republican? If it be decided that it is, Congress *can not,* constitutionally, refuse her admission into the Confederacy. What her domestic institutions are, whether her inhabitants practice polygamy, monogamy, or the Shaker doctrines of non-intercourse of the sexes, is something that does not really concern Congress, or call for any action on their part. The moment they should assume the right to dictate to the inhabitants of a state or territory, what they shall believe and practice, and what they shall not, and remodel the constitution of such state or territory to suit their peculiar views, when it is already republican in every feature, they practically abrogate republicanism and institute an oligarchy in its stead.

This writer truly remarks that theological tenets cannot be made the subject of investigation, either by the legislative or judicial authorities; but he certainly spoils the sentiment by immediately stating that polygamy, which, he says, we choose to hold as a religious principle, can be extirpated without entrenching upon our religious freedom. We who know the feelings and views of the inhabitants of Utah, know that it cannot be. This institution is conscientiously believed in and practiced by them as a portion of their religion, they knowing it to be of divine origin. If the editors of the *Alta* could prove what they so freely assert, that it is a revolting pretence of ours that polygamy is expressly ordained by the Almighty, then there might be some weight attached to their ideas relative to the course Congress ought to pursue towards us. They might then be sustained in saying that it would not be entrenching upon our religious point of view, the Latter-day Saints have everything on their side, and polygamy can be indisputably proved to be a divine institution—blasphemous though it be in the estimation of the editors of the *Alta* to utter it—on the authority of that Book, recognized by Christendom as sacred. As for the national escutcheon being stained by the admission of Utah into the Union, the editors of the *Alta* know better. They know, and were they honest they would acknowledge it, that so far as morality and virtue are concerned, Utah is incomparably superior to her monogamic sisters. They have excellent opportunities of knowing that the rank and festering corruption that is fastening itself on the very vitals of monogamic communities, producing and fostering the most terrible evils, is unknown in Utah. And every other individual can know it that will take any pains to investigate.

The editors say that we tell them flatly that we will come in "priestly tyranny, polygamy and all," or else we will not come in at all. Regarding it as we do, as a portion of our religious belief, are we not justified in saying that we will not submit to be curtailed or dictated to in these matters? The practice of this doctrine is neither unconstitutional nor unscriptural, why, then, should our form of belief in this point be dictated to us? The editors of the *Alta* say that this portion of it is revolting and horrible, that it is contrary to the laws of God, Man and nature. It may be contrary to the laws of some communities of men, who prohibit it, and sanction and legalize the diabolical crimes of prostitution and whoredom; but we have yet to be shown the law of God, or of nature, that is violated in its practice. The "Mormons" have repeatedly said, that were the practice of this system of marriage wrong, could it be shown unto them that it is contrary to the laws of God, they would forsake it instanter; but they will die contending for their rights, before they will be coerced into this or that practice to suit the whim or views of any man or community of men. If their belief be incorrect, show it to them, and do not resort to extraordinary and unconstitutional measures to compel them to believe as you do. If it be as repugnant to Christianity as you, Messrs. Editors of the *Alta,* pretend to say it is, and you are well satisfied of its evils, you have no need to alarm yourselves about the admission of Utah into the Union. Let her be admitted by all means, "priestly tyranny, polygamy and all," and the superiority of your institutions, practices, etc. if they be superior, and consonant with pure Christianity, will soon destroy every vestige of barbarism and debauchery there may exist in her midst.

We have noticed in our experience since the revelation of polygamy, that the honest, the virtuous and the pure of both sexes, when they hear it explained, never raise any objections against it; but the adulterous, the corrupt and the depraved, almost invariably protest in indignant terms against its proclamation or practice. They can see no propriety in such a principle, and they deride the most noble and holy of the ancient servants of God because they believed and practiced it. Whether the writer of the article to which we have alluded can be reckoned in the latter category or not, we do not pretend to say; but, whenever we hear such bitter denunciations of this doctrine and its believers, we set their author down as either ignorant or impure.

LET THEM WAG THEIR TONGUES OF SLANDER

One of Cannon's favorite arguments was that polygamy was preferable to the "prostitution and whoredom" that he believed was necessarily present in any society that did not sanction plural marriage. This reflected the common nineteenth-century view that male nature required prostitutes to protect the virtue of "decent" women. A dozen years later, J. H. Beadle offered these observations concerning the Mormon's "solution" to prostitution:

> Public prostitution is, of course, comparatively unknown, but that private immorality, and that of the most loathsome character, prevails extensively, (and) is well known to all who care to inquire . . . This, then, is the self-proclaimed task of Mormonism: to save a few by reducing all to a level; to abolish prostitution by legalizing concubinage; to promote conjugal purity by multiplying the husband's temptation and opportunity, and to improve the condition of woman by making her a mere life-giving machine.[72]

In arguing that this "private immorality," this "moral ulcer of polygamy" could be excised without negatively affecting the fundamental theology of the LDS church as then understood, the *Alta California* and like-minded newspapers betrayed a fundamental misunderstanding of that theology. Polygamy was not perceived by the Mormons as something tangential to the core of the restored Gospel of Jesus Christ. Rather, it was considered a fundamental tenet of their religion, crucial to eternal glory. As one early traveler heard it simply explained, "the more wives, the more salvation."[73] Even in their humor, the Mormons held to this belief, especially during the Utah Reformation, which was also the period of greatest commitment to plural marriage.[74] This is beautifully demonstrated in the following verse from a song of that period, titled "The Reformation:"

> Now, sisters, list to what I say,—
> With trials this world is rife,
> You can't expect to miss them all,
> Help husband get a wife!
> Now, this advice I freely give,
> If exalted you would be,
> Remember that your husband must
> Be blessed with more than thee.

---

[72] Beadle, *Life in Utah,* 292, 373.

[73] Schiel, *Journey through the Rocky Mountains,* 86.

[74] O'Dea, *The Mormons,* 245–46.

Then, oh, let us say,
God bless the wife that strives
And aids her husband all she can
To obtain a dozen wives.[75]

For his part, Brigham Young could never quite understand why polygamy was such an issue for the Gentiles. In a letter to Cannon, written 30 May 1856, Young bemoaned the fact that polygamy was all the Gentile world seemed to know or care about when it came to Mormonism. "The only thing interesting, that comes from Utah," he complained, "is awful disclosures about polygamy, and a general hostility to the Government." He continued:

> Matters remain much as usual with us. As for news I suppose that we shall still be labelled "Nothing important from Utah." You know it takes war, murder, blood, thunder, and earthquakes to make any thing interesting to satisfy the ever-craving, blood-thirsty, depraved taste, that insatiate public maw, which is only gratified with the most thrilling narratives, horrible and bloody tragedies and melancholy catastrophies. If the mails come laden with such direful news, then it is satisfied, and the news is interesting; but if peace, union, and a calm prosperity prevails, it is branded as above, "Nothing important from Utah." The only thing interesting, however, that comes from Utah, is awful disclosures about polygamy, and a general hostility to the Government. I do not know that the world will ever tire upon these *interesting* subjects, they seem so pleased with them that they continually serve them up, dish after dish, course after course, and like the Indian at the feast who had taken sucketash every time, when asked the fifth, and last time, what he would have, replied that he would take a little more sucketash. So with the world, they have great delight in false and calumnious statements made about Mormons, and polygamy appears to form their chief attraction. Let them wag their tongues of slander and misrepresentation, we know the reason why they prefer falsehood to truth, it is a sweet morsel to them now; but the time will come when the refuge of lies will be swept away, as with the besom of destruction; when they will be glad to represent the truth as it is, and award unto the Saints their just rights, but it will not be their privilege. Such characters will most probably perish in their own iniquity, and sink into oblivion, while truth will increase and spread abroad, and rise higher, and the Saints become purer and better until the victory is won, all things overcome and the kingdoms be broken in pieces and become the kingdom of our Lord and of his Christ. I am glad that you are wielding so effective a weapon in this great cause, and that you may be prospered therein is my most earnest prayer.[76]

[75] *Deseret News*, 26 November 1856, reprinted in Green, *Mormonism*, 217.

[76] Young to Cannon, 30 May 1856, *Western Standard*, 12 July 1856, 3.

Chapter 7

"THE BEST NEWS FROM THIS PLACE IS THE REFORMATION"

The Reality of Rhetoric

As economic and social pressure built in Utah during the mid-1850s, leaders of the Church of Jesus Christ of Latter-day Saints were increasingly interested in—even obsessed by—the need for general reformation. What is now known as the Utah Reformation began in September 1856 and lasted well into 1857.[1] It was a kind of Pentecostal revival—an attempt by Brigham Young and other leaders—most particularly his counselor, Jedediah M. Grant—to account for the dire economic conditions in Zion, where plague and drought had devastated the harvests of 1855 and 1856.

Although the news Cannon preferred to write was the *good* news of the restored gospel, he was not above passing on the *bad* news as well, including the following excerpt from the *Deseret News,* which made the conditions of the famine of 1855–1856 all too clear:

> In addition to the drouth and destruction by insects last season, to the severity of the past winter and consequent heavy loss of stock, and to the destitution we are still suffering, the long continued dry weather, the scant supply of water at command for irrigation, the entire destruction of crops by grasshoppers in Cache county, and the like destruction in portions of Box Elder and Utah counties, the general ravages of tobacco and other

---

[1] The best general treatment, as yet unpublished, is Peterson, "The Utah Reformation," but see also his following essays: "Brigham Young and the Mormon Reformation," "The Mormon Reformation of 1856–1857," and "Like a Fire in My Bones." For additional informative chapters on the Utah Reformation, see Werner, *Brigham Young,* 398–417 and Bigler, *Forgotten Kingdom,* 121–40. Furniss, *The Mormon Conflict,* contains much useful information as does Larson, "The Mormon Reformation," 45–63; Sessions, *Mormon Thunder*; Alexander, "Wilford Woodruff and the Mormon Reformation of 1856–1857," 25–29; Searle, "The Mormon Reformation of 1856–1857"; and Orme, "The Causes of the Mormon Reformation of 1856–1857." For further commentary on nineteenth-century revival movements, see Smith, *Revivalism and Social Reform.*

worms upon potatoes and corn, and the parching of whole fields of grain before the heads are filled are far from promising a surplus of food for the Saints now here and the thousands already on their way to the mountains. Strong faith in the wisdom of the providences of the Almighty, great skill, strict obedience to the commandments of the Lord and the counsels of His servants, the most rigid economy and untiring well-directed industry may enable us to escape starvation until a harvest in 1857. But those who have not the above named essential qualifications, and who do not intend to strive for them, will be apt to have their feelings sorely chafed and their stomachs severely pinched, ere plenty again gladdens our quiet homes. And until the lapse of at least another year emigrants and others will fall in their dependence upon Utah for sustenance, and will run great risk of starving unless they bring their supplies with them, and that too not in gold, silver and merchandize with a view to exchange advantageously, but in such an amount of provisions as they may need until August 1857, and for how much longer we are not informed.[2]

Joseph Fielding's diary vividly confirmed the dire predictions of the *Deseret News,* capturing the conditions that helped fire the excesses of the Reformation.

The last Summer was indeed A hard time with the poor Saints through the Lack of Bread. We lived chiefly on Weeds which we gathered from the Fields or the Roads. This was oweing to the destruction caused by the Grasshoppers the previous year. We had not the usual supply of Water. I sowed about 13 Acres of wheat took much Pains with it gave it all the Water I could get for it but did not reap more than 70 bushels from it, and planted 3 Acres of Corn but did not get more than 40 Bushels.

This was in the Harvest of 56, but our hardest time was previous to it. The Pastures were dried up so that it was very difficult to sustain our Cattle. It [w]as as though the Lord had commanded the Clouds that they should not rain. In short the Lord has withheld his wanted Blessings from us for the last 2 or 3 years but still I did not see the Cause of it till Brother Brigham began to call upon us to repent, declaring he would have A Reformation.

---

[2] "News from Utah; Prospects," *Western Standard,* 13 September 1856. For editorials in which Cannon addressed the famine of 1855–1856, see "The Alta and Its Correspondent," *Western Standard,* 22 March 1856; "Distress at Salt Lake," *Western Standard,* 5 April 1856, reprinted in *Writings from the "Western Standard,"* 65–66; and "Two Versions of a Story," *Western Standard,* 21 June 1856, reprinted in *Writings from the "Western Standard,"* 129–43. For a recent analysis of Utah's forgotten famine, see Carter, "Fish and the Famine of 1855–56." One practice of the Latter-day Saints that sprang from necessity during this period and which is still encouraged today is the monthly fasting of two meals. Members donate the cost of those missed meals—or more, when one can afford it—for the use of the poor. This is one of the keystones of the remarkable welfare program of the Church of Jesus Christ of Latter-day Saints. See Arrington, *Great Basin Kingdom,* 148–56.

His Councilors took the same then the 12 and others joined in Cry[ing] Repent, make Restitution. Then the Sacrement which before has been administered every Sabath, was withheld, and there was no Preaching but Repentence, and Reformation, even to all, for all had sinned and were sleeping and that on the Brink of Destruction; all must make Restitution inasmuch as we had injured anyone, in any way. Some Questions were offered to us by which we might try our selves and which we were required to answer and A Curse pronounced on anyone that should lie.[3]

To Get the Spirit of Reformation

In addition to the crop failures of 1855 and 1856 (a sign taken by many as a manifestation of God's displeasure), the Reformation was fueled by the increasing friction between the Mormons and the federal government and other outsiders. Swept up in millennial zeal, many believed that the Second Coming of Jesus Christ would take place as soon as His saints had prepared the way. In this surge of religious fervor, virtually every Mormon in Utah Territory was re-baptized to signify a renewed commitment to the principles of the gospel. While the call for reformation aroused the Saints to greater faithfulness to the gospel, the persistent and often shrill call to repentance that Mormon leaders issued from Salt Lake added to the general distrust many Westerners felt toward the Mormons.

The Reformation was a period of considerable mercy and forgiveness in which the Mormons truly strived to become Saints.[4] That spirit of love was not always evident in the rhetoric of the day, however, and George Q. Cannon must have found it particularly difficult to defend his brethren in Great Salt Lake City when they made injudicious statements that were published in their own newspaper, the *Deseret News*. Discourses by Mormon leaders were reviewed by Brigham Young and edited—especially for language—before being published in the *News*, but many of these impassioned sermons still reeked of hellfire and brimstone.

---

3 Joseph Fielding Diary, 1849–1859, 3 May 1857, MS 1567, LDS Archives, 161–64. Scott Kinney transcription.

4 "The notion that forbearance and forgiveness were dominant Reformation themes is one that has by and large eluded the analysis of many scholars who have studied this era, probably because it, at least on the surface, seems to run counter to the prevailing image of the Reformation as a time of sternness and unbending severity." Peterson, "Brigham Young and the Mormon Reformation," 254.

The rhetoric that inspired the Reformation attracted considerable notice in the California press. While they delighted in printing Brigham Young's colorful speeches, few editors had any grasp of the complex stew of politics, economics, and religious devotion that fueled the movement.

Current events, notably the handcart episode of 1856, complicated the story coming out of Utah. Cannon sometimes chose to remain silent; perhaps he was too busy responding to some other newspaper, or he may have felt it would be best to not comment on the handcart disaster. Undoubtedly, he was limited by the lack of credible and specific reports. In any event, when the official organ of California's Democratic party used selected Mormon discourses by Brigham Young from the *Deseret News* to highlight the handcart debacle, Cannon chose to hold his fire.

"BEAUTIES OF MORMONISM,"
DEMOCRATIC STATE JOURNAL, 14 JANUARY 1857.

THE HANDCART TRAINS.—Have any of you suffered while coming here? Yes. How many of you sisters present buried your husbands, or your fathers, or mothers, or children, on the plains? How many of you brethren buried your wives? Have you suffered, and been in peril and trouble? Yes, you had to endure anguish and pain from the effects of cholera, toil and weariness. Do you live your religion when you get here after all the trouble, afflictions and pains you have passed through to come to Zion? and to a pretty Zion! Men and women start across the plains for this place, and are they willing to wade through the snow? Yes. To travel through snow storms? Yes. To wade rivers? Yes. What for? To get to Zion. And here we are in Zion, and what a Zion! where it is necessary for the cry of reformation to go through the land, both a spiritual and temporal reformation. God is more merciful than man can be, and it is well for us. Again, when I consider the backsliding of the people and their sins, I will not ask God to be more merciful and have more sympathy towards me, than I have for my brethren and sisters.

Some of those who have died in the handcart companies this season, I am told, would be singing, and, before the tune was done, would drop over and breathe their last; and others would die while eating, and with a piece of bread in their hands. I should be pleased, when the time come, if we could all depart from this life as easily as did those, our brethren and sisters. I repeat, it will be a happy circumstance, when death overtakes me, if I am privileged to die without a groan or struggle, while yet retaining a good appetite for food. I speak of these things, to forestall indulgence in a misplaced sympathy.

You have heard the brethren relate their trials through Iowa; it is a wicked place. Those regions of the country are the locality of the afflictions that

> have come upon this people. Take Missouri, Illinois and Iowa, and they are the places where we have been affelicted and driven. What can we expect from those people, anything but hell out of doors?
>
> Count the living and the dead and you will find that not half the number died in brother Willie's hand cart company, in proportion to the number in that company, as have died, in past seasons by the cholera in single companies traveling with wagons and oxen, with carriages and horses, and that too in the forepart of the season. When you called to mind this fact, the relations of the sufferings of our companies this season will not be so harrowing to your feelings. With regard to those who have died and been laid away by the roadside on the plains, since the cold weather commenced, let me tell you they have not suffered one hundredth part so much as did our brethren and sisters who have died with the cholera.[5]
>
> We are not in the least discouraged about the hand cart method of traveling. As to its preaching a sermon to the nations, as has been remarked, they are preached pretty nigh to destruction already. We do not care whether the hand cart scheme preaches to them or whether it be by the teachings of the Elders of Israel. They are so bound up with their friends and so priest ridden that they canot burst through their chains; and they will have to remain so until Jesus devises some other means to save them, for the great majority will not hear and obey.

Despite Young's equivocations, well over two-hundred members of the Willie and Martin handcart companies perished on the plains of Wyoming. Although earlier and subsequent handcart trains proved to be both efficient and cost-effective, this was the greatest disaster in America's move west from the Missouri River, claiming seven times as many lives as the Donner tragedy. With better planning and stronger leadership, it could have been avoided completely. Nonetheless, whether from fear of autocratic leaders or—as often reported—from a united faith in a great cause, few of the survivors were ever known to complain of their sufferings.

The handcart system was Brigham Young's idea—an innovation that was not only cheaper, but faster, than ox trains—so it is perhaps understandable why he downplayed the disaster. When he first learned that

[5] Between sixty-eight and seventy-seven of the 421 members of the Willie handcart company died of exposure and starvation. Cholera was an awful death, but it generally had the advantage of being quick. One expert set the Willie company mortality rate at sixteen percent, four times the best expert's estimates of general mortality rates for overland companies. See Grayson, "Human Mortality in a Natural Disaster: the Willie Handcart Company"; and Unruh, *The Plains Across*, 408.

Artist's retrospective rendering of the terrible privations encountered by the Willie and Martin handcart companies of 1856. From Stenhouse, *Rocky Mountain Saints.*

hundreds of converts were still on the blizzard-swept plains in early October, Young wrote Cannon: "They inform us that there are still 970 souls back on the plains with hand-carts, besides ninety wagons. We hope for their sakes, if no other, the present fine warm weather may continue, as many of them are bound to be quite late."[6]

In his next monthly letter to Cannon—one that Cannon chose not to publish—Young was no longer hoping for "fine warm weather," but had realized the enormity of the situation on the plains and had begun to fix the blame elsewhere:

> A portion of our emigration this year are very late, not having yet arrived—they have encountered severe storms on the Sweetwater, but having forwarded to them a large amount of assistance in teams, wagons, provisions, clothing and men, we trust that their journey may be accomplished without any great degree of suffering or loss of life. We were not aware of their being upon the plains until the arrival of F. D. Richards, Daniel Spencer and others of the returning missionaries who arrived in this city on the 4th Ulto. It was a great mistake to start them

[6] Young to Cannon, 4 October 1856, *Western Standard,* 15 November 1856, 2.

> across the plains so late in the season, a fault that must be remedied in future.[7]

It was true that Franklin D. Richards and Daniel Spencer—not Brigham Young—were the ones who decided to push ahead in spite of the lateness of the season, a decision that earned them the public opprobrium of Young.[8] Levi Savage pointed out that it was too dangerous to proceed that late in the year, but was "rebuked by the other elders for lack of faith [and] was overwhelmed with the religious fanaticism and blind faith of others who thought the very elements would be changed or influenced."[9] As Nathan Tanner Porter, who accompanied the handcarts as an assistant to Hodgett's independent company, noted, "I was not in the council above mentioned as I was not invited by those in charge . . . my own feelings according to my judgment was not in harmony with the decision of the council; nevertheless, I felt it my duty to comply with the request of those who were placed to direct the work in which I was engaged."[10]

Even though it was the decision of the church authorities on the scene and not Brigham Young to push ahead so late in the season, most anti-Mormon writers of the time laid the blame for this complex problem directly on his shoulders.[11]

In early November, Brigham Young addressed the Saints in Utah, threatening anyone in the future with excommunication if they started immigrants across the plains "after a given time." He also made it excruciatingly clear that he would accept none of the blame for the handcart disaster, calling down God's wrath upon anyone who complained.[12]

> If any man or woman complains of me or of my Counselors, in regard to the lateness of some of this season's immigration, let the curse of God be on them and blast their substance with mildew and destruction, until their names are forgotten from the earth. I never thought of my being accused of

[7] Young to Cannon, 4 November 1856, LDS Archives.

[8] Young, "Counsel Concerning Immigration—Benefits to be Derived from an Early Start—Crossing the Plains with Handcarts, etc.," 2 November 1856, *Journal of Discourses,* 4:66–70.

[9] Stenhouse, *The Rocky Mountain Saints,* 317.

[10] Porter, *Nathan Tanner Porter's Family Record,* 94–95.

[11] See, for example, Young, *Wife No. 19,* 208.

[12] "Remarks by President Brigham Young, Tabernacle, Nov. 2, 1856," *Deseret News,* 12 November 1856.

> advising or having any thing to do with so late a start. The people must know that I know how to handle money and means, and I never supposed that anybody had a doubt of it.[13]

By the time the survivors had finally made it into Salt Lake Valley, Young had apparently decided to downplay the tragedy, believing that the full truth of the matter would only hurt the cause of Mormonism. Instead, he provided Cannon with the interpretation he no doubt hoped would find its way into print:

> Notwithstanding the companies now out and the two last arrived—handcart Companies were caught in the cold and storms, owing to far too late a start from Florence, yet the relief so promptly, freely, liberally and timely sent from here was so blest in rescuing them that but few, comparatively, have suffered severely, though some had their feet and hands more or less frosted; yet the mortality has been much less than attends well fitted animal trains traveling in good season.[14]

It May Seem Strange That Reformation Is Needed

To facilitate the Reformation, home missionaries (the precursors to today's home teachers) were sent to each family with a list of questions to be put to each adult member of the LDS church. The editor of the *Bulletin* found this "catechism" to be not only a source of amusement but further evidence of patriarchal tyranny.

"Mormon Catechizing," *Daily Evening Bulletin*, 29 August 1857.

> As our article of yesterday concerning the great Reformation that was reported to be going on last winter at Salt Lake, may have caused some curiosity among the readers of the *Bulletin* to know what were the nature of the questions the Mormon missionaries in their capacity of father confessors, put to the Saints, we have procured a copy of some of them, together with a portion of the instructions by which they were accompanied. They will also be interesting as exhibiting the kind of sins which the heads of the church expected to find among its members, and thus give some insight into the habits and situation of the people of Utah, and the influence which the church leaders assume to exercise over them. We may add also that these

13 "Remarks by President Brigham Young, Tabernacle, Nov. 2, 1856," *Deseret News*, 12 November 1856.

14 Young to Cannon, 7 December 1856, LDS Archives. For more on the tragedy, see Hafen and Hafen, *Handcarts to Zion*; Bartholomew and Arrington, *Rescue of the 1856 Handcart Companies*; John Chislett's narrative of the Willie Company in Stenhouse, *Rocky Mountain Saints*, chapter 37; and Carter, "The Mormon Handcart Companies."

questions have been exhibited to a number of Mormons and read by them, and they freely admitted that these were the questions put, but the women enquired of all stated that there were many other questions which we have not obtained. Here they are, however, as we have them:

1. Have you committed murder by shedding innocent blood, or consenting thereto?

2. Have you betrayed your brethren or sisters in any thing?

3. Have you committed adultery by having connection with a woman that was not your wife, or a man that was not your husband?

4. Have you taken and made use of property not your own, without the consent of the owner?

5. Have you cut hay where you had no right to, or turned your animals into another person's grain or field without his knowledge or consent?

6. Have you lied about, or maliciously misrepresented any person or thing?

7. Have you borrowed any thing that you have not returned or paid for?

8. Have you borne false witness against your neighbor?

9. Have you taken the name of the Deity in vain?

10. Have you coveted anything not your own?

11. Have you been intoxicated with strong drink?

12. Have you found lost property and not returned it to the owner, or used all diligence to do so?

13. Have you branded an animal that you did not know to be your own?

14. Have you taken another's horse or mule from the range, and ridden it without the owner's consent?

15. Have you fulfilled your promises in paying your debts, or run into debt without prospect of paying?

16. Have you taken water to irrigate with, when it belonged to another person?

17. Do you pay your tithing promptly?

18. Do you teach your family the Gospel of Salvation?

19. Do you speak against the brethren, or against any principle taught in the Bible, Book of Mormon, Book of Doctrine and Covenants, Revelations given through Joseph Smith, the Prophet, and the Presidency of the Church as now organized?

20. Do you pray in your family night and morning, and attend to secret prayer?

21. Do you wash your body and have your family do so, as often as health and cleanliness and circumstances will permit?[15]

22. Do you labor six days, and rest or go to the house of worship on the seventh?

23. Do you and your family attend ward meetings? [Each ward of the city has its own religious organization.]

---

[15] According to John Moon Clements, even Brigham Young had difficulty complying with an earlier version of this article of faith: "Do you wash your bodies once a week. (President Young) said that he did not he had tried it. He was well aware that this was not for everybody." See Sessions, *Mormon Thunder*, 220–21. Perhaps this aversion to bathing resulted in the more flexible revision, which must have been quite a compromise for the fastidious Grant.

24. Do you preside over your family as a servant of God, and is your family subject to you?

25. Have you labored diligently and earned faithfully the wages paid you by your employers?

26. Do you oppress the hireling in his wages?

27. Have you taken up and converted any stray animal to your use, or in any manner appropriated one to your benefit, without accounting therefor to the proper authorities?[16]

* * * * * * * *

In answer to the above questions, let all men and women confess to the persons they have injured and make restitution or satisfaction. And when satisfaction has been made to the people injured, the Bishop, Teachers, Missionaries, and the other officers of the church, are not at liberty to pry into sins that are between a person and his or her God, but let such person confess to the proper authority, that the adversary may not have an opportunity to take an advantage of human weakness and thereby destroy souls.

Hesitation in answering these and similar questions, would be sure to lead to a further examination which would soon bring out the person's real feelings towards the church authorities, and perhaps cause them to put a black mark against his or her name.

It is more than a little ironic that the very nature of this reformatory "catechism"—apparently originated by the fiery reformer, Jedediah M. Grant during his first reformation visit to the settlements in northern Utah—underscored the deep commitment to morality embraced by the Mormon people. Moreover, with the possible exception of question 19, which asked whether the member "speaks against the brethren," this catechism argues against the charges made by the *Bulletin* that the entire purpose of the Reformation was to ferret out those who opposed Brigham Young. In spite of what many considered an unwarranted invasion of privacy, the primary objective of this and other revivals in Mormon history was to promote confession, repentance, and recommitment to the faith. In this respect, at least, the Utah Reformation was remarkably successful. Nonetheless, this did not stop later anti-Mormon writers like Fanny Stenhouse from characterizing the catechism (an example of which she did not include in her exposé) as "obscene."[17]

---

[16] Over time, this catechism evolved into slightly different formats. For a similar list, but limited to only seventeen questions, see Brooks, *John Doyle Lee,* 193–94. Davis Bitton provides a useful discussion of how the various versions of the Reformation catechism fit into the history of Mormon religious instruction in "Mormon Catechisms."

[17] Stenhouse, "*Tell it All,*" 314.

If this catechizing was, at times, "obscene," it could also be humorous, as illustrated through the following exchange between Wilford Woodruff and an unnamed elder. "After explaining to a certain individual that he considered it a privilege to be re-baptized, the man professed his immunity from sin:

> In all the trials incident to the pilgrimage and pioneer life, have you never sworn nor used bad language?'
>
> 'No sir,' was the prompt reply.
>
> 'Have you never broken the Sabbath day?'
>
> 'No sir,' came the quick response.
>
> 'Have you never cheated your neighbor in trade?'
>
> 'No sir,' thundered the unrepentant man.
>
> 'Then for heavens sake, go off and do something. You are the only perfect man I ever saw, and hope never to see another in this life.'[18]

Some apostates used the catechism to justify their defections. Joseph Morris, whose revelations named him—rather than Brigham Young—as the "Prophet, Seer and Revelator" for the church, was a prime example. "To bolster his claims to righteousness, he went through the long list of questions asked of those in the reformation, all of which he answered properly, at least to his own satisfaction."[19]

Albert Carrington, editor of the *Deseret News,* anticipated how both the Gentile press and many of the Saints would react to the idea of a Mormon Reformation:

> To the world it may seem strange that reformation is needed where there are none to molest us in our religion, in a country throughout whose broad borders there is not a single brothel, grogshop, or gambling hall; where murders, assassination, highway robberies, arson, husband and wife killing and other high crimes are unknown to our court records; and where even one lawyer could not make a living, at fair rates, by attending to the whole of the small amount of litigation among this numerous people. And, perhaps, some saints have deemed reform uncalled for at present, not being sufficiently faithful to at all times see afar off.
>
> But when we are of like passions with other people, and when commodious buildings are multiplied, when numerous fields are enclosed and the comforts and luxuries of life accumulate around us, we are prone to slacken the faith and energy engaged in producing them, and to measurably forget our indebtedness for the peculiar privileges and blessings in our possession.

---

[18] Cowley, *Wilford Woodruff,* 373.

[19] Anderson, *Joseph Morris and the Saga of the Morrisites,* 15.

> Prosperity and ease tempts to remissness in duty, to neglect of secret and family prayer, to unlawful indulgence of thought, word and act, to laying aside weapon after weapon and shield after shield of the gospel armor, until there is little or no defence against the assaults of the adversary. Hence the necessity for reformation, and we rejoice that the people are so zealous in a work of so much importance.[20]

Like a Fire in My Bones

Writing to Cannon in early October 1856, Young announced the beginnings of the Reformation, which was "Springing up in many of the settlements." "Now that much of the chaff of the winters threshing floor has been floated off by the Summer breezes, we trust that the Saints who are really Such will awake from their lethargy and lay hold with an increased faith and energy," Young wrote, using one of his favorite metaphors. "And not only obtain but retain the Holy Ghost in their bosums Sufficient to enable them to walk humbly before the Lord of Hosts, and render more effective Service in his Cause."[21]

In several of his letters to Cannon, many of which were published in the *Western Standard,* Apostle Wilford Woodruff spoke glowingly of the movement. In his October letter he proclaimed:

> We have had much excellent preaching lately by the First Presidency and others. Prest. Young has come out boldly and told this people in the name of the Lord, they must repent and be baptized for the remission of their sins. Several wards have gone forward en masse, been baptized and renewed their covenants before the Lord; and I believe the fire of a universal reformation in this Territory has been lit and will continue to burn, until a permanent foundation for good works has been laid in our midst. We must say since the organization of this church our ears have never been saluted with more pointed, Godlike sermons, than have flowed lately from Pres. Young and his Counsellors.[22]

The initial focus of the Reformation was largely on health and cleanliness. Editorializing in the *Deseret News,* Albert Carrington praised in particular the effect the home missionaries were having in this respect:

---

[20] *Deseret News,* 22 October 1856.

[21] Young to Cannon, 4 October 1856, in *Western Standard,* 15 November 1856.

[22] Woodruff to Cannon, 4 October 1856, in *Western Standard,* 15 November 1856. For additional insights on Woodruff and the Reformation, see Alexander, "Wilford Woodruff and the Mormon Reformation of 1855–57," 25–39.

> The cheerfulness with which the Home Missionaries are met, the crowded meetings attending their appointments, the full and frank confessions, the manifestations of the Spirit and the general and hearty response to the summons to renew covenants all clearly show forth an anxious desire to keep the commandments of God and abide the counsels of his servants. . . .
>
> Some housewives esteem themselves models of neatness when their parlors and visiting dresses are kept scrupulously clean, though at the same time hurly burly may prevail in their kitchens, dirt accumulate under beds, behind doors and in bye corners, and their every day and out-of-sight clothing be entirely too untidy to pass a correct inspection. And some men fancy that they are using their time, means and energies to the utmost advantage to the cause, when building commodious dwellings, enclosing large fields and increasing their stock, without providing privies for their families, even though there be no bush, rock, or other hiding place, within a mile.
>
> It may be urged that these are small matters, but small matters are the main ingredients of this life, especially with the great majority; and our understanding of a reform, of making Israel an example in every good thing, extends to correct thought, word and action at home, as well as abroad; before and with one's family, as well as with friends and strangers.[23]

As the Reformation gained steam, Jedediah Grant, in particular, left no question that moral as well as physical filth was to be rooted out of the Mormon community, with mercy toward none but the fully repentant:

> If the Bishops and Teachers will go to work, together with every officer in the church, we can soon find out those who are not disposed to do right; and let their names be written down, and let the offence and place of residence be written against the name, that we may know who are living in sin, where they live and what their offences are . . .
>
> Let the whole people take warning; and let every man and woman in Israel, understand that the indignation of the Almighty rests upon that person who fails to expose iniquity. And let the wrath of God be upon any officer of the church that knows of abomination, unless he comes out and makes known that abomination. . . .
>
> I want to see the people wake up and reform, forsake all the evil habits and everything that is dark, loathsome and impure. I want to see them eschew all dirt, and filth and degradation, and cease profaning the Sabbath and the name of the Lord God of Israel; I want to see them become at least as moral and temperate as any people in the gentile world, as we call it. I tell you that the gentiles would be shocked at the filth and dirt of some of the sons and daughters of Israel, and feel offended to associate with them; I mean that portion of the gentiles that are pure in their moral habits . . .

[23] "Reformation," *Deseret News,* 5 November 1856.

> Some people talk of wild fire; I would rather have wild fire than no fire at all. I would like you to come up to the light of the Almighty, and if you want to pray to God, if you want to shout and make heaven and earth ring, drive the devil out of doors; chase darkness from your houses and from your families, and raise the banner of the Lord Jesus Christ in your households and the flag of God in your city, and say, in the name of the Lord Jesus Christ, I will do right and root up everything that is wrong.[24]

It did not take long for Cannon to hear from his correspondents in Utah about the effects of the Reformation. James McNight wrote of Brigham Young's "most piercing exhortation" in which he had informed the Saints that "thro' the pride, and vanity, and deceit of the world, [they had] lost the Spirit of Almighty God, and become dead, dead!" Agreeing with his prophet, McNight exclaimed, "Those who are too pure to enter upon this work of reformation, should take passage to some more congenial sphere." He then concluded his letter by informing Cannon and his readers that the First Presidency was setting the example for reformation: "Presidents Young, Kimball and Grant, with their families have been rebaptized, and renewed their covenants unto God, and have called upon all the Saints to prepare themselves to follow their example, by cleaning themselves inside and outside, their homes, and their yards, repenting of their sins, and obtaining the Holy Ghost. There is a 'shaking among the dry bones,'" he concluded, "and life is manifesting itself among the Saints."[25] "Reformation is all the theme here," wrote Samuel Pitchforth from Nephi City, "and the Saints are rejoicing under the cry of wake up! WAKE UP!"[26]

Soon the Reformation had even taken root in California, as Cannon told Brigham Young in January 1857.

> Our hearts have been filled with joy in reading of the reformation that has been commenced at home, and the outpouring of the spirit on the people. We have felt its influence here, and I do feel thankful to my Heavenly Father that He poured his Spirit upon you to arouse us to a sense of our condition; for I can now realize that I was permitting my mind to be engrossed so much with business etc. that I was becoming careless. But I desire to repent,

---

[24] "Discourse by President Jedediah M. Grant, Tabernacle, 2 November 1856, *Deseret News,* 11 December 1856.

[25] McKnight to Cannon, 2 November 1856, *Western Standard,* 13 December 1856. The allusion to the dry bones is found in Ezekial 37.

[26] Pitchforth to Cannon, 10 January 1857, *Western Standard,* 28 February 1857.

> I desire to live my religion and enjoy the revelations of the Lord Jesus, and be fitted to magnify my priesthood and discharge the duties devolving upon me, that my garments may be spotless of the blood of all men. I can testify that since I have sought more diligently to do these things I have had more power and more of the Spirit than I have since my arrival in this place. The Saints here have all partaken of this feeling also, and we nearly all have been baptized. The meetings continue to increase in interest, and all feel to rejoice and praise the Lord for having placed a prophet in his church through whom the people may be warned . . .[27]

"At the rate I was progressing when this spirit of reformation found me," Cannon confessed to Young a month later, "I never could have entered into the Celestial Kingdom of our Father." He assured his leader, "Never in my life have I felt so much of this feeling as I have for the last few months; it is like a fire in my bones and I feel to prophesy unto this people continually and warn them of the judgments and calamities about to be poured upon the wicked."[28]

As Woodruff suggested, the Reformation was indeed a thorn for some of the less valiant Saints. Whatever its faults, this period of purging helped separate the wheat from the chaff among their numbers. Take the case of Gladden Bishop and his fellow dissenters. Bishop represented a relatively minor schism within Mormonism, but those who were looking forward to the dissolution of the LDS kingdom saw it as potentially the beginning of the end. Among these were the editors of San Francisco's *Golden Era,* J. MacDonough Foard and Rollin M. Daggett.

"Row among the Saints—Probable Result," *Golden Era,* 10 May 1857.

> The Saints are in trouble. The shield of holiness which Young preaches to his followers is an impenetrable bulwark against the hostile encroachments of the Gentiles, is pronounced by the same high authority impotent, as a protection to the "Chosen" when they turn their arms against themselves. Too monstrous even for the easy morals of the Mormons themselves, Polygamy has at length created a breach in their ranks, which bids fair to crumble to the earth the whole fabric of Mormonism, and thus spare the

[27] Cannon to Young, 3 January 1857, LDS Archives.

[28] Cannon to Young, 19 February 1857, LDS Archives. A handy way to access this and the pertinent portions of other letters between Cannon and Young related to the Reformation is Peterson, "'Like a Fire in My Bones,'" 107–15.

government the disagreeable duty of forcibly purging Utah of a community of knaves, traitors and fanatics.

Common sense should have taught Joe Smith, that with polygamy as a tenet of Mormonism, the religion would foster within itself the seeds of its ultimate destruction, and fall to pieces, if let alone, from sheer social rottenness. Polygamy has done its work, and Mormonism has reached the acme of numerical strength and prosperity, and henceforward cannot but decline in both; and in fifty years, the faith will be known as an ingenious trick of an ambitious Yankee, who lived in the early part of the nineteenth century, and who died with a city under his control of his own creation.

Although the Mormon papers are comparatively silent in regard to the Gladdenite disaffection, affairs in Salt Lake cannot be disguised. The Saints are in open rebellion, and Brigham Young, despairing of reconciling the factions, or restoring himself to authority, is making an effort to shake the dust from his feet and flee from this modern Sodom. We learn from private sources, that it is his intention to leave Salt Lake as soon as it is practicable, with a few followers, and settle on Vancouvre's Island. This was ascertained by a letter written by Young to the chief of the Utah Indians, requesting him to join the expedition with a few hundred of his tribe, and escort the party to the Pacific. The letter was translated to the chief by a Mormon residing with the tribe, but fearful of treachery, the Indian handed it for perusal to a member of a U.S. Surveying party, by whom it was copied.

With the hegira of Brigham, polygamy will receive a death blow in Utah, and with him will vanish the awe in which the Elders and Seventies are held by the people. Then the Saints will begin to think and dare to be skeptical, and Mormonism will go the way of all the creations of man.

"THE TWO PROPHETS," *WESTERN STANDARD*, 15 MAY 1857.

The Golden Era of the 10th inst., contains a remarkable prediction of the Prophets Foard and Daggett, which is too important to pass unnoticed. Read, ye Latter-day Saints, ponder, and weep. . . .

And this, then, is to be the fate of Mormonism. After all our toil, suffering, labor, self-denial and devotion to its cause; after indulging so long in delightful anticipations, and delusive visions of its future prosperity and magnificence, are all our hopes to be dashed to the ground? Are all our expectations doomed to disappointment? Alas! alas! that we should have been so deceived. How cruel of you Messrs. Era, so rudely to dash from our lips the delicious draught we were sipping. How heartless, to tear down from before our eyes the enchanting scene which inspired our enraptured souls, and leave to us only the naked, stern reality, and the bitterness of despair. If Mormonism had reached its "acme" and would consequently not be likely to deceive any more victims, why did you not suffer us to continue our vain and delusive, but glorious dreams of happiness and prosperity. We certainly did not expect such unkind treatment from our brethren of the cloth. But the fate of Mormonism is decided and it's no use we suppose to repine. All we can do now, is to calmly await the fulfillment of this prophecy, and then hide our heads in shame and mortification.

But some how or other we have got the impression that we have as good a right (and perhaps a little better) to prophecy as our cotemporaries, and also that our predictions are worthy of as much credit as theirs, and that their fulfilment is a little more probable. Had they used any argument, or given any reason for their statements, we would have met argument with argument, we would have answered reason with reason, but as they have simply prophesied, we shall content ourselves with placing prophecy against prophecy. You have predicted, Messrs. Editors, the complete overthrow and extinction of "Mormonism" in less than fifty years. We predict, with the utmost assurance, that in that time, it will have progressed and prospered faster than any other society or nation the world ever saw, that it will have spread over a great portion of the globe, that its principles will be believed in, and its founder honored as a prophet of God by the majority of the inhabitants of most enlightened nations, that it will be as firmly established as modern Christianity is at the present time, that its representatives and ministers will be as much respected and honored as the ministers of any earthly government now are, and that many of its believers and disciples will hold some of the most important and distinguished positions in the governments of the world. At the expiration of that period, we, if we live and if not, our children, can decide who was the true prophet.

"Common sense," say these sapient gentlemen, "should have taught Joe Smith, that with polygamy as a tenet of Mormonism, the religion would foster within itself the seeds of its ultimate destruction, and fall to pieces, if let alone, from sheer rottenness." "Common sense," is a very favorite term with people now-a-days, and more especially with those who possess the least share of it themselves. Every thick pated, shallow brained fool when he lacks argument, or can't think of any thing else to prate about, pompously talks about "common sense," which according to their practical definition of it, means, the ability to see through a solid stone wall, to perceive a sinister purpose and a malicious motive in every thing which everybody does, and to draw the most ridiculous, impossible and unphilosophical conclusions, from the most absurd and false premises.

True common sense always accompanies true philanthropy, it enables its possessors to discover existing evils and to devise their present remedy, and also teaches that important maxim, "mind your own business." If the editors of the Era possessed a little more of this excellent quality, they would find that they had plenty to occupy their attention at home, without interfering in the affairs of Utah. Let them devise some remedy for the evils which exist in our midst in San Francisco, and throughout the State. Talk about the social corruption of Utah, why there are thousands in your own enlightened, civilized, Christianized State, who are dying, not of figurative, but literal rottenness. The testimony of physicians will show that civilized society is actually "falling to pieces from sheer rottenness," that the very fountain and issue of life is corrupted, that the race is degenerating, and, unless something is done to check the onward progress of vice and crime, the period of human life will become more and more abbreviated, until children will be ushered into the world only to be carried almost immediately to their graves. Pull the beam out of your own eye, gentlemen, then, perhaps, you will find the fault was in yourselves instead of the Mormons. . . .

"The Saints are in trouble." What joyful news for the world. It is so refreshing in this era of peace and harmony to hear of the prospect of discord and bloodshed anywhere. We have been so long without anything like anarchy, confusion, bloodshed, murder or war to relieve the monotony of the dull round of existence, that it really is quite cheering to hear of the probability of a little stir in any quarter, especially when it is so far distant that we are not in any personal danger. But Utah is the only place we suppose where there is any trouble. San Francisco was never in trouble. Oh no. Kansas never had any trouble—of course not. There is no trouble between the North and South; no discord and confusion in our Legislatures; no quarrelings and contentions, disgraceful scenes, fights and murders in our Congressional halls; no prospect of war anywhere but in Utah.

Yes, according to to [*sic*] the Era, the fate of Utah and the Mormons is sealed—Brigham Young has fled to Vancouver's Island, all is uncertainty and confusion at Salt Lake, the power of the priesthood is broken, the influence and awe of the leaders are destroyed, the delusion is dispelled, polygamy is ended, the Saints can now think and act for themselves, (never having, of course, done so before) and they will soon be scattered over the face of the land as sheep without a shepherd, seeking their homes in the various States from which they came.

But we are not told how this wonderful intelligence was received, excepting, that they have learned from private sources, that Brigham Young wrote a letter to an Indian Chief requesting him to accompany him with a few hundred warriors, to the Pacific coast on his way to Vancouvers' Island, that this letter was translated to the Indians by a Mormon, then fell into the hands of a United States surveying party who copied it, and then, we presume, told some one else about it, who whispered it round, and in this extremely private way, we expect the Era has received its information. About as likely a story as some of those contained in the Arabian Nights, concerning the adventures of Sinbad the sailor.

As to Brigham Young going to Vancouver's Island, we presume that report has originated in his contemplated visit to the northern settlements in Utah. But it would be nothing surprising to us if he should visit quite a number of places besides Utah before he dies, for, as we have before said, Mormonism is destined to stand and increase and we calculate yet, to colonize, not only Vancouver's Island, but the whole world.[29]

This whole story is evidently hatched up by some ignorant "catch penny," or designing knave; but were it all true, it would no more prove Mormonism to be false, than the discords, contentions, and civil wars which existed among the Israelites when Moses was leading them from Egypt to the land of Canaan, would prove Moses to be an impostor, and that they were a deluded people, or a gang of thieves, marauders and cut-throats. "Common sense," if these gentlemen were possessed of any, as well as the experience of the last twenty-seven years, would teach them that such balderdash and croakings were utterly powerless to impede the progress of Mormonism.

The leader of the "Gladdenites," Gladden Bishop, had served as president of the Westfield, New York, branch of the LDS church but was subsequently involved in a series of heretical activities. At least twice, Bishop was tried before a High Council.[30] Apparently he was forgiven on both occasions after confessing the error of his ways. On 11 March 1842, Gladden was again tried and then disfellowshipped for "having received, written, and published certain 'revelations' and doctrines not consistent with the Doctrine and Covenants of the Church."[31] Following a stay among the followers of James Strang[32] in Wisconsin, Bishop found his way to Utah where, as recorded in Brigham Young's unfortunately provocative address, he and his anti-polygamy followers were threatened: "I say again, you Gladdenites, do not court persecution, or you will get more than you want, and it will come quicker than you want it. I say to you Bishops, do not allow them to preach in your wards. Who

[29] Notwithstanding Cannon's hope, Brigham Young's April–May 1857 trip to the Salmon River mission in what was then southern Oregon Territory was to be his last excursion outside Utah.

[30] The minutes of the second trial on 27 September 1835 appear in Smith, Jr., *History of the Church,* 2:284–85.

[31] Ibid, 4:550.

[32] Strang, a fascinating figure who attracted ten of the eleven living *Book of Mormon* witnesses to his camp, had himself crowned king over his followers and was later assassinated by same. An excellent biography is Van Noord's *King of Beaver Island: The Life and Assassination of James Jesse Strang.*

broke the roads to these valleys? Did this little nasty Smith, and his wife?[33]

This warning was immediately followed by President Young's recitation of a "dream" in which he met two apostate ruffians and used his bowie knife to "cut one of their throats from ear to ear, saying, 'Go to hell across lots.'"[34] Such sermons did little to discourage sensational claims of "blood atonement" at the hands of Brigham's Destroying Angels.

Three weeks later Young was more conciliatory and specifically assured Bishop and his followers that they were free to pursue their own religious practices so long as they did not "disturb the peace of their neighbors in any way, but by then Bishop had left Utah for good."[35] The anti-Mormon press was much more interested in the first speech than in the second. Bishop ended up in Little Sioux, Iowa, where he died sometime before 1878. His few remaining followers then gravitated toward the Reorganized Church of Jesus Christ of Latter Day Saints, now known as the Community of Christ.[36]

The other issue raised by the *Era* was that Brigham Young and a few of his followers were about to make an escape to the Northwest. In the midst of the Reformation, Brigham Young did leave Salt Lake on 24 April 1857 with 141 people "to rest their minds, to invigorate their bodies" and to examine the country on a three-hundred mile trek to the north.[37] As word of his departure reached the West Coast, several newspapers reported that the Mormon leader had fled Utah for Vancouver Island. Other observers were more perceptive: "Brigham Young (as heretofore reported) had gone North with his expedition, fully equipped, with three months' provisions, and a train of eighty wagons," a Mr. Wilkins wrote on 11 July 1857 from Placerville. "Various rumors

---

[33] Without providing his first name, Benjamin G. Ferris states that "Smith the Gladdenite" alarmed Young by making several converts from Mormonism in the winter of 1852–1853. See Ferris, *Utah and the Mormons,* 327.

[34] Young, "Joseph, a True Prophet—Apostates—Dream, etc.," 27 March 1853, *Journal of Discourses,* 1:83.

[35] Young, "Saints Subject to Temptation...Devils without Tabernacles," 17 April 1853, *Journal of Discourses,* 2:125–26.

[36] Shields, *Divergent Paths of the Restoration,* 29. For additional interesting information on Gladden Bishop, see Ferris, *Utah and the Mormons,* 326–34, and Saunders, "Francis Gladden Bishop and Gladdenism."

[37] *Deseret News,* 10 June 1857. For details on this odd venture, see Bigler, *Forgotten Kingdom,* 142–45.

were afloat as to its object. The most important and conclusive is that he has gone in search of a locality to defend the faithful against the expected troops from the East. He exhorts all the saints, if it comes to fight, to kill each his man, and his salvation is secured."[38]

Rather than going to Vancouver Island, Young and his company of 140 notables had journeyed to the Salmon River Lamanite Mission at Fort Limhi, today spelled "Lemhi," near present-day Salmon, Idaho. Young left Great Salt Lake City on 24 April 1857 and returned a little over a month later. Young later suggested this journey to the Saints' northernmost settlement was essentially a sight-seeing trip, but it appears that he was exploring the country for a possible northern exodus, should such an escape become necessary.[39]

Cannon understood that the trip was more than a mere excursion, but certainly not an escape from mutinous Saints: "I trust that your trip North has both refreshed and benefited yourself and the brethren who accompanied you," he wrote his prophet, "and that the nucleus of a flourishing and permanent settlement has been planted."[40]

To Cut the Throats of Apostates: Blood Atonement

There is no question that the Utah Reformation encouraged zealotry that led to manifestations of religious excess—what Beadle called the "black chapter in the annals of Utah."[41] Central to this excess was the doctrine of "blood atonement," which held that some sins were so serious they could only be atoned for through the blood of the guilty party. "The time is coming when justice will be laid to the line and righteousness to the plummet; when we shall take the old broad sword and ask, 'Are you for God?'" Brigham Young preached in early 1856, "and if you

[38] *New York Herald,* 14 August 1857, 3/2, copied from the *Sacramento Union.*

[39] Bigler, *Forgotten Kingdom,* 142–45; and Cooley, ed., *Diary of Brigham Young,* 2n2.

[40] Cannon to Young, 19 June 1857, LDS Archives. For Brigham Young's account of this journey, in which he rather disappointedly referred to the northern area as "a sterile, barren, desert country, filled with belts of rock and sand," see *Journal of Discourses,* 4:323–27. For brief accounts of the Salmon River mission, which ended in disaster, see Gottfredson, *History of Indian Depredations in Utah,* 89–100.

[41] Beadle, *Life in Utah,* 177. While virtually all of the anti-Mormon writers of the period focused heavily on the excesses of the Utah Reformation, Ann Eliza Young's firsthand experiences are of particular interest. See especially Chapter X of her *Wife No. 19.* (An alternative manner of accessing her story is through Wallace, *The Twenty-seventh Wife.*)

are not heartily on the Lord's side, you will be hewn down."[42] The prophet's provocative comments were surely calculated to frighten backsliders into conformity rather than to give Utah ruffians a license to kill, but this strange doctrine was open to interpretation: "Will you love that man or woman well enough to shed their blood? That is what Jesus meant. He never told a man or woman to love their enemies in their wickedness, never."[43]

Even more violent in his language was the firebrand of the Reformation, Jedediah Grant, second counselor to the prophet:

> I want the Gentiles to understand that we know all about their whoredoms and other abominations. If we have not invariably killed such corrupt scoundrels, those who will seek to corrupt and pollute our community, I swear to you that we mean to, and to accomplish more in a few hours, towards clearing the atmosphere, than all your grand and traverse juries can in a year.[44]

Faced with such strong language by their spiritual and temporal leaders, it would be surprising if some Mormons did not act on such counsel, particularly if they were already looking for justification to "cut off" an enemy. That some did so is inescapable, as revealed in the following editorial in the *Daily Bulletin*, one Cannon did not refute. Whether he decided to let it pass uncontested because he did not have access to enough of the facts, or because he did not feel he could defend such actions, is a matter of conjecture.

"A MORMON REFORMATION," *DAILY BULLETIN*, 28 AUGUST 1857.

During the past winter it became very evident to the church authorities at Salt Lake, that among the people they had collected together, there existed a wide spread spirit of disaffection, and many persons were making preparations to leave the Territory in the Spring, with the object of freeing

---

[42] Young, "The Necessity of the Saints Living Up to the Light which Has Been Given Them," 2 March 1856, *Journal of Discourses*, 3:226.

[43] Young, "To Know God...Atonement by the Shedding of Blood," 8 February 1857, Ibid, 4:219–20. One authority on the Reformation has speculated that "while Brigham probably entertained a theoretical notion of an ideal future theocratic society that would require individuals to atone for grievous sin, he clearly recognized that such a practice would be illegal according to existing statutes. Furthermore, it is doubtful that Young, characteristically patient and forgiving with regard to foibles of most church members, ever envisioned that such a penalty would be meted out to anyone excepting, perhaps, a hard-bitten apostate who had betrayed Mormonism's ideals." Peterson, "The Mormon Reformation of 1856–1857," 67, 84n69.

[44] *Deseret News*, 12 March 1856.

themselves from the priestly and tyrannical control to which they were there subjected. The leading men among the Mormons were naturally anxious to check the further spread of sentiments which weakened their authority, and to prevent an emigration, which, besides immediately diminishing the population, would do more than anything else to contradict the stories industriously circulated abroad by their missionaries, concerning the universal contentment and prosperity prevailing at Salt Lake.

After consultation as to what were the best means to adopt for this purpose, it was determined that the first thing necessary before any other steps were taken, was to "sift the people thoroughly," and find out how far such feelings had spread, and with what number they had to deal. To accomplish this and to give the movement a religious character, what they were pleased to style a "reformation" was determined on. A cry was accordingly raised that there was a great neglect of religious duties, that worldliness was on the increase and a stirring up of the people was necessary. Accordingly, two home missionaries were set to work in each ward of the city, and others for the settlements, to visit the people in their houses, catechise [*sic*] them and their families and see precisely how they stood towards the Church; and two elders were also set apart as teachers. Each of these missionaries was furnished with a list of questions, which it was his duty to put as a father confessor, though not restricted entirely to the formula, if others were necessary, to ensure full and satisfactory answers, which he was to report at head quarters.

Certain it is, that those who knew themselves to be obnoxious to the elders, believed they were especially pointed at, and the opinion was generally entertained that, when the black sheep were thus set apart, a general massacre would ensue in the settlements, and those who attempted to escape would be "attacked by the Indians," or otherwise cut off. This belief drew the disaffected more closely together, and gave them a strength and importance they would not otherwise have possessed. The atrocity of the measure also inspired a horror of the church leaders in the breasts of many others, which still further augmented the number of those who were anxious to get away. And this belief in the intention to massacre the apostates was not without foundation, but was based on conversations among leading men, which were overheard by persons they did not distrust, and on various sinister hints or expressions, carelessly let fall by those who expected to take part in the movement. As a single instance, the substance of one of these conversations may be given:

All through the Mormon settlement there exist secret religious societies known as the "Seventies."[45] The members are bound by oaths to

---

[45] The "Seventies" were, and still are, an office within the higher or Melchizedek priesthood. Apparently the editor of the *Bulletin* confused them with the semi-mythical Danites. Still, as Nels Anderson pointed out, the Saints "needed no vigilantes to keep order, for they had the priesthood, and the priesthood was so constituted that there was no problem of authority and control." See *Desert Saints*, 83.

> obey all orders of their superiors without question. A young man from one of the other settlements, a leader in one of these companies, was on a visit to his friends in Salt Lake, and a number of the neighbors had dropped in to see him. The conversation turned on the church troubles. One of his relatives, an old man high in authority in the church, expressed the hope "that the apostates might be enabled to get away from the valley in peace." The young man replied: "Why, you don't know anything about the Reformation that is going on. I have always been opposed to the shedding of blood, but I tell you we may as well make up our minds to it first as at last. We have got to cut them off, root and branch, and the 'Seventies' are the ones who will have to do it. The 'Seventies' are all 'minute men.'" It was then agreed by several of those present, that "it was better to cut the throats of apostates, than to let them go out into the world and injure the church." This conversation, which was reported to the disaffected, occurred about three weeks before the massacre at Springville, where three apostates intending to leave Salt [Lake] were killed, and two badly wounded. This occurrence, and the comments that were made upon it, convinced them that the work had indeed already begun . . .
>
> The missionaries, meanwhile, had been about their work, asking their questions, teaching, and making their reports to their masters. The information they obtained was far from satisfactory. A sad state of morale was exhibited, and before the catechizing was half through, over three thousand confessed adulterers were on the list of sinners, besides others guilty of smaller and larger offences. Worse, however, for them than this, they found that the heresies had been allowed to remain undisturbed so long, that the number of actual apostates, and those ready to become such, had grown so large, that the success of any measure against them, such as had been thought of, was very uncertain, and that concealment of the cause and object of so many deaths would be impossible, while they would be exposed to the detestation and hatred of the civilized world, and a strong desire excited for their own extermination. These considerations, and the fact that their intended victims seemed aware of the plotting, caused them to abandon the idea of a general massacre, and wait for time and opportunity to apply other remedies. It remains to be seen how long the "destroying angels" will remain inactive.

The three apostates were William R. Parrish and his two sons—William Beason (sometimes rendered as Benson or Beetson), 22, and Orrin, 18. Only Orrin escaped being murdered the evening prior to their intended departure to California. (A third person—Gardner

"Duff" Potter—was also killed, but he was probably acting as a decoy for the assailants.) Although no one was ever brought to justice for these killings, the local bishop and mayor were both charged, according to T. B. H. Stenhouse, with "deliberating in a council of elders against this man Parrish, and with having put the machinery to work that brought about his death." Stenhouse then remarked, "It is to be hoped that of all this they are innocent, for it is painful to see men who have every quality calculated to command respect dragged into such frightful positions."[46] Bancroft did not explore the incident in detail and B. H. Roberts made only a passing comment, observing that with respect to this and other such atrocities, "whatever was done in that kind was done on the responsibility of the guilty individuals. . . . The law of God has not lodged the right of capital punishment with the church. . . . What the law of God does not authorize the church to do, it has not authorized individuals to do."[47] Roberts' comments responded to numerous anti-Mormon publications (which often reported the facts incorrectly) alleging that this and similar murders were ordered by church leaders to assure the blood atonement of members or former members who had committed serious sin.

The belief in blood atonement resulted in the Territory of Utah providing defendants convicted of capital offenses with the options of execution by firing squad or beheading in addition to hanging, thereby maximizing the likelihood that their blood would be shed literally. Although the Church of Jesus Christ of Latter-day Saints has since abandoned this doctrine and the state no longer offers beheading, death by firing squad continues in Utah as a legal alternative to capital punishment via lethal injection.[48]

---

[46] Stenhouse, *The Rocky Mountain Saints,* 461–69.

[47] Roberts, *Comprehensive History,* 4:176n.

[48] For an overview of Utah's peculiar bloodletting option for capital punishment, see Gardner, "Mormonism and Capital Punishment." For the most extensive commentaries on this subject by LDS authorities, consult Penrose, *Blood Atonement as Taught by Leading Elders of the Church*; and Smith, *Blood Atonement and the Origin of Plural Marriage.* See also Field, "Mormon Blood Atonement," 262–67, along with West, "Notes and Comments," 643–47. Norman, "A Kinder, Gentler Mormonism," 10–14, discusses some of the modern implications of the doctrine. The last person to be executed in Utah by firing squad to date was John Taylor, who was executed by a police firing squad on 26 January 1996 for the 1989 rape and murder of an 11-year-old girl.

The Mormon Car Is *Still* Going Ahead

The Mormon Reformation provided the Saints with an opportunity to prove their devotion to their religion while separating the devout sheep from the apostate goats. Early in 1857, Young proudly discussed "the work of reform":

> It is rather warm for the wicked, and we expect when spring comes there will be a scattering out of such as cannot abide righteousness and the purifying influences of the Spirit of God. Let them go, it is better for us to have them leave now in times of peace than to have them fail us in times of trouble, when, peradventure, their treachery might cost some of us our lives. We hope the fire will continue to burn and grow hotter, until wickedness and iniquity shall be consumed, and truth triumph over the whole earth.[49]

By April 1857 Young's prediction began to come true as disaffected members and non-Mormons began to leave Utah in significant numbers, much to the delight of the prophet: "The way Lawyers, loafers, special pleaders, apostates, officials, and filth has been cast out is a caution to all sinners, that here they would be in the wrong place."[50] Wilford Woodruff reported that "since the opening spring has washed away with the tide of emigration some half hearted Saints, the moral elements feel considerably clearer."[51] A gleeful Hosea Stout commented in April 1857, "The fire of the reformation is burning many out who flee from the territory afraid for their lives. This is scriptural. 'The wicked flee when no man pursue,' and so with an apostate Mormon he always believes his life in danger and flees accordingly."[52]

Not all left freely, however, and various accusations—predominantly vague and typically unsubstantiated—only provided additional evidence of Young's supposed tyranny. Newspapers all across the country were only too happy to report such accusations as undisputed fact, and the California papers were particularly quick to pick up these stories since the golden state was often the immediate destination of those who fled Zion.

The LDS colonies in Carson Valley, then part of Utah Territory, became a center of conflict between Mormons and their foes. Originally

---

[49] Young to Cannon, 7 January 1857, *Western Standard*, 21 February 1857, 2.

[50] Young to Cannon, 4 July 1857, LDS Archives.

[51] Woodruff to Cannon, 4 June 1857, *Western Standard*, 17 July 1857, 3.

[52] Brooks, ed., *On the Mormon Frontier*, 2:625.

known as Mormon Station, Carson Valley's Genoa lay at the gateway to the Sierra Nevada on the northern route to California in present-day Nevada. According to Dale Morgan, "As an outpost of Zion, the settlement in Carson Valley from the beginning had a doubtful reputation. Saints might go there, but there was no organized mission; none had been 'called' to settle Carson Valley. Besides, that valley was too near the gold fields."[53] Understandably, it collected plenty of Gentiles and apostates and was often a hotbed of opposition to Brigham Young and his policies.

As early as 1852 efforts were made to annex Carson Valley to California, rather than to have it remain within the immense Utah Territory, then nearly twice the size of Texas. In January 1857 non-Mormon residents sent a formal petition to Congress toward that end. Among other arguments, the petitioners claimed that "the territorial laws are not administered with justice, but that those who are not Mormons, and not 'zealously affected' towards that faith, are subjected to gross persecutions, by which they are often impoverished, and that the will and fanaticism of the leading elders bear heavily upon the 'Gentile minority' in the Territory of Utah." They complained that the county's probate judge, Apostle Orson Hyde, had brought one of his plural wives, whom the non-Mormons regarded as "no better than the 'scarlet lady,'" to the valley. Congress denied the petition, but only because it was felt that California was already too large and that "some measure of wider scope is necessary to effect a radical cure of the moral and political pestilence which makes Utah the scandal of the American people."[54]

This petition from a Utah settlement, coupled with various rumors—many of which were magnified considerably by the time they had passed through Carson Valley—convinced many California newspapers not only of the tyranny purported to exist in Utah, but that the Mormon people were beginning to rebel against the autocratic rule of their leaders. The *Daily Herald* interpreted an innocuous phrase from the *Deseret News* commenting on his spring trip to the north as a sure sign that Brigham Young was in trouble. The *Deseret News* reported:

---

[53] Morgan, *The Humboldt*, 203.

[54] "Carson Valley, Utah—Annexation to State of California—and Eastern Boundary of California," 20 January 1857, House Report 116 (34–3).

. . . the departure of the Missionaries and of Gov. Young and his party, in addition to the common business movements and transactions of the citizens, made things appear lively and interesting to every beholder, showing conclusively that the Mormon car was still going ahead, and that the backing out of a few faint hearted, irresolute, and corrupt persons, had not impeded its progress in the least. The only difference is, the car runs a little faster after being divested of some of the useless rubbish that was aboard, and its speed will be still further increased after a few more passengers quietly step off.[55]

"Later from Salt Lake," *Daily Herald*, 14 June 1857.[56]

By the arrival of the Senator we have dates from Salt Lake City to April 29th. We condense the following summary of the news from the *Los Angeles Star*, copied by that paper from the *Deseret News*. . . .

[The *Herald* quoted several extracts from the *Deseret News*, mentioning the departure of a few dissidents and emphasizing the prevalent tranquillity in Salt Lake City and the continuing success of the church's missionary work.]

The above intelligence is copied, as stated above, from the *Deseret News*, in which anything calculated to prejudice Mormonism in the eyes of the world, would not, as we have heretofore explained, be admitted. It will be observed that is [*sic*] stated "that the Mormon car is *still* going ahead," an expression that would not be employed if there had recently been nothing to retard its progress. In fact, it is admited [*sic*] that it has met with obstacles, and these obstacles are stated to be "the backing out of a few faint and corrupt persons." This, coupled with the statement "that all is now peace and quietness," proves conclusively the correctness of the rumors of trouble in the Mormon camp, received *via* Carson Valley. There has been trouble, but it would seem that tranquillity now prevails.

"Late Intelligence from Utah," *Western Standard*, 19 June 1857.[57]

The steamer Senator arrived from the south on Saturday last with the Utah mail, containing dates to the 6th of May. This mail has been looked for by some of our city cotemporaries with some little anxiety, as it was confidently expected that news would be received confirmatory of the numerous rumors and stories which have been circulated concerning the dissensions at Great Salt Lake City, the flight of Governor Young and the complete overthrow and dispersion of the people. So confident was one of the leading weeklies that "the Great Utah drama" was drawing to a close, that one of the editors wrote quite an imaginative leader on its closing

[55] "News from Utah," *Western Standard*, 19 June 1857, 3.

[56] For a similar editorial, see *Daily Herald*, 23 May 1857.

[57] Reprinted in Cannon, *Writings from the "Western Standard,"* 449–51.

> scene a week or two ago, and concluded by stating that the internal troubles and difficulties which existed would, "of course, end in the disorganization of the Church in Utah, and its branches all over the world." How woefully such persons have been deceived in their expectations can be ascertained by a perusal of the news contained in our columns. Instead of troubles and difficulty, breaches of the peace, murder, rapine, etc., we are informed that everything moves on smoothly and tranquilly, the streets are filled with wagons and teams going and coming from the country loaded with marketable commodities, and all kinds of business are being carried on with the usual diligence and perseverance characteristic of the people. The plastering of the wall around the Temple Block was progressing rapidly, and large numbers of men were busily engaged in hauling and hewing stone for the Temple.
>
> The Herald of Sunday labors strongly, however, to prove by the editorial of the Deseret News that they have had considerable trouble in Utah, and that all the rumors received via Carson Valley were correct. The assurance given by the editor of the News "that the Mormon car is still going ahead," would not be employed, thinks the astute Herald, if there had recently been nothing to retard its progress! They are determined to have the people of Utah in trouble and difficulty anyhow; and because the News does not thus report matters there, the editor is accused of suppressing the truth and publishing only such items as will not prejudice "Mormonism" in the eyes of the world! If the columns of the News were only filled with details of crimes of every description committed daily and weekly in Great Salt Lake City—if its columns, instead of being devoted to the publication of truthful and heavenly principles, were lined with doctor's advertisements and notices of nostrums for the cure of foul and loathsome diseases engendered by corrupt practices, then probably all would be right in the estimation of these censors; the situation of Utah society would then be on a par with that which they set up as a model for the Latter-day Saints to copy after, and would be, in their opinion, comparatively unexceptionable.

If the press believed and reported that rank-and-file Mormons were in a state of rebellion, they were even more inclined to believe that the lives of both Mormon apostates and Gentiles of all persuasions were in jeopardy, no matter how eloquently George Q. Cannon argued to the contrary. None of these charges was new. Remy and Brenchley reported that during their visit to the Great Salt Lake in 1855, non-Mormons warned them that they were in constant danger and would be fortunate if they were allowed to leave with their lives. Their experience, however, was quite different:

> We have wandered about night and day in the most populous places, and in the most solitary defiles of the mountains, and we have never experienced the least molestation. Not one of the crimes which were related to us could sustain a close investigation. . . . While reserving to ourselves the right to relate without reserve the evil we were eyewitnesses to, we feel pleasure and yield to a sense of justice in declaring that the Mormons are not wicked nor immoral, as they have often been represented to our too credulous minds. . . . They are industrious, honest, sober, pious, and it is just to say, since we believe it to be the case, even chaste in their polygamic relations.[58]

Jacob Hamblin recalled at least one incident in which he was specifically directed by Brigham Young to help fleeing Gentiles get to California in safety:

> Late in the autumn of 1857, a company came along on their way to California. They brought a letter from President Brigham Young, directing me to see this company and their effects safely through to California. They were mostly merchants who had been doing business in Salt Lake City, and, anticipating difficulty between the people of Utah and the United States army, were fleeing to the Eastern States by way of California and the Isthmus of Panama. . . .
>
> I found a man who had been traveling alone, also in pursuit of the company, with a view of getting through with it to California.
>
> When I found him he was already in the hands of the Indians, and stripped of his clothing. They were making calculations to have a good time with him, as they expressed it, that is, they intended to take him to their camp and torture him.
>
> The stranger, seeing I had influence with the Indians, begged me to save his life, and said if I would do so he would serve me as long as he lived.
>
> I replied that I did not wish any reward for saving him.
>
> In answer to his inquiry, I informed him that I was a 'Mormon.'
>
> 'Well,' said he, "I am not a Mormon, but I wish you would save my life.'
>
> I assured him that it made no difference to me whether he was a 'Mormon' or not. I told the Indians to bring back his clothing, which they did, except his shoes, and I took him along with me to the company.[59]

Had the "Apostle in Buckskin" been at his home at the Mountain Meadows at the time of the infamous massacre, many believe he would have prevented it. John D. Lee, however, argued that Hamblin would

[58] Remy and Brenchley, *A Journey to Great-Salt-Lake City,* 1:216–217.

[59] Little, "Jacob Hamblin," in Nibley, *Three Mormon Classics,* 237–38. For more on this incident, see Corbett, *Jacob Hamblin, the Peacemaker,* 119, 121.

have been an eager participant in the murders and cited his involvement in the robbery of the stock of the next emigrant train to come through southern Utah.[60] In this exposé, published by his defense attorney after Lee was executed for his involvement in the massacre, Lee regaled his readers with tales of Mormon crimes against apostates and Gentiles. Nonetheless, in his journals, Lee recorded an incident in which a Mormon attempted unsuccessfully to defect to the U.S. Army yet later left Utah Territory for California—Danites and Avenging Angels notwithstanding.[61]

When Young's replacement, Gov. Alfred Cumming, offered military protection to all who "considered themselves unlawfully restrained of their liberties" at the conclusion of the Utah War, no more than 200 (including children) took him up on the offer.[62] Even then, the governor claimed the majority of those who left Utah admitted that their primary motive was not the tyranny of the Mormon priesthood but their own economic reversals.[63]

In the Spirit & Favor of God

As the Mormons consolidated their position in the Great Basin and apostates, dissenters, and backsliders seemed to be on the run, Brigham Young appeared more confident than ever that his dream of statehood would be realized. By July 1857, most of the fires of the Reformation had burned themselves out, but not without a price. While the efforts of Young, Grant and other Mormon leaders resulted in much needed spiritual reform, it was too often stimulated by irresponsible rhetoric that fed Puritanical fanaticism, sometimes leading to criminal behavior. The

[60] Lee, *Mormonism Unveiled,* 270–72 and 375–77.

[61] Cleland and Brooks, eds., *A Mormon Chronicle,* 162, 321n30.

[62] The number of apostates who chose to leave Utah is difficult to estimate, but several hundred dissenters abandoned Zion every year during the mid-1850s. For an excellent overview of the subject and an account of the military support provided these refugees, see Aird, "Escape from Zion: The United States Army Escort of Mormon Apostates, 1859."

[63] Furniss, *The Mormon Conflict,* 187. By Furniss' count, only eighty-nine adults left with the military escort. Although these statistics are often cited to show the lack of dissent in Utah, they may better reflect a lack of confidence in Governor Cumming's ability to protect those who accepted his offer. Judge Elias Smith contemptuously commented that "the Pretender" Cumming was "emphatically an individual of small calibre." Next day, Smith noted that apostates must "have lost their senses or they would not seek protection from such an impotent source." See Thomas, ed., *Elias Smith's Journal,* 25, 26 April 1858.

"unsolved" Parrish murders were among the best documented examples of such uninvestigated extralegal activity. Reports of such crimes understandably influenced President Buchanan in his decision to send federal troops to Utah Territory.

As the Reformation waned, Young's attention turned to a variety of ambitious enterprises, as he also focused on the looming prospect of a military confrontation with the U.S. government. In a newsy letter to Cannon written on Independence Day, the governor chatted about missionary efforts, Utah's new mail contract, the success of the "handcart missionaries" he had sent east that spring to prove that the system worked, and his plans to establish the Brigham Young Express and Carrying Company, also known as the Y.X. Company.

This last enterprise was a little-noted tribute to Young's far-ranging vision. As early as April 1856, he had announced plans to locate settlements from Kanesville, Iowa, to Carson Valley "with a view of establishing a daily express through the entire route."[64] After Hiram Kimball won the U.S. mail contract, Young dispatched men in spring 1857 to build an extensive network of stations and supply depots at prime trail locations such as Deer Creek, Devils Gate, and Wood River. He envisioned a freight and mail delivery service that might have controlled the economic life of much of the West. The government cancelled Kimball's contract on 10 June 1857, resulting in the loss of the $125,000 invested in the operation.[65] America had to wait five years until Russell, Majors & Waddell's Central Overland California & Pike's Peak Express Company implemented part of Young's vision as the legendary Pony Express.

Young ended his letter with the optimistic prediction that "we will be admitted into the Union as a *free* and Sovereign State." But statehood would elude the Mormons for another thirty-nine years.

BRIGHAM YOUNG TO GEORGE Q. CANNON, 4 JULY 1857,
BRIGHAM YOUNG COLLECTION, LDS ARCHIVES.

President's Office G.S.L. City U.T.
July 4 1857

Dear Bro Geo. Q. Cannon

Your letter of May 19th I received 1st inst, with mail from San Bar-

[64] Brigham Young to F. D. Richards, 11 April 1856, *Millennial Star*, 26 July 1856, 466.

[65] Furniss, *The Mormon Conflict*, 51–53.

nadino. When I gave California the "delightful Sobriquette" of "Hell" I felt that the people would soon be tired of it, but I could hardly think that they would so soon "kiss the rod" which has smitten them. The Lord has indeed fulfilled the promises made to His Elders; "that, as their day, their strength should be."

I heartily approve the course which you have taken to promote the spreading of the Gospel, and the upbuilding of the kingdom of God. That there are thousands of honest in heart who have never heard the gospel, the enclosed (copy) letter as one of the many which I receive, will bear ample testimony. I would advise you to send an Elder in accordance with the wish of Mr. Wright, as I believe he would be the instrument in Gods hand of doing great good in that section of country.

In relation to the emigration from California, do not advise persons to emigrate who would not serve God when they get here, as such are only a drag to those who are faithful, and the more we have of them the poorer we are. You had better, as I have no doubt you have done, and will do, tell the Saints what they may expect when they get here, that is, to hold themselves & all that they possess in readiness to forward the interests of God's kingdom, even to the laying down of their lives should the exigencies of time require them.

My nephews John Y. Green, Joseph W. Brigham H. & Seymour B. Young, with several other missionarys for the "States" "Canada" & "England" left here April 23, to cross the plains with Handcarts, from what I have heard I think that they made the trip to Florence N.T. [Nebraska Territory] within 40 days.

The Public works are progressing rapidly, there are between 3 and 400 hands employed working upon the Temple and 30 heavy teams rolling in the stones for that building. Many fine buildings are contemplated, some are in course of erection. Hands in gangs are improveing our Streets & Sidewalks. The trees about the City are increasing in size, and takeing our circumstances into consideration, we can in almost every thing (rottenness excepted) defy the whole world to produce an equal for this people. The Territory this season has taken an emetic and the way Lawyers, Loafers, Special pleaders, Apostates, Officials, and filth has been cast out, is a caution to all Sinners that here they would be in the wrong pew.

When the harvest of '56 has been gathered into our graneries, it was the opinion of those most competent to decide that bread would be scarce before another harvest, contrary to our expectation grain has never been so plentiful at this season of the year. And the crops from present appearances will be better this summer than has previously ever been the case. In Davis Co. grain cutting has already commenced. I learn from the Rio Virgin that the cotton, Indigo & other crops are looking well, and I hope the time is at hand when these with all other staple articles can be procured without sending our means out of the Territory and enriching the Gentiles.

That portion of the Saints who have had sufficient faith to withstand the scourgeings of the few past years are now living in the enjoyment of peace quietness prosperity and in the spirit & favor of God in their holy religion, and contrary to all former experience, is multiplying with their increase of blessings.

The Y.X. Co. is in a flourishing condition, we are sending out from 40 to 65 animals every mail, which we wish to increasingly continue until we get the road stocked with 1800 horses & mules. We have sent Elders A. O. Smoot & N. V. Jones with 80 men, to locate permanent stations in the Black Hills, which we design as resting places to those of our emigration who have not means to come through, or who may be too late as was the case last fall.[66] Of course we shall plentifully supply them with provisions &c.

The Eastern mail arrived 23 ult, conducted by F Little & E Hanks. The excitement concerning us seems rather on the increase in the States. I regret exceeding to hear of the death of Bro Parley, but the Lords not my will be done. The day will come when the kingdom of God will be triumphant, and none will dare to raise their hand against those who bear His name.

Bros G.A. Smith, J.M. Bernhisel & T.O. Angel arrived the 29 of May, passing by mail. The Doctor think[s] that although there is much enmity to us, in the minds of the people, that by being quiet a while we will be admitted in to Union as a *free* & Sovereign State.

Brigham Young

---

[66] This station, located at Deer Creek, near today's Casper, Wyoming, was abandoned during the Utah War. The last comment reveals that Young was trying to correct the conditions that led to the handcart disaster.

Chapter 8

"The Kingdom That Daniel Saw"

Autocracy, Theocracy, and Theo-Democracy in Deseret

Although polygamy was the issue that captured the popular imagination in the newspapers of the day, an even larger problem—particularly among those who either held or sought political power—was the perceived autocracy of Brigham Young and the theocratic government the Saints so obviously favored. Americans saw polygamy as "foreign" in nature, and they held any political structure that appeared to be at odds with republican values and democratic ideals highly suspect. Not only were many of the Mormon converts foreigners, but their entire way of life was considered alien to the American experience. This only added to the suspicion and profound discomfort felt by the Mormons' neighbors in the West.

A Kingdom That Will Sway the Sceptre of Power

A fundamental principle of the American Republic was and is the separation of church and state. To what extent did such a separation exist among the Mormons and what were the resulting implications for those not of their faith? One of the earliest observers of Deseret, Capt. Howard Stansbury, insisted that "justice was equitably administered alike to 'saint' and 'gentile.'" Nevertheless, he noted that given the lack of separation between church and state in early Utah it would be impossible to separate the "spiritual administration of the church" from the temporal government: "This intimate connection of church and state seems to pervade every thing that is done. The supreme power in both being lodged in the hands of the same individuals, it is difficult to separate their two official characters, and to determine whether in any one instance they act as spiritual or merely temporal officers."[1]

Mormons made a private distinction between the church as a religious entity (governed by the priesthood) and the political kingdom of God (directed by the Council of Fifty), so some apologists argued strenuously that a clear separation between church and state existed. This in spite of the fact that the president of the church (whether Joseph Smith, Brigham Young, or John Taylor) directed the activities of both entities, and the leaders of one group closely matched the men who led the other.[2] Arguably, the Mormon concept of separation of powers had been skewered from the time of the Nauvoo charter, which had granted the Saints extraordinarily sweeping powers.[3]

Thomas O'Dea examined the church/state issue relative to the Latter-day Saints from the perspective of sociology. He argued that

> the Mormons had not thought out the implications of their basic position with regard to relations between church and state. They had, from the start, accepted the republican convictions and prejudices of their milieu, while at the same time they acted in terms of the solidarity of the new, total, religious-secular community they had created . . . The fact is that the Mormons never worked out consistently the political implications of their religious philosophy. Its theocratic and separatist aspects were counterbalanced by democratic and patriotic motives which were equally genuine and equally well grounded in Mormon doctrine.[4]

David L. Bigler, on the other hand, suggests that the Saints understood the implications of how the church and the state were to interact perfectly—the entire purpose of manmade government was to serve the interests of the Church of Jesus Christ:

> Conceived in Nauvoo and established by Brigham Young and his followers in the Great Basin, the Kingdom of God was the literal fulfillment of Old Testament prophecy. It was the stone which the Prophet Daniel saw cut out of the mountain without hands that would break in pieces and consume all other kingdoms and stand forever. [Dan. 2:28-45.] It was an irresistible

---

[1] Stansbury, *Exploration and Survey*, 130–31.

[2] See Hansen, *Quest for Empire*, and Bigler, *Forgotten Kingdom*.

[3] Avery, *From Mission to Madness*, 9.

[4] O'Dea, *The Mormons*, 99, 171. For insight into LDS perspectives, as well as Cannon's feelings on this subject—particularly as they developed in later years—see Cook, "George Q. Cannon's Views on Church and State."

> movement that would fill the whole earth as a condition of the Lord's coming again. With a zeal unknown to most faiths today, those who carried its banner created a society that, in its original form, resembled a determined effort to create so perfectly the conditions on which Christ's coming depended that the Lord would have no choice but to make His appearance.[5]

Given the Saints' unique understanding of the relationship between church and state, it is little wonder that disestablishment-minded outsiders perceived the Mormons as traitors to fundamental American ideals.[6] Although the Saints insisted they were loyal Americans, even they sometimes described their activities as treasonable, at least in the eyes of the world. At the 1852 dedication of Salt Lake's "New Tabernacle"— built in only four months "in the most inclement season of the year" to provide "a commodious place" to worship "without the fear of being driven from our seats by wet and cold, or of standing exposed to the weather"—Brigham Young proclaimed:

> The Lord God Almighty has set up a kingdom that will sway the sceptre of power and authority over all the kingdoms of the world, and will never be destroyed, it is the kingdom that Daniel saw and wrote of. It may be considered treason to say that the kingdom which that Prophet foretold is actually set up; that we cannot help, but we know it is so, and call upon the nations to believe our testimony. The kingdom will continue to increase, to grow, to spread and prosper more and more. Every time its enemies undertake to overthrow it, it will become more extensive and powerful; instead of its decreasing, it will continue to increase, it will spread the more, become more wonderful and conspicuous to the nations, until it fills the whole earth. If such is your wish, identify your own individual interest in it, and tie yourselves thereto by every means in your power. Let every man and every woman do this, and then be willing to make every sacrifice the Lord may require; and when they have bound up their affections, time, and talents, with all they have, to the interest of the kingdom, then have they gained the victory, and their work is complete, so far as they understand.[7]

The "kingdom" was the *political* Kingdom of God, not simply the church *per se.* Joseph Smith in 1844 organized "The Kingdom of God and His Laws with the Keys and Power[s] thereof and Judgment in the

[5] Bigler, *Forgotten Kingdom,* 363. See also Daniel 2.

[6] For a helpful summary of the legal evolution of the establishment clause in the First Amendment, see Gordon, *The Mormon Question,* 6–8, 77–81.

[7] "A Discourse Delivered by President Brigham Young at the Opening of the New Tabernacle, Great Salt Lake City, April 6, 1852," *Journal of Discourses,* 1:198.

Hands of His Servants, Ahman Christ" to usher in the millennial reign of Christ. Also known as the Council of Fifty, its ultimate objective was to rule the entire earth under the direction of Jesus Christ. Historian D. Michael Quinn has insisted that "the Council was not a challenge to the existing system of law and government, but functioned in roles familiar to American political science: special interest lobby, caucus, local political machine, and private organization governed by parliamentary procedures."[8] Because those procedures assured freedom of speech and the right to dissent, Andrew F. Ehat has argued that the Council was a "theo-democratic republican form of government and not a theocratic tyranny."[9] Nonetheless, as events progressed, the Kingdom was perceived by the majority of anti-Mormon leaders as an even greater threat to Jacksonian pluralism and American democratic ideals than polygamy or economic communitarianism and thus became the primary impetus for anti-Mormon persecution through the nineteenth century.[10]

Governor Lilburn Boggs' retrospective rationale for his infamous "extermination order,"[11] which effectively drove the Saints from Missouri in 1838 and 1839, was that "they had instituted among themselves a government of their own, independent of and in opposition to the government of this State."[12] Though he can hardly be regarded as a credible witness—notwithstanding his earlier roles as assistant president of the church and major general of the Nauvoo Legion—John C. Bennett argued as early as 1842 for the "existence of a vast and deep-laid scheme, upon [the Mormons'] part, for conquering the states of Ohio, Indiana, Illinois, Iowa, and Missouri, and of erecting upon the ruin of their present governments a despotic military and religious empire, the

---

[8] Quinn, "The Council of Fifty and Its Members, 1844 to 1945," 164. For a discussion of the various names by which the Council was known, see 167n11.

[9] Ehat, "'It Seems Like Heaven Began on Earth,'" 263.

[10] See Lyman, *Political Deliverance*, and Hansen, *Quest for Empire*.

[11] "Your orders are, therefore, to hasten your operations with all possible speed. The Mormons must be treated as enemies, and must be exterminated or driven from the State if necessary for the public peace—their outrages are beyond all description. If you can increase your force, you are authorized to do so to any extent you may consider necessary." Missouri General Assembly, *Document Containing the Correspondence, Orders, &c., in relation to the disturbances with the Mormons*, 61. See also Smith, Jr., *History of the Church*, 3:175, for a slightly different version.

[12] Quoted in Bennett, *The History of the Saints*, 308. This directive was not officially rescinded until Christopher S. Bond's Executive Order of 25 June 1976, in which the governor of Missouri also extended the state's apologies to the Mormon people.

head of which, as emperor and pope, was to be Joseph Smith."[13] Similarly, Thomas B. Marsh, at that time still the senior Mormon apostle, claimed in an affidavit that "The plan of said Smith, the prophet, is to take this State, and he professes to his people to intend taking the United States, and ultimately the whole world."[14] Even the generally sympathetic William Chandless opined in 1857 that the religion was "the worst of tyranny, since it is an oligarchy working under and deadening the forms of a democracy. I think this the very worst feature of Mormonism."[15] Later, J. H. Beadle acknowledged that "it is not the social, immoral, or polygamic features that so chiefly concern us, but the hostile, the treasonable and the mutinous."[16]

The very serious efforts to bring about a new political kingdom notwithstanding, the Mormons were not above having a little fun flirting with the idea of treason. This song, composed with tongue firmly planted in cheek by one of their popular poets, the *original* James Bond, captured these sentiments in 1852:

> For Mormons always vote one way
> And soon a voice they'll get,
> And unison will bless the day
> That shines on Deseret.
> But never mention what we've said
> For this particular reason,
> That if you do, we're good as dead,
> Because you know, IT'S TREASON![17]

YOUNG AND HIS CUT-THROAT MINIONS

The question of "Mormon disloyalty and tyranny" is a difficult one, even today. Did President Buchanan have sufficient justification for sending federal troops to quell what was widely perceived as a general rebellion against the U.S. government? Although the Mormons claimed

---

13 Ibid., 6.

14 Missouri General Assembly, *Document Containing the Correspondence, Orders, &c., in relation to the disturbances with the Mormons,* 58; and Thomas Marsh, affidavit, 24 October 1838, cited in LeSueur, *The 1838 Mormon War in Missouri,* 136.

15 Chandless, *A Visit to Salt Lake,* 178.

16 Beadle, *Life in Utah,* 401.

17 *Deseret News,* 21 November 1852.

fierce loyalty to their country (and more particularly to its "divinely inspired" constitution), they perceived no contradiction in roundly criticizing the "damned rascals" that had either been appointed or elected to office. Consider these comments by Jedediah M. Grant:

> They will threaten us with the U.S. troops! Why your impudence and ignorance would bring a blush to the cheeks of the veriest camp follower among them. We ask no odds of you, you rotten carcasses, and I am not going to bow one hair's breadth to your influence. I would rather be cut into inch pieces than succumb one particle to such filthiness. . . .
>
> What is it that maddens the devils? Simply that we are determined to do right, and to set at defiance wickedness and wicked men, and to send them to hell across lots, as quick as we can.
>
> I do not ask any odds of them myself, I never have. If they behave themselves as white men ought to behave, we will treat them as such.
>
> The armies of our nation will have plenty to do without attending to us; they will need us to help them. Yes, instead of bringing their armies to fight the people in Utah, they will need Utah's armies to help them. They are threatening war in Kansas on the slavery question, and the General Government has already been called upon to send troops there. Well, all I have to say on that matter is, "Success to both parties."...
>
> To send men here as spies to watch us! Curse the spies and those who send them, and all who sustain the system of whorehouses and the debauchery of the innocent and unsuspecting, and all who threaten that the United States are going to drive and kill the "Mormons"...
>
> Have we been disloyal to our country? Have we, in one instance, violated her institutions? No. We are lawful and loyal citizens of the government of the United States, and a few poor, miserable, pusilanimous [*sic*], rotten, stinking rebels, come here and threaten us with the armies of the United States. We wish all such characters to understand that, if the generals and armies and those who wish to send them, are as corrupt as those who threaten us, and as vile as most of those heretofore sent here, we defy them, and the sooner we come in contact with them the better.[18]

In his journal, Wilford Woodruff commented that in the above speech, President Grant "rained down pitchforks and forked lightening figuratively speaking upon the Gentiles who were working wickedness upon this people and defiling the females. He spoke very plain and pointed."[19]

---

[18] "Exposing Wickedness... Aside in the Courts," 2 March 1856, *Journal of Discourses,* 3:235.

[19] *Wilford Woodruff's Journal,* 72.

The Mormons saw the U.S. constitution as greater than the government of the United States, and because of their devotion to that document, they saw themselves as more loyal and patriotic to the truest principles of America than anyone else.[20] That was not how others saw them. While the editors of the *Golden Era* were out of step with most of their journalistic colleagues in suggesting that statehood for Utah was justifiable, they were troubled by their perception that Brigham Young was a corrupt despot, ruling over his minions through a network of blood-atoning spies.

"THE NEW STATE OF DESERET," *GOLDEN ERA*, 18 MAY 1856.

The latest advices from Salt Lake bring the intelligence of the adoption of a State Constitution by the citizens of Utah, which was to have been submitted to the people for approval on the 7th of April. The delegates, assembled from all portions of the territory for the purpose of framing the instrument, signed it without an exception, and the greatest harmony prevailed throughout the sitting of the convention. Hon. Geo. A. Smith and Hon. John Taylor, editor of the *Mormon*, were chosen to proceed to Washington and lay the Constitution before Congress, and urge the immediate admission of Deseret into the Union.

The unexpected haste with which all this has been accomplished, is no doubt a wise stroke of policy of the wily Brigham. As Governor of Utah, he holds the office of temporal ruler by appointment, and is at any time subject to removal as the Governor of the State of Deseret; however, with the provisions relating to the office acknowledged by its Constitution, he can remain in power as long as the people see proper to entrust it to his keeping. It is necessary to Mormonism in its present stage of its existence, if not in the future, that the Governor of Utah, whether a State or Territory, should be, if not the head of the Church, at least an influential member of it; and it is neither savory to the ambitious Brigham, nor to the Mormon leaders themselves, to be at the mercy of the Administration. Were any one but a Mormon now Governor of Utah, with sufficient power to enforce the decrees of justice and maintain free religious tolerance, it is not too much to say that at least one-third of the professors of the Mormon faith, now watched by the spies of the Church, and threatened at the least exhibition of disaffection with assassination, would renounce the religion which fear alone holds them unwilling converts to, and hurl defiance to Young and his

[20] Nonetheless, it is fascinating to note that in 1844, Joseph Smith directed the Council of Fifty to amend the United States' Constitution to become the "voice of Jehovah." See Ehat, "'It Seems Like Heaven Began on Earth,'" 259–60.

cut-throat minions. We know that a man of property dare not leave the Territory; and if he does, it is at the sacrifice of all he owns. To guard against the contingency of the appointment of a governor over Utah, adverse to Mormonism, is the main secret of the present movement. However, this has nothing to [do] with the right of the admission of Deseret into the Union as a State. Its population is sufficient, and if its Constitution be not found objectionable, Congress cannot but grant its request.

The provisions of the Constitution are similar to those of most of the States. In fact, its framers seem to have drawn it up with the view of securing its immediate sanction by Congress and the ends [?] of its adoption. The gubernatorial term of office is four years; In relation to religious tolerance, we find the following:

> Sec. 3. All men shall have a natural and inalienable right to worship God according to the dictates of their own consciences; and the General Assembly shall make no law respecting an establishment of religion, or prohibiting the free exercise thereof, or to disturb any person in his religious worship or sentiments, and all persons demeaning themselves peaceably, as good members of this State, shall be equally under the protection of the laws; and no subordination or preference of any one sect or denomination to another shall ever be established by law, nor shall any religious test be ever required for any office or trust under this Constitution.

Thus the Constitution leaves the matter of polygamy unsettled. If Deseret is to be admitted into the Union—and the Constitution urges nothing against it—this obnoxious tenet of the Mormon faith will be left to the decision of the Supreme Court of the United States, for in it are involved principles of fundamental morality too sacred to pass unheeded, and rights of property which will sooner or later require for adjudication a direct opinion from the highest sources in regard to the validity of this religious bigamy. Here is the rock upon which this cherished tenet will split. The children of but the first wife will be considered legitimate in the eyes of the law, and the fruits of subsequent marriages during her life, will not be accorded equal rights with the children of the first as heirs to property. The fear of legal disinheritance may yet compel our Mormon friends to do what morality and decency in vain might plead for. We shall see.

"Despotism in Utah," *Western Standard*, 31 May 1856.[21]

It is a mystery to us, how men, occupying prominent positions as journalists, and who profess to be well posted up in the history of the times, can give utterance to the idea, which we occasionally see advanced, that the people of Utah are completely bound, hand and foot, body and soul, under a tyrannical despotism, without the power to extricate themselves from that

[21] Reprinted in Cannon, *Writings from the "Western Standard,"* 120–23.

position, by leaving the territory, or doing anything else that is the inalienable right of freemen to do, unless it meets the mind of their superiors in the Church. To assert, as a weekly paper of this city (the *Golden Era*) lately has done, that the professors of the "Mormon" faith are under the constant surveillance of the spies of the Church, or, that the threat of assassination deters them from exhibiting the disaffection which they feel, and prevents them from hurling defiance at "Young and his cut-throats minions," is simply preposterous, and totally at variance with everything reliable that has been written or told about the people. What men can expect to gain by perpetrating and publishing such malignant perversions, that every one, who is in the least informed on these subjects, must know to be such, we cannot divine. Such reckless fabrications betray a malicious and contemptible spirit, as their originators must be aware that they are utterly false. Who does not know that there are hundreds of men leaving Great Salt Lake country, every season, for the east and the west? And if there are any there who wish to leave, they are as much at liberty to do so as they would be were they in California; and yet this paper says that one-third, at least, of the professors of the "Mormon" faith would, if they did not have the fear of assassination before their eyes, renounce the religion to which they are held unwilling converts. A few weeks ago it was stated, in this paper to which we allude, that nine-tenths of the converts to "Mormonism" were knaves, etc.; now, it appears, the editors have had more recent intelligence, for, by some means, not set forth by them, "one-third, at least, of the Mormons" have become suddenly transformed, in their estimation, from knaves to honest men, and are now only kept from renouncing "Mormonism" through the fear of the omnipresent spies of the Church. A few weeks ago the "Mormons" were, with scarcely an exception, if we may believe them, a pack of cut-throats, subsisting by plunder, etc.; but now, they have suddenly ascertained that the minions of Governor Young are the only cut-throats, and have obtained information through which they know that there are men of property in Utah who dare not, on the peril of their lives, or the sacrifice of all they own, leave the Territory. We cannot conjecture how these different statements of theirs can be reconciled, or how they can escape the charge of falsification; unless, indeed, they consider they are licensed to say everything bad about the "Mormons" they possibly can, without the slightest regard to facts or testimony. To draw the long bow, and to deal as largely in romance as they evidently do, when they attempt to write about "Mormonism" requires a good memory,—if not gifted with that necessary qualification, a reperusal of their previous articles is necessary, or they will inevitably lose their credit for consistency among reflecting and discerning men.

We are aware that, in noticing these foolish and untruthful statements, we are bestowing more attention on them than they deserve; but emanating from the quarter whence they do—from a paper professing to be the leading weekly in the State—they demand exposure. With the "Mormons," themselves, such statements pass unheeded,—even those who have never lived among the people have sufficient penetration to understand, at a glance, the spirit by which they are dictated; and all, who bestow any reflection on the subject, must perceive that such a state of things cannot possibly exist. The Territory of Utah is not walled in, nor completely secluded from outside influences and intercourse. Since the first discovery of the gold in California, there has been a constant stream of emigrants passing through Utah to this State, and if any portion of its inhabitants were disposed to leave, they have had abundant opportunities of doing so. These gentlemen state that they *know* a man of property dare not leave this Territory; will they cite us to the instance where they have been unlawfully detained there? Were they fully conversant with "Mormonism," they would know, that, instead of measures being taken to prevent the disaffected, whether men of property or otherwise, from leaving Utah, the people have always felt that the community has been benefited by their absence, and would, therefore, never be guilty of interposing force to deter them. We think that it would be a good plan for writers, who are striving so zealously to give the people all the knowledge they can about the despotism under which the "Mormons" are living, to give their readers, at the same time, a little insight into the secret of the "Mormons'" unity, and their freedom from litigation, broils and bloodshed. It is universally conceded that, with all their "corruption" and "fanaticism," they enjoy these blessings to an unparalleled extent; and we conceive that it would be a work of philanthropy to make known the causes which produce these results. Will not some individual, out of the numbers who profess to know all about the "Mormons," step forward and do this? The State of California is noted for the number of its *pious, self-sacrificing and Christian* ministers, who are devoting the whole of their time in endeavoring to suppress vice, inculcate virtue and institute a better order of things; but it is remarkable that, with all their labors, and the vast outlay of money there is made to carry out their plans, they are immeasurably behind the "Mormons" in accomplishing the objects to which they profess they are devoting their lives. Their labors have been useless and unfelt.

Comparisons are proverbially odious; but we can scarcely refrain from instituting a comparison between the situation of the two people—the people of California and the people of Utah. The land of one filled with bloodshed, crime and violence; while the other is enjoying a complete immunity from these evils, and order and harmony everywhere visible in all their proceedings. Probably some of these writers on "Mormonism and the Mormons," can explain the cause of this palpable difference. If despotism produces the good order and harmony witnessed among the "Mormons," we have an idea that it would not be a bad move to engraft a sufficient amount of it into our republican institutions, in this country, to produce similar results. If men would but reflect, there would be no need for lengthy argument to prove to them that these absurd and ridiculous statements, made about the "Mormons," are false. Can an evil tree bring forth good fruit? Will a pure stream proceed from an impure fountain? Is it possible that Utah, if her inhabitants were as wicked, and her government as despotic, as they are represented to be, would have less crime and bloodshed committed within her borders, from the time of her settlement up to the present, than there has been frequently committed in one week in this State? We leave it for just and virtuous men to decide.

Our Duty to Crush You Out!

The inclusion of Section 3 in the proposed constitution of the State of Deseret was a particularly shrewd move by the Mormons. While acknowledging that "social and religious unity led to the establishment of a theo-democracy in which Church and State fused in common administration," Gustive Larson points to this provision as evidence that the Saints were seriously committed to the protection of the "traditional rights of religious worship."[22] Still, there can be little doubt that the primary rationale behind this language was—as suspected by the *Golden Era*—the protection of polygamy.

In his response to the *Era,* Cannon quoted scripture: "By their fruits ye shall know them."[23] If conditions were so bad in Utah, he reasoned, why was there so much more crime elsewhere? This was a favorite argument of Cannon's—that the "crimes" of Mormonism could hardly be compared with the crimes of the "enlightened" Gentile world. One writer perceptively responded to this note of self-righteousness: "It is a prime principle in their creed that all mankind but themselves are on the swift road to ruin, and they are never so well pleased as in listening to statements in regard to 'the great increase of crime and immorality in the States.'"[24] Many explanations—beyond relative commitments to religious principles—can be posited when comparing crime in San Fran-

[22] Larson, *Prelude to the Kingdom,* 80.

[23] This idea is expressed not only twice in the Bible, Matt. 7:17 & Luke 6:43, but also in *The Book of Mormon,* 3 Nephi 14:20 and Moroni 7:5.

[24] Beadle, *Life in Utah,* 307.

cisco to crime in Utah. Large numbers of single young males, representing numerous cultures and civilizations and living in relative anonymity, contributed to an especially fertile breeding ground for crime on the West Coast.

Nonetheless, the editors of most California newspapers seemed to prefer the crime and disorder of a free society like San Francisco to the theocratic dictatorship they saw in Utah. As Mormon settlements expanded, the *Golden Era* became increasingly anxious. It was bad enough that the Mormons had gained a foothold in San Bernardino, but their missionaries seemed to be everywhere and there was no end in sight to the supply of foreign converts.

"UTAH—MORMON IMMIGRATION," *GOLDEN ERA*, 6 SEPTEMBER 1856.

We are surprised that California journals do not advert more frequently to the subject of the rapidly increasing immigration of Mormons to the fertile valleys of Utah and the lower counties of California. Many of our Atlantic contemporaries, though far less liable to the baneful influence growing out of the peculiar social predilections of the Mormons, give to the subject a much greater importance than do our own newspapers. While Great Salt Lake City is the focus of this pernicious "ism," it is apparent to all who watch its progress, that it is gradually radiating towards the shores of the Pacific. In San Bernardino the faith of the "martyred Smith" has its thousands of zealous converts, while in many of the most central agricultural districts of the States, we hear of numerous settlements of this sect, whose dogmas are so glaringly subversive of good society and domestic purity. We are not among those who would persecute and stigmatize these unfortunate and deluded people, so long as they confine themselves within the limits of Utah, but when we find them sending forth agents to make proselytes in California, we deem it a duty we owe society to lend our aid in "crushing out" an evil so portentous to the future welfare of our people and the fair fame of our State.

The rapidly increasing immigration from Europe and the Eastern States to Utah, is to us a forerunner of internal difficulties almost as perplexing, and perhaps more lasting, than those which have grown out of the question of slavery. Already has Utah asked for admission into the Union as a sovereign State, with the implied guarantee to her people of being allowed to worship God in their own peculiar way—with a code of morals forming a sad exception to those recognized by other States.

In our opinion Congress has remained too long silent upon the anomalous condition of affairs in Utah—a silence which has doubtless led the

Mormons to believe that the Government intends no interference with them for the foul stain which their doctrines of polygamy would forever place upon a territory naturally susceptible of being made one of the most prosperous in the Union. Too long have they been left quietly alone to augment their numbers and train a vast rising generation in the vilest precepts, and amid social spectacles more degrading than those which characterise the harems of the East. If Utah come into the Union as a State, let it be with the understanding that all traces of polygamy and other demoralizing customs now in vogue there, be totally obliterated.

"GOLDEN ERA—BANEFUL INFLUENCES," *WESTERN STANDARD,* 13 SEPTEMBER 1856.[25]

The silence of the California journals on the subject of the rapidly increasing immigration of the "Mormons" to the fertile valleys of Utah and the lower counties of California, has become a matter of so much concern to our neighbors of the *Golden Era,* that they have taken it upon themselves to read their *confreres* a lecture on the subject, stirring them up to their duties, and setting up for their example the conduct of their Atlantic contemporaries, who, "though far less liable to the baneful influences growing out of the social predilections of the Mormons," advert frequently to the subject. We really hope that the exhortation of the *Era,* will have due weight with California journalists, and that they, as well as the editors of the *Era,* will, for the future, keep the subject before the people. It is an exhaustless theme—one that can be dwelt upon without becoming stale or threadbare. These gentlemen seem to have just awakened to a sense of the danger which they are in. "Mormonism," though acknowledging Great Salt Lake City as its grand centre, is still spreading on the right and left, and, in the language of the *Era,* "it is apparent to all who watch its progress, that it is gradually radiating towards the shores of the Pacific." They are afraid that it will overwhelm them,—that it will accomplish all that its adherents have foretold it should. But now, as the danger is so imminent, arises the question as to the best mode to be adopted to stop its farther progress. What shall be the plan? The editors of the *Golden Era* have chosen, and shamelessly made public, the means they have determined to adopt. . . .

Oh, no! we would not be guilty of persecuting and stigmatizing you, unfortunate and deluded "Mormons"—we would not discharge the duty, which, in our opinion, we owe to society, by *crushing you out,* so long as you confine yourselves within the limits of Utah; but, if you ever put your foot outside of the boundaries of your territory, if you ever are guilty of sending forth agents to make proselytes in California, if you ever attempt to

[25] Reprinted in Cannon, *Writings from the "Western Standard,"* 200–204.

extend your peculiar predilections over here, *then* we shall deem it our duty to *crush you out!* If there is any force in language, this is the only inference that can be drawn. . . . To prove to their readers that they really wish this idea to be conveyed, they express surprise that their contemporaries do not persecute, stigmatize and attempt to crush out the "Mormons" more than they do; and, not content with expressing surprise at this, they endeavor to incite them to adopt this course; the spirit of their article recommending it as the only course to be pursued to deliver "the fair fame of our State" from the blighting and baneful influences of "Mormonism." Whether their persecution will have the effect to crush us out or not, time will prove; we, however, have no fears about the result. The *Golden Era* and its editors do not fire heavy enough shot either to crush out or prevent "Mormonism" from radiating to the Pacific, and from the borders of the Pacific westward, until it will circumscribe the earth, and imbue men of every nation with its peculiar social predilections.

"Already has Utah" say they, "presented herself for admission into the Union as a sovereign State, with a constitution in which is the implied guarantee to her people of being permitted to worship God in their own peculiar way—with a code of morals forming a *sad* exception to those recognized by other States;" Utah, therefore, must be attended to. Congress has been too long silent on the subject. The "Mormons" have been left too long alone to augment their numbers. They have been left too long to train a vast rising generation in the vilest precepts, and amid social spectacles the most degrading. We are contiguous to them. We are pure! We are holy! Our children hear no vile precepts, witness no degrading social spectacles! Vice raises not its hideous head in our midst! Crime, rapine and murder are unknown to our borders! She is our neighbor—our borders join. We shall be corrupted! The advances of her people must be stopped; they *shall* be stopped, if we have the power to do it. Their presumption in daring to apply for admission into the Union with a constitution that guarantees unto them the right of worshiping God in their peculiar way, is too monstrous. A Californian, a Chinaman or a Hindoo may have this privilege, but for a "Mormon" to expect such a privilege—bah! the idea is too absurd, and the "Mormons" are fools for thinking of such a thing. . . .

If California cannot produce villains who, for a few pieces of gold, would sell the life of their dearest friend and relative, she contains plenty who would unhesitatingly murder them in cold blood for the same object. Will intercourse with the "Mormons" have a tendency to increase these evils? The question needs no answer; all that is necessary is to look at Utah; if they do not exist there, if crimes of this and every other description are unknown there, we may safely conclude that instead of "Mormon" intercourse having the effect to deteriorate the morals of their neighbors, it will have a tendency to elevate them. Paint Utah as black as you can, set forth, in as glowing language as you can command, the iniquities of her inhabitants, yet you cannot make her equal to her neighbors in all that is recognized by good men as evil. Talk about the baneful influences of "Mormonism" destroying, or in any way injuring, the purity of California morals! The idea is ridiculous; and, were it not so gravely advanced, it would excite our risibilities. We are very much averse to the practice of instituting comparisons; in self defence, however, we are sometimes compelled to adopt them. Compare the criminal records of Utah with those of California, or with those of any other State or Territory in the Union, and how infinitely superior she is to them all,—if we admit that freedom from crime and wrong constitutes superiority. It was only a few days ago that one of the daily papers in this city, in speaking of the commission of crime throughout the State, remarked,—"Villainies are become more frequent in California than in any other civilized country on earth; they are, in fact, events of every-day occurrence." And yet the editors of the *Golden Era* think that the "fair fame of our State" can be sullied by intercourse with the "Mormons." Truly they have strange ideas relative to "fair fame."...

The infusion of "Mormon" principles and element into California character would have the same effect here that it has in Utah—it would abolish prostitution; it would remove from the sight and hearing of California youth scenes that were never witnessed by the rising generations of "Mormons" in Utah, and of which they have no conception; it would give security to life and property; it would end the interminable amount of litigation with which the courts in this country are cursed; it would give dignity to labor and thus promote industry; it would in short, do all for California that it has done for Utah, by causing peace, good order and union to abound in her borders. These are the influences which attend the radiation of "Mormonism," and we leave it to all honest and good men to decide whether they are "baneful" or beneficial.

A Filthy and Debasing Immoral Hypocrisy

Again and again, George Q. Cannon leaned on what he felt was one of his strongest arguments in defense of Mormonism in general and polygamy in particular: the existence of prostitution in supposedly civilized places like San Francisco. Whether due to the positive effects of polygamy or simply the social controls that are inherent in an isolated, theocratic community, prostitution was virtually unheard of in Utah Territory—at least until federal troops arrived.

Remy and Brenchley supported Cannon's views on morality in Utah:

> At night not a woman is to be met with in the streets, which is worthy of remark among people where the number of women exceeds that of men, and where it might be assumed that polygamy would lead to greater freedom of manners. It is a strange spectacle and one full of interest, this society so laborious and so sober, so peaceable and so orderly, when one considers the different elements of which it is composed, and the classes from which it generally springs.[26]

The Jewish-Portuguese artist who accompanied Frémont to Utah in 1853 and 1854 made a similar report in his book, first published in 1857:

> During a residence of ten weeks in Great Salt Lake City, and my observations in all their various settlements, amongst a homogeneous population of over seventy-five thousand inhabitants, it is worthy of record, that I never heard any obscene or improper language; never saw a man drunk; never had my attention called to the exhibition of vice of any sort. There are no gambling houses, grog shops, or buildings of ill fame, in all their settlements. They preach morality in their churches and from their stands, and what is at strange as it is true, the people practise it, and religiously believe their salvation depends on fulfilling the behests of the religion they have adopted.[27]

Those who could not see any virtues among the Mormons because of an intense aversion to polygamy were quick to dismiss such positive reports:

> It will not do here to judge from appearances. A man stopping here for a few days, or even weeks, would be very apt to go away impressed with the idea that it was a prosperous and happy community. He finds a city which has been built up within a brief period; he sees a certain degree of commendable industry; he hears the saints addressing each other as brothers and sisters, seeming to live together in great harmony; and pursues his journey to California or Oregon, without obtaining a glimpse of the "dead men's bones and rottenness" which lie festering beneath this whited sepulchre.[28]

As the *Weekly Chronicle* made clear early in 1857, whatever problems or benefits polygamy or Mormon theocracy might entail, Utah's political

---

[26] Remy and Brenchley, *A Journey to Great-Salt-Lake-City*, I:199. The authors listed seventeen nationalities or ethnic groups living together peaceably in the Mormon capital.

[27] Carvalho, *Incidents of Travel and Adventure in the Far West*, 209.

[28] Ferris, *The Mormons at Home*, 122–23.

destiny became hopelessly entangled in questions of morality and patriotism.

UNTITLED EDITORIAL, *WEEKLY CHRONICLE*, 7 MARCH 1857.[29]

. . . In company with some of these territories asking for admission as States, doubtless the Ishmaelitish dwellers of Utah will present themselves. They have ere this asked the privilege. If they present themselves with a Republican Constitution, how can they be rejected? Are they to come in with all their harems complete, their disgusting orgies in full rehearsal, their lechery free to indulge its exercise, their brothels endorsed by act of Congress as well as sanctified by their own hideous creed? If there be no other tangible ground upon which such a blot as a Mormon State upon our flag can be prevented, is not a sufficient reason found in the fact that to admit Utah with its system of priesthood, which virtually abolishes all civil power, and constitutes the whole government an all-ruling hierarchy, would be a violation of the plain spirit of the Constitution of the United States, which in its first amendment declares that "Congress shall make no law respecting an establishment of religion?" If Congress admit a State whose entire government is religious, in which all other departments are mere agents to the priesthood, will it not violate this provision? For the law of admission would be a law really respecting the establishment of religion.

Aside from this, however, the moral aspect of such a question is enough to deter all decent men from voting for such a bill. To admit the grand seraglio of Utah as a State, would be an insult to every pure mind in the country. There is not a decent woman in the land who might not feel ashamed at the act. It would be an endorsement of the grossest sensuality, and would place every State under the necessity of recognizing the validity of the Mormon concubinage system whenever a case might arise within their jurisdiction touching a Mormon claim. For the Constitution of the United States declares that "full faith and credit shall be given in each State to the public sets, records, and judicial proceedings of every other state." Thus if Brigham Young, Grand Priest and Grand Goat of the State of Utah, should claim for instance in the State of Massachusetts, any thing in right of Abigail or Mehitable as his wife, the courts of the Old Commonwealth would be forced to admit his claim, although they had proof that Abigail or the other, was the sixty-eighth wife, or woman of this lecherous old concubinist. Such an obligation to recognize a filthy and debasing immoral hypocrisy, is beyond the right of Congress to force upon the mil-

[29] The date printed on the masthead of this issue is 8 March 1856. Similar problems occur in subsequent issues. The year is corrected to 1857 directly over the editorial, but the day is still erroneously noted as 8 March rather than 7 March.

lions of our thirty odd States. It would be a violation of the whole recognized civil, moral and religions sentiment of our people.

"'Mormons' Rights.—Republicanism," *Western Standard,* 13 March 1857.[30]

How easily the difficult question relative to the admission of Utah into the Union might have been solved, had the people of that territory only inserted some anti-republican feature into their constitution. Had this been done, a vast amount of calculation and scheming would have been saved those who are averse to her admission. But her constitution is eminently republican, and she cannot be rejected on that ground. The first amendment to the Constitution of the United States declares that "Congress shall make no law respecting an establishment of religion." Whether, then, the inhabitants of a territory possessing the requisite qualifications, and petitioning for admission into the confederacy, be Christians or infidels, believers in Mohammed or Vishnu, is a matter with which Congress can have nothing to do. The question at issue is, do they present themselves with a republican constitution? It is not,—What is their belief? It is not,—Are they Christians? but it is,—Are they republicans? Are they loyal, willing to adhere to the Constitution and the laws of our country? If they are, admit them; and leave their religion, and every practice flowing from that religion which does not interfere with the laws and Constitution of the United States, and which does not conflict with the rights of their fellow-men, to them and their God. Freedom of conscience—the liberty to worship God as they please—is the inalienable right of all men. Despotism and tyranny may debar them from exercising it; but it is still their right, and a right, too, which all are justified in contending for so long as life endures. It was to guarantee to all men this precious right that, in the designs and wisdom of an All-wise Providence, this Government was established. It is the great principle underlying the whole fabric of pure republican government, and the sacrilegious wretch who would put forth his hand to destroy it, and would use his influence to deprive his fellow-men of its enjoyment, merits the execrations of every lover of liberty.

A leading article in the *Chronicle,* about a week ago, catechetically advances the idea, that if there be no other tangible ground upon which the claims of Utah for admission into the Union can be rejected, sufficient can be found in the fact that its system of priesthood virtually abolishes all civil power, and constitutes the whole government an all-ruling hierarchy. If Congress, this writer asks, admit a state whose entire government is religious, in which all other departments are mere agents to the priesthood, will it not violate the provision, made in the first amendment of the Constitution, that "Con-

[30] Reprinted in Cannon, *Writings from the "Western Standard,"* 361–64.

gress shall make no law respecting the establishment of religion"? This writer is mistaken when he asserts that Utah's system of priesthood virtually abolishes all civil power; on the contrary, it increases its efficiency. Neither religion nor the respect due to the priesthood is in the least incompatible with republicanism and the observance of civil law administered by its officers. It is true that, in Utah, holders of civil office generally hold the priesthood; but being republicans, we cannot imagine why this should detract from their worth, capability or the effective discharge of their civil duties.

The idea is absurd and directly contrary to the spirit of the Constitution, that because the people of Utah are religious, or many of them ministers of religion, Congress, in admitting their territory as a state, is making a law respecting the establishment of religion. In admitting Utah, Congress does not recognize her system of belief, but her republicanism—Congress does not violate the provisions respecting the establishment of religion, but honors and enforces that portion of it which says, that the free exercise thereof shall not be prohibited.

There is another objection which the *Chronicle* advances, and which it thinks would be a violation of the whole recognized civil, moral and religious sentiment of the people, and beyond the right of Congress to force upon the millions of our thirty odd States. That is, if Brigham Young should claim, for instance, in the State of Massachusetts, anything in right of one of his wives, the courts of the old commonwealth would be forced to admit his claim. Though she might be his sixty-eighth wife and they had proof of the fact, they would be compelled to accede to the claim, as the first section of the fourth article of the Constitution of the United States declares that "full faith and credit shall be given in each State to the public acts, records, and judicial proceedings of every other State." But why should this be an objection? True, every State would be under the necessity of recognizing the validity of the Latter-day Saints' system of marriage; but this would not be an endorsement of their religion, but of their republican right to regulate their own domestic institutions.[31] By the people of Utah marriage is viewed as a religious ordinance of vital importance. Polygamy is practiced by them not for the gratification of lust, (had this been their motive they might have accomplished it by the more popular mode of prostitutes and brothels,) but as a law of God; they firmly and conscientiously believe that it was revealed by Him to Abraham and other worthies for their obedience, and that they have received a similar command. Its practice nei-

[31] Ironically (though not surprisingly), the Church of Jesus Christ of Latter-day Saints has rejected modern applications of this argument. In 1998 the church publicly opposed potential legalization of homosexual marriages in Hawaii and Alaska, and in 2000, members in California successfully supported the controversial "Definition of Marriage Act," which specifically defined marriage as "between a man and a woman."

ther conflicts with nor contravenes the laws or Constitution of the United States; and it being a portion of the religion of the Latter-day Saints, neither the Commonwealth of Massachusetts nor any other State of the Confederacy has any right whatever to meddle with it. The people of Utah never will submit to have their religion, their system of morality or their domestic institutions dictated unto them by an oligarchy, though it may be composed of millions; they will either be admitted into the Union on a republican footing, with equal rights with the inhabitants of other States, or they will not enter at all. Their liberty and religious rights are as dear to them as they possibly can be to any other people, and they will go to as great lengths and sacrifice as much to preserve them.

The Counsel and Commandments of God

As Utah became further embroiled in the national conflicts of the 1850s that eventually led to civil war, it became hopelessly entangled in partisan sectionalism. Utah's leaders sympathized with the interests of the South and its advocacy of popular sovereignty, which would let the Mormons settle questions related to polygamy without the interference of the federal government. The Saints tried to avoid taking a public stance on slavery, but as the only slave territory in the nation, Utah's status and politics made it a hot political potato.

"Utah Matters," *Weekly Chronicle*, 4 July 1857 [sic].[32]

A gentleman who claims to be posted in political matters, prophecies that within one year Utah will be a State in this Confederacy, without the recognition of the polygamy institution in its Constitution; and he also believes that in the same instrument there will be no slavery prohibition clause, as the doctrines of the Mormon Church expressly recognize the inferiority of the African race. It is thought that the mighty Brigham will receive a revelation (as all his revelations are received) within a few months to the effect that the institution of polygamy among the "Saints" is no longer required, that being an indispensable requisite to the admission of that Territory as a State. The apostles and elders have already been summoned to Salt Lake to hear some important communication (from above?) and this is likely to be the revelation referred to, as Brigham Young and Dr. Bernheisel are extremely anxious for seats in the U.S. Senate. Should this Territory and New Mexico be admitted with pro-slavery Constitutions, they will form a powerful combination against Free State advancement; and though a large

[32] The correct date is 27 June 1857, though it is printed as 4 July.

majority of the people of Utah being foreigners, are opposed to slavery, the edict of the Church will be sufficient to settle that matter. Slavery already exists to a moderate extent in that Territory.

The "revelations" to the head of the Church are not promulgated with any degree of haste. The existence of polygamy was solemnly denied by the Mormon Elders in the civilized world, for years after it was practiced at the head-quarters of the Church, and exposed by the press. This may in some instances have been done honestly, as the head of the Church does not in all cases allow "poor curses" that he sends out on missions (*vide* his address April, 1856) to know too much. There are plenty of documents to prove the above denials, and there is a little doubt that among decent people at a distance the same deception is practiced to this day in regard to new "principles" advanced by the fifty-wife prophet, the plea being that the ideas are of so "stupendous" a character that new converts to the faith are not prepared by sufficient training of their minds to receive them as yet. By the same rule the proxy system, which is no worse than polygamy, the marriage of brother and sister, and other horrors may be in the Church this day, though not given out publicly, policy requiring for the present the denial of their existence. As far as the secrets of the Church are concerned, those of a Free Mason's lodge were never kept more inviolate. One half has not yet been revealed to the world, nor will be, except at such times as may suit the convenience of the leaders. The papers of the Church are not published for the purpose of expounding all of the doctrines of the Church, and they dare not do it, even if (as is not probably the case) they knew of all the great "principles" that the world and the newly converted Mormons are not prepared to receive. Setting aside the many absurd and foolishly false stories that are now going the rounds concerning these people, there is enough of the real, well-substantiated truth to give matter for grave reflection.

"Admission of Utah—Vain Anticipations," *Western Standard*, 3 July 1857.[33]

An original article appeared in the *Chronicle* of Friday last[34] on Utah matters, in which the writer publishes the prophecy of a gentleman posted in political affairs, to the effect that within one year Utah will be a State in this Confederacy, without the recognition of the institution of polygamy in its constitution. This, it is thought, will be repudiated by President Young receiving a revelation that polygamy is no longer required, that being an indispensable requisite to the admission of the territory of Utah as a State. To complete the absurdity of this prophet's hypothesis, he thinks it likely that it is a revelation of this character that is to be revealed because the apos-

[33] Reprinted in Cannon, *Writings from the "Western Standard,"* 462–65.

[34] The article in question was actually printed 27 June 1857, the previous Saturday.

tles and elders have been summoned to Salt Lake City. How a man, laying any claim to common sense and given to the exercise of his reasoning faculties, can be deluded into the publication of such ideas for the public to peruse, is strange to us. Were as baseless a theory to be advanced upon any other subject than that of "Mormonism" the originator would be subjected to ridicule. As we have often said, there is not the slightest occasion for the word, polygamy, to be mentioned in the constitution of Utah, nor in the discussion of the question of her admission into the Union. The discussion of the question will neither be shortened by the repudiation nor protracted by the advocacy of polygamy by the Latter-day Saints. If Utah have claims to admission into the Confederacy as an independent State, they are equally as valid with the belief and practice of the doctrine of polygamy by her people, as though they believed and practiced monogamy. Under no circumstances can Congress legitimately make the belief or practice of that principle an objection against her entrance into the Union. The people of Utah are aware of this, and, therefore, will never submit to be deprived of the rights which they, in common with every citizen of these United States, possess. Had they and their leader, without regard to the commandments of God, been inclined to conciliate or seek the favor of man by making these concessions, they would have done so years ago. They have suffered mobbings, plunderings, and perils of every description, many have lost their lives and the remainder have been expatriated, for their adherence to the principles of their religion. If conformation to the popular prejudices, and the repudiation of every doctrine opposed thereto, had been the object—instead of obedience to the counsel and commandments of God—what a vast amount of fearful and bloody persecution might have been saved! If love of life and all its comforts, was insufficient to induce them to recant their belief in their religion or any of its principles, then how unreasonable it is to suppose that a desire to become a State would prompt to do it. Men permit themselves to be deceived in their estimate of the Latter-day Saints, by the idea that they are actuated by sordid or licentious motives in their movements. They have not bestowed that amount of reflection upon the subject which they might and which it really demands, when they give utterance to such an idea. The entire history of "Mormonism," from its inception until the present time, teems with evidences of the falsity of such an idea. They have sacrificed everything for the sake of their principles. Sordid or licentious motives would never prompt men to take a similar course to theirs. These would cause men to float with the stream of popular feeling; their course has ever been against it.

The article contains many ideas relative to the asserted course pursued by the head of the Church in keeping back the new principles and revelations from the new converts and the world; and thinks it quite likely that many of the "poor curses" sent out on missions deny the existence of these principles honestly, as they may not be aware of their being revealed. Paul says that milk is suitable for babes—those unskilful in the world of righteousness; but strong meat belongeth to them that are of full age. It may be that the experience of the head of the Church in Utah has taught him the truth of these remarks of Paul, and he has been constrained to put them into practice. But do not the Latter-day Saints have an extraordinary amount of confidence in the truth and impregnability of their system when they appoint such "ignoramuses" to advocate and defend their doctrines against the learning of the world? With other systems and creeds—particularly when strong opposition is expected—they put forward their talented and intelligent men to combat with their opponents and to propagate their ideas. If the "poor curses" and "ignoramuses" of the Latter-day Saints are so successful in disseminating and defending the principles of "Mormonism," and bringing such large additions to the Church yearly, what may not be expected from those who know the whole of its principles? Every principle that the present missionaries teach has been repeatedly proved to be invulnerable. They have been individually and collectively assailed by priest and layman learned and unlearned; but from every ordeal they have ever emerged brighter and more attractive. If this has been the result of the advocacy of "Mormonism" by those who only know its principles in part, how much greater and more apparent would the results be if those thoroughly acquainted with it were to be its defenders!

The idea, however, that the head of the Church keeps the members in ignorance of the principles which are revealed, only excites a smile on the part of those acquainted with the operations of "Mormonism." If men be in ignorance of its principles, it is not because of deception practiced upon them by the head; but because they do not take the proper course to have their ignorance dissipated. The gospel of Jesus Christ, or "Mormonism," as it is termed, teaches men that the Lord is accessible to all who humbly seek him in the appointed way. The head of the Church is not the only privileged person, though he stands as prophet, seer, and revelator to the people. No man that is faithful to his God and his religion, whether he be in Utah or called by duty to minister in foreign lands, will be unprepared for the reception of principles which are being revealed to the head of the Church. He possesses that Spirit which Jesus said should lead men into all truth. That Spirit, if sought after, and cherished, reveals these principles to him, and he thereby becomes a living witness of their truth. This is what constitutes the potency of "Mormonism," or, more properly, the gospel, and is the means by which its believers are bound and cemented together from the head downward. Elders faithful in their callings, then, are not kept in ignorance by the head of the Church not letting them know too much.

Historical perspective gives special poignancy to the *Chronicle*'s supposition that a new revelation abandoning polygamy would be an inevitable and convenient precursor to statehood. This was an idea that would come up over and over again. Two years later Horace Greeley—the crusading founder and editor of the *New York Tribune*—predicted that "there will be a new revelation, ere many years, whereby the saints will be admonished to love and cherish the wives they already have, but not to marry any more beyond the natural assignment of one wife to each husband."[35]

Schuyler Colfax, speaker of the U.S. House of Representatives, made the same suggestion directly to Brigham Young in 1865:

> he had hoped the prophets of the church would have a new revelation on the subject, which should put a stop to the practice . . . Mr. Young responded quickly and frankly that he should readily welcome such a revelation; that polygamy was not in the original book of the Mormons; that it was not an essential practice in the church, but only a privilege and a duty, under special command of God; that he knew it had been abused; that people had entered into polygamy who ought not to have done so, and against his protestation and advice. At the same time, he defended the practice as having biblical authority, and as having, within proper limits, a sound, moral and philosophical reason and propriety.[36]

Young's remarkable response, if recorded correctly, suggests a softening in the Mormon position, but it was not until 1890 that the "new revelation" finally came.[37]

Rebellion Has Been Its Creed and Practice

An observant California editor noted that the Mormons often referred to their president and governor as "Brother Brigham," while William Chandless was fascinated that the Mormons habitually referred to their leader by his first name:

> Mormons are fond of great titles. So now and then they speak of "the governor," or even "his excellency the governor;" more commonly of Brigham,

[35] Greeley, *An Overland Journey*, 241.

[36] Bowles, *Across the Continent*, 111.

[37] Albert D. Richardson's version of this exchange suggested no such conciliatory tone in the prophet's response: "Brigham and his supporters earnestly insisted that it was a part of their religion with which Government had no right to interfere; and were indignant at our suggestion . . ." Richardson, *Beyond the Mississippi*, 350.

A beardless Brigham Young, from a daguerreotype taken in 1855. From Remy and Brenchley, *A Journey to Great-Salt-Lake City*.

or brother Brigham, or occasionally, with some want of reverence, of "the old boss." But in every Mormon family he is prayed for morning and evening, the words being usually the same, "Bless thy servant, Brigham, bless him in so and so, &c.; bless his counsellors, brother Kimball and brother Grant," &c. The two last cannot dispense with their surnames; this privilege seems a prerogative of the prophetic crown. Joseph and Brigham have shaken off their chrysalis, Smith and Young.[38]

Regardless of whether they called him Brother Brigham or Governor Young, California newspapers loved to attack the man they viewed as a Rocky Mountain tyrant who ruled as chief of "a Hierarchy of cheats."

UNTITLED EDITORIAL, *WEEKLY CHRONICLE*, 11 JULY 1857.[39]

Since the time when Joe Smith ceased to chop wood at fifty cents a cord, and took to whacking fools, making Latter-day Saints out of the Latter-day rascals, and building up a Hierarchy of cheats to rule a church of enthusiasts, fanatics and hypocrites, the Mormon humbug has been an individual curse, a public nuisance. The most holy impulses and instincts of many have been seized upon, and their religious tendencies made the means of making them the mere puppets of Mormon prophets, priests and kings. Many honest minds have been perverted to their ruin, while a few cheats have reaped the temporal benefits of the great imposture.

---

[38] Chandless, *A Visit to Salt Lake*, 189. A book by Eugene England reflects this enduring affection for Brigham Young in its very title: *Brother Brigham.*

[39] The correct date is 4 July 1857.

At the start, Mormonism was bad enough and repugnant enough to morality and common sense; yet it has grown constantly worse, just as its owner has increased. When its doctrine of plurality of wives was first promulgated the public mind was shocked; but it did not stop there. The plurality has no limits, and to this in practice, if not in promulgated theory, the lecherous goats of that nauseous gang have added that of "proxy," or a substitution of husbands—of paramours, rather—so that the absent husband's wife has another furnished her by the Holy Church during her husband's absence. Bigamy, plurality, proxy, incest, are each and all a portion of Mormon creed and practice.

Rebellion has been its creed and practice ever since they gathered at Nauvoo. Brigham Young has preached it in their temple; his paper has published his threats, his defiance, his denunciations of the Federal Government, and all others except that which he professes to hold direct from Heaven. Mr. Fillmore knew this when he appointed him Governor of Utah; Mr. Pierce knew this while he continued him Governor. Brigham has made murder one of the principles of his religious government, and instituted his "Danite Band" or "Destroying Angels," whose business it is made, under terrific oaths, to exercise this part of their religious ceremonies—the sacrifice of whomsoever the heads of their Church designate as victims.

Most honest minds may often be perverted to most dreadful acts through their religious instincts. This is undoubtedly the case with many Mormons. They fully believe the Mormon creed, and whatever "Brother Brigham" says, is to them gospel, prophecy, revelation. For such we feel pity. It is the hypocrites who thus mislead and use them, that are the culpable ones who should be punished. And many think the time has nearly come when they will be. For Fillmore and Pierce are, neither of them, any longer President, thank God and the people, and Mr. Buchanan seems determined to decide who is to rule, he or Brigham Young. But will he be able to do so through his new Governor, General Harney and his twenty-five hundred troops?[40] We think not.

In the first place, all honest Mormons believe that their government is a hierarchy ordained by and derived directly from Heaven, that the office of Head of the Church is an inheritance, an heirship above all earthly rule, never to end till Christ shall come again, and Brigham as that Head is above all Presidents and rulers. All Mormons who do not thus believe, affect the faith for their own purposes. Consequently Brigham's word is law, and when any particular necessity arises, he can have a convenient "revelation," which of course leaves no room for cavil, question or disobedience.

Using this power over the minds of his deluded people, he has forced them to not only pay their tithes and other contributions professedly for the

---

[40] For more on these events, see Chapter 11.

service of the church, amounting in all to about one-third of all their income, but all their possessory rights in lands, chattels and property of all kinds have been legally made over to the "Trustee in Trust of the Church of Christ of Latter-day Saints" as "consecrations" to the Lord.[41] Brigham Young being that Trustee, is supreme owner of all property in Utah. He holds it all in trust—lands, cattle, houses, pasturage, woodlands, goods, personal property—all. We understand that these "consecrations" have all been legally executed in accordance with the laws of the Territory enacted under the authority delegated by Congress in the act under which Utah was organized. Not only this, but the crops are all at Brigham's command, and he can control every bushel of grain raised in the Territory and order it into granaries, to be dispensed only as he may direct. He is more absolute with the people of Utah than is Alexander among the Russians; for the Mormon Government is carried to the utmost point of perfection from the Head, Brigham, throughout all its gradations of office, the "Twelve," Seventies, etc., all based upon the one idea of its divine institution, its eventual universal supremacy, and in all its details fashioned so that the whole force of the organization shall be directed through its head to its complete triumph.

Now, shrewd, cunning and unscrupulous as Young is, and possessing this power, how will he exert it in meeting the present demonstration of the Federal Government? No one need think that he will attempt an armed resistance. He is aware that such a course would be his ruin. For the idea that he can raise a large force of warriors sufficient to cope with the forces of the United States, is baseless. Utah does not contain fifty thousand people. He might stand one campaign, but the ruin of his crops would starve out his whole territorial harem before he could make a second. He will probably pursue a very different course.

He will be very patriotic. He will celebrate the Fourth of July with great parades, with patriotic orations, odes and fire crackers. He will welcome the new Governor, General Harney and the U.S. troops. He will offer no resistance to the complete establishment of the U.S. Courts. But he will be Governor and complete ruler still. For it must be recollected that all the jurors will be Mormons; no juror will be allowed to be on a panel except such as Brigham secretly indicates, and every trial will be by them decided just as he wishes. He will thus have complete control of the civil government, and that, too, under the laws of the Territory. What can a U.S. Judge, Marshal and Attorney do, although backed up by General Harney and his troops, against such an organization as he controls thus, where the entire jury are his in soul, body, conscience, life, faith, hope and action?

He may refuse to sell the troops one bushel of grain, one pound of sup-

---

[41] An excellent study of Brigham Young's application of the "Law of Consecration" is Arrington *et. al., Building the City of God.* See also Arrington's classic *Great Basin Kingdom.*

plies of any kind, and starve them out or force them to draw their supplies a thousand miles over the desert; or he may demand an exhorbitant price, and thus reap an immense harvest of gold from the very forces sent to upset him. If he sees fit to trade, that army of two or three thousand men will soon require an expenditure of a million of dollars in Utah, and enrich Brigham and his saints to that amount. If he prefers otherwise, he can keep his grain and provisions generally garnered upon the plea that he is preparing for the large immigration of Mormons he is expecting, or to anticipate a possible famine. If they be taken by force, he will trump up a formidable array of claims which the United States Government will have to pay. Thus, the very array made and sent against him will turn to his pecuniary advantage.

Our Government will offer safe conduct out of Utah to all who wish to go. This is the very thing Brigham wants, for it will relieve him of all the discontented, dissatisfied, rebellious spirits about him, and leave him only those who are devoted soul and body to the Mormon faith, and who believe in him as the mouth-piece of God. Thus he will be immeasurably strengthened, his power made compact, and his influence infinite with his people.

Then let the new Governor, or Gen. Harney, or any other of the "Gentiles" make a mis-step, and see how they will fare before the Courts where the law is to be vindicated and the facts adjudged by a jury of Mormons. The fact is, Brigham has the inside track, and he is shrewd enough to keep it, and this whole martial array against him will amount to about as much as the Japan Treaty of Commodore Perry, to the United States, while it will consolidate Brigham's power, fill his treasury, and leave the Mormons more prosperous than they have ever before been.

"The 'Mormons' on the Inside Track," *Western Standard*, 10 July 1857.[42]

A long article appeared in the *Chronicle*, of Friday last, on the Utah question, from which we make some extracts. The writer . . . is correct in his conjecture when he asserts that Governor Young will not attempt an armed resistance if the Administration should send a new Governor, General Harney and twenty-five hundred troops to Utah—measures, by-the-bye, which had not been definitely adopted at the last advices. Why should he offer resistance? If the administration of justice is the object for which these troops and Governor are to be sent, then Governor Young and the "Mormons" have nothing to fear. As to the remark that they will become very patriotic when they hear of the march of these regiments, it was dictated by a mean, ignoble spirit. Let Governor Young and the "Mormons" manifest the most lofty and disinterested patriotism, and the writer of this sentence

[42] Reprinted in Cannon, *Writings from the "Western Standard,"* 475–78.

would seek to detract from the merit of such actions by attributing them to sinister motives. He knows very well, if he knows anything about the "Mormons" and their system, that they never have lifted their hand against the constituted authorities, and they never will.[43] But lest the "Mormons" should get any credit for forbearance—lest the eyes of the public should be opened to see the "Mormons" in their true light—they must be told by this writer that the "Mormons" have ever been rebellious, and that it will not be on account of their love for the Constitution and laws that they maintain peace; but because they are cunning enough to perceive that resistance would be useless at present. No man who does not himself act from cunning, despicable motives, would ever think of attributing the actions of others to such a cause.

So far as patriotism is concerned, the "Mormons" have never indulged in any other feeling. They have no need to resort to empty parade, orations or odes, to show to God and the world that they love their country and its Constitution. The patience and lofty heroism which they have exhibited in the midst of the severest trials, submitting to every indignity and making every sacrifice rather than assail or violate the Constitution of their country, will be embalmed in the archives of history, and be viewed by future generations with admiration. No man can point to a single act of the "Mormons," from the rise of the Church until the present time, that can be termed unpatriotic. And if that patriotism be measured by the style in which the fourth of July is celebrated, then it needs no future celebration to prove that they are patriots. The stories about the rebellion in Utah, circulated so extensively of late, are fast melting away. They are rapidly sharing the fate of those which have preceded them; the characters of their fabricators are becoming too well known for them to pass current long. Being false they must perish. Arrange it any way they please, as it is truly said,—Brigham has the inside track and knows how to keep it. But has it been or will it be by cunning? Did Governor Young and the "Mormons" depend on cunning alone they would have been worsted years ago. Shrewdness and cunning alone would have proved but poor auxiliaries in delivering them so frequently from the machinations of such hosts of crafty enemies. Nothing but eternal wisdom and Almighty power could have done it. By this aid they have kept *right* and *truth* on their side, and, therefore, have had the "inside track." By this aid they will continue to have the weather-gage of their enemies, and everything will be overruled for their good.

---

[43] Though virtually no blood was shed during the Utah War, Cannon was wrong in arguing that Brigham Young would not offer armed resistance to federal forces. In 1857 the Nauvoo Legion may have been larger than the Utah Expedition, and though perhaps outgunned by the federal troops, they were armed and prepared for battle if need be. Lot Smith's burning of the federal supply trains at the point of a gun would have to qualify as "armed resistance."

Our Departed Liberty

In arguing that the Mormons had never indulged in any other feeling than patriotism, Cannon chose to overlook the ambivalence toward their country many Mormons had themselves expressed. Witness this occasional poem, written by Eliza R. Snow, then one of Joseph Smith's plural wives, in 1840:

ODE
For the Fourth of July

Shall we commemorate the day
Whose genial influence has pass'd o'er?
Shall we our hearts best tribute pay,
Where heart and feeling are no more?

Shall we commemorate the day
With freedom's ensigns waving high,
Whose blood stain'd banner's furl'd away—
Whose rights and freedom have gone by?

Should we, when gasping 'neath its wave,
Extol the beauties of the sea?
Or, lash'd upon fair freedom's grave,
Proclaim the strength of Liberty? . . .

Columbia's glory is a theme
That with our life's warm pulses grew,
But ah! 'tis fled—and, like a dream
Its ghost is flutt'ring in our view! . . .

PROTECTION faints, and JUSTICE cow'rs—
REDRESS is slumb'ring on the heath;
And 'tis in vain to lavish flow'rs
Upon our country's fading wreath!

Better implore His aid divine,
Whose arm can make his people free;
Than decorate the hollow shrine
Of our departed liberty![44]

[44] Reprinted in Taylor, *The Kingdom or Nothing*, 68–69.

But in spite of any such ambivalence, many of their earliest visitors, such as Lt. John W. Gunnison, understood the Mormons to be anything but traitors to their country:

> Though this people fled to a foreign country to enjoy the liberty that persecution denied them in the states, as soon as they found their adopted land had come under the jurisdiction of the stripes and stars—which their own valor had helped to win in the army of the Pacific against Mexico,—they embraced the earliest opportunity of declaring their adherence to the great charter of liberty and national glory, and announced to the world that it was given to our patriot fathers by divine inspiration, and that they will uphold and defend it, though all the original parties shall secede and trample it under foot. . . . The government is frequently proclaimed corrupt, and dangerous to liberty, in party declamation; the writers and speakers being ready to defend it, however, with their life-blood.[45]

His commanding officer agreed completely: " a more loyal and patriotic people cannot be found within the limits of the Union."[46]

Finally, the artist and daguerreotypist Solomon Carvalho, who spent nearly three months with the Mormons through the winter of 1853 and 1854 as a member of Frémont's final western exploring expedition, made it clear that Young came across as anything but autocratic:

> I never could have imagined the deep idolatry with which he is almost worshipped. There is no aristocracy or presuming upon position about the Governor; he is emphatically one of the people; the boys call him Brother Brigham, and the elders also call him Brother Brigham. They place implicit confidence in him, and if he were to say he wanted a mountain cut through, instantly every man capable of bearing a pick-axe would commence the work, without asking any questions, or entertaining expectation of payment for services.[47]

To understand Mormon loyalty to the constitution—at least in those days—one must note that they perceived it as a divinely inspired document whose purpose was to serve as a means to a greater end. Ultimately, they believed Christ would rule personally on the earth, with all governments, including that of the United States, being made subject to Him and to His people, the Latter-day Saints. By affording them freedom of

[45] Gunnison, *The Mormons, or, Latter-day Saints,* 83–84, 154.

[46] Stansbury, *Exploration and Survey,* 144.

[47] Carvalho, *Incidents of Travel and Adventure in the Far West,* 273–74.

religion, they expected that the constitution could be a valuable, if temporary, tool for the Kingdom of God (Deseret) as it prepared the world for millennial rule.

If that process required the leadership of a benevolent dictator, so be it. After all, when Jesus Christ returned to the earth he was not expected to rule through popular or even representative democracy. "It is said of the Almighty," wrote S. W. Richards, "that, 'He speaks and it is done,' and brother Brigham's actions are so much like this, that one might think they had learnt their lessons in the same school and of the same teacher."[48] The apostle John Taylor was reported in 1853 to have envied the government of China, arguing that "it was better in the end for the wiser and more learned to care for the affairs of a people than that the people themselves should bicker about everything."[49]

It was therefore not surprising that the Mormons would perceive themselves as loyal to the highest ideals of the constitution while many of their fellow Americans viewed them as being rebels and even traitors to those same ideals. There was truth in both views. In describing the political loyalties of Peter Haws, Remy and Brenchley stated that in spite of his quarrels with Brigham Young, Haws

> had renounced his allegiance to the British crown to become a naturalized American, had in fact no other feeling of nationality than that which he derived from his religious opinions; that is to say, he was neither English nor American, but solely and simply Mormon. Far from vaunting the American nation as the first in the world, he took pleasure in undervaluing it, and predicted the disruption of the Union on account of the depravity of its Government. There was nothing possible or good upon the earth save a theocratic government, which the Mormons alone possess; so that they have at the same time the full truth and the perfection of political systems.[50]

Wallace Stegner—one of the great twentieth-century writers on the Mormon contribution to the settling of the American West—noted that

> Mormonism was in several ways—and its persecutors rightly felt it so—antipathetic to the unlicked democracy out of which it grew. Far from separating church and state, it made them synonymous. ("Theoretically," said

48 Richards to Cannon, 6 March 1857, *Western Standard,* 17 April 1857, 3.

49 Schiel, *Journey through the Rocky Mountains,* 78–79.

50 Remy and Brenchley, *A Journey to Great-Salt-Lake City,* 1:142-43.

> Apostle Franklin D. Richards in 1880, "Church and State are one. If there were no Gentiles and no other Government there would be no Civil Law.") Instead of celebrating the free individual, it celebrated the obedient group. For the will of the people it substituted the will of God as announced by the priesthood. . . . What they went to build in the Great Basin was not a state, not a republic, but a Kingdom.[51]

Even today, many members of the Church of Jesus Christ of Latter-day Saints seem caught between two worlds:

> In fact, we as American Mormons are constantly compelled in our acts of everyday living to mediate between the two cultures that nourish and sustain us: those of liberal, democratic, individualistic America and those of authoritative, consensus, communal, Mormondom—what Mormons understand to be the kingdom of God. And these cultures are in their most fundamental premises antithetical to each other—the first tends toward chaotic, narcissistic materialism; the second toward harmonious, mutually responsible, asceticism.[52]

Religion and politics rarely mix well—especially in a democracy. In spite of the clear aversion so many Americans felt toward Mormon polygamy, there is good evidence that it was not so much polygamy that got in the way of statehood, as it was their peculiar form of self-government. "As a religious community, the Latter-day Saints might have been able to ask for the free exercise of their religious views and would probably have been granted it on the free soil of America," Jacob Schiel wrote in 1859, "but as a political body inhabiting a territory of the United States with institutions like theirs, it was inevitable that they should come into conflict very soon with the government of the United States."[53]

---

[51] Stegner, *The Gathering of Zion*, 4.
[52] May, "Still a Puzzle," 83.
[53] Schiel, *Journey through the Rocky Mountains*, 90–91.

Chapter 9

"The Villainous, Wholesale Calumniator" Judge Drummond and The Friends of the Court

Much of the bad press experienced by the Church of Jesus Christ of Latter-day Saints in the mid-nineteenth century can be attributed directly to the stormy relationship between the Mormons and a succession of federal appointees. From the perspective of the LDS church, those who did not succeed in Utah left their positions because of personal immorality, general incompetence, or their failure to milk Utah and the federal government. The Saints considered these men undisciplined, unqualified carpetbaggers of the worst sort.[1] On the other hand, the "runaway judges" and other appointees who left their posts in Utah felt they were never allowed to succeed. Instead of being loyally supported by those whom they had come to serve, they believed their authority was constantly undermined by Mormon leaders who cast unwarranted aspersions upon their character. The truth lies somewhere in between.

The first non-Mormon federal appointees to Utah Territory lasted less than two months. Sen. Stephen A. Douglas, then a political ally of the Mormons, recommended Chief Justice Perry Brocchus to Brigham Young as "an accomplished gentleman—a sound lawyer—a man of strict honor and of high order of talents."[2] The Saints took a different view of the judge. Shortly after his arrival, Brocchus gave a speech at a general session of conference in which he tried "to correct erroneous opinions in regard to the [U.S.] Government" with calm and dispassionate "remonstrances." The Mormon audience heard him attack their

---

[1] For an overview of the difficulties with federal appointees during this period, see Cooley, "Carpetbag Rule—Territorial Government in Utah," 107–29.

[2] Douglas to Young, 9 April 1851, LDS Archives. Citation courtesy of Ardis Parshall.

patriotism and question the virtue of their women. Brigham Young responded with a thinly veiled threat against his life.[3] When the legislature did not choose him as its territorial delegate, Brocchus, his associate Lemuel G. Brandebury, Indian Agent Henry Day, and Secretary of State Broughton D. Harris headed back east, taking with them a host of complaints and the $24,000 that had been appropriated by Congress for the new territory. In his *History of Utah,* which was heavily influenced by Mormon perspectives, Bancroft stated that "Judge Brocchus especially was a vain and ambitious man, full of self-importance, fond of intrigue, corrupt, revengeful, hypocritical."[4]

The accusations of the departed justices created problems for the Saints, but there were enough mitigating factors (not the least of which was Brocchus' insult to the women of Utah and Harris's departure with the territorial funds) that the furor soon died down. With the exit of the federal judges in 1851, the territorial legislature immediately granted criminal—as well as civil—jurisdiction to the county probate courts. This was a major departure from past practice in all of the other states and U.S. territories, where the probate courts were confined to the adjudication of such civil matters as the resolution of wills and estates. As noted by Sarah Barringer Gordon, "Scholarly studies of the probate and church courts have concluded that they generally were administered fairly and impartially. To outsiders, however, the overlap between church and state in Utah was evidence that the church really held the reins of secular power."[5] The questionable constitutionality of the legislation resulted in an ongoing power struggle with the federal district courts that was not resolved until 1874 with the passage of the Poland Act.[6]

Lazarus H. Reid and Leonidas Shaver initially replaced the "runaway judges," with Benjamin G. Ferris as territorial secretary. As noted, Ferris

---

[3] This fiasco resulted in an illuminating exchange of letters between Brocchus and Young subsequently published as "Information in reference to the condition of affairs in the Territory of Utah," House Exec. Doc. 25 (32–1), 1852, Serial 640. The appendix of Bigler, ed., *A Winter with the Mormons,* reprints this document. For Brocchus's letter to President Fillmore, Jedediah Grant's (Thomas Kane's?) version of the judge's otherwise unrecorded speech, and Brigham Young's response, see Mulder and Mortensen, *Among the Mormons,* 250–53, 257–61; and Roberts, *Comprehensive History,* 3:520–44. See also Arrington, *Brigham Young: American Moses,* 227–30 and Furniss, *The Mormon Conflict,* 21–32.

[4] Bancroft, *History of Utah,* 456.

[5] Gordon, *The Mormon Question,* 95. For an early discussion of the probate court system in Utah, see Tullidge, *Tullidge's Histories,* 2:320–341.

[6] Allen and Leonard, *The Story of the Latter-day Saints,* 257–63; and Bailey, *Holy Smoke,* 56–59.

admitted that he came out of mere curiosity and then stayed only half a year, gathered material for his book, *Utah and the Mormons,* and returned east. Neither Shaver nor Reid—both of whom enjoyed a fairly amicable relationship with the Saints—lived long. Shaver's death, perhaps due to an opium addiction, was sudden, giving rise to unwarranted rumors that the Mormons had poisoned him. Fortunately for the Saints, Reid died on a visit to his home in Bath, New York, forestalling rumors of Danite intrigue.[7]

One of the next three judges to be appointed by the president to Utah Territory was John Fitch Kinney, a man who appeared to admire and respect the Mormon people.[8] He had known them in Iowa, where he was considered a "Jack Mormon," a term used in those days to suggest a Gentile friendly to the LDS church. "Rotund, of vinous aspect, and of medium height, dull-witted, brusque in manner, and pompous in mien," H. H. Bancroft noted, "he was a man whom Brigham knew well how to use."[9] Kinney served as chief justice of the federal courts in Utah from 1854 to 1857 and again from 1860 to 1863 when he was unanimously elected as Utah's territorial delegate to congress. Much of Kinney's early support for the Mormons was simple duplicity, as he privately condemned them in confidential correspondence to the U.S. government.[10] Nonetheless, he had a change of heart. After numerous political appointments and business dealings in Nebraska and California, Kinney elected to make his home in Utah, dying there in 1902. One anti-Mormon writer even claimed that Kinney "joined the Mormons, [and] was baptized in the holy Jordan," but this was not the case.[11]

While Kinney seemed—at least on the surface—to get along well with the Mormons, his two associates, George P. Stiles and, most especially, W. W. Drummond, did not. Stiles had been a prominent member of the church in Nauvoo, serving as city attorney and joining Almon Babbitt and other city council members in advocating the destruction of the anti-Mormon *Nauvoo Expositor.* President Franklin Pierce named him

---

7 Roberts, *Comprehensive History,* 3:518.

8 For Kinney's first term in Utah, see Homer, "The Federal Bench and Priesthood Authority: The Rise and Fall of John Fitch Kinney's Early Relationship with the Mormons."

9 Bancroft, *History of Utah,* 489.

10 Furniss, *The Mormon Conflict,* 54.

11 Beadle, *Life in Utah,* 197. For an excellent summary of Kinney's checkered career in Utah, see Homer, "The Federal Bench and Priesthood Authority."

as associate justice for Utah Territory in 1854, but he was at best an "indifferent" member of the church and was finally excommunicated in December 1856 for adultery. From that point on, there was considerable friction between Stiles and his former brethren, resulting in an altercation in his court that led to the burning of his law library and charges that the Mormons had destroyed federal court records.

This Prostitute Sitting on the Bench

While many of the federal officials sent to Utah were honorable, fair-minded individuals, W. W. Drummond seemed to personify charges that the men sent to govern Utah Territory were corrupt, vindictive, and immoral. He quickly earned the opprobrium of the Mormons through his opposition to the probate courts and for his flagrant disrespect for local moral sensibilities. Like many in the nation, Drummond erroneously assumed that the Mormons' embrace of polygamy was symptomatic of a pervasive licentiousness. Consequently, he brought his mistress, Ada Carrol (born Mary Ridgley, married to Charles Fletcher and later exposed as a Washington, D.C., prostitute), with him to Utah. He even allowed this "wife" to share the bench with him as he sat in hypocritical judgment on the Mormon people.

The annals of Mormon history are replete with unsavory anecdotes about Drummond. Bill Hickman, a sometime Mormon attorney, among other professions, told an interesting story of the judge and his "lady:"

> About this time Judge W. W. Drummond had been holding a term of the District Court, and had with him a woman whom he had picked up in Washington, leaving his wife and family, and had this prostitute sitting on the bench with him when trying a case of murder. She was writing billets[12] and passing to him while on his judicial bench. I heard this in Salt Lake City a few days before leaving for Filmore, and made an assertion on the street that if I had a murder case before him, and he had that woman on the bench, I would kick them both out of the house. He heard this before I got to Filmore, and issued a bench warrant for my arrest for contempt of court. I heard of it when I got in town, and said if he served such a writ on me I would horsewhip him. It was not served.[13]

[12] From the French "billets doux," literally "sweet notes," or love letters.

[13] Hickman, *Brigham's Destroying Angel*, 111.

Drummond attacked the Mormons first through the California and later the Eastern newspapers, hiding behind various *nomes de plume* including "Amicus Curiae," or "friend of the court." It did not take Cannon long, however, to determine this "friend's" identity. W. W. Drummond lodged a number of complaints against the Mormons and his letters were ready fodder for the California press, prompting George Q. Cannon's inevitable rebuttals and vigorous counterattacks in the *Western Standard.*

"POLYGAMY IN UTAH, FILLMORE CITY, UTAH, SEPT. 15TH, 1856," *DAILY HERALD,* 24 NOVEMBER 1856.[14]

EDITOR OF THE SAN FRANCISCO HERALD:—*Dear Sir:*—As it may be a matter of interest to the gentile world to know how fast our people are in Utah Territory, I will give you briefly a list of the standing among the women of the members of the last Legislature, that is their names and the number of wives, to-wit:

Of the Members of the Council, 13 persons:

Heber C. Kimball, President of Council	57
Daniel H. Wells, Councilman, (cross-eyed)	19
Albert Carrington, (cripple and near-sighted)	21
Orson Pratt (cripple and near-sighted)	7
Wilford Woodruff, (cripple and near-sighted)	12
John Stoker, (cripple and near-sighted)	8
Lorin Farr, (cripple and near-sighted)	3
Lorenzo Snow, (cripple and near-sighted)	25
Leonard E. Harrington, (cripple and near-sighted)	3
Benjamin F. Johnson, (cripple and near-sighted)	4
Isaac Moorley, (72 years old)	5
John A. Ray, (from Texas)	2
George A. Smith, (cripple and near-sighted)	5
Grand total, men 13, women	171

House of Representatives, 26 members:

J. M. Grant, Speaker, has	6
W. W. Phelps, (printer of Morgan's book)	7
A. P. Rockwood, (an old man)	8
Edwin D. Woolley, (a small man)	5
J. W. Cummings, (a cripple)	10
Hosea Stout, (lawyer, from Kentucky—3 dead)	1

[14] The following list was subsequently reprinted in *Harper's Weekly,* 10 January 1857.

S. W. Richards, (young and hansome [sic] lawyer)	15
Jessie C. Little, (lawyer, of Boston, Mass.)	3
Wm. Snow, (Vermont laborer)	8
P. H. Young (older brother of Brigham—tailor)	5
C. V. Spencer, (of Mass., quite small,) has but	2
Ezra S. Benson, (old and homely,)	15
James C. Snow, (quite poor)	3
Aaron Johnson, (has three sisters, and altogether)	6
Lorenzo H. Hatch, (wagon maker,)	2
Jacob G. Bigler, (farmer,)	10
George Peacock, (farmer,)	10
John Eldridge (phrenologist—two dead,)	1
Isaac C. Haight, (coal digger,)	12
Jesse N. Smith, (lawyer,)	2
John D. Parker, (old and deaf,)	3
Jesse Hobson, (ox teamster,)	10
J. C. Wright, (hotel keeper,)	5
James Brown, (dairyman,)	7
Enoch Reese, (farmer, etc.)	2
W. A. Hickman, (one of the Danites,)	3
Total	157

To which add officers of the House, to wit:

Thomas Bullock, (Clerk, and an Englishman,)	4
J. Grimshaw, (Assistant Clerk, and an Englishman)	5
Chandler Holbrook, (Foreman, and deaf,)	4
Jacob F. Hutchinson, (Messenger)	2
Joel H. Johnson, (Chaplain,)	7
Total	22

To which add 68 for the number then living of Governor Young's wives, and you have the whole number of females thus represented by the members of the Legislature, officers of same, and his Excellency, amounting to 420; or, in other words, 40 men have 420 wives. These, Mr. Editor, are sober truths, and in what they will end is for the dark and doleful future.

AMICUS CURIAE.

"'Amicus Curiae' Versus Cripples," *Western Standard*, 29 November 1856.[15]

That highly veracious (?) sheet, the *San Francisco Herald,* in its issue of Monday last, published a communication purporting to have been written

[15] Reprinted in Cannon, *Writings from the "Western Standard,"* 260–61.

at Fillmore city, under the date of Sept. 15th, 1856, the writer of which attempts to give a list of the members and officers of the last Utah Legislature, with the number of wives belonging to each individual. The *Bulletin*, of the same evening, in commenting upon this choice production, says,—"As to the truth (?) of its statements we have no means of judging." Had the editor of the *Bulletin* but reflected a moment, we are of the opinion that he would have written differently, as, from his experience, he should have every means of judging of the truth of any statement made through the columns of the *Herald.* We have never seen the time, during our residence here, that any statement of importance it published could be relied upon. Its editor and correspondents have ever delighted in hyperbole, whether in dilating on the proceedings of the Vigilance Committee or any other subject of moment. Particularly has this been the case when "Mormonism" or the "Mormons" have been alluded to. To publish a sober, truthful article in that sheet, on this subject, would be next to impossible, and something, we presume, the public have never yet beheld. There is such an air of improbability about this communication, however, to which we allude, that the most credulous cannot believe it. To represent nine, out of the thirteen members of the Legislative Council in Utah, to be cripples and near-sighted, and yet to have, in the aggregate, 171 wives, is a *leetle* too strong, even for the readers of the *Herald.*[16] In preparing such an article for San Francisco consumption, the writer ought to have consulted the editor as to the most suitable style; his experience has been so extensive in dishing up articles of this kind, that his advice could scarcely have failed to benefit. It is really cruel for this *"Amicus Curiae"* to cripple men and make purblind so many hale, hearty, active, farseeing men in one communication; if he had no mercy for them, he ought at least to have spared the feelings of their 328 wives. If they had been has [*sic*] imbecile and near-sighted, during his residence in Fillmore, as he has represented them to be, we are inclined to think that his time there would have been much more agreeably spent than, if rumor speaks correctly, it was. Two runaway judges and a secretary from Utah Territory told, once, just such "sober truths" as these published by *"Amicus Curiae,"* and, like him, thought "the dark and doleful future" would be apt to reveal the end of this state of things which they described. But they proved themselves, as *"Amicus Curiae"* will certainly prove himself, to be dullards in descrying what the future would bring forth, so far as the "Mormons" and their religion are concerned.

---

[16] To its credit, the *Daily Evening Bulletin* of 24 November 1856 noted this problem: "The great number of 'members of the Council' who are described as 'cripple and near-sighted,' will probably make some people entertain doubts as to the reliable character of the writer." Cannon did not respond to the *Bulletin's* inclusion of this letter within its pages, choosing instead to focus on the more gullible *Herald.*

THE RECENT OUTRAGES OF THE PEOPLE OF UTAH

As the fires of the Reformation burned white hot in Utah, on 29 December 1856, a mob broke into the law offices of Associate Supreme Court Justice George P. Stiles and his apostate partner, Thomas S. Williams. The mob, largely composed of Mormon lawyers, destroyed their personal libraries and records. "Last night the Law library of Judge Stiles & T. S. Williams was broken open and the books and papers thereof taken away," Hosea Stout (one of the culprits) recorded. "A privy near by was filled with books a few thousand shingles and laths added and the concern set on fire and consumed. *Sic transit Lex non Scripti*" [thus passeth away the unwritten law].[17]

Federal hegemony again came under attack during February 1857 at a hearing in Judge Stiles's court on the authority of federal and territorial courts. Mormon attorneys claimed that the federal judges had "no jurisdiction to try cases arising under the laws of the Territory" and objected to federal courts "continually ruling our laws nugatory by their decisions." Tempers flared, and Hosea Stout noted that "several laid off their coats while two gentiles not wishing to take a hand in the contest" left the courtroom. Feelings ran high, for "this was a contest for the supremacy of our laws."[18]

Among the most damning of Drummond's many accusations was his story of how the Mormons had seized and burned these federal court records. If this was not treason, many reasoned, what was?

"MORE OUTRAGES OF BRIGHAM YOUNG," *DAILY HERALD*, 25 FEBRUARY 1857.

EDITOR OF THE SAN FRANCISCO HERALD:—I wish to call your attention to a few of the recent outrages of the people of Utah Territory, and particularly to the course of Brigham Young, the Governor of Utah, who has taken an oath to support the Constitution of the United States; and as Governor of Utah Territory, to see that the laws are faithfully observed and executed. Has he ever done it? Look at the facts and see: In March last, William A. Hickman, Alexander McKea [sic], Thos. J. Johnson, and others, broke open the door of the District Clerk's office in Salt Lake City, on Saturday night before the sitting of the District Court, and took therefrom the papers, records and documents belonging to the Court; and after Judge Kin-

[17] Brooks, ed. *On the Mormon Frontier*, 613.

[18] Ibid., 621–22.

ney instructed the Grand Jury it was their duty to enquire into the offence, and bring the offenders to justice, this man Young instructed the Grand Jury that it was a Gentile Court, and as such, the Saints of God had nothing to do with the matter, and that if the d—d Gentiles had business to settle, they most [*sic*] do it some place other than in Utah Territory. Nothing was done with the offenders.[19] Again, a man by the name of Baker, (a Mormon,) was tried for murdering a dumb boy, in Judge Drummond's court, at Fillmore city; and although the proof showed one of the most aggravated cases of murder, the Grand Jury, (all Mormons of course,) brought in a verdict of murder in the second degree; this was on Wednesday, and although the sentence was pronounced on Baker, and he started towards the Penitentiary, yet, before the sixth Sabbath he had a full and complete pardon from Gov. Young, and really never went as far as the Penitentiary; but on the other hand, accompanied Gov. Young to church on the Sabbath next after his trial and conviction. The reason assigned for this pardon was that he was a Saint, and a d—d Gentile Judge should not have the pleasure of seeing one of the Saints of God put in prison for the murder of so useless a being as a dumb boy. That if people were so unfortunate as to have children that could not speak, they were incapable of becoming Saints, and it was a blessing to kill them off and save the parents the trouble of bringing them up, and that God required a human being to talk before he could pray.

Again, I have to chronicle one of the most daring and insulting national crimes ever committed in the United States, and that, too, under the direct care and control, and under the immediate order and direction of this man Young. Early in January, and just in advance of the meeting of the Supreme Court, a party of Mormons in high standing in the Church, and under the advice of Brigham Young, repaired to the office of the Hon. G. P. Stiles, one of the United States District Judges, the law office of T. S. Williams, Esq., and the office of the Clerk of the Supreme Court, and took therefrom *all the papers* belonging to the Supreme Court, consisting of *records, dockets, opinions* filed away, together with nine hundred volumes of the laws, furnished by the Federal Government for the use of the Territory of Utah. The reason given for this treasonous act was that Congress would not admit them as a State, and that they would not allow the Federal officers to remain in the Territory; and that what officers were now in the Territory must leave as soon as grass grows or he will send them to hell, across lots. Now, sir, can you find a parallel to this act of treason since the organization of the American Colonies, if so, please note the time and place.

It seems now to be a settled fact that the laws of Congress cannot be carried out or put in force in this territory—the only law known or obeyed, is

[19] Alexander McRea was Utah Territorial Marshal. Thomas S. Johnson was a client of Hosea Stout in "a very excitable case" involving cattle.

the law of the Church, and that is the will of Brigham Young, who most clearly is the most brutal tyrant now on earth, and in point of treasonous designs, without an equal. . . .

At this time, sir, there are five young men lingering out a weary life of misery and wretchedness, groaning beneath heavy loads of iron, in the damp and dismal cells of the Utah Penitentiary, for no crime known to the laws other than expressing opinions of disapprobation of the doctrines of Mormonism, which here is the blackest crime a man can commit. It is worthy of remark that these young men are not Mormons, but were passing, on their way to California, from Missouri. Poor fellows! they are doomed to a sickly and torturing death, and that, soon, for it is not possible to survive such brutal treatment very long. Quite recently a young man by the name of Lewis was convicted of assault and battery, and sentenced to five years imprisonment in the Penitentiary; and while on the way to the prison, a band of ruffians took him away from the officer and deprived him of his ______, and then put him into the prison to die. These things are too common to be endured much longer; and unless the Federal Government speedily lends aid unto her officers now in this territory, the miserable ends of both Mormons and officers of the government can be better anticipated than told.

Please insert this in your valuable paper, for the benefit of its many readers.

SALT LAKE CITY, Jan. 7, 1857 AMICUS CURIAE

"THE FEDERAL RECORDS OF UTAH," *DAILY HERALD*, 26 FEBRUARY 1857.

MR. JOHN NUGENT—*My Dear Sir:* In your paper of this date, I notice an article over the signature of "Amicus Curiae," relative to affairs in Utah Territory, and among other things your correspondent speaks of the books, records, etc. having been taken from the office of the Clerk of the Supreme Court, from the office of Judge Stiles, etc., but does not say what became of the books, records and other things belonging to the office of the Clerk of the Supreme Court. The facts, sir, are that they were burned up in the City of Great Salt Lake, and no notice taken of the outrage by any one in authority at that place. While the matter is being made public, it is just as well to tell what was done with the records, etc., of the Supreme Court, and the library furnished by the United States for the benefit of the Federal officers of that Territory. I very much doubt, sir, whether an outrage of that character was ever thought of in "bleeding Kansas." Please place this in the columns of the HERALD, that the whole history of that infamous insult may go out together.

Respectfully, your obedient servant,
W. W. DRUMMOND
February 25, 1857

"Base Artifice to Injure the 'Mormons'," *Western Standard,* 28 February 1857.[20]

In the *Herald* of Wednesday, "Amicus Curiae," who distinguished himself a few months ago by writing a silly article giving a *crippled* account of the members of the Legislature and their wives, has another long article, headed "More outrages of Brigham Young." In this latter article he proceeds to call the attention of the editor of the *Herald* to "a few of the recent outrages of the people of Utah and particularly to the course of Brigham Young,". . . The article is evidently written with the most base and malicious intentions, and is the production of a man who, if we may judge by the spirit of his article, would have no higher pleasure than to see the dogs of war let loose upon the "Mormons" and them exterminated from the face of the earth. The article is dated January 7th, at Great Salt Lake City, but was without doubt written in this city, as the editor of the *Herald's* proclivities for such slanders are too well known to admit of the supposition, for one moment, that he would keep so sweet a morsel on hand for two weeks after the arrival of the mail. The public are expected, of course, to innocently gulp down the whole story without questioning; dating the letter at Great Salt Lake City would make the article have a more telling effect, and was an artifice perfectly justifiable, in the estimation of the writer, to be used in creating prejudice against Brigham Young and the Latter-day Saints. To corroborate and give the statements a greater semblance of truth, on Thursday another communication appeared, over the signature of W. W. Drummond, confirming and giving additional items relative to the fate of all the records, books, etc. . . .

It was not intended, of course, that the public should know that "Amicus Curiae," the Great Salt Lake correspondent of the *Herald,* and W. W. Drummond are one and the same personage; yet, every person who will examine both communications, the structure of the sentences, etc., will scarcely fail to be convinced that the effusions of "Amicus Curiae" and that of W. W. Drummond emanated from the same pen. We have the best of reasons for concluding that both communications originated here, and if they did, how contemptible a subterfuge to practice to bring indignation upon the "Mormons!" It was a most brave device and excellently planned! "Amicus Curiae," at Great Salt Lake City, omitted to mention the fate of the books, records, etc., abstracted from the office of the Clerk of the Supreme Court in Utah by a party of "Mormons" in high standing, under the immediate direction of Brigham Young, but the omission is easily corrected; W. W. Drummond, United States District Judge of Utah, steps into the witness stand in San Francisco, and completes "the whole history of the infamous insult," by informing the editor of the *Herald* that they were burned,

[20] Reprinted in Cannon, *Writings from the "Western Standard,"* 355–57. (In *Writings,* Cannon incorrectly listed the month as February, rather than January.)

> yes, "sir, burned up in the city of Great Salt Lake, and no notice taken of the outrage by any one in authority at that place!" Thus the convenient omission of this item by the mythical "Amicus Curiae," gives an opportunity for the testimony of another to be introduced, who confirms one part of the story and tacitly conveys the idea that the remainder is equally true; and thus the uninitiated are left to imagine that there are two persons, one in Great Salt lake City and the other in San Francisco, who testify to the same things!
>
> Such low and disgraceful measures to injure the Governor and the people of Utah are unworthy of any man who lays the slightest claim to respectability and truth, and they will sooner or later recoil on the heads of those who originate them. . . .

Cannon saw through Drummond's ruse. After traveling to Carson City to hear a case, Judge Drummond fled Utah in spring 1857 and was residing in California at this time. Contrary to what he had told numerous people—including the brother of his wife, who lived in Salt Lake—he had never divorced Jemima Richards Drummond. While he was in California, this fact was finally discovered and he felt it would be imprudent to return, even if the Mormons had not discovered the true identity of "Amicus Curiae." He did not officially resign his position as federal judge until he arrived in New Orleans on 30 March. His letter of resignation contained further indictments of Brigham Young and the Mormons, including the false charges that they had been instrumental in the recent murders of Almon W. Babbitt, secretary of Utah Territory, and Captain Gunnison and his surveying party.

Drummond seriously misrepresented the facts when he claimed that district court records were destroyed. It is possible his error was an honest one inasmuch as the gang had *pretended* to burn government records while in fact burning Judge Stiles' books. Honest or not, this error was widely believed. It wasn't until 2 May 1858, shortly after arriving in Utah, that Governor Cumming said he had examined "the records of the supreme and district courts, which I am now prepared to report as being perfect and unimpaired" and "the legislative records and other books belonging to the office of the secretary of state, which are in perfect preservation."[21]

[21] U.S. House, "Cessation of Difficulties in Utah," Serial 959. Still the controversy raged on: "The public records of this Territory are in a state of inglorious confusion, notwithstanding the assertion made by Gov. Cumming," *New York Times* correspondent James W. Simonton wrote from Great Salt Lake City in 1858. "How Gov. Cumming, in view of these facts, was able to reconcile his conscience to his report that these records are in a perfect state of preservation, I cannot tell you." See "Public Records in Utah Territory All in Confusion," *Evening Bulletin*, 30 September 1858, 1/1.

There may be some truth to Drummond's contention that it was difficult for Gentiles to be dealt with justly in Utah and that Mormons were often let off by their juries of peers. Doubtless with some reason, non-Mormons often felt it impossible to get a fair and impartial hearing from an all-Mormon jury. Nonetheless, one of the most severe critics of the Utah courts conceded there were cases in which justice prevailed : "For instance in the winter of 1863–64, Jason Luce, a Mormon, was tried, convicted, and shot, for the murder of a gentile in Salt Lake City."[22] Though inconclusive, modern scholarship has suggested there is "insufficient proof that between 1855 and 1872 the judges and juries of the Utah County Probate Court manipulated judicial proceedings and therefore worked a dual brand of justice upon those who pled their cases before them."[23]

One of Drummond's most spectacular allegations was that the Mormons took sacred vows during their Temple ceremony against the government of the United States. Today's members of the Church of Jesus Christ of Latter-day Saints who have participated in the temple rites would find little similarity between the oaths they have taken (none of which could possibly be construed as a challenge to civil authority or an oath of vengeance) and those alleged by Ann Eliza Young to have been taken by their pioneer ancestors in 1875:

> The women promised entire subjection to their husbands' will; the men that they would take no woman as a wife without the express permission of the priesthood. We all promised that we would never question the commands of our authorities in the church, but would grant them instant obedience; we swore also to entertain an everlasting enmity to the United States government; and to disregard its laws so far as possible; we swore that we would use every exertion to avenge the death of our Prophet Joseph Smith and his brother Hyrum upon the Gentile race, and to teach our children to foster this spirit of revenge also.[24]

Ann Eliza Young was not only a bitter apostate, but by her own admission, had only been to the Endowment House on a single occasion—when she received her own special ordinances, or endowment. Based on the balance of her book, it could be argued that her memory was highly

22 Waite, *The Mormon Prophet and His Harem,* 117.

23 Gee, "Justice for All or for the 'Elect'?: The Utah County Probate Court, 1855–72", 146.

24 Young, *Wife No. 19*, 368.

selective, and it is likely that her recollection was colored by the equally damning (though second-hand) versions described by Beadle five years earlier.[25] Perhaps the most accurate early exposé of the LDS temple ceremonies— though also distorted by his biases—was provided by John Hyde, Jr., who experienced them on at least two occasions. He conflated two of the above "oaths" into one: "We were, therefore, sworn to cherish constant enmity toward the United States government for not avenging the death of Smith, or righting the persecutions of the Saints."[26]

As one particularly objective non-Mormon has summarized this issue,

> These rites were once painted in lurid terms or surrounded by hints and innuendo in the writing of some apostates, but there is actually nothing more to them than a ritualization of the beliefs that Joseph taught at Nauvoo, most of which are part of Mormon belief and published and taught openly in Mormon religious literature today . . . There has been much discussion as to whether or not an oath against, or at least interpretable as unfriendly to or violating the sovereignty of, the United States of America was ever given at these ceremonies later in Utah. However, even if such charges be true, this is long past and was not really an essential part of the ceremonies themselves.[27]

There can now be little doubt that the temple ceremony, beginning in 1845 and continuing (though with increasingly softened language) through 1927 contained an oath to avenge the blood of the prophets Joseph and Hyrum Smith and to pray for such vengeance at the hands of God.[28] One participant testified that the oath said, "You and each of you do covenant and promise that you will pray, and never cease to pray, Almighty God to avenge the blood of the prophets upon this nation, and that you will teach the same to your children and your children's children unto the third and fourth generations."[29]

His apostle son recorded George Q. Cannon himself saying "that he

---

[25] Beadle, *Life in Utah*, 496–97.

[26] Hyde, *Mormonism: Its Leaders and Designs*, 97. The earliest published exposé of the temple rites was by Van Deusen, *The Mormon Endowment: A Secret Drama, or Conspiracy, in the Nauvoo Temple, in 1846*. For a treatment of the larger Biblical context of "oath making," see Whittaker, "A Covenant People," 196–216.

[27] O'Dea, *The Mormons*, 58–59.

[28] See *The Inside of Mormonism*; Buerger, *The Mysteries of Godliness*, 133–38; and Tanner and Tanner, *Evolution of the Mormon Temple Ceremony: 1842–1990*, 22–26.

[29] Buerger, "The Development of the Mormon Temple Endowment Ceremony," 52–53. The source, Walter M. Wolfe, had been a professor at Brigham Young Academy and was testifying sometime during the Smoot Hearing, 1904–1906.

understood when he had his endowment in Nauvoo that he took an oath against the murderers of the Prophet Joseph as well as other prophets, and if he had ever met any of those who had taken a hand in that massacre he would undoubtedly have attempted to avenge the blood of the martyrs."[30]

A Picture of Beastly Barbarity

Throughout Cannon's years editing the *Western Standard,* news from Utah Territory provided anti-Mormons with a host of charges, both true and false, to level against the Saints. "For the Mormons have had enemies, both bitter and unscrupulous, during the whole course of their history," historian Dale Morgan observed, "enemies who have delighted to seize upon real or imagined irregularities of which the Saints have been guilty, to make all the lurid capital possible to be made from them."[31]

An event took place in September 1856 that provided more grist for the mill of W. W. Drummond. A Cheyenne war party butchered Almon W. Babbitt, secretary of Utah Territory, as the colorful and controversial Mormon politician raced across the plains west of Fort Kearny. Babbitt, whose raging alcoholism and questionable personal morality put him at odds with Brigham Young, had refused a military escort through dangerous Indian country, knew the risk he was taking and, according to the warriors who split his skull, fought "like a grizzly bear." U.S. military officers were convinced Indians had killed Babbitt, but when Orrin Porter Rockwell appeared at Fort Laramie on 19 September with some of Babbitt's livestock attached to his five wagons, rumors immediately sprang up that "the Mormon destroying angel had notched another victim."[32]

Many of Drummond's allegations were groundless while some had merit. Regardless of the accuracy of his sensational accusations, his prolific letter writing generated, especially in California, renewed enthusiasm for attacks on Mormonism by the Western press. One newspaper, the *Alta California,* recalled the Missouri persecutions by once again floating the suggestion that the Mormons should be exterminated.

---

[30] Abraham H. Cannon Diary, 6 December 1889, 205.

[31] Morgan, *The Great Salt Lake,* 282.

[32] Schindler, *Orrin Porter Rockwell,* 230–37. For a fuller treatment of Babbitt, see Ridd, "Almon Whiting Babbitt, Mormon Emissary." For interesting insights into Babbitt's difficulties with church leadership, see Melville, "Brigham Young on Politics and Priesthood," 488–89.

"The Utah Problem," *Alta California*, 21 May 1857.

Perhaps no man who has occupied the Presidential chair of our nation, has ever entered upon his duties, with more intricate national questions before him, and more important measures to be passed upon, than is exhibited in the opening of Mr. Buchanan's administration. Leaving out the agitation of sectional questions, involving the rights of the people of the north and the south, there is a spot away in the heart of the continent, where an institution has obtained a foothold, the acts of the leaders of which, growing every day more and more astounding in their unparalleled outrageousness, are assuming an alarming degree of importance in the eyes of the nation at large. The Utah problem is one more difficult of solution, than all the other political questions of the day; not because there is not a marked unanimity of sentiment in condemnation of it, but because of the proper treatment necessary to remove this fixed and corroding incubus from the body politic.

The [30 March 1857] letter of Judge Drummond to the U.S. Attorney General, Mr. Black, reveals a detail of wrongs and outrages perpetrated by Brigham Young and his myrmidoms [*sic*], that is enough to rouse the ire of every honest American heart, and thrill us with horror to think that such a foul stain blots the fair land which we rejoice to call our birthright.

There are positive assertions made over the signature of the Hon. Judge, that "the male members of the church acknowledge no law save that of the Holy Priesthood, which comes to the people through Brigham Young." That there "are a set of men set apart by special order of the church to take both the lives and property of all who question the authority of the church." That the records and papers of the United States Court have been destroyed by order of Brigham Young. That federal officers are abused and insulted, and the authority and institutions of our country are vilified and spit upon in the most loathsome and wicked manner. As a proof of this latter charge, we give the following statement in the Judge's own language:

> After Moroni Green had been convicted in the District Court, before my colleague, Judge Kinney, of an assault with intent to commit murder; and afterward, on appeal to the Supreme Court, the judgment being affirmed and the said Green sentenced to the penitentiary, Brigham Young gave a full pardon to the said Green before he reached the penitentiary; also, that the said Governor Young pardoned a man by the name of Baker, who had been tried and sentenced to ten years imprisonment in the penitentiary for the murder of a dumb boy by the name of White House, the proof showing one of the most aggravated cases of murder that I ever knew being tried; and to insult the Court and Government officers this man, Young, took this pardoned criminal with him in proper person to church on the next Sabbath after his conviction,

> Baker, in the meantime having received a full pardon from Governor Brigham Young. These two men were Mormons. . . .
>
> * * * * * * *
>
> After a careful and mature investigation, I have been compelled to come to the conclusion—heart-rending and sickening as it may be—that Capt. John W. Gunnison and his party of eight others were murdered by the Indians in 1853, under the order, advice and directions of the Mormons; that my illustrious and distinguished predecessor, the Hon. Leonidas Shaver, came to his death by drinking poisonous liquors, given to him under the order of the leading men of the Mormon Church in Great Salt Lake City; that the late Secretary of the Territory, A. W. Babbitt, was murdered on the Plains by a band of Mormon marauders, under the particular and special order of Brigham Young, Heber C. Kimball, and J. M. Grant, and not by the Indians, as reported by the Mormons themselves, and that they were sent from Salt Lake City for that purpose and that only; and as members of the Danite band, they were bound to do the will of Brigham Young, as the head of the church, or forfeit their own lives.

However strong may be the denial of these assertions by the Mormons and their sympathizers, the evidence is introvertable[*sic*], accumulating as it has for several years past, by the reports of every one who has spent any time among them, until it is backed up by the solemn reiteration of one high in the confidence of the government, and whose untarnished reputation would of itself alone have sustained the charges.

Side by side with these sickening outrages, follow the accounts of the beastly barbarity that is displayed in the social relations of their every day life:

> "If a father has a child, fair and innocent, whom he loves and cherishes, and if she captivates the fancy of some leading Mormon, she will be taken from her home by the decree of the elders, and given up by the ceremony of "sealing" to become the fortieth or fiftieth wife to an old villian [*sic*], while her predecessors, who have grown old in the same guilty and abominable connection become his household or cornfield servants. It often happens that a man is sealed to two women at the same ceremony, and cases are not rare when one of the wives so acquitted is lost by a divorce before breakfast next morning.
>
> "The account given by Judge Drummond, of many of these connections, were [*sic*] sometimes a mother and two or three of her daughters were all sealed to the same man, presents a picture of beastly barbarity. Could a correct idea of these horrible transactions be made known throughout the country, a crusade would be preached against this foul horde, that would soon put an end to their sway."

In discussing this matter, we feel an inability to suggest any other remedy for this growing evil, other than a resort to physical force and the bringing of the military arm of the nation into requisition, even though it waged a war of total extermination to the horde of villians [*sic*]. Yet we feel a confidence that the present administration will use the extent of its power camly [*sic*], firmly, and with true discretion, and that it will devise some means to check its alarming progress.

The existence of a superior power here, in their immediate neighbors, as it were, prevents the probability of the Mormon colony at San Berna[r]dino from ever becoming sufficiently powerful to carry out their measures with such a high hand as does Brigham Young and his sattelites [*sic*]. But being made acquainted with their brutal tenets, we know that it is only an unavoidable fear that prevents the enactment of such scenes among the priesthood of San Bernardino.

So far as forming an ingredient in deciding upon the political destinies of our State, they have exercised all the trickery and cunning that they dared, and the charge stands uncontradicted and incontrovertible, that they sold their suffrages for a price, in the campaign of 1855, to the highest bidder, after passing through a regular course of diplomatic negotiation, in disposing of the aggregate vote, for the most advantageous price. To expatriate this class of people from sharing in the formation of the laws of the commonwealth, to deny to them the right of suffrage or political communion with us, is to our mind, but a mild treatment. Intolerance is no part of our creed, neither is a social and political communion with men who reduce themselves below the level of beasts, in accordance with our desires. Respect for the institutions and form of our government, veneration for the memory of those who gave us this glorious heritage, teaches us to revolt against this inhuman and wicked association; and when its disgusting tenets are cloaked in the holy garb of religion, we view it in the light of grossest sacrilege to attempt to vindicate its existence. How long must it be tolerated, and what is the key to the "Utah problem?"

"EXTERMINATION.—A BLOOD-THIRSTY EDITOR," *WESTERN STANDARD*, 22 MAY 1857.[33]

The editor of the *Alta California*, in a long leader in yesterday's issue, works himself into a perfect rage over the "Utah problem," and indulges in the most foolish and intemperate language upon that subject. The text which he has taken, is the letter of Judge Drummond to Mr. Attorney General Black. This Drummond letter we have already referred to in another column.[34] But the *Alta* says,—"However strong may be the denial of these

[33] Reprinted in Cannon, *Writings from the "Western Standard,"* 411–15.

[34] This reference is to another editorial in the same issue, "Ex-Judge Drummond and His Slanders." In addition to repudiating Drummond's charges of Mormon complicity in several murders, Cannon

assertions by the Mormons and their sympathizers, the evidence is incontrovertible,[35] accumulating as it has for several years past, by the reports of every one who has spent any time among them, until it is backed up by the solemn reiteration of one high in the confidence of the Government, and whose untarnished reputation would of itself alone have sustained the charges." We have denied these assertions—emphatically and indignantly denied them—and can produce the evidence of gentlemen as high in the confidence of the Government, and of as untarnished a reputation as Judge Drummond, to support us in our denial. The editor of the *Alta* has either a very treacherous memory or he has willfully misrepresented, when he says that the reports, for several years past, of every one who has spent any time among the "Mormons" has been confirmatory of the slanders of Drummond. We are willing to compare testimony with testimony, to meet authority with authority on this subject, without the slightest fear as to the result. We will neither appeal to the testimony of Latter-day Saints nor of those who are known as their sympathizers; but we will take that of gentlemen whose social position and standing and public reputation are immeasurably superior to Drummond's, and we will prove by them that he has willfully and maliciously defamed both Governor Young and the people of Utah.

As we have not space in this article to give lengthy extracts—and as the charges preferred are principally against Governor Young—we will merely quote from a memorial forwarded to President Pierce, and signed by several prominent United States civil and military officers, as well as other gentlemen of unblemished reputation, whose opportunities of obtaining a knowledge of Governor Young's character and the nature of his influence over the people were equal, if not superior, to those of Judge Drummond. The object of the memorial was the reappointment of Brigham Young, as Governor and Superintendent of Indian affairs for Utah. They state:—

> "*Whereas,* Governor Brigham Young possesses the entire confidence of the people of this Territory, *without distinction of party or sect;* and from personal intercourse, we find him to be a firm supporter of the Constitution and laws of the United States, and a tried pillar of republican institutions; and, having repeatedly listened to his remarks, in private as well as in public assemblies, do know he is the warm friend and able supporter of constitutional liberty, *the rumors in the States to the contrary notwithstanding.* * * *
>
> And it being our unqualified opinion—based upon the personal acquaintance which we have formed with Governor Young, and from our observation of the results of his influence and administration in this

---

exposed the judge's cowardice through his publication of an anti-polygamy address purportedly delivered to the Grand Jury of Carson County. Drummond gave no such speech.

35 Cannon corrects the original rendering of "incontrovertible" as "introvertable" without calling attention to the original error. Although angry with the *Alta's* editor, he was not reduced to pettiness.

> Territory, that he possesses in an eminent degree every qualification necessary for the discharge of his official duties, and unquestioned integrity and ability—that he is decidedly the most suitable person that can be selected for that office."

The italics are ours. The name of J. T. Kinney, Chief Justice of the United States Supreme Court,[36] heads the list as Chairman, followed by those of E. J. Steptoe, Lieut. Col. United States Army; Major Reynolds, Capt. Ingalls, and several other officers, with that also of Hon Leonidas Shaver, Assistant Justice of the United States Supreme Court. If having an "untarnished reputation," and being "high in the confidence of the Government," are the qualifications giving weight to and sustaining the testimony of Judge Drummond, how overwhelmingly conclusive must be the calm, unbiased and incontrovertible testimony of these gentlemen. They had no revenge to gratify, no spleen to vent in recommending Brigham Young to the Executive as a man eminently worthy of the office of Governor; but this can not be said of the man who has maligned him. Will the editor of the *Alta* be liberal and honest enough to acknowledge, after he reads this (which is not a tithe of the evidence that can be adduced,) that he was either mistaken when he said that the reports of every one who has spent any time among the people of Utah are similar to these assertions of Drummond's, or that he has been guilty of willful perversion? We shall see.[37]

But it was not to allude to Drummond and his slanders particularly that we commenced this article. It was to call public attention to the sentiments given utterance to by this creature who aspires, in his character of editor, to mold and control public sentiment. After indulging in a long and bitter tirade against the "Mormons" because of their alleged crimes, he says:—

> "In discussing this matter, we feel an inability to suggest any remedy for this growing evil, other than a resort to physical force and the bringing of the military arm of the nation into requisition,—*even though it waged a war of extermination to this horde of villains.*"

In alluding to this sentiment *we* feel *our* inability to express our detestation of and utter contempt for the man who would give publicity to such a suggestion. Condemn the Latter-day Saints and recommend their extermination for practicing crimes, and yet immediately have recourse to a crime of such magnitude that, in comparison with it, the worst crimes the "Mormons" ever were accused of sink into insignificance! Even were Drummond's statements true, of how light a hue are the crimes of which he says they are guilty, compared to this fiendish and inhuman one recommended

[36] Cannon errs here. Kinney's middle initial was "F" rather than "T" and he was of course a justice of the Utah—not the federal—Supreme Court.

[37] The *Alta California's* editor did not allude to the memorial signed most prominently by John F. Kinney, Drummond's "colleague," in whose court Moroni Green was convicted of assault.

by the moral (?) editor of the *Alta California* to the people and Government. In a leading article published by him of little more than a month ago (April 17th) on the subject of "Mormonism," he says:—

> "Violence then is not to be thought of as a means of eradicating this pernicious error. Such a course would be no less impolitic than unjust. It would be impolitic, because, as we have seen, it would tend to strengthen rather than invalidate the evil at which it was aimed; *and it would be unjust,* because *the great mass of the Mormons are not only sincere in their faith, but many of them are comparatively moral and upright in their lives."*

We give his own language verbatim. Mark the portion we have italicized. By his own words shall this chameleon-like editor be judged and condemned: one month ago the "Mormons" were not only sincere in their faith, but many of them were comparatively moral and upright in their lives, and yet now he suggests as the only course to be pursued toward them, their total extermination!!! If they are a "horde of villains" because Judge Drummond asserts that they have committed crimes, of how deep a dye must we conclude the villainy of the editor of the *Alta California* to be, when we have his own published words to show that he desires nothing less than the total extermination of a people *sincere in their faith, and moral and upright in their lives?* We leave it for every just man to answer. . . .

We have barely space to rapidly glance at the many foolish ideas advanced by this editor in the article to which we allude, but enough has been touched upon to set off in a strong light some of the many inconsistencies with which it abounds. A man such as this man evidently is, so destitute of moral and just principles—if this article be a fair expression of his feelings—ought never to be permitted to occupy a position where he could influence the popular mind; for if his prejudices should be roused, whether by a just cause or not, he would disregard constitutions, laws, order and everything else that might stand between him and the accomplishment of his purposes; it would matter not whether the anticipated victims were "Mormons" or anti-Mormons, Christians or Pagans, Jews or Moslems, if they were in the minority and he thought he would be safe, his principles would never prevent him from urging their massacre.

"A Mormon's Estimation of Gentiles," *Alta California*, 25 May 1857.

An obscure sheet is published weekly in this city, called the Western Standard, (we advertise its existence gratis,) and is devoted to the advocacy of the moral and religious teachings of Mormonism. The editor of the journal referred to, has gone stark, staring, raving mad over an editorial in the Alta a few days since, condemning the disgusting and criminal practices of the priesthood at Salt Lake, headed by that human hyena, Brigham

> Young. He condemns the editor of the Alta as "a creature who aspires, in his character of editor, to mould [*sic*] and control public sentiment," and alludes to our suggestions for the employment of the military arm of the government, if by no other means could the evil be exterminated, in reaching Brigham Young and his myrmidons, as "fiendish and inhuman." He goes further, and says "Of how deep a dye must we conclude the villainy of the editor of the Alta California to be, when we have his own published words to show that he desires nothing less than the total extermination of a people sincere in their faith and moral and upright in their lives." This rabid editor has undoubtedly graduated with high honors from Brigham Young's tutilage [*sic*]. Billingsgate is evidently his standard of argument, and his perception of "morality" authorizes the extreme exercise of the passion for free love, and the general commingling of the sexes, without regard to consanguinity.
>
> He looks upon anything against Mormonism, or upon the character of one who exposes its immorality, and wages crusade against its practices, as one "so destitute of moral and just principles, that he ought not to be permitted to occupy a position where he could influence the popular mind." The character and tone of the article referred to, is of a piece with Brigham Young's sermon's [*sic*], and no doubt we have been consigned, ere this, by the juggling practices of Mormon mummery to the lowest degree of their peculiar punishment for the utterance of such heresy. . . .
>
> Looking upon Mormonism as we do, as the abomination of the present day, we shall continue, whenever occasion offers, to expose its iniquities, and endeavor to attract the attention of our government to the evils which it is planting upon our soil—and to call upon that power to sustain its own dignity at least, and by all proper means prevent the spread of this modern religious scourge.

Uncharacteristically, Cannon allowed the *Alta* to have the last word in this round of the California newspaper wars. Perhaps he had come to feel that there were some wars that simply could not be won. More likely, his attention was diverted at the time toward another journalistic foe.

Drummond himself had written the decision in the Moroni Green case, which remitted the costs of the prosecution due to extenuating circumstances. The judges—feeling that Green had acted in self-defense—joined with many others in petitioning Governor Young to pardon the young man. Tullidge subsequently rebutted Drummond's charge that Young had granted a pardon over the wishes of the court, as well as the allegation that "five or six young men from Missouri and Iowa" were imprisoned by the Mormons without cause.[38] Witnesses such as Stansbury felt Mormon court decisions "were remarkable for their fairness and impartiality," whether applied to Saint or Gentile.[39]

Although the poisoning of Judge Shaver is highly unlikely, Drummond was not the only one to make that allegation.[40] Nonetheless, even anti-Mormon classics questioned the allegation: Stenhouse, disavowed "any ground for such a suspicion" and even Beadle argued that he had likely died as a result of being deprived of opium. The physicians at the inquest attested to the judge's addiction to that drug, which was likely at least a contributing factor to his demise.[41]

Cannon was correct with respect to the massacres of Babbitt and Gunnison. Drummond's sensational charges notwithstanding, Captain Gunnison and Almon Babbitt were killed by Indians, and in neither case was Mormon complicity clearly demonstrated. Nonetheless, it is understandable that some would have imagined Mormon involvement in the death of Babbitt, who had been disfellowshipped no fewer than four times before finally being excommunicated from the church in 1854. His stormy relationship with Brigham Young led the latter to proclaim, upon hearing of Babbitt's death, "thank God for that I will acknowledge the hand of the Lord in *that* at all events."[42]

Although it is probable Brigham Young helped the Pahvants accused of the Gunnison Expedition murders to escape justice to preserve a rather tenuous peace, there is no hard evidence of Mormon complicity in the murders themselves, but this did not deter writers from repeating such charges for years to come. One eminent and refreshingly objective writer pointed out in 1862 the inherent irony in accusing the Mormons of Gunnison's murder:

> Like his C.O., Lieutenant Gunnison is accused of having favoured the New Faith, and yet, with all the inconsistency of the odium theologicum [those who hate all things religious] the Faithful are charged with his subsequent

[38] See Deputy Clerk of the U.S. Supreme Court for Utah Curtis E. Bolton's rebuttal to Drummond via his 26 June 1857 letter to President Buchanan in Whitney, *History of Utah,* 1:583–84 or Tullidge, *History of Salt Lake City,* 135–36. Regrettably, this letter did not reach Buchanan before he had decided to send federal troops to Utah Territory.

[39] Stansbury, *Exploration and Survey,* 130.

[40] See Waite, *The Mormon Prophet,* 24; and Green, *Mormonism,* 247–48.

[41] Stenhouse, *Rocky Mountain Saints,* 279; Beadle, *Life in Utah,* 170; *Deseret News,* 4 July 1855.

[42] Quoted, but without specific attribution, in Van Wagoner and Walker, *A Book of Mormons,* 9.

> murder; the only motive of the foul deed being that the Saints dreaded future disclosures, and were determined, though one of their number had been sent to accompany Captain Stansbury as assistant, to prevent other expeditions.[43]

Though some Mormons were critical of Gunnison's book, it was a remarkably fair treatment of the Latter-day Saints. The author thought they were a deluded people who had embraced false doctrines, but he characterized them as a persecuted people and urged the government not to impose its "foreign control" upon them. His analysis of Mormon theology was incomplete and incorrect in many respects, and like many of his day, he accepted the now-discredited Spaulding manuscript theory (which argued that Joseph Smith or Sidney Rigdon had plagiarized an unpublished 1812 novel) as the true origin of *The Book of Mormon.* Published a year prior to his murder, the book's observations on the Mormon people were remarkably sympathetic. Of the many accounts published on the Latter-day Saints during this period, Gunnison's surely did them much more good than harm.

Anti-Mormon writers persisted in reporting Judge Drummond's accusations as incontrovertible fact. Even when all the investigations had been completed and enough time had passed to convince virtually everyone that the Indians had committed these murders, one of these critics found a way to still lay the blame at the feet of Brigham Young. In 1909, Josiah Gibbs argued that Young had been too easy on the Indians, suggesting that had it not been for his "it is cheaper to feed the Indians than to fight them" policy, the attack on Gunnison would have never taken place.[44] Although virtually all historians have now absolved Brigham Young of any responsibility for either of these massacres, there is still an occasional—though ultimately unconvincing—attempt to suggest Mormon complicity, at least in the case of Gunnison.[45] Arguably, if a party of emigrants passing through Utah had taken the advice of local authorities and left the Indians alone, the chain of events that resulted in the Gunnison massacre would have never happened.

---

[43] Burton, *The City of the Saints,* 250n.

[44] Gibbs, *Lights and Shadows of Mormonism,* chapter 23.

[45] For the latest such effort, see Fielding, *The Unsolicited Chronicler.* Fielding's is a one-sided and often careless treatment; tellingly, he did not list Arrington's scholarly *Brigham Young: American Moses* in his bibliography.

Drummond's allegation regarding the ease of divorce in Utah, however, was on solid—if hypocritical—ground. Initially, divorce was relatively difficult, particularly when sought by the man, and had to be approved personally by Brigham Young. Nonetheless, divorce became much more common among post-Reformation polygamists once the difficult reality of sharing a husband and supporting more than one wife set in. Even Young himself had to suffer the indignity of having a former wife publish one of the more popular anti-Mormon books of the period.[46] Not surprisingly, one especially virulent anti-Mormon writer who lived among the Saints for nine years collecting (and embellishing) every sordid story she could find capitalized on the relatively high divorce rate by claiming "It is a common thing to find women living in polygamy who have been divorced three or four times from as many different husbands."[47]

The more moderate J. H. Beadle wrote, "I met one woman who had been divorced and re-married six times, and an old Mormon once pointed out to me a woman who had once been his wife, and had been divorced and re-married nine times."[48] At one point requests for divorce became so frequent that Young started charging ten dollars per approved divorce in an apparently unsuccessful effort to discourage such easy separations. "He boasted once in a sermon, that he made enough this way, 'by their d——d foolishness, to keep him in spending money.'"[49] Even Carlie, the daughter of Brigham Young who later married George Q. Cannon, was a divorcee.[50]

A Peculating Thief and a Foul Calumniator

Cannon elected not to sustain his newspaper war with the *Alta California*, but he was hardly finished with Drummond—particularly when the facts concerning the supposedly burned federal documents came out

---

[46] Young, *Wife Number 19*.

[47] Paddock, *The Fate of Madame La Tour*, 342.

[48] Beadle, *Life in Utah*, 350.

[49] Ibid, 391.

[50] For an amusing account of a divorce countenanced by President Young, see Chandless, *A Visit to Salt Lake*, 236–37. For discussions of polygamous divorce, see Campbell and Campbell, "Divorce Among Mormon Polygamists: Extent and Explanation," 4–23; Embry, *Mormon Polygamous Families*, 175–82; and Young, *Isn't One Wife Enough?*, 226–40.

and Drummond's own deviations from marital norms were revealed. Following are two editorials written over a period of three months in response to Drummond's continuing efforts to malign the Mormons:

"JUDGE DRUMMOND OF UTAH," *WESTERN STANDARD*, 3 JULY 1857.

We have had occasion to allude to this worthy who professes to hail from Chicago, and who has made quite a lion of himself in the newspapers.

The Oquawka [Illinois] Plaindealer contains an article which is conclusive that the Judge should have very little to say about immoralities in Utah, or indeed anywhere else.

The Plaindealer states that at the time he was appointed Judge he was a resident of that town.

> "And if his private history were written it would unfold a career of as cruel and inhuman treatment to a family, as could be found in the annals of infamous husbands. The press in this place well knew his perfidy, but, out of regard to the feelings of his family, remained silent. After Drummond's resignation, and return to the States, he seemed to evince no desire to visit his family. When it was announced through the press that he was in Chicago, Mrs. Drummond proceeded thither to seek an interview with him; and although she stopped at the same hotel, and remained one night while he was there, he managed to screen himself from her sight, and the next morning stealthily got aboard of the train and came to this place, and took two of his children with him. His wife remained a week in Chicago seeking in vain for her faithless husband; and then returned home to have a more bitter pang added to her already broken heart, to find that her children had been spirited away, she knew not where."

We have known Drummond to be all that his family knew him to be, and which they very naturally wished to conceal from the public; but neither they nor we are in possession of any secret; wherever the wretch has been he has exhibited his real nature, he has left his blasting mark, and thousands know him to be what he is. Before he left Utah he well knew that the people of that Territory would expose his abominations, and he took the first opportunity to write against them to damage their character, and, as he hoped, thereby to invalidate their testimony; but has he succeeded? Verily no! He has lied, he has made numerous unfounded charges, which have been published and republished, again and again, all over the Union, and by which he has, doubtless, stirred up the worst feelings of the people against the Mormons, and very nigh succeeded in placing the administration at Washington in a dilemma; but when the present clouds that now indicate a raging storm against the Mormons, shall have passed away and the morrow bring with it clearer times, then will Drummond wither before the brightness of Truth—the tangible, incontrovertible facts, which a new Governor or "Special Commissioners" will discover if they examine impartially the evidence *pro* and *con.*

The Oquawka *Plaindealer* has not published his timely revelation of this scapegrace to favor the Mormons; but from a sense of justice to the public, and none need suspect that we have a friend in the Chicago *Weekly Tribune*—as it is our unscrupulous enemy—the *facsimile* of our New York cotemporary of the same name.[51] The fatality that rushes on the criminal to the great imprudent act which reveals his crime, has followed the *"horse-trader"* Judge and villainous wholesale calumniator of Utah, who would have rejoiced in the massacre of thousands of unoffending persons for the purpose of covering up his dark deeds, but he has at length got to the end of his rope.

(Will not our cotemporaries in this city and State, many of whom have been quite eager to republish Drummond's slanders against the Mormons, manifest enough fairness to give place to the above extract from the Chicago *Weekly Tribune.* Let the public have an opportunity of knowing the character he bears at home in Illinois; they then, perhaps, can judge of how much credence there is to be attached to his statements in regard to the Mormons. This will be giving the public a glance at the other side of the story. Ed W. S.)

UNTITLED EDITORIAL, *WESTERN STANDARD,* 4 SEPTEMBER 1857.

The law of attraction and repulsion is not more certain in its operation than that extreme measures re-act upon themselves. This is illustrated in the case of the late Utah Gentile officials, who by their own conduct rendered themselves obnoxious to the citizens of that Territory. Drummond insulted the people by introducing among them a strumpet as his wife and seating her by his side upon the judicial bench—Stiles, and his confederates by their drunkenness, gambling, lewdness, and efforts to stir up litigation, and Burr by his total disregard of the rights of the people in turning his animals into grain fields and such like conduct, his manifest dishonesty with the Federal Government and his employees, and his publication in the New York papers of most abominable calumnies against the people of whose hospitality he was constantly partaking, and which, if credited by the Government, were calculated to lead to the shedding of innocent blood. By these and kindred means these hombres (we cannot call them gentlemen,) succeeded in rendering themselves absolutely detestable to the people of Utah, and so aroused the insuppressable indignation of the latter, that they considered it wisdom to leave the Territory.

When Drummond came to California, his plan was to electioneer for the Democratic party, and at the accession of the new administration to claim

[51] A notation preceded this article: "we take particular pleasure in laying before our readers the following, which we clip from the Chicago *Weekly Tribune,* of May 28th." Contrary to most Eastern newspapers, Horace Greeley's *New York Tribune,* though hardly a friend of Mormonism, roundly criticized the decision to send troops to Utah. See Roberts, *Comprehensive History,* 4:405–407, 416–17.

the gubernatorial office in Utah. To this end he was all butter and honey to the Mormons in this State, but vinegar and gall when in conversation with Gentiles on the Mormon Question. To us personally he complimented Gov. Young and the citizens of Utah, while at the same time he was endeavoring to wound the Mormon community through the press over an anonymous signature. Proceeding eastward at close of the election, and finding his chances less than he had calculated, he renewed his energies even to desperation, solemnly affirming to statements of a most serious character, and which he knew to be totally false. These statements, coming as they did from a Justice of a Federal Court, carried with them an authority which was irresistible to those who were unacquainted with the Mormon character, and well nigh started the whole country from its propriety. But the re-action was certain, and is already beginning to develope itself. Events entirely beyond the reach of the Mormons have transpired, which have brought upon him the execrations of all honest men as one of the basest of wretches that ever disgraced the name of husband and father. Following in the train of this, comes the honest and authoritative testimony of Mr. C. E. Bolton, Clerk of the Supreme Court of Utah, who makes affidavit to the U.S. Attorney General, that the records, etc., which Drummond had reported to have been destroyed by the Mormons, and from which arose the recent cry of "Mormon treason," were safe in his possession, and had not been molested. Capt. H. W. Wharton of C Infantry, stationed at Fort Kearney, N. T., comes forward next in order, and shows beyond a doubt, that the Cowdy and Margetts party were murdered by the Cheyennes, and not by Mormons. Mrs. Babbitt closes the refutation of Drummond's calumnies, in a letter to the N. Y. Herald, in which she shews by the testimony of Major Hoffman who is in command at Fort Laramie, that Secretary Babbitt was killed by the Cheyennes as was first reported. The affair of the Gunnison massacre was tried in Utah in the presence of Col. Steptoe, and was clearly proven to have been done by Indians. Thus the lies and impure ambition of that base man, Drummond, which he hoped would elevate him to higher office, have dragged him from the seat of justice and buried him beneath the pile of his own infamy. These testimonies will appear in the Standard next week.

Judge Stiles having originally been a "Jack (!) Mormon," that is, as here interpreted, having married a Mormon woman for what he could make out of her and the Mormons and knowing the forbearance of the Saints with evils they could not legally remove, presumed upon their patience by making his office a gambling hole, drinking shop and devils' den generally, and used his official position to involve the people in disastrous litigation, until the community was outraged to that degree, that they abated his pest-house as a nuisance. He may bring the people of G. S. L. City to trial on his case as soon as he pleases—they are ready to unmask him before the world.

Surveyor Burr, when he went to Utah per appointment, doubtless thought it a capital opportunity to glut his lust for gold by cheating the treasury of the United States. He was going a long way off, and the stupid Mormons would never penetrate the surface of his operations, and by a general scheme of swindling the Government and his employees, he could return from his appointment independent of the world! The evidence before the world shews that such must have been his cogitations. But human projects are apt to fail, especially when their accomplishment depends upon connivance at by [*sic*] Mormons. They suffered him to proceed until he became so conscious of the power they had over him, that as a matter of self-defence he planned their destruction, that in their fall the evidence of his guilt might be destroyed. This was the cause of those outrageous libels which were published in the New York Times, etc., and were well calculated to bring down upon the Saints the heated anger of the Government and the world. But the citizens of Utah discerned in him the peculator, liar and soulless plotter; and when the evidence of these became too palpable to be denied with any show of success, they gave him to understand that they were aware of his rascality, and knew how desirous he was to become their executioner. This denouement put him upon his fears, and, leaving the Territory he hastens to Washington to tell his story first; but the truth follows in due time, and he like Drummond stands before the world in his true colors—a peculating thief and a foul calumniator. The testimony of Stiles and his confederates to exonerate him from the charges against him will avail him nothing. They have their reasons for making common cause with him. . . .

The history of Washington appointees in Utah proves, that, with a few honorable exceptions, Gentiles of real worth and suitability have not as yet exercised official functions in that Territory. The fact is, and we are not ignorant of it, that the Utah offices have all along went begging among the small-fry politicians, and were only accepted as a dernier resorts to replenish empty purses. The results of such unfit appointments are before the public and the Government, to the effect, we hope, of enlightening both upon Utah affairs, and the nature and extent of her requirements. Of the recent appointees we have nothing unkind to say. Time, which impartially tries all things, will try them also. If they prove to be good and capable men, they will meet with a ready support from the people, and will receive that honor which is due to their station. If they bring with them the desire which should animate rulers, namely, to promote the peace and welfare of the people—to protect and encourage virtue and morals, and to punish their opposites; their efforts to that end will be duly seconded and acknowledged. Utah has resources, and the right kind of a white population to develope them. All they ask is what they are undeniably entitled to—peace, their just share of territorial appropriations from the Federal treasury, and an accept-

> able government. With these, though isolated as she is, she will prosper and accomplish her mission of political sovereignty.

While President Buchanan's decision to send federal troops to Utah Territory was based on many factors, including allegations of treason and rebellion that had been accumulating for years, W. W. Drummond probably had as great an impact on that decision as any other single person or event.[52] No wonder he became the man the Mormons most loved to hate, perhaps second only to Gov. Lilburn W. Boggs, author of the infamous Missouri extermination order.

Nor was Drummond held in contempt only by Mormons. Jules Remy and Julius Brenchley were appalled by the judge's immorality and veniality (he was noted for lending money at usurious rates and being a notorious gambler), writing that he had openly declared to them that "Money is my God, and you may put this down in your journals if you like."[53] Another critic of Judge Drummond was one "SIGMA," who wrote a stinging exposé of Drummond in the 11 July 1857 edition of the San Francisco *Weekly Chronicle*, noting his infidelity and lies. Though a self-professed "most hearty hater of Mormon doctrine," the well-informed SIGMA could not abide the slanders of Drummond against the Mormon people and rushed to their defense, all the time remaining within the comfortable protection of anonymity.[54]

An indication of the antipathy with which the Saints held Drummond, and yet another example of the unyielding rhetoric of the Utah Reformation, is the imprecation pronounced upon the former judge by President Heber C. Kimball from the Bowery in July 1857:

> There is a poor curse who has written the bigger part of those lies which have been printed in the States; and I curse him, in the name of Israel's God, and by the Priesthood and authority of Jesus Christ; and the disease that is in him shall sap and dry up the fountain of life and eat him up. Some of you may think that he has not the disease I allude to; but he is full of pox from

---

[52] John Taylor argued this point in some detail in 1882. See "Discourse by President John Taylor," 9 April 1882, *Journal of Discourses*, 23:54–56. Schindler, *Orrin Porter Rockwell*, 243–44n61, made the same argument.

[53] Remy and Brenchley, *A Journey to Great-Salt-Lake City*, 1:469.

[54] "Judge Drummond," *Weekly Chronicle*, 11 July 1857. For an early, yet fairly comprehensive, treatment of Drummond from the LDS. perspective (including the opinions of many non-Mormons), see Roberts, *Comprehensive History*, 4:200–06.

> the crown of his head to the point of its beginning. That is the curse of that man; it shall be so, and all Israel shall say, Amen. (The vast congregation of Saints said, 'Amen.') He is laying plans to destroy us, and is striving with his might to stir up the Government of the United States and the President to send troops here to bring us into collision and destroy this pure people—man, woman, and child. May God Almighty curse such men, (Voices all through the congregation: "Amen!") and women, and every damned thing there is upon the earth that opposes this people.[55]

The Mormons followed Drummond's downward slide until 1885, "carefully noting in their records his conviction for fraud, indictment for perjury, and at last his sentence in New York to a house of correction for stealing stamps from a mail box in order to get enough money for a drink."[56] The former judge "died in a Chicago grogshop" on 20 November 1888—an ironic end to a man who worshipped money.[57]

---

[55] Kimball, "The Latter-day Kingdom. . .Love to His Servants," 12 July 1857, *Journal of Discourses,* 5:32

[56] Furniss, *The Mormon Conflict,* 54–55.

[57] Schindler, *Orrin Porter Rockwell,* 244n61.

Chapter 10

"The Hoary-headed Reverend Seducer"

The Assassination of Parley P. Pratt

Throughout the early years of the West, the frontier press and federal officials accused the Mormons of numerous assassinations. These allegations, though almost always devoid of proof, thrived in the pages of nineteenth-century yellow journalism for years—especially as the truth of the massacre at Mountain Meadows seemed to confirm every dark suspicion and every silly story. Cornelia Paddock, who resided in Utah in the 1880s with her husband, a member of the anti-polygamy Utah Commission, included an affidavit in her emotional exposé of Mormonism which alleged that none other than George Q. Cannon had attempted to induce one Adolph Razins to kill Almon W. Babbitt in early March 1855. According to Paddock, Razins claimed that it was Cannon's position that Babbitt's blood needed to be shed to atone for his transgressions against the LDS church. Whatever his opinion might have been at the time regarding Babbitt, the young Cannon, who by then had held no ecclesiastical position higher than a common missionary, was hardly in a position to be arranging blood atonements on behalf of the Mormon hierarchy.[1]

Paddock's best-selling book is an especially fine example of the extremes in bathos and unsubstantiated allegation to which some anti-Mormon writers were willing to stoop in their attempts to disenfranchise polygamists and end theocracy in Utah. Other examples of such yellow journalism include Froiseth, *The Women of Mormonism* and the almost totally fictional Ward (pseud.), *Female Life among the Mormons.* While rabidly anti-Mormon, the exposés by Fanny Stenhouse and Ann Eliza Webb Young were much more substantial, though they borrowed heav-

---

[1] Paddock, *The Fate of Madame La Tour,* 305–06.

ily from one another and told some very tall tales. As an example of how irresponsible some of the most popular anti-Mormon authors of the period could be, note that "Maria Ward" reconstructed the martyrdom of Joseph Smith by having him shot off of a horse by a jealous husband. She—or, according to Fanny Stenhouse, *he*—charged the Mormons with responsibility not only for the deaths of the "Gunison" [*sic*] party, but also of the Donner party, even though that tragedy took place a year before the Mormons reached the Rocky Mountains.[2]

A Martyr to the Cause of Truth

While the Mormons were constantly accused of assassinating their enemies, often on the shallowest of evidence, some of the most influential leaders of the fledgling church had themselves fallen victim to assassins: first Joseph and Hyrum Smith and then, in 1857, the popular apostle, Parley P. Pratt.

Parley Parker Pratt was one of the most prolific of early Mormon writers. His *Voice of Warning,* published in 1837, was arguably the most important non-canonical contribution to the development of Mormon doctrine and his most important work, *The Key to the Science of Theology,* published in 1855, but mostly written during his time in California, was the church's earliest comprehensive synthetical work. It underwent over a dozen editions and is still considered one of the great classics of Mormon theology.[3]

Largely because of his voluminous writings, Pratt held a place of special affection in the hearts of most Mormons, but this was especially true for George Q. Cannon. It was Pratt who first introduced the restored Gospel of Jesus Christ to Cannon's uncle, John Taylor, who then brought Mormonism to his sister's family in England. It was Pratt who hired the young Cannon to assist him as a copyist for his autobiography, and it was Pratt who asked Brigham Young to send Cannon back to California to head up the printing of *The Book of Mormon* in the Hawaiian language. It was also Pratt who turned over responsibility for the

[2] Ward, *Female Life Among the Mormons,* 137, 438–43. Other sensational anti-polygamy novels of this period include Victor, *Mormon Wives;* Belisle, *Mormonism Unveiled;* and Bel, *Boadicea.*

[3] For a discussion of these and other early works by Pratt, see Crawley, "Parley P. Pratt: Father of Mormon Pamphleteering."

Parley Parker Pratt, within a few years of his assassination, from a steel engraving. From Whitney, *History of Utah, Vol. I.*

Pacific Mission as well as the *Western Standard* to his protégé and friend, George Q. Cannon.

During the newspaper's brief history, Cannon saw to it that the writings of Parley P. Pratt were featured prominently in the *Western Standard.* In the 21 June 1856 issue, for example, Cannon reprinted one of Pratt's numerous defenses of plural marriage, "Marriage and Morals." Pratt's final publication to find its way into the *Western Standard* and other Mormon newspapers of the day was an attempt at poetry, in which he reflected on his life at the half-century mark. Following are the final stanzas:

P. P. PRATT, "MY FIFTIETH YEAR,"
WESTERN STANDARD, 26 JUNE 1857.

I have wandered far—I have wandered wide,
From Maine to the wild Missouri's tide;
And over the ocean's sea-girt isles
Full many a weary thousand miles.
I have trampled the deserts' burning sands
And the snow-clad mountains of unknown lands.
'Mid the crystal waters of Deseret

I have pulled the oar and cast the net.
I have climbed the steeps 'mid the golden ore,
And roamed o'er the lone Pacific shore.
I have plowed its bosom many-a-day
To visit the nations far away.
I have stood on Chili's distant shore,
Where the Polar Star is seen no more.
I have gazed on the Andes' heights of snow,
And roamed 'mid the flowery plains below.[4]
I have toiled with the great in freedom's cause
And assisted to give to a State its laws.
I have lain in a dungeon, bound in chains
And been honored in Courts where Justice reigns.
In a thousand joys, and a thousand fears
I have struggled on through my fifty years.
And now, by the law of God, I am free;
I will seek to enjoy my Jubilee.
I will hie me home, to my mountain dell,
And will say to the "Christian" world;—farewell.
To retire in peace is all I ask.
   Another fifty years will full prove
Our message true, and all our motives, love.
Then shall a humble world in reverence bow
And hail the prophets so rejected now.
To Zion's temple, and to Zion's King.
I will be there and celebrate the day
Till twice ten fifties shall have passed away.[5]

It was not Pratt's destiny to "retire in peace." He would live only one month and a day beyond his fiftieth birthday.

The high melodrama of the apostle's assassination seemed tailored for the popular press. On the western border of Arkansas, Hector H. McLean murdered Pratt on 13 May 1857 after the Mormon apostle journeyed to Indian Territory in an attempt to help a woman he consid-

[4] For a summary of Pratt's largely unsuccessful missionary visit to Chile, see Whittaker, "Parley P. Pratt and the Pacific Mission," 54–57.

[5] While Pratt established himself among the earliest of Mormon poets (his first poem was published in 1835), "My Fiftieth Year" is not likely to appeal to modern tastes. Pratt had more success as a lyricist. Some of the hymns he wrote are still widely sung in meetings of the Church of Jesus Christ of Latter-day Saints today. These include "An Angel from on High, The Long, Long Silence Broke"; "As the Dew, from Heav'n Distilling"; "Come, O Thou King of Kings"; "Father in Heaven, We Do Believe"; "Jesus, Once of Humble Birth"; and "The Morning Breaks, the Shadows Flee." For a list of all Pratt's hymns, see Proctor and Proctor, eds., *The Autobiography of Parley P. Pratt,* 614–15.

ered his wife, Eleanor Jane McComb McLean Pratt, reclaim her children. She had become Pratt's twelfth wife while estranged—but not legally divorced—from her abusive first husband, Hector McLean.

Eleanor McLean first encountered members of the LDS church in San Francisco in 1851. It is possible she met Parley P. Pratt sometime between 11 July and 5 September of that year or between 21 May and 39 July 1852, following his return from a mission to Chile. She claimed, however, that they met during his year of writing and publishing in San Francisco between 2 July 1854 and 20 June 1855 when he was presiding over the Pacific Mission. Regardless of when she met Pratt, her marriage to Hector McLean was in trouble long before then. They had first separated while living in New Orleans in 1844 and continued to experience marital problems after moving to San Francisco. Rather than leave him and move to San Bernardino as she had apparently intended, she was persuaded by the San Francisco Mormons to stay with him, to treat him well, and by tender persuasion gain his permission for baptism. (It was then, and still is, against church policy to baptize a woman against the wishes of her husband.)

Although she was not apparently baptized until 24 May 1854, Mr. McLean had given written permission for his wife to join the Mormon faith in November 1851. Still, he would not allow her to talk of her new religion or sing Mormon hymns in his presence. Nor would he give permission for the baptism of his children. Notwithstanding, Eleanor had the two eldest children, Fitzroy and Albert, secretly baptized by Parley P. Pratt on 27 August 1854. She also spent much time in 1854 caring for Pratt and his sick wife, Elizabeth. It is not clear to what extent Mrs. McLean entertained romantic feelings for Pratt at that time or, if she did, whether they were reciprocated. But her growing dedication to Mormonism, coupled with her decision to have her children baptized without her husband's permission, exacerbated an already bad marriage.

In January 1855, Hector secretly sent the children from San Francisco to New Orleans to live with their maternal grandparents, safe from the influence of Mormonism. According to Eleanor, he locked her in her room so she could not retrieve her children until they were safely en route. Two weeks later, Eleanor followed them to New Orleans, leaving Hector behind in San Francisco. Eleanor's parents had turned against her and despised her new faith. They questioned her sanity and refused to give her possession of her children. Dejected and lonely, she traveled to Utah cooking for an overland company, arriving in September 1855. She sought out old acquaintances and was taken in by the family of Parley P. Pratt. Two months later, they were married "for time and all eternity."

Although Pratt's "marriage in Utah to the legal wife of another man in 1855 was not prohibited by territorial law, his actual or potential cohabitation with her in Missouri and Arkansas in 1857 was contrary to statutes in those states."[6] The McLeans had been separated for two years before Brigham Young sealed Eleanor to Parley in Great Salt Lake City on 14 November 1855.[7] According to Eleanor, the McLeans had a stormy marriage, exacerbated by Hector's drunkenness and physical and emotional abuse. Though still legally married to McLean when she was sealed to Pratt, she felt justified in her decision. She considered that she was no longer McLean's wife inasmuch as she had not shared a bed with him since the night he had beaten her and cast her into the streets of San Francisco. Moreover, the Mormons believed that with the advent of the eternal marriage covenant, civil marriages were not binding anyway.[8]

A year after Eleanor became Pratt's twelfth plural wife, she and her new husband devised a strategy to retrieve her children. In November 1856 they arrived in St. Louis, where they separated—Parley to take care of church business in the East and Eleanor to return to her parents' home in New Orleans. They planned to reunite on the frontier, once Eleanor had escaped with her children, and join a train of Mormon emigrants to return to Zion.

Seeking to win possession of her children, in New Orleans Eleanor pretended to have rejected Mormonism. In Utah she "had seen much suffering from the famine, and had seen also the error of her ways! Said she had been mad, had now left the Mormons," but she "still insisted that the Mormons were good people, and Brigham and his associates in office were true Prophets."[9] Eventually she won her parents' trust and

---

[6] Quinn, *The Mormon Hierarchy: Origins of Power,* 572. Quinn is partly in error: the couple never cohabited in Arkansas.

[7] Pratt, "Eleanor McLean and the Murder of Parley P. Pratt," 234.

[8] See, for example, Pratt's own teachings on this point in his *Key to the Science of Theology,* chapter 17. While Mormon scripture (D.C. 132:15) specifies that marriages not performed by priesthood authority are binding for this life only, it was an easy next step for some to conclude that therefore they weren't really binding at all when compared to "celestial marriage."

[9] "Sad Story of Mormonism," *New Orleans Bulletin,* in *The Mormon,* 14 March 1857, 2/7.

fled with her two youngest children to Texas, apparently leaving her son, Fitzroy, behind. As soon as he heard that Eleanor had disappeared, Hector McLean left San Francisco. McLean hunted for Pratt up and down the Ohio and Mississippi river valleys, almost catching the apostle in Missouri, where Pratt was under indictment for an alleged murder dating from the Mormon War of 1838. McLean intercepted a letter Pratt had sent to Eleanor in Texas and finally tracked down his wife and captured Pratt in Indian Territory.[10]

Pratt was arrested on the weak charge that he and Eleanor had stolen the clothing of the children. A federal court in Van Buren, Arkansas, found no evidence to hold Pratt and quietly set him free. McLean and his friends pursued and then brutally shot and stabbed to death the unarmed apostle.[11]

Elder William H. Shearman, one of Cannon's missionaries who had been proselyting in the gold fields since 1855, transferred to the office to assist the staff and wrote the initial California editorial on Pratt's murder.[12] Given his close relationship to Pratt, it is entirely possible that Cannon was too overcome with grief to put his own thoughts to type. Shearman did not address the question of bigamy on the part of Pratt. He was either unaware of Pratt's twelfth and final marriage or chose to ignore that Parley and Eleanor were arguably man and wife.[13]

Shearman's *Western Standard* article discussed the assassination in flowery detail, reveling in the type of blood-atonement rhetoric that contributed to the excesses of the day.[14] A lengthy extract from a letter by "Mrs. McLane" appeared in the same issue. Three days later both articles were exposed to a much wider reading public than had been afforded through the pages of the *Western Standard*. Cannon's old nemesis,

---

[10] Roberts, *A Comprehensive History*, 2:166; and Pratt, "Eleanor McLean and the Murder of Parley P. Pratt," 234–41.

[11] Details of the apostle's murder are taken from Ibid; Appendix A of Proctor and Proctor, eds., *Autobiography of Parley P. Pratt*; and the 4 July 1857 letter from D. E. to Cannon, *Western Standard*, 10 July 1857, 3.

[12] See Cannon to Young 19 May 1857, LDS Archives.

[13] Adding to possible confusion was the curious fact that the widow signed her published letters at this time first as "Mrs. McLean" and later as "Eleanor McComb"—reverting to her maiden name—and not as Mrs. Pratt. Even in a private letter to Parley's brother Orson, written just nine days after the murder, she signed herself "Eleanor J. McLean." See *Millennial Star*, 4 July 1857.

[14] Although generally less inclined to engage in the type of "personal journalism" prevalent on both the East and West coasts, the *Deseret News*, in Salt Lake, was also promoting this kind of rhetoric at the time. See McLaws, *Spokesman for the Kingdom*, 73–77.

the *Alta California,* chose to reproduce Shearman's editorial and Eleanor's letter—initially without much commentary—on its editorial page.

"A Mormon Editor's Opinion on the Killing of a Seducer—Letter from Mrs. McLean," *Alta California,* 6 July 1857.

Supposing that our readers will be desirous of seeing what the Mormons say in relation to the reverend seducer Parley P. Pratt, we transfer to our columns, from the *Western Standard,* of yesterday,[15] the following extraordinary production, containing a letter from Mrs. McLean, the wife of the injured husband. Want of space prevents any comments at present. We shall refer to the whole subject matter at an early day.

"Assassination of President P. P. Pratt," *Western Standard,* 3 July 1857.

By this mail was brought the melancholy and heart sickening intelligence of the murder of our beloved brother, President Parley P. Pratt.[16] This diabolical transaction will no doubt be the signal for a general jubilee throughout California, as it has already been in the East, and will be a cause of congratulation and rejoicing among all those who hate the servants of God. Their triumphing, however, will be but short. God will, ere long, come out of his hiding place and vex the nations in his sore displeasure. He will make requisition for blood. He *will* require the lives of His servants at the hands of their murderers. He has sent them Apostles and Prophets and they have slain them, crying, "their blood be upon us and our children." Their request will be granted, for verily upon *this* generation shall come all the righteous blood which has been shed from the time of Jesus until the present. We extract the following particulars from a letter we received from Mrs. McLane [*sic*], giving an account of the murder and the circumstances attending it.

> "My heart sickens at thought of the scenes of blood and desolation through which I have been called to pass in the brief space of one month. I came to my father's in December last and took my children and journeyed to Texas, where I remained until the 13th of April, when I engaged passage in a wagon with a man who was going to Nebraska. He had a wife and three children—was not a Mormon. We had travelled three hundred miles, and were in the Creek nation when the father of the children met us with a strong force of armed men. At the moment

[15] The correct date of the article in the *Western Standard,* reprinted accurately by the *Alta California,* is 3 July 1857.

[16] Although Pratt was an apostle in the church, and therefore was normally referred to as "Apostle" or "Elder Pratt," (the latter term also being applied to any male missionary—then and now) he was also the former president of the Pacific Mission. It was in this capacity that he endeared himself to the California Saints and it was through this calling that Shearman, apparently, wanted to memorialize him.

he met us there was but one man with him, to whom he pointed, and said, "That is an officer madam." I looked at the man and said, "Are you an officer, sir?" He made no reply. I repeated but he did not reply. The father then dragged me out, threw me on the ground—got hold of the dear children, and no entreaties could avail, they were soon out of sight and I have not seen them since, only at a distance.

"In about two hours after their shrieks had died away in the distance, a man stating he was "the Marshal" rode up and read a paper to me, charging me in connexion with P. P. Pratt, James Gammell and Elias Gammell with larceny of clothing belonging to Albert and Annie McLean to the amount of ten dollars.[17] He said I was his prisoner and must go to Van Buren, Arkansas for trial.

"The next day when on the way we met a company of soldiers who had P. P. arrested. We were carried to Van Buren, a distance of over a hundred miles, and brought before the court only to be told, "There is nothing found against you, *you may depart.*" When Parley was released from the prison, McLean took after him, and two men accompanied him, and a little later the rabble. Twelve miles from the town they got up with him, fired six balls which only made holes in the skirt of his coat. One of the men then headed Parley's horse, which threw him entirely in the power of McLean, who then stabbed him twice; one of the wounds went direct to his heart and he fell from his horse. But the fiend was not satisfied, after leaving him once for dead, he came back and when close to him fired, which made a wound on his neck but would not have taken his life. After all this he lived two hours and a half and answered to many questions made by persons who came to the spot, and saw him die. This is the testimony of the man who lives near the place and saw it all (the name Winn.) I went the following day under the protection of Mr. Hays, the Marshal, to Mr. Winn's house, where I saw the dead body of the 'Beloved Parley,' saw his precious blood dripping from his heart.

"A young brother who had been preaching in the Creek nation, and happened to be with br. Parley when arrested was also arrested and put in chains with him, but released as soon as we reached Van Buren. This young man (Higginson) went with me to see the body buried, and the Marshal assisted to roll the body in fine white linen, which we did after the gentlemen had put on him a clean pair of garments. He was still quite limber and looked natural. He looked well when we had done, but in the afternoon he greatly changed. I could not stay to see him put in the grave, but br. H. said he would, and then escape in the night."

---

[17] In nineteenth-century America, because of the common law principle of coverture, it was not uncommon to assume that the male head of the house owned all family property. Interestingly, Beadle decried a situation in Utah where Mormon authorities arrested a man for helping a woman remove a trunk of clothing from the residence she formally shared with her ex-husband. See *Life in Utah*, 204.

> The murderer, will, of course, receive the congratulations of his friends and *accomplices,* while his name will be extolled by the press from one end of the land to the other, and the deed, will not only be justified, but applauded as a richly merited act of retributive justice. The world, will, for the present, say that the victim of this cold-blooded murder died as an adulterer and paid the just penalty of his crimes, even as the Jews said that Jesus died as a traitor and a blasphemer and according to their law had rendered himself worthy of death. But, thank God, there is a higher tribunal than popular opinion—We are willing to rest our case in the hands of our great "Advocate" and "Judge." We appeal to the Court of Heaven, and there, if not before—in the presence of an assembled world, and before an innumerable company of angels and the church of the firstborn, shall the innocence and purity of this martyred servant and Apostle of the Lord Jesus be established—the decision given by human courts on earth be ratified, and it shall be said, "THERE IS NOTHING FOUND AGAINST YOU, you have been faithful unto death, enter now into the joy of your Lord and be crowned with glory, honor, immortality and eternal life! . ."
>
> While the name of his assassin shall be first execrated, then die, rot and be forgotten forever—Parley's will be embalmed in the hearts of millions and will be handed down to posterity as that of a noble philanthropist and a martyr to the cause of truth.

The Best Act of My Life

Not only Shearman and Cannon, but Parley P. Pratt himself, interpreted the assassination as a martyrdom. Pratt's final words—uttered to non-Mormons as he bled to death—were: "I die a firm believer in the Gospel of Jesus Christ as revealed through the Prophet Joseph Smith, and I wish you to carry this my dying testimony. I know that the Gospel is true and that Joseph Smith was a prophet of the living God, I am dying a martyr to the faith."[18]

Although the editor of the *Alta* held back on his commentary when he reproduced Shearman's editorial and Eleanor's letter, he kept his promise to refer to the entire matter "at an early day." In hindsight, his comments on Shearman's blood-atonement rhetoric and the resulting likelihood of white Indians seeking revenge upon emigrants traveling through Utah were, all too sadly, remarkably on target. Cannon

[18] Peel, Dying Remarks of Parley P. Pratt, LDS Archives, cited in Pratt, "Eleanor McLean and the Murder of Parley P. Pratt," 227.

employed yet another editorial for the sake of damage control, clarifying that "retributive vengeance" would come through the Lord, and not through "Saints disguised as Indians." Four months later the massacre at Mountain Meadows proved him wrong.

Finally, the *Daily Evening Bulletin* weighed in on the entire affair, dismissing the "benighted" Eleanor as a poor, deluded lunatic. That editorial—to which Cannon did not respond—ends with a warning to its readers to protect themselves and their families against the trickery and deceit of the Mormon missionaries who had been sent to California to win both converts and, presumably, additional wives.

"THE KILLING OF PRATT—LETTER FROM MR. MCLEAN,"
ALTA CALIFORNIA, 9 JULY 1857.

We published a few days since, a very extraordinary article from the Mormon *Standard* of this city, a paper established and set up on this outpost, by Brigham Young, for the purpose of correcting the errors into which we ignorant Gentiles fall, in relation to the true character of Mormomism [*sic*]. This article was in relation to the killing of that hoary-headed seducer, Parley P. Pratt, who had exemplified the beauties of the system of which he was one of the most prominent and learned expounders, by stealing from her husband the affections of a wife, robbing him of his children and "sealing" to himself in an adulterous union, as his seventh wife, the wife of another, the mother whose duties were owed to her family. The tool of Brigham Young, who publishes this treasonable and filthy sheet in this community, denominates the just retribution, which at the hands of an injured husband, has overtaken the lecherous old villain, Pratt, as a "murder," and blasphemously compares him and his death to our Saviour and his crucifixion, and calls down the vengeance of the Almighty upon his "murderer," at the same time giving rather strong hints that the blood of "Parley" will be avenged, and that right soon.

Whether the hot blood which must now be seething and boiling in the veins of Brigham Young and his satellites, at Salt Lake, is to be cooled by the murder of Gentiles who pass through their territory, whether the "destroying angels" of Mormomdom [*sic*], are to be brought into requisition to make reprisals upon travelers, or whether, as has been done before, "Saints" disguised as Indians are to constitute themselves the supposed ministers of God's vengeance in this case, we are not informed, but have no doubt that such thoughts, such intentions as these, are prevalent among those saintly villains, adulterers and seducers, of Salt Lake, who, did they receive their just deserts, would be where Parley Pratt is now, in a world, where hypocrisy and saintly fraud will not pass current.

It is not for us here, to enter coolly upon any argumentation, to justify the course which Mr. McLean took to rid the world of as great a scoundrel as ever infested it. There are occasions and circumstances under which it seems that an injured, wronged, ruined in peace of mind, and heart-broken man has a God-given right to take the satisfaction of his deep wrongs into his own hand. There are cases which the law cannot reach, cases which deserve the severest punishment; and if there ever was such a one, this of Mr. McLean's is it. Bulwer, in one of his plays, only utters a sentiment which is implanted deeply in our natures, that "when dishonor enters our homes, law dies, and murder takes the angel form of justice." The wronged husband has practised upon this precept, and the civilized world will, we believe, applaud the set.

We have been permitted to examine a letter from Mr. McLean, written to a relative in this city, after the shooting of Pratt, and which details, with heartfelt earnestness, the trials and troubles, and anxieties, endured by him in his search for his children. Most of the particulars, however, do not differ from those which have been already given, and we therefore only publish below, Mr. McLean's own account of the closing scenes in this tragedy. The narrative commences after he had secured the children from his wife:

> "On leaving Fort Gibson, the Marshal made a demand on the Commander for a command of soldiers, to aid him to make the arrests, which he directed to follow him the next day. The Commander complied, and started my best and true friend, Capt. [Lewis Henry] Little, off that morning with a company. My friend, Mr. Shaw, who had been for some time trying to come across Pratt's whereabouts, happened to ascertain that Pratt, or a person calling himself Parker, had that morning—(the day Capt. Little left to follow the U.S. Marshal)—crossed the Arkansas river about two miles from the Fort, in company of a young Englishman. It struck him at once that this was none other than Pratt, and his Mormon spy of North Fork. He pursued him and soon overtook Capt. Little and his command, and instantly informed him that he believed Pratt was ahead of them going the same way. Capt. L. quickened his march, and soon came up with Pratt, and arrested him. Capt. L. told me that as soon as he did so, and informed him that it was at my instance, that he never saw consternation until then—the fellow fairly wilted.
>
> "The day Capt. Little left Fort Gibson, myself and the children, and a dozen of my Masonic friends, who gathered from all parts of the territory to aid me should the government not take any notice of my grievances, they got to North Fork simultaneously with the Marshal. The Marshal and E. J. [Eleanor Jane] also started that morning to Fort Gibson. We met the Captain and his command about half-way, resting at a

spring, and having Pratt a prisoner, in the centre of a circle of soldiers.[19]

"He, I am told, had pretty sorrowful greetings for his "seventh" wife when she presented herself, and the two met. Pratt was tied with his own rope, and the end of it given to a soldier, and the party marched off to Fort Gibson.

"To avoid a contact, I, with my friends, proceeded to the Creek Agency, where we were hospitably received by friend Whitfield and his lady. I started the following morning for Fort Gibson, with an escort of my Masonic brethren, and got there in safety. Remaining with the children at Fort Gibson two nights, I met with an excellent opportunity of accompanying one of the officers and his lady to Fort Smith. He drove his wife and the children in his carriage, and I rode his horse, and on getting there took us to his father-in-law's (Major Elias Rector) house, where we were kindly and cordially received, and where I had the children until I left the place. On going to Van Buren, the next morning, with Major Rector and Capt. Cahel, his son-in-law, and my devoted friend, we formed a great assemblage of people awaiting the opening of the United States Circuit Court, and found that my affairs had created the most intense excitement. I soon found that the parties could not be punished, as I had not sufficient evidence to convict them. Various propositions of revenge and redress were offered and proposed to me by the best men of the place and surrounding country, but I kept my purposes to myself. That day, the Marshal arrived with his prisoners, and locked Pratt in jail at his own request, and took E. J. to the hotel.

"The next day they were called into court, and I as a witness. The officers of the court paid such deference to my feelings that they dismissed Eleanor before calling upon me to testify. I was allowed to state the history of my grievances, and to read the evidences of my wrongs to the court, and to about five hundred spectators. In fact, the court-room was crowded. I exceeded any previous effort of my life at relating to others the burden of my soul's anguish. I was kindly permitted to implicate the scoundrel in court, Parley Parker Pratt, as the principal cause of all my sorrows. I succeeded admirably in producing the most intense excitement; I really twice thought the crowd were about making a move to lay hold of him and tear him to pieces. The Commissioner concluded it necessary, in order to save him from mob violence, to adjourn the further hearing until 4 P.M. of that day.

"The crowd reluctantly permitted him to be locked up again in jail; and when 4 P.M. arrived, the court-room was crowded long before the

[19] Remarkably, McLean was able to persuade U.S. soldiers to intervene in what was essentially a domestic dispute. See Ball, *Army Regulars on the Western Frontier*, 242n67.

time, and the yard in front likewise. The Commissioner not deeming it prudent to bring him out then, postponed the case until after breakfast the next morning—under pretence of having some witnesses for the defence to summon in the meantime. I knew they could have none, and that it was done to slip Pratt off quietly that night. My friends, anticipating this result, kept a watch all night on the jail, and the Marshal, fearing an attack, kept a watch also. So Pratt could not be gratified—"allowed to depart at the twelfth hour."

"About 8 o'clock the following morning, instead of being called into court, his horse was taken round to the jail, and he was released—mounted and "put." Friends, soon after missing him, came and apprised me of it, got me a horse—I pursued him; they followed and overtook me, and we overtook Pratt, and *I killed him.*

"I am not able to say how you will view the act, but I look upon it as the best act of my life. My duty to myself, demanded it; my duty to my children, demanded it; my duty to my relations, demanded it; and my duty to society, demanded it. And the people of West Arkansas agree with me in this view of the commission of the deed.

"I was permitted to leave Fort Smith, five miles from Van Buren, where I had the children, two days after, in a carriage with my children, about noon of the day."

Thus fell at the hands of a deeply injured man the hoary-headed seducer of his wife—the robber of his children. And who of us shall blame him, or say that, under the circumstances, we would have acted otherwise? We know of cases in this city, where, through the meddling interference of Mormon missionaries, other families have been broken up, other wives estranged from their husbands, family ties dissolved, and misery entailed upon all the victims of this accursed system. A few such examples as have been made in the case of Pratt will have a tendency to put a stop to these interferences, and where the evidence is as strong as it was in this case, we do not believe that the world would do else than justify a similar course of action.

"THE BEGINNING OF THE END," *ALTA CALIFORNIA,* 15 JULY 1857.

Dark clouds are gathering above the home of the "Saints"—the Zion in the wilderness—and by the news recently received from there, it seems that some of them are breaking with terrible force above the heads of those who dare act in opposition to the rule of the great high priest and prophet of Mormondom,[20] Brigham Young.

[20] The "expressive epithet 'Mormondom' was . . . first used in the New York Herald and made to signify, in this connection, that the Mormon Church should be tolerated with all other Churches, but that the 'Mormon theocracy' must be invaded and overthrown." See Tullidge, *History of Salt Lake City,* 140. Curiously, Tullidge himself had earlier appropriated this term in a positive context for the title of his *Women of Mormondom.*

The news received by the late arrival, by way of Carson Valley, is really the most important of any which has come to us from Salt Lake, since the time the polygamists settled there, and the seeds of dissension, which must necessarily have been sown in such an organization as was then effected, have germinated and ripened. Brigham Young's band of "destroying angels" are at their hellish work of murder, and, thug-like, are "putting out of the way," as they term it, the "apostates" to the faith and practice of the "Saints." Armed opposition to the expected attempt to enforce the laws of the United States, is openly advocated, and murder has become a prominent and customary means of punishing disobedience to the decrees of the tyrants and despots who rule with their individual wills the deluded people who have been induced to go to that hell upon earth—the city of Salt Lake. This is only what might have been expected, and is what we long ago predicted. No system of religious faith, however strong a hold it may have upon a community, can long keep it reconciled to such an unnatural system of society as has been established among the Mormons. Human nature is the same through all the world, and the artificial forms and modes of life which may be established by human authority cannot alter it. When men and women, fathers and mothers, see their families broken up, the innate sense of virtue eradicated, and their daughters taken from them, to gratify the beastly desires of the hypocritical scoundrels, who as priests and prophets enforce their decrees, it is but natural they should rebel and endeavor to throw off the chains in which they have been bound.

Mormondom is, we believe, upon the wane. Carefully concealed as are the facts, by those who are interested in the support of this foul system, there can be no doubt that there is a great degree of dissatisfaction among the residents of the wilderness Zion. Men have arisen there, who are not willing to submit patiently and uncomplainingly to the tyranny of Brigham Young, and others are disgusted with the system of polygamy, and already it is understood that quite a prominent faction of the "Saints" are desirous of abolishing it entirely.

That there has been a considerable emigration from Utah during the past year, we firmly believe; and that if proper facilities are afforded, a much larger one will immediately take place, we have no doubt. There is a schism in the church, and dissatisfaction in the society of Utah; the people there see that the United States government is no longer willing to submit to the defiance, outrage and insult which Brigham Young and his minions have put upon it. The recent killing of the hoary-headed seducer Pratt cannot fail to serve as a warning to others who, like him, affect to believe that it is a part of their religious duty to dissever the bonds of marriage, and break up and ruin families, and from all the signs, we are inclined to believe that Mormonism is ripe for dissolution—ripe and ready to fall and putrefy with its own innate rottenness. The recent proceedings at Salt Lake are but "the beginning of the end," and if, as is reported, (although we have since seen it contradicted,) a large military force has been ordered to Utah, we believe that the result will inevitably be a rooting out of the peculiar principles and practices which have distinguished the Mormons from other people. Now, it seems, the "destroying angels" are authorized to murder those who, disgusted with the state of society there, are desirous of leaving the unholy, polluted city; but a government force would, of course, furnish protection to such, as well as protection to the officers of the law who would punish the guilty murderers. When that force marches to Utah, we hope, too, that a band of missionaries will go with it. Our religious societies raise a large amount of funds each year, to send the heralds of Christianity and civilization to the remotest corners of the globe, and yet we have here, upon our own soil, a reproach and a disgrace to us and the age we lie in, a community of people sunk in a state of beastly degradation and heathenism, compared to which the worship of wooden gods is harmless. Now no one dare utter a loud word in opposition to the faith, and practice, and decrees of the Mormon prophets at Salt Lake; but when Gen. Harney and his forces reach there, the right of free speech, so dear to American citizens, will be sustained, and then an excellent and wide field will be opened for missionary labors. Let missionaries go there, and publicly, at the corners of the streets and in their houses, reason with the people, and show them the iniquity of the system in which they have been entangled. An army of soldiers and an army of missionaries can do a great work in Mormondom now.

"Assassination of President P. P. Pratt," *Western Standard,* 17 July 1857.[21]

Our article on the assassination of President Parley P. Pratt, published in the issue of the 3rd inst.,* has called forth numerous notices, not very complimentary, from our contemporaries. Many of them denounce our language as "extraordinary," "impudent," "infamous," "wicked," "blasphemous," etc., because we call the base and cowardly deed by which his life was taken, a MURDER. Exceeding all others in the loudness of his vociferations and the bitterness of his denunciations on this subject, is the editor of the *Alta California.* The wholesome rebukes we have administered to him, and the freedom with which we have exposed his flagitious conduct—his treasonable and defiant course towards the General Government, and his imbecile and foolish attempts to excite indignation against, and to bring about the extermination of a people whom he had previously called "sincere in their faith and comparatively moral and upright in their lives"—have aroused his vindictiveness, and he seeks to give it vent in a truculent and venomous article,

[21] Reprinted in Cannon, *Writings from the "Western Standard,"* 465–69.

* The article here referred to was from the pen of Elder William H. Shearman [Cannon's note].

containing extracts from a letter written by the assassin of President Pratt, in the *Alta* of the 9th inst. If there were anything wanting to complete and fully establish McLean's infamy, to seal his damnation in the mind of every just and honorable man who is acquainted with the circumstances of this case, this letter would effectually supply the deficiency. Who is there that possesses any of the finer feelings of humanity, whose heart is not steeled with hatred against "Mormonism" and the Latter-day Saints, that can read his letter without being disgusted with the fiendish exultation and malignity that pervade it? What man not actuated by a spirit of base and demoniacal revenge would egotistically boast, in speaking of his course at elder Pratt's trial, as follows:—"*I succeeded admirably in producing the most intense excitement,* I really twice thought the crowd were about to make a move to lay hold of him and tear him to pieces." Or that would relate in a cold-blooded, boasting manner that he, while surrounded by his abettors, killed a man, whom he knew to be friendless and defenseless. But the editor of the *Alta* thinks this all right, and applauds and glories in the deed, and the spirit in which it was done. We will inform that person, however, that in taking this course he has approved of, and consented to, the shedding of innocent blood. As true as the Lord lives, that blood will be required at the hands of him who shed it; and at the judgment seat of Him who will award to every man the reward or punishment of his acts in the flesh, those who have applauded and gloried in the cruel deed will not be found guiltless. A retributive vengeance will be administered; but it will not, as the editor hints, be administered by saints disguised as Indians. The indignation and wrath of an offended God will be poured out, and the guilty ones shall yet learn, to their sorrow, that they cannot shed the blood of His servants with bitter impunity; and he who has said, "Vengeance is mine; I will repay,"[22] shall yet cause them to experience His hot displeasure.

Parley P. Pratt, an apostle of Jesus Christ, was a holy and pure man, and was innocent of the things with which he has been charged. We state that we *know* when we state this. Charge upon charge has been circulated by his enemies and the enemies of the gospel, to malign his memory, and to give the color of justification to his murder. The *Alta* says that he stole from her husband the affections of a wife; robbed him of his children, etc. Others have accused him of invading the sanctity of the family circle and robbing it of its finest ornament, by abducting a wife and children. These charges are utterly false, and the men who originated them knew them to be so. Parley P. Pratt did not steal the affections of Mrs. McLean from her husband; he did not invade the sanctity of their family circle; he did not abduct her and her children; but he did all in his power to preserve peace in that family, to prevent

[22] This was the same inscription written on the cedar cross atop the cairn the army erected at Mountain Meadows in 1859, which Brigham Young read and allegedly had destroyed on his visit in 1861.

a rupture, and to mollify the feelings of animosity which prompted McLean to pursue the intolerant and abusive course which he did towards his wife because of her religion. Respectable and truthful men and women are in this country who can testify that President Pratt's counsel was the only influence that caused Mrs. McLean to endure, so long as she did, the harsh and violent treatment of her husband. It was her husband's own conduct that alienated her affections and drove her from him. It was her husband's own conduct, in abducting her children and sending them to New Orleans without her knowledge, that caused her to leave this city; and even then she left in pursuit of her children, to recover them. This is well known here by all who know anything in relation to the case; and yet many editors, with a total disregard of truth, have stated that she eloped with Parley P. Pratt to Utah!

In a long and ably written vindication of her course, written by herself, and published in the Van Buren (Arkansas) *Intelligencer,* the whole of which we have not space in this number to republish, she corroborates by her testimony, in the following language, what we have stated:—

> "I am free to declare, before angels and men, that Parley P. Pratt was innocent of the charges made against him. If the deeds of men were registered on their faces, it would be known and read of all men that H. H. McLean drove me from him, and that his own acts blighted and consigned to eternal death all the delicate ties that existed between us, and that before 'Mormonism' crossed our pathway. That I would fain have been separated from him while yet living in New Orleans, I will name as living witnesses, my father, J. S. McComb, and my brothers, E. C. McComb and J. J. McComb, and Mr. John McDougal. These all know that I sought their counsel while living in New Orleans, to know whether I must continue to endure the degrading influence of a man who would continue to sip at the wine cup, and thereby unfit him for the society of his family. That my statements are correct in reference to our separation in California, I will name as witnesses, Captain Thomas Grey and family, Mr. Samuel Webb and family, and my neighbors and friends in general in the city of San Francisco. That Mr. McLean put me by violence into the street at night and locked the door against me, Captain Gray [*sic?*] and Dr. Bush are witnesses, and I presume Mr. McLean himself would not deny that I then declared that I would no more be his wife, however many years I might be compelled to appear as such for the sake of my children. I presume that Mr. McLean would lay it as a complaint against me that I never afterwards came to his bed.
>
> * * I would appeal to every man and woman of refined sensibility to know whether a virtuous woman and faithful mother is so humble a thing that she should come again to the bosom of a man who had by violence thrust her from him and exposed her to insult and

> injury in the streets of a wicked city. Whosoever takes the affirmative differs from the writer of this,
>
> E. J. McCOMB, once E. J. McLEAN."

We should ever feel condemned did we not also lift up our voice and wield our pen in defense of the memory and reputation of this martyred servant of Jesus Christ. We have known him long and well, and we, with thousands of others know, that he was incapable of the actions attributed to him by those who are engaged in traducing his memory. We know that his heart beat with the noblest and holiest impulses, and that the great aim of his life, from his boyhood up, was to save and redeem his fellow men from the thraldom of sin and wickedness. The actions of his whole life bear testimony to the truth of this. Those who hate the work of God may rejoice at his death; but the time is not far distant when they, with the lies they have fabricated, will be swept away, and the worth of this servant of the Lord be fully recognized.

In the comments of the editor of the *Alta* upon this atrocious deed, we notice another statement that our self-respect will not suffer us to pass by unnoticed. He says:—

> "We know of cases in this city, where, through the meddling interference of Mormon missionaries, other families have been broken up, other wives estranged from their husbands, family ties dissolved, and misery entailed upon all the victims of this accursed system. A few such examples as have been made in the case of Pratt, will have a tendency to put a stop to these interferences, and where the evidence is as strong as it was in his case, we do not believe that the world would do else than justify a similar course of action."

When the writer penned that statement he wrote a deliberate falsehood. He does not know of cases of this kind in this city. The interference of "Mormon missionaries" has not broken up other families, has not estranged wives from their husbands, has not dissolved family ties, and has not entailed misery upon those who have embraced this system. This charge is as false as his other charges, which he, from time to time, makes. As to his suggestions relative to the course to be taken towards the "Mormons," we despise them and the threats which they convey alike with himself. We have no doubt but it would afford him immense gratification to see every "Mormon missionary" murdered, as was elder Pratt. Even were so good a pretext not to be had as has been trumped up in his case, yet, if it were thought that the world would only justify such deeds, advocates for the adoption of such a course would not long be wanting. But this poor creature may fume, and fret, and threaten, and grow indignant in vain. "Mormonism" will still flourish. Murdering its adherents and advocates will only have the tendency it ever has had, to spread it abroad and establish it more firmly in the earth.

"Frightful Effects of Mormonism," *Daily Evening Bulletin*, 18 July 1857.

Mrs. McLean, whose husband killed Parley P. Pratt, publishes in the Van Buren *Intelligencer* two columns of incoherent raving, which clearly establish the fact of her insanity, and show, beyond cavil, the necessity of her confinement in an asylum where she can receive medical treatment and be under wholesome restraint. The first part of her letter is devoted to a narration of the trouble between herself and husband, her efforts to get her children, and the incidents of her attempted escape to Salt Lake. In this portion of the epistle she is tolerably rational and clear; though an occasional gleam of her besetting hallucination breaks forth. In the last half of her letter, which she devotes to Pratt, the infirmity of her mind constantly appears. This benighted woman evidently regarded the coarse, sensual imposter, as a canonized saint; and deemed it a privilege to abase herself before him, and perform the most menial services for his personal comfort and luxury. In this way, by leading estray [*sic*] the weak of the other sex, the designing old hypocrite covers his back and fills his belly—arraying himself in fine linen, and faring sumptuously every day upon the produce of other men's labor.

Mrs. McLean still adheres to her idol. She says:

> In behalf of the dead I have to testify that whatsoever relation existed between us was of my own seeking. When he kept house with his wife, Elizabeth, in San Francisco, I often sought his society; and, if any censure me, let them censure me for the strongest impulses of my nature.
>
> * * *
>
> This man was a fountain of light and intelligence at which thousands might drink, and yet the stream flowed *clear, pure and free.*
>
> I am willing to acknowledge that I have often sought his door at the dawn of day, when his wife was sick, to take some *meat, bread and fruit,* upon which they might subsist until the following morning.

Thus this woman unblushingly admits that she has often, in the obscurity of the morning, stolen from home with the food furnished by her husband for the sustenance of his family, and conveyed it to the Elder, who yet lay indolently in bed with one of his eight wives, waiting to be fed by such means. She was not content with providing for the "Beloved Parley and his wife Elizabeth" at their own house, but insisted on her husband receiving them at his home. She says:

> Neither do I deny that I much desired from time to time to have him entertained at our house, even as I gladly entertained my husband's brethren. We had unoccupied rooms and beds, and a profusion of the good things of life, while he was poor and a stranger, and as unpopular as a certain Nazarene who once pilgrimized through the land of Judea and could not find a place to lay his head.

By this it will be seen that this poor deluded creature looked upon Parley as a parallel to Jesus Christ; and thought herself another Martha sent to minister to his wants. She continues:

> I do not deny that I washed his feet, combed his hair and often walked that he might ride. Neither do I deny visiting with him a number of families in St. Louis, who thought it a greater honor to entertain him than they would to entertain any king or potentate living upon the earth.
>
> I also confess that it pained me to see him in chains, and fain would have bathed his wrist where the cursed iron chafed his skin.

As may be well supposed, all these acts of sinful folly, which were not unknown to her husband, did not tend to the furtherance of peace or harmony in the family. Remonstrances on the part of the husband thus outraged often took a violent shape; and on one occasion Mrs. McLean alleges he put her out of the house at night, and locked the door upon her. We do not justify such an act; but must say, that the conduct of his wife had been such as to raise a feeling of desperation that would go far towards excusing it. When McLean found that his wife had had his children baptized by Pratt, in the Mormon Church, and was inculcating upon their minds the infamous doctrines which has estranged his wife from him, he sent them home to *her* parents. What followed afterwards, our readers already know.

When Mrs. McLean reaches that part of her narrative where the "beloved Parley" is slain, her feeling is too intense for prose. After reciting a number of the hardships she has endured for her faith, she continues:

> But this was nothing to what I was yet to see! Have I not yet seen *his heart's blood dripping from the wound of the deadly knife?*
>
> Six pistol balls could not avail
> To make his holy visage pale.
> But the fierce and deadly knife
> Pierced his heart and took his life.
>
> Oh! Parley dear, we love you well—
> Yea, more than mortal tongues can tell,
> And we know you'll come again,
> With us to live, with Christ to reign.
>
> Oh. God of Israel, let the cry
> Of Parley's blood come up on high,
> And let his wounds before thee plead
> For wrath on him who did the deed.

When we recollect that "him who did the deed" was her husband, whom she had sworn at the altar to love and cleave unto, was the father of her children, and the man whose happiness she had destroyed, and whose hearth she had made desolate, the extent of her insanity can be realized.

This story is not without its moral, and one that is capable of practical and profitable application. Mr. McLean and his family were respectable, prosperous and happy, before the Mormon missionaries thrust themselves upon the acquaintance of the wife and mother. The feeble intellect and undisciplined mind of the woman was no match for the cunning casuistry and studied sophisms of Pratt, a man of large brain, who had spent years in studying out schemes of deception, and made a living by practicing upon the weak traits of female character. Under his skillful and systematic attacks her reason gave way, and Pratt, gaining an ascendancy over her, found her ever afterwards a willing disciple and pliant tool, to be used for his profit, advantage and gratification. There are hundreds of persons, of both sexes, perhaps, but particularly females, who would have been as malleable in the hands of Pratt as was Mrs. McLean. And the Mormons are still sending missionaries among us, some perhaps as able as Pratt. These men continue to tamper with the peace of families as did Pratt. Let the public be warned against them. When found lurking about the homes of decent people, they should be treated like noxious reptiles. Every good man should beat them from his door, and clean his house after contamination by their presence as if they were reeking with a contagion more filthy and fatal than the small-pox

This Heaven-daring Deed

As he made clear in his own boastful letter to the newspapers, Hector McLean regarded the killing of Parley P. Pratt as "the best act of my life." Elder Shearman predicted that the world outside of Mormonism would agree and that McLean would "receive the congratulations of his friends and *accomplices,* while his name will be extolled by the press from one end of the land to the other, and the deed, will not only be justified, but applauded as a richly merited act of retributive justice." Indeed, according to George Higginson and George Crouch, who were in Arkansas at the time and very familiar with the circumstances of Pratt's death,

After perpetrating this heaven-daring deed, McLean returned to Van Buren and made it known. After remaining in town several hours, and walking the streets with impunity, he was escorted by a number of the citizens of Van Buren to the boat, and took his leave of the place. Verily, we had long thought that the blood-thirsty mobocrats of Missouri and Illinois were without a parallel in the world, but we now yield the palm to the church-going citizens of Van Buren, for they have proven to the world that they are a den of murderers and assassins.[23]

[23] 17 May 1857 letter from Higginson and Crouch to the editor of *The Mormon,* 20 June 1857, and reprinted in the *Western Standard,* 31 July 1857, 3.

Most of the country at this time subscribed to a common law principle that pretty much gave a man *carte blanche* to avenge himself on anyone who violated the honor of his wife or sister. This was particularly true in Utah, where this principle was often referred to as "mountain justice." In 1851, for example, George A. Smith was successful in getting fellow Mormon Howard Egan acquitted for having killed one James Monroe, who had seduced (and impregnated) Egan's wife while Egan was in California.[24] Since the citizens of Van Buren, Arkansas in no way recognized the validity of polygamous marriages, it is understandable why they would have sided with Hector McClean as the wronged husband.

"Mountain justice" notwithstanding, Eleanor Pratt and other Mormons who knew Hector McLean claimed he was a brutish drunkard who cared nothing about his children but only used them as a pawn to punish his wife for having embraced both Mormonism and one of its leading apostles. By his own admission, McLean was a cold-blooded assassin.[25] That he won the sympathies of most of his countrymen and was vindicated by so many newspapers of the day underscores the deep prejudice that existed against Mormonism in the middle of the nineteenth century. Little wonder that at the same time McLean was murdering Pratt, the president of the United States was ordering federal troops to Utah.

[24] For more on the Egan case, together with B. H. Roberts' defense of this practice, see Roberts, *Comprehensive History*, 4:135–36.

[25] California newspapers painted a different picture of McLean's character, as did apostate John Hyde: "I made the acquaintance of Mr. M'Lean in California, where he was universally respected and esteemed as an honorable and an upright man; deeply devoted to his wife, and tenderly attached to his children." Hyde, *Mormonism*, 80.

Chapter 11

"The Mormons Must Be Crushed Out"

War and Rumors of War

Virtually all the events, accusations, and perceptions concerning Utah that appeared in California newspapers during the mid-1850s combined to convince President James Buchanan that the Mormons were in a state of treasonous rebellion. While he was criticized both then and now for not having sent a commission to Utah Territory to ascertain firsthand the true situation, by 1857 the circumstantial evidence against the Mormons was overwhelming. As a result, Buchanan resolved not only to replace Brigham Young as territorial governor, but to send Young's replacement with a large army of federal troops as a *posse comitatus*[1] to assure a peaceful transition of power.

Given the political objections to sending troops, coupled with the difficulty in finding a suitable appointee as governor, Buchanan did not make a final decision to deploy the army until about 20 May.[2] Months later, in his annual message to congress, the president first articulated his reasons for sending armed forces to Utah Territory:

> All the officers of the United States, judicial and executive, with the single exception of two Indian agents, have found it necessary for their own personal safety to withdraw from the Territory, and there no longer remains any government in Utah but the despotism of Brigham Young. This being the condition of affairs in the Territory, I could not mistake the path of duty. As Chief Executive Magistrate, I was bound to restore the supremacy of the Constitution and laws within its limits. In order to effect this purpose, I appointed a new governor and other federal officers for Utah, and sent with

[1] An armed force called up by proper civil authority to enforce the law.

[2] Furniss, *The Mormon Conflict*, 63. For a discussion of the political maneuverings behind the president's retreat from his previous commitment to popular sovereignty, see Neff, *History of Utah, 1847 to 1869*, 451–55.

> them a military force for their protection, and to aid as a *posse comitatus,* in case of need, in the execution of the laws.[3]

Historians and other commentators have suggested a host of ulterior motive theories—most of them conspiracy-oriented—for that decision. Leonard J. Arrington posits several possibilities of varying credibility:

> Although Buchanan was active in pressing and defending the expedition, the prime mover would appear to have been Secretary Floyd, who kept the letter of General Scott advising against the immediate expedition secret from the president. Was Floyd, a Virginian, and southern-sympathizer, trying to put the army out of action and deplete the federal treasury as the secession movement was gaining momentum? Did businessmen and patronage-hungry politicians who expected to profit from the large contracts unduly influence Floyd and other administration leaders? Or were the president and secretary really interested in demonstrating federal supremacy to the obstreperous Kansans and others, like the Mormons, who were giving "popular sovereignty" a bad name? At a time when rumblings of secessionism were being heard, in other words, was the anxious dispatching of the Utah Expedition intended to serve as a vivid demonstration of the resolution that would be shown in putting down any states-rights rebellion?[4]

Were there really no ulterior motives? Was it simply the case that President Buchanan's "health, personal style, and reactions to pressure were such as to make it quite possible that the temptation to yield to the public demand for military action against Utah was irresistible during the first quarter of 1857"?[5] What was the true state of Utah at the time? Was it as Cannon and the majority of Mormons perceived it, a "refuge from Babylon, presided over by a God-designated prophet"? Or was it as the more moderate Gentiles and backsliding Mormons saw it, "an isolated land of modest opportunities, controlled by an astute, usually benevolent, occasionally ruthless autocrat"? Was there any truth to the allegations by the most bitter anti-Mormons and apostates that Utah was "a dangerous anomaly in mid-nineteenth-century America, one ruled by a fanatical tyrant"?[6]

---

[3] Moore, *The Works of James Buchanan,* 10:152.

[4] Arrington, *Great Basin Kingdom,* 172.

[5] MacKinnon, "125 Years of Conspiracy Theories," 228. MacKinnon systematically considers and then rejects each of the possibilities raised by Arrington.

[6] Poll and MacKinnon, "Causes of the Utah War," 16–17.

To Resist the Forces That May Be Sent by Uncle Sam

The final skirmishes of George Q. Cannon's newspaper wars in California began with a seemingly innocuous announcement in the *Western Standard* of that season's plans to "gather" to Zion. The gathering had been going on for years, with organized wagon or handcart trains established to help new converts emigrate to Utah, but the growing tensions between the U.S. government and the Saints suggested to many a secret urgency behind this latest call of "Ho! For Salt Lake."

"Ho! For Salt Lake," *Western Standard,* 10 April 1857.

To the Saints in northern California who intend removing to Salt Lake City this season, we have a word of counsel. We expect to organize and send off two companies; one about the 21st of June, and the other some time in August: and all those who intend gathering, are desired to make it known to us as soon as possible, stating their whereabouts, the number of their family, and the amount of their means. Let none think of gathering on their own account, and in disorder, as has hitherto been too much the case with the brethren who have emigrated from this State; but remember that *organize* is a word. Write to us immediately and post us up correctly upon your situation, in order that we may know who it is that lacks and what they lack.

Quite a number of Saints are now ready, or will be by the time the season opens, and it is advisable for them to be on their way by that time, and for all to go with them who can. Others will have to harvest their crops and dispose of them before they can leave. These will compose the second company, and will start by the 21st of August. An agent will be appointed to purchase teams etc., and to superintend the general business of the emigration: and if the brethren living in the country parts, will give us information of the prices of mules etc., in their neighborhoods, it will make his duties less difficult, and will save money to the company. Finally, brethren, whatever information you may have to give upon all matters connected with this year's emigration, give it to us at once.

You will hear from us again upon this subject.

"Ho! For Salt Lake," *The Pacific,* 16 April 1857.

The *Western Standard* of last week, heads an article of advice to those who intend removing to Salt Lake this year with the above caption. We have heard it rumored that orders have been privately sent to the members of this singular sect directing them all to concentrate in Utah as soon possible. It is supposed that expecting trouble with the U.S. Government, they are taking means to increase their effective force in this way, to enable them to resist the forces that may be sent by Uncle Sam to secure the due execution of the laws of the United States in that territory.

"'PACIFIC'S' REASON FOR MORMON EMIGRATION,"
WESTERN STANDARD, 17 APRIL 1857.

Our neighbor of the *Pacific*, whose acuteness in discovering "mares' nests" we have alluded to occasionally, has made a most wonderful discovery this last week, which confirms to an astonishing extent the previous impressions we entertained of his perspicacity. He has discovered in our article of last week headed "Ho! for Salt Lake" a latent design against the Government of the United States! . . .

Mr. Brayton is morbidly sensitive at present on every thing connected with "Mormonism," and seems to be haunted with a continual fear lest it should succeed. His late efforts to deal it a death blow, have excited him. His imagination has become so distempered that he can discover nothing in the immigration to Utah but a design against the General Government. We should advise the gentleman, before he goes any farther, to inquire whether this is a new movement of the Mormons, or have they been expecting trouble with the U.S. Government for the past quarter of a century, that has caused them to take this means of increasing their effective force? The people of Utah have neither violated nor interfered with the due execution of the laws of the United States; they, therefore, have no cause to anticipate a visit from Uncle Sam. Were they in the position of the editor of the *Pacific*, and had unblushingly contended that they had the right to depose the regularly constituted courts, transcend the metes and bounds prescribed by the constitution, and administer justice irrespective of the forms of the law, they might be apprehensive of a visit from the old gentleman's forces. But this, (to their honor be it spoken when we remember what has been done in neighboring communities,) they can not be charged with.

In this instance, at least, the editor of the *Pacific* was more prescient (or realistic) than Cannon. It was only two months later that Brigham Young would acknowledge learning of a "secret" movement of 2,500 soldiers plus suppliers, teamsters, and the usual camp followers sent to Utah to suppress a "Mormon rebellion." Subsequently and incrementally, Young issued a general call to all Saints to return to Utah to defend against what he feared would be a repeat of the Missouri expulsion.

Initially the Mormon leader's calls for a gathering to Utah were simply aimed at consolidating the strength of the Saints in the Salt Lake Valley.

Writing to Cannon in April, he expressed his chagrin that so many of them preferred to remain among the temptations and comforts of California:

> The disposition on the part of some to prefer San Bernardino to Head Quarters is probably the result of ignorance, fear & avarice: They seem not to be aware that we should gather to *learn* the laws of the Lord & of His ways: They are afraid perhaps of the cold experienced in this more Northern climate; and probably believe they can become rich, in less time in San Bno. than they could here, having learned, no doubt, that, here, cash is scarce.[7]

Two months later, however, Brigham Young seemed to be re-thinking the call to gather. Writing to Cannon in early July 1857, he was quite clear that he did not want all of the Saints to gather to Utah after all. He knew that many in California were only lukewarm in the faith and, given the mounting tensions with the government, Young wanted only those who were fully committed "to hold themselves & all that they possess in readiness to forward the interests of God's Kingdom, even to the laying down of their lives should the exigencies of time require them."[8]

As rumors concerning the Mormons continued to circulate, calls for government intervention escalated. One of the favorite rumors of the anti-Mormon press was that the rank-and-file Utahns had turned against their leaders, forcing Brigham Young to flee for his life. As noted, Young's northern tour to Fort Limhi in spring 1857 was the apparent source of such tales. The non-Mormon population of Carson Valley, Nevada, was an especially fertile ground for such rumors, as revealed in the following brief notice in the Placerville paper, the *Mountain Democrat.*

"FROM CARSON VALLEY," *MOUNTAIN DEMOCRAT,* 11 APRIL 1857.

> Messrs. H. Aldrich and W. Wood, arrived in this city on Thursday, direct from Carso[n] Vallley [*sic*]. . .
>
> A report was present in the Valley to the effect that a serious dissension had arisen among the Saints, at Salt Lake City. It is said that Brigham Young has been compelled to flee the city, to save himself from the fury of his flock. The difficulty had its origin in matters relating to the administration of the Church property, we belive [*sic*].

---

[7] Young to Cannon, 4 April 1857, LDS Archives.

[8] See Young to Cannon, 4 July 1857, in Chapter 7. Note that the typed transcript in LDS Archives is erroneously dated 4 June.

"False Reports about the 'Mormons,'" *Western Standard,* 17 April 1857.[9]

If some of the many reports that are put in circulation relative to Governor Young and the "Mormons" were true, what a vast amount of perplexing trouble would be ended. How easily the "Mormon problem" would be solved! How quickly the oft-repeated and troublesome question,—"Who shall be Governor of Utah" would be answered! But, unfortunately for the hopes of its enemies, "Mormonism" still lives—still pursues the even tenor of its way, and will undoubtedly accomplish all that its adherents predict concerning it. The latest report we have noticed in circulation, comes to us in the Placerville *Democrat,* having been brought from Carson Valley by Messrs. H. Aldrich and W. Wood. [Cannon quotes from the *Mountain Democrat's* report.] To the people of Great Salt Lake City this will be news. They imagine that they are at peace, and that His Excellency, Governor Brigham Young, is in their midst, publicly addressing them from time to time in their meetings. But who that desires to hear of the downfall of "Mormonism" would believe that the "Mormons" know anything about their own affairs? The Latter-day Saints may write and publish as much as they please about the peace and union that prevail in their midst; but who will believe it? Let a report be published, however, about dissensions and strife, tyranny and want existing there, and how greedily it is swallowed! It is published and republished until it goes throughout the length and breadth of the land. What a jubilee would be held if the above report were only true! What congratulations would be indulged in! No difference how much blood would be shed, how much suffering endured, if the "Mormons" would only quarrel among themselves and commence a war of extermination upon each other. Every apprehension would then be removed, and the constant dread which is now felt lest the Latter-day Saints should be too strong to be managed, would be ended. For the want of real dissensions and troubles and the breaking up of the "Mormons," they endeavor to console themselves with fictitious ones; these for the time being, answer very well; for when they become stale and are no longer believed, others can be manufactured to suit the exigency. Hope, by this means, is kept alive in their breasts; and they perish whilst cherishing and leaning upon the flattering suggestion, that "Mormonism" and the "Mormons" will fall to pieces before long. Thousands of rumors of this kind have been in constant circulation for these past twenty-seven years, and though their falsity has been abundantly and repeatedly exposed, yet men will rely upon them as heaven's truth, and still pertinaciously assert that there must be foundation for them. And, judging by the past, they will continue to circulate and believe in these rumors and reports so long as they live, though having the continual evidence before their eyes of the spread and increase of "Mormonism."

---

[9] Reprinted in Cannon, *Writings from the "Western Standard,"* 387–88.

A Gibbet Rather than a Bed of Roses

In spring 1857, the mood of the nation—and especially of the West—was that the "treasonous" attitudes and actions of the Mormons had to be punished. At a minimum, Brigham Young had to be replaced as territorial governor. But whom should the president send to Utah in his place? This became a "knotty question" indeed.

"The Knotty Question of Utah," *Western Standard*, 1 May 1857.[10]

> One of the most troublesome questions now presenting itself to the new Administration is that of the Governorship of Utah. It is perfectly clear that if the Federal Government attempts to enforce its power in Utah, there will be armed resistance by Brigham Young. Gen. Pierce foresaw this, and so sneaked out of the responsibility of any steps to put down the bold defyer of American law. The selection of a Governor who shall be willing to risk his life and reputation in the effort to subjugate Utah to law and decency, is a difficult task.
>
> Hitherto no suitable man has been found. Meantime, the President keeps the Kansas-like-Governorship on hand to tender to importunate applicants for place who, like Fayette McMullen of Virginia, have more impudence and self-conceit than brains, and who, also like him, are sure to peremptorily decline a position which promises a gibbet rather than a bed of roses. If there is any consideration which might have been expected to tempt Fayette to go to Utah, it was its system of polygamy; but even that was insufficient to overcome his dread of Brigham's fanatical assassins.

The above we clip from the Washington correspondence of the *Evening Bulletin.* We do not vouch for the accuracy of the statement about the Governorship of Utah having been offered to any individual, though we find, in the New York correspondence of the same paper, that the office has been refused by two or three civilians. It is next to impossible to obtain anything reliable relative to Utah or its affairs from the correspondence of anonymous letter writers; but, assuming a portion of it to be true, and that the position has actually been tendered to certain parties and by them refused, it shows to us that the very means men have taken to injure "Mormonism" are now recoiling on their own heads. "There has no suitable man been found," says this letter writer, "who is willing to risk his life and reputation in the effort to subjugate Utah to law and decency." Visions of gibbets and the extreme danger of being put out of the way by Brigham's "fanatical assassins" present themselves to the minds of some of those to whom the

[10] Ibid. 400–02.

position has been tendered. That the dread of these dangers must have been of a most terrible nature, everybody must know who is in the least acquainted with the character of a professional politician and the eagerness with which he hunts for and accepts office, or they would never have been deterred from accepting this position.

There are politicians who do not dread in the least any evil results from a residence in Utah as its Governor; but they are too shrewd and sensible to accept the position, even were it offered, as they are fully convinced that the office is magnified with dignity and the duties honorably discharged by the present incumbent; and, moreover, they know that he is the *unanimous choice of the people to be governed!* There are others, however, to whom the inhabitants of Utah are terrible; a more than mortal dread fills them at the bare thought of being thrown in the midst of the "Mormons," and they would refuse a position of this kind, were they tendered it, from motives of fear. Why should this dread of the "Mormons" be indulged in? Have this people ever failed to show due respect or pay the highest honor to any Federal officer, who conducted himself in a gentlemanly and honorable manner, and confined himself to the discharge of the duties of his office? Let the testimony of Capt. Stansbury, Judge Reed [*sic*], Judge Shaver, Col. Steptoe, and also that of Judge Kinney, given before both branches of the Utah Legislature, on the evening of the adjournment of the session of 1854-5, in the presence of the Territorial and Federal officers residing there, be adduced in answer to this. These gentlemen were Federal officers, and their testimonies give the lie direct to the numerous statements made by the corrupt to the prejudice of the people of Utah.

The fact is, Governor Young, the "Mormons" and "Mormonism" have been atrociously misrepresented and belied, and the majority of the conductors of public journals have taken so much [*sic*] pains to spread these falsehoods and to suppress everything correct and truthful, that a great fear and terror has taken possession of the minds of many in regard to them. Men have painted "Mormonism" so blackly, and described Governor Young as being such a monster, that they are actually getting scared of the phantoms of their own creation. They have dwelt on these subjects so much and so long that they begin to believe the imaginations of their own brains to be true, and that it is as much as a man's life is worth to put his foot in Utah, especially if he hold a Federal office. They are ready to flee when no man pursueth. We have been looking for the day when the inhabitants of Zion would be terrible; but we scarcely expected it to come about in this manner. Letter writers and editors are doing more than they imagine to make Joseph Smith a true prophet.[11]

---

11 "And it shall be said among the wicked: Let us not go up to battle against Zion, for the inhabitants of Zion are terrible; wherefore we cannot stand." *Doctrine and Covenants* 45:70.

To Find Any Man Competent to Succeed Him

Regardless of the workable, if not entirely positive, relationships some federal appointees had enjoyed with the Mormons, it was not long before the entire nation was aware that President Buchanan was having difficulties finding the right man to replace Brigham Young. Small wonder, given the tales of conflict (often exaggerated, as in the case of Drummond) from other former Utah officials. Among the most recent as well as longest-standing lodgers of such complaints was the surveyor general, David H. Burr. Burr had gone to Utah with excellent qualifications: he had been surveyor general of both New York and Delaware, was the former geographer to the U.S. House of Representatives, and had made the first map of the explorations of Jedediah Smith. When Utah Territory was created in 1850, Congress declined to extend the system of land preemption to it. Federal law required surveying Utah Territory before settlers could hope to obtain legal land titles, but the Saints had their own church-devised system of distributing land. Their lack of title to the property they occupied added to their distrust of virtually all federal appointees:

> Many Mormons looked upon Burr's survey—a necessary step toward private land ownership—as a potential threat, knowing that title to the lands they had occupied was tenuous in the absence of Mexican grant, Indian treaty, or congressional enactment. Some tried to impede the surveyor's work, and Burr reported to superiors that he had been threatened with violence and that Mormons were encouraging Indians to resist the surveying parties. By the spring of 1857, Burr gave up his work in Utah, claiming that he had been denounced from the pulpit and that his life was in danger. He asserted that his associates had been beaten and threatened with death. Mormon leaders denied Burr's claims and accused Burr of conspiracy to defraud the public.[12]

Hosea Stout, a Mormon attorney who apparently participated in the theft and alleged destruction of government records that led to the departure of Judge Stiles and other government officials, described Burr's role in precipitating that event in his journal for February 1857. According to Stout, Burr raised objections to recent court rulings con-

[12] Campbell, *Establishing Zion,* 227. See also Bigler, *Forgotten Kingdom,* 135–36 for more on Burr's view. Cannon printed several accusations against Burr in the 11 September 1857 edition of the *Standard.*

firming the primacy of territorial over federal law, which then prompted a Mormon attorney to call him a "cowardly cur who wished to attact [*sic*], our laws clandestinely but had not courage to do it openly." This exchange, in which "feelings were very high," resulted in the departure of Burr, among others.[13]

David H. Burr wrote several anonymous and inflammatory letters to eastern newspapers.[14] Burr's reported experience doubtless served to discourage others—including prospective governors—from serving in Utah Territory. His letter to the General Land Office commissioner alleging that "*these people repudiate the authority of the United States in this country, and are in open rebellion against the general government*" may have helped influence Buchanan's decision to send in the troops, though it is unlikely the letter reached Washington until after the cabinet had acted.[15]

Meanwhile, newspapers such as the *Daily Evening Bulletin* simultaneously engaged in speculation as to who would be the new governor and criticized Buchanan for dragging his feet. They wanted a solution to the "Mormon problem" and they wanted it now. But as historian Norman F. Furniss pointed out, "If the army should arrive first, without civil officers, the Mormons could with some reason claim that they were being invaded by a hostile force sent solely to destroy them, and war, not a pleasant possibility to Buchanan, might ensue." The delay in deploying the troops to Utah was largely a result of the difficulty Buchanan encountered in finding a competent individual willing to accept what could only be "a political death-trap" as the new governor of Utah Territory. Several promising candidates declined the office, including the administration's first choice, Benjamin McCulloch of Texas, and Upper Missouri River Indian Superintendent Alfred Cumming. The only men eager to win the appointment were notorious anti-Mormons, including, of course, William Drummond.[16] As rumors leaked out through the eastern press, the California newspapers were eager to reprint the more interesting letters and editorials, often adding their own commentary:

---

[13] Brooks, ed., *On the Mormon Frontier,* 622

[14] Neff, *History of Utah,* 443.

[15] Burr to Hendricks, House Exec. Doc. 71, 118–20, March 28, 1857, as quoted in Bigler, *Forgotten Kingdom,* 135. William P. MacKinnon discusses the timing of the various letters that may have influenced Buchanan's decision in "The Buchanan Spoils System and the Utah Expedition."

[16] Furniss, *The Mormon Conflict,* 57, 96.

"MORE OF UTAH MATTERS," *DAILY EVENING BULLETIN*, 16 JULY 1857.

Ex-Governor Philip Frank Thomas, of Maryland, has also declined the Utah governorship. It is thought that Col.[17] Cummings [*sic*], who has once declined, may now be induced to accept. Emery D. Potter, of Ohio, has accepted one of the Utah judgships [*sic*], and the other has been offered to a Mr. Eckles, of Indiana, who it is believed will also accept. Thos. H. Dunn, of Mississippi, will probably be appointed U.S. Marshall for the Territory. David H. Burr, late U.S. Surveyor General of Utah, has arrived at his home in this city [Washington, D.C.], having been compelled to leave by the threats against his life. He states: That the Mormon Legion is poorly equipped, and that one thousand United States troops would effectually over-awe them. Before he left Utah the Mormons had not heard of the intention of the Government to send a force thither, but they frequently laughed at the idea of the Government compelling them to obey the Federal laws, and cited the failure of the Government to put down the disturbances in Kansas as evidence of its inefficiency. He supposed that one-third or half of the Mormons, who are disgusted with Brigham's tyranny, would rise against him were they protected by the United States troops. Mr. Burr does not apprehend that the Mormons will show fight. It is the duty of every good Mormon to obey the Church as the higher law, and hence the opinion is entertained that Brigham Young may leave the Territory with a large force of deluded followers, provided he can find some other seat for his Government. Mr. Burr says that Salt Lake is the meanest settlement that he ever beheld, everything having the appearance of abject poverty. Young's word is law, and the oppressions of the Mormons are cruel, and without remedy from the present rulers. There are about fifty "Gentiles" only in the Territory, and they are the objects of bitter persecution.

"LETTER FROM WASHINGTON: SUMMARY OF POLITICAL NEWS," *DAILY EVENING BULLETIN*, 16 JULY 1857.

UTAH AFFAIRS—DUPLICITY OF THE ADMINISTRATION

We still receive daily assurances that the President has undertaken to deal resolutely with Brigham Young and his Mormon vassals, but I confess that I have strong suspicions of his sincerity. One of the first questions which engaged his attention after his inauguration was that relating to the Utah rebellion. Four months have nearly elapsed, and still all law and decency are marked by the continuance of Young in the gubernatorial office, while we are gravely told that it is impossible, in this wide land, to find any man com-

[17] Cumming was not a commissioned officer. This was an honorific title commonly and informally bestowed on the frontier for men who served in such positions as Indian superintendent, wagon road superintendent, guide, scout, wagon boss, etc.

petent to succeed him who is willing to accept the place! We are told, too, that a force of 2,500 men, under Gen. Harney, has been ordered to Utah to support the new Governor and establish the law. For myself, I believe this is another executive lie—a quibble—a tub to the whale, designed to allay the storm of public sentiment in behalf of vigorous measures, without really doing *anything* for the present. Certain it is, that no order of troops to Salt Lake has been published. On the contrary, the old orders distributing in other directions every company of troops otherwise available to that service have been acted upon.

I enclose an extract from the St. Louis *Republican,* showing that this is true, and that the Cheyenne Expedition is already entered upon. Notwithstanding all the protestations of Mr. Buchanan to the contrary, he is dishonestly endeavoring to further postpone the issue, in the idle hope that internal dissensions in Mormondom will work its own overthrow, and so relieve him from the necessity of dealing with the troublesome question. If public sentiment refuses to be lulled into security, but continues to insist on action, the troops which have started for the Cheyenne country can and may be diverted from that service and ordered to Salt Lake. In that is the only probability of anything being done this summer.

Ben McCulloch and the President—
Ben is to be Married and Can't Go

Major Ben McCulloch has been in Washington and was again urged by the President to take the Governorship at Utah. Ben declined persistently, urging that with the cut-throat idea which the country had of him, he would be expected to hang Brigham Young and a half a dozens of his fellow-apostles without Judge or Jury, and to thrash the whole Mormon community once a day at least. As it is not at all probable that the rebels would give him any pretext for such vigorous measures, when they should find themselves in the presence of a strong force, the Major foresaw that he would fail to answer public expectations, and so would lose vastly in popular estimation. The President was not inclined to let the Major off on this plea, which he deemed insufficient to justify a patriot in declining public service. Ben then suggested that there was another reason personal to himself, which he had not deemed necessary to mention.

"The fact is," said Ben, "there's a lady in the case: I am to be married this fall, in fulfillment of a duty already neglected too long; and I fear if I neglect it longer I shall get on the old bachelor list."

Old Buck pricked up his ears at this, uttered a sigh at the thought of his own neglected opportunities, and "caved in." "Why," said he, "didn't you tell me that before? What's the use of saving your best argument until the last? Stay at Home? Certainly! Better far marry one wife than neglect it for the purpose of governing men with forty. Wish you joy, Major; my respects to the lady, and be sure to tell her that I would never knowingly have attempted to take you from her side to send you in such dangerous company."

"Disappointed Letter Writers," *Western Standard*, 24 July 1857.[18]

The last mail from the east, instead of bringing, as was confidently anticipated, the news of the definite appointment of a Governor for Utah and the departure of Gen. Harney and his troops for that Territory, only brings the oft-repeated story that it has been proffered and again declined. Some of our contemporaries begin to think that newspaper correspondents have been premature in stating that prompt and decided action had been taken against the "Mormons." They now are willing to acknowledge that, up to the latest advices, it was extremely doubtful whether any orders had been issued from the Department for the movement of any military force in the direction of Utah. All the glorification and rejoicing they have indulged in, have thus far proved to be entirely destitute of good foundation. The "Mormons" are not yet annihilated, and the prospect for such a consummation seems to be more distant than it did a few months ago. The Washington correspondent of the Evening *Bulletin* waxes quite indignant on this subject in his letter to that paper, and accuses the Administration of duplicity. . . .

This correspondent has given his readers the strongest assurances for some time back that this question would be summarily disposed of, by the appointment of a military Governor, backed by the presence of General Harney and his troops. Because his statements have not been carried out, he now seeks to prejudice the people against the Administration by charging the President with duplicity. We were satisfied that the poor soul knew nothing about what the intentions of the President and the Cabinet were on the subject, and his remarks only confirm us in our opinion. Newspaper correspondents must write something, if it be nothing more than the coinage of their own imaginations. It would not be policy to say that they knew nothing about a subject which occupies so much of the public attention as does Utah. Better pander to corrupt and vitiated taste by manufacturing something that would be likely to suit,—marking out, for instance, a course of policy, and stating that the Executive had decided to adopt it. If it should not be carried out, the correspondent need not lose any credit for misleading the public; he can charge the Executive with duplicity and the adoption of a temporizing policy. Newspaper correspondents have written enough on this single subject within the last few months to stamp their communications as worthless and erroneous. They have proved themselves to be ignoramuses.

---

[18] Reprinted in Cannon, *Writings from the "Western Standard,"* 292–93.

Nothing Remains But an Appeal to Arms

The man President Buchanan finally persuaded to replace Brigham Young as territorial governor was Alfred Cumming, former mayor of Augusta, Georgia, and superintendent of Indian affairs on the Upper Missouri. According to Norman F. Furniss, Cumming had in some way won the "sponsorship" of Mormon agent Thomas L. Kane.[19] (While this seems improbable, it would further explain Kane's subsequent journey to Great Salt Lake City to help broker a peaceful resolution to the ensuing conflict.)

Col. William Selby Harney (known by his enemies as "squaw-killer" because of his slaughter of Indian women and children in the 1856 battle of Ash Hollow on the Oregon Trail) was the original commander of the first 1,500 troops sent to quell the "Utah rebellion." Harney recognized a logistical and tactical disaster in the making and became sorely needed in Kansas.[20] He was replaced by Col. Albert Sidney Johnston, who was later breveted brigadier general as the leader of the Utah Expedition, known in Utah ever since as "Johnston's Army." Ironically, Johnston denounced Mormon rebellion but died as a Confederate general in the Civil War—leading his own army of rebels at the battle of Shiloh. By the time the Utah Expedition finally ended, a total of 5,602 troops had been sent to the territory to put down the perceived insurrection at a cost estimated between fifteen and forty million dollars.[21]

"War with the Mormons," *Daily Evening Bulletin*, 22 June 1857.

We think it pretty evident from the signs of the times that there will be a collision between the forces of the Government and the Mormons of Utah. However much this is to be regretted, we must confess that we know no way of preventing such a misfortune, should Brigham Young adhere to his high-handed policy, and continue his open defiance of the Constitution and laws of the nation. What the final result of such a war will be, does not admit of much doubt. In time, the Mormons must be crushed out. But this is not going to prove so easy a task, even with the vast resources at the com-

---

[19] Furniss, *The Mormon Conflict*, 96.

[20] Ball, *Army Regulars on the Western Frontier*, 161.

[21] For a fine overview and documentary history of the Utah War, see Hafen and Hafen, eds., *The Utah Expedition*. Currently the definitive narrative study is Furniss, *The Mormon Conflict*. Other useful treatments include Arrington and Bitton, eds., *The Mormon Experience*, 164–70; Poll and MacKinnon, "Causes of the Utah War Reconsidered," 16–44; and Bigler, *Forgotten Kingdom*, 141–58. Of particular interest will be William P. MacKinnon's forthcoming book in this series.

An artist's rendition of the massive Utah Expedition of 1857.
From Stenhouse, *Rocky Mountain Saints.*

mand of the Government, as some people imagine. The numerical force of the Mormons is already formidable. The peculiar tenets of their religious belief, which give their saints and prophets entire supremacy, will insure union of design and integrity of action. The distance of their territory and its inaccessibility—surrounded as it is by deserts and mountains—renders operations against them tedious, difficult and dangerous; while the cry of persecution that will be raised by them must be expected to attract some sympathy, and perhaps succor, to their aid from abroad. Besides, the military power of the United States has never been directly employed to any extent in enforcing the laws; and a resort to this extremity, even in so necessary a case as the one in point, will doubtless shock the sensibilities of many people, who having so enlarged an idea of liberty, naturally feel a strong aversion to coercion by force.

Notwithstanding all these difficulties, we think there should be no hesitation on the part of the Administration in its course. Indeed, the greater the difficulty the more need of prompt and decisive action. Six years ago, Brigham Young could have been removed without trouble; now, the task is one of extreme labor; and in six years more, it may be one of extreme danger. The population of the Territory is rapidly increasing by accessions of deluded victims from every part of the world; and it will be found much easier to subdue hundreds, than to wait until their strength has grown into thousands. Experience has shown us that it is vain to expect Brigham Young to moderate his pretensions—his impudence increases with every arrival of immigrants and each accession of strength. Nothing remains but an appeal to arms; let it come; and upon the heads of those who have brought it on, shall the responsibility rest.

If operations are begun, however, everything depends upon their being decisive and vigorous. If a demand be made upon Brigham, it should be positive and imperative, and backed by a formidable military force, to render any equivocation or dilly-dallying on his part out of the question. Should it become necessary to resort to arms, no timid blow should be struck—it must be one that will strike terror to the centre of Mormondom, and teach them at the start what they will have to depend upon. Nothing could be more unfortunate than to permit them to gain an advantage at the first. A victory over a body of United States troops would puff these fanatical people, shut up in their fastnesses, with confidence and pride that would prolong the war for years. They would imagine that the days of miracles had returned, and that the Lord of Hosts had delivered their enemies into their hands, as He did the enemies of His people of old. Such a catastrophe, therefore, should be carefully guarded against; no small force should be marched against Utah; every preparation should be made for a desperate struggle with a hardy people; the whole strength of the Confederacy should be brought to bear; and when the traitors saw that it was useless to contend, and had suffered one or two vigorous repulses, they would doubtless give up the point—permit Brigham Young to be deposed—and return to their allegiance to the legally appointed Governor of the President's choosing, consent to the reorganization of the United States Court, and pay proper respect to its officers and mandates.

We know very well that there are many people of judgment who seriously question the policy of attacking Brigham with arms. These look upon Mormonism as a fanaticism, and declare that fanaticism was never yet crushed out by force. They say that whenever it has been attempted in history, it has ended in failure—as it did in England in the case of the Puritans. But such men overlook altogether the main feature of the contest. The government is not called on to interfere because of any religious belief or tenet held by the Mormons. We do not wish to invade Utah because the people there believe in Joe Smith's bible, or marry fifty wives, but because they have rebelled against the Constitution and laws of the land. If a man commit murder, there is no reason for excusing him in the fact that he happens to believe in a different religion from ours. His religion neither makes him the more nor the less guilty. It is the same in cases of treason. Therefore, it seems to us the height of absurdity to urge the President to let Brigham Young go unpunished, merely because he is a false prophet, a teacher of polygamy, and an encourager of incest. But there is one way in which these matters will be brought in. The mischievous doctrines and beastly practices of these people will cut them off from the sympathies of the world. The relation of their brutalities has already raised against them a storm of hatred throughout christendom. And the voice of Brigham Young, crying persecution, will be drowned by the shrieks of young girls and the curses of women, sacrificed in that Pandemonium of wickedness, Salt Lake City.

"The 'Mormon Problem' and the 'Bulletin,'" *Western Standard*, 26 June 1857.[22]

... in an evening paper—the *Bulletin*—a few days ago, headed "War with the Mormons," . . . the editor dilates at some length on the course which ought to be taken with the people of Utah. . . .

For a man occupying the position of this editor, to jump at the conclusions he evidently does in thus speaking about the people of Utah, he must either be dishonest and determined to consider them guilty however strong the evidence of their innocence may be, or extremely gullible. Mr. King's experience as a journalist during the past year in this city, ought to have taught him better than to pursue the unwise course he has in this instance, in endeavoring to arouse a spirit of excitement and indignation in the public mind. He ought to stop, at least for a moment, and inquire whether there is not another side to the stories in circulation about "Mormon" treason and outrage, and not gulp down all that is said to their prejudice as unimpeachable and indisputable truths. All the evidence he has before him in regard to the alleged treasonable acts of the "Mormons," is that emanating from our enemies. And yet, on the strength of these one-sided statements, he proceeds to denounce the people of Utah, in language which reminds us forcibly of the blood-thirsty appeals of the infamous Marat,[23] as traitors to the Constitution and laws of this nation, and invokes the General Government to exert its power and crush us. Shame upon such a man, who is so lost to all sense of propriety, so dead to all the feelings of reason and humanity as to pursue such a course! Must the people of a whole Territory, thousands of whom have as just a claim on the protection and fostering care of the General Government as the most favored citizens of these United States, be condemned unheard, to the fate suggested by this editor? If so, farewell to liberty, farewell to justice, and farewell to the liberal institutions purchased by the blood and sufferings of the revolutionary fathers!

---

[22] Reprinted in Cannon, *Writings from the "Western Standard,"* 454–59.

[23] Jean Paul Marat (1743–93) was a physician and newspaper editor during the French Revolution who had a hand in inciting the September massacres. Charlotte Corday assassinated Marat while he was writing in his bath, a scene made famous by the painter Jacques Louis David.

But what if this course, which the editor of the *Bulletin* recommends to be pursued towards the "Mormons," should be adopted by the public towards himself, where would he be to-morrow? Mr. King has been assailed, and grave and serious charges fulminated against him by those who are as much entitled to credit and hold equally as respectable positions in society as the defamers of Utah and the Latter-day Saints. What would be the opinion we would be compelled to entertain of him and his character, were we to read and listen to all that his opponents have to say, and not pay any attention to his denial of these vile charges? We should conclude that a more unscrupulous and corrupt man, and one more unfit to be countenanced or associated with, could scarcely be found. But he denies the truth of these charges—says the men who circulate them are unworthy of credence, and thinks that his denials and protestations ought to have weight and be heard. Thousands of men, whose words have never been impeached, whose lives have been pure and unblemished, and whose greatest and only *crime* has been that of believing "Mormonism," deny the statements and charges circulated to the injury of the people of Utah, and yet this editor will neither believe nor think their statements worthy of the slightest consideration or notice; but will, nevertheless, urge upon the General Government the propriety of crushing them out! How inconsistent a course for a man in his position to pursue! "We do not wish," says Mr. King, "to invade Utah because the people there believe in Joe [Joseph] Smith's bible, or marry fifty wives; but *because they have rebelled against the Constitution and laws of the land.*" If, for the supposed or asserted commission of this crime, an appeal to arms is to be had, Utah invaded and the "Mormons" crushed out by an overwhelming force of Federal troops, then, to be just and to execute the penalty impartially upon all who are guilty, a detachment of those troops had better invade the domicile of the gentleman who makes the suggestion, and execute the summary vengeance upon him which he prescribes for the Latter-day Saints. For it is a fact, patent to every reader of the *Bulletin* since the present editor has had control of its columns, that he has openly advocated undisguised resistance to the Federal authorities, and made insane appeals to the people to resist any intervention they might offer in the local affairs of this city. The most bold and fearless expressions uttered by Governor Young and the other "Mormons," and which have been garbled and colored by our enemies, appear mild and loyal compared with many of the sentiments given utterance to by him in his leaders of last summer and fall. And could he then have had as much influence over the people of this city as Governor Young always has had over the people of Utah, we are of the opinion that his criminality would not have been confined to threats.

But this action, Mr. King asserts, was taken to maintain the rights of man, to teach corrupt office holders the lesson that there was a point beyond which it would be worse than cowardice for a suffering and long-oppressed people to endure. If this be granted, what then becomes of his rodomontade[24] against the "Mormons?" Have the "Mormons" no rights to maintain? Are they to suffer uncomplainingly and unresistingly every wrong that can be inflicted upon them, without seeking for the redress to be obtained by the exercise of their legal and guaranteed rights and privileges? They have neither violated the constitution and laws of the Territory of Utah nor of the United States in the course they have taken. They have not incarcerated for long weary weeks Judges of their own electing; they have not openly defied the power of the Federal Government nor arrayed themselves against it. But they have contended for their rights; they have told the corrupt and unprincipled men who have been too often imposed upon them, regardless of any of their likes or dislikes, that they should not have unbridled license to practice their whoredom and abominations in their midst, neither would they submit to their high-handed oppression; they have given them to understand that though "Mormons," yet they are freemen. If this be wrong, then every man who contends for the blessings of freedom is a transgressor; if this be treason, then every man who ever lifted his voice against tyranny and oppression was a traitor. The gentleman either deceives himself or endeavors to deceive his readers when he states that it is not for the belief in the doctrines taught and practiced by the "Mormons," but for rebellion against the Constitution and laws of the land that he wishes to invade Utah. If interrupting the Court in its proceedings, taking possession of records, threatening its Judge and forcing him to fly, constitute the rebellion of the "Mormons"—for these are the rebellious acts they are falsely accused of committing—then, we again assert, the editor of the *Bulletin* either deceives himself or his readers, when he says that for these acts, and not for their religion, he would have Utah invaded and the "Mormons" crushed out; because all these acts, or others equally culpable, he himself has connived at and abetted. Courts have been interrupted; a Judge has been incarcerated, threatened, his life demanded; and other overt acts committed in the loyal city of San Francisco, which he has openly encouraged and defended. It cannot be, then, for rebellious acts of this description that he wishes Utah invaded by the Federal troops; he surely is not so inconsistent. It must be a religious crusade that he wishes commenced.

Once again, Cannon skillfully pointed out the contradiction between the support the California press offered the vigilantes and their condemnation of Mormon defiance of federal officials, who had now

[24] Named for the proclivities of a character in Matteo Boiardo's *Orlando Innamorato*, a rodomontade is a vain and bragging speech.

deployed the army to assert their authority. Understandably, the Mormons condemned this "invasion":

> We know those aspersions to be false, but that avails us nothing. We are condemned unheard and forced to an issue with an armed, mercenary mob, which has been sent against us at the instigation of anonymous letter writers ashamed to father the base slanderous falsehoods which they have given to the public; of corrupt officials who have brought false accusation against us to screen themselves in their own infamy; and of hireling priests and howling editors who prostitute the truth for filthy lucre's sake.[25]

If such accusations appear to be the result of hyperbole or paranoia, consider the sentiment expressed by one of America's foremost journalists, Horace Greeley, of the *New York Tribune.* "If the Mormons are ready to set themselves up as God's chosen people, standing in the place of the Israelites of old, there is scarcely less disposition in other quarters to regard them as a sort of modern Canaanites whose infamous wickedness affords sufficient warrant even for their utter extermination."[26]

In his "War with the Mormons" editorial, editor Thomas S. King provoked the ire of Cannon by unabashedly suggesting that "In time, the Mormons must be crushed out." Still, neither he nor many others felt it would be an easy task. "Should a war take place between the Mormons and the United States," wrote the editor of the San Francisco *Herald,* "it will be one of the most protracted and bloody the country has ever engaged in, and would require an immense outlay to bring it to a termination."[27] As King observed, the geography of Utah, coupled with its distance from the East, provided the Mormons with a natural defense—an advantage not lost on the Saints. One Mormon hymn, published by John Jacques at the height of the crisis, delighted in the natural security to be found in the land of God:

> We thank thee for the deserts
> And for the canyon bold,
> For all our rocky bulwarks,
> And for the piercing cold,

[25] Excerpt from a "Proclamation by the Governor" in which Brigham Young decreed martial law on 15 September 1857. Although extant variants of the proclamation bear the date 5 August 1857, Young did not instruct Daniel H. Wells to write it until 29 August. See Cooley, ed., *Diary of Brigham Young, 1857,* 68, 82–83. No contemporary evidence supports the existence of a circulated August version of the proclamation, which appears to be the result of either a printer's error or a forgery.

[26] Greeley, the *New York Tribune,* 30 January 1858.

[27] *San Francisco Daily Herald,* 19 October 1857, 2/2.

And that thou dost surround us
With heavy mantling snows,
For these are our defenses
Against our Christian foes.[28]

THE UNITED STATES TROOPS ARE GOING TO KILL US ALL

Natural fortifications notwithstanding, Brigham Young had been aware of the movement of the federal troops since at least 23 June when the Eastern mail confirmed the rumors of press reports on 29 May announcing the president's decision to send an army to Utah. On the twenty-fourth of July 1857, the tenth anniversary of Brigham Young's entrance into the Salt Lake Valley, their prophet publicly apprised the Utah Mormons of the movement of troops. As Cannon later learned of the event from Wilford Woodruff,

> Elders A. O. Smoot, O. P. Rockwell and Judson Stoddard arrived from the States, bringing the intelligence that the Mail Contract had been taken from Mr. Kimball—that Col. Cummins [*sic*] was appointed Governor, and a full branch of Judges and other Officers were appointed, to be accompanied by 2500 troops as a small body guard, and 700 teams and wagons laden with baggage and provisions for 15 months. To a people quietly engaged minding their own business, living in strict obedience to the laws of their country, and ever having proved themselves devoted and loyal to its Constitution, this was certainly a startling announcement![29]

In the same mail came another letter by John G. Chambers, confirming the rumor of what appeared to be a planned invasion: "The government of the United States (it is reported) are now sending 2500 troops and government officials and missionaries to put the Mormons right in Utah! I suppose they have believed all the false reports and rumors respecting us, and are acting upon such to carry out certain designs, the ultimatum of which is to exterminate us from this our mountain home."[30]

---

[28] *Deseret News,* 30 December, 1857 quoted in Neff, *History of Utah,* 473. Note again the distance the Mormons of that day desired to place between themselves and their "Christian" critics and enemies. Today the Church of Jesus Christ of Latter-day Saints battles long and hard to convince the world that they, along with Catholics and Protestants, are Christians.

[29] Woodruff to Cannon, 4 August 1857, *Western Standard,* 18 September 1857, 3. Woodruff—and virtually all other sources—omitted the name of the passenger Rockwell and Stoddard had brought to Utah: Eleanor McLean Pratt. See Thomas, ed., *Elias Smith's Journal,* 23 July 1857.

[30] Chambers to Cannon, 3 August 1857, Ibid.

It was probably not until he had received these letters that Cannon finally abandoned his desperate hope that the "invasion" was little more than an ugly rumor. David H. Burr's assessment of the relative weakness of Mormon military power was essentially correct, but they were more than ready to fight. An anonymous letter to the *Evening Bulletin* revealed that they quickly concluded American soldiers and politicians were committed to exterminating the Latter-day Saints.

"LETTER FROM A SALT LAKE MORMON,"
EVENING BULLETIN, 18 AUGUST 1857.

The annexed are extracts from a letter written from Great Salt Lake City, bearing date 28th June last. The writer is a young man, who is said to have a nice little piece of property at San Bernardino, which he is willing to sell to get arms to fight against his country. He says:

> The report is, that John Taylor is in prison. I've not heard the particulars about it. Ephraim Hanks had to flee for his life from Independence, Missouri, on account of a story that Judge Drummond told about him. He accused Hanks of the murder of Capt. Gunnison, and said he (Hanks) cut his heart out and stamped on it with his feet, which is a notorious lie, for John Toben [*sic*] told me all about it. He was out with Gunnison, and left him the day before he was killed. Bill Hickman had to swim the Missouri river and come home.[31]
>
> I've joined the Light Artillery, but I have no horse rigging nor weapons; and if you can sell my place in San Bernardino for a horse and a Colt's revolver or two, and an old sword, or something that will get them, and send them to me, they may be the means of saving my life, for I expect a row here before long. The United States troops are going to kill us all off; but I think they will smell h__l before they accomplish it. There is nobody scared here that I know of, for they think the sooner they come the better. And so do I, for there has not been much fun since I've been home.

[31] John Taylor followed Brigham Young as the third president of the LDS church. Ephraim Hanks was a Mormon mountaineer who figured prominently in the rescue of the 1856 handcart companies. Tobin was a convert from the Stansbury expedition who was later attacked by whites, possibly fellow Mormons, en route to California. The infamous Bill Hickman had been a bodyguard to Joseph Smith and an Indian fighter and lawman under Brigham Young prior to numerous criminal accusations and his excommunication in 1868. To save his own skin in a plea bargain, Hickman told his story to the anti-Mormon writer, J. H. Beadle. This resulted in a wildly popular ghostwritten exposé of all things Mormon, which Hickman later disavowed: *Brigham's Destroying Angel: Being the Life, Confession, and Startling Disclosures of the Notorious Bill Hickman, the Danite Chief of Utah.* In 1857, however, Hickman was in excellent standing with Brigham Young and served as an officer in the Nauvoo Legion. A recent treatment on Hickman, though lacking in specific documentation, is Hilton, *"Wild Bill" Hickman and the Mormon Frontier.*

The anonymous young Mormon quoted above was not the only one to rattle sabers in the direction of the federal troops. On the contrary, he was merely repeating the threats and boasts of his leaders. Writing to Cannon on 4 August, Brigham Young not only confirmed Cumming's appointment, but he began directing a series of sarcastic comments at the federal troops marching to the Great Basin. He also counseled Cannon to begin releasing the missionaries in California, and the call to return home in anticipation of a conflict with the U.S. Army had begun.

YOUNG TO CANNON, 4 AUGUST 1857, LDS ARCHIVES.

Dear Brother,

Since the Y.X. Company commenced operations we have had sufficient news from the States to satisfy any reasonable person. A. O. Smoot and Judson Stoddard arrived in this city July 23 having left Fort Leavenworth July 4th. Did we look thro the eyes of the world, I am not sure but that their tidings would be somewhat startling.

The Government have at last hit upon the long sought-for plan to extinguish "Mormonism." What that plan is we can form no idea except from the effects growing out of it, which are these: One Mr. Cummings of St. Louis, Mo. is appointed Governor, a fellow by the name of Worrel is Post Master, besides the list contains a Secretary, Judges, U.S. Marshal, and Surveyor & Attorney Generals, all of course from the ranks of our most bitter enemies. Then there are 2500 regulars coming with them as a body-guard to execute their commands, to sustain them in their exalted positions. This grand cavalcade were to make their debut on the plains of the 15th ult. The soldiers were going to march here on foot, and were to be accompanied by 400 mule teams to haul their luggage. W. H. Russell of Mo. has contracted to freight 15 months provision to this place, for their use, and furnish them with 7000 head of beef Cattle.

The mission of these "War-Dogs" is of course peaceful, as that saintly Squaw killer, General Harney, is supposed commandant of the expedition; and the current report is, that he has committed himself on the peace side, by openly avowing that he felt no hostility to the settlers of Utah further than myself and about 29 others, and all those who believe as we do. A Jubilee[32] is to be declared, means and protection are to be afforded to all who wish to return to the States. In fact the Mormons are going (?) to be *christianized,* civilized and victimized by the "virtuous, highminded (?) Officers" of 'uncle Sam's' *regulars.* To offset this there is a strong probability that

[32] The same term was used in Texas and other southern states to describe the day in 1865 that they learned of their freedom.

the troop will not reach further than Laramie this fall, and a still *stronger* probability that they will *not get here*. . . .

Let as many of the Saints as possible come through to the valley this fall. Release those of the Elders who have been laboring there for any great length of time. Induce as any of our young men to return as possible as their parents are exceedingly anxious to see them. The Saints who come through the north route had better supply themselves with efficient arms and keep strong guards, as the Indians on that rout are said to be exceedingly hostile. . . .[33]

May God ever bless you with all his faithful servants, and enable us to triumph over all our enemies, is my prayer in the name of Jesus Christ. Amen.

THE DEVIL'S MYRMIDONS

Second-hand stories traveling east and west became increasingly extravagant until rumor had it that Col. Edwin V. "Bull" Sumner had arrested Brigham Young, Prophet of the Lord and tenuous governor of Utah Territory, for treason. The parenthetical note included at the end of the dramatic announcement made obvious to Thomas S. King, editor of the *Bulletin*, that something was wrong with his Oroville correspondent's information. Still, he did not hesitate to print it—as a "flaming telegraphic dispatch," no less—thereby encouraging the perpetuation and embellishment of the story by other California newspapers such as the *Herald*. Naturally, it also drew the wrath of the ever-vigilant Cannon.

"IMPORTANT NEWS FROM SALT LAKE.
BRIGHAM YOUNG ARRESTED FOR TREASON.
YOUNG CARRIED OFF A PRISONER BY COL. SUMNER TO WASHINGTON," *DAILY EVENING BULLETIN*, 22 AUGUST 1857.

Oroville, 22d August, 1857

Mr. J. J. Bush arrived here last Thursday with a large train, consisting of 174 men, 4 women, 17 wagons, 800 head of cattle and 500 mules. Mr. Bush came in by the Honey Lake route. He reports a large immigration on the way. His train left Salt Lake on June 27th; and reports that Col. Sumner with 86 dragoons, of Company G., U.S. Army, arrived in that city on June 25th, at 7 P. M., and took Brigham Young prisoner, on a charge of treason and other crimes, and started with him for Washington city, within two hours after his arrival, meeting with no opposition on the part of the Mormons. [There must be some mistake about this news. On 25th June Col.

[33] For the following three paragraphs of this letter, see "Late News from Utah," *Western Standard*, 18 September 1857, in the following chapter.

Sumner was supposed to be in Kansas. We have seen letters from Salt Lake, dated 2d July, in which mention is made of Brigham Young being seen in that city, and well. Perhaps the date should be 25th *July*—which would allow time for an arrival here from Salt Lake. Our telegraphic dispatches say June, but the operator, or the party sending the message, may have made a mistake.—Ed. BULLETIN.]

"LATE NEWS FROM UTAH," *WESTERN STANDARD*, 18 SEPTEMBER 1857.

We wonder whether the editor of the S. F. *Bulletin*, since the arrival of the Utah mail, has ordered its special correspondent at Oroville to make particular inquiries as to the whereabouts of that J. J. Bush, upon whose testimony a flaming telegraphic dispatch appeared in the columns of the *Bulletin* about two or three weeks ago, announcing the arrest of Governor Young on a charge of treason and other crimes, by Col. Sumner, and his departure with him as prisoner to Washington city. Knowing the proclivities of the editor of the *Bulletin* so well, we should scarcely think that he would let so good an opportunity escape him as now presents itself of lampooning Mr. Bush for the grievous and heinous sin of lying. How you could dilate, Mr. King, on the evil consequences of hoaxing an editor! Or, was Mr. Bush a myth, manufactured expressly for the occasion by "Our Special Correspondent," as a means of swelling the treasury of the Evening *Bulletin* by the proceeds of the sale of a few papers?

Our latest dates from Utah, by the mail, are to August 5th. They inform us that President Young was still there, and in the enjoyment of good health. Peace prevailed, and every thing was moving on harmoniously. In a letter written by himself, he says:

> "The harvest is most abundant; there is sufficient grain in the Territory for several year's [*sic*] consumption. The Saints are renewing their diligence and faithfulness before the Lord. The Public Works are moving on cheerfully. For account of our 24th ult. recreations, home news, and the tone of feeling here, I refer you to the *Deseret News.*
>
> "Unfortunately for the raciness of my letter I have no accounts to forward you of murder, riots, rapes, crim. Cons ["criminal connections," or illicit sex], or any of the thousand and one interesting little circumstances which usually render an editor's private correspondence so spicy. This is what makes the devil mad; this is why all hell is fired up with wrath; and why the devil's myrmidons—beside whom he is a gentleman—are continually howling, "exterminate the Mormons." In spite of the devil and all his imps Mormonism will triumph; the power of God will make the nations writhe on couches of their own choosing.
>
> "We will stand by the revelations of God, and the Constitution of the United States, and let those who invade them tremble, for the vengeance of a just God will surely come upon them, and His curse will blot their names from the Book of Life."

"TOPICS OF THE DAY," *DAILY HERALD*, 23 AUGUST 1857.

The news published last evening, in relation to the arrest of Brigham Young by Col. Sumner, at Salt Lake City, on a charge of treason, and his conveyance to Washington, may have some truth in it. The date, however, upon which it is reported the arrest has been made, is unquestionably incorrect. Col. Sumner is reported to have arrived at Great Salt Lake City on the 25th June, at 7 P.M., with eighty-five dragoons—took Young in custody, and started with him for Washington two to three hours afterwards. By the last mail from the South, we received files of the *Deseret News* to the 1st of July, and in it not one word was said about these events. The *News*, we admit, is a very unreliable paper; but we hardly think that it would suppress so important a fact as the arrest of Young on a charge of treason—and his removal from the Territory, particularly—as no end could be observed for such suppression. It might, however, have been the 25th of July. Our reason for believing that there may be some truth in the report is, that, on the 8th of June, Col. Sumner, with his baggage train, was met by a party of Mormons, few miles east of Plum Creek, on his way to Fort Laramie, where he expected to receive instructions, to govern his further movements. . .

The statement, therefore, that Col. Sumner was in Kansas on the date upon which Brigham Young is reported to have been arrested is incorrect; for, as appears from the above extract, on the 8th of June he was only six days' journey from Fort Laramie. He arrived there, probably, on the 16th of June, and remained, awaiting instructions. The mail leaves Independence, Missouri, on the 1st of every month, and reaches Fort Laramie on or about the 14th. He could, therefore, have received the instructions to arrest Young by the July mail, on the 14th of that month, and immediately started for Salt Lake, which is about ten days' journey from Fort Laramie. This could fix his arrival there on or about the 25th of July, which is supposed to be the correct date, and the news could have reached Oroville—the point from which the news was telegraphed here—on the 22d of August. We trust that the report is correct. In prompt and vigorous action will alone be found the solution of the Mormon problem.

"A STARTLING REPORT," *WESTERN STANDARD*, 28 AUGUST 1857.

Another of those *startling rumors* which have been so common of late, relative to affairs in Utah, has made its appearance in the interior and city papers. We have had rumors unnumbered from that region previous to this that have been very exciting; but this exceeds them all. California papers have had Governor Young strictly guarded by his friends to prevent his assassination by those who, dissatisfied with his "tyranny" and indignant at his "heaven-daring assumptions," had rebelled against his authority. They have had him surrounded by enemies, and the community of which he is the head split up into factions and in danger of disrupture through dissensions. They have had him fleeing to Oregon with a chosen band of devoted followers to escape from the impending difficulty with the General Government and the disaffected of his own people. They have had him entrenched in the midst of Great Salt Lake City, surrounded by thousands of faithful adherents, and breathing out threats and defiance against the Federal Government. They have had him in almost every conceivable position; but they have somehow or other contrived to extricate him from all these disagreeable predicaments—have delivered him from his violent and vindictive enemies—have brought him back without any trouble from Oregon whither he had fled; and by a few strokes of the pen have terminated the Utah war—nipped the rebellion in the bud, and spared Government the necessity of sending Harney with his troops across a weary stretch of wilderness of eleven or twelve hundred miles in extent!

. . . That this is another "sell," is clear enough. There is a letter in this office written by Prest. Young, and dated July 4th, at which time all was peace and quietness, and no troops had entered Utah up to that time. But why should we dwell upon a report which is so ridiculous and utterly false, and which was, evidently, coined for the purpose of selling a few newspapers? That in the hurry and excitement of the moment the *Bulletin* should have been so deceived is not impossible but that this *sell* should be soberly sucked in by the *Herald* was rather unexpected! How is it br. Nugent, have you less penetration than we were giving you credit for? Of the entire editorial fraternity of San Francisco, Messrs. Conklin and Halkin of the *Town Talk*, who appear to make it a rule, to admit nothing in their paper of which they would afterward be ashamed, were the only ones to advance independently and refute the wretched lie.

This last fable, however, is not without its moral. It came to the public quite as straight and as well attested as the many which have preceded it. The *North California*, published at Oroville, the place where the report originated, says:

> "This news is very startling, and we have seen nothing in the late news from the East which would warrant us to expect any such *coup d'etat* [*coup de main*] on the part of the Government. If it were a mere rumor, we should place but little credence in it; but our informant professes to have been present, and gives the dates, and most minute particulars, without the slightest ambiguity."

Put this with the testimony of other eye witnesses to events which never occurred! and it will show, that the public has all along been humbugged about Utah, by lying anti-Mormon witnesses; and further, it will prove, that a true knowledge of affairs among the Saints can be obtained only through Mormon journals and by Mormon testimony.

Breathing a Spirit of Defiance

One might question Cannon's absolute reliance upon "Mormon journals . . . and testimony," but the story of Young's arrest was either an act of wishful thinking that got out of hand or a complete fabrication. While Young and a large number of Mormons would later be indicted for treason by a federal grand jury sitting in Green River County (Fort Bridger), no one had been arrested. All was indeed relatively quiet, if not well, in Zion—at least for the time being—and Cannon took obvious pleasure in exploiting patently false reports to the contrary. Witness the comments to Young that Cannon penned on 31 August:

> Yours of the 4th of July came safely to hand by the last mail, and we were much pleased to hear by it of the continued peace and prosperity enjoyed by the Saints in the Valleys and the good prospects there were of an abundant harvest. It is indeed gratifying to learn that the excitement and uneasiness which fills the communities in the adjacent States and Territories, do not in the least affect the tranquillity of the people of God. This completely nonpluses priests, editors and others, who are anxiously desiring the downfall of "Mormons." They have calculated every mail to hear something "very important" from Utah, at least to hear of the people there being filled with fear and apprehension relative to the threatened visit of Harney and his troops; mail after mail has arrived, however, containing naught but assurances of the continued peace and harmony of the society in the Valleys, and showing that the Saints are neither disturbed in their feelings nor dismayed at the fuss, excitement and threats so commonly indulged in by their enemies. They can not account for this upon any principle with which they are acquainted, and to console themselves from their disappointment, assert that the real situation of affairs must be suppressed! It is astonishing to us, as a people; they greedily swallow the most absurd lies, and prefer them, all the time, to plain straightforward, reasonable truth. The latest lie in circulation here, is one concerning your arrest, on a charge of treason, by Col. Sumner, with 86 dragoons, and his departure with you in custody for Washington, "*unmolested by the Mormons*"! This happened on the 25th of June, and as you did not seem to be aware of it on the 4th of July, the date of your letter, I send you the news. What Gen. Harney, with three thousand men, was scarcely thought able to accomplish, Sumner with eighty-six men, has performed with ease and without the loss of a drop of blood![34]

---

[34] Cannon to Young, 31 August 1857, LDS Archives.

In spite of his very real concerns about the whereabouts and mission of Sumner, one can readily imagine Brigham Young chuckling at Cannon's humor. Nonetheless, bizarre rumors persisted and proliferated. If Brigham Young was not being arrested for treason, he was surely beating the tar out of the federal troops.

"TOPICS OF THE DAY," *DAILY HERALD*, 16 SEPTEMBER 1857.

It is hardly necessary for us to reiterate our entire disbelief of the news received at Placerville by way of Carson Valley, and published yesterday, in which it is reported that General Harney had experienced defeat at the hands of Brigham Young's Legionnaires. Leaving out of consideration the almost impossibility for his troops to have reached a point where such a conflict could have taken place, the General is a soldier too well tried and experienced to suffer himself to be drawn into an ambuscade, or to be betrayed; for under no other circumstances could such a result as reported have taken place. However, these startling rumors have the effect of drawing attention to the present and future state of affairs in Utah. . . .

The probability of a peaceable termination of the present disgraceful licentiousness and disaffection at Salt Lake, is not very encouraging. The rumors we hear from that quarter crowd on us with increased seriousness. Harangues are delivered by Young and his confidential adherents, breathing a spirit of defiance, mingled with vague threats and in all of them the advent of General Harney and his troops is looked upon with dislike and ill-concealed terror. The *Deseret News* bears a strong resemblance to an army bulletin, so crowded is it with the orders of militia commanders in relation to newly formed military companies, and there are many other circumstances going to show the Mormons are determined to make a demonstration of resistance. If they perceive such would be ineffectual in presence of the troops who will be among them, what measures they will take, and how treachery, or worse, is to be guarded against, becomes the duty of the civil and army authorities to take into consideration. We cannot believe the reports that the Mormons would deliberately attempt to poison, or by cowardly means destroy the lives of soldiers, or others, on the grand scale referred to in the letter of our Los Angeles correspondent, published a few days since, but still there are reasons sufficient why every measure of precaution should be adopted. Intelligence from Carson Valley and San Bernardino both agree in stating that the Mormons in those places are disposing of their property, with the intention of leaving forthwith for Utah, and it is also stated, this movement is in accordance with instructions received from Brigham Young. Whether this change of residence is to keep out of the way of expected retaliation, or to reinforce the Mormons at Salt

> Lake, in anticipation of collision with the troops, or from some other cause, we are left only to infer. We have the most perfect confidence in the skill, sound judgment and bravery of Gen. Harney and the soldiers under his command. They will be equal to any emergency; and, seconded with the advice and discretion of Governor Cumming and the Territorial officers just appointed, the country may rest satisfied the Mormon difficulty will be settled by extinguishing the gross abuses that exist among them, and the re-establishment of morality and good government. Let us add, in all sincerity, the hope that this desirable end, which must, regardless of all consequences, be attained, may be brought about without bloodshed. The condition of affairs at Salt Lake can no longer be tolerated, and if the dictates of self-interest, and only a scintilla of common sense obtain in Mormon councils, they will acquiesce in the judgment of Christendom, that it is time their distinctive dogmas should be abandoned. The world is too far advanced to allow the precepts of morality to be outraged; and moreover, the character of the country, deeply involved in this question, imperatively requires to be vindicated. This must be done at all hazards, and no fear need be entertained for the result. The days of Mormonism at Salt Lake are numbered.

The reference to the letter "published a few days since" appeared over the pseudonym of one "Viandante,"[35] who, together with other absurd allegations, reported that Mormon missionaries in China had learned to manufacture a special tea which included an "insidious but fatal poison." "These poisons are of various kinds," Viandante continued. "Some are so slow that long periods elapse before they take effect, while at the same time their fatality may be precipitated by the admixture of other poisons." In fact, he argued, "one poison within the knowledge and possession of Brigham, possesses qualities that remain inert in the human system for years before its fatal consequences are developed." He then went on to imply such poisons would be used on the U.S. troops who would all be doomed by Brigham to a "homestead, six feet by two, in his romantic valley."[36]

By September, neither Cannon nor Young found any humor in rumors that troops were marching toward the Salt Lake. Any hint of extermination, whether that word was used specifically or not, evoked a profound sense of understandable paranoia among the Mormons. Extermination held special meaning for the Mormons, who had been

---

[35] Italian for "traveler," especially by foot.

[36] "Our Los Angeles Correspondence . . .," *San Francisco Herald,* 14 September 1857, 2/4.

subjected to the horrendous persecutions resulting from Missouri Gov. Lilburn W. Boggs' infamous order of 1838, regarding extermination.[37] Once again that ugly word was on the tongues of the enemies of Mormonism, with the editors of several California newspapers at the forefront.

As the *Herald* suggested, Brigham Young had indeed begun to show a "spirit of defiance" and had been showing it for quite some time. While many of his "vague threats" were made for political reasons, there is little question that he intended—at least initially—to go down fighting. "I wish to avoid hostilities ~~as long as~~ with the United States, but before I'll See this people Suffer as they have done heretofore ~~and permit the bones of myself and family to bleach with those of my brethren and Sisters, on these mountains~~," he vowed in his private diary on 12 July 1857. "I will draw my sword, in the name of Isreal God, ~~and Slay~~ and say to my brethren let our Swords fall upon our enemies."[38]

As the U.S. Army began to enter the eastern counties of Utah Territory in fall 1857, it remained to be seen how Brigham Young would use his sword.

[37] Missouri General Assembly, *Document Containing the Correspondence, Orders, &c., in relation to the disturbances with the Mormons,* 61; and the Governor to General Clark, 27 October 1838, cited in LeSueur, *The 1838 Mormon War in Missouri,* 152.

[38] Cooley, ed., *Diary of Brigham Young, 1857,* 42. Spelling, capitalization, and strikethroughs are reproduced from the original handwritten text.

Chapter 12

"A Horrible Massacre of Emigrants"
Vengeance at Mountain Meadows

The Reformation may have been a period of much-needed spiritual reform, but it was also a time of irresponsible rhetoric that fed the kind of Puritanical fanaticism which sometimes led to criminal behavior. The "unsolved" Parrish murders were among the best-documented examples of such extralegal activity and they understandably influenced President Buchanan in his decision to send federal troops to Utah Territory.

The most infamous example of "holy murder" in Utah history, however, is the massacre that took place on 11 September 1857 at Mountain Meadows, a southern Utah oasis that Parley P. Pratt called a "little mountain paradise" and "all togather the most beautiful place in all the rout" to California.[1] Here a complex mixture of the worst elements of Danite vigilantism and "white Indian" depredation, confusion over the doctrine of blood atonement, a desire to avenge the death of Parley P. Pratt and perhaps earlier church martyrs, unquestioning obedience to religious/militia authority, and siege-mentality paranoia springing from war hysteria resulted in the slaughter of 120 innocent men, women, and children. Alongside the martyrdom of Joseph and Hyrum Smith, this was without question the single greatest calamity in the history of Mormonism. It was also the greatest incident of organized mass murder of unarmed civilians in American history prior to the bombing of the Oklahoma City federal building and the destruction of New York's World Trade Center, the latter of which also ironically occurred on "9/11."

[1] Stanley and Camp, eds., "A Mormon Mission to California in 1851," 65.

The frightful story of the Mountain Meadows massacre has been given considerable attention elsewhere.[2] Suffice it to say that acting on what they believed was the mind and will of Brigham Young,[3] officers of the Iron County Brigade of the territorial militia, the Nauvoo Legion, organized and launched an "Indian" attack on the Fancher-Baker wagon train. The company was made up almost entirely of emigrant families from western Arkansas, not far from the spot where Hector McLean had murdered Apostle Parley P. Pratt.[4] That the party had left Arkansas two weeks before Pratt's death and therefore was wholly uninvolved in that affair did nothing to spare them from the war hysteria and spirit of vengeance burning white-hot in isolated, hard scrabble southern Utah. Mormons disguised themselves as Indians and, as dawn broke over the emigrant camp, actively participated in the assault.

After a grueling five-day siege, under cover of a flag of truce, Mormon zealot John D. Lee convinced the beleaguered emigrants they would only be safe if they surrendered their arms to the Mormons. In the greatest act of treachery imaginable, Lee marched his charges back to the California Road, where militia commander Maj. John Higbee ordered his men, "Do your duty!" Mormons and Indians killed every man, woman, and older child, sparing only seventeen children deemed too young to be credible witnesses. After twenty years of investigations and cover-ups, John D. Lee was tried twice and executed at Mountain Meadows as the single scapegoat. He chose to die by firing squad, having foresworn beheading. Those above Lee in the church/militia chain of command—who ultimately shared responsibility with Lee for this unfathomable

[2] For years, the definitive treatment has been Brooks, *The Mountain Meadows Massacre.* Backus, *Mountain Meadows Witness*; Bigler, *Forgotten Kingdom,* 159–80; and Bagley, *Blood of the Prophets,* summarize the evidence that has come to light in the fifty years since Brooks. Of particular interest will be the forthcoming book on this event by three historians employed by the LDS Church: Richard Turley, Glen Leonard and Ronald Walker. Titled *Tragedy at Mountain Meadows,* it is to be published by Oxford University Press.

[3] Young always denied having anything to do with the massacre. (See, for example, Young to Kane, 15 December 1859, Kane Collection, Special Collections, BYU.) In fact, speaking of the event two years later, Young wrote to Cannon that "from the little I can or ever have learned of that affair, I feel sanguine that when the truth is safely arrived at it will be found that had it not been for a few whites being near by at the time, not a child or animal would have been saved alive, as the Indians were exceedingly exasperated with the conduct of that and other emigrating companies." Young to Cannon, 5 May 1859, Brigham Young Papers, Univ. of Utah. For Young's possible role in the events leading to the massacre, see Bagley, *Blood of the Prophets,* 90–94, 112–14, 136–37.

[4] Bigler, *Forgotten Kingdom,* 159–60.

While period depictions of what the massacre at Mountain Meadows may have looked like often yielded to melodrama, none could approximate the true horror of that great tragedy. From Clampitt, *Echoes from the Rocky Mountains.*

crime against humanity—escaped justice, at least by earthly tribunals.[5]

Early rumors of the massacre began circulating within weeks after a trailing wagon train, led by William C. Dukes, arrived in California from southern Utah. By then, orders from Young had finally come down to leave the emigrants alone: "Go with all speed, spare no horse flesh. The emigrants must not be meddled with, if it takes all Iron County to prevent it. They must go free and unmolested."[6] But this command came too late for the Fancher train. The Dukes company complained that the Mormons stole most of their stock, but they bypassed Mountain Meadows and were allowed to come to California where their story was immediately picked up by the Los Angeles *Star* and other papers.[7]

---

[5] For a fairly one-sided account of Lee's trials, see Fielding, ed., *The Tribune Reports of the Trials of John D. Lee.*

[6] "The Lee Trials," *Deseret News,* 16 September 1876, 544.

[7] See reports in the *Star* beginning 3 October 1857 and continuing for over two months.

To Be Thus Charged with an Atrocious Crime

Cannon was so used to hearing unsubstantiated accusations made against the Mormons that the earliest report of the massacre at Mountain Meadows must have seemed little more than another nasty rumor. Nor was it represented as much more than that. The final line of the first brief article in the Los Angeles *Star* dismissed the entire report: "Although the rumor was generally believed in San Bernardino, we confess our unwillingness to credit such a wholesale massacre."[8]

One week later, *The Star* had determined that the rumors were all too true: "We were unwilling at first to credit the statement and hoped that rumor had exaggerated the facts, but the report has been confirmed, and the loss of life is even greater than at first reported." In a long article, which included a letter from J. W. Christian of San Bernardino with a carefully edited Mormon account of the murders, *The Star* concluded that the Mormons must have been behind the entire affair:

> The writer seems to intimate that the Mormons will be held responsible for the murder, and in this respect he is fully borne out by present indications, for a general belief pervades the public mind here that the Indians were instigated to this crime by the "Destroying Angels" of the church, and that the blow fell on these emigrants from Arkansas, in retribution of the death of Parley Pratt, which took place in that State.[9]

Editor John Nugent of the *Herald* agreed:

> We are lo[a]th to believe that the Mormons, as bad as they may be, could have instigated this massacre; but when we reflect that ... the persons murdered were from the State in which the Sainted Parley received the reward for his crimes, it is impossible to divert the mind from the suspicion that others besides the Indians had a hand in this horrible butchery.[10]

The editors were correct. Although not always recognized as such, perhaps the most significant contributing factor to the Mountain Meadows massacre was the assassination of Parley Parker Pratt.[11] The

---

8 "Rumored Massacre on the Plains," *Los Angeles Star,* 3 October 1857, 2/3.

9 "Horrible Massacre of Emigrants!! Over 100 Persons Murdered!! Confirmation of the Report," Ibid., 10 October 1857, 2/2–3.

10 "Topics of the Day," *San Francisco Herald,* 12 October 1857, 2/1.

11 Although B. H. Roberts argued to the contrary, both Stenhouse and Bancroft concluded that Pratt's assassination was a factor. Juanita Brooks provided ample evidence that the Mormons knew of Pratt's death prior to the massacre. Will Bagley concluded that the events at Mountain Meadows were a calculated

Mormons had learned of the murder of their beloved Parley even before the Baker-Fancher train arrived in Utah, and that report, combined with war hysteria, Reformation rhetoric, and rumors both true and false led to the horrific destruction of the emigrants. The question of whether or not Brigham Young was in any way involved in the massacre has generated heated controversy for almost a century and a half, but he reportedly evoked the Lord's vengeance while destroying the monument the U.S. Army burial party had charitably raised over the emigrants' grave at Mountain Meadows.[12] If one can believe John D. Lee, Young was not particularly moved by compassion when he had a private conversation with Lee after his visit to the site of the massacre on 24 May 1861:

> Pres. Young Said that the company that was used up at the Mountain Meadowes were the Fathers, Mothe[rs], Bros., Sisters & connections of those that Muerders the Prophets; they Merited their fate, & the only thing that ever troubled him was the lives of the Women & children, but that under the circumstances [this] could not be avoided.[13]

On the other hand, according to Young's most eminent biographer, when Lee earlier informed Young of the massacre (claiming it was carried out entirely by the Indians), "the details were so gruesome that Brigham Young wept."[14]

By mid-October, George Q. Cannon had seen a copy of *The Star's* 10 October account. Stunned as he must have been from the tragic news, he could not believe the reports. Appropriately, he urged the public to withhold opinion until all the facts were known.

"MASSACRE OF EMIGRANTS—RECKLESS AND MALIGNANT SLANDERS," *WESTERN STANDARD*, 23 OCTOBER 1857.

An extra of the Los Angeles *Star* contains an account of a horrible massacre of emigrants, which took place at the Mountain Meadows, near the rim of the Great Basin, between the 10th and 12th of Sept. The details, so far as known, have been given in a letter written by J. Ward Christian of San

act of revenge for Pratt's murder. See Roberts, *Comprehensive History*, 4:155n; Stenhouse, *Rocky Mountain Saints*, 428; Brooks, *Mountain Meadows Massacre*, 57–58; and Bagley, *The Blood of the Prophets*.

[12] Brooks, *Mountain Meadows Massacre*, 183n16. Brooks also cites evidence suggesting the monument may have still been standing (or re-erected) three years later.

[13] Cleland and Brooks, eds., *A Mormon Chronicle*, I:314. The phrase, "Vengence is mine and I have taken a little" appears in the description of Young's 25 May 1861 visit to the cairn at Mountain Meadows in Wilford Woodruff's diary.

[14] Arrington, *Brigham Young: American Moses*, 259.

Bernardino, under date of Oct. 4th, to a gentleman in Los Angeles, and is published in the *Star.* The company consisted of about 130 or 135 men, women and children, and included some forty or forty-five capable of bearing arms. They were on their way from Missouri and Arkansas to this State.[15] The causes which have led to this massacre, are given as follows by Mr. Christian, he having obtained them from Elders Wm. Matthew and Wm. Hyde, who were on their way to San Bernardino and several days' journey in the rear of this train:

"The train camped at Corn Creek, near Fillmore city, where there is an Indian village, the inhabitants of which have raised a crop of wheat, and they, not knowing the value of coin, were severely cheated. They wanted a blanket for a sack of wheat, but they gave them fifty cents, and told them that amount would buy a blanket. They also had an ox with them which had died, and they put strychnine in him for the purpose of poisoning the Indians; and also put poison of some description in the water which is standing in holes. This occasioned several deaths among them, within a few days after the departure of the train. And upon this, it seems, the Indians gathered themselves together, and had, no doubt, chosen the places of attack and arranged everything before the train arrived at the place where they were murdered."

It appears from what can be gleaned from the Indians, that the encampment was attacked about daylight in the morning by the combined forces of all the various tribes in that section of the country. The majority of them were slain at the first onset; the remainder placed themselves in the best position for defence that their circumstances would allow; but before they could complete their arrangements, there were but few left who were capable of bearing arms. Sheltered by their wagons and a ditch they had dug for protection, these few continued for one or two days to fire upon the Indians; but it was of no avail; the Indians were so securely secreted, that, according to their own statement, there was not one of them killed, and but few wounded. A flag of truce, borne by a little girl, was then sent out by the emigrants, and they gave themselves up to the mercy of the Indians, who immediately rushed in and slaughtered all of them, with the exception of fifteen infant children, that have since been purchased, with much difficulty by the "Mormon" interpreters.

These are all the particulars which have yet come to light relative to this

---

[15] Dale Morgan warned Juanita Brooks as she began writing about Mountain Meadows, "you consistently speak of the Fancher party as Missourians, whereas it has long been established that they were Arkansans, the only question being whether a few Missourians may have been with the party." See Morgan to Brooks, 7 September 1942, Brooks Papers, Marriott Library. Despite enduring legends of "Missouri Wildcats," decades of research by descendants have identified almost ninety of the victims from Arkansas, but only "Lee's Victims," *San Jose Pioneer*, 21 April 1877, 1/6, mentioned "the Reeds from Missouri, comprising Reed senior and his family, and his son and family."

dreadful affair. But corrupt editors have not been idle in manufacturing and circulating the most base and damnable suspicions about this occurrence.

"Trifles light as air,
Are, to an Anti-Mormon editor, confirmation strong
As proofs of holy writ."

The fact that the massacre occurred somewhere within the boundaries of Utah, and the fact also that the train was from Missouri and Arkansas—States against which, we are gratuitously informed, the "Mormons" entertain the most intense hatred—are deemed a sufficient foundation upon which to base an accusation of guilt against the Mormons. It is incredible, and utterly inconsistent with civilized human nature, in these editors' view of the case, for the emigrants to cheat the Indians, or to poison their water and the carcase of an ox. This is too hard a story to believe. But mark the difference, when there exists the slightest possible chance of attributing the most foul and atrocious deeds to an innocent people, because they are "Mormons," and live in the Territory where they are committed. It is not incredible to think that the "Mormons" either perpetrated themselves or instigated the Indians to perpetrate the murder of upwards of a hundred men, women and children, because, forsooth, they hailed from the States of Missouri and Arkansas! This is not too hard a story to believe—it does not tax the credibility of these very incredulous gentlemen in the least. They can believe this without the slightest shadow of evidence; but transactions which every season's emigration witnesses—the cold-blooded murder and poisoning of Indians, can not be believed, because, if believed, the "Mormons" could not be charged as the instigators of the massacre.

Inconsistent as it may seem with "civilized human nature," every man who has affected to discredit the story of the poisoning of the water and the carcase of an ox by the emigrants, must *know* that it is a practice of common occurrence on the plains, especially among "border ruffians," to shoot down every Indian they can get sight at, and to leave the poisoned carcases of cattle as a means of entrapping the unsuspecting savage. If they had been killed in any other territory than Utah, the story would have been believed without hesitation; and it would have been said, that the emigrants provoked a most fearful retribution by their own acts.

We appeal to every honest, intelligent man to view all the facts of the case as they have thus far come to light, and ask, Is it not enough to drive any people mad, to be thus charged with an atrocious crime of this kind, when they know they are as innocent of it as the child unborn—and when they know, also, that their accusers are no more warranted by the evidence before them in accusing them, than they would be in fastening a similar charge on the inhabitants of San Francisco? As if the feelings of the people were not already sufficiently hostile against the people of Deseret, a venal and incendiary press must seek to add fuel to the flame, and raise a feeling of embittered hatred against "Mormonism" and the "Mormons" in the breast of every man who will be influenced by them, or who will not take the trouble to think and investigate for themselves. What cause is there for wonder at our talking as plainly and independently as we do, when this state of feeling is so universally prevalent on all hands? Though we were filled with the most intense love for our compatriots, yet this persistent determination on their part to fasten upon us the commission of the most foul and unnatural crimes, regardless of all evidence and all our protestations of innocence, is sufficient to finally extinguish it. And the instance above is only one out of a numerous list that might be adduced; it is but another illustration of that utter disregard of justice and honor which has been continually exhibited by journalists and others in their treatment of the "Mormons." How long they expect we can endure such things, and not arise and resent them, we do not know; but such creatures may yet learn that there is a limit even to Mormon forbearance and endurance.

Ending this editorial with a thinly veiled threat was probably not the wisest course of action under the circumstances. Cannon's final editorials suggest a deepening sense of frustration and militancy against all who would attack Mormonism, even if they were only reporting what others were alleging. Clearly, Cannon was tired of defending what for many was simply indefensible and after all, what really was the point with a federal army on its way to Utah? Perhaps it was this anger and fatigue—as much as any blind sense of loyalty—that kept the young editor from perceiving clearly the dreadful truth of the massacre.

Inflict on Them Condign Punishment

The initial reports of the massacre at Mountain Meadows did untold damage to the Mormon cause, but as the weeks went on, reports confirming both the tragedy and the likelihood of Mormon complicity flooded the California press. Perhaps nothing was as damning as the eyewitness accounts of George Powers and P. M. Warn.

"The late Horrible Massacre," *Los Angeles Star*, 17 October 1857, 2/2–4.

In the early part of the week, an intense excitement pervaded out citizens on learning that parties had arrived in town, who corroborated the statements previously made in regard to the horrible massacre of *one hundred and eighteen persons,* on the Salt Lake route to California; and placards were posted throughout the city, calling a public meeting of the citizens to be held at the Circus Pavilion, on the Plaza, on Monday evening, to hear the statements of the parties alluded to, and to adopt such measures, in view of the facts, as should be deemed advisable. Accordingly, at the time appointed, a very large number of our citizens assembled, deeply impressed by the awful tragedy which had been enacted on the borders of our State, and anxious that such a representation of the facts in the case should be made to the authorities in Washington, as should compel them to take immediate steps to discover the perpetrators and instigators of the foul outrage, and inflict on them condign punishment. We need not here more particularly refer to the proceedings of the meeting, as they are reported elsewhere; but as we have obtained the statements of Messrs. Powers and Warn, the gentlemen above alluded to, which contain the nearest approach to an account of the massacre that can be given at present, we prefer to add them here, rather than in the report of the meeting.

The statements were drawn up, at the dictation of the parties, by Mr. W. A. Wallace,[16] who read them to [t]he meeting, and from whom we obtained them, through the chairman of the meeting, Mr. G. N. Whitman.

These documents exhibit a deplorable picture of the working of Mormonism, which, if correct, show the leaders of this sect to be actuated by the most atrocious designs towards their fellow-citizens of the Union. We hope for the sake of our common humanity, that the character of this people may be redeemed from the black catalogue of crime here preferred, and that it will yet appear that they are not the fiends incarnate they are represented, but that they used all possible diligence to prevent the late massacre, and that they act in good faith to preserve the lives of such of their fellow citizens as, from necessity or choice, travel through their Territory—the common property of the citizens of the Union.

As each will draw his own conclusions from the narrative, without further comment we give the statements of Messrs. Powers and Warn, regarding the late Massacre of the Plains.

Mr. George Powers, of Little Rock, left Arkansas, and with his train arrived at Salt Lake in August. He says:

We found the Mormons making very determined preparations to fight the United States troops, whenever they may arrive. On our way in, we met three companies of 100 men each, armed and on the road towards the pass above Fort Bridger. I was told at Fort Bridger, that at Fort Supply, twelve miles this side of Fort Bridger, there were 400 armed Indians awaiting orders; they also said that there were 60,000 pounds of flour stored at Fort Bridger for the use of their army. We found companies drilling every evening in the city. The Mormons declared to us that no U.S. troops should ever

[16] William Allen Wallace had been editor of the *Los Angeles Star* until 1856.

cross the mountains; and they talked and acted as if they were willing to take a brush with Uncle Sam.

We remained in Salt Lake five days, and then pushed on, hoping we might overtake a larger train, which had started ten days ahead of us, and which proved to be the train that was massacred. We came on to Buttermilk Fort near the lone cedar, 175 miles, and found the inhabitants greatly enraged at the train which had just passed, declaring that they had abused the Mormon women, calling them w—s, &c, and letting on about the men.[17] The people had refused to sell that train any provisions, and told us they were sorry they had not killed them there; but, they knew it would be done before they got in. They stated further, that they were holding the Indians in check until the arrival of their chief, when he would follow the train and cut it in pieces.

We attempted to purchase some butter here; the women set it out to us, and as we were taking it away, the men came running and charging, and swore we should not have it, nor anything else, as we had misused them. They appeared to be bitterly hostile, and would hardly speak to us. We were unable to get anything we stood in need of. We camped at this place but one night.

At Corn Creek, we found plenty of Indians, who were all peaceable and friendly. We learned nothing of the train, except that it had passed that place several days before, and we were glad to find we had gained so much on them. The next place where we heard of the Train was on our arrival at Beaver, 230 miles from Salt Lake. Here we learned, that when the train ahead were camped at Corn Creek, which was thirty-five miles back, and at which place we found the Indians so friendly, an ox died, and the Indians asked for it. Before it was given to them, a Mormon reported that he saw an emigrant go to the carcass and cut it with his knife, and as he did so, would pour some liquid into the cut from a phial. The meat was eaten by the Indians, and three of them died, and several more were sick and would die. The people of Beaver seemed also to be incensed against the train, for the same reason as before reported. I asked an Indian, at Beaver, if there was any truth in the poisoned meat story; he replied in English, that he did not know, that several of the Indians had died and several were sick; he said their water melons made them all sick, and he believed that the Mormons had poisoned them.

We laid by at Beaver several days, as the Bishop [Philo T. Farnsworth] told us it was dangerous for so small a company as ours to go on. Our train consisted of only three wagons, and we were hurrying on to join the larger one.

While waiting here, the train of Wm. Mathews and Sidney Tanner of

---

[17] Powers' account of the conflict at today's Holden, Utah, would appear to provide contemporary validation of Fancher party provocations chronicled in Utah lore, but "the train" might have been one of the outfits led by Nicholas Turner or William C. Dukes.

San Bernardino came up, and I made arrangements to come on with them.[18] We came on to Parowan, and here we learned that the train ahead had been attacked by the Indians, at the Mountain Meadows, fifty miles from Parowan, and had returned upon their road five miles to a spring, and fortified themselves. We then drove out of Parowan five or six miles, and camped at what is called the Summit [on 8 September 1857].

Next morning an express arrived from Mr. Dame, President of Parowan, requesting us not to proceed any further that day if we pleased; also that Mathews and Tanner should return to Parowan, and bring me along with them.[19] We returned, and a council was held, at which it was advised by Mr. Dame, that I should go back to my own train, as they did not wish to have strangers in their train. He also stated, that at two o'clock that morning [9 September 1857], he had received an express from the train ahead, stating they were surrounded by Indians, who had killed two or three of their number, and asking for assistance. While we were talking, an express came in from Beaver, stating that the Indians had attacked my train in the streets of that place, and were fighting when he left. One reason given, was that ten miles the other side of Beaver, an emigrant train had shot an Indian, which greatly enraged them; that the people of Beaver went out in the night and brought the emigrants in, and were followed by the Indians, who made the attack after their arrival.[20]

On the receipt of this news, another private council was held; after which I was called in and told, that in consequence of the fight behind, it would be for their advantage to bring me through, provided I would obey council and the rules of the train. To this I assented, being anxious to get on, and asked what was required of me. Mr. Dame replied, that in passing through the Indian country, it might be necessary for me to be laid flat in the wagon and covered with blankets, for two or three days, as the Indians were deadly hostile to all Americans; that if I was seen, it would endanger the safety of the whole train. My friend Mr. Warn, was told that he could also go on upon the same conditions.

At Parowan, it seems, when it was "for their interest" to bring us through, the Elders had no control over the Indians; while at Buttermilk Fort, they were able to restrain them, as they declared, under great provocation.

---

[18] Mormon freighters William Mathews and Sidney Tanner were members of the San Bernardino Stake High Council. Mathews was a counselor in the stake presidency. He allegedly had brought arms and ammunition to Utah. On returning to San Bernardino, he reported, "the ammunition we will make every exertion to get as soon as we can but we have to work exceedingly carefull to avoid suspicion." See Mathews to Young, 7 October 1857, LDS Archives.

[19] Col. William Dame was president of Parowan Stake and commander of the Iron County Brigade of the Nauvoo Legion.

[20] For this attack on the Dukes-Tanner train, see Brooks, *The Mountain Meadows Massacre,* 115–16.

On Friday, the 18th [11th] day of September, we left Parowan, and arrived at Cedar City, some eighteen miles, about one o'clock. During the afternoon, *an express arrived from the Indians,* stating that one of their warriors had run up and looked into the corral, and he supposed that "only five or six of the emigrants were killed yet." These were the words of the express-man. The same night, four men were sent out from Parowan, to go and learn what was the fate of the train, and, as they pretended, to save, if possible, some of its members.

I omitted to mention, in the proper place, that Mr. Dame informed me that the attack on the train commenced on Monday, the 14th of September.[21] I asked him if he could not raise a company, and go out and relieve the besieged train. He replied, that he could go out and take them away in safety, but he dared not; he dared not disobey counsel.

On Saturday [12 September], at twelve o'clock, we left Cedar City. About the middle of the afternoon, we met the four men who were sent out the night previous, returning in a wagon. Mathews and Tanner held a council with them apart, and when they left, Mathews told me the entire train had been cut off; and as it was still dangerous to travel the road, they had concluded it was better for us to pass the spot in the night. We continued on, without much conversation, and about dusk met Mr. Dame, (I did not know that he had left Cedar City) and three other white men, coming from the scene of the slaughter, in company with a band of some twenty Indian warriors. One of the men in company with Mr. Dame, was Mr. Haight, President of Cedar City. Mr. Dame said they had been out to see to the burying of the dead; but the dead were not buried. From what I heard, I believe the bodies were left lying naked upon the ground, having been stripped of their clothing by the Indians. These Indians had a two-horse wagon; [it was] filled with something I could not see, as blankets were carefully spread over the top. The wagon was driven by a white man, and beside him there were two or three Indians in it! Many of them had shawls, and bundles of women's clothes were tied to their saddles. They were also all supplied with guns or pistols, besides bows and arrows. The hindmost Indians were driving several head of the emigrants' cattle. Mr. Dame and Mr. Haight, and their men, seemed to be on the best of terms with the Indians, and they were all in high spirits, as if they were mutually pleased with the accomplishment of some desired object. They thronged around us, and greeted us with noisy cordiality. We did not learn much from them. They passed on, and we drove all night in silence, and at daylight camped, and were told we were three miles beyond the scene of the slaughter. We lay by here two or three hours to rest, and then drove all day, twenty miles, at night camping on the Santa Clara River, near the Chief Jackson's village.

---

[21] Powers almost surely had his dates off a week, since the best evidence indicates the attack on the Fancher party took place on 7 September and the massacre on 11 September 1857.

Next morning, after driving a few miles, we stopped to water. Jackson and his band soon came to us; and in a few minutes pointed out Mr. Warn as an American [that is, a non-Mormon]. The Mormon boys denied it, but the Indians were dissatisfied, and appeared restive. The Chief came up and accused me of being an American; appeared mad; stepped round; shook his head, and pulled his bowstring. He then sent several men on our road ahead. Mr. Mathews advised us to leave there as quick as possible, as it was getting dangerous.

At Jackson's, we engaged Mr. Hatch to go on to the Muddy as an interpreter.[22] It was a fortunate circumstance for us that this Mr. Hatch arrived at our camp at the very moment that we were wishing for him most. Mr. Mathews told me he was an Indian missionary, and of great influence among them. He could do more with them than anybody else; and if he could not get me over the road, nobody could. Mr. Tanner had declared that he would not go on without Mr. Hatch, and pretended to be afraid of the dangers of the road.[23]

Next morning, Mr. Hatch left us and went on to the Muddy. About a day's drive, the other side of the Muddy, we met him returning in company with two young men, brothers Young, horse-thieves, who were escaping from justice in San Bernardino;[24] having been assisted in getting away by those who had them in custody. Mr. Hatch stated, that when he reached the Muddy he found the young boys, in company with an emigrant who had escaped the massacre. That on his arrival, there was not an Indian in sight, and that he had to give the whoop to call them from concealment. He said in continuation, without appearing to notice the discrepancy, that on his arrival he found the Indians hotly pursuing the three men; and that they jumped upon the emigrant and killed him before his eyes, before he could interfere to prevent it. He said he threw himself between the boys and the Indians, and had great difficulty in saving them. The Indians were in a great excitement, as he said, but that as Mathews and Tanner were Mormons, they could pass without danger.

We arrived at the Muddy the day after we met Mr. Hatch, and the Young boys. We found here 30 or 40 Indians, and the mail riders from Los Angeles, who had come in that morning. The Indians were very friendly, and shook hands with everybody. No expression of hostility to Americans was heard, but that was accounted for on the ground that this was a Mormon train.

[22] U.S. Army Maj. James H. Carleton reported that Indian missionary Ira Hatch "talks Pah-Ute like a native" but concluded that he helped murder one of the last survivors of the massacre. See Clark, ed., *The Mountain Meadows Massacre*. For a more sympathetic portrait, see Robinson, *The Life of Ira Hatch*.

[23] Warn told the *Alta California* correspondent that mail carrier Bill Hyde joined the Mathews-Tanner train two days out of San Bernardino. Hyde told Warn that Jackson had "a little book or journal of one of the emigrants in which was written the name, 'William B. Jones, Caldwell County, Missouri.'" See "Later from the South: The Murders at Mountain Canon Confirmed," *Alta California*, 27 October 1857, 1/4.

[24] Brothers Henry T. and Cau Young were allegedly non-Mormon horse thieves.

At the Vegas we found another band of Indians. The chief asked our interpreter whether our captain had brought him no word from Brigham Young, whether he was nearly ready to fight the Americans yet; adding that he was ready, had got his arrows poisoned, &c &c.

At the Cotton Woods, 15 miles from the Vegas, the chief, called Brigham Young, said he was afraid of the emigrant train behind, and wished to know if they would shoot.

On the 1st October, we arrived at San Bernardino, and I was advised by Mr. Mathews, who I learned, was a President or Elder in that place, not to associate with the damned apostates, that they were cut throats of the worst character. If I wished, they would give me constant work at their mill in the mountains, and I must be careful not to talk too much of what I had seen.

Whilst in San Bernardino I heard many persons express gratification at the massacre. At the church services on Sunday, Capt. [Jefferson] Hunt occupied the pulpit, and among other things, he said that the hand of the Lord was in it; whether it was done by white or red skins, it was right![25] The prophesies concerning Missouri[26] were being fulfilled, and they would all be accomplished.

Mr. Matthews said the work had just begun, and it should be carried on until Uncle Sam and all his boys that were left, should come to Zion and beg for bread.

I did not stay in San Bernardino, because it did not appear to be a free country, for I am an American, and like freedom of thought and speech.

Thus far the narrative of Mr. Powers.

On being asked, if he did not at any time express any feeling, in the company, at the wholesale massacre of his countrymen. He replied, it was not safe to express an opinion. The men he was with were unscrupulous, and would not have hesitated to kill him for any unguarded words. When the Indians passed by him, wearing the garments of American women, and seeming to exult in their crimes, his blood boiled, but he dared not speak; and after they were gone, he asked Matthews, with earnestness, why it had been done. Matthews replied, that he must not grieve or take on, for the women were all prostitutes, that their bodies had been examined by President Dame, and this ought to console him. Matthews rejoiced greatly at the massacre, and considered it the beginning of long delayed vengeance.

Mr. Tanner regretted it, and seemed to be deeply grieved.

It is supposed that one hundred and eighteen (118) persons were killed of whom fifty six (56) were men, and that fifteen (15) children were taken

[25] LDS leader Jefferson Hunt served as senior captain in the Mormon Battalion and represented San Bernardino in the California State Legislature.

[26] Numerous "prophecies" concerning the Lord's ultimate vengeance upon those who had persecuted the Mormons in Missouri in 1838 had circulated for years, thereby mitigating in the minds of some Mormons the circumstances of and responsibility for the massacre at Mountain Meadows.

back to Cedar City —of whom, not one was over six years old. It was reported, that but one Indian was killed.

Mr. P. M. Warn, of Bergen, Genesee county, New York; who was a fellow-traveler with Mr. Powers, on that fatal journey, corroborates the statements of Powers, so far as he was acquainted with the facts, and gives the following additional particulars, which did not come under the observation of Mr. Powers:

Mr. Warn states that there was a coolness between himself and Mr. Matthews, arising from the frankness with which he expressed his opinions, and in consequence of this, he was not treated with as much confidence as Mr. Powers.

Mr. Warn arrived at Salt Lake, via Independence, on the 7th of April last, and remained until the 26th [of August 1857], on which day he started for California, as a passenger in Matthews and Tanner's train. He states, that on his journey through the settlements, which was a week or ten days subsequent to the passage of the murdered train, he every where heard the same threats of vengeance against them, for their boisterousness and abuse of Mormons and Mormonism, as was reported, and these threats seemed to be made with the intention of preparing the mind to expect a calamity, and also when a calamity occurred, it should appear to fall upon transgressors, as a matter of retribution.

Mr. Warn says according to his memorandum, "On the 5th of September we encamped at Corn Creek. Here I had conversation with the Indian agent, concerning the poisoning of the ox. He said that six Indians had died; that others were sick and would die. Upon one of them, the poison had worked out all over his breast, and he was dead next morning, as reported. Afterwards, I conversed with an Indian, said to be the war chief Ammon, who spoke good English.[27] I inquired how many of his tribe had died from eating the poisoned animal. He replied not any—but some were sick. He did not attribute the sickness to poison, nor did he give any reason for it. His manner, and that of all his people towards us, was not only friendly, but cordial; and he did not mention the train which had been doomed. Besides the Mormon train, there were camped at this place two or three emigrants trains, amounting to fifteen or eighteen wagons, with whom the Indians were as friendly as with ourselves. From Corn Creek, nothing of importance occurred more than is related by Mr. Powers, until we arrived at Cedar City. Here the four men, spoken of by Mr. Powers, (and among whom I recognized Mr. Dame,) arrived at our camp; they wished to get fresh animals, that they might go on that night to the besieged party. This was on Friday night, the night on which the slaughter was completed. They rested an hour or two,

[27] Ammon was one of many purported brothers of the legendary Wakara and was a senior leader of the Ute nation.

and took refreshments. In the conversation which ensured, one our party said, "be careful, and don't get shot, Mr. Haight." Mr. H. replied, "we shall have no shooting;" emphasizing the *we*, and throwing up his head, as if he meant to imply that the shooting would be all over before he arrived. They left us in good spirits.

One reason that may be assigned for the massacre of this train, is, that it was known to be in possession of considerable valuable property, and this fact excited the cupidity of the Mormons. It was said, they had over 400 head of stock, besides mules, &c. They were well supplied with arms and ammunition, an element of gain which enters largely into all Mormon calculations. The train was composed of families who all seemed to be in good circumstances, and as they were moving to California, their outfit indicated that they might be in possession of considerable funds. The men were very free in speaking of the Mormons; their conduct was said to have been reckless, and they would commit little acts of annoyance for the purpose of provoking the saints. Feeling perfectly safe in their arms and numbers, they seemed to set at defiance all the powers that could be brought against them. And they were not permitted to feel the dangers that surrounded them, until they were cut off from all hope of relief.

Mr. Warn states, in speaking of the emigrant who escaped and was killed at the Muddy, that at Painter Creek, some six or seven miles on the other side of the place of massacre, a Mormon told him that one of the little girls who was taken back, and who is about six years old, said that she saw her mother killed by an arrow, and that her father had escaped to California.[28] This was before Hatch joined the train. The matter of the escaped was talked over by the Mormon captains, and Mathews made the remark, "If the man comes into our train, he shall not be received!"

The Powers and Warn narratives, along with additional testimony from S. B. Honea, filled four columns on the front page of the *Alta California* one morning in late October, further inflaming anti-Mormon sentiment in San Francisico. William Wallace, the *Alta's* Los Angeles correspondent who wrote as "Yo Mismo" [I Myself], again evoked the word that had haunted Mormon history: extermination. He ended his report with a summary of events in San Bernardino. "Public attention has been much engrossed by these outrages, and almost everyone of those particularly who have been on the Salt Lake road generally winds up with 'Let Government call for volunteers—I should like to take a

[28] Family historian Burr Fancher identified the three messengers who escaped Mountain Meadows as John H. Baker, Tilghman Cameron, and Hampton Fancher. All three were tracked down and killed. See Fancher, *Westward with the Sun*, 255.

turn at those fellows!' Were a call made, half of our population would respond, so bitter is their experience."[29]

THEY HATE US YET THEY FEAR US

Despite an avalanche of bad news, George Q. Cannon, Defender of the Faith and protector of his people, continued to stay the course. In the final issue of the *Western Standard*, published in the midst of closing down the office prior to his return to Great Salt Lake City, Elder Cannon made a last valiant effort to defend the Mormons against this latest round of accusations. He did not have enough information to argue the facts, and what facts he did have seemed to work against him. But even if he had more concrete information at hand, there was little he could have truthfully said in defense of "Deseret" or the people of Utah. Instead, he used his considerable rhetorical skill to remind his readers how often the Mormons had been falsely accused in the past. Once again, he put the world on notice that neither he nor his brethren were going to turn the other cheek.

"KILLING OF IMMIGRANTS—MORMONS FALSELY ACCUSED— FURTHER ENDURANCE NO LONGER A VIRTUE," *WESTERN STANDARD*, 6 NOVEMBER 1857.

After this, we presume, there will not be a white man killed, or an emigrant train attacked between the Sierra Nevada and the Western or Southern States, on any route, but what will be credited to the Mormons. They may be as innocent as angels, but that will make no difference; the determination is apparent to heap upon them the odium of every such deed. The published estimate of one man, Abbot, which has obtained considerable circulation lately, is, that the Mormons and Indians have killed five hundred immigrants on the road between Salt Lake and California during this year alone. Trains have been attacked by Indians led on by white men, and the white men were, of course, concluded to be Mormons. One statement says that they were known to be Mormons, because they swore. The statement made by Mr. Honea,[30] who came by way of the Southern Utah route, via San Bernardino,

[29] "Later from the South: The Massacre at Mountain Canon Confirmed," *Alta California*, 27 October 1857, 1/5.

[30] "More Outrages on the Plains!!," *Los Angeles Star*, 24 October 1857, 2/1–2. For a corroboration of S.B. Honea's account, signed by William C. Dukes and twenty-six other men in his wagon train, see their letter to the editor of the *Los Angeles Star*, dated 3 November 1857, and the deposition by William Webb, both published 7 November 1857, 2/1–3.

and whose testimony is adduced as evidence that the Mormons were the instigators, if not the perpetrators of the massacre at Mountain Meadows—goes to prove that the Mormons were distinguished from the Gentiles, by the Indians on that route, by their not swearing. This person says that the Mormon interpreters urged them to refrain from swearing, as the Indians would know that they were not Mormons, if they did not take this precaution. The swearing, therefore, of those white men who were among the Indians on the Northern route, is not an evidence that they were Mormons, but rather that they were Gentiles; moreover, it is preposterous to suppose that, if they were Mormons, they would let expressions drop, such as we see reported that immigrants have heard, which would lead those whom they attacked to recognize them as Mormons. If they were Mormons disguised as Indians, and they considered such disguise necessary for the concealment of their identity, they would be very sure to let nothing escape them that would cause suspicion to fall upon them; but if they were rascals who wished suspicion to be diverted from themselves and to fall upon the Mormons, it is quite reasonable to suppose that they would disguise themselves as Indians, and also be sure to let some expression fall from them that would lead those whom they assailed and whose minds were already filled with suspicion and fear about the people of Utah, to suppose that the Mormons were leading on and instigating the Indians to plunder and murder them.

The course that editors and others in California have taken in their treatment of the Mormons, has given all the encouragement needed to scoundrels of every grade to rob, murder and attack trains with impunity between here and Salt Lake. They have seen the disposition which is every where manifest to charge the Mormons with the commission of every conceivable crime, and have had every opportunity of knowing that all that is necessary to escape detection is to arrange their plundering schemes in such a manner that suspicion will fall on that people. Let the story be started that the Mormons have had a hand in any wickedness, and there is an end to investigation. A question is never asked about the rebutting testimony; it is enough to know that the Mormons are the accused party, and it is at once concluded that, of course, the allegations must be true. Every penny-a-liner in the country then immediately begins to threaten and pile abuse on to the Mormons, and has any number of suggestions to make for their extermination.

This is literally the truth, and it must be familiar to every reader of public journals in California. We have had an illustration of it before us this past week or two in the reports that have obtained circulation relative to the massacre of the company of emigrants at the rim of the Great Basin, or Mountain Meadows. No sooner was it known that a massacre had taken place, than it was charged to the Mormons. Innocent or guilty, it made not a particle of difference, they had to bear the onus of the butchery. With such a state of feeling—such a pre-disposition to saddle them with the bloody deed whether or no, testimony of a damning character was not long wanting to fully confirm all that they had been charged with. Could it not have been found on earth, the lower regions would have been raked to obtain it.

But it was found and the thousand-tongued press heralded it forth. Every circumstance, however trivial; every word, however idly spoken; every look, however innocently given, was misconstrued, and a list of charges based upon them against the people of Deseret which find a place in the columns of every newspaper, and are industriously blazoned throughout the civilized world. What if they should prove to be baseless and utterly false, who cares? They are only Mormons that will suffer. It is not worth while to make an inquiry relative to any rebuttal that may be offered of charges against them; if they were successfully rebutted, the refutation would not attract notice. Is not this the idea indulged in, we ask? Examine the case in point. Sift the evidence that these charges are based upon. It is said that the Mormons killed or caused this train to be killed, because they were from Arkansas, and Parley P. Pratt was murdered in Arkansas. It is said that the train was blotted out because they had property, and the Mormons coveted it. It is said that they were Gentiles, and the Mormons had said that they would be the means of killing every Gentile—of cutting off every train.

Who are the witnesses that testify that the Mormons committed this bloody deed, or were the instigators of it? Are they not Gentiles? Did not the majority of them come from Arkansas? Had they no property? If any one or all of these motives prompted the Mormons to kill off or to instigate the extirpations of the train alluded to, how happened it, in the name of all that is just, that those parties escaped, who are now cited as witnesses and who followed on the trail of the murdered train?—How happened it that they were assisted by the Mormons, escorted into their fort when attacked by Indians, protected and guided by them through the exasperated red men, when to all their other motives for murder was added the additional one of concealment? Had they killed or caused to be killed the first train for the motives assigned, who would think, if they would reflect upon it for a moment, that they would let others equally as objectionable pass by unmolested, especially when they knew that they would not fail to charge them with the slaughter?[31] But the enlightened press (?) do not condescend to notice these things. It would be treating the Mormons like white men—like freemen, equally entitled with themselves to all the rights of American citizens.

In one corner of the paper in which these accusatory statements were published (the Los Angeles Star,) we perceived a little notice which stated

[31] Though Cannon would have been in no position to know this, the obvious answer to his questions is that the directive from Brigham Young to let the emigrants pass through to California unmolested came too late for the Baker-Fancher train, but not too late for the Duke train and other emigrant parties.

that the editor had received from Mr. J. Ward Christian of San Bernardino, a long statement of the late attack, by the Indians, on the emigrant train on the Salt Lake road, differing materially from that which he had already published; and, perhaps, he would insert it in his next issue. Scarcely a paper that has published all the statements from which this materially differed, has noticed the existence of such a statement. Coming from San Bernardino, it must be justificatory of the Mormons, and therefore, must be ignored.—Every other accused party may have the benefit of a doubt; but a Mormon—Never. They are fearful that the unfavorable impressions which they wish made on the public mind in respect to the Mormons, should be weakened; therefore, every statement that would increase the hatred of the masses against "Mormonism" and the Mormons, has been carefully published, and duly compiled in the summary of news sent on the steamer to the East; but the exculpatory evidence is not once alluded to.—This was the course they pursued with the Drummond slanders, until their author's character was so completely exposed that he was a stench in the nose of every virtuous man. And when the time arrives, as it most assuredly will, that the utter falsity of these charges will also be made apparent, the exposure will be quietly hushed up and no more be said about it than can possibly be helped.[32]

Our contemporaries think that a crisis is approaching. In this we agree with them. It is time that there should be a change of some kind; we care but little what it may be. With the Lord to uphold the cause of the just, it can not be any worse than it has been. For ourself we are sick and weary of enduring such treatment as we, in common with our co-religionists, have endured for years past. We have borne the yoke so long that our patience is nearly exhausted. This continual abuse and piling on of false charges—this eternal whine about Mormon treason, Mormon aggressions, Mormon licentiousness, with these oft-repeated threats of whipping us into an abjuration of our principles and of exterminating us, we are tired of hearing. We know that the Mormons in Deseret are an industrious, peaceable, god-fearing people, and that they have been most foully abused and villified. All they have asked or now ask, is justice; all they desire is their guaranteed rights. These they never have had; but we, as one individual whose interests are wholly identified with theirs, feel that the time has arrived when it is but right that they be demanded, and if needs be, contended for.

Cannon could not have been more wrong about the massacre at Mountain Meadows. The truth of the matter was more than he would have imagined and it continued to be more than he could ever—at least publicly—accept. For many years, the official position of the LDS church seemed to be "the less said the sooner done."

[32] Ironically, this is precisely what happened in the Mormon press.

Following on the heels of the Mountain Meadows massacre and the Utah War, Mormon rhetoric changed considerably. John D. Lee noted three speeches in one week early in 1859 in which Apostle Amasa Lyman "addressed the Saints on the Subject of avenging the blood of the Prophets; which he said never would be done by Butchering each other, but to the contrary by implanting in the mind & cultivating the opposite principle, until man ceace to sin & be as one Family &c."[33]

Much later, a Utah historian would attempt to separate the doctrine of blood atonement from actual homicide: "Quite foreign to this theological concept was the idea that a man of his own volition might weigh another individual in the balance, adjudge him guilty, and administer the death penalty. Such a deed would properly constitute an act of murder."[34] But until the Mormons were finally subdued by the reality of an invading army, the unfortunate rhetoric of the Reformation continued to provide the anti-Mormon press with more than enough evidence to convince many readers that the Mormons, just like the savage Indians, were a danger to civilization. Small wonder that so many Gentiles who were involved with the settling of the American West both loathed and feared their Mormon neighbors. As Cannon put the matter to Young on 30 October 1857, "The late news from the South concerning the massacre at Mountain Meadows, has caused considerable feeling and excitement. They hate us yet they fear us."[35]

They Were Resolved to Wreak a Terrible Revenge

The Mountain Meadows massacre would torment Brigham Young throughout the remaining twenty years of his long life. During those twenty years it often fell to George Q. Cannon to defend his religion and its beloved prophet from charges of Mormon involvement. When he did respond, he perpetuated the story that the Indians had acted alone in righteous vengeance.

History is silent as to Cannon's personal reaction to the evidence of the massacre he encountered at Mountain Meadows as he took the southern route home to Salt Lake. "George Q. Cannon and I were both

[33] Cleland and Brooks, eds., *A Mormon Chronicle*, 201–02.

[34] Neff, *History of Utah*, 413.

[35] Cannon to Young, 30 October 1857, LDS Archives.

in California at the time of the massacre," Charles W. Wandell, a former California Mormon missionary and correspondent for the *Western Standard,* recalled a decade after his departure from Mormonism. "We both passed over the bloody ground within a few days of each other, and within three months of its occurrence; we both knew from the statements of the brethren in Southern Utah that it was Governor Young's militia that did the job!"[36]

There is no extant journal available that records Cannon's reaction to what he may have seen at Mountain Meadows or heard in towns like Cedar City and Parowan. But how could he have been anything other than horrified to learn that the worst imaginings of his enemies—at least in this case—had apparently come true? Years later, Sarah Dunn Thornton recalled the terrible night her family spent at Mountain Meadows during the evacuation of San Bernardino as she traveled to Great Salt Lake City with Cannon and other Californian Saints.[37] She claimed she had watched as apostles Orson Pratt, Orson Hyde, John Bull, and George Q. Cannon "washed their hands in a stream of water, said they were innocent of such a deed and knew the Church had sanctioned no such thing."[38]

Sanctioned or not, Juanita Brooks long ago argued that Mormon authorities, themselves under siege by the federal government, protected the murderers and covered up the crime at Mountain Meadows for almost two decades.[39] As editor of the *Deseret News,* it fell to George Q.

[36] Wandell to Joseph Smith III, 26 September 1874, typescript, Henry A. Stebbins Papers, P24, f38, Community of Christ Library-Archives, 2. Wandell's initials identify several of the letters he wrote to the *Western Standard,* while he apparently signed others using the pseudonyms "Americanus," "Mormonus," and "Mormon Citizen." See Newton, *Hero or Traitor: A Biographical Study of Charles Wesley Wandell,* 80n78. Wandell had "resigned" his LDS membership in 1864.

[37] It is estimated that as many as 3,000 California Saints (or somewhere between 50 to 80 percent of the California Mormon population) removed to Utah in anticipation of the Utah War. Cowan and Homer, *California Saints,* 210, 212. However, many—if not all—of the outlying settlements may soon have collapsed even were it not for the impending invasion. See Rosenvall, "Defunct Mormon Settlements: 1830–1930," 57.

[38] Thornton, Incidents in the Life of Sarah Elizabeth Dunn Thornton, in Hammond Family Papers, Special Collections, BYU. Joseph—not John—Bull, Cannon's assistant, was never an apostle and at the time, neither was Cannon. Thornton also recalled that the people at Jacob Hamblin's ranch told her family "that John D. Lee and his men disguised as Indians had come upon the train of emigrants and mercilessly murdered them."

[39] "Brigham Young was accessory after the fact, in that he knew what had happened, and how and why it happened," wrote Brooks. "Evidence of this is abundant and unmistakable, and from the most impeccable Mormon sources." See Brooks, *The Mountain Meadows Massacre,* 219.

Cannon to publish the last official denial that Mormons had participated in a crime that has never ceased haunting his people.[40]

"MOUNTAIN MEADOW MASSACRE,"
DESERET NEWS, 1 DECEMBER 1869.

In the delivery of the lecture "Six Months in Utah," by Mrs. St. Clair on Tuesday last at the Theatre, there was an allusion made by the lecturess to what is known as the "Mountain Meadow Massacre." There was nothing in her treatment of this point in her lecture that was offensive to her audience; but she evidently was unfamiliar with the facts, and as a general misapprehension exists abroad in relation to them, simple justice demands that they be correctly stated. Our silence upon this subject is frequently construed as an evidence of the inability of the people of this Territory to defend themselves against the cruel charges which have been made against them in connection with that tragedy.

It is almost a pity to break this silence now, for there is a class of anti "Mormon" writers whose entire stock of trade consists of the "Mountain Meadow Massacre," and a few other acts of violence which have occurred in this Territory, and upon which they ring constant changes, holding the "massacre" over our heads somewhat as an old schoolmistress could a rod over a naughty child. We scarcely know how these threats and menaces sound to people who live outside this Territory; but they only excite either amusement or contempt here where the facts are understood.

After Governor Alfred Cumming had reached this city and was fairly installed in office—considerable having been said about the massacre of a company of emigrants at Mountain Meadows the previous Fall—ex-Governor Young urged upon the Governor and U.S. District Attorney [Alexander] Wilson the propriety of taking steps to investigate this occurrence. In the wish for a thorough examination he was seconded by the entire community, for all felt that most cruel and unjust aspersions had been cast upon them. To render what aid he could President Young proffered to go with the Federal officers to the vicinity of the outrage, and use every effort in his power to aid the matter to the uttermost, and discover the guilty ones. But this was no part of the policy of the Judges who were then here nor the attachés of the camp. Such a course would settle the question; but they were interested in keeping it open.

---

[40] Juanita Brooks, *Ibid.*, 213, credited the editorial to Cannon, but the text is strikingly similar to George A. Smith to Mr. St. Clair, 25 November 1869, Historian's Office Journal, MS 2737, LDS Archives, 941–49. Whether Smith's letter was used as the basis for the unsigned *Deseret News* editorial of six days later or whether the editorial had been written well in advance of publication and then became the basis for the Smith letter is unknown. In any event, Cannon was the editor of the *Deseret News* at that time and therefore was ultimately responsible for the editorial he published.

At Provo, in the Spring of 1859, a Grand Jury on U S business undertook the investigation of the "Mountain Meadow Massacre." They requested the U S District Attorney, Mr. Wilson, a citizen of Pennsylvania, to be present with them and examine the witnesses. Two Indians, Mose and Looking-glass, had been committed for the crime of rape perpetrated upon a white woman and her daughter, a girl of ten years. In the midst of the investigation of the Mountain Meadow case, the Judge, John Cradlebaugh, called the Grand Jury into the court room and administered to the members an abusive lecture, and summarily discharged them! At the same time, he turned the savages, Mose and Looking-glass, loose upon the community. The Grand Jury protested, but in vain, against this unwarrantable proceeding by the Court. District Attorney Wilson, also reported that he was present at the deliberations of the Grand Jury, and, at the request of its members, had examined the witnesses and that the Jury were proceeding in the matter efficiently. Thus ended the attempt to have the transaction investigated judicially.

From the earliest years that white men traveled through the country now incorporated in the southern portion of this Territory and the northern part of Arizona, outrages upon the Indians were frequent. When Colonel Fremont passed through the southern desert in 1842, his party killed, without any provocation, several Pah-Ute Indians near the Rio Virgen. When New Mexico was organized, Governor [James] Calhoun, Superintendent of Indian Affairs recommended, to the Department at Washington, the extermination of the Pah-Utes. Emigrants passing through by the southern route to California had also frequently shot them whenever they came in sight. To such an extent had this custom prevailed that when President Geo. A. Smith and party made the settlement at Parowan, Iron Country, in January, 1851, then 200 miles from settlements on the North and upwards of 500 on the South, a delegation of Pah-Utes from New Mexico, now Arizona, visited him and besought that the indiscriminate shooting of Indians by emigrants should cease, as they were disposed to be friendly and wished to trade with them. President Smith, of course, could only speak for his own people.

From all that is known respecting the company of Arkansas emigrants, who were killed at Mountain Meadows, they conducted themselves in a hostile manner towards the Indians wherever they saw them. At Corn Creek, Millard Co., President George A. Smith, who was coming for a visit to the southern settlements in company with several friends, found a company of emigrants camped; they had about thirty wagons and a considerable herd of stock. He and his party crossed the creek and camped about forty yards from them. Three of the company visited his camp, and one was introduced as the Captain of the company. After inquiring where President Smith and party were from, he asked if there was any danger to be feared from the Indians who were camped near by. He was told that if his company had committed no outrage upon the Indians, there was no danger. Next morning early, while President S. and party were hitching up, the Captain of the emigrant company again joined them. He pointed to an ox which had died during the night, and wished to know if the Indians would eat the animal. He was told they would; that they were in the habit of eating cattle that died, and that if he would give it to them, they would be thankful. As President S. was starting, one of his party asked him what the Captain was doing over at the dead ox with a bottle in his hand. He replied that he was probably taking a drink.[41]

The Indians ate the ox and ten of their number died. It had, without doubt, been poisoned. A portion of these Indians were Pahvantes and other were Pah-Utes, who lived in the vicinity of the Mountain Meadows, and were on a visit to the Pahvantes. There is reason to believe that this company poisoned the spring also, for thirty head of cattle which drank of its waters died with every symptom of poisoning. The Pah-Ute Indians who survived, returned home with the news of the death of their companions. But the company that had occasioned their death was not lost sight of. Another outrage had been added to the long list which had been accumulated from the days when Fremont had passed through their country, and they were resolved to wreak a terrible revenge. They rallied all the neighboring [3] Indians, and when the emigrants reached "Cane Spring" in the Mountain Meadows, they attacked them.

After the attack was made the first intimation of it received at Parowan was by Indian runners to Oawauup, a chief of the Pi-edes, in that vicinity, who was summoned to assist them. From the Pi-edes, the citizens learned something about a difficulty between the Indians and a company of emigrants and succeeded in keeping them from joining the Pah-Utes. Rumors still arriving that a battle was going on, a party of citizens from Cedar started for the purposed of relieving the travelers; but arrived too late. They succeeded, however, in rescuing a few children, who had been preserved by the Indians, agreeably to their custom, when victorious, of keeping children to trade.

Another company, which was following the Arkansas company, fired upon some Indians near Beaver and wounded one of them. The Indians

---

[41] In his letter to St. Clair, George A. Smith wrote, "while we were hitching up to continue our journey, I was again waited upon by the Captain of the emigrant company, who pointed out to me an ox which had died during the night, enquiring if the Indians would eat the animal. I answered, Yes; and informed him that they were in the habit of eating the cattle that died, and that if he would give it to them, they would be thankful. As we were starting, Elisha Hoops asked me what the Captain was doing over at the dead ox with a bottle in his hand. I informed Hoops that I had advised the Captain to give the Indians the ox and that he was probably taking a drink." Smith's detailed story contradicted his earlier accounts of meeting the Fancher party. According to emigrant George Davis, the Dukes train regarded the poison story as "a fabrication, on the part of the Mormons to clear themselves of suspicion, and to justify the Indians in murdering that company of emigrants." Davis believed William Mathews started the story. See "Letter from San Bernardino," *San Francisco Bulletin,* 12 November 1857, 2/3.

appeared determined to destroy them, and they probably would have done so, had not Col. Dame, of Parowan, sent a detachment of militia, who pacified the Indians to some extent, and guarded the company on their road some three hundred miles.

The above is a brief outline of the circumstances connected with this massacre. The determined policy of the enemies of the people of this Territory has been to not investigate this transaction. During the years 1858-9 an army of several thousand men were stationed in the Territory without any employment. The Federal Judges who were here at that time were the open and avowed enemies of the people, and is it probable that, with such a force to back them, if there had been the least probability of incriminating the "Mormons," they would have suffered so good an opportunity to pass? The fact is, the newspaper rumors concerning this affair answered a better purpose than investigating, in affording an excuse for keeping up the expense of sustaining troops where they were not needed.

There has never been a time when President Young and the people have not been ready to give every aid in their power to have this occurrence rigidly examined.

Chapter 13

"Faithfully Warning the People"
Cannon's Parting Shots

Years after his tenure as the editor of the *Western Standard*, George Q. Cannon prepared his favorite editorials for publication in book form. He did so primarily for the sake of his posterity. The final editorial he selected for inclusion in *Writings from the "Western Standard"* was one he had written six weeks prior to his departure for Utah. It was not his last editorial, but it was, quite possibly, his best:

"Freedom or Slavery.—Which Is Preferable?"
Western Standard, 18 September 1857.[1]

Rumors have obtained circulation within the last few days in Sacramento and this city, that Gen. Harney and 2,500 troops, while on their journey to Great Salt Lake City, had been met and driven back with a loss of 600 men. The rumor is so utterly baseless, and the impossibility of such a collision taking place is so easily perceived, that it has been universally discredited. Yet it has had the effect to draw forth several leaders from the pens of our contemporaries, and among the rest a very long and malignant one from the editor of the San Francisco *Herald*. In his article on this subject this editor attempts to foreshadow the policy of the Administration, and the plan of action which has been decided upon by the new Governor and the myrmidons who accompany him on his way to Utah. If he really does reflect the policy to be pursued toward the people of Utah—and after making every deduction for his known rancor and spite we still have enough left to make us think that to some extent he does—the army now on their way to that Territory, is but little, if any, better than a mob, organized under pretence of law. We had hoped, notwithstanding the suspicious appearance of this movement and our knowledge that it was entirely uncalled for, that a liberal, high-minded policy would be pursued in the selection of a suitable man for Governor and in the instructions given to the troops. But, if the editor of the *Herald* may be relied upon, the contrary is the case, and the Administra-

[1] Reprinted in Cannon, *Writings from the "Western Standard,"* 506–12.

tion has suffered its power to be converted to the carrying out of the nefarious schemes of corrupt and designing men. It is with the express and avowed purpose of waging a deathless warfare against "Mormonism"—the influence of Governor Young, and the union which pervades the society of Utah, that the new Governor and troops are going there. This writer says:—

> "Governor Cumming is charged with the duty of checking and finally overthrowing the detestable practices that prevail in Utah, and on which are balanced Mormonism and Young's power."

This sentence condenses the whole policy in a nutshell. Every feature which distinguishes "Mormonism" from the cursed and effete systems of the day, is to be obliterated. The virtuous practices of its believers, which in the opinion of this moral editor, are "detestable," are to be "checked and finally overthrown." If resistance be offered, and the people of Utah should not submit to the inauguration of the Christian (?) practices of unlimited, licensed whoredom and adultery in the stead of the ancient, heaven-approving, Bible-sustaining practice of polygamy, then the cannon and the bayonet are to be used as irresistible arguments in Christianizing, (?) civilizing, (?) and, if they persist in their resistance, victimizing the "Mormons!"

. . . The word now is, that "Mormonism" must be put down at all hazards—regardless of all consequences. The choice is to be made between a renunciation of "Mormonism" and death. If a stubborn adherence be exhibited, blood must be shed; for, says the editor of the *Herald*, (and who would doubt his authority?) it is now time that our distinctive dogmas should be abandoned,—self-interest demands it, common sense demands it, Christendom demands it, and the character of the country demands it! How dare the "Mormons," then, think of demurring, and lose sight so far of their self-interest as not to travel in the broad road with the crowd? Could they see with the eyes of the editor of the *Herald*, they would give full scope to the passions—throw open the marriage bed to the defiler, prostitute their sisters and daughters, poison the very fountains of existence, and give unbridled license to every species of corruption that would sow the seeds of disease and death broadcast through their land. But they do not see the propriety of receiving and permitting the practice of such a system of morality, though it be supported by the new Governor and his troops, and the judgment of Christendom. "Mormons" have, from the very first, been very blind to what the world call their self-interest. The first step they took in "Mormonism" called for the sacrifice of self-interest; and self-interest has been immolated on the altar of duty to God from that day to this. They have also been peculiarly tenacious of their right to worship God according to the dictates of their own consciences. They were so when they were but a handful, and they are no less so now. No six nor six hundred United States officials, though backed by ferocious General Harney and his 2,500 or 3,000 troops, or by the whole regular army of our revered Uncle Sam, will be able to force them to relinquish their heaven-born right of practicing the precepts of their religion according to the revelations of God and the Constitution of their fathers. They will not be dictated to in these matters by others, be they few or many. It is a right, for the correct exercise of which they are accountable to God and to him alone; and cursed be the man that would deprive them of it. How indicative it is of the degeneracy of the age, and the absence of the spirit of liberty, when an editor can unblushingly and publicly declare in these free states that the day has come when the inhabitants of a United States Territory can no longer have the right to enjoy liberty of conscience—to declare that 100,000 freemen must frame their creed and practice their religion according to the ideas of a half-a-dozen politicians, who, by hook or by crook, have contrived to get appointed to the Federal offices in that Territory, or be visited by the full weight of the resources of the General Government! Such an indignity was never offered to the Thirteen Colonies by the tyrannical ministers of the third George. For less than this, and other indignities and wrongs which we have endured, the colonists declared themselves free and independent, and broke the yoke which the tyrants sought to impose upon them; and shall freemen—men reared under the shade of the tree of liberty, sons of those revolters against oppression, and in whose breasts the spirit of freedom was born, and which has "grown with their growth and strengthened with their strength"—do less?

If the policy foreshadowed by the editor of the *Herald,* in the article to which we have alluded, be the policy to be practiced by the new officials on their arrival in Utah—and upon the supposition that it is we make our remarks—we, as one individual, one believer in "Mormonism," one who knows and appreciates the sweets of liberty, say, NO! Not while we breathe the free air of our Creator—not while the heavens shine above us, and the earth remains beneath our feet, will we ever submit to it. In this we speak for ourself—not for the people of Utah. We have pleaded, humbly and imploringly pleaded, in common with our brethren, for peace. We have diligently sought and labored for the salvation of the children of men. We have not encroached on the rights or privileges of any; but we have been encroached upon. We have submitted to it. Not once or twice, but repeatedly. When smitten on one cheek, we have turned again and again the other to the smiter. To escape from this oppression we were willing to exile ourselves in a far-off wilderness—a country so sterile and repelling that no other people would occupy it; but have we been permitted to dwell there unmolested? We were while there were crickets to fight, while starvation and want stared us in the face, and the prospect was promising of our having to succumb to them. But no sooner had we reared comfortable homes, demonstrated that the country was inhabitable, and surrounded ourselves with the appliances of civilized life and comparative wealth, than the old system of oppression was recommended; and, at last, the unceasing efforts of our oppressors have succeeded in persuading the Administration to lend itself to the scheme of crushing out a people who have ever been loyal subjects, and who have done more during the last ten years toward developing the resources of the country and adding to the conveniences of traveling than any other community of thrice its size!

The determination evidently is that we shall renounce our so-called errors, or be exterminated. The word extermination is not used in the article above referred to—though it has been used time and again in other articles on this subject—but accepting the language used at its standard meaning, it is as plain as a pikestaff that this is the result which we may expect, if the policy adopted can be successfully carried out and Harney's troops do not all desert him before he reaches Utah. If rumor may be relied on, and we have it from accredited sources, they have commenced putting their plan of operations into effect on the plains—pressing "Mormon" emigrants into their service, oppressing the men, and abusing and practicing their devilish arts upon the women. What the result will be we cannot precisely say; but, as sure as the Lord lives, such high-handed outrages will not go unpunished. We do not know what steps the people of Utah will take in the matter; we know, however, that they will act prudently, wisely, and righteously, and do all in their power to prevent a collision. (In fact, we have been informed that the people of Utah, instead of aiding the deserters from Harney's command in their escape, have arrested two, and intend holding them in custody until he arrives.) But if the collision be forced upon them—if the determination be to compel them to cease the practice of their religion, to deprive them of their rights and privileges as freemen, to make them slaves in fact—then we, were we in Utah, would say,—Let it come; with God to defend the right, we will risk the consequences. We would say,—Let the rugged defiles of the Rocky Mountains become a second Thermopylae, where the sons of illustrious sires will contend for the precious rights bought by the blood of their fathers and bequeathed to them as the most inestimable boon that they could bestow. We would say,—Rather than part with our religion, we, with God's assistance, will part with life; rather than live a slave, to fawn and cringe and bend the knee at another's beck—to endure the slavery of the mind, a slavery far more ignoble and debasing than the slavery of the body—we will die, nobly contending for the God-given right of freedom of conscience. Better far do this, than stand tamely by and be robbed of our dearest rights or suffer extermination; for if we should fall, others might live, and be victorious, and our children could then enjoy what we contended for. These are our feelings to-day, and we pray God they may ever be,—we wish no other. We boldly avow them, confident that they will meet the approval of every friend of justice and liberty. As for the disrupture, the overthrow, or the crushing out of "Mormonism," such an event need not be looked for nor thought of; neither need there be any speculations indulged in relative to the extermination of its believers. The editor of the *Herald* deceives himself and those who believe what he writes, when he says that "the days of Mormonism at Salt Lake are numbered." The cannon are not cast, the muskets or rifles not made, the powder and ball not manufactured, nor the men to use them either born or conceived, that will destroy "Mormonism." Mark our words, gentlemen, it will live, though all earth and hell array themselves against it.

Following the issue in which Cannon's extraordinary "Freedom or Slavery" editorial appeared, there was a lapse of four weeks and then the paper appeared with no advertising and only two pages instead of the customary four. Cannon apologized for the "suspension of three weeks." Apparently he had been so involved in helping his family and other Saints under his care prepare for the return to Utah Territory that he had lost track of one of those four intervening weeks:

After a suspension of three weeks [issues], the "STANDARD" again makes its appearance. Its non-appearance has given rise to various surmises, and elicited many polite inquiries from our contemporaries and many have come to the conclusion that we had entirely deserted the field. We have been so busily employed in other duties that we were compelled to suspend the publication of the paper; this is also the only apology we have to offer to our readers this week for the appearance of only a half sheet.[2]

The phrase, "deserted the field," is telling, for surely Cannon perceived himself as a soldier on the field of battle, pinned down by enemy fire, facing a highly uncertain future that might include imminent defeat or strategic retreat. He continued to fight, again lashing out at other San Francisco newspapers as he sought to defend the rights of the Mormons to live their religion as they chose.[3]

---

[2] *Western Standard,* 23 October 1857.

[3] See especially the unsigned editorial in the *Western Standard,* 23 October 1857.

Every Indignity and Wrong

Two more weeks would pass before another issue of the *Western Standard* was published on 6 November 1857. This, Cannon's last issue for this newspaper, appeared as a full sheet, or four pages. Although it again contained no advertising, it did include Cannon's final fusillades.

In his leader, Cannon reviewed the latest news about the situation in Utah, noting that government troops had apparently reached Fort Laramie and that by all appearances, "the 'Mormons' were making preparations for a fight" by fortifying Fort Bridger. Commenting on the newspaper editors who had expressed disbelief that the Mormons would be so foolhardy as to engage in armed resistance, Cannon first commended the *Chronicle* for having acknowledged the previous persecutions of the Mormons and the generally non-violent manner in which they had borne their afflictions:

> The *Chronicle* of this city in an editorial last week, speaks the mind of many on this subject, only the editor candidly owns—an acknowledgment so truthful and unpalatable that very few ever make it, and one that we are surprised he should publish—that inhuman atrocities have been perpetrated upon us in days past. He says:
>
>> "We have heard Mormon bluster before. When the Church was expelled from Missouri, where even to this day it is believed by them that the stakes of Zion have been set, weak in numbers though it was, the inhuman atrocities perpetrated by the border people should certainly have aroused a spirit of resistance, and prompted the defense of wives and children, had a defensive attitude been advisable. So also when the leader and prophet Smith was killed at Carthage, Illinois, his death it was predicted would create civil war; but they went not to battle, and have ever since been growing stronger for it. When they broke up their establishment at Nauvoo, and turned their faces toward the wilderness, instead of evincing a vindictive and hostile feeling toward the U.S. Government, they responded to its call for volunteers, and enrolled a large number of their young men in a battalion for service in this country during the Mexican war. Thus it will be seen their policy has been from the beginning, non-resistance."

Cannon was grateful for this unaccustomed admission of the Saints' relative docility in responding to the mob violence that both state and federal governments had previously allowed to come down upon them, but he was quick to point out that such forbearance could not be counted upon in the future:

> What preparations have been made by the people of Deseret to defend themselves, or whether any have been made, we know not. But men deceive themselves when they think that their expressed determinations are but idle bravado, and that they will continue to suffer as they have heretofore done from the beginning, without making any effort to save themselves. The course that the Mormons have taken for the past twenty-seven years, when rightly and unprejudicedly viewed, has been such as to satisfy the most zealous advocates of the doctrine of non-resistance; we also know that it has been such to satisfy the Lord. If it were not so, we would still continue to submit to every indignity and wrong until He should say that it was enough.

Doubtless Cannon had in mind a revelation received by Joseph Smith in 1833 that counseled the Saints to endure an enemy's attacks against themselves and their families three times. Then "if he shall come upon you, or your children, or your children's children, unto the third and fourth generation: I have delivered thine enemy into thine hands . . . and if thou reward him according to his works, thou are justified, if he has sought thy life, and thy life is endangered by him; thine enemy is in thine hands, and thou art justified."[4]

True enough, Cannon seemed to be saying, the Saints have generally practiced non-violence in the past, but there is a limit to everything. His editorial continued as he speculated about conditions in Utah, justifying the reports of impending armed resistance:

> They may well feel that the time for action has arrived, and that they must make every preparation in their power to avert the contemplated catastrophe. To supinely await the blow, which is to rob them of their rights and privileges and enslave or destroy them, and not make an effort to ward it off, when they know it is coming and are aware of the consequences, would be in the highest degree reprehensible. The choice which is offered is, renunciation of the principles which they have obeyed, knowing them to be heaven's truths, and for the love of which they have already suffered so much, or extermination.

In another article in the final issue, Cannon chastised especially the editors of so-called religious newspapers for fanning the flames of

[4] *Doctrine and Covenants of the Church of the Latter Day Saints: Carefully Selected from the Revelations of God,* 75:5. (*Doctrine and Covenants,* 98:23–31 in modern LDS editions.)

hatred against the Mormon people. A particular target was the *Pacific Christian Advocate,* an Oregon Territory newspaper affiliated with the Methodists. Cannon had locked horns with its editor, Thomas H. Pearne, previously and now condemned him for advocating new laws designed to prohibit Mormon Elders from preaching within Oregon Territory so long as they continued to believe in polygamy. "Let such a man as (Pearne) have the power," Cannon argued, "and religious freedom would be unknown." And then, perhaps to demonstrate that he had still retained his sense of humor in spite of everything, Cannon attacked Pearne's objections to polygamy:

> Now, we would ask Mr. Pearne, if, when he dies, he expects to go to heaven? And if he does—which we take for granted, he being a Methodist preacher—whether he intends to let the angels carry him, as the Savior says they did Lazarus, into Abraham, the polygamist's bosom? Or, does he intend to object to such an arrangement, and urge upon the Lord of heaven and earth the propriety of passing laws which will oust Father Abraham from the exalted and honorable station occupied by him?[5]

Cannon appreciated the fact that not all "religionists" were against him and in the same article, he praised A. C. Edmunds, the editor of the *Star of the Pacific* (a Sacramento newspaper associated with the Universalist church), for his liberality. Cannon printed an extract from that paper he felt "deserved republishing":

> Much anxiety is felt at present as to what the Mormons intend doing. We see it stated that they are making great preparations to resist by force of arms the legalized authorities of Uncle Sam. Now, it is not our purpose to defend the Mormons, or to screen them from censure where censure should fall; but this we do say, they are bitterly and cruelly persecuted, and that, too, without any just cause or provocation.
>
> The Mormons, as a class, are not so base as many represent them. They, like us, are human, with human sympathies, with likes and dislikes. And because they differ from us in sentiment, is it a reason sufficient to warrant us in sending an armed force, and, under the point of the bayonet, compel them to bow to our God and live up to the requirements of our creed? It matters not how black and how foul a person's character may be, we are not justifiable in meting to them the measure of their guilt in the spirit of revenge.
>
> The Mormons are a devoted people; they are bound to each other by ties of the strongest sympathy, and the first violent step taken to sever that tie,

5 "Mormonism," *Western Standard,* 6 November 1857.

will be the first to arouse the intense feelings of their hearts, and cause them to resist to the last, any force, or any means, by which their rights are invaded and the peace and the quietness of their families disturbed. Does not the Lion[6] protect her whelps, and should the Mormon show less sympathy for the cherished endearments of their homes, than the king of the forest?

This spirit of revenge, savors too much of partialism. It is the spirit that crucified our Savior; and which is now seeking to drive a deluded people from their dear bought homes. Is there no sympathy for a persecuted people? Is there no human heart to plead their cause? Yea, no human voice may be raised in their behalf, but the voice of Immanuel rings thro' the broken arches of crumbling ages, saying come unto me all ye that are weary and heavy laden and I will give you rest. Let us remember that the people, in whose blood we seek to wash our hands, are our brethren, children of the same Father, and heirs of the same promise. Return thy sword to its scabbard and learn to love a people whom God loves, and to bear the iniquities of a people who are under the same moral law, and to whom judgment will be meted out in the full measure of justice.[7]

To Debate With You the Principles of Mormonism

Thanks to a few courageous editors, such as Edmunds, who defended the Mormons in spite of their perceived theological aberrations, Cannon's was not the only voice literally crying in the wilderness, arguing that the Mormons were "more sinned against than sinning." What a difference it could have made if more early commentators on Mormonism had adopted the journalistic ethics of William Chandless: "Before entering on the subject it may be as well to remark that I shall never intentionally speak with irreverence of what any Christian church or sect may hold sacred; nor on the other hand indulge in sneers at the faith I am writing of—still less in the vulgarity of nick-naming its author or propagators, whatever may be their real or supposed character."[8] Nonetheless, the voice of George Q. Cannon was in the definite minority, and it was a voice that would soon be silenced—at least in San Francisco.

For months after learning of the army's approach, Brigham Young continued to assure his followers that God would not allow troops to enter the valley. Being of a practical "God-helps-them-that-help-them-

[6] Among the Mormons, Brigham Young's nickname was "The Lion of the Lord."

[7] "Mormonism," *Western Standard*, 6 November 1857.

[8] Chandless, *A Visit to Salt Lake*, 156.

selves" mindset, with increasing urgency he called home Saints living outside of Utah. If he were going to take on the U.S. Army he needed all the troops he could muster, including George Q. Cannon. Writing to Cannon in early September, Young made clear that he believed war with the American government was imminent. After reporting on the latest intelligence concerning the Utah Expedition's freight wagons and a rumor that General Harney had killed one of his officers in a duel, Young prepared Cannon for the inevitable:

> You had better so arrange your business that should open hostilities commence between us and the U.S. that you can leave at a moment's notice, as when the torch is once lighted it will be the signal for a general crusade against 'Mormonism.' You might sell all your publishing apparatus, and every thing you could not move at once, and with the proceeds, hire your printing done. You had better send sister Cannon home with the first company, from San Bernardino, if there are none coming the north route.
>
> In fact take every precaution which prudence suggests—that when you can 'fight' no longer you may be able to beat a safe retreat. . . . May God bless and prosper you continually, make you adequate to every duty, and gather you to these vallies to enjoy the society of your friends, in the name of Jesus Christ Amen.[9]

The dutiful Cannon began to "beat a safe retreat" by arranging for his wife and son to return to Utah. Even though he continued publishing the *Western Standard,* he must have felt that his own days in California were numbered, especially after receiving Young's letter of 7 October. Young discussed the possibility of sending Cannon to Hawaii to supervise the binding and sale of the Hawaiian *Book of Mormon* and to help a skeleton crew of missionaries launch a newspaper for the islands. Young then reiterated his earlier warning while bringing Cannon up to date on the latest troop movements:

> As heretofore advised, you will doubtless keep yourself in readiness for a sudden move in case of emergency. By advices on the 5th inst. we learn that the U.S. Troops for Utah were on Ham's Fork and moving at the rate of some 10 miles a day towards Fort Hall. The commanding officer had not arrived, and it was not known who or where he was. Our brethren vacated and burned down Forts Supply and Bridger on the 3rd. inst. Lieut. Gen'l Wells and Elders Taylor and Geo. A. Smith had their head quarters 4 miles this side of Cache Cave in Echo Kanyon on the 5th, and all things were

[9] Young to Cannon, 4 September 1857, LDS Archives.

> moving in a manner plainly indicating the hand of the Lord extended for the welfare of His cause and people, which will ever be the case, so the Saints but live their religion.

Brigham Young encouraged the California Saints to hasten to Utah, suggesting that they bring with them as many guns and as much ammunition as they could get away with: "It is presumed that all saints in California, who desire to come to Utah, and continue to live as Saints, are making every reasonable effort to speed their way hither, 'armed and equipped as the law directs'. Should any such prefer the milder climate of the southern settlements in Utah, they are at liberty to settle therein."[10]

Before the year was out, Cannon would leave California to help the Mormons prepare for what appeared to be an impending war with the United States. He had already sent his wife, Elizabeth, and his seven-month old son, John Q., home to Utah under the protection of his brother.[11] (At Cannon's request, David Cannon had been sent to California by Brigham Young as a missionary to assist his older brother.) Shortly after his family's departure, toward the end of November, Cannon was visited by Apostles Orson Pratt and Ezra T. Benson. Traveling incognito, the apostles were accompanying missionaries who were returning home from England, taking the long route through California to avoid both the snow and entanglements with the federal troops. Pratt and Benson convinced Cannon that it was time for him to return to Zion, where he would soon accept new responsibilities in the Mormon army of defense and editor of the relocated "Deseret News."[12]

Cannon had been less than enthusiastic about coming to California in the first place. In his letter to Brigham Young of 31 August 1855, he had noted that "Times are hard in this country at the present time and but little prospect of them improving. Those of the church in this country who have any of the leaven of truth about them are anxious to get away, and all are exerting themselves for this end."[13] Still, Cannon had done his best to fulfill his calling and after working day and night to settle his

---

[10] Young to Cannon, 7 October 1857, LDS Archives.

[11] Cannon's first son and namesake was born shortly after their arrival in California but died 14 November 1856 at the age of nine months and sixteen days. Adjacent to the obituary, printed in the issue appearing the following day, was a poignant article titled "Afflictions Tend to Make Us Wiser."

[12] Flake, *George Q. Cannon: His Missionary Years,* 123. Cannon took over from Albert Carrington and edited the *News* for only four months, while located at Fillmore City, but returned as editor in 1867–1873 and again—at least in name—from 1877–1879. McLaws, *Spokesman for the Kingdom,* 95–96.

business affairs and store the press, he, too, was ready to get away. "I leave San Francisco without a sign of regret;" he wrote in his journal, "I feel clear from the blood of this people; I have labored diligently, labored to lay before them the principles of salvation by means of the press and public preaching, but to all the offers of salvation they have turned a deaf ear, and they have treated all our testimonies and warning as idle tales."[14] Perhaps shaking dust from his feet as he left, George Q. Cannon arrived home just nineteen days after his family, on 19 January 1858, prepared to accept any new assignment from the "Brethren" in defense of Zion.

Until They Take Their Final Sleep

Although the Mormons never engaged federal troops in battle, as commander-in-chief of Utah's territorial militia, Brigham Young ordered the Nauvoo Legion to harass the army and attack its supply trains. "In those orders," Maj. Joseph Taylor recalled, "I was, with my command, to stay the progress of the expedition, by stampeding their cattle, burning their grass, &c., and not to take life, only in case of self defence."[15] Mormon historians have made much of militia Lt. Gen. D. H. Wells' orders to "take no life, but destroy the trains," that Taylor was carrying when he was captured on 4 October. These instructions, they argue, show that the Latter-day Saints were committed to avoiding violence if at all possible. Nonetheless, Brigham Young's orders reveal that while he did seek to avoid a military conflict, he was ready to fight if the army advanced toward Utah's settlements.

The Mormons pursued an aggressive strategy. Porter Rockwell's small command rustled more than a thousand government cattle, while a raiding party under Maj. Lot Smith burned three wagon trains carrying enough provisions to feed the federal expedition for at least two months.[16] The Mormons torched the grasslands in advance of the army, and General Wells ordered the destruction of the valuable Mormon civilian outposts of Fort Supply and Fort Bridger.

13 Cannon to Young, 31 August 1855, LDS Archives.

14 Cannon, "George Q. Cannon: The Mission to California," 514.

15 Knecht and Crawley, eds. *History of Brigham Young*, 195.

16 For more on the fascinating life of Lot Smith, with particular emphasis on his later years, see Peterson, "'A Mighty Man Was Brother Lot.'"

Winter stopped the army at the ruins of Fort Bridger, and that fall they did not cross the line in the snow that Brigham Young had drawn at the approaches to the Salt Lake Valley. U.S. Army soldiers and Nauvoo Legionnaires spent a tense winter staring each other down from the windy bluffs overlooking Blacks Fork, but despite many close confrontations, no blood was spilled except for a handful of casualties resulting from accidental gunshot wounds and drunken garrison brawls. Fortuitously, Thomas L. Kane, who had long taken an intense personal interest in the welfare of the Mormons, arrived in Utah in February 1858. He came as an unofficial emissary of President Buchanan and offered hope that the crisis could be resolved without violence. By spring, an Indian attack on their northern outpost at Fort Limhi shattered any Mormon hopes to rally the Indians to their cause, and Brigham Young agreed to support Kane's peace overtures. In a daring move, Kane persuaded the new governor, Alfred Cumming, to accompany him to Great Salt Lake City without a military escort. Using a mixture of charm, flattery, and intimidation, the Mormons quickly won over the pliant, probably alcoholic Cumming, who had not enjoyed the winter he had spent with the army.[17]

Brigham Young realized he was about to be overpowered and that engaging in war with the United States of America could only lead to disaster for him and the Latter-day Saints. Instead, he ordered the "Move South," which emptied northern Utah and Great Salt Lake City (thereby garnering considerable public national sympathy), and prepared to torch everything that would burn as a final act of defiance. Maj. Ben McCulloch, a determined, no-nonsense veteran of both the Texas Revolution and the Mexican War who had declined to serve as Utah's governor, was appointed as peace commissioner to Utah along with L. W. Powell. McCulloch was a U.S. Marshal for east Texas as well as the the former head of the Texas Rangers and Powell was the former governor and senator-elect of Kentucky. The commissioners met with Governor Cumming at Camp Scott on 29 May 1858. There, they informed him that James Buchanan had extended a presidential pardon to the Mormons for "seditions and treasons heretofore by them committed," a pardon Brigham Young would grudgingly accept, all the while insisting

[17] This analysis is derived from David L. Bigler's *Forgotten Kingdom*, 181–89.

that he and his people had done nothing to require a pardon. Just as the South justified secession from the Union as an act necessary to preserve the constitution, so the Mormons continued to justify their actions on the highest of patriotic principles. Thanks in large part to the diplomacy of Thomas L. Kane, the anticipated conflict between the U.S. Army and the Saints never advanced beyond the skirmishing stage.

Despite his tactical defeat and the loss of his multiple federal offices, Brigham Young emerged from his confrontation with the U.S. government still firmly in control of Utah and with his stature as a national figure greatly enhanced. At the end of his service in Utah, someone asked Governor Cumming how his successor would get along. "Get along? well enough, if he will do nothing. There is nothing to do," he replied. "Alfred Cumming is Governor of the Territory, but Brigham Young is Governor *of the people*. By ——, I am not fool enough to think otherwise."[18] Even two of the twentieth-century's most severe anti-Mormon writers had to acknowledge that "Not a shot was fired, yet the Mormons were victorious."[19]

But were they? In spite of the Saints' tendency—then and now—to perceive the Utah War as a David vs. Goliath encounter in which they came out the winners, statehood, economic prosperity, and national acceptance would prove to be elusive goals for decades to come.[20] And George Q. Cannon, the seasoned newspaperman from California, would be at the center of the church's continuing quest for legitimacy.

The Best and Most Effective Weapons They Have

The pages of the *Western Standard* reveal that George Q. Cannon was a strong-willed, sometimes acerbic, even occasionally petulant man who showed no mercy to his many journalistic opponents. As stated in his editorial "How We Oppose," published on 4 September 1857, Cannon was well aware that "all experience teaches that men use in warfare, whether physical or mental, the best and most effective weapons they have." That Cannon's most effective weapons in the California Mormon

[18] Stenhouse, *The Rocky Mountain Saints*, 445.

[19] Kelly and Birney, *Holy Murder*, 141.

[20] See William P. MacKinnon, "Epilogue to the Utah War: A Military Campaign's Impact and Legacy."

newspaper wars of 1856 and 1857 were his words no one can doubt. While he occasionally stooped to argument *ad hominem* himself, for the most part he appealed to reason, demanding that his opponents produce facts rather than mere accusations, evidence as opposed to convenient rhetoric. As he proved in California, this fearless young journalist was the best and most effective weapon the Mormons had to defend their controversial American religion.

When it came to defending Zion, Cannon did not hold back. As he concluded in his "Shifting the Responsibility" editorial of 21 February 1857, "The day is past, and we thank the Lord for it, for us to sit tamely by and have detraction and unmeasured abuse heaped upon us without daring to resent it or to hurl the falsehoods back in the teeth of the men who utter them." The threats against Mormonism were serious and very, very real. It was the mission of George Q. Cannon to do everything in his power to disabuse the public of its misconceptions and prejudices toward his religion.

Cannon's pugilistic editorial style was not unique; it was the general style of the day. A generation later, the editor of the *San Francisco Chronicle* looked back on the 1850s and evoked that rowdy newspaper scene:

> The writer who could tell the truth in the plainest fashion possible and who could give the hardest knocks shared popularity with the stump orator who voiced the grievances of the crowd at the frequently held indignation meetings. This being the situation, it would have been astonishing if the publishers of newspapers had not aimed to secure an editor whose philippics rivaled those of Demosthenes, and pioneers of an observant disposition at a later day told that the reader did not look in the News, the Herald, the Alta, or any of the live sheets half so much for intelligence as to see who was being "lambasted."[21]

How effective was George Q. Cannon in his "take no prisoners" approach to newspaper warfare? Cannon himself was very optimistic about his efforts as he reflected on the success of the *Western Standard* at the conclusion of the first six months of its existence:

> "Mormonism" is rapidly assuming such a position in the earth that every auxiliary which can be brought to aid in diffusing correct ideas in relation to it and its objects, is absolutely needed; and we sanguinely look forward to the day when "Mormon" presses will be so numerous, that those who have

[21] Young, *Journalism in California*, 14.

the slightest desire to arrive at correct conclusions in relation to it, can do so with very little difficulty. . . . The press has its mission to perform in aiding to consummate this glorious victory; already it has performed much, and much more yet remains for it to perform. Every press, that is converted to the dissemination of truth, is a host within itself in breaking down the ranks of error. It is an instrument peculiarly adapted, in the work of God, to the wants of the age, in counteracting the influence of the pernicious literature with which the earth is flooded, and in spreading the knowledge of that kingdom, which the prophet informs us, should fill the whole earth. For years, our enemies had every advantage over us; they could publish the most gross and diabolical slanders about us, and we had to submit to them. True, we might deny them, and demonstrate their untruthfulness and inconsistency; but our denial and all our remonstrances were comparatively unheard, and, so far as its influences upon us were concerned, the press appeared to be, peculiarly and exclusively, an anti-Mormon engine. That day, however—and we thank God for it—is past, and there is no longer any necessity for us to submit tamely to have the lie crammed down our throat, without the power to reject the nauseating dose. We can now meet our enemies on their own ground, with their own weapons, and, with God to defend the right, we have nothing to fear from the contest.[22]

At least one of his contemporaries, arguably the most renowned Western newspaper editor of the day, paid significant homage to George Q. Cannon and the *Western Standard.* In his remarkable "History of California Newspapers," published in a special edition of the Sacramento *Union* on 25 December 1858, E. C. Kemble, Sam Brannan's old apprentice, provided a historical perspective on the Mormon paper:

The *Western Standard* was the name of a weekly paper started in 1855, under the auspices of G. Q. Cannon, who was alike publisher and editor. It was discontinued in the Summer [Fall] of 1857. It was distinguished for an ardent advocacy of the peculiar doctrines of the Latter Day Saints, which it was ready to discuss and defend in season and out of season. Quite many were the wars which it waged with the secular and religious press concerning the polygamic faith, the designs of Brigham Young towards the United States Government, and the general institutions of Mormondom. When the Mormon trump was sounded, calling the faithful to the City of the Saints in 1857, the *Standard* was discontinued, and the editor rejoined his brethren in that memorable locality.

[22] "Interest Attached to Mormonism," *Western Standard,* 23 August 1856; reprinted in Cannon, *Writings from the "Western Standard,"* 185–86.

Without question, Cannon more than met his enemies on their own ground, not only defending the LDS church against newspaper wars initiated by the Gentile press, but obviously starting a few of his own. He may have caused many of his non-Mormon readers and even a few of the editors of rival newspapers to think twice about their prejudices and preconceptions, but his polemics undoubtedly changed the minds of very few. If he is to be judged by the extent to which he turned nineteenth-century America away from its aversion to polygamy and theocratic government, he, among others, was an abject failure. That was a battle no one could have won:

> By 1857 facts and fancies had become so embellished by lurid tales and fertile imaginings that practically every crusading editor and sin-conscious divine would have considered himself remiss in duty not to have expounded publicly on the 'Mormon Menace.' The only question seems to have been which retributive measure might be most effective in dealing with the 'heretical brigands' who were fast populating the west with converts and offspring.[23]

If one is to judge George Q. Cannon by how well he fought the good fight and how successful he was in bolstering the faith of his fellow Mormons, one must recognize his tremendous success. That he retained his marvelous, ironic, sometimes sarcastic sense of humor through it all is commendable in itself. The Fourteenth General Epistle of the Church, promulgated by Brigham Young and his counselors, summarized their perceptions of Cannon's success early in 1857:

> In California the *Western Standard* is faithfully warning the people, under the able care and guidance of br. George Q. Cannon, who has also published the Book of Mormon in the Hawaiian language. The publication of that paper has proved very useful and beneficent in correcting public opinion, and in exercising a salutary influence over the few to be found in that land who are seekers after truth. Gold is the shrine at which they bow, and the truth emanating from High Heaven's King has but few admirers. The *Standard*, however, will be able to sustain itself, mostly through the aid of the Saints, and will continue to be issued so long as it shall be considered beneficial in aiding the cause of truth in that region.[24]

---

[23] Bailey, *Holy Smoke*, 14.

[24] "Fourteenth General Epistle of the Church," *Western Standard*, 21 February 1857. Indeed, subscriptions to the *Western Standard* were taken out almost exclusively by church members.

California was not exactly the godless wasteland the first presidency pictured — the chroniclers of *The Annals of San Francisco* devoted fifteen pages to their city's churches alone, concluding that "not all, nor nigh all the citizens of San Francisco are lost to everything but reckless dissipation."[25] But as Young and Cannon noted, many Californians of that day were a "hard case." Whether still mining for gold or trying to build their fortunes through other ventures, the priorities of most were strictly of this world and conversions to Mormonism were few. Still, from the outset, Cannon had expressed his faith in the enterprise. Referring to characters in *The Book of Mormon,* Cannon had written to Young that "The success of Alma in as wicked as Ammonihah, gives me hope that even in San Francisco there may an Amulek, a Zeezrom and others who may be constrained to acknowledge the power of the spirit of truth sufficiently to become obedient to its mandates."[26]

The Amuleks and Zeezroms were few and far between. When a convert was found—particularly on the rare occasion when he or she was anything short of penniless—the event was noteworthy. Consider the following excerpt from Brigham Young's letter of 4 July 1857, referring to a new convert who had already made a significant tithing contribution to the LDS church:

> I heartily approve the course which you have taken to promote the spreading of the Gospel; and the upbuilding of the kingdom of God. That there are thousands of honest in heart who have never heard the gospel, the enclosed (copy) letter; as one of the many which, I receive; will bear ample testimony. I would advise you to send an elder in accordance with the wish of Mr. Wright, as I believe he would be the instrument in God's hand of doing great good in that section of country.[27]

To be sure, there were converts and the newspaper wars Cannon both started and encouraged may have had a positive effect. "We shall be able

[25] Soulé, Gihon, and Nisbet, *The Annals of San Francisco,* 701.

[26] Cannon to Young, 3 December 1855, LDS Archives. Amulek was a *Book of Mormon* prophet who converted Zeezrom, a skeptical lawyer who was "the foremost to accuse Amulek." See Alma 11:31. The city Ammonihah was, like San Francisco, noted for its wickedness.

[27] Young to Cannon, 4 July 1857, LDS Archives. Even in his most private reflections, Young seemed to appreciate Cannon less for his tough editorial stances (by his own admission, Young was not much of a reader) than for his leadership as president of the mission. "Bro Geo Q is doing a great work in California," he wrote in his diary on 1 July 1857, "in building up churches, & establishing the Gospel." See Cooley, ed., *Diary of Brigham Young, 1857,* 35.

to baptize several between this and the conference in October [1857]," Missionary Elder Henry G. Boyle, who had labored extensively in Sonoma, Napa and Yolo counties, assured Cannon. "If Editors will keep up the Newspaper war against us so as to draw the attention of the people to our principles, we shall get along first rate; for since they commenced their crusade against us and our principles, I know our meetings as a general thing have been better attended." Perhaps even one of the converts was a journalist employed by none other than the *Daily Evening Bulletin.* In the same letter, Boyle gushed that

> One of the *Bulletin's* correspondents informed me the other day, that he intended to be baptized—that he was satisfied that Mormonism was true, and that it was superior to any thing that he had ever met with—and further, that his attention had been attracted to our principles by the amount of stuff that appeared in the colums [*sic*] of the *Bulletin* against us, and that investigation convinced him of the correctness of our principles; as it will every honest mind.
>
> The people think that any thing which causes so much fuss in the world is worthy of investigation; and to investigate is to become acquainted with the truth, and the Holy Spirit that accompanies it, will work their [*sic*] way into the hearts of all those that are honest, and the others we care not for: we only love and value folks according to their love of the truth.[28]

Still, converts were very hard to come by. "Mormonism in California is an up hill business," Elder Boyle had earlier complained from Dry Creek in Mendocino County, "and more so now than at any previous time since California became a State." Most of the Californians he met had come there to get rich, often at considerable sacrifice. "You might as well try to get access to the contents of their great iron safes," Boyle lamented, "as to try to reach their hearts by the power of truth."[29]

Cannon's greatest success on this mission was not with converts and those few church members under his jurisdiction, but with himself, as he grew in intellectual and spiritual maturity. He arrived in San Francisco at the age of only twenty-eight, having enjoyed great success as a missionary in Hawaii but with relatively little experience as a writer and leader of church affairs in a sophisticated environment. He faced a challenge from which many older and wiser men would (and at least one

[28] Boyle to Cannon, 18 August 1857, *Western Standard,* 28 August 1857, 3.

[29] Ibid., 1 October 1856, *Western Standard,* 11 October 1856, 3.

did) readily shrink. He left that "Sodom of the Pacific"[30] twenty months later as a man who had developed critical reasoning and writing skills unusual in one twice his age, fully prepared for the increasingly heavy and eventually apostolic responsibilities awaiting him.

---

[30] Now a popular euphemism used by political and religious conservatives for San Francisco, Cannon used the phrase as early as 22 November 1856 in an editorial, "Truth's Boldness—Error's Servility." "Yes," he remarked, "right here in San Francisco, the most notoriously corrupt city for its size in the United States, the Sodom of the Pacific, where crime and villainy have ever been better paid and more respected and honored than virtue, where it is no uncommon occurrence for four and five applications to be made for divorce in one day, the cry is raised about 'the corruptions of the Latter-day Saints!'" One cannot but wonder what Cannon would think of his old "home away from home" today.

Afterword

A Man Who Had Knocked about the World
Cannon after California

As 1857 drew to a close, George Q. Cannon joined the floodtide of Mormon refugees from San Bernardino that fled the increasing hostility of their neighbors and answered Brigham Young's call to return to Zion. As part of the move south, the *Deseret News* was relocated from Great Salt Lake City to Fillmore, with the now very experienced George Q. Cannon as its new editor, serving in that capacity from April to September. This would be the first of many critical assignments Cannon would fulfill after his return to Zion on behalf of his church.

Brigham Young summoned Cannon to Salt Lake in late 1858. The prophet had changed tactics. Rather than have Cannon take on the world as a newspaper editor, he would now send him out into the world to influence editorial opinion in the major eastern journals by working behind the scenes. Young characterized this as "quite a delicate mission, but relying upon your known character of sagacity, wisdom, ability, and, above all, humility and integrity, we feel that you will be successful and accomplish, through the blessing of the Lord, the purpose and objects of your mission."[1]

The newspaper editors of Cannon's day were in many ways quite different from their modern counterparts. As shown by Jeffrey L. Pasley,[2] a primary function of nineteenth-century newspapers was not simply to report but to create the news. Newspapers, possibly even more than the fledgling national political parties, were the most powerful political institutions of the land. Together, they helped establish "imagined com-

[1] Young to Cannon, 15 September 1858, LDS Archives, cited in Bitton, *George Q. Cannon: A Biography*, 94.

[2] Pasley, *"The Tyranny of Printers": Newspaper Politics in the Early American Republic.*

munities," whether among the citizens of Utah through their own press, or the nation as a whole as it learned of and reacted against the values and beliefs of Mormonism.[3]

With the guidance of Thomas L. Kane, then living in central Pennsylvania, Cannon enjoyed moderate success as a lobbyist. Though a non-Mormon, Kane continued to play an important—if often ambiguous—role as an agent of the church. Under Kane's tutelage, Cannon soon learned that the real source of access to editorial opinion was money, particularly if something as unpopular as Mormonism was to be defended. Fortunately, Young told Kane, "Bro George has command of all the funds you may deem requisite for the accomplishment of his work."[4] Cannon would devote a great portion of the rest of his life quietly using his powers of persuasion—as well as church funds—to influence newspaper editors and politicians to look more favorably upon Utah and the Mormons. "Be wise and discreet," Young directed his business agent, Horace Eldredge, so that in concert with Cannon and Kane he could "move the whole world [although] no one will know who has done it."[5]

Brigham Young informed Cannon in 1859 he had been appointed to serve as an apostle, appropriately to fill the long-standing vacancy occasioned by the untimely death of his friend and former California mentor, Parley P. Pratt.[6] "Your election has not been made public in our papers, nor as yet in the Tabernackle," advised Young, "lest it might in some way militate against the operations in which you are at present engaged."[7] Cannon responded, describing how the news filled him with fear and dread but also joy:

> I know that I scarcely need to say to you how peculiar my feelings were on reading in your letter of my appointment to fill the vacancy in the quorum of the twelve, occasioned by the death of Bro. Parley. You know, I am sure, much better what they were and are than I can write them. I had to steal aside

[3] See Anderson, *Imagined Communities: Reflections on the Origin and Spread of Nationalism,* and Nord, *Communities of Journalism: A History of American Newspapers and Their Readers.*

[4] Young, Letter to Colonel Kane, 22 October 1858, Beinecke Library.

[5] Young to Eldredge, 20 October 1858, Eldredge Letters, Beinecke Library.

[6] According to one account, when Pratt helped Apostles Charles C. Rich and Amasa Lyman set the young Cannon apart as President of the Pacific Mission back in 1855, Pratt had prophesied that one day Cannon would fill his place in the Quorum of the Twelve Apostles. Sauls, "The Life of George Q. Cannon," 12.

[7] Young to Cannon, 3 November 1859, Special Collections and Manuscripts, Harold B. Lee Library.

> to give vent to my feelings and hide the tremor that shook my frame. I trembled with fear and dread, and yet I was filled with joy—fear and dread when I reflected on my weakness and unworthiness and the great responsibility that rested upon one holding the apostleship, and joy to think of the goodness and favor of the Lord and the love and confidence of my brethren. Never shall I forget, I trust, the feelings and desires I then had. May the Lord give me grace and strength to magnify this Holy Priesthood and calling to the glory of His name and the salvation of His Israel, is my earnest prayer.[8]

After presiding over the European Mission, Cannon was asked to return in 1862 to serve as an unseated "senator" from Deseret in the LDS church's continuing bid for statehood. The statehood petition was denied, but the first federal anti-polygamy legislation, the Morrill Act of 1862, was enacted. Cannon returned to England the following year where he found himself sole president of the European Mission. It is here that he encountered Charles Dickens, who would later record his impressions of Cannon (though without mentioning him by name) in *The Uncommercial Traveler,* first published in 1898:

> The Mormon Agent . . . was pointed out to me. A compactly-made handsome man in black, rather short, with rich-brown hair and beard, and clear bright eyes. From his speech, I should set him down as American. Probably, a man who had "knocked about the world" pretty much. A man with a frank open manner, and unshrinking look; withal a man of great quickness. I believe he was wholly ignorant of my Uncommercial individuality, and consequently of my immense Uncommercial importance.[9]

During his stint as editor of the *Standard,* Cannon had defended the Church of Jesus Christ of Latter-day Saints, earning Dickens' observation that he was a man who had "knocked about the world"—in more ways than one. Without question, the doctrine that caused the greatest difficulty for the Mormons, and the one Cannon most often had to defend, was "the Principle"—the doctrine of plural marriage.

For many of the LDS church's political (as opposed to religious) opponents—at least some of whom were personally, if privately, comfortable with the idea of maintaining a sexual relationship with more

---

[8] Cooley, "A Brigham Young Letter to George Q. Cannon, 1859," 108n9, citing Cannon to Young, 13 December 1859, LDS Archives.

[9] Dickens, *The Uncommercial Traveler,* 225. By this time Cannon had apparently become so Americanized that Dickens did not recognize him as a fellow Englishman.

than one woman—the real issue was not polygamy but the political kingdom of God the Mormons hoped to establish on the earth to usher in Christ's second coming. One critic admitted this quite openly:

> Those of us who understand the situation were not nearly so much opposed to polygamy as we were to the political domination of the Church. We realized, however, that we could not make those who did not come actually in contact with it, understand what this political domination meant. We made use of polygamy in consequence as our great weapon of offense and to gain recruits to our standard. There was a universal detestation of polygamy, and inasmuch as the Mormons openly defended it we were given a very effective weapon with which to attack.[10]

Perhaps more than anyone else, the Mormons themselves recognized the truth of the situation:

> It has often been said that the abandonment of polygamy by the 'Mormons' would be the worst misfortune that could happen to their maligners. Nothing would be so disastrous to the . . . ambitious wirepullers and their pious and profane toadies and tools, than the abolition of the theory and practice which they pretend to be anxious to suppress. Everybody who understands the situation knows that the local plotters care nothing whatever for polygamy, except as a popular cry in their interest. What they want and all they are after is possession of the Territory, its offices and its treasury.[11]

Regardless of motive, virtually every attack on Mormonism was directly or indirectly connected with the attempt to live the old-time religion of Abraham and other Old Testament patriarchs. Predictably, Cannon had his own entanglements with this inflammatory doctrine.

In spite of his strident defense of polygamy, Cannon had remained monogamous while in California. That changed as he married a total of five additional women: Sarah Jane Jenne (in April 1858), Eliza Lamercia Tenny (1865), Martha Telle (1868), Emily Hoagland Little (1881), and Caroline Young Croxall (1884), one of the many daughters of Brigham Young. If the purpose of polygamy was to assure a large progeny, it certainly worked for Cannon. Although he had only three living children at the age of forty—the eldest a boy of ten—by 1927 he had 239 living descendants, with twenty-six deceased.[12]

---

[10] "Autobiography of Frederick T. Dubois," 29, quoted in Hansen, *Quest for Empire*, 170.

[11] *Deseret News*, 15 March 1887, quoted in Taylor, *The Kingdom or Nothing*, 381.

[12] Cannon, "Tell Us Some More About Your Funny Family," 2, 1.

Through his extraordinary church service, reinforced by familial relationships, Cannon received additional callings of significant stature in the LDS church, serving first as a secretary to Brigham Young, and later as his counselor in the First Presidency. Cannon enjoyed the distinction of having served as counselor to four presidents of the church: Brigham Young (1873–1877), John Taylor (1880–1887), Wilford Woodruff (1889–1898) and Lorenzo Snow (1898–1901). Had Snow died just a few months earlier, Cannon would have become the sixth president of the church rather than his fellow-counselor, Joseph F. Smith.[13] It is not an exaggeration to say that George Q. Cannon was the most powerful political figure in the LDS church from the time of Brigham Young's death in 1877 to the admission of Utah as the forty-fifth state in 1896. Perhaps more than anyone else, he helped move Mormonism into the American mainstream.

As a politician, Cannon was elected and re-elected five times to congress as Utah's delegate over ten years, stepping down only when denied his seat in the House after passage of the anti-polygamy Edmunds Act of 1882. During his years of service in Washington on behalf of the church, when he felt it was fitting to be diplomatic or even at times deferential, he was without peer. "His forte, in secular affairs, was statecraft," Mormon historian/apostle Orson F. Whitney observed, "and in the field of diplomacy, Utah, among all her gifted sons, has not seen his equal."[14] As an example of this diplomatic talent, note the following (successful) request to Brigham Young, inserted as part of a long postscript and written the day after the birth of his son in San Francisco, whom he described as "a young eleven pounder Cannon":

> I have thought for some time of asking your counsel about the propriety or wisdom of my youngest brother, David Henry, being appointed a mission to this country. . . . However, I would not for the world, Bro. Brigham, have him come out here should you have the slightest doubt about the wisdom or propriety of him doing so. I have never presumed to hint such a thing to him, so that if it is not wisdom, it will be the same as though it had not been mentioned or thought of.[15]

---

[13] By that time, it had become clear that the senior member of the Quorum (Council) of the Twelve Apostles was the automatic successor to a deceased church president. Cannon was immediately senior to Smith, but did not live long enough to assume the presidency.

[14] Whitney, *History of Utah*, 4:663.

[15] Cannon to Young, 30 January 1856, LDS Archives.

Throughout his life, George Q. Cannon remained absolutely true to the faith, even suffering from life on the "underground" as a polygamist on the run from government prosecution. Beginning in late January 1885, Cannon joined President John Taylor in hiding from federal marshals who hoped to make an example of all polygamists by arresting their two most important leaders. Over the next year they would move from one hiding place to another, often traveling at night and wearing a variety of disguises. This did not stop Cannon from writing articles for the *Deseret News* and other Mormon publications, nor did it keep him from occasionally addressing the Saints at well-guarded church meetings. But the toll on both him and Taylor was tremendous.

In February 1886 a $500 reward was offered for information leading to the arrest of George Q. Cannon. (Even though Cannon was a counselor to President Taylor, the reward for the aging prophet was only $300.) In an attempt to flee to the Mormon colonies in Mexico, Cannon shaved off his beard and caught a train for San Francisco. Someone recognized him and before long he was on his way back to Utah under the custody of Marshal E. A. Ireland.

During the return trip, Cannon either momentarily escaped or—as he later insisted—fell off the back of the train while trying to get a breath of fresh air. He was badly injured and was soon recaptured as he walked along the railroad tracks, dazed from his fall. If the report from the marshal was accurate, he was found in possession of a loaded pistol as well as bread and water, indicating he was not only trying to escape but had help in doing so. That he was walking along the tracks, however, suggests either he had not planned his escape route very carefully or he was too stunned from the fall to think clearly.

Charged with the misdemeanor of "u.c." (unlawful cohabitation), Cannon's bond was set at $45,000—an enormous sum in those days. Nonetheless, because he was considered much more valuable to the church than even that exorbitant amount, the decision was made that he would forfeit the bond. Samuel W. Taylor made the insightful comment that Cannon's decision to jump bail seems to belie the argument made by B. H. Roberts and others that he was too much of a law-abiding citizen to have attempted to escape from the train.[16] He and dozens of

[16] Taylor, *The Kingdom or Nothing*, 356n3.

George Q. Cannon (seated) in fall 1888 at the Utah Territorial Penitentiary during his imprisonment for unlawful cohabitation. The prisoner on the left is John Walton Price. The second man from the right is Bishop James C. Hamilton.
Courtesy, Utah State Historical Society.

other Mormon polygamists simply felt they had to obey the "higher law" of church authority over that of the American government. Finally, in September 1888, a little over a year after the death of John Taylor, the political climate seemed propitious for Cannon to plead guilty to the two counts of unlawful cohabitation. The church's most notable prisoner of conscience was fined $450 and sentenced to 175 days in the Utah Territorial Prison.[17]

The role Cannon played in the writing of the document that would eventually lead to the abandonment of polygamy by the Church of Jesus Christ of Latter-day Saints is less than clear. Some have argued that Cannon was the real author of the Manifesto of 1890, but Frank J. Cannon, who otherwise tried to downplay his father's commitment to polygamy, stated that President Wilford Woodruff "told me he had

[17] See Bitton, *George Q. Cannon: A Biography*, chapter 8. For a full study of another prominent Mormon's life in prison for unlawful cohabitation, see Larson, *Prisoner for Polygamy*.

written it himself, and it certainly appeared to me to be in his handwriting."[18] Regardless of the actual authorship, the document gave every indication that the LDS church, its property escheated and its members disenfranchised, was finally on the verge of renouncing the practice of plural marriage.

> Inasmuch as laws have been enacted by Congress forbidding plural marriages, which laws have been pronounced constitutional by the court of last resort, I hereby declare my intention to submit to those laws, and to use my influence with the members of the Church over which I preside to have them do likewise.
>
> There is nothing in my teachings to the Church or in those of my associates, during the time specified, which can be reasonably construed to inculcate or encourage polygamy; and when any Elder of the Church has used language which appeared to convey any such teaching, he has been promptly reproved. And I now publicly declare that my advice to the Latter-day Saints is to refrain from contracting any marriage forbidden by the law of the land.[19]

George Q. Cannon—and most of his fellow apostles—did not view the "manifesto" as anything other than a ploy to reduce federal pressure on the church while awaiting the second coming of Jesus Christ—an event he and most Mormons of the day believed was imminent.[20] Not only was he aware of several post-manifesto polygamous marriages, but Cannon was often the person to whom President Woodruff—who needed to maintain what today might be called "plausible deniability" in such matters—delegated the responsibility to authorize such unions. Most of these rites were performed in Mexico, with others secretly carried out in Canada as well as throughout the United States. Permission for such marriages after 1890 was not given easily, but recent scholarship demonstrates that Cannon continued to approve polygamous unions under both Presidents Woodruff and Snow.[21]

Cannon did not live to see the LDS church completely submit to gov-

---

[18] Cannon, *Under the Prophet in Utah,* 100. See also Quinn, "New Plural Marriages," 44–46.

[19] The Manifesto appears today as Official Declaration 1 toward the end of all modern LDS editions of the *Doctrine and Covenants.* For an enlightening and well researched discussion of the evolution of Woodruff's Manifesto from a "tactical retreat" to what later was viewed as a revelation from God, see Hardy, *Solemn Covenant.*

[20] For an insightful analysis of these events, see Dan Erickson's "Joseph Smith's 1891 Millennial Prophecy," 1–34; and his *As a Thief in the Night: The Mormon Quest for Millennial Deliverance.*

[21] For the most thorough treatments of the controversial issue of post-manifesto polygamy, see Van Wagoner, *Mormon Polygamy: A History*; and Carmon Hardy, *Solemn Covenant.* Of additional particular interest is Quinn, "LDS Church Authority and New Plural Marriages, 1890–1904." Scholarly treatments on the

ernment pressure, if not the will of God, through the "Second Manifesto," issued 7 April 1904 by Joseph F. Smith following his appearance at the Reed Smoot hearings in Washington, D.C. Unlike the 1890 pronouncement, this document made it painfully clear that those who failed to comply with the federal anti-polygamy laws would face excommunication:

> Inasmuch as there are numerous reports in circulation that plural marriages have been entered into contrary to the official declaration of President Woodruff, of September 26, 1890, commonly called the Manifesto, which was issued by President Woodruff and adopted by the church at its general conference, October 6, 1890, which forbade any marriages violative of the law of the land, I, Joseph F. Smith, president of the Church of Jesus Christ of Latter-day Saints, do hereby affirm and declare that no such marriages have been solemnized with the sanction, consent, or knowledge of the Church of Jesus Christ of Latter-day Saints; and I hereby announce that all such marriages are prohibited, and if any officer or member of the church shall assume to solemnize or enter into any such marriage he will be deemed in transgression against the church, and will be liable to be dealt with according to the rules and regulations thereof and excommunicated therefrom.[22]

One of George Q.'s numerous sons, Frank J. Cannon, found it convenient to remember his father as a fierce supporter of the original Manifesto and a latter-day foe of polygamy. Frank, a Utah politician and chief editorial writer for the anti-Mormon *Tribune*—and a reprobate who was eventually excommunicated—had a vested interest in selective memory and was absolute in his insistence that his father fully supported the Manifesto of 1890: "I knew from my father's personal assurance—and from his constant practice from that time to the day of his death—that he was acting in good faith."[23] On the other hand, there is considerable evidence of George Q. Cannon's complicity in the 1896 plural marriage

effects of polygamy and other factors on Utah's bid for statehood can be found in Hansen, *Quest for Empire*; Larson, *The "Americanization" of Utah for Statehood*; Lyman, *Political Deliverance*; and Gordon, *The Mormon Question*.

[22] Roberts, *Comprehensive History*, 6:401. As was later demonstrated through the Smoot hearings, President Smith had been disingenuous in his declaration that "no such marriages have been solemnized with the sanction, consent, or knowledge of the Church . . . ." Nonetheless, it was the leadership of Joseph F. Smith that finally brought an end to church-sanctioned polygamy.

[23] Cannon and O'Higgins, *Under the Prophet in Utah: The National Menace of a Political Priestcraft*, 135. As the subtitle makes clear, this book is a fierce attack on the LDS hierarchy—particularly Joseph F. Smith—that came following the death of George Q. Cannon and on the heels of the LDS church's lack of support for Frank J. Cannon's re-election as one of Utah's first senators. Nonetheless, throughout the book, Cannon shows great love and respect for his father, and seems convinced—though Carmon Hardy argues that he was hypocritical in making such an argument—that George Q. was unsupportive, if not (continued)

of his apostle son, Abraham H. Cannon, to Lilian Hamblin. It is likely (though conclusive proof is lacking) that the second counselor to President Woodruff, Joseph F. Smith, officiated at Abraham's post-Manifesto marriage, probably off the coast of California.

In spite of Frank's protests, it is apparent that his father went to his grave in 1901 with the understanding that the church had not yet fully capitulated, and that his predictions regarding the permanence of polygamy would still be fulfilled, once the current difficulties with Washington had been resolved. In this, Cannon was mistaken. Then as now, most faithful Mormons believed it was the Lord who introduced the practice of polygamy, beginning with Joseph Smith in the 1830s, and it was the Lord who rescinded it through Smith's successors. Most Latter-day Saints recognized the extenuating circumstances that prompted this change in policy: the religion could no longer contend against the monogamous traditions of the rest of Victorian America while enduring the financial ruin being imposed upon it by the federal government via the escheatment of church property provisions in the Edmunds-Tucker Bill of 1887.[24] Whatever the reason, the LDS church finally gave up the practice if not the doctrine of a fundamental principle of the gospel that Cannon and others had believed would never be rescinded.

Cannon made various arguments in defense of polygamy, but two are particularly obnoxious to today's feminist sensibilities. The first is that for whatever reason (priesthood authority was the one most often cited), women cannot enter into the highest degree of "heaven" unless they are first attached to a man. (The LDS church taught then, as now, that *neither* a man nor a woman can gain the highest degree of the Celestial Kingdom unless sealed to an eternal mate.) Still, as Capt. Howard Stansbury and many Mormons understood, "it is the doctrine of the church, that no woman can attain to celestial glory *without the husband,* nor can *he* arrive at full perfection in the next world without at least one wife: and the greater the number he is able to take with him, the higher will be his seat in the celestial paradise."[25]

The second argument, which was a particular favorite of Cannon's, was

---

completely unaware, of plural marriages solemnized after 1890. Despite Frank J. Cannon's bias, the journal of his apostle half-brother Abraham corroborates many of the details in his sensational book.)

[24] For details on this and other federal legislation directed against the Mormons, see Firmage and Mangrum, *Zion in the Courts.*

[25] Stansbury, *Exploration and Survey,* 137.

that whether because of weak, female nature or natural disinclination in the male toward monogamy, polygamy was necessary to eliminate the evils of prostitution. The fact that there was relatively little prostitution in polygamous Utah—the little that did emerge, primarily the result of non-Mormon miners and garrisoned U.S. soldiers—but a great deal in cities like San Francisco, was viewed as *prima facie* evidence in support of this position.[26]

But one need not embrace such sexist arguments for polygamy to gain some understanding of, if not sympathy for, the estimated 30,000 to 50,000 Mormon "fundamentalists" who steadfastly continue in the Principle to this very day, even though doing so has cost them their membership in the Church of Jesus Christ of Latter-day Saints. The powerful prose of George Q. Cannon, designed to appeal to the reason as well as to the emotions of his day, makes clear how difficult it was for many Saints to give up this deeply held conviction. One rank-and-file polygamist, present in the tabernacle when the Manifesto was read to the Saints for their sustaining vote during the October Conference of 1890, recorded in his journal:

> Heard the Manifesto read, issued by Pres. Woodruff; and saw the conference vote to sustain it. There were no hands raised against it, but I thot it was a very slim vote, considering the multitude assembled. My own feelings were very peculier, and I could not concicusly vote, and saw a good many others in the same way; some with tears in their eyes. A very solem feeling pervailed in the meeting.[27]

At least one general authority, historian B. H. Roberts, joined those who refused to give their sustaining vote to the Manifesto: "When the crisis came I felt heart-broken but remained silent. It seemed to me to be the awfulest moment in my life, my arm was like lead when the motion was put; I could not vote for it, and did not."[28]

As distasteful as the Manifesto was to so many of the faithful, it nonetheless helped assure the temporal salvation of the church while providing the impetus that would at long last result in Utah's statehood. In this, too, Cannon played such a critical role that his biographer, Davis

---

[26] For an overview of contemporary arguments both for and against polygamy, see Bancroft, *History of Utah*, 375–96. A surprisingly cogent contemporary argument against the points Cannon consistently raised in defense of polygamy is in Waite, *The Mormon Prophet and His Harem*, 221–43. A convenient compilation of positive anecdotes from those who practiced polygamy in the 19th century is found in Whelan, *More Than One*.

[27] Broadbent, Journal.

[28] Walker, "B. H. Roberts and the Woodruff Manifesto," 365, cited in Hardy, *Solemn Covenant*, 135.

Bitton, has called him the "Father of Utah Statehood."[29]

Few individuals in the history of America have wielded as much political power over such a long period of time as did George Q. Cannon. To be sure, much of this power was exercised behind the scenes, but for nearly thirty years, Cannon held a variety of elected positions that provided him front-door access to many of the most powerful men in Washington.

At the young age of thirty-five, Cannon was shocked to find himself elected by a wishful general assembly as one of two U.S. Senators from the projected "State of Deseret." While he and his cohort, William H. Hooper, were allowed to watch the proceedings on the floor of the House and even managed interviews with the Secretary of State, nearly every Senator, and even with President Abraham Lincoln, he soon learned that Utah's 1862 bid for statehood was doomed.

This did not stop the would-be State of Deseret from submitting annual petitions for statehood. Nor did it stop the Mormons from re-electing Cannon five times as territorial delegate to congress until the Edmunds bill disqualified him from further service. In his final speech to the House of Representatives, Cannon mustered all of his rhetorical skill, letting his colleagues know that he had been defrauded of his rights and denied his seat not by the constitutionally required two-thirds vote, but by the simple majority that had passed the Edmunds Act:

> But I ask you, you gentlemen, all of you, who say the people of Utah shall obey the law, will you who say we should comply with the law, religion or no religion, will you set us the example of smiting law down here, in what ought to be the temple of justice! Will you do this! . . . will you deny us equity, and say we shall not have it because there are allegations made against Utah Territory; because they are falsely accused of every thing that is vile, and charged with being bad men, just as the first Christians were when Nero burned them, made torches of them, and justified himself in doing so—will you, because of the alleged bad character of the people of Utah, be guilty of this great wrong![30]

Cannon's formal political career may have been over, but he continued to broker deal after deal in Washington as well as in Utah, as he and his fellow Mormons continued to work for statehood, a dream that was finally realized in 1896.[31] Reflecting on his influence upon congres-

[29] This is the title of chapter 10 in Bitton, *George Q. Cannon: A Biography.*

[30] Quoted in Ibid., 256.

sional affairs, Orson F. Whitney noted that Cannon

> had made it a point to acquaint himself with all departments and functions of the government, also with the names, personal history and constituencies of every member in both houses of the national legislature, and his retentive memory and quick recollection enabled him to give information upon those points at a moment's notice. It was no uncommon thing, when one member was asked by another some question, to hear the response: "I don't know; ask Mr. Cannon from Utah; he seems to know everybody." He was regarded by his associates as a wise statesman, and admired as one of the ablest speakers in the House. While a "silent member," as a delegate was expected to be, he wielded great influence, and on more than one occasion, when accorded cheerful permission, made his ringing eloquence felt for the good of the people whom he represented.[32]

The people of Utah entrusted to George Q. Cannon numerous high church callings and political appointments. But he gained considerable prominence as a businessman, as well. Cannon served as director of the Union Pacific Railroad and the Bullion-Beck and Champion Mining Companies; president of Utah Sugar, Utah Light and Power, and the Brigham Young Trust Companies; vice president and director of Zion's Cooperative Mercantile Institution and Zion's Saving Bank and Trust Company; and founder of his own publishing concern, George Q. Cannon and Sons, today's Deseret Book. It is not an exaggeration to assert that besides Joseph Smith and Brigham Young, George Q. Cannon was the most powerful and influential figure in nineteenth-century Mormonism.

Even though Cannon was never successful in convincing his congressional colleagues of the benefits of polygamy, his predictions concerning Mormonism as a whole have been fulfilled—perhaps not according to his timeline and certainly not to the full extent envisioned by him—but fulfilled nonetheless. Consider one of his bolder pronouncements, appearing in his *Western Standard* editorial of 15 April 1857:

> We predict, with the utmost assurance, that in that time [fifty years], it will have progressed and prospered faster than any other society or nation the world ever saw, that it will have spread over a great portion of the globe, that its principles will be believed in, and its founder honored as a prophet of God by the majority of the inhabitants of most enlightened nations, that it will be

---

[31] For specific details on Cannon's central role in winning statehood for Utah, see Lyman, *Political Deliverance.*

[32] Whitney, *History of Utah,* 4:661–62.

> as firmly established as modern Christianity is at the present time, that its representatives and ministers will be as much respected and honored as the ministers of any earthly government now are, and that many of its believers and disciples will hold some of the most important and distinguished positions in the governments of the world. At the expiration of that period, we, if we live and if not, our children, can decide who was the true prophet.

As prescient as much of the above may be with respect to the scope and influence of the Church of Jesus Christ of Latter-day Saints in the world today, Cannon should not be judged for the accuracy of his predictions. Though repeatedly sustained by the faithful as such, he never claimed to be a prophet. And while he is considered a great leader by modern Mormons (though most are regrettably unacquainted with the majesty of his early writings), he deserves special credit as one of the most humorous, irascible, and brilliant newspaper editors of his day. This is all the more remarkable since the largely self-taught Cannon dropped out of formal schooling at the age of thirteen. According to family legend, when his parents objected to this decision, "the determined boy replied that learning was not a matter of going to school; it was the result of an inner hunger."[33] Clearly, George Q. Cannon was a very hungry young man.

Where, one might ask, are the George Q. Cannons of today? To be sure, men and women of such polemical persuasion are no longer as needed as they were in his age. Gross invective was the order of the day in the 1850s, even in the "established" press, and this warranted—if not demanded—a like response by this Defender of the Faith. Today, only the fringe elements of anti-Mormon sentiment are as reckless and indiscreet as their literary brothers of Cannon's time, often launching their attacks from the safe anonymity of the internet.

To be sure, there are still objections to Mormonism from numerous fronts. But those who would attack or criticize the Church of Jesus Christ of Latter-day Saints today are usually more subtle, preferring to file lawsuits or write books and articles carrying the appearance of scholarly objectivity. For its part, the LDS church generally responds in kind, relying on a cadre of attorneys and faithful scholars to confront hostility with gentility.

Perhaps the biggest contrast between Cannon's day and our own is the advent of the public relations industry, where the media is managed,

[33] Evans and Cannon, eds., *Cannon Family Historical Treasury*, 86.

George Q. Cannon in his prime, photographed by Charles Roscoe Savage. Courtesy, Utah State Historical Society.

rather than attacked.[34] The modern LDS church owns newspaper, television, radio, and other media outlets, and its leaders have become increasingly adroit at presenting its image, capitalizing on appearances on "Sixty Minutes" and "Larry King Live" to downplay the differences between Mormonism and orthodox Christianity, assuring the world that the Mormons are no longer—if indeed they ever were—a threat.

The Church of Jesus Christ of Latter-day Saints has become a world presence—just as Cannon predicted—and enjoys respect, if not admiration, from many quarters. Though its American members tend to be politically conservative and overwhelmingly Republican, they no longer vote in a bloc, except in the case of an occasional "moral" issue. In this, today's church has clearly distanced itself from the ideas of Brigham Young in 1871: "I would say to the political world, if they were before me, that the opposition they are so anxious to promote contains the seeds of the

[34] For insight into the church's handling of the media, see Lythgoe, "Marketing the Mormon Image," 15–20.

destruction of the government that we live in. This is the plant or tree from which schism springs; and every government lays the foundation of its own downfall when it permits what are called democratic elections."[35]

In his bid for unity, President Young was benignly autocratic, as evidenced by the following offhand remark he recorded in his diary for 14 July 1857: "Decided who Should be candidate for representing G. S. L. next Session in the Legislature." Fifteen years later, notwithstanding the fact that opposition parties had become established in the territory, Young sent forth the following instructions to all bishops and stake presidents in support of his beloved friend, George Q. Cannon: "Be awake and prepared for the Coming Election, vote for Ticket with Geo. Q. Cannon Delegate to Congress with all your strength and *cast not a single vote for any other Candidate* and use every exertion to poll a strong unanimous vote."[36]

Because Mormons rarely vote in organized blocs today, the LDS church is seldom perceived as a major political threat, despite its wealth and influence. Today's church can afford to take the high road, ignoring rather than grappling with its opposition. True to the vision of Apostle Bruce R. McConkie, the caravan rolls on, more or less oblivious to the dogs snapping at the heels of the faithful.

For all of these reasons, there is probably no need for polemicists such as the young George Q. Cannon in today's Church of Jesus Christ of Latter-day Saints. Nor is he likely to be remembered by many for his early years as the editor of the *Western Standard,* overshadowed as they were by his subsequent career as a business executive, political catalyst and church leader. But Cannon's fiery editorials of 1856 and 1857 are worthy of historical memory. If nothing else, we must acknowledge the value of good writing and sound reasoning. Cannon was not without error, but the worst of his writing was infinitely superior to much of what passes for reasoned argument today. Perhaps just as importantly, he wrote with a flair and faithful sense of purpose rarely encountered at the beginning of the twenty-first century. The power and mastery of the early writings of George Q. Cannon reveal that something quite extraordinary was lost with the passing of the editor of the *Western Standard* and the fiesty little newspaper through which he took on his world.

---

35 Young, "The One-Man Power . . . Priesthood and Government, etc.," 8 April 1871, *Journal of Discourses,* 14:93.

36 Cooley, ed., *Diary of Brigham Young, 1857,* 44, 45n49.

Appendix

THE NEWSPAPERS AND THEIR EDITORS

Over the twenty months that George Q. Cannon edited the *Western Standard,* he referred to no fewer than two dozen newspapers, most of them based in California, in his editorials. This study has focused on the ten central and northern California newspapers and one from Los Angeles that Cannon most often engaged in editorial combat. This appendix provides historical context for each of these newspapers and their editors and outlines their professed editorial policies.

ALTA CALIFORNIA

The *Alta California* was the Golden State's first daily newspaper and the one that probably best reflected the prevailing values of the day. The founding editors—all Democrats—were Edward Gilbert (the former commander of the town garrison in 1847), former lieutenant George C. Hubbard of the New York Volunteers, and Samuel Brannan protegé, Edward C. Kemble. In their "salutatory" in the maiden issue of 4 January 1849, these San Franciscans set themselves up as a force to help bring California from the chaos associated with the gold rush to a society of law, liberty, justice, humanity, and education:

> This press will be independent of all parties, cliques and persons. The cause which it will assert is the cause of California . . . In doing this, it is believed that this paper will not be controlled by unworthy or sordid motives, that it will not be swerved by sectional or local jealousies, and that, however much it may err in judgment, it will never degrade itself by becoming a channel through which prejudice or envy may vent its personalities or sarcasms.

Furthermore, the editors promised that while they would not be "sparing of rebuke where we think it merited . . . attacks upon private character or conduct" would not be tolerated.

Edward Gilbert and Edward C. Kemble. *Courtesy, California History Section, California State Library.*

As noted in chapter 1, one of Parley P. Pratt's biographers erroneously claimed the *Alta California* had given Pratt "a favorable write-up." In truth, the *Alta California* was critical of Mormonism from the outset but sympathetic to the members of the new church who had endured so many hardships. Doubtless this early compassion toward the Mormon people stemmed largely from Edward C. Kemble's early association with Sam Brannan, who later counseled against the founding of the *Alta,* believing the venture would be impractical. Kemble had worked for Brannan—setting type for two Mormon newspaper, *The Prophet* and *The Messenger,* which Brannan had edited in New York along with Joseph Smith's brother, William, and Parley and Orson Pratt. Though apparently never a Mormon, Kemble came to San Francisco with Brannan on the *Brooklyn* in 1846, where he edited and eventually owned the *California Star* and later was publisher and editor of both the *Star and Californian* (formed by the marriage of California's first two newspapers) and the *Alta California.* Kemble came to be regarded as one of the most prominent newspapermen in early California and was later associated with the *Placer Times* and the *Sacramento Daily Union.*[1]

After the departure of Kemble for New York in 1854, the editor's job eventually fell to the much less tolerant E. Gould Buffum, another veteran of the New York Volunteers and author of the popular *Six Months in the Gold Mines,* "one of the earliest and most vivid accounts of the excitement, the hardships, and the rewards of placer mining."[2] As the chief editor from April 1856 through November 1857, Buffam's *Alta* editorials against the Mormons

[1] For more on Kemble and the early history of California newspapers, see his lengthy article, "The History of California Newspapers," *Sacramento Daily Union,* 25 December 1858; the foreword to Helen Harding Bretnor's reprinting, *A History of California Newspapers, 1846–1858*; Fred Blackburn Rogers' foreword to the facsimile reprint of *The California Star;* and his edition of *A Kemble Reader: Stories of California, 1846–1848.*

[2] Buffum, *Six Months in the Gold Mines,* Introduction, University Microfilms reprint edition.

became even more strident. Given its fierce opposition to the religion, it is ironic that Mormon lobbyists later targeted the *Alta California,* along with other major national newspapers, as a potential recipient of "financial incentives" as a reward for helping Utah achieve statehood. In 1887 Hiram B. Clawson, the husband of several of Brigham Young's daughters and one of Utah's most active thespians and businessmen, apparently suggested that the *Alta's* support could be had for $2,500 down with another $10,000 "to remain quiet" once statehood was a reality. Judging from the tenor of the *Alta's* subsequent editorials, it appears such an offer was either never made or was rejected.[3]

DAILY CALIFORNIA AMERICAN

John Rollin Ridge.
Courtesy, California History Section, California State Library.

The successor of the Sacramento *State Tribune* and the precursor to today's very prominent Sacramento *Bee,* the *Daily California American* was first published on 2 June 1856. Its initial owners were Samuel J. May, John Rollin Ridge, and James Allen, who also served as its chief editor until January of the following year, when Ridge took over. Never financially successful (it was said to have lost more than $15,000 during its first six months of operation), the paper soon folded, in February of 1857.

A native of Boston, May had earlier been a part-owner of the *Sacramento Democrat State Journal,* where he shared in writing the editorials before moving on to the *Tribune.* Following the demise of the *Daily California American,* May and Ridge became editors of the *Sacramento Bee.* Ridge was born in Georgia—his father a Cherokee chief who, together with his grandfather, was killed in a tribal quarrel. Ridge began his newspaper career as the editor of the Marysville *California Express* in 1851. After succeeding Allen as the chief editor of the *Daily California American,* Ridge went on to edit another Marysville paper, the *National Democrat.*

James Allen, a Pennsylvanian, began with the Marysville *Herald* in 1850 before moving on to the *State Tribune* in 1855. After his time with the *California American,* Allen owned and edited several other papers, including the Marysville *News* and the Marysville *National Democrat.* Allen served as Marysville's mayor

---

[3] See Lyman, *Political Deliverance,* 80.

and was appointed to the position of California State Printer. He also edited the North San Juan *Hydraulic Press* and at the time of his death in 1863, he was the editor of the Virginia City *Nevada Washoe Times.*[4] As was customary for independent newspapers of the day, the owners of the *American* prided themselves in remaining free from political or religious influences. In their lead editorial of 22 November 1856, they proclaimed:

> The incalculable benefit of a purely conducted public press ought to be evident to all good citizens. It is the only present safeguard of their rights. Public sentiment should speak through it in tones of thunder. It should have a voice that would make every hollow-hearted knave in power, or attendant upon power, tremble to the very center of his craven soul. Such beings should be made to feel that they are vulnerable, that they are responsible to the people, and that public opinion will not tolerate them.
>
> Let honest men, then, come forward, and lending their influence and their means to uphold the dignity of a free press, say to its conductors, "Go on, and fear not; we are with you, and *vox populi vox dei,* forever!"

Daily Evening Bulletin

The stormy history of San Francisco's *Daily Evening Bulletin* is of particular interest, for it illustrates the very real dangers controversial newspaper editors of the day often faced. The paper was started on 8 October 1855, by C. O. Gerberding and Company, with James King, of William—a member of the first vigilance committee in 1851—as editor. Gerberding, a German, began his career as a newspaperman with the New York *Courier and Enquirer;* he purchased outstanding shares of the *Bulletin* in January 1858, selling that interest shortly after to James W. Simonton. Simonton, who had earlier served as the Utah correspondent to the *New York Times*—a paper he helped found—came to the *Bulletin* with considerable previous experience with the Mormons. The other original partner, Abel Whitton of Maine, started with the San Francisco *Legal Intelligencer* and went on to publish the San Francisco *Christian Recorder.*

In James King's salutatory, he "announced that he had been driven into the experiment of publishing, and that 'no one could be more fully sensible of the folly of a newspaper enterprise.'"[5] He was referring to the high expense-to-profit ratio of newspapers in that day, but his statement came to be prophetic in ways he had surely not imagined. King's brief and tragic story, the end of

[4] [Kemble], "The History of California Newspapers," *Sacramento Daily Union,* 25 December 1858, 7 and Bretnor, ed., *A History of California Newspapers,* 361–62, 372, 320.

[5] Young, *Journalism in California,* 15.

Thomas S. King.
Courtesy, California History Section, California State Library.

which sparked the Second Vigilance Committee of 1856, is told in Chapter Two.

Following James King's relatively short stint as editor of the *Bulletin,* he was followed by his brother, Thomas S. King, who was primarily responsible for the foment of increasingly bitter denunciations of Mormonism with which Cannon so forcefully disagreed. Though he responded to only a portion of the attacks published by the *Bulletin,* Cannon probably devoted more energy to fighting Thomas King than any other editor of the day.

During the Utah War of 1857–1858, the *Bulletin* printed more first-hand coverage of the conflict than any other American newspaper except the *Times* and the *Tribune* of New York. Thomas King retired from the *Bulletin* four years after the assassination of his brother and died in Buffalo, New York, in 1911.[6]

DAILY HERALD

Launched in June 1850 with Edmund Randolph and John Nugent as editors, the San Francisco *Daily Herald* was successful from the outset, particularly once it had more or less assured itself as the exclusive advertiser for many of the city's merchants including—as Cannon sarcastically noted—purveyors of questionable nostrums. It suffered severe financial reversals when its editor, John Nugent, lashed out against the popular Vigilance Committee.

According to Kemble, Nugent, who became the paper's sole proprietor by buying out his attorney partner, was "a bold, caustic writer, and a bitter and relentless enemy (who) rushed with all his soul into the political quarrels of the time, and made himself a reputation at once." The paper employed the notorious filibuster, William Walker, and with its strongly Southern sympathies became "noted for its partisan [Democrat] zeal in behalf of its friends, and its malignant bitterness towards its enemies."

Nugent was involved in two duels with members of the City Council, Alderman Cotter and Thomas Hayes. Although wounded both times with compound fractures first to his leg and later to his arm, Nugent fully recovered

[6] Bretnor, ed. *A History of California Newspapers,* 344, 378, 354.

John Nugent.
Courtesy, California History Section, California State Library.

but gave up editing the *Herald* after the vigilante movement subsided. He continued to lend his name to the newspaper, which he brought into the camp of the Democratic party. Nugent left the newspaper business and became the United States Commissioner to the Fraser River.

Irish journalist Mattias Gibert Upton, who began his career with the New York *Herald,* then edited the paper until moving on to the *Alta* where he became the principal writer and editor. Upton was an editorial writer for the San Francisco *Bulletin* in 1872 or 1873, remaining with that paper until the end of his career.[7]

Democratic State Journal

The *Journal* was the first newspaper in the state set up specifically to advance the political agenda of the Democratic administration. It began publication in Sacramento in February 1852 and ceased publication, after a series of changes in ownership, in July 1857 when it was sold under attachment to its printers. A primary reason for the *Journal's* demise was that it, like the *Daily Herald,* took the unpopular position of opposing the Second Vigilance Committee.

One of its original publishers was Vincent E. Geiger (another editor who came to blows with a rival), who went on to become the Indian agent at the Nome Lackee Reservation until he was censured in 1861 for his indenture of Indians. He died in Valparaiso, Chile, in 1869, after he allegedly "killed a man at Red Bluff, and has since been a fugitive from justice." Although he did not pass through Salt Lake City and expressed virtually no opinions of the Mormons at the time, Geiger kept the first section of one of the earliest and best overland journals.[8]

The other original owner was Benjamin Franklin Washington, who left the paper to become the editor-in-chief of the San Francisco *Daily Times and Transcript* in 1854. While the paper went through a succession of owners, in 1856 its pub-

[7] [Kemble], "The History of California Newspapers," *Sacramento Daily Union,* 25 December 1858, 3; Bancroft, *History of California,* 6:661, and Bretnor, ed., *A History of California Newspapers,* 366, 385–86

[8] Potter, ed., *Trail to California: The Overland Journal of Vincent Geiger and Wakeman Bryarly.*

Benjamin Barnard Redding.
Courtesy, California History Section, California State Library.

lishers were Benjamin Barnard Redding and Daniel J. Thomas, with John White as chief editor. Redding went on to become the mayor of Sacramento, state printer, and California's secretary of state. White had been the editor and proprietor of the Sonora *Herald,* editor of the Stockton *San Joaquin Republican,* and one of the publishers of the Stockton *Times,* the pioneer journal of the San Joaquin Valley.[9]

Golden Era

The *Golden Era* commenced publication in San Francisco on 19 December 1852, edited and published by J. MacDonough Foard and Rollin M. Daggett. Its mission, as announced in virtually every issue, was to serve the people as "A Weekly California Journal of Literature, History, News, Science and General Information: Devoted to the Interests of the State, and the Instruction and Amusement of its People." It also claimed part of its *raison d'être* was "to suppress vice [and] to elevate the standard of morality." Given the national moral standards of 1856, this inevitably meant a declaration of war on the Mormon principle of polygamy. Although apparently independent of any religious or political affiliation, the *Golden Era,* which became the leading California weekly of its day, was one of the most vociferous critics of the *Western Standard.*

Ironically, the *Golden Era* was quick to agree with the *Chronicle* in "deprecating the almost entire want of courtesy and fellowship governing the actions of the members of the press towards each other in this city." Clearly seeing themselves as being above the fray, the editor-owners of the *Golden Era* rather sanctimoniously noted the following:

> For more than three years past, the mutual cut-throat policy has been the only one recognized in the editorials as well as the business conduct of the newspapers in this city, and such a thing as unanimity or harmony of sentiment has been almost unknown in their management. They have not only degraded themselves in the eyes of the public by securing patronage through

[9] [Kemble], "The History of California Newspapers," *Sacramento Daily Union,* 25 December 1858, 7; and Bretnor, ed., *A History of California Newspapers,* 343, 389, 371, 390.

Rollin M. Daggett.
Courtesy, California History Section, California State Library.

> illegitimate means, but have attempted to enhance their individual popularity by proving their neighbors unworthy of confidence. The result of this has been a loss of influence to the press, and of all respect for its conductors. They have harped upon each other's dishonesty until the public have learned to believe them. This has been carried to a shameful extent, and not only the press but the people have been sufferers by it.[10]

Foard was an important figure in California literary journals, beginning his career at age twenty-one with the *Golden Era.* After 1860 he was associated with G. B. Densmore in publishing the *Golden City*; he also wrote for *Call* and the Sacramento *Transcript* and was associated with numerous San Francisco newspapers until his death in 1892. His partner, Rollin Daggett, was even younger—only nineteen—when these two young men launched the *Golden Era.* Daggett went on to edit the Virginia City *Territorial Enterprise* and became active in Nevada politics. He died at the age of seventy-one after serving as U.S. Minister to Hawaii.[11]

Mountain Democrat

Of all the newspapers cited in this study, the *Mountain Democrat* is the sole survivor. As such, it is California's oldest newspaper still in publication. Originally founded as the *El Dorado News* in June 1851, Thomas Springer moved the paper from Coloma to Placerville in December, renaming it the *El Dorado Republican.* Springer sold the business in 1854 (along with its subscription list and press) to Daniel Webster Gelwicks and William A. January, who gave the paper its present name to reflect their preference for the pro-slavery orientation of the Democratic Party of that day.[12]

In its inaugural edition of 25 January 1854, the editors expressed their willingness to take on anyone with whom they disagreed—in that case, the editors of two rival Democratic newspapers, the *Argus* and the *Advocate.* Predictably, the *Mountain Democrat* fearlessly took on all comers and was more than eager to attack the historically anti-slavery, pro-polygamy Mormons.

[10] "The San Francisco Press," *Golden Era,* 1/ June 1856.

[11] Bretnor, ed., *A History of California Newspapers,* 341, 334.

Daniel Webster Gelwicks.
Courtesy, California History Section, California State Library.

Gelwicks began his support for the Democratic party through the *Coloma Miners' Advocate,* which he published and edited beginning in 1852, and the Coloma *Empire County Argus* before moving on to the *Mountain Democrat.*[13]

THE PACIFIC

"A weekly journal devoted to religion, education and useful intelligence," *The Pacific* first appeared in August 1851 in San Francisco and was apparently still in publication as late as 1928. As an organ of the Congregationalists, *The Pacific* had clergymen from both the Congregational and Presbyterian churches contributing regularly to its pages and was later recognized as "the oldest and most prosperous religious paper on the coast."[14] Although never as influential as some of its competitors, the *Pacific* was the largest religious newspapers in California, with a subscription list of four thousand in 1856, two-thirds of whom were reported by the staff as being outside its denominational constituency.[15] The motto "First Pure, Then Peaceable—without Partiality and without Hypocrisy" appeared prominently on its masthead. Perhaps it is because of its strong denominational affiliations that the primary editor of the paper, Isaac H. Brayton, devoted so much space to condemning the Mormons.

SPIRIT OF THE AGE

Volume 1, number 1 of Sacramento's Spirit of the Age, appeared on 6 December 1855, three months before the advent of the Western Standard. ceasing publication in August 1856 (though Kemble recalls it as continuing through early 1857). In the lead editorial in its first issue, the editors, J. A. Mitchell and George Holbrook Baker, made the typical claim of fierce inde-

[12] Raffety, "Mountain Democrat Sole Gold Rush Survivor." Gelwicks was so much against the abolitionists that he is quoted elsewhere on the paper's current web site as referring to President Lincoln in 1858 as an "unadulterated nigger worshiper." Little wonder that he disliked the Mormons, whose perceived early pro-abolitionist sentiments were a primary cause of their expulsion from Missouri.

[13] Bretnor, ed., *A History of California Newspapers,* 343–44.

[14] [Kemble,] "The History of California Newspapers," *Sacramento Daily Union,* 25 December, 1858, 6.

[15] Norton, "'Like a Thousand Preachers Flying,'" 197.

pendence: "Our motto is Independent in every thing, Neutral in nothing. We have no friends to reward, no enemies to punish; but without respect of persons or things we shall pitch into all who may deserve without regard to influence, patronage or power they may wield." Indeed, the editors promised solemnly that it would be their "pride to fire away on the public and administer such rebuke, criticism or ridicule, as shall tend to exalt virtue and bring down vice. . . ."

In making this claim, the editors were only too aware that this was precisely what most newspapers of the time advocated, but they truly saw their paper as something different. "We are aware there are news papers (a most proper name) that contain nothing but the stereotyped opinions and news of the day; whose opinions are bought and paid for at so much a square . . . [but] We belong to no man, party, sect or clique and none belong to us." The editors saw themselves as truly "of the people" and even promised to distribute issues of their paper free to anyone who could not afford the weekly subscription price of twenty-five cents.

George H. Baker had trained as an artist in New York before coming to California in 1849 via Mexico. He engaged in a variety of enterprises and was active as a lithographer as well as a journalist. In addition to the *Spirit of the Age*, Baker edited the Folsom *Granite Journal* and possibly the Granite Hill *Miners' Exposé*.[16]

Los Angeles Star

Founded in 1851 as the first newspaper in southern California, the Los Angeles *Star* functioned as a mouthpiece for the Democratic party that dominated local politics. Scots-Irish forty-niner Henry Hamilton brought *The Star* in 1856 from William Allen Wallace, who went on to write for the *Alta California* as its southern California correspondent, Yo Mismo. As Democrats, both men were generally sympathetic to the Mormons, whom correspondent C. W. W. (probably *Western Standard* contributor Charles Wesley Wandell) called "good and useful citizens," although as early as 1852 the paper argued "they should be made to respect and conform" to American laws. *The Star* considered the Mormon settlement at San Bernardino "an ornament to the state" and approvingly noted Assemblyman Jefferson Hunt's proposal to create a new state called "Columbia" from California's southern counties.

Hamilton, long-time editor of the Calaveras *Journal*, printed many of the early writings of Ina Donna Coolbrith, the niece of Joseph Smith who later became California's poet laureate. As a member of the pro-southern "chivalry"

[16] Bretnor, ed., *A History of California Newspapers*, 333.

wing of the Democratic party, he worked so tirelessly to promote the candidacy of James Buchanan that a competitor, *El Clamor Público,* nominated the racist editor as ambassador to Mozambique. Ironically, during the succession crisis of 1860 Hamilton advocated creating an independent nation on the West Coast, but in 1857 Utah's defiance of the federal government terminated the paper's friendly relations with the Mormons. As the first journal to report the Mountain Meadows massacre, *The Star* called on the government to "strangle the monster" responsible for the crime.[17] In a typically ambiguous threat, Brigham Young told San Bernardino Stake President William Cox to warn *The Star's* editor that "unless he ceases publishing such infernal lies about Utah and her people, his lies may to his utter astonishment, become truths."[18] Hamilton escaped Mormon vengeance, but his rabid support of the Confederacy during the Civil War led to his brief imprisonment at Alcatraz. He sold *The Star* in 1873 and it ceased publication in 1879. Hamilton went on to pioneer the citrus industry in the San Gabriel Valley, where he died in 1891.[19]

Weekly Chronicle

The weekly edition of the *California Chronicle,* launched in November 1853, enjoyed a fairly short run of four years, beginning in December 1854, but it enjoyed the largest circulation in the state. This San Francisco newspaper was originally edited and published by Frank Soulé, who had previously been associated with the *Alta.* One curious fact about this newspaper is that Soulé rarely got the date right. Well into 1857, the masthead continued to show a date of 1856. Moreover, many of the issues, including those containing several of the editorials and articles quoted herein, were dated one week late.

Frank Soulé. *Courtesy, California History Section, California State Library.*

During the excitement following the assassination of James King, of William (which Soulé first characterized as a justifiable homicide rather than

[17] Rice, *The Los Angeles Star,* 48, 96–97, 103, 158, 193; and Robinson, "A California Copperhead: Henry Hamilton and the Los Angeles *Star,*" 40, 42.

[18] Young to Cox, 4 December 1857, LDS Archives.

[19] Robinson, "A California Copperhead," 44, 50.

murder), Soulé originally opposed the reorganization of the Vigilance Committee. Immediately, advertising contracts were cancelled and the following day, Soulé reversed course, singing the praises of the vigilantes.

By summer 1857, the paper had become an organ of the Republican party and Soulé withdrew as editor, turning that responsibility over to J. H. Purdy and others. From September to the end of that year, the lead articles were all written by E. C. Kemble. By the beginning of the following year, he had resigned to become editor of the Sacramento *Union*. The *Chronicle* folded in spring 1858.[20]

Of some interest to those who would understand the professed editorial policies of the *Weekly Chronicle* is a column in which the editor responded to a reader who wanted the newspaper to criticize governmental officials for alleged corruption more vigorously. He summarized the paper's position as follows: "Or in the case of official misconduct, or of abandoned characters running for office, we shall, *if the proofs thereof are furnished us*, make such use of the facts as the good of the community may require; *reserving the right in all cases where the facts are not within our own personal knowledge of divulging our authority when called upon*" [emphasis added].[21] It remains to the reader to determine how well this newspaper, or any of the other papers in this study, successfully withheld judgement about the Mormons until all the facts were firmly established.

Soulé was an influential figure in California politics and journalism. He got his first break as a journalist when he was named as the editor of the *Alta California* from October 1850 until May of the following year while Kemble was back East. Today he is best known as the primary author, with John H. Gihon and James Nisbet, of *Annals of San Francisco, Containing a Summary of the History of the First Discovery, Settlement, Progress and Present Condition of California*, published in 1855.[22]

---

[20] [Kemble,] "The History of California Newspapers," *Sacramento Daily Union*, 25 December 1858, 6.

[21] "What Some People Expect Editors to Do," *Weekly Chronicle*, 4 July 1857, 6.

[22] Bretnor, ed., *A History of California Newspapers*, 380.

Bibliography

This bibliography is confined to those works mentioned in the notes and omits numerous secondary sources consulted but not cited.

Books

Allen, James B. and Glen M. Leonard. *The Story of the Latter-day Saints.* S.L.C: Deseret Book Co., 1976.

Anderson, Benedict. *Imagined Communities: Reflections on the Origin and Spread of Nationalism.* London and N.Y: Verso, 1981, 1993.

Anderson, C. LeRoy. *Joseph Morris and the Saga of the Morrisites.* Logan, Utah: Utah State Univ. Press, 1988.

Anderson, Nels. *Desert Saints: the Mormon Frontier in Utah.* Chicago: The Univ. of Chicago Press, 1942.

Andrus, Hyrum L. *Joseph Smith and World Government.* S.L.C: Deseret Book Co., 1958.

Arrington, Leonard J. *Brigham Young: American Moses.* N. Y.: Alfred A. Knopf, Inc., 1985.

_________. "Centrifugal Tendencies in Mormon History." In *To the Glory of God: Mormon Essays on Great Issues,* Eds. Truman G. Madsen and Charles D. Tate, S.L.C: Deseret Book Co., 1972.

_________. *Great Basin Kingdom: An Economic History of the Latter-day Saints, 1830–1900.*
Cambridge: Harvard Univ. Press, 1958. Reprinted, S.L.C: Univ. of Utah Press, 1993.

___________, and Davis Bitton. *The Mormon Experience: A History of the Latter-day Saints.* N.Y: Alfred A. Knopf, 1979.

___________, Feramorz Y. Fox and Dean L. May. *Building the City of God: Community and Cooperation Among the Mormons.* S.L.C: Deseret Book Co., 1976.

Avery, Valeen Tippetts. *From Mission to Madness: Last Son of the Mormon Prophet.* Urbana and Chicago: Univ. of Ill. Press, 1998.

Backus, Anna Jean. *Mountain Meadows Witness: The Life and Times of Bishop Philip Klingensmith.* Spokane, Wash: The Arthur H. Clark Co., 1995.

Bagley, Will. *Blood of the Prophets: Brigham Young and the Massacre at Mountain Meadows.* Norman, Univ. of Okla. Press, 2002.

___________, ed. *Scoundrel's Tale: The Samuel Brannan Papers.* Spokane, Wash: The Arthur H. Clark Co., 1999.

Bailey, Paul. *Holy Smoke: A Dissertation on the Utah War.* L.A: Westernlore Books, 1978.

________. *Jacob Hamblin, Buckskin Apostle.* S.L.C: Publishers Press, 1948.

________. *Sam Brannan and the California Mormons.* L.A: Westernlore Press, 1953.

Ball, Durwood. *Army Regulars on the Western Frontier, 1848–1861.* Norman: Univ. of Okla. Press, 2001.

Bancroft, Hubert Howe. *History of California.* 7 vols. S.F: History Company, 1886. Reprinted, Santa Barbara: Wallace Hebbard, 1963.

________. *History of Utah, 1540–1886.* S.F: The History Company, 1889.

________. *Popular Tribunals.* 2 vols. S.F: History Company, 1887. Reprinted, N.Y: Arno Press, n.d.

Bartholomew, Rebecca and Leonard J. Arrington. *Rescue of the 1856 Handcart Companies.* Provo, Utah: Charles Redd Center for Western Studies, 1992.

Batchelor, Mary, Marianne Watson and Anne Wilde. *Voices in Harmony: Contemporary Women Celebrate Plural Marriage.* S.L.C: Principle Voices, 2000.

Beadle, J. H. *Life in Utah; or, the Mysteries and Crimes of Mormonism, Being an Exposé of the Secret Rites and Ceremonies of the Latter-day Saints, with a Full and Authentic History of Polygamy and the Mormon Sect from its Origin to the Present Time.* Philadelphia: National Publishing Co., 1870.

Belisle, Orvilla. *Mormonism Unveiled; or, A History of Mormonism from Its Rise to the Present Time.* London: Charles Clarke, 1855.

Bell, Orvilla. *Boadicea; The Mormon Wife. Life Scenes in Utah.* Baltimore: Arthur R. Orton, 1855.

Bennett, John C. *The History of the Saints; or, An Exposé of Joe Smith and Mormonism.* Boston: Leland and Whiting, 1842. Reprinted, Urbana and Chicago: Univ. of Ill. Press, 2000.

Bigler, David L. *Forgotten Kingdom: The Mormon Theocracy in the American West, 1847–1896.* Spokane, Wash: The Arthur H. Clark Co., 1998.

__________, ed. *A Winter with the Mormons: The 1852 Letters of Jotham Goodell.* S.L.C: Tanner Trust Fund, 2001.

__________ and Will Bagley, eds. *Army of Israel: Mormon Battalion Narratives.* Spokane, Wash: The Arthur H. Clark Co., 2000.

Bitton, Davis. *George Q. Cannon: A Biography.* S.L.C: Deseret Book Co., 1999.

________. *The Ritualization of Mormon History and Other Essays.* Urbana and Chicago: Univ. of Ill. Press, 1994.

Bowles, Samuel. *Across the Continent: A Summer's Journey to the Rocky Mountains, the Mormons, and the Pacific States, with Speaker Colfax.* Springfield, Mass: Samuel Bowles & Co., 1866.

Brodie, Fawn M. *No Man Knows My History: The Life Story of Joseph Smith, the Mormon Prophet.* N.Y: Alfred A. Knopf, 1945.

Brooks, Juanita. *John Doyle Lee: Zealot, Pioneer Builder, Scapegoat.* Glendale, Calif.: The Arthur H. Clark Co., 1961.

________. *The Mountain Meadows Massacre.* Stanford, Calif.: Stanford Univ. Press, 1950. Revised Edition, Norman: Univ. of Okla. Press, 1962.

__________, ed. *On the Mormon Frontier: The Diary of Hosea Stout, 1844–1861.* S.L.C: Univ. of Utah Press, 1964. Reprint Edition, 1982.

Brown, Richard Maxwell. *Strain of Violence: Historical Studies of American Violence and Vigilantism.* N.Y: Oxford Univ. Press, 1975.

Browne, Charles F. *The Complete Works of Charles F. Browne, Better Known as "Artemus Ward."* London: Chatto and Windus, 1887.

Buerger, David John. *The Mysteries of Godliness: A History of Mormon Temple Worship.* S. F.: Smith Research Assoc., 1994.

Buffum, Edward Gould. *Six Months in the Gold Mines.* Philadelphia: Lea and Blanchard, 1850. Reprinted Ann Arbor: Univ. Microfilms, Inc., 1966.

Bunker, Gary L. and Davis Bitton. *The Mormon Graphic Image, 1834–1914: Cartoons, Caricatures, and Illustrations.* S.L.C: Univ. of Utah Press, 1983.

Burton, Richard F. *The City of the Saints And Across the Rocky Mountains to California.* London: Longman, Green, Longman, and Roberts, 1862.

California Star, The. Berkeley, Calif: Howell-North Books, 1965.

Campbell, Eugene E. *Establishing Zion: The Mormon Church in the American West, 1847–1869.* S.L.C: Signature Books, 1988.

Cannon, Elder George Q. *Writings from the Western Standard, Published in San Francisco, California.* Liverpool: George Q. Cannon, 1864.

Cannon, Frank J. and Harvey J. O'Higgins. *Under the Prophet in Utah: The National Menace of a Political Priestcraft.* Boston: C. M. Clark Publishing Co., 1911.

Cannon, George Q. *The History of the Mormons: Their Persecutions and Travels.* N.p: (c. 1890).

Cannon, George Q. *My First Mission.* (See Nibley, Preston. *Three Mormon Classics.*)

Carvalho, Solomon Nunes. *Incidents of Travel and Adventure in the Far West with Col. Frémont's Last Expedition.* N.Y: Derby & Jackson, 1857. Reprinted, Philadelphia: The Jewish Publication Society of America, 1954.

Chandless, William. *A Visit to Salt Lake; Being a Journey Across the Plains and a Residence in the Mormon Settlements at Utah.* London: Smith, Elder and Co., 1857. Reprinted N.Y: AMS Press, 1971.

Clark, Robert A., ed. *The Mountain Meadows Massacre: A Special Report by Brevet Major James Henry Carleton.* Spokane: The Arthur H. Clark Company, 1995.

Cleland, Robert Glass and Juanita Brooks, eds. *A Mormon Chronicle: The Diaries of John D. Lee, 1848–1876.* San Marino, Calif.: The Huntington Library, 1955.

Compton, Todd. *In Sacred Loneliness: The Plural Wives of Joseph Smith.* S.L.C: Signature Books, 1997.

Cooley, Everett L., ed. *Diary of Brigham Young, 1857.* S.L.C: Tanner Trust Fund, Univ. of Utah Library, 1980.

Corbett, Pearson H. *Jacob Hamblin, the Peacemaker.* S.L.C: Deseret Book Co., 1952.

Corrill, John. *A Brief History of the Church of Jesus Christ of Latter-day Saints, (Commonly Called Mormons;) Including an Account of Their Doctrine and Discipline; with the Reasons of the Author for Leaving the Church.* St. Louis: Printed for the Author, 1839.

Cowan, Richard O. and William E. Homer. *California Saints: A 150-Year Legacy in the Golden State.* Provo, Utah: Religious Studies Center, B.Y.U., 1996.

Cowley, Matthew. *Wilford Woodruff: History of His Life and Labors as Recorded in His Daily Journals.* S.L.C: The Deseret News, 1909.

Dary, David. *Red Blood & Black Ink: Journalism in the Old West.* N.Y: Alfred A. Knopf, 1998.

Daynes, Kathryn M. *More Wives Than One: Transformation of the Mormon Marriage System, 1840-1910.* Urbana and Chicago: Univ. of Ill. Press, 2001.

Dickens, Charles. *The Uncommercial Traveler and Reprinted Pieces Etc.* Oxford: Oxford Univ. Press, n.d.

Doctrine and Covenants of the Church of the Latter Day Saints: Carefully Selected from the Revelations of God and Compiled by Joseph Smith Junior, Oliver Cowdery, Sidney Rigdon, Frederick G. Williams, [Presiding Elders of said Church.] Kirtland, Ohio: 1835. (See also subsequent editions published by the Church of Jesus Christ of Latter-day Saints.)

Doyle, Arthur Conan. *Angels of Darkness: A Drama in Three Acts.* N.Y: The Baker Street Irregulars, 2001.

________. *A Study in Scarlet.* London, Ward, Lock and Co., 1888. Reprinted with original illustrations, N.Y: Hart Publishing Co., 1976.

Drury, Clifford M. *Marcus and Narcissa Whitman and the Opening of Old Oregon,* 2 vols. Glendale, Calif: The Arthur H. Clark Company, 1973. Reprinted Seattle: Northwest Interpretive Association, 1994.

Embry, Jessie L. *Mormon Polygamous Families: Life in the Principle.* S.L.C: Univ. of Utah Press, 1987.

England, Eugene. *Brother Brigham.* S.L.C: Bookcraft, 1980.

English, Thomas Dunn. *The Mormons; or, Life at Salt Lake City.* N.Y.C: S. French, 1858.

Erickson, Dan. *As a Thief in the Night: The Mormon Quest for Millennial Deliverance.* S.L.C: Signature Books, 1998.

Evans, Beatrice Cannon and Janeth Russell Cannon, eds. *Cannon Family Historical Treasury,* S.L.C: Publishers Press, 1967.

Fancher, Burr. *Westward with the Sun.* Bend, Oregon: Fancher & Associates, 1999.

Ferris, Benjamin G. *Utah and the Mormons. The History, Government, Doctrines, Customs, and Prospects of the Latter-day Saints, from Personal Observation during a Six Months' Residence at Great Salt Lake City.* N.Y: Harper and Bros., 1854.

Ferris, Mrs. B. G. *Female Life among the Mormons, A Narrative.* London: C. H. Clarke, 1855.

________. *The Mormons at Home; with Some Incidents of Travel from Missouri to California, 1852–3, in a Series of Letters.* New York: Dix & Edwards, 1856.

Fielding, Robert Kent, ed. *The Tribune Reports of the Trials of John D. Lee for the Massacre at Mountain Meadows, November, 1874–April, 1877.* Higganum, Conn.: Kent's Books, 2000.

________. *The Unsolicited Chronicler: An Account of the Gunnison Massacre, Its Causes and Consequences—Utah Territory, 1847–1859.* Brookline, Mass: Paradigm Publishers, 1993.

Flake, Lawrence R. *George Q. Cannon: His Missionary Years.* S.L.C: Bookcraft, 1998.

________. "George Q. Cannon's Mission to California, 1855–1857." *Regional Studies in Latter-day Saint Church History: California.* Eds. David F. Boone, *et. al.* Provo, Utah: Department of Church History and Doctrine, Brigham Young Univ., 1998.

Ford, Gov. Thomas. *A History of Illinois, from its Commencement as a State in 1818 to 1847. Containing a Full Account of the Black Hawk War, the Rise, Progress, and Fall of Mormonism, the Alton and Lovejoy Riots, and Other Important and Interesting Events.* Chicago: S. C. Griggs & Co., and N.Y: Ivison & Phinney, 1854.

Froiseth, Jennie Anderson. *The Women of Mormonism, or The Story of Polygamy as Told by the Victims Themselves.* Detroit, Mich: C. G. G. Paine, 1886.

Furniss, Norman F. *The Mormon Conflict, 1850–1859,* New Haven and London: Yale Univ. Press, 1960.

Gibbs, J. F. *Lights and Shadows of Mormonism.* S.L.C: Salt Lake Tribune Publishing Co., 1909.

Golder, Frank J., Thomas A. Bailey, and J. Lyman Smith, eds. *The March of the Mormon Battalion from Council Bluffs to California, Taken from the Journal of Henry Standage.* N. Y: The Century Company, 1928.

Gordon, Sarah Barringer. *The Mormon Question: Polygamy and Constitutional Conflict in Nineteenth Century America.* Chapel Hill and London: Univ. of N. C. Press, 2002.

Gottfredson, Peter, ed. *History of Indian Depredations in Utah.* S.L.C: 1919.

Greeley, Horace. *An Overland Journey, from New York to San Francisco, in the Summer of 1859.* N. Y: C. M. Saxton, Barker & Co., 1860.

Green, Nelson Winch. *Mormonism: Its Rise, Progress, and Present Condition. Embracing the Narrative of Mrs. Mary Ettie V. Smith, of her Residence and Experience of Fifteen Years with the Mormons; Containing a Full and Authentic Account of their Social Condition—their Religious Doctrines, and Political Government.* N.Y: H. Drayton, 1858. Reprinted, Hartford, Conn.: Belknap & Bliss, 1870.

Gunnison, Lieut. J. W. *The Mormons, or, Latter-day Saints, in the Valley of the Great Salt Lake: a History of their Rise and Progress, Peculiar Doctrines, Present Condition, and Prospects, Derived from Pesonal Observation During a Residence Among Them.* Philadelphia: J. B. Lippincott & Co. 1852.

Hafen, Leroy R. and Ann W. Hafen. *Handcarts to Zion: the story of a Unique Western Migration, 1856–1860, with contemporary journals, accounts, reports; and rosters of members of the Ten Handcart Companies.* Glendale, Calif: The Arthur H. Clark Co., 1960.

__________, eds. *The Utah Expedition, 1857–1858: A Documentary Account of the United States Military Movement under Colonel Albert Sidney Johnston, and the Resistance by Brigham Young and the Mormon Nauvoo Legion.* Glendale, Calif: The Arthur H. Clark Co., 1982.

Hansen, Klaus J. *Quest for Empire: The Political Kingdom of God and the Council of Fifty in Mormon History.* East Lansing: Mich. State Univ. Press, 1970.

Hardy, Carmon. *Solemn Covenant: The Mormon Polygamous Passage.* Urbana and Chicago: Univ. of Ill. Press, 1992.

Hickman, William A. *Brigham's Destroying Angel: Being the Life, Confession, and Startling Disclosures of the Notorious Bill Hickman, the Danite Chief of Utah. Written by Himself, with Explanatory Notes by J. H. Beadle, Esq., of Salt Lake City.* N.Y: Geo. A. Crofutt, 1872.

Hilton, Hope A. *"Wild Bill" Hickman and the Mormon Frontier.* S.L.C: Signature Books, 1988.

Hinckley, Gordon B. *Standing for Something: 10 Neglected Virtues that Will Heal Our Hearts and Homes.* N.Y: Times Books (Random House), 2000.

Hollon, W. Eugene. *Frontier Vioilence: Another Look.* N.Y.C: Oxford Univ. Press, 1974.

Homer, Michael W. "The Mormon Subplot in A *Study in Scarlet* and *Angels of Darkness,*" in Doyle, Arthur Conan. *Angels of Darkness: A Drama in Three Acts.* N.Y: The Baker Street Irregulars, 2001.

Howe, Eber D. *Mormonism Unvailed* [*sic*]: *Or, A Faithful Account of That Singular Imposition and Delusion, From Its Rise to the Present Time. With Sketches of the Characters of Its Propagators, and a Full Detail of the Manner in Which the Famous Golden Bible Was Brought Before the World. To Which Are Added, Inquiries Into the Probability That the Historical Part of the Said Bible Was Written By One Solomon Spalding, More Than Twenty Years Ago, and By Him Intended to Have Been Published as a Romance.* Painesville, Ohio: By the author, 1834.

Jackson, Kent. P., ed. *Manuscript Found: The Complete Original "Spaulding Manuscript."* Vol. 11, Religious Studies Center Specialized Monograph Series. Introductory essay by Rex C. Reeve, Jr. Provo, Utah: Religious Studies Center, BYU, 1996.

Jessee, Dean C., ed. *Letters of Brigham Young to His Sons.* S.L.C: Deseret Book Co., 1974.

Knecht, William L. and Peter L. Crawley, eds. *History of Brigham Young, 1847–1867.* Berkeley, Calif: MassCal Associates, 1964.

Hyde, John, Jun. *Mormonism: Its Leaders and Designs.* N.Y: W. P. Fetridge & Co., 1857.

Inside of Mormonism, The. A Judicial Examination of the Endowment Oaths Administered in All the Mormon Temples, by the United States District Court for the Third Judicial District of Utah, to Determine whether Membership in the Mormon Church is Consistent with Citizenship in the United States. S.L.C: The Utah Americans, 1903.

Jenson, Andrew. *Latter-day Saint Biographical Encyclopedia* 4 vols. S.L.C: Andrew Jenson History Co., 1920.

Jones, Daniel W. *Forty Years Among the Indians, a True Yet Thrilling Narrative of the Author's Experiences Among the Natives.* S.L.C: Juvenile Instructor Office, 1890.

Journal of Discourses, 26 vols. London: Latter-Day Saints Book Depot, 1854–1886.

Kane, Thomas L. *The Mormons.* Philadelphia: King & Baird, 1850.

Kelly, Charles and Hoffman Birney. *Holy Murder: The Story of Porter Rockwell.* N.Y: Minton, Balch & Co., 1934.

Kelly, William. *An Excursion to California over the Prairie, Rocky Mountains, and Great Sierra Nevada, with a Stroll through the Diggings and Ranches of that Country.* 2 vols. London: Chapman & Hill, 1851.

Kemble, Edward C. *A History of California Newspapers, 1846–1858: Reprinted from the Supplement to the Sacramento Union of December 25, 1858,* edited by Helen Harding Bretnor. Los Gatos, Calif: The Talisman Press, 1962.

Lambert, Charlotte P. *Printing in California, 1846–1856.* [San Francisco:] Lawton Kennedy, n.d.

Landon, Michael N., ed. *The Journals of George Q. Cannon, Vol. I: To California in '49* . S.L.C: Deseret Book Co., 1999.

Larson, Carl V. *A Database of the Mormon Battalion: An Identification of the Original Members of the Mormon Battalion.* S.L.C: U.S. Mormon Battalion, Inc., 1997.

Larson, Gustive O. *The "Americanization" of Utah for Statehood.* San Marino, Calif: The Huntington Library, 1971.

_________. *Prelude to the Kingdom: Mormon Desert Conquest, a Chapter in American Cooperative Experience.* Francetown, N.H: Marshall Jones Company, 1947.

Larson, Stan, ed. *Prisoner for Polygamy: The Memoirs and Letters of Rudger Clawson at the Uintah Territorial Penitentiary, 1884–87.* Urbana and Chicago: Univ. of Ill. Press, 1993.

Lee, John Doyle. *Mormonism Unveiled; Including the Remarkable Life and Confessions of the Late Mormon Bishop, John. D. Lee; (Written by himself.) and Complete Life of Brigham Young, Embracing a History of Mormonism from its Inception down to the Present Time, with an Exposition of the Secret History, Signs, Symbols, and Crimes of the Mormon Church.* St. Louis, Mo: Moffatt Publishing Co., 1881.

Leonard, Glen M. *Nauvoo: A Place of Peace, a People of Promise.* S.L.C: Deseret Book Co., and Provo, Utah: Brigham Young Univ. Press, 2002.

LeSueur, Stephen C. *The 1838 Mormon War in Missouri.* Columbia: Univ. of Mo. Press, 1987.

Linn, William A. *The Story of the Mormons, from the Date of their Origin to the Year 1901.* N.Y: Macmillan, 1902.

Little, James A. *Jacob Hamblin.* (See Nibley, Preston. *Three Mormon Classics.*)

Lotchin, Roger W. *San Francisco, 1846–1856: From Hamlet to City.* N.Y: Oxford Univ. Press, 1974.

Ludlow, Daniel L., ed. *Encyclopedia of Mormonism,* 4 vols. N.Y: Macmillan Pub. Co., 1992.

Lyman, Edward Leo. *Political Deliverance: The Mormon Quest for Utah Statehood.* Urbana and Chicago: Univ. of Ill. Press, 1986.

________. *San Bernardino: The Rise and Fall of a California Community.* S.L.C: Signature Books, 1996.

(Mackay, Charles/Henry Mayhew). *The Mormons, or Latter-day Saints: A Contemporary History.* London: 1851.

McLaws, Monte Burr. *Spokesman for the Kingdom: Early Mormon Journalism and the "Deseret News," 1830–1898.* Provo, Utah: Brigham Young Univ. Press, 1977.

Moore, John Bassett, ed. *The Works of James Buchanan, Comprising his Speeches, State Papers, and Private Correspondence.* Ten Volumes. Philadelphia and London: J. B. Lippincott Co., 1910.

Morgan, Dale. *The Humboldt: Highroad of the West.* N.Y: Farrar & Rinehardt, 1943. Reprinted edition, Lincoln and London: Univ. of Nebraska Press, 1985.

Mulder, William and A. Russell Mortensen. *Among the Mormons: Historic Accounts by Contemporary Observers.* N.Y: Alfred A. Knopf, 1958. Reprinted edition, 1973.

Mullen, Kevin J. *Let Justice Be Done: Crime and Politics in Early San Francisco.* Reno and Las Vegas: Univ. of Nevada Press, 1989.

Neff, Andrew Love. *History of Utah, 1847 to 1869.* S.L.C: Deseret News Press, 1940.

Newton, Marjorie. *Hero or Traitor: A Biographical Study of Charles Wesley Wandell.* Independence: John Whitmer Historical Association, 1992.

Nibley, Preston. *Three Mormon Classics.* S.L.C: Stevens & Wallis, Inc., 1944.

Noord, Roger Van. *King of Beaver Island: The Life and Assassination of James Jesse Strang.* Urbana and Chicago: Univ. of Ill. Press, 1988.

Nord, David Paul. *Communities of Journalism: A History of American Newspapers and Their Readers.* Urbana and Chicago: Univ. of Ill. Press, 2001.

Nye, Bill. *Forty Liars, and Other Lies.* Chicago and N.Y: Belford, Clarke & Co., 1884.

Oaks, Dallin H. and Marvin S. Hill. *Carthage Conspiracy: The Trial of the Accused Assassins of Joseph Smith.* Urbana: Univ. of Ill. Press, 1975.

O'Dea, Thomas. *The Mormons.* Chicago: Univ. of Chicago Press. Paperback edition, 1964.

Paddock, Mrs. A. G. *The Fate of Madame La Tour, a Tale of Great Salt Lake.* N. Y: Fords, Howard, & Hulbert, 1882.

Peterson, John Alton. *Utah's Black Hawk War.* S.L.C: Univ. of Utah Press, 1998.

Peterson, Paul H. "Brigham Young and the Mormon Reformation." In *Lion of the Lord: Essays on the Life & Service of Brigham Young,* Eds. Susan Easton Black and Larry C. Porter, S.L.C: Deseret Book Co., 1995.

__________."'Like a Fire in My Bones': The Reformation Correspondence between Brigham Young and George Q. Cannon." In *Regional Studies in Latter-day Saint Church History: California.* Eds. David F. Boone, *et. al.* Provo, Utah: Department of Church History and Doctrine, Brigham Young Univ., 1998.

Poll, Richard D. *Quixotic Mediator: Thomas L. Kane and the Utah War.* Ogden, Utah: Weber State College Press, 1985.

Potter, David Morris, ed. *Trail to California: The Overland Journal of Vincent Geiger and Wakeman Bryarly.* New Haven and London: Yale Univ. Press, 1945. Paperback edition, 1962.

Powell, Allan Kent, ed. *Utah History Encyclopedia.* S.L.C: Univ. of Utah Press, 1994.

Pratt, Parley P. *Key to the Science of Theology, Designed as an Introduction to the First Principles of Spiritual Philosophy, Religion, Law and Government, as Delivered by the Ancients, and as Restored in this Age, for the Final Development of Universal Peace, Truth and Knowledge.* Fifth Edition. S.L.C: George Q. Cannon & Sons Co, 1891.

Proctor, Scot Facer and Maurine Jensen Proctor, eds. *Autobiography of Parley P. Pratt, Revised and Enhanced Edition.* S.L.C: Deseret Book Co., 2000.

Quinn, D. Michael. *The Mormon Hierarchy: Extensions of Power.* S.L.C: Signature Books, 1997.

________. *The Mormon Hierarchy: Origins of Power.* S.L.C: Signature Books, 1994.

________. *The New Mormon History: Revisionist Essays on the Past.* S.L.C: Signature Books, 1992.

Reid, J. M. *Sketches & Anecdotes of the Old Settlers and the New Comers, The Mormon Bandits and Danite Band.* Keokuk, Iowa: R. B. Ogden, 1876.

Remy, Jules and Julius Brenchley. *A Journey to Great Salt Lake City by Jules Remy, and Julius Brenchley, M.A.; with a Sketch of the History, Religion, and Customs of the Mormons, and an Introduction on the Religious Movement in the United States.* 2 vols. London: W. Jeffs, 1861.

Rice, William B. *The Los Angeles Star, 1851–1864: The Beginnings of Journalism in Southern California.* Ed. by John W. Caughey. Berkeley: Univ. of Calif. Press, 1947.

Richardson, Albert D. *Beyond the Mississippi: From the Great River to the Great Ocean. Life and Adventure on the Prairies, Mountains, and Pacific Coast . . .* .Hartford, Conn: American Publishing Co., 1867, 1869.

Ricketts, Norma B. *The Mormon Battalion: U.S. Army of the West, 1846–1848.* Logan, Utah State Press, 1996.

Roberts, Brigham H. *A Comprehensive History of the Church of Jesus Christ of Latter-day Saints,* 6 vols. S.L.C: Deseret News Press, 1930.

________. *The Mormon Battalion: Its History and Achievements.* S.L.C: The Deseret News, 1919.

Robinson, Ezra C. *The Life of Ira Hatch, Famous Indian Missionary and Scout.* n.p.: By the Author, n.d.

Robison, Parker Pratt, ed. *Writings of Parley Parker Pratt, One of the First Missionaries and a Member of the First Quorum of the Twelve Apostles of the Church of Jesus Christ of Latter-day Saints.* S.L.C: Parker Pratt Robison, 1952.

Rogers, Fred Blackburn, ed. *A Kemble Reader: Stories of California, 1846–1848.* S. F: The California Historical Society, 1963.

Rosenvall, Lyn A. "Defunct Mormon Settlements: 1830–1930," in Jackson, Richard H., ed. *The Mormon Role in the Settlement of the West.* Provo, Utah: Brigham Young Univ. Press, 1978, 1980.

Royce, Josiah. *California: From the Conquest in 1846 to the Second Vigilance Committee in San Francisco, A Study of American Character.* Boston and N.Y: Houghton, Mifflin and Co., 1886.

Schiel, Jacob B. *Journey through the Rocky Mountains and the Humboldt Mountains to the Pacific Ocean.* Thomas N. Bonner, trans. and ed. Norman: Univ. of Okla. Press, 1959.

Schindler, Harold. *Orrin Porter Rockwell: Man of God, Son of Thunder.* S.L.C: Univ. of Utah Press, 1966, 1993.

Sessions, Gene A. *Mormon Thunder: A Documentary History of Jedediah M. Grant.* Urbana: Univ. of Ill. Press.

Shields, Steven L. *Divergent Paths of the Restoration.* Bountiful, Utah: Restoration Research, 1982.

Shipps, Jan. *Sojourner in the Promised Land: Forty Years among the Mormons.* Urbana and Chicago: Univ. of Ill. Press, 2000.

Smith, Andrew F. *The Saintly Scoundrel: The Life and Times of Dr. John Cook Bennett.* Urbana and Chicago: Univ. of Ill. Press, 1977.

Smith, Joseph, Jr. *The Book of Mormon: An Account Written by the Hand of Mormon, Upon Plates Taken from the Plates of Nephi.* Palmyra, N.Y: E. B. Grandin, 1830. (See also subsequent editions, listing Joseph Smith, Jr. as translator, rather than author.)

________. *History of the Church of Jesus Christ of Latter-day Saints. Period 1. History of Joseph Smith, the Prophet, by Himself.* Ed. by Brigham H. Roberts. 6 vols. S.L.C: Deseret News, 1902–1912.

Smith, Timothy L. *Revivalism and Social Reform: American Protestantism on the Eve of the Civil War.* N.Y: Harper and Row, 1965.

Soulé, Frank, John H. Gihon, M.D., and James Nisbet. *The Annals of San Francisco; Containing a Summary of the History of the First Discovery, Settlement, Progress and Present Condition of California, and a Complete History of All the Important Events Connected with its Great City: To Which Are Added, Biographical Memoirs of Some Prominent Citizens,* N.Y: D. Appleton & Company, 1855. Reprinted as Dorothy H. Higgens, ed. *The Annals of San Francisco by Frank Soulé, John H. Gihon, M.D., and James Nisbet; Together with the Continuation, through 1855*; Palo Alto: Lewis Osborne, 1966.

Stampp, Kenneth M. *America in 1857: A Nation on the Brink.* N.Y., Oxford: Oxford Univ. Press, 1990.

Stanley, Reva. *A Biography of Parley P. Pratt: the Archer of Paradise.* Caldwell, Idaho: Caxton Printers, 1937.

Stansbury, Howard. *Exploration and Survey of the Valley of the Great Salt Lake of Utah, Including a Reconnoissance [sic] of a New Route Through the Rocky Mountains.* Philadelphia: Lippincott, Grambo & Co, 1852. Reprinted, Wash., D.C.: Smithsonian Institution Press, 1988.

Stegner, Wallace. *The Gathering of Zion: The Story of the Mormon Trail.* N.Y: McGraw-Hill Book Co., 1964.

Stellman. Louis J. *Sam Brannan: Builder of San Francisco.* N.Y: Exposition Press, 1953.

Stenhouse, Fanny. *"Tell it All": the Story of a Life's Experience in Mormonism.* Hartford, Conn: A. D. Worthington & Co., 1874.

Stenhouse, T. B. H. *Rocky Mountain Saints: A Full and Complete History of the Mormons, From the First Vision of Joseph Smoith to the Last Courtship of Brigham Young. . . .* N.Y: D. Appleton and Co., 1873.

Stone, Irving. *Men to Match My Mountains: The Opening of the Far West, 1840–1900.* N.Y: Doubleday and Co., 1956.

Taggart, Stephen G. *Mormonism's Negro Policy: Social and Historical Origins.* S.L.C: Univ. of Utah Press, 1970.

Taylor, Samuel W. *The Kingdom or Nothing: The Life of John Taylor, Militant Mormon.* N. Y: Macmillan Publishing Co., Inc., 1976.

Thomas, Sarah C., ed. *Elias Smith's Journal* 3 vols. SL.C: 1984. Copy available at Utah State Historical Society, 921 SM5th 1984.

Tullidge, Edward W. *History of Salt Lake City.* S.L.C: Star Printing Co., 1886.

________. *Tullidge's Histories, Vol. II.* S.L.C: Juvenile Instructor, 1889.

________. *The Women of Mormondom.* N.Y: Tullidge and Crandall, 1877.

Twain, Mark (Samuel Langhorne Clemens). *Roughing It.* Hartford, Conn: American Publishing Co., 1872. Facsimile reprint, N.Y: Hippocrene Books, n.d.

Tyler, Sergeant Daniel. *A Concise History of the Mormon Battalion in the Mexican War, 1846–1847.* S.L.C., 1881. Facsimile reprint, S.L.C: Publishers Press, 1996.

Unruh, John D., Jr. *The Plains Across: The Overland Emigrants and the Trans-Mississippi West, 1840–60.* Urbana, Chicago, London: Univ. of Ill. Press, 1979.

Valentine, Alan. *Vigilante Justice.* N.Y: Reynal & Company, 1956.

Van Deusen, Increase McGee. *The Mormon Endowment: A Secret Drama, or Conspiracy, in the Nauvoo Temple, in 1846.* Syracuse, N.Y: N. M. D. Luther, printer, 1847.

Van Wagoner, Richard S. *Mormon Polygamy: A History.* S.L.C: Signature Books, 1986.

_________ and Steven C. Walker. *A Book of Mormons.* S.L.C: Signature Books, 1982.

Vattel, Emmerich de. *Le Droit des Gens; ou, Principes de la loi naturelle, appliques a la conduite & aux affaires des nations & des souverains.* A. Leide : Aux depens de la Compagnie, 1758. Reprinted as *The Law of Nations; or, Principles of the law of nature, applied to the conduct and affairs of nations and sovereigns.* Northampton, Mass: Simeon Butler, 1820.

Victor, Metta Victoria Fuller. *Mormon Wives, A Narrative of Facts Stranger than Fiction.* N.Y: Derby and Jackson, 1856.

Waite, Mrs. C. (Catherine) V. *The Mormon Prophet and His Harem; or, An Authentic History of Brigham Young, His Numerous Wives and Children.* Cambridge, Mass: Riverside Press, 1866.

Wallace, Irving. *The Twenty-seventh Wife.* N.Y: Simon and Schuster, 1961.

Ward, Maria N. (pseud.). *Female Life Among the Mormons; A Narrative of Many Years' Personal Experience, by the Wife of a Mormon Elder, Recently from Utah.* N.Y: J. C. Derby, 1855.

Werner, M. R. *Brigham Young.* N.Y: Harcourt, Brace and Co., 1925.

Whelan, Shane LeGrande. *More Than One: Plural Marriage, a Sacred Heritage, a Promise for Tomorrow.* Bountiful, Utah: Zion Publishers, 2001.

White, David A., ed. *News of the Plains and the Rockies, 1803–1865,* Volume 3, *Missionaries, Mormons, 1821–1864; Indian Agents, Captives, 1832–1865.* Spokane: The Arthur H. Clark Co., 1997.

Whitney, Orson F. *History of Utah.* 4 vols. S.L.C: George Q. Cannon and Sons, 1904.

Whittaker, David J. "Brigham Young and the Missionary Enterprise." In *Lion of the Lord: Essays on the Life & Service of Brigham Young.* Eds. Susan Easton Black and Larry C. Porter, S.L.C: Deseret Book Co., 1996.

_________. "A Covenant People." In *The Seventh Annual Sidney B. Sperry Symposium: The Doctrine and Covenants,* Provo, Utah: College of Religious Instruction, Brigham Young Univ., 1979.

Wilford Woodruff's Journal. S.L.C: Pioneer Press, n.d.

Winther, Oscar Osburn, ed. *A Friend of the Mormons: The Private Papers and Diary of Thomas Leiper Kane.* S.F: Gelber-Lilienthal, Inc., 1937.

Young, Ann Eliza. *Wife No. 19, the Story of a Life in Bondage, Being a Complete Exposé of Mormonism, and Revealing the Sorrows, Sacrifices, and Sufferings of Women in Polygamy.* Hartford, Conn: Dustin, Gilman & Co., 1875.

Young, John P. Young. *Journalism in California.* S.F: Chronicle Publishing Co., 1915.

Young, Kimball. *Isn't One Wife Enough?* N.Y: Henry Holt and Co., 1954.

Zboray, Ronald J. *A Fictive People: Antebellum Economic Development and the American Reading Public.* N.Y. and Oxford: Oxford Univ. Press, 1993.

Periodicals

Aird, Polly. "Escape from Zion: The United States Army Escort of Mormon Apostates, 1859." *Nevada Historical Society Quarterly* 44:3 (Fall 2001).

Alexander, Thomas G. "Wilford Woodruff and the Mormon Reformation of 1855–57." *Dialogue: A Journal of Mormon Thought* 25:2 (Summer 1992).

Alter, J. Cecil. "The Mormons and the Indians." *Utah Historical Quarterly* 12 (January-April 1944).

Anderson, Richard Lloyd. "Atchison's Letters and the Causes of Mormon Expulsion from Missouri." *BYU Studies* 26 (Summer 1986).

Arrington, Leonard. "'In Honorable Remembrance': Thomas L. Kane's Services to the Mormons." *BYU Studies* 21 (Fall 1981).

Bitton, Davis. "Mormon Polygamy: A Review Article." *Journal of Mormon History* 4 (1977).

Buerger, David John. "The Development of the Mormon Temple Endowment Ceremony." *Dialogue: A Journal of Mormon Thought* 20:4 (Winter 1987).

Bush, Lester E., Jr. "Mormonism's Negro Doctrine: An Historical Overview." *Dialogue: A Journal of Mormon Thought* 8:1 (Spring 1973).

________. "The Spalding Theory Then and Now." *Dialogue: A Journal of Mormon Thought* 10:4 (Autumn 1977).

________. "Writing 'Mormonism's Negro Doctrine: An Historical Overview' (1973): Context and Reflections, 1998." *Journal of Mormon History* 25:1 (Spring 1999).

Campbell, Eugene E. and Bruce R. Campbell, "Divorce Among Mormon Polygamists: Extent and Explanation." *Utah Historical Quarterly* 46:1 (Winter 1978).

Cannon, Charles A. "The Awesome Power of Sex: The Polemical Campaign against Mormon Polygamy." *Pacific Historical Review* 43 (February 1974).

Cannon, George O. "Twenty Years Ago." *Juvenile Instructor* 4 (January 16, 1869).

Cannon, Joseph J. "George Q. Cannon: The Mission to California." *Instructor* LXXIX (November 1944).

Cannon, Kenneth L. II, "A Strange Encounter: The English Courts and Mormon Polygamy." *BYU Studies* 22 (Winter 1981).

Carter, D. Robert. "Fish and the Famine of 1855–56." *Journal of Mormon History* 27:2 (Fall 2001).

Carter, Lyndia McDowell. "The Mormon Handcart Companies" *Overland Journal* 13:1 (Spring 1995).

Christy, Howard A. "Open Hand and Mailed Fist: Mormon-Indian Relations in Utah, 1847–52." *Utah Historical Quarterly* 46:3 (Summer 1978).

________. "'What Virtue There is in Stone' and Other Pungent Talk on the Early Utah Frontier." *Utah Historical Quarterly* 59:3 (Summer 1991).

Clark, James R. "The Kingdom of God, the Council of Fifty, and the State of Deseret." *Utah Historical Quarterly* 26:2 (April 1958).

Cooley, Everett L. "A Brigham Young Letter to George Q. Cannon, 1859." *Brigham Young Univ. Studies* 25:3, (Summer 1985).

________. "Carpetbag Rule—Territorial Government in Utah." *Utah Historical Quarterly* 26:2 (April 1959).

Cornwall, Rebecca Foster and Leonard J. Arrington, "Perpetuation of a Myth: Mormon Danites in Five Western Novels, 1840–90." *Brigham Young Univ. Studies* 23:2 (Spring 1983).

Crawley, Peter. "Parley P. Pratt: Father of Mormon Pamphleteering." *Dialogue* 15:3 (Autumn 1982).

Cummings, B. F. Jr. "Shining Lights." *The Contributor* XVI, (December 1894).

Ehat, Andrew F. "'It Seems Like Heaven Began on Earth': Joseph Smith and the Constitution of the Kingdom of God." *BYU Studies* 20:3 (Spring 1980).

Erickson, Dan. "Joseph Smith's 1891 Millennial Prophecy: The Quest for Apocalyptic Deliverance." *Journal of Mormon History* 22:2 (Fall 1996).

Field, Kate. "Mormon Blood Atonement." *North American Review* 140 (September 1886).

Gardner, Martin R. "Mormonism and Capital Punishment: A Doctrinal Perspective, Past and Present." *Dialogue: A Journal of Mormon Thought* 12:1 (Spring 1979).

Gee, Elizabeth D. "Justice for All or for the 'Elect'?: The Utah County Probate Court, 1855–72." *Utah Historical Quarterly* 48:2 (Spring 1980).

Gentry, Leland H. "The Danite Band of 1838." *BYU Studies* 14 (Summer 1974).

Grayson, Donald K."Human Mortality in a Natural Disaster: the Willie Handcart Company." *Journal of Anthropological Research* 52:2 (Summer 1996).

Hart, Edward L. "John Hyde Junior—An Earlier View." *Brigham Young Univ. Studies* 16:7 (Winter 1976).

Homer, Michael W. "The Federal Bench and Priesthood Authority: The Rise and Fall of John Fitch Kinney's Early Relationship with the Mormons." *Journal of Mormon History* 12 (1986–1987).

________. "'Recent Psychic Evidence': The Visit of Sir Arthur Conan Doyle to Utah in 1923." *Utah Historical Quarterly* 52:3 (Summer 1984).

Johnson, Jeffery Ogden. "Determining and Defining 'Wife': The Brigham Young Households." *Dialogue: A Journal of Mormon Thought* 20:3 (Fall 1987).

Jorgensen, Lynne Watkins. "John Hyde, Jr., Mormon Renegade." *Journal of Mormon History* 17 (1991).

Larson, Gustive O. "An Industrial Home for Polygamous Wives." *Utah Historical Quarterly* 38:3 (Summer 1970).

________. "The Mormon Reformation." *Utah Historical Quarterly* 26:1 (January 1958).

Lythgoe, Dennis L. "Marketing the Mormon Image: An Interview with Wendell J. Ashton." *Dialogue* 10 (Spring 1977).

MacKinnon, William P. "125 Years of Conspiracy Theories: Origins of the Utah Expedition of 1857–58." *Utah Historical Quarterly* 52:3 (Summer 1984).

________. "The Buchanan Spoils System and the Utah Expedition: Careers of W. M. F. Magraw and John M. Hockaday." *Utah Historical Quarterly* 31 (Spring 1963).

May, Dean L. "Still a Puzzle—the Mysterious Place of Mormonism in American Culture." *Sunstone: Mormon Experience, Scholarship, Issues, & Art* 118 (April 2001).

McConkie, Bruce R. "The Caravan Moves On." *The Ensign* (November 1984).

Melville, J. Keith. "Brigham Young on Politics and Priesthood." *BYU Studies* X:4 (Summer 1970).

Morgan, Dale L. "Washakie and the Shoshoni." *Annals of Wyoming* 25–27 (Part I, July 1953; Part II, January 1954; Part III, July 1954; Part IV, April, 1955; Part V, October 1955).

Munkres, Robert L. "The Plains Indian Threat on the Oregon Trail before 1860." *Annals of Wyoming* (October 1968).

"National Press Club Told about Church." *Church News*, week ending 18 March 2000.

Norman, Keith E. "A Kinder, Gentler Mormonism: Moving Beyond the Vioilence of our Past." *Sunstone: Mormon Experience, Scholarship, Issues, and Art* 14:4, Issue 78 (August 1990).

Norton, Wesley. "'Like a Thousand Preachers Flying': Religious Newspapers on the Pacific Coast to 1865." *California Historical Quarterly* 56:3 (Fall 1977).

Oaks, Dallin H. "Suppression of the *Nauvoo Expositor*." *Utah Law Review* 9 (Winter 1965).

O'Neil, Floyd A. and Stanford J. Layton. "Of Pride and Politics: Brigham Young as Indian Superintendent." *Utah Historical Quarterly* 46:3 (Summer 1978).

Orme, Michael. "The Causes of the Mormon Reformation of 1856–1857." *Tangents* (Spring 1975).

Peterson, Charles S. "'A Mighty Man Was Brother Lot': A Portrait of Lot Smith—Mormon Frontiersman." *Western Historical Quarterly* 1:4 (October 1970).

Peterson, Paul H. "The Mormon Reformation of 1856–1857: The Rhetoric and the Reality." *Journal of Mormon History* 15 (1989).

Poll, Richard D. "The Mormon Question Enters National Politics, 1850–1856." *Utah Historical Quarterly* 25:2 (April 1957).

Poll, Richard D. and William P. MacKinnon. "Causes of the Utah War Reconsidered." *Journal of Mormon History* 20:2 (Fall 1994).

Pratt, Steven. "Eleanor McLean and the Murder of Parley P. Pratt." *Brigham Young Univ. Studies* 15:2 (Winter 1975).

Quinn, D. Michael. "The Council of Fifty and Its Members, 1844 to 1945." *BYU Studies* 20 (Winter 1980).

________. "The Flag of the Kingdom of God." *BYU Stuies* 14:1 (Autumn 1973).

________. "LDS Church Authority and New Plural Marriages, 1890–1904." *Dialogue: A Journal of Mormon Thought* 18:1 (Spring 1985).

"Rev. John Hyde, The." *The Intellectual Repository and New Jerusalem Magazine* XXII:262 (October 1, 1875).

Robinson, John W. "A California Copperhead: Henry Hamilton and the Los Angeles *Star*." *Dogtown Territorial Quarterly* 32 (Winter 1997).

Scott, Patricia Lyn. "Mormon Polygamy: A Bibliography, 1977–92." *Journal of Mormon History* 19 (Spring 1993).

Stanley, Reva Holdaway and Charles L. Camp, eds. "A Mormon Mission to California in 1851: From the Diary of Parley Parker Pratt." *California Historical Society Quarterly* 14:1–2 (March and June 1935).

Walker, Ronald D. "Raining Pitchforks: Brigham Young as Preacher." *Sunstone* 8:3 (May-June 1983).

________. "Thomas L. Kane and Utah's Quest for Self-Government, 1846–1851." *Utah Historical Quarterly*, 69:2 (Spring 2001).

__________ and Ronald K. Esplin. "Brigham Himself: An Autobiographical Recollection," *Journal of Mormon History*, 4 (1977).

West, Joseph Anthony. "Notes and Comments on 'Mormon Blood-Atonement,'" *North American Review* Vol. 143 (December 1886).

Whittaker, David J. "The Bone in the Throat: Orson Pratt and the Public Announcement of Plural Marriage." *Western Historical Quarterly* 18 (July 1987).

________. "Early Mormon Polygamy Defenses." *Journal of Mormon History* 11 (1984).

________. "Parley P. Pratt and the Pacific Mission: Mormon Publishing in 'That Very Questionable Part of the Civilized World,'" in Bitton, Davis, ed., *Mormons, Scripture, and the Ancient World, Studies in Honor of John L. Sorenson.* Provo, Utah: Foundation for Ancient Research and Mormon Studies, 1998.

__________."Placing the Keystone: George Q. Cannon's Mission of Translating and Printing the Book of Mormon into the Hawaiian Language," forthcoming.

________. "Toward a Reconstruction of Mormon and Indian Relations, 1847–1877." *BYU Studies* 29:4 (Fall 1989).

________. "The Web of Print: Toward a History of the Book in Early Mormon Culture." *Journal of Mormon History* 4 (Spring 1997).

NEWSPAPERS

California American, Sacramento, California.

California Star, Yerba Buena (San Francisco), California.

Daily Alta California (Alta California), San Francisco, California.

Daily California American, Sacramento, California.

Daily Evening Bulletin, San Francisco, California.

Daily Herald, San Francisco, California.

Democratic State Journal, Sacramento, California.

Deseret News, Salt Lake City, Utah.

Deseret Weekly, Salt Lake City, Utah.

Golden Era, San Francisco, California.

Harper's Weekly, New York City, New York.

Latter-day Saints' Millenial Star, Liverpool, England.

Los Angeles Star, Los Angeles, California.

The Messenger, New York City, New York.

The Mormon, New York City, New York.

Mountain Democrat, Placerville, California.

National Intelligencer, Washington, D.C.

Nauvoo Expositor, Nauvoo, Illinois.

New York Herald. New York City, New York.

New York Post, New York City, New York.

New York Tribune, New York City, New York.

The Pacific, San Francisco, California.

Pacific Christian Advocate, Oregon Territory

Pathfinder and Post, San Francisco, California

Philadelphia American, Philadelphia, Pennsylvania.

Sacramento Daily Union, Sacramento, California.

The Seer, Washington, D.C. (Baltimore, Maryland).

Spirit of the Age, Sacramento, California.
St. Louis Luminary, Saint Louis, Missouri.
Star of the Pacific, Sacramento, California
Weekly Chronicle (California Chronicle), San Francisco, California.

THESES, DISSERTATIONS, AND PAPERS

Bitton, Davis. "Mormon Catechisms." *Task Papers in LDS History*, No. 15, S.L.C: Historical Dept. of the Church, 1976.

Burgess-Olson, Vicky. "Family Structure and Dynamics in Early Utah Mormon Families, 1847–1885." Ph.D. diss., Northwestern Univ., 1975.

Cook, Lyndon Watson. "George Q. Cannon's Views on Church and State." M.A. thesis, Brigham Young Univ., 1977.

Flake, Lawrence R. "George Q. Cannon: His Missionary Years." Ph.D. diss., Brigham Young Univ., 1970.

Grow, Matthew. "Parley P. Pratt and the San Francisco Press, 1854–55." A paper presented to the Mormon History Association in Cedar City, Utah, 19 May 2001, copy in possession of editor.

Jones, Shirley Greenwood. "Brigham Young's Rhetoric: A Critical and Cultural Analysis of Key Sermons in Five Rhetorical Events." Ph.D. diss., Univ. of Utah, 1992.

Keele, Reba Lou. "A Doctrinal Group Counterattacks: An Analysis of the Oral Rhetoric of the Mormons in the Utah War, 1855–1859." M.A. thesis, Purdue Univ., 1974.

MacKinnon, William P. "Epilogue to the Utah War: A Military Campaign's Impact and Legacy." A paper presented to the Mormon History Association in Cedar City, Utah, 18 May 2001.

O'Neil, Floyd A. "A History of the Ute Indians of Utah until 1890." Ph.D. diss., Univ. of Utah, 1973.

Parshall, Ardis E. "The Many Voices of Brigham Young." A paper presented to the Sunstone Symposium 2001, audiocassette SL 01 #351, in possession of the editor.

Peterson, Paul H. "The Mormon Reformation." Ph.D. diss, Brigham Young Univ., 1981.

Ridd, Jay Donald. "Almon Whiting Babbitt, Mormon Emmissary." Master's thesis, Univ. of Utah, 1953.

Saunders, Richard L. "Francis Gladden Bishop and Gladdenism: A Study in the Culture of a Mormon Dissenter and His Movement." Master's thesis, Utah State Univ., 1989.

Searle, Howard Claire, "The Mormon Reformation of 1856–1857." Master's thesis, Brigham Young Univ., 1956.

PAMPHLETS AND DOCUMENTS

Burr to Hendricks, March 28, 1857, House Exec. Doc. 71, 118–20

Dubois, Frederick T. "Autobiography of Frederick T. Dubois." Typescript in Idaho Historical Society. House Exec. Doc. (35–2), II, pt. ii.

Missouri General Assembly. *Document Containing the Correspondence, Orders, &c., in relation to the disturbances with the Mormons; and the evidence given before the Hon. Austin A. King, judge of the Fifth judicial circuit of the state of Missouri, at the Court-house in Richmond, in a criminal court of inquiry, begun November 12, 1838, on the trial of Joseph Smith, jr., and others, for high treason and other crimes against the state.* Fayette, Mo: Printed at the Office of the Boon's Lick Democrat, 1841.

Penrose, Charles W. "Blood Atonement as Taught by Leading Elders of the Church of Jesus Christ of Latter-day Saints." S.L.C: Juvenile Instructor Office, 1884.

Proclamation of Governor Brigham Young, 15 September 1857, *The Utah Expedition*, 35th Cong., 1st Sess., 1857–58, Serial 956, House Exec. Doc. 71, 34–35.

Sauls, Elizabeth Cannon. "The Life of George Q. Cannon." Provo, Utah: 1956.

Smith, Joseph Fielding, Jr. "Blood Atonement and the Origin of Plural Marriage." S.L.C: 1905.

U.S. House. "Cessation of Difficulties in Utah." House Exec. Doc. 138 (35-1), 1852, Serial 959.

U.S. House, Committee on Territories. "Carson Valley, Utah—Annexation to State of California—and Eastern Boundary of California." 20 January 1857. House Report 116 (34–3).

U.S. House. "Information in Reference to the Condition of Affairs in the Territory of Utah." House Exec. Doc. 25 (32-1), 1852, Serial 640.

U.S. Senate. "Message of the President of the United States, Communicating, in compliance with a resolution of the Senate, information in relation to the massacre at Mountain Meadows, and other massacres in Utah Territory." Sen. Exec. Doc. 42 (36–1), 1860, Serial 1033.

MANUSCRIPTS

Note: The Library-Archives of the Family and Church History Department of the Church of Jesus Christ of Latter-day Saints is abbreviated as "LDS Archives."

Brigham Young Addresses, Speech by Gov. Young in Joint Session of the Legislature. 5 February 1852. LDS Archives.

Broadbent, Thomas. Journal of Thomas Broadbent, typescript copy in possession of the author.

Brooks, Juanita. Papers. MS 486, Manuscripts Division, Marriott Library, Univ. of Utah.

Cannon, Abraham H. Journal of Abraham H. Cannon. Special Collections, Brigham Young Univ.

Cannon, David H. to Cannon, Georgius Y., 7 January 1921. In possession of Mary Barnes Pearson.

Cannon, George Q. Journal of George Q. Cannon No. 1, May 10 1855–February 1865, California, LDS Archives.

Cannon, George Q. to Wells, Daniel H., 4 March 1857. Brigham Young Office Files, LDS Archives.

________. to Young, Brigham, 27 July 1855, Ibid.

________. 31 August 1855. Ibid.
________. 1 October 1855. Ibid.
________. 3 December 1855. Ibid.
________. 31 January 1856. Ibid.
________. 1 March 1856. Ibid.
________. 26 May 1856. Ibid.
________. 27 September 1856. Ibid.
________. 3 January 1857. Ibid.
________. 19 February 1857. Ibid.
________. 19 May 1857. Ibid.
________. 19 June 1857. Ibid.
________. 31 August 1857. Ibid.
________. 30 October 1857. Ibid.

Cannon, Georgius Young. Tell Us Some More About Your Funny Family. Special Collections, Harold B. Lee Library, Brigham Young Univ.

Eldredge, Horace Sunderlin. Letters from Brigham Young and Other Papers. Western Americana Collection, Beinecke Rare Book and Manuscript Library, Yale Univ.

Hamblin, Jacob. Journal, 1854–1859. Utah State Historical Society, A 567–1.

Hamelin, Joseph P., Jr. Journal, 1849. WA MSS 239. Western Americana Collection, Beinecke Rare Book and Manuscript Library, Yale Univ.

Porter, Nathan Tanner. Nathan Tanner Porter's Family Record. LDS Archives; photocopy in the possession of the editor.

Pratt, Orson to Young, Brigham, 31 Oct., 1845. *Journal History,* LDS Archives.

Pratt, Parley P. to Young, Brigham, Feb., 1855. LDS Archives.

Rothwell, William Renfro. Papers. WA MSS 409, Western Americana Collection, Beinecke Rare Book and Manuscript Library, Yale Univ.

Temple, William Bedford, to "Wife and Littleones," 2 June 1850, Mss #1508, Oregon Historical Society.

Thornton, Sarah Elizabeth Dunn. Incidents in the Life of . . ., in Hammond Family Papers, Special Collections, Harold B. Lee Library, BYU.

Wandell, Charles W. to Joseph Smith III, 26 September 1874, typescript, Henry A. Stebbins Papers, P24, f38, Community of Christ Library-Archives.

Young, Brigham to Bernhisel, John M. 4 November 1856. Brigham Young Office Files, LDS Archives.

Young, Brigham to Cannon, George Q., 30 October 1855. Brigham Young Office Files, LDS Archives.

________. 29 November, 1855. Ibid.
________. 30 January 1856. Ibid.
________. 3 April 1856. Ibid.
________. 29 April 1856. Ibid.
________. 30 May 1856. Ibid.
________. 27 September 1856. Ibid.
________. 4 October 1856. Ibid.

________. 4 November 1856. Ibid.

________. 7 December 1856. Ibid.

________. 7 January 1857. Ibid.

________. 31 January 1857. Ibid.

________. 4 April 1857. Ibid.

________. 4 June 1857. Ibid. (Incorrectly noted on typescript copy as 4 July.)

________. 4 August 1857. Ibid.

________. 4 September 1857. Ibid.

________. 7 October 1857. Ibid.

________.15 September 1858. Ibid.

________. 5 May 1859. Brigham Young Papers, Marriott Library, Univ. of Utah.

________. 3 November 1859. MS 577, Special Collections and Manuscripts, Harold B. Lee Library, Brigham Young Univ.

Young to Cox, William. 4 December 1857. Brigham Young Office Letterbooks, 1851–1879, LDS Archives.

Young, Brigham to Kane, Thomas L. 15 Dec., 1859. Kane Collection, Special Collections, Harold B. Lee Library, Brigham Young Univ.

Young, Brigham to Colonel Kane. WA MSS S-1023 Y84, Western Americana Collection, Beinecke Rare Book and Manuscript Library, Yale Univ.

Online Sources

FamilySearch Ancestral Internet Genealogy Service: www.familysearch.org.

Fielding, Joseph. Diary. Saints Without Halos: A Mormon History Web Site: http://saintswithouthalos.com/pri/jfi_d_147-181.htm.

King, Larry—Interview with Gordon B. Hinckley, aired 8 September 1998; transcript courtesy of CNN at www.cnn.com.

Raffety, Michael. "Mountain Democrat Sole Gold Rush Survivor." *Mountain Democrat* web page: http://www.mtdemocrat.com/demohistory/DEMOHST.html.

Index

The Editor

Roger Robin Ekins, a fifth-generation member of the Church of Jesus Christ of Latter-day Saints, was born in Salt Lake City, Utah. After serving a mission in Argentina and a four-year hitch in the U.S. Army Reserves, he graduated Phi Beta Kappa from the University of Utah in 1970 with an Honors Baccalaureate of Arts in English and in 1972 with a Master's in Creative Writing. In 1976 he earned his Ph.D. in Higher Education from the Union Graduate School (Union Institute and University).

Dr. Ekins has served in a series of administrative and teaching positions. These include Director of the Open Community Learning Center and Assistant Professor of English at Staten Island Community College, City University of New York; Dean of Student Life and Faculty Fellow in English and Education at Johnston College, University of Redlands; Dean of Student Development and Director of the Honors Program at the University of Maine at Augusta; and Dean of Instruction at Butte College in Oroville, California, where he is currently chair of the Honors Program and teaches literature, writing and the history of ideas.

A President Emeritus of the California Humanities Association, which awarded him the Charles D. Perlee Award, Dr. Ekins serves on the National Honors Advisory Committee of the University of Utah and on the editorial board of his local newspaper, the *Paradise Post.* His previous publications include poetry, fiction, and essays. *Defending Zion* marks his first book-length venture as well as his first publication in Mormon Studies, long a topic of deep interest. He lives and fly-fishes in Paradise, California, with his wife, the former Helen Kaye Leonard. They are the parents of three children: Sarah, Adam, and Rachael.